Living Liturgy™

Living Liturgy™

Spirituality, Celebration, and Catechesis for Sundays and Solemnities

Year A • 2011

Joyce Ann Zimmerman, CPPS
Kathleen Harmon, SND de N
Christopher W. Conlon, SM

LITURGICAL PRESS
Collegeville, Minnesota

www.litpress.org

Design by Ann Blattner. Art by Julie Lonneman.

ISSN 1547-089X

ISBN 978-0-8146-2748-8

CONTENTS

☩ CONTRIBUTORS

Joyce Ann Zimmerman, CPPS, is the director of the Institute for Liturgical Ministry in Dayton, Ohio, and is the founding editor and columnist for *Liturgical Ministry*. She is also an adjunct professor of liturgy, liturgical consultant, and frequent facilitator of workshops on liturgy. She has published numerous scholarly and pastoral liturgical works. She holds civil and pontifical doctorates of theology.

Kathleen Harmon, SND de N, is the music director for programs of the Institute for Liturgical Ministry in Dayton, Ohio, and is the author of the *Music Notes* column for *Liturgical Ministry*. An educator and musician, she facilitates liturgical music workshops and cantor formation programs, teaches private voice lessons, and has been a parish liturgical music director. She holds a graduate degree in music and a doctorate in liturgy.

Christopher W. Conlon, SM, is a Marianist priest who works with faculty and staff and has taught Scripture at the University of Dayton. He has been an educator for over a half century and is a highly respected homilist, a frequent workshop presenter, and a spiritual director. He holds a graduate degree in religious education and the licentiate in theology.

USING THIS RESOURCE

Many of us often live by putting the cart before the horse. This saying is particularly apropos for this twelfth volume of *Living Liturgy*™. We writers are suggesting that readers put the cart before the horse in preparing for the Sunday eucharistic celebration. That is, we advise that readers prepare the readings and live the gospel the *week before* the Sunday celebration. By such preparation we are primed to hear the readings, be challenged by the homily, be moved to pray for the church and world's needs at the prayer of the faithful, be ready to hear and respond to the story of salvation recited at the eucharistic prayer, be eager to be dismissed to live what we have celebrated.

This year, however, there may be another kind of way *Living Liturgy*™ puts the cart before the horse. We begin team meetings and writing a full two years before the year of publication of any given volume. At this time we know that the church in the United States is completing its work on the third edition of the Roman Missal. However, we do not know when this will be available as a published Missal or when the official promulgation date will be. Hence, it is quite possible that the text for the opening prayer may not be the translation used at Sunday Mass (if the new Missal is in use). Nor may some of the section headings agree with those used in the new Missal. So we ask the readers to please be patient during this transition period.

A third way we put the cart before the horse concerns the music suggestions on the Catechesis page: because a number of the music suggestions made in *Living Liturgy*™ are drawn from resources published annually, some suggestions made at the time a volume of *Living Liturgy*™ was written and printed may no longer appear in the resources cited. Our intention here is not to provide a complete list of music suggestions for each Sunday or solemnity (these are readily available in other publications) but to make a few suggestions with accompanying catechesis; thus, we hope this is a learning process.

All this being said, *Living Liturgy*™ still continues its original purpose: to help people prepare well for liturgy and live a liturgical spirituality (that is, a way of living that is rooted in liturgy) that opens their vision to their baptismal identity as the Body of Christ and shapes their living according to the rhythm of paschal mystery dying and rising. The paschal mystery is the central focus of liturgy, of the gospels, and of every volume of *Living Liturgy*™.

A threefold dynamic of daily living, prayer, and study continues to determine the basic structure of *Living Liturgy*™, captured in the layout under the headings "Spirituality," "Celebration," and "Catechesis." This threefold dynamic is lived by the three authors; this is why each year the new volume is fresh with new material. The features don't always change (and there are no new features for this year), but the content does.

During Ordinary Time of the 2011 liturgical year, we read from Matthew's gospel, with a special focus on God's kingdom among us in the life and ministry of Jesus. Matthew is also careful about showing Jesus as the new Moses who fulfills the Old Testament prophecies about the coming of the Messiah and the coming of a new age. We are living now in this new age. Let us live it well, according to the Good News revealed in Christ: Emmanuel, God is with us!

PREPARATION FOR SUNDAY: PUT THE CART BEFORE THE HORSE

TRANSITION TO NEW ROMAN MISSAL

MUSIC SUGGESTIONS

PASCHAL MYSTERY STILL CENTRAL FOCUS

SPIRITUALITY, CELEBRATION, AND CATECHESIS

GOD'S KINGDOM IS AMONG US

✝ INTRODUCTION to the Gospel of Matthew

In order to understand Matthew's gospel better, it is helpful to recall that the first Christians were convinced that Jesus' Second Coming and the end of the world would occur in their lifetime. So, as a result, at first they were not really concerned about passing on the Good News to future generations. However, as decades passed and most of the original followers had died (and the end of the world had not happened!), there was a concern about having a more permanent record of the life, death, and resurrection of Jesus—something written that could be passed on. Consequently, in the 70s, 80s and 90s the gospels were written. They were accounts of what Jesus did and said, based on the memory and lived experience of a particular community of his followers.

What each gospel writer put into his account was governed by the needs, the problems, and the trials and challenges of the community for which they were writing. The Gospel of Matthew was probably written by a Jewish scribe, a person who was very familiar with the Hebrew Scriptures. He was writing for the Jewish followers of Jesus who had continued to attend the synagogue regularly—their religion was still the Jewish religion, with belief in Christ and his teachings a further revelation of their inherited beliefs and traditions. Then around the year AD 70 (when the city of Jerusalem was completely destroyed by the Romans and the Pharisees took over as the ruling group), the Jewish Christians were expelled from the synagogue and treated like enemies of the Jewish God. These Jewish Christians did not understand why God had allowed their city and temple to be completely destroyed so that "not a stone remained on a stone." They were told by these same Pharisee leaders that not only was Jesus of Nazareth not the Son of God but he was a sinner who violated the Sabbath and other Jewish practices. Matthew "answers" this charge by presenting Jesus as the new Moses who, for example, came out of Egypt to lead his people and who gave a new covenant on the Mount of the Beatitudes.

Matthew's gospel addresses these issues in an anecdotal literary form. Matthew presents Jesus by having him do "Moses-like" things. Like Moses, he comes into Israel from Egypt to lead the people out of slavery. Like Moses, he goes up on a mount to give the people new rules of behavior (the Beatitudes). He is the Son of God who, like Moses, had miraculous powers (for Jesus, especially, to heal, cure, and forgive), and who brought hope to many people. Unlike Moses, he is also the Messiah who would be tortured and killed but who would rise from the dead and whose Spirit would continue to live in those who follow him. This Jewish Scribe gospel writer backs up what he says about Jesus by frequently quoting passages from the Hebrew Scriptures, passages that foretold the different things that would happen to the Messiah—things that did not always fit the image of the messiah that the people had.

This Synoptic Gospel is structured in such a way that the central theme, the main point around which the gospel revolves, is that the kingdom of God (chapter 13 on ". . . the kingdom of God is like . . .") is among us when we live the spirit of the Beatitudes (chapter 5) and not the way of the Pharisees (chapter 23). Scripture scholar Jack Dean Kingsbury, in his book *Matthew as Story* (Augsburg Fortress, 1998), identifies three phases in the Gospel of Matthew, each one identified by the phrase, "From that time on, Jesus began to preach . . ." This phrase alerts the reader to a change in phase: the beginning from 1:1 to 4:16; the middle phase (the kingdom phase), 4:17 to 16:20; and the end phase, 16:21 to 28:20.

Matthew's gospel begins with a statement from Isaiah: "Emmanuel . . . God is with us" (1:23). The gospel ends with a similar statement of God's continuing presence—after the resurrection the gospel writer brackets the entire story when he records Jesus' final words: "I am with you always, to the close of the age" (28:20b). Matthew's gospel invites us to hear and believe the word of God, beginning with the apostles and continuing down to us and to the end of time. We are to open ourselves to God's continuing presence—"Emmanuel . . . God is with us . . . always, to the close of the age." Jesus' "great commission" (28:19-20a) makes clear that we who hear and believe are invited to go out and share this marvelous Good News with "all nations."

LITURGICAL RESOURCES

BofB	*Book of Blessings*. International Commission on English in the Liturgy. Collegeville: Liturgical Press, 1989.
GIRM	*General Instruction of the Roman Missal* (2002).
GNLYC	General Norms for the Liturgical Year and the Calendar
ILM	Introduction to the Lectionary for Mass
L	*Lectionary*
NT	New Testament
OT	Old Testament
SC	*Sacrosanctum Concilium*. The Constitution on the Sacred Liturgy. Vatican II.

MUSICAL RESOURCES

BB	*Breaking Bread*. Portland, OR: Oregon Catholic Press, annual.
CBW3	*Catholic Book of Worship III*. Ottawa, Ontario: Canadian Conference of Catholic Bishops, 1994.
CH	*The Collegeville Hymnal*. Collegeville: Liturgical Press, 1990.
G2	*Gather*. 2nd edition. Chicago: GIA Publications, Inc., 1994.
GC	*Gather Comprehensive*. Chicago: GIA Publications, Inc., 1994.
GC2	*Gather Comprehensive*. 2nd edition. Chicago: GIA Publications, Inc., 2004.
HG	*Hymns for the Gospels*. Chicago: GIA Publications, Inc., 2001.
JS2	*JourneySongs*. 2nd edition. Portland, OR: Oregon Catholic Press, 2003.
LMGM	*Lead Me, Guide Me*. Chicago: GIA Publications, Inc., 1987.
OFUV	*One Faith/Una Voz*. Portland, OR: Oregon Catholic Press, 2005.
PMB	*People's Mass Book*. Schiller Park, IL: World Library Publications, 2003.
PS	*Psallite*. Collegeville: Liturgical Press.
RS	*Ritual Song*. Chicago: GIA Publications, Inc., 1996.
SS	*Sacred Song*. Collegeville: Liturgical Press, annual.
S&S	*Spirit and Song*. Portland, OR: Oregon Catholic Press.
VO	*Voices As One*. Schiller Park, IL: World Library Publications, 1998.
VO2	*Voices As One*, vol. 2. Schiller Park, IL: World Library Publications, 2005.
W3	*Worship*. 3rd edition. Chicago: GIA Publications, Inc., 1986.
WC	*We Celebrate*. Schiller Park, IL: World Library Publications, 2004.
WS	*Word and Song*. Schiller Park, IL: World Library Publications, 2005.
GIA	GIA Publications, Inc.
LTP	Liturgy Training Publications, Inc.
OCP	Oregon Catholic Press
WLP	World Library Publications

NOTE: Because a number of the music suggestions made in *Living Liturgy*™ are drawn from resources published annually, some suggestions made at the time this volume of *Living Liturgy*™ was produced may no longer appear in the resources cited.

Season of Advent

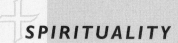

SPIRITUALITY

GOSPEL ACCLAMATION
Ps 85:8

℟. Alleluia, alleluia.
Show us Lord, your love;
and grant us your salvation.
℟. Alleluia, alleluia.

Gospel

Matt 24:37-44; L1A

Jesus said to his disciples:
"As it was in the days of Noah,
 so it will be at the coming of
  the Son of Man.
In those days before the flood,
 they were eating and drinking,
 marrying and giving in
  marriage,
 up to the day that Noah entered the
  ark.
They did not know until the flood came
 and carried them all away.
So will it be also at the coming of the
 Son of Man.
Two men will be out in the field;
 one will be taken, and one will be
  left.
Two women will be grinding at the mill;
 one will be taken, and one will be
  left.
Therefore, stay awake!
For you do not know on which day your
 Lord will come.
Be sure of this: if the master of the
 house
 had known the hour of night when
  the thief was coming,
 he would have stayed awake
 and not let his house be broken into.
So too, you also must be prepared,
 for at an hour you do not expect, the
  Son of Man will come."

Reflecting on the Gospel

Philosopher and poet George Santayana, famous for his aphorisms, gave us this one, which is quite apropos for this Sunday's gospel: "Those who cannot learn from history are doomed to repeat it." In the "days of Noah" there was great wickedness in the world—so much so that God chose to destroy the wicked and only save the righteous Noah and his family (see Gen 6–9). Jesus sees far into the future and remarks that "so it will be at the coming of the Son of Man." From the very beginning of history to the very end of history we humans have a short-sighted vision of life, a vision that all too frequently only sees ourselves and our selfish desires. Jesus invites us to shed our short-sightedness and have a clearer vision of what our life is really about.

Jesus' warning, "Stay awake!" has to do with having clear vision. We are to see what in our lives needs to change. We are also to see how our good living now is already preparation for the "coming of the Son of Man" who will arrive "at an hour [we] do not expect." Thus the day will come when all people will climb the mountain of the Lord and encounter a new vision of what it means to walk in the ways of God. War and enmity will cease. Jesus is challenging us to enter this vision even now while we are still climbing. This clear vision is assured only when we "put on the Lord Jesus Christ" (second reading). With this clear vision we can have the hope and trust that by living in Christ we will be among those who are taken into eternal glory at the Second Coming.

Advent always begins by looking to the second coming of Christ. But Advent is not simply about looking into the future; Christ came in the past and is coming to us now. No matter how we talk about Christ's coming (whether at his first coming at the incarnation, at his second coming, or at his coming to us now in word and sacrament and each other), we are always talking about *salvation*. Isaiah invites Israel to salvation collectively, as a nation; Paul invites the Christian Romans to salvation by practicing personal morality; Jesus invites all of us to salvation by staying awake, that is, having the vision to make the right choices that prepare us for his coming. The choice between war or peace, darkness or light, immorality or goodness is ours. The consequences of our everyday choices are urgent: we will be either taken or left behind. Let's not allow history to repeat itself!

Living the Paschal Mystery

Isaiah admonishes the people of his time to "climb the LORD's mountain . . . that he may instruct us in his ways." We are thus not at a loss about how we walk in the light and remain righteous: we listen to God's instructions. Instruction in doing God's will comes more formally through the readings and homily at Sunday Mass or through catechetical instructions. But this is not the only way God teaches us right living. God's instructions also come through people who may ask for our help (giving us the choice to put another's good ahead of our own) or numerous everyday situations when we are faced with making moral choices (such as whether or not to put in an honest day's work). The issue is to *listen* and see in these practical situations how God is broadening our vision. Our listening means staying awake. Advent will bring us many choices; how we respond is practice in being prepared.

Focusing the Gospel

Key words and phrases: coming of the Son of Man, Stay awake, be prepared, hour you do not expect

To the point: Jesus' warning, "Stay awake!" has to do with having clear vision. We are to see what in our lives needs to change. We are also to see how our good living now is already preparation for the "coming of the Son of Man" who will arrive "at an hour [we] do not expect." Clear vision is assured when we "put on the Lord Jesus Christ" (second reading).

Connecting the Gospel

to the first and second readings: We children of earth sink so easily into the routine of human history as it plays out both in our daily personal lives and on the world scene: "As it was . . . so it will be" (gospel). These readings call us to wake up (gospel and second reading), to climb the mountain of new vision (see first reading), and see that God does something new through the "coming of the Son of Man."

to our experience: It is so easy to get caught up in our daily routine that our vision of anything beyond immediate concerns tends to be blurred. Jesus calls us to a vision that includes not only the purpose of our own lives but even the very end of the world.

Connecting the Responsorial Psalm

to the readings: In the first reading Isaiah offers us the vision of a future in which all nations stream to the dwelling place of God, listen to God's instruction, and choose to live God's ways of peace and justice. In the gospel Jesus warns that we must keep ourselves ready at all times for the fulfillment of this vision (i.e., the day when the Son of Man will come). In the second reading Paul declares that the hour of fulfillment is now, and we must act accordingly.

Being ready for the final coming of God's kingdom, then, is not a passive state but an active one. And part of this activity, declares the responsorial psalm, is choosing to journey joyfully toward the God who is coming: "Let us go rejoicing to the house of the Lord." As the second reading and gospel show us, such a journey is no small undertaking, for it will require twists and turns in our manner of living. But its rewards will be great and the journey itself will bring joy.

to psalmist preparation: In singing this psalm you express the joy one feels in journeying toward God. This joy has a price, however, for to travel toward God means to leave behind one's present dwelling place. In your own life right now where is God calling you to "make a move"? How will making this move prepare you for the final coming of Christ? How in singing this psalm can you encourage the assembly to make this journey with you?

ASSEMBLY & FAITH-SHARING GROUPS

- For me, Jesus' command to "Stay awake" means . . .
- A few examples of when I have "stayed awake" to Christ's coming in my daily living are . . .
- I am using this Advent to grow in my preparedness for when "the Son of Man will come" by . . .

PRESIDERS

Occasions within my ministry that cause me to wake up to Christ's coming are . . . ; a recent example when I gently helped another to wake up is . . .

DEACONS

To "walk in the light of the Lord" (first reading) challenges me to . . . ; my ministry helps others to do this when . . .

HOSPITALITY MINISTERS

I enable those assembling to let go of their daily routine and wake up to the new vision offered in the liturgy when I . . .

MUSIC MINISTERS

Music ministry requires staying awake to many details. What helps me stay awake to the coming of Christ in these details is . . .

ALTAR MINISTERS

My service guides me to "conduct [myself] properly as in the day" (second reading) by . . .

LECTORS

My manner of proclamation calls the community to be alert to new vision offered in the liturgy when . . .

EXTRAORDINARY MINISTERS OF HOLY COMMUNION

Each communicant who approaches offers me a new vision of God's presence in that . . . I am able to perceive this new vision when I . . .

3

Model Act of Penitence

Presider: Today, the first Sunday of Advent, Jesus commands us to stay awake for his coming. Let us open our eyes to the new vision he offers us as we celebrate this Eucharist . . . [pause]

Lord Jesus, you are Son of God and Son of Man: Lord . . .

Christ Jesus, you will come in glory: Christ . . .

Lord Jesus, you are the Light that dispels darkness: Lord . . .

Homily Points

• A person climbing a mountain must pay attention to many details and difficulties along the route. Often the climb is tedious and strenuous. At the summit, however, a vista so overpowering and awesome opens up that the struggles of the climb recede into oblivion. Immediacy, details, short vision give way to the glory of timelessness, expansive vista, and broader vision.

• Our journey of discipleship as we prepare for the final coming of Christ is similar to climbing a mountain. The work is hard and long. Our vision tends to be focused on immediate concerns. Jesus challenges us to wake up now to a broader vision: to put off unseemly conduct and look beyond immediate concerns to his final coming.

• The key to a broader vision is to keep our eyes on Christ as the center of our lives. We do this, for example, by seeing a plea for help in the eyes of a neighbor in need and taking the time to respond, or by being patient when someone is annoying or frustrating us. Preparing for the coming of Christ means that we recognize Christ in ourselves as well as in those around us every day and respond as he would.

Model Prayer of the Faithful

Presider: God never fails to help us on our journey to final glory. Let us make our needs known to this God in whom we trust and have hope.

Response:

Lord, hear our prayer.

Cantor:

we pray to the Lord,

That the church proclaim a vision of goodness and fidelity that helps us on our journey to glory . . . [pause]

That civil leaders diligently make the cities and nations of the world safe and peaceful for all . . . [pause]

That, through our generous care, the sick and disadvantaged come to hope and trust in God's presence . . . [pause]

That each of us here grow in putting on Christ, that we may be prepared for his coming . . . [pause]

Presider: God of salvation, you desire that all people share eternal life with you: hear these our prayers that we might be wakeful and prepared for the coming judgment of your Son. We pray through that same Son, Jesus Christ our Lord. **Amen.**

OPENING PRAYER

Let us pray

Pause for silent prayer

All-powerful God,
increase our strength of will for doing
    good
that Christ may find an eager welcome at
    his coming
and call us to his side in the kingdom of
    heaven,
where he lives and reigns with you and the
    Holy Spirit,
one God, for ever and ever. **Amen.**

FIRST READING

Isa 2:1-5

This is what Isaiah, son of Amoz,
    saw concerning Judah and Jerusalem.
        In days to come,
    the mountain of the LORD's house
        shall be established as the highest
            mountain
        and raised above the hills.
All nations shall stream toward it;
    many peoples shall come and say:
"Come, let us climb the LORD's
    mountain,
    to the house of the God of Jacob,
that he may instruct us in his ways,
    and we may walk in his paths."
For from Zion shall go forth instruction,
    and the word of the LORD from
        Jerusalem.
He shall judge between the nations,
    and impose terms on many peoples.
They shall beat their swords into
    plowshares
    and their spears into pruning hooks;
one nation shall not raise the sword
        against another,
    nor shall they train for war again.
O house of Jacob, come,
    let us walk in the light of the LORD!

RESPONSORIAL PSALM
Ps 122:1-2, 3-4, 4-5, 6-7, 8-9

℞. Let us go rejoicing to the house of the Lord.

I rejoiced because they said to me,
   "We will go up to the house of the LORD."
And now we have set foot
   within your gates, O Jerusalem.

℞. Let us go rejoicing to the house of the Lord.

Jerusalem, built as a city
   with compact unity.
To it the tribes go up,
   the tribes of the LORD.

℞. Let us go rejoicing to the house of the Lord.

According to the decree for Israel,
   to give thanks to the name of the LORD.
In it are set up judgment seats,
   seats for the house of David.

℞. Let us go rejoicing to the house of the Lord.

Pray for the peace of Jerusalem!
   May those who love you prosper!
May peace be within your walls,
   prosperity in your buildings.

℞. Let us go rejoicing to the house of the Lord.

Because of my brothers and friends
   I will say, "Peace be within you!"
Because of the house of the LORD, our God,
   I will pray for your good.

℞. Let us go rejoicing to the house of the Lord.

SECOND READING
Rom 13:11-14

Brothers and sisters:
You know the time;
   it is the hour now for you to awake from
      sleep.
For our salvation is nearer now than when
      we first believed;
   the night is advanced, the day is at
      hand.
Let us then throw off the works of
      darkness
   and put on the armor of light;
   let us conduct ourselves properly as in
      the day,
   not in orgies and drunkenness,
   not in promiscuity and lust,
   not in rivalry and jealousy.
But put on the Lord Jesus Christ,
   and make no provision for the desires of
      the flesh.

About Liturgy

Liturgy broadens our vision: For many it seems as though liturgy unfolds the same way week after week except for the obvious changes in the readings, homily, and music. In fact, each liturgy offers many choices for celebration. The choices we make about liturgy help us to climb the mountain of holiness and have a clearer vision of God's will for us.

Assembly: Obviously, the basic choice for each person is simply deciding to come to Mass. Beyond this, each of us must choose to participate fully, actively, and consciously. This means that we surrender ourselves to God's transforming action during the liturgy. We join our voices with others in singing God's praises. We *actively listen* to the instructions in God's ways. We enter deeply into the prayer of the liturgy. Perhaps the most persistent choice is to remain focused on the prayer at hand, gently bringing ourselves back to attention whenever our minds wander.

Presider: The presider (or in some cases the liturgy director) chooses the form of the introductory rites, the preface, the eucharistic prayer, greetings and introductions, which form of the final blessing to use. The presider also chooses to be present to the people before and after the liturgy. For our part we respond to that presence when we go out of our way to compliment him when he has prayed and preached well. We also respond when we choose to pay attention—stay awake—to the prayers that are being prayed.

Music director: The music offers many opportunities for choices and self-surrender. Besides choosing which hymns to sing, the music director also chooses appropriate service music and prepares cantor, choir, and assembly for their important music roles, always with the needs of the liturgy and the assembly in mind. For our part, we choose to join in the singing. We choose to focus on the cantor and enter into the singing of the responsorial psalm. When the assembly needs to be prepared to sing something new, we choose to pay attention and learn.

About Liturgical Music

Music suggestions: The Lectionary focus during the first two weeks of Advent is not on the infant Jesus' coming in Bethlehem but on the resurrected Christ's final coming in judgment at the end of history. The songs we sing these two weeks need to express this focus, while songs oriented toward the coming of the newborn Jesus need to be saved for the final two weeks of Advent.

Examples of song texts, found in various resources, that focus on the final coming of Christ are "The King Shall Come When Morning Dawns"; "Wake, O Wake, and Sleep No Longer"; "Lift Up Your Heads, O Mighty Gates"; "Soon and Very Soon"; "Hail to the Lord's Anointed"; "Clear the Voice"; and "In the Day of the Lord." Some examples of appropriate choral pieces are Andre Thomas's setting of the spiritual "Keep Your Lamps" [Hinshaw HMC-577]; Alan Hommerding's creative setting of the same, titled "Keep Your Lamps Trimmed and Burning" [WLP 005739]; and Scot Crandal's "Waken, O Sleeper," for SATB choir, assembly, and handbells [OCP 11118CC].

NOVEMBER 28, 2010
FIRST SUNDAY OF ADVENT

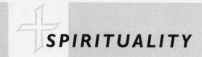

SPIRITUALITY

GOSPEL ACCLAMATION
Luke 3:4, 6

℟. Alleluia, alleluia.
Prepare the way of the Lord, make straight his
    paths:
all flesh shall see the salvation of God.
℟. Alleluia, alleluia.

Gospel   Matt 3:1-12; L4A

John the Baptist appeared, preaching
    in the desert of Judea
and saying, "Repent, for the
    kingdom of heaven is at
    hand!"
It was of him that the prophet Isaiah
    had spoken when he said:
    *A voice of one crying out in the
        desert,*
    Prepare the way of the Lord,
        make straight his paths.
John wore clothing made of camel's
    hair
    and had a leather belt around his
        waist.
His food was locusts and wild honey.
At that time Jerusalem, all Judea,
    and the whole region around the
        Jordan
    were going out to him
    and were being baptized by him in
        the Jordan River
    as they acknowledged their sins.

When he saw many of the Pharisees
    and Sadducees
    coming to his baptism, he said to
        them, "You brood of vipers!
Who warned you to flee from the
    coming wrath?
Produce good fruit as evidence of your
    repentance.
And do not presume to say to
    yourselves,
    'We have Abraham as our father.'
For I tell you,
    God can raise up children to
        Abraham from these stones.

Continued in Appendix A, p. 263.

Reflecting on the Gospel

This gospel is filled with great imagery that brings to it both "color" and concreteness. John is described as a kind of wild man who wears "clothing made of camel's hair" and eats "locusts and wild honey." He is surely a man of the desert. On the other hand, the Pharisees and Sadducees—no doubt men of the city with good breeding—are called a "brood of vipers." Vipers are light-colored, dark-patterned venomous snakes with long fangs that reach out to poison their victims. What a contrast! John, the wild man, is the one chosen to "[p]repare the way of the Lord." The others mislead, making straight paths crooked with their haughty living that produces no good fruit. The integrity of John's living gave his words power, which drew many to turn to live their lives with the same integrity.

The harshness of John the Baptist's preaching to some Pharisees and Sadducees in this gospel—"You brood of vipers!"—is a scathing judgment, indeed. John's harsh language, unrelenting judgment, and uncompromising challenge demand a wholehearted response: Repent! Repentance always changes one's life. Changing our lives is very concrete and visible: "Produce good fruit as evidence of your repentance."

Repentance, at root, means to change one's mind. Only then can we act according to God's plan, thus changing our lives. Further, although the gospel brings our attention to personal repentance—and this is absolutely essential—the first two readings remind us that repentance, as personal as it must be, always implicates the broader community. Herein is the deeper challenge of the readings: to repent not simply to save ourselves but to be motivated to repentance because our own change of mind and accordant actions also affect others and help bring them to salvation. When each of us changes our mind—repents—by conforming our will to God's, then there will be "no [more] harm or ruin" but rather the peace and harmony described by Isaiah; when we repent together, then we will "think in harmony" and will, with "one voice," glorify God, as St. Paul encourages us to do.

Repentance brings not the poison of striking vipers but the "[g]ood fruit" of counsel, strength, knowledge, and delight in the Lord (see first reading). Repentance brings the favorable judgment that not only invites us to the kingdom of heaven but *is* the peace and harmony portraying the already "at hand" of God's reign.

Living the Paschal Mystery

The gospel challenges us not to dismiss the Pharisees and Sadducees of the gospel too quickly. John's harsh judgment of them must bring us to look at what is within us that opposes God's ways and Christ's coming. One good way to discover what within us needs to change is to *listen* to the judgments others are making about us. Whenever we hear negative things about ourselves we tend to be hurt, and this is quite natural. Perhaps the hurt would be eased if we remember that such judgments may reveal to us ways we need to repent. Here is the paschal mystery reality of our lives: true, we *already* share in the new life of Jesus' resurrection; at the same time we have *not yet* rid ourselves of all that opposes God's ways and for which we must repent.

Focusing the Gospel

Key words and phrases: Repent, acknowledged their sins, Produce good fruit as evidence

To the point: John's harsh language, unrelenting judgment, and uncompromising challenge demand a wholehearted response: Repent! Repentance always changes one's life. Changing our lives is very concrete and visible: "Produce good fruit as evidence of your repentance."

Connecting the Gospel

to the first and second readings: Repentance brings us into conformity with God's plan of salvation and leads us to the kingdom of peace and harmony described by Isaiah and Paul.

to experience: We tend to think repentance is only about our individual relationship to God. The harmony the second reading speaks of and the first reading alludes to implies that repentance always has a social dimension.

Connecting the Responsorial Psalm

to the readings: Both Isaiah (first reading) and John the Baptist (gospel) deliver a message of judgment. God's kingdom of justice, peace, and harmony will not be established before the ruthless who burden the poor and oppress the lowly have been cut down. The readings, then, offer hope but also bear a warning. One is coming who will establish God's kingdom, but this same One will also destroy whoever stands in the kingdom's way.

The verses from Psalm 72 describe the One who is to come, this King (Christ) appointed by God and endowed with God's judgment. In singing it we express our certainty that the future God has promised will come to pass. We sing the hope of which Paul speaks. But the words of Isaiah and John the Baptist remind us that we also sing our own judgment. We cannot sing of hope for God's reign without also acting to bring that reign to reality, and this means opening ourselves to God's judgment and choosing whatever repentance is required of us. May we sing Psalm 72 with full awareness of what we are praying.

to psalmist preparation: The King of whom you sing in this responsorial psalm is Christ who will come at the end of time to establish definitively God's kingdom of peace. In what ways do you long for his coming? In what ways do you act to hasten his coming?

ASSEMBLY & FAITH-SHARING GROUPS
- When I hear John's harsh language, my first inclination is . . .
- If John were here today the challenge he would place upon me is . . .
- Some "good fruit" that is evidence of my repentance is . . .

PRESIDERS
The most fruitful way I call the assembly to repentance is . . . they call me to repentance when . . .

DEACONS
My service requires using the challenging words of John when . . . It calls for the comforting words of Isaiah when . . .

HOSPITALITY MINISTERS
My welcome is a voice crying out to make straight the path to God when . . .

MUSIC MINISTERS
Doing music ministry challenges me to change my ways of behaving by . . .

ALTAR MINISTERS
My serving at the altar prepares for the way of the Lord by . . . ; my serving others prepares the way of the Lord by . . .

LECTORS
Proclaiming the word of God to the assembly challenges me to repentance in that . . .

EXTRAORDINARY MINISTERS OF HOLY COMMUNION
The "good fruit" that the Eucharist is nourishing in me during this Advent is . . . ; I share this good fruit with others whenever I . . .

Model Act of Penitence

Presider: John the Baptist calls us in today's gospel to repent and make straight our way to the Lord. We pause at the beginning of this liturgy to open ourselves to God's saving mercy . . . [pause]

Lord Jesus, you judge us justly and lead us to your kingdom: Lord . . .

Christ Jesus, you are the glory of God who calls us to new life: Christ . . .

Lord Jesus, you gather the nations into harmony and peace: Lord . . .

Homily Points

• We naturally recoil from or react against what we perceive as harsh criticism. We want to protect ourselves. Yet we all have had experiences when criticism has led us to look at ourselves more clearly and change our way of behaving. Sometimes the difference in our response is because of the person who levels the criticism. Sometimes the difference is because of a new dawning of insight into ourselves.

• Something about John, harsh as his message was, drew large crowds to come to him for baptism. It was not enough to listen to his words and undergo his baptism, however. Genuine repentance had to be made evident in the good action of everyday living.

• Today we are the crowd hearing John's harsh words calling us to repentance. During this season of preparing for Christmas, we often get testy with each other because we are overly busy, tired, and under pressure. The good fruit of our own repentance is stepping back, assessing ourselves and reactions, and putting ourselves on the straight path of changing whatever behavior impedes God's vision of peace and harmony.

Model Prayer of the Faithful

Presider: Let us make our needs known to our good God, so that our repentance may bear fruit.

Response:

Lord, hear our prayer.

Cantor:

we pray to the Lord,

That all members of the church hear John's call to repent and bear fruit in their daily living . . . [pause]

That all people of the world live according to God's ways, bringing peace and harmony to all . . . [pause]

That the poor and hungry receive the good fruit that truly satisfies . . . [pause]

That each of us assembled here grow in wisdom, understanding, counsel, strength, and knowledge as we await the coming of God's kingdom . . . [pause]

Presider: God of salvation, you hear the prayers of those who call to you: grant us the courage to repent and bear fruit in our daily living. We ask this through Christ our Lord. **Amen.**

OPENING PRAYER

Let us pray

Pause for silent prayer

God of power and mercy,
open our hearts in welcome.
Remove the things that hinder us from
    receiving Christ with joy,
so that we may share his wisdom
and become one with him
when he comes in glory,
for he lives and reigns with you and the
    Holy Spirit,
one God, for ever and ever. **Amen.**

FIRST READING

Isa 11:1-10

On that day, a shoot shall sprout from the
        stump of Jesse,
    and from his roots a bud shall blossom.
The spirit of the LORD shall rest upon him:
    a spirit of wisdom and of
        understanding,
a spirit of counsel and of strength,
    a spirit of knowledge and of fear of the
        LORD,
    and his delight shall be the fear of the
        LORD.
Not by appearance shall he judge,
    nor by hearsay shall he decide,
but he shall judge the poor with justice,
    and decide aright for the land's afflicted.
He shall strike the ruthless with the rod of
        his mouth,
    and with the breath of his lips he shall
        slay the wicked.
Justice shall be the band around his waist,
    and faithfulness a belt upon his hips.
Then the wolf shall be a guest of the lamb,
    and the leopard shall lie down with the
        kid;
the calf and the young lion shall browse
        together,
    with a little child to guide them.
The cow and the bear shall be neighbors,
    together their young shall rest;
    the lion shall eat hay like the ox.
The baby shall play by the cobra's den,
    and the child lay his hand on the adder's
        lair.
There shall be no harm or ruin on all my
        holy mountain;
    for the earth shall be filled with
        knowledge of the LORD,
    as water covers the sea.
On that day, the root of Jesse,
    set up as a signal for the nations,
the Gentiles shall seek out,
    for his dwelling shall be glorious.

RESPONSORIAL PSALM
Ps 72:1-2, 7-8, 12-13, 17

R̶. (cf. 7) Justice shall flourish in his time, and fullness of peace forever.

O God, with your judgment endow the king,
  and with your justice, the king's son;
he shall govern your people with justice
  and your afflicted ones with judgment.

R̶. Justice shall flourish in his time, and fullness of peace forever.

Justice shall flower in his days,
  and profound peace, till the moon be no more.
May he rule from sea to sea,
  and from the River to the ends of the earth.

R̶. Justice shall flourish in his time, and fullness of peace forever.

For he shall rescue the poor when he cries out,
  and the afflicted when he has no one to help him.
He shall have pity for the lowly and the poor;
  the lives of the poor he shall save.

R̶. Justice shall flourish in his time, and fullness of peace forever.

May his name be blessed forever;
  as long as the sun his name shall remain.
In him shall all the tribes of the earth be blessed;
  all the nations shall proclaim his happiness.

R̶. Justice shall flourish in his time, and fullness of peace forever.

SECOND READING
Rom 15:4-9

Brothers and sisters:
Whatever was written previously was
  written for our instruction,
  that by endurance and by the
    encouragement of the Scriptures
  we might have hope.
May the God of endurance and
  encouragement
  grant you to think in harmony with one
    another,
  in keeping with Christ Jesus,
  that with one accord you may with one
    voice
  glorify the God and Father of our Lord
    Jesus Christ.

Continued in Appendix A, p. 263.

About Liturgy
Advent and Lent—two sides of the same coin? The gospel for this Sunday sounds like it might also be a good gospel to use for Lent—Repent! Although we usually think of preparedness and expectation as describing what Advent is really all about—and this within a quiet joyfulness—we are also reminded that Advent begins by looking to the Second Coming and the final judgment. The repentance of Advent is interpreted within this context; thus repentance is one way we prepare and expect.

The liturgical seasons don't unfold the paschal mystery in any chronological or historical manner. The wholeness of the mystery is always incorporated in the various themes for each season of the church year. There is a special convergence between the beginning of Advent and Lent because of the repentance motif. Repentance brings us face-to-face with the *not yet* of the mystery, that we are still sinful humanity in need of redemption. At the same time, both seasons also bring us to the gift of salvation: Advent in that it opens into the celebration of the incarnation and the coming of our Savior into our midst; Lent in that it opens into the celebration of Easter and the joyful new life of the risen Christ and of the baptized.

Advent and Lent aren't the two sides of the coin—dying and rising are. Advent and Lent each find themselves on both sides of the coin. Both seasons invite us to death and to resurrection.

About Liturgical Music
Music suggestions: As we continue looking toward the final coming of Christ during this second week of Advent, some examples of hymns that combine confidence in his coming with openness to God's judgment and willingness to repent of behaviors that impede the coming of the kingdom are "On Jordan's Bank" [BB, CH, JS2, RS, WC, W3]; "Comfort, Comfort, O My People" [BB, JS2, RS, WC, W3]; "Awake, Awake: Fling off the Night" [CBW3]; and "The Advent of our God" [CBW3, CH, WC]. CBW3 and WC suggest different tunes for this last hymn. The energy and joy of ST. THOMAS, used in CBW3, would make a good entrance song, while the introspective containment of POTSDAM, used in WC, would be more suitable for the presentation of the gifts. A choral piece worth repeating if used last Sunday would be Scot Crandal's "Waken, O Sleeper" [OCP 1118].

DECEMBER 5, 2010
SECOND SUNDAY OF ADVENT

✚ SPIRITUALITY

GOSPEL ACCLAMATION
cf. Luke 1:28

℞. Alleluia, alleluia.
Hail, Mary, full of grace, the Lord is with you;
blessed are you among women.
℞. Alleluia, alleluia.

Gospel   Luke 1:26-38; L689

The angel Gabriel was sent
    from God
    to a town of Galilee called
        Nazareth,
    to a virgin betrothed to a
        man named Joseph,
    of the house of David,
    and the virgin's name was Mary.
And coming to her, he said,
    "Hail, full of grace! The Lord is with
        you."
But she was greatly troubled at what was
        said
    and pondered what sort of greeting this
        might be.
Then the angel said to her,
    "Do not be afraid, Mary,
    for you have found favor with God.
Behold, you will conceive in your womb
        and bear a son,
    and you shall name him Jesus.
He will be great and will be called Son of
        the Most High,
    and the Lord God will give him the
        throne of David his father,
    and he will rule over the house of Jacob
        forever,
    and of his Kingdom there will be no end."
But Mary said to the angel,
    "How can this be,
    since I have no relations with a man?"
And the angel said to her in reply,
    "The Holy Spirit will come upon you,
    and the power of the Most High will
        overshadow you.
Therefore the child to be born
    will be called holy, the Son of God.

Continued in Appendix A, p. 264.

See Appendix A, p. 263, for the other readings.

Reflecting on the Gospel

This is a lofty festival, indeed. This feast celebrates God's extraordinary favor of choosing Mary to be the mother of Jesus and preserving her from all sin: "before the foundation of the world" Mary was "holy and without blemish" (second reading). Is this too lofty for us simple folk living lives reflecting both sin and grace? Is Mary too holy to be a model of holiness for us? The gospel for this solemnity shows us otherwise. Mary is truly a human like us, for she struggled to understand Gabriel's greeting. Mary is a model of holiness not because she never struggled but because she was ever faithful to God's will, opening herself to receiving God's abundant offer of divine presence.

When Gabriel appeared and greeted Mary as one who would become the mother of God's Son, she surely struggled with what this meant. However, because she believed God's promise, "[t]he Lord is with you," she was able to say, "May it be done to me." So it is with us: we too are most able to follow God's will and grow in holiness when we believe that God is with us. Saying yes to God doesn't begin with our will; it begins with the revelation that God loves us so much as to want to be with us. Believing in the divine presence is the key to choosing to do God's will. It is the key to being holy. The incredible good news of this gospel is that even in the midst of our struggle to be faithful to God and say our own yes, God takes up residence *within* us too! Through Christ we are God's adopted sons and daughters (see second reading), called to be holy and enjoy God's intimate presence to us.

In the first reading Adam and Eve move from innocence to guilt because of their wrong choice and, consequently, removed themselves from God's presence ("I hid myself"). The consequence of their wrong choice meant not only that they were expelled from the Garden of Paradise with its easy intimacy with God but that all of their descendants struggle with God's presence and intimacy as well. Their sin had consequences for all of humanity. Mary's choosing to say yes also has consequences for all of humanity: through her, the Savior of the world was born; through her, divinity was wed with humanity and new life burst forth. Similarly, our own choice to say yes has consequences for humanity: it is through the yes of each one of us that God chooses to make the risen life of the Son present in our world today. Divinity continues to be wedded to humanity through us, and for this, Holy Mary, Mother of God is truly the model for our own holy living.

Living the Paschal Mystery

On this solemnity we move from the stern message of John the Baptist (the second week of Advent) to the tender mercy of God bestowed on Mary and on all of humanity through her yes. We ourselves won't be visited by an angel to assure us of God's presence and encouragement to live holy lives. That assurance comes through our continued choices to do God's will.

We do God's will when we look to the needs of others and respond with the same tender mercy as God showers on all of us. By emptying ourselves for the sake of others we are filled with God's presence and holiness. We do God's will when we don't let the struggles and challenges of everyday living swerve us from being faithful to God's will. Rather than a stumbling block, struggles are an avenue of faithful choice to say yes because God is within and among us. "May it be done to me" flows from "The Lord is with you."

Focusing the Gospel

Key words and phrases: troubled, pondered, How can this be, May it be done to me

To the point: When Gabriel appeared and greeted Mary as the one who would become the mother of God's Son, she struggled with what this meant. However, because she believed God's promise, "[t]he Lord is with you," she was able to say, "May it be done to me." So it is with us: we too are most able to follow God's will and grow in holiness when we believe that God is with us.

Model Act of Penitence

Presider: Mary was conceived in her mother's womb without any blemish of sin. In this way God prepared her to be the fitting temple for the Son Jesus. Let us open ourselves to God's mercy and prepare ourselves to be fitting temples to receive that same Son Jesus . . . [pause]

Lord Jesus, you are Son of God and Son of Mary: Lord . . .

Christ Jesus, your kingdom has no end: Christ . . .

Lord Jesus, you dwell within us: Lord . . .

Model Prayer of the Faithful

Presider: Let us pray for the grace always to say yes to God's will and to be holy all the days of our life.

Response:

Cantor:

That all members of the church respond faithfully to whatever God asks . . . [pause]

That leaders of nations embody God's will in their judgments and actions . . . [pause]

That all those in need receive the fullness that God's presence promises . . . [pause]

That each one of us model our lives after the self-surrender of Mary . . . [pause]

Presider: Tender and merciful God, you chose Mary to bear the Savior of the world: hear these our prayers that one day we might enjoy everlasting life with Mary and her Son, our Lord Jesus Christ. **Amen.**

FOR REFLECTION
• God is asking me to . . . and I struggle because . . .
• As with Mary, God takes up residence within me whenever I . . .
• "May it be done to me" is most difficult for me to say when . . . is easiest to say when . . .

Homily Points

• "Holy" is probably not an adjective most of us would use to describe ourselves. Yet, as with Mary, God "chose us . . . to be holy" (second reading).

• "How can this be?" It can be because of who our God is, and in whose image we have been created. Holiness is a gift offered by God. Like Mary, we must respond to God with, "May it be done to me according to your will." Holiness is a gift requiring a response.

✢ SPIRITUALITY

GOSPEL ACCLAMATION
Isa 61:1 (cited in Luke 4:18)

R⁊. Alleluia, alleluia.
The Spirit of the LORD is upon me,
because he has anointed me
to bring glad tidings to the poor.
R⁊. Alleluia, alleluia.

Gospel Matt 11:2-11; L7A

When John the Baptist heard in
   prison of the works of the
   Christ,
he sent his disciples to Jesus
   with this question,
"Are you the one who is to
   come,
or should we look for another?"
Jesus said to them in reply,
"Go and tell John what you hear and
   see:
the blind regain their sight,
the lame walk,
lepers are cleansed,
the deaf hear,
the dead are raised,
and the poor have the good news
   proclaimed to them.
And blessed is the one who takes no offense
   at me."

As they were going off,
   Jesus began to speak to the crowds about
   John,
"What did you go out to the desert to see?
A reed swayed by the wind?
Then what did you go out to see?
Someone dressed in fine clothing?
Those who wear fine clothing are in royal
   palaces.
Then why did you go out? To see a prophet?
Yes, I tell you, and more than a prophet.
This is the one about whom it is written:
   Behold, I am sending my messenger
      ahead of you;
      he will prepare your way before
      you.
Amen, I say to you,
   among those born of women
   there has been none greater than John
      the Baptist;
   yet the least in the kingdom of heaven is
      greater than he."

Reflecting on the Gospel

When we limit what we are looking for, we limit what we might find. If we are only looking for coins with a metal detector, we may miss finding a primitive tool from the Iron Age. If we are only looking for a six-figure-salary job, we may miss the job that can be at hand and pay our immediate bills. If we are looking for a movie-star type Mr. or Ms. Right, we may miss an opportunity to spend a lifetime with someone who loves us deeply and faithfully. Life is limitless when our horizon of vision is expanded to include the unexpected and extraordinary.

The gospel this Sunday has two central characters—John the Baptist and Jesus. The gospel says marvelous things about both characters: Jesus works to reverse the sad plight of humanity; John is a prophet privileged to announce the coming of the Messiah. With this third Sunday in Advent our attention is turned explicitly toward the Christmas mystery. But rather than an infant, we encounter the adult Jesus who is already about his saving ministry. If we are only looking for a baby in a manger, we will not be able to recognize what the gospel is truly asking us to see: Jesus the Messiah, who brings about a reversal of human plight. We who see and acknowledge this Jesus are blessed as John was blessed.

Israel was patiently awaiting a conquering Messiah who would be their earthly king. The surprise of the gospel is who the Messiah truly is—the tender and merciful servant who reaches out to those in need. In Jesus, the *whole* vision of God for a world of peace and harmony comes to fruition. An alternative world is present in the coming of this Jesus Messiah, a world far surpassing the wealth and might and power of earthly expectations. The world Jesus brings is a world in which all are blessed beyond what we look for or see—even beyond imagination.

The crowds went out in the desert to see a prophet; Jesus assures them they saw even more, and he extols John's greatness. Now, here is the real shock of the gospel and the blessing: as great as John is—the one who follows Jesus—even the very least of these is still greater than John! *We* are those blessed ones who inherit the "kingdom of heaven," those of us who take up Jesus' tender and merciful servant ministry and continue to bring sight and healing and proclaim the Good News to all those *we* meet. Now it is our ministry to reverse the sad plight of humanity by helping others see in Jesus the One who brings blessing.

Let us see John for who he really was—the messenger pointing to the Messiah. Let us see Jesus for who he really is—the Messiah-king whose power is in his being the tender, merciful servant. Let us see ourselves for who we really are—God's blessed and beloved who, when we minister as Jesus did, are even greater than John. Yes, seeing is believing—but only when we look beyond to the blessedness breaking upon us.

Living the Paschal Mystery

The patience admonished in the second reading is needed for us to look beyond our limited vision and see what God offers us in Christ Jesus. If we limit our expectations to a baby born long ago in a manger, we will not be able to see Jesus as the "glory" and "splendor" of our God who is present among us—and *within* us—and whose presence continues to save. Through patience—first, with ourselves—we gradually learn to look beyond the immediate demands of the cares of our everyday lives to see the possibilities for change in our lives and in the lives of others.

Focusing the Gospel

Key words and phrases: works of the Christ, look for, see, blessed

To the point: When we limit what we are looking for, we limit what we might find. If we are only looking for a baby in a manger, we will not be able to recognize what the gospel is truly asking us to see: Jesus the Messiah, who brings about a reversal of human plight. We who see and acknowledge this Jesus are blessed.

Connecting the Gospel

to first reading: Isaiah in the first reading promises the reversal of human plight that is fulfilled in the gospel's description of the "works of the Christ." Isaiah further promises the joy and gladness that come with the coming of God's reign.

to experience: We ourselves are blessed by the reversal of human plight that Jesus' ministry brings; for example, we are freed from the captivity of narrow vision or weak hope, lifted up when we stumble out of confusion or fear, and healed from our own alienation.

Connecting the Responsorial Psalm

to the readings: When in 587 BC the Israelites were conquered by Babylon and carried off into exile, the experience threw them into a crisis of faith: was their God not stronger than pagan gods? Even more painful was the question: did God not really care about them? Psalm 146 was written after Israel had been freed from Babylon and had rebuilt the temple in Jerusalem. In verses omitted by the Lectionary, the psalm advises against placing trust in earthly powers and blesses those who place their hope only in the Lord. The psalm reasserts Israel's faith that God can be counted on forever and does indeed care, in a litany of ways, for those in need.

In some ways we stand in the same position as Israel. We have the promise of salvation gloriously described in the first reading. We have the witness of the saving works of Jesus detailed in the gospel. Yet we need to remain strong (first reading), to "be patient" (second reading), and to examine what it is we are looking for (gospel). Psalm 146 reminds us that what must hold our vision and ground our hope is God alone, God who will "come and save us," not in the way of earthly power but in the way of mercy and compassion.

to psalmist preparation: In what ways does this psalm strengthen your faith in God's promise of salvation? In what ways does it encourage you—and the assembly—to remain strong (first reading) and to be patient (second reading) as you await the coming of Christ?

ASSEMBLY & FAITH-SHARING GROUPS
- The works I have seen that make me believe that Jesus is the Messiah are . . .
- An example of when my expectations of who Jesus is blinded me to his advent is . . .
- I know I acknowledge Jesus because . . . I experience being truly blessed because of this in that . . .

PRESIDERS
When I heed Jesus' words, "Go and tell . . . what you hear and see," my ministry looks like . . .

DEACONS
My service is a participation in the "works of the Christ" when . . .

HOSPITALITY MINISTERS
My hospitality helps others recognize Jesus as "one who is to come" whenever I . . .

MUSIC MINISTERS
"Go and tell John what you hear and see." What the assembly hears in my singing is . . . What they see in my behavior is . . .

ALTAR MINISTERS
My acts of service at the altar witness to the assembly that I acknowledge Jesus in my life in that . . .

LECTORS
My proclamation of the word speaks to the assembly about Jesus when . . . about the reversal of human plight when . . .

EXTRAORDINARY MINISTERS OF HOLY COMMUNION
In distributing Holy Communion, what I see in the communicants is . . . what I hear in their response of "Amen" is . . .

Model Act of Penitence

Presider: The gospel today asks us, what is it we come to see? Let us open our hearts to Jesus' coming in word and sacrament and prepare ourselves to embrace him . . . [pause]

Lord Jesus, you are the Messiah who proclaims Good News: Lord . . .

Christ Jesus, you are the One for whom John was to prepare the way: Christ . . .

Lord Jesus, you are the Savior whose coming we await: Lord . . .

Homily Points

• A group of tourists on a bus heard someone exclaim, "Oh, look!" and everyone looked toward the horizon way out beyond the bus, missing the grizzly bear walking within ten feet of the side of the road. It is so easy for us to miss seeing what is right under our noses. This is no less true of our looking for the coming of the Messiah.

• We recognize Jesus when we open our eyes to see the evidence of his presence in the new things that are happening. In the gospel, Jesus made the blind see, the lame walk, etc. Today these same reversals are happening through our blessedness—Jesus working within and among us.

• Jesus is the promised One who changes the way things are. His presence today is made visible through our actions: our including those who feel alienated, our encouraging a student or child to come to full potential, our sensitivity to those suffering from AIDS. Jesus' reversals of the human plight were dramatic and hard not to see. Jesus' saving mission is just as present today when we do the little, often unseen, everyday good actions that are consistent with our blessedness.

Model Prayer of the Faithful

Presider: We are confident to make our needs known to the God who makes our salvation visible in the works of Jesus.

Response:

Lord,———— hear our prayer.

Cantor:

we pray to the Lord,

That the church embody faithfully the good works of Jesus . . . [pause]

That all people of the world seek and find salvation . . . [pause]

That those who suffer physically, mentally, or emotionally receive God's blessed healing . . . [pause]

That each of us spend Advent by opening ourselves to see the many comings of Jesus . . . [pause]

Presider: Gracious God, you bless those who come to you with longing: hear these our prayers that we might one day share in the blessedness of eternal life. We ask this through our Savior, Jesus Christ our Lord. **Amen.**

OPENING PRAYER

Let us pray

Pause for silent prayer

Lord God,
may we, your people,
who look forward to the birthday of Christ
experience the joy of salvation
and celebrate that feast with love and
    thanksgiving.

We ask this through our Lord Jesus Christ,
    your Son,
who lives and reigns with you and the
    Holy Spirit,
one God, for ever and ever. **Amen.**

FIRST READING

Isa 35:1-6a, 10

The desert and the parched land will exult;
    the steppe will rejoice and bloom.
They will bloom with abundant flowers,
    and rejoice with joyful song.
The glory of Lebanon will be given to
    them,
    the splendor of Carmel and Sharon;
they will see the glory of the LORD,
    the splendor of our God.
Strengthen the hands that are feeble,
    make firm the knees that are weak,
say to those whose hearts are frightened:
    Be strong, fear not!
Here is your God,
    he comes with vindication;
with divine recompense
    he comes to save you.
Then will the eyes of the blind be opened,
    the ears of the deaf be cleared;
then will the lame leap like a stag,
    then the tongue of the mute will sing.

Those whom the LORD has ransomed will
    return
    and enter Zion singing,
    crowned with everlasting joy;
they will meet with joy and gladness,
    sorrow and mourning will flee.

RESPONSORIAL PSALM
Ps 146:6-7, 8-9, 9-10

R̸. (cf. Isaiah 35:4) Lord, come and save us.
or:
R̸. Alleluia.

The LORD God keeps faith forever,
   secures justice for the oppressed,
   gives food to the hungry.
The LORD sets captives free.

R̸. Lord, come and save us.
or:
R̸. Alleluia.

The LORD gives sight to the blind;
   the LORD raises up those who were
      bowed down.
The LORD loves the just;
   the LORD protects strangers.

R̸. Lord, come and save us.
or:
R̸. Alleluia.

The fatherless and the widow he sustains,
   but the way of the wicked he thwarts.
The LORD shall reign forever;
   your God, O Zion, through all
      generations.

R̸. Lord, come and save us.
or:
R̸. Alleluia.

SECOND READING
Jas 5:7-10

Be patient, brothers and sisters,
   until the coming of the Lord.
See how the farmer waits for the precious
      fruit of the earth,
   being patient with it
   until it receives the early and the late
      rains.
You too must be patient.
Make your hearts firm,
   because the coming of the Lord is at
      hand.
Do not complain, brothers and sisters,
   about one another,
   that you may not be judged.
Behold, the Judge is standing before the
      gates.
Take as an example of hardship and
      patience, brothers and sisters,
   the prophets who spoke in the name of
      the Lord.

About Liturgy
Veneration of the altar and the presence/coming of the Lord: When the entrance procession reaches the sanctuary space and the ministers have made their reverence of the altar, the presider (and deacon) approach the altar and kiss it. We are occupied with singing the entrance hymn, so we probably don't pay too much attention to this profound gesture. Yet it is fraught with meaning.

This gesture dates at least to the fourth century and probably has its origin in ancient culture; often families would kiss the table before a meal began as a kind of greeting. Thus, one interpretation of the veneration of the altar by a kiss is that the presider is greeting Christ who is present among the assembly. In ancient times this gesture of the presider kissing the altar was directly linked to the exchange of the kiss of peace among the faithful.

At its dedication the altar was anointed with holy chrism and thus became a symbol of Christ's presence. We begin liturgy, then, with a gesture that reminds us of Christ, and we are at the same time reminded that we are the Body of Christ, now gathered around the Head who is present. We also prepare ourselves for the coming of Christ in both word and sacrament. So there is a kind of "already" and "not yet" at play in the veneration of the altar with a kiss. Christ is present, yet we anticipate Christ still to come.

About Liturgical Music
Music suggestions: This is the Sunday to begin using Advent hymns that prepare us for Christ's coming in the incarnation. Appropriate texts are those that speak of the birth of Christ, of his coming as a child, of his identity as Emmanuel (i.e., "God with us"). Some suggestions include "O Come, O Come, Emmanuel"; "O Come, Divine Messiah"; "Savior of the Nations, Come"; "Creator of the Stars of Night"; "Come, O Long Expected Jesus"; "People, Look East"; "Awake, Awake, and Greet the New Morn"; "Emmanuel"; "O Child of Promise, Come"; and "Proclaim the Joyful Message."

✠ SPIRITUALITY

GOSPEL ACCLAMATION
Matt 1:23

℟. Alleluia, alleluia.
The virgin shall conceive, and bear a son,
and they shall name him Emmanuel.
℟. Alleluia, alleluia.

Gospel

Matt 1:18-24; L10A

This is how the birth of Jesus
    Christ came about.
When his mother Mary was
    betrothed to Joseph,
  but before they lived together,
  she was found with child
    through the Holy Spirit.
Joseph her husband, since he was
    a righteous man,
  yet unwilling to expose her to shame,
  decided to divorce her quietly.
Such was his intention when, behold,
  the angel of the Lord appeared to him
    in a dream and said,
  "Joseph, son of David,
  do not be afraid to take Mary your
    wife into your home.
For it is through the Holy Spirit
  that this child has been conceived in
    her.
She will bear a son and you are to
    name him Jesus,
  because he will save his people from
    their sins."
All this took place to fulfill what the
    Lord had said through the prophet:
  Behold, the virgin shall conceive
    and bear a son,
  and they shall name him
    Emmanuel,
  which means "God is with us."
When Joseph awoke,
  he did as the angel of the Lord had
    commanded him
  and took his wife into his home.

Reflecting on the Gospel

We often make a distinction between a "house" and a "home." A house is a building with heat and light and furniture and people moving about—all very impersonal. A home, by contrast, is more than walls and carpets and appliances. A home is very personal: the colors suit the people who live there; the style of furniture reflects a particular taste; there are family pictures to remind all those who enter of the relationships that have created the home dwellers, now and in the past. If a family lives in the home, there are usually toys scattered about signaling play time; TV might be tuned into WB for the youth; the parents might be sitting at the kitchen table with a cup of coffee discussing the day. A home is centered on the people who live there. A home embraces not so much what the people do but who and how they are.

This Sunday's gospel is about an engaged couple, Mary and Joseph, who are about to make a home together. Joseph is in a quandary—his betrothed is pregnant, and not by him! We can only imagine his inner turmoil and his sense that his dream home has been smashed before he and his beloved ever move in together. For a carpenter who no doubt lovingly put personal touches into their new home, this must have been especially devastating.

Then the absolutely unexpected happens: an angel appears and reassures him—restoring his dream home. Responding to the angel's admonition not to be afraid, Joseph does more than take Mary into his home as a wife. He also is making a dwelling place for "Emmanuel . . . God is with us." At the center of this home will be the child not yet born (in the context of this gospel scene), but who is named "God with us" and revealed as the One who would "save his people from their sins." Salvation comes about because God is active in many and surprising ways. A virgin conceives. A husband is obedient to the message of his dreams. Here is the Gift that changes a house to a home.

This story, which begins with the yes of Joseph and Mary, continues through history with our yes to opening ourselves to God's dwelling among us. The birth of this child isn't simply a historical event that happened long ago but is a present experience of "God is with us." Though unnamed in the gospels, we are to be the Josephs who dream dreams and the Marys who give birth to this child who saves. "This is how the birth of Jesus [comes] about": *we* make a home for Emmanuel whenever we make a home for those around us. *We* are now to be the risen presence of Christ in our world, we are to make his gospel known, and we are to do all that God commands us too. This is how "God is with us." This is how we live, truly, in our dream home.

Living the Paschal Mystery

Christmas—the mystery of Emmanuel, "God is with us"—isn't a day or season on our calendars. It is the mystery of our making incarnate the God who loves us and saves us by our being obedient to God's will and living the presence of this Savior all year long. Each of us is God's betrothed overshadowed with the grace of the Holy Spirit. Each one of us carries within ourselves this "God is with us" and savior. Each of us has the capacity to embrace divine indwelling. Each of us is God's home.

Focusing the Gospel

Key words and phrases: Joseph . . . do not be afraid, take . . . into your home, Emmanuel

To the point: Responding to the angel's admonition not to be afraid, Joseph does more than take Mary into his home as a wife. He also is making a dwelling place for "Emmanuel . . . God is with us." This story, which begins with the yes of Joseph and Mary, continues through history with our yes to opening ourselves to God's dwelling among us.

Connecting the Gospel

to the second reading: Through Christ we receive the "grace of apostleship" and the "obedience of faith." Thus, like Joseph and Mary, we are enabled to become the dwelling place of Emmanuel, God with us.

to experience: Approaching the Christmas mystery, we too must heed the angel's invitation. In the ongoing story of Jesus' presence in the world, each of us must continually choose to receive him into our home and into our heart.

Connecting the Responsorial Psalm

to the readings: The readings and responsorial psalm for this Sunday reveal that everything we have comes to us from God: "the earth and its fullness" (psalm); God's presence even when not asked for (first reading); all grace, peace, and holiness (second reading); and above all, the very gift of Jesus, Savior and Emmanuel (gospel). We can ascend to God (psalm) because God so continuously and graciously descends to us (the readings). For our part we need only turn our hearts away from whatever is vain (psalm), in other words, from whatever outside of God is mistakenly perceived to be the source of life and satisfaction (even when, as in the first reading, that masquerades as piety). Let us, like Mary and Joseph, open our hearts so that the Lord may enter.

to psalmist preparation: As you prepare to sing this responsorial psalm, spend some time reflecting on when your heart turns to God and when your heart turns away from God to what is "vain." Who or what helps you get your heart back on track so that God may enter in?

**ASSEMBLY &
FAITH-SHARING GROUPS**
- The birth of Jesus Christ comes about *in me* whenever . . .
- To receive Jesus into my "home," I need to . . .
- My life witnesses to *Emmanuel* ("God is with us") whenever I . . .

PRESIDERS
My preaching opens others to welcome Emmanuel, "God is with us," whenever . . .

DEACONS
My service flows from the Emmanuel dwelling within my home/heart whenever . . .

HOSPITALITY MINISTERS
My hospitality incarnates for the gathering assembly "God is with us" whenever I . . .

MUSIC MINISTERS
I experience "God is with us" in my music ministry when . . .

ALTAR MINISTERS
Joseph set aside *his* plans to serve Mary. Some personal plans I need to set aside to better serve others are . . .

LECTORS
The prophet Isaiah challenged Ahaz to be open to God's sign, but he resisted. How I usually receive the challenge to remain open to God is . . . ; I am most likely to resist when . . .

**EXTRAORDINARY MINISTERS
OF HOLY COMMUNION**
Eucharist announces and makes present *Emmanuel*, "God is with us." My daily life is a living Eucharist for others whenever I . . .

Model Act of Penitence

Presider: In today's gospel, an angel invites Joseph to take Mary into his home. Let us set aside the busyness of this season and make room in our hearts to welcome Christ's presence in word and sacrament . . . [pause]

Lord Jesus, you were conceived in Mary by the Holy Spirit: Lord . . .

Christ Jesus, you are Emmanuel, "God is with us": Christ . . .

Lord Jesus, you dwelt in the home of Joseph and now dwell in our hearts: Lord . . .

Homily Points

• In most cases, putting up the Christmas decorations in our home necessitates moving things around. Furniture is moved to accommodate the Christmas tree. The buffet is cleared off to make room for a seasonal centerpiece. Our schedules are shifted to have the time to prepare our homes for Christmas. So it is with preparing our hearts for the coming of Emmanuel. We've got some shifting to do.

• Imagine the shifting in his life that Joseph had to do! He said yes to taking as his wife a woman already pregnant. He said yes to a new in-breaking of God's presence. He said yes to going wherever God called him. The continuation of the story demands that our own yes to God be no less expansive and expensive.

• Our own continuing the story is expansive in these ways: our expectations of what God wants of us are stretched; God's call comes to us in surprising modes; God's presence is sometimes encountered through the most unlikely people. Each of these shifts costs an expenditure of the heart—a self-giving surrender to the mystery of God's desire to dwell within and among us.

Model Prayer of the Faithful

Presider: Let us pray for our needs to the God who dwells within us.

Response:

Cantor:

That the church always proclaim the good news of the abiding presence of "God is with us" . . . [pause]

That all peoples of the world respond yes to whatever God asks . . . [pause]

That those without a dwelling place find warmth and comfort . . . [pause]

That each of us generously expend our hearts for the good of others . . . [pause]

Presider: God who dwells within, your presence brings us confidence and courage: hear these our prayers that one day we might enjoy everlasting glory with you. Grant this through that same Son, Jesus Christ our Lord. **Amen.**

OPENING PRAYER

Let us pray
[as Advent draws to a close, that Christ will truly come into our hearts]

Pause for silent prayer

Lord,
fill our hearts with your love,
and as you revealed to us by an angel
the coming of your Son as man,
so lead us through his suffering and death
to the glory of his resurrection,
for he lives and reigns with you and the Holy Spirit,
one God, for ever and ever. **Amen.**

FIRST READING
Isa 7:10-14

The LORD spoke to Ahaz, saying:
    Ask for a sign from the LORD, your God;
    let it be deep as the netherworld, or high
        as the sky!
But Ahaz answered,
    "I will not ask! I will not tempt the
        LORD!"
Then Isaiah said:
    Listen, O house of David!
Is it not enough for you to weary people,
    must you also weary my God?
Therefore the Lord himself will give you
        this sign:
    the virgin shall conceive, and bear a son,
    and shall name him Emmanuel.

RESPONSORIAL PSALM
Ps 24:1-2, 3-4, 5-6

R⁊. (7c and 10b) Let the Lord enter; he is king of glory.

The LORD's are the earth and its fullness;
    the world and those who dwell in it.
For he founded it upon the seas
    and established it upon the rivers.

R⁊. Let the Lord enter; he is king of glory.

Who can ascend the mountain of the LORD?
    or who may stand in his holy place?
One whose hands are sinless, whose heart
    is clean,
    who desires not what is vain.

R⁊. Let the Lord enter; he is king of glory.

He shall receive a blessing from the LORD,
    a reward from God his savior.
Such is the race that seeks for him,
    that seeks the face of the God of Jacob.

R⁊. Let the Lord enter; he is king of glory.

SECOND READING
Rom 1:1-7

Paul, a slave of Christ Jesus,
    called to be an apostle and set apart for
        the gospel of God,
    which he promised previously through
        his prophets in the holy Scriptures,
the gospel about his Son, descended from
        David according to the flesh,
    but established as Son of God in power
    according to the Spirit of holiness
    through resurrection from the dead,
        Jesus Christ our Lord.
Through him we have received the grace
    of apostleship,
    to bring about the obedience of faith,
    for the sake of his name, among all the
        Gentiles,
    among whom are you also, who are
        called to belong to Jesus Christ;
to all the beloved of God in Rome, called
    to be holy.
Grace to you and peace from God our
    Father
    and the Lord Jesus Christ.

About Liturgy

Advent expecting: The General Norms for the Liturgical Year and the Calendar simply describe Advent as "a period for devout and joyful expectation" (no. 39). Naturally, with this Fourth Sunday of Advent our expectation is heightened. Christmas is almost here! Yet we can so easily fool ourselves; once Christmas Day arrives we might think our expectation is ended. Actually, it's only begun!

Christian living is characterized by expectation: Christ continually comes in the most unexpected ways. Jesus' birth so long ago unleashed a new and startling presence of God in our midst. Since that time our expectation never ceases: we live for Christ's comings. The surprise of the Good News of salvation is that God comes to dwell among us, to be at home with us. Our wildest dreams, our most heartfelt expectations are fulfilled in the birth of this Savior, Emmanuel, "God is with us."

Christmas environment: During the day on Christmas Eve the sacred space will be prepared for the celebration of the incarnation. One principle to keep in mind is that this is a *sacred* space. Department store decorations may be beautiful in our living rooms, but generally this is not what enhances our sacred space so that the assembly can truly be drawn into the mystery we celebrate. Simple colors and fresh greens that speak to us of the new life that was given birth not just two thousand years ago but again and again within us are far more fitting. Lights can be effective since this is the season when we celebrate the Light come into the world to dispel darkness. But, again, our sacred space ought not compete with our neighborhoods for the best-decorated house! A million lights won't do it; we only really need one Light.

About Liturgical Music

Music suggestions: Three hymns well suited for this Sunday are "Lift Up Your Heads, O Mighty Gates"; "Let All Mortal Flesh Keep Silence"; and "Savior of the Nations, Come." The first is based on the responsorial psalm of the day (Ps 24) and sings about our hearts open wide to receive Christ. Its strong 4/4 meter makes it appropriate for the entrance procession. The text of the second, from the fourth-century Liturgy of St. James, interrelates Christ's transcendence and his fleshly incarnation. The modal melody conveys a mystical quality that fits the text. This hymn could be sung either at the preparation of the gifts or during Communion. The text of the third hymn was originally ascribed to St. Ambrose (4th c.) and now appears in many variations. Its style and meter would be appropriate for the entrance, the preparation of the gifts, or the recessional.

Season of Christmas

Blessed be He Whom
our mouth cannot adequately praise . . .
For praise Him as we may, it is too little.
But since it is useless
to be silent and to constrain ourselves,
may our feebleness excuse
such praise as we can give.

—St. Ephraim the Syrian
Nineteen Hymns on the Nativity of Christ in the Flesh
Hymn II

SPIRITUALITY

The Vigil Mass

GOSPEL ACCLAMATION

R⁷. Alleluia, alleluia.
Tomorrow the wickedness of the earth
    will be destroyed:
the Savior of the world will reign over us.
R⁷. Alleluia, alleluia.

Gospel

Matt 1:1-25; L13ABC

The book of the genealogy of
    Jesus Christ,
  the son of David, the son of
    Abraham.

Abraham became the father of
    Isaac,
  Isaac the father of Jacob,
  Jacob the father of Judah and
    his brothers.
Judah became the father of Perez and
    Zerah,
  whose mother was Tamar.
Perez became the father of Hezron,
  Hezron the father of Ram,
  Ram the father of Amminadab.
Amminadab became the father of
    Nahshon,
  Nahshon the father of Salmon,
  Salmon the father of Boaz,
  whose mother was Rahab.
Boaz became the father of Obed,
  whose mother was Ruth.
Obed became the father of Jesse,
  Jesse the father of David the king.

Continued in Appendix A, p. 264,
or Matt 1:18-25 in Appendix A, p. 265.

See Appendix A, p. 265, for the other readings.

Reflecting on the Gospel and Living the Paschal Mystery

Key words and phrases: became the father of, was born Jesus, name him Jesus, did as the angel of the Lord had commanded him, named him Jesus

To the point: This Savior whose birth we celebrate ushers in a new story for humankind, one that tells of changed relationships that are made possible by the mystery of the incarnation, the story we remember this day. With the incarnation there is a new marriage of divinity and humanity, of heaven and earth. There is a new family. And we are part of that family of God.

Reflection: Of all times of the year, perhaps Christmas is the most cherished "family time." People travel from far and near to get together. And when they do, often it is to talk about the "good old days," or to talk about relatives of years gone by, or to talk about missing those who could not be present. Whatever the conversation, one thing is clear: these gatherings are hardly silent! The children are running around having a boisterous good time with their cousins; the adults are moving from circle to circle chattering up a storm. Talk, talk, talk is the order of the day. It would be unthinkable to gather as a family and then be silent! Stories are always part of a holiday family gathering; and, sometimes, when it's a really, really good family story, even the children come drifting in one by one to listen. There is a kind of silent, awed attention as details are relayed and the story unfolds.

The readings for this Vigil Mass of Christmas tell a story and include a lot of talking, too, among members of the extended family of Israel. In fact, the first reading opens with the strong declaration, "I will not be silent . . . I will not be quiet"! This Scripture talk, however, is quite focused: it is about naming. The gospel twice mentions that Mary and Joseph will name their first-born Son "Jesus." As the second reading intimates, this is no ordinary name. It means "savior," and "he will save his people from their sins" (gospel).

This Savior whose birth we celebrate ushers in a new story for humankind, one that tells of changed relationships that are made possible by the mystery of the incarnation, the story we remember this day. As the first reading says, we "shall be called by a new name" that God speaks. The new name reflects so well sentiments of this festival: joy ("My Delight") and family intimacy ("Espoused"). With the incarnation there is a new marriage of divinity and humanity, of heaven and earth. There is a new family. And we are part of that family of God.

As we well know, family membership has its demands. The readings remind us not only of our new name but also of how we remain faithful to the family name we inherit from God. Jesus was born in the lineage of David, who was a great king because he was "a man after [God's] own heart" and carried out God's will (see second reading). The gospel tells of the righteousness of Joseph, who turns from divorcing Mary to receiving her into his home, "as the angel of the Lord had commanded him."

To carry a family name proudly, one must be obedient to the values and laws of the family. We proudly carry our divine family name—Christian—and we, like David and Joseph and Mary, are called to be obedient to God's values and laws. In this way is Jesus truly our Savior, and the Savior of all the world.

SPIRITUALITY

Mass at Midnight

GOSPEL ACCLAMATION
Luke 2:10-11

R. Alleluia, alleluia.
I proclaim to you good news of
     great joy:
today a Savior is born for us,
Christ the Lord.
R. Alleluia, alleluia.

Gospel

Luke 2:1-14; L14ABC

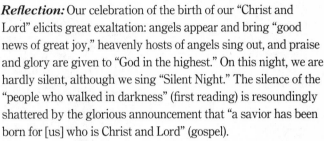

In those days a decree
     went out from Caesar
     Augustus
   that the whole world
     should be enrolled.
This was the first enrollment,
   when Quirinius was governor of
     Syria.
So all went to be enrolled, each to his
     own town.
And Joseph too went up from Galilee
     from the town of Nazareth
   to Judea, to the city of David that is
     called Bethlehem,
   because he was of the house and
     family of David,
   to be enrolled with Mary, his
     betrothed, who was with child.
While they were there,
   the time came for her to have her
     child,
   and she gave birth to her firstborn
     son.
She wrapped him in swaddling clothes
     and laid him in a manger,
   because there was no room for them
     in the inn.

Continued in Appendix A, p. 266.

See Appendix A, p. 266, for the other readings.

Reflecting on the Gospel and Living the Paschal Mystery
Key words and phrases: Christ and Lord, infant . . . in a manger

To the point: Though the angel reveals the exalted status of Jesus as "Christ and Lord," he is actually born humbly as an "infant . . . in a manger." Ironically, the humblest of God's instruments, humanity, becomes the means of accomplishing God's greatest deed—salvation.

Reflection: Our celebration of the birth of our "Christ and Lord" elicits great exaltation: angels appear and bring "good news of great joy," heavenly hosts of angels sing out, and praise and glory are given to "God in the highest." On this night, we are hardly silent, although we sing "Silent Night." The silence of the "people who walked in darkness" (first reading) is resoundingly shattered by the glorious announcement that "a savior has been born for [us] who is Christ and Lord" (gospel).

Though the angel reveals the exalted status of Jesus as "Christ and Lord," he is actually born humbly as an "infant . . . in a manger." In the silence of the night was born this Savior who, by giving "himself for us to deliver us" (second reading), showed through the silence of poverty and unassuming lowliness how we might become a people "eager to do what is good" (second reading). Ironically, the humblest of God's instruments, humanity, becomes the means of accomplishing God's greatest deed—salvation.

The angel proclaims to the shepherds that "a savior has been born for" us. Even on Christmas—that great feast of joy and light and glory, and shouting out in the silence of God's gift—we cannot dwell only in lofty heights. We are reminded that this child has come to be Savior. We ourselves are now to be the sign of God's gift and we are so when we "do what is good." The goodness we do is a reflection of God's blessings and goodness toward us. Our very actions for the sake of others are proclamations of the "good news of great joy" that the birth of this child brings.

Doing what is good can be something so simple as sitting back and truly reveling in the joy of the children at this magical time of the year. It can be taking some extra time with them to build up their fragile and forming egos so that they can grow to full stature as children of God. It can be searching out the shy person who stands off alone at a Christmas party and engaging him or her in conversation. It can be doing more for the poor than throwing money in the Salvation Army buckets, perhaps by spending some time at a soup kitchen or visiting a lonely elder.

The silence of poverty, despair, darkness, gloom, and isolation that we hear and read about in our broken world is only broken by each one of us doing the kind of good that shouts out God's glory. Christmas is to be a joyous celebration, to be sure. But it also stands as a reminder that this infant born in such lowly estate is a Savior who makes possible the joy and peace that come only from doing good for others. Christmas happens every day that we ourselves incarnate God's love and goodness, light and joy, judgment and justice. The incarnation pledges that God dwells among us, and we are a sign of that presence in whatever good we do.

Surely God's greatest deed is salvation—and what a privilege it is for humanity to share in this great deed! No wonder on this night we break the silence: our joy cannot be contained at the wonder of the gift that God has given to us.

✠ SPIRITUALITY

Mass at Dawn

GOSPEL ACCLAMATION
Luke 2:14

℟. Alleluia, alleluia.
Glory to God in the
     highest,
and on earth peace to
     those
on whom his favor rests.
℟. Alleluia, alleluia.

Gospel

Luke 2:15-20; L15ABC

When the angels
     went away from them to heaven,
     the shepherds said to one another,
     "Let us go, then, to Bethlehem
     to see this thing that has taken place,
     which the Lord has made known to
          us."
So they went in haste and found Mary
     and Joseph,
     and the infant lying in the manger.
When they saw this,
     they made known the message
     that had been told them about this
          child.
All who heard it were amazed
     by what had been told them by the
          shepherds.
And Mary kept all these things,
     reflecting on them in her heart.
Then the shepherds returned,
     glorifying and praising God
     for all they had heard and seen,
     just as it had been told to them.

See Appendix A, p. 267, for the other readings.

Reflecting on the Gospel and Living the Paschal Mystery

Key words and phrases: angels went away, Let us go, went in haste, made known the message, glorifying and praising God

To the point: The shepherds could not keep silent because of the amazement of what happened to them. God's *angels* spoke to *them*! This happening cannot be contained. This message must be told, now as then. This "glorifying and praising God" must be shouted, now as then. So, we are now the shepherds who do the announcing and praising.

Reflection: Teachers have sometimes been known to confess that when they are asked a question to which they don't know the answer, they make up one. Truth be told, many of us probably do something similar on occasion. When we hear these Christmas gospels proclaimed, we might think that either the gospel writers had great imaginations or were surely making all this up. Who can believe that angels appear to humans? Who can imagine that scruffy shepherds leave their flocks to find some infant and are led to prayer? Who can envisage a baby being born in an animal trough? Surely, such preposterous details are the fodder of a great story.

Yet these gospels we hear are not merely stories. They are the wondrous proclamation of God's "kindness and generous love" (second reading) and the promise that we might "become heirs in hope of eternal life." They are the concrete expression of God's mighty deeds on our behalf. In hindsight, after over two millennia of realizing the import of the message the shepherds "made known," each year during our Christmas celebrations we are given another opportunity to be reawakened to the reality that all the imagination in the world cannot serve to capture this mystery. And so each year we celebrate again God's mercy bestowed upon us in faith and joy, with the imagination and mirth of little children.

If we could reimagine the Christmas story from our twenty-first century perspective, what might it look and sound like? Would we be willing to be the angel to announce to outcasts—the poor, imprisoned, downtrodden, those who suffer injustice, those who are hungry and deprived of life's necessities, those who do not meet our expectations of religious, social, economic, sexual status—that God has come among us? Would we leave our responsibilities—family, workplace, social engagements—to search for the most helpless among us with the enthusiasm and hope of those given a great gift? Would we be willing to recognize in the homeless or uneducated or powerless the presence of our saving God?

"All who heard" the shepherds' message "were amazed." Here is the utter amazement about which the gospel speaks: in the simplicity of who and what is familiar, in who and what is happening all around us, our amazing God is present. This Christmas gospel reminds us that God speaks in and through anyone at all. No one is excluded from being presented with God's message of kindness, generosity, and mercy.

The shepherds could not keep silent because of the amazement of what happened to them. God's *angels* spoke to *them*! This happening cannot be contained. This message must be told, now as then. This "glorifying and praising God" must be shouted, now as then. So, we are now the shepherds who do the announcing and praising. We are the shepherds who proclaim "to the ends of the earth" (first reading), to anyone and everyone, that God's graceful presence is not only among us but within us.

✢ SPIRITUALITY

Mass during the Day

GOSPEL ACCLAMATION
R̴. Alleluia, alleluia.
A holy day has dawned upon us.
Come, you nations, and adore the Lord.
For today a great light has come upon the earth.
R̴. Alleluia, alleluia.

Gospel

John 1:1-18; L16ABC

In the beginning was the Word,
　　and the Word was with God,
　　and the Word was God.
He was in the beginning with God.
All things came to be through him,
　　and without him nothing came to be.
What came to be through him was life,
　　and this life was the light of the
　　　　human race;
the light shines in the darkness,
　　and the darkness has not
　　　　overcome it.

A man named John was sent from God.
He came for testimony, to testify to the
　　light,
　　so that all might believe through him.
He was not the light,
　　but came to testify to the light.

Continued in Appendix A, p. 267,
or John 1:1-5, 9-14 in Appendix A, p. 267.

See Appendix A, p. 268, for the other readings.

Reflecting on the Gospel and Living the Paschal Mystery

Key words and phrases: life was the light, the light shines, true light, we saw his glory

To the point: As Jesus is the light of the world, so it is with us. If the darkness is not to overcome the light, then we ourselves must be that light, revealing God's truth and glory. This gospel seems to lack the imaginative details of other Christmas gospels. At the same time it announces what no one could imagine: "From [God's] fullness we have all received."

Reflection: Christmas morning is a joy for all, but it is especially so for little children. They come running into where the Christmas tree is piled with gifts, and their faces light up with a transparency that breaks the silence of waiting and shouts out expectation and excitement. At church these same little faces might light up with the otherworldly fascination of the crèche, the blare of trumpets and tingle of bells, the lights and greetings and silent awe of the Christmas prayer. The alternative opening prayer for the Mass during the Day says it all: "Make us a people of this light."

The gospel for this Mass lacks the imaginative details of the other Christmas gospels. Rather than angels appearing to shepherds, we have the adult John testifying to the adult Jesus, the "true light . . . coming into the world." Rather than a newborn infant lying in a manger, we have the exalted Word whose sound brought forth creation and life at the beginning, before there was even time. Rather than the darkness of deep night and an inglorious birth, we have the very glory of God incarnated within and among us. Yet the details of this gospel are without equal, unparalleled in the wildest imagination, as unthinkable as the most outlandish story. This gospel reveals not only the Son who was begotten by the Holy Spirit (see second reading) but also the Son who is King (see first reading) and through whom we are able to see God. No human imagination can make up such details! No human storytelling can equal the great story of salvation God announces to us this day!

Light enables us to see. It is so easy for us to have light today: pay our electric bill, and flip the switch; put kindling in the fireplace, and light a match; flick a lighter, and light a candle. But this light of human making only lets us see what is right before us. The gospel tells of another light, one over which we have no control. This Light enables us to "see" the "refulgence of [God's] glory" (second reading); indeed, it enables us to "see" the God who has been revealed to us through Christ Jesus.

As Jesus is the light of the world, so it is with us. If the darkness is not to overcome the light, then we ourselves must be that light, revealing God's truth and glory. This gospel announces what no one could imagine: "From [God's] fullness we have all received." Because we have been graced, we ourselves are the light of the world. We ourselves—by our goodness and truth—announce to the whole world that the Word made flesh dwells among us.

Far from living in an imaginary world, this gospel calls us to the stark reality of all too much darkness and the responsibility to bring light so others can see clearly and truthfully; it calls us to the awesome reality that in coming to dwell among us, the Word-Light dwells-shines within us; it calls us to the glory of being called "children of God." As with children taken up in awe and excitement, let that light radiate from our faces pure joy.

Model Act of Penitence

Presider: We gather in awe to pause at so wondrous a mystery, that the Son of God becomes one with us. Let us raise grateful hearts to God, and open ourselves to the mystery before us . . . [pause]

Lord Jesus, you were born the Savior, Christ and Lord: Lord . . .

Christ Jesus, your appearance fills the whole world with glory: Christ . . .

Lord Jesus, you are the eternal Word born in a humble manger: Lord . . .

Model Prayer of the Faithful

Presider: With hearts brimming with joy we lift our prayers to our wondrous God.

Response:

Cantor:

That the church always bring joy and peace to a world still laboring in darkness . . . [pause]

That all peoples of the world share equitably in the abundant gifts of God . . . [pause]

That the poor, lonely, and weary be lifted up by the glory and joy of this holy Christmas . . . [pause]

That each of us here respect and love in each other the divine life that we share . . . [pause]

Presider: Glorious God of salvation, you sent your Son to be born of Mary and dwell among us: hear these our prayers that we may one day share in your everlasting glory. We ask this through our Savior Jesus who is Christ and Lord. **Amen**.

FOR REFLECTION
• What brings me to silence and awe when I ponder the Christmas mystery is . . .
• Light and peace radiate from me when . . . I am drawn to share this with others by . . .
• The parts of the Christmas story that elicit great joy in me are . . . ; ways I share this joy with others are . . .

Homily Points

• Children love stories, especially when they are read to them. They never seem to grow tired of a story, even when it is read to them over and over. We hear the Christmas story over and over. Yet, what we hear is not the *same* story. The Christmas story must be heard and lived anew in our lives every day.

• The Christmas story tells of Joseph doing as the Lord commands him, of angels appearing and announcing the glory of the Lord, of shepherds making haste to adore the babe in a manger, of the Word made flesh and dwelling among us.

• This story is ever new when we hear it as *our* story, with fresh insight into how we, in our everyday lives, do as God commands, announce the glory of the Lord, make haste to discover where Christ is to be found, and open ourselves to the Word dwelling within us.

✢ SPIRITUALITY

GOSPEL ACCLAMATION
Col 3:15a, 16a

℟. Alleluia, alleluia.
Let the peace of Christ control your hearts;
let the word of Christ dwell in you richly.
℟. Alleluia, alleluia.

Gospel   Matt 2:13-15, 19-23; L17A

When the magi had departed,
    behold,
    the angel of the Lord appeared to
        Joseph in a dream and said,
    "Rise, take the child and his
        mother, flee to Egypt,
    and stay there until I tell you.
Herod is going to search for the
    child to destroy him."
Joseph rose and took the child and his
    mother by night
    and departed for Egypt.
He stayed there until the death of Herod,
    that what the Lord had said through
        the prophet might be fulfilled,
    Out of Egypt I called my son.

When Herod had died, behold,
    the angel of the Lord appeared in a
        dream
    to Joseph in Egypt and said,
    "Rise, take the child and his mother
        and go to the land of Israel,
    for those who sought the child's life
        are dead."
He rose, took the child and his mother,
    and went to the land of Israel.
But when he heard that Archelaus was
    ruling over Judea
    in place of his father Herod,
    he was afraid to go back there.
And because he had been warned in a
    dream,
    he departed for the region of Galilee.
He went and dwelt in a town called
    Nazareth,
    so that what had been spoken through
        the prophets might be fulfilled,
    He shall be called a Nazorean.

Reflecting on the Gospel

Seating around a family dinner table is always interesting. And when there is extended family present, it is even more interesting. Adam, Hugh, and Alex all want to sit next to Grandpa, but he has only two sides! Tricia wants to sit next to her favorite aunt, but so do Tasha and Sid. Somehow, someone has the wisdom to sort this out and everyone gets seated. While sometimes arguments can break out over who sits next to whom, this is also a very warming scene. Wanting to "sit next to" is an expression of a loving relationship where admiration is met with respect, need is met with care, desire is met with responsiveness. These are really the best times for our families—when love is shown and trust is forged.

Much about our family life today (especially as presented by the media) reminds us of sorrow and struggles, difficulties and hardships. At first glance this feast might be discouraging for some: how can the holy family of Jesus, Mary, and Joseph be a model when they were all so obviously graced by God? Indeed, the child is the Son of God! Nevertheless, this gospel story shows that this holy family underwent distress and peril too. Twice in the gospel God sends an angel to command Joseph, "Rise, take the child and his mother . . ." Alert and listening, Joseph perceived the danger threatening his family and acted to protect them.

In this is holiness: listening for God's voice, heeding whatever God asks of us, and acting faithfully for the good and well-being of others. Holiness, then, doesn't mean the absence of difficulties and tension (if so, who would be holy?) but the willingness to grow in our ability to hear God's directions for our lives. God takes the initiative in guiding us so that the divine plan for our holiness is fulfilled. We need to be alert to listen and respond.

Following God's initiative and doing God's will isn't something automatic or mindless. We won't have dreams in which an angel speaks God's will to us clearly. Most of us have to discern God's will in the myriad of motives and circumstances that surround our everyday lives. If we practice the virtues extolled in the first two readings we will have the ground from which to discern good choices for doing God's will. Living virtuously is already a discernment of God's will. This is how we are holy: being open to God's initiatives and responding with graciousness and courage.

Living the Paschal Mystery

Shortly after birth this newborn child is caught in controversy and difficulties—a foreshadowing of his whole life. This gospel account clearly lays out for us that the kingdom of this world is already, at Jesus' birth, at odds with the kingdom of God. Already we see the death/resurrection conflict of the mystery that defines Jesus' life, and our own life as baptized disciples.

Our motivation for seeking holiness as a family and caring for, forgiving, loving, teaching, and admonishing one another is that God always does this for us. We are not asked to extend to each other what God hasn't already extended to us. Our dying to self is modeled first by Jesus; the new life of holiness is his gift to us.

Focusing the Gospel

Key words and phrases: angel of the Lord appeared; Rise, take the child and his mother; angel of the Lord appeared

To the point: Twice in the gospel God sends an angel to command Joseph, "Rise, take the child and his mother . . ." Alert and listening, Joseph perceived the danger threatening his family and acted to protect them. In this is holiness: listening for God's voice, heeding whatever God asks of us, and acting faithfully for the good and well-being of others.

Connecting the Gospel

to the first two readings: The first two readings present us with the best-case scenario of how holy families might live. But, realistically, many people experience family life otherwise. Holiness doesn't mean the absence of difficulties and tensions but the willingness to grow in our ability to care for, to forgive, to love, to teach, and to admonish one another.

to experience: Holiness is not a matter of achieving perfection or flawlessness. It is our continual growth in being open to God's presence and our willingness to respond to divine overtures.

Connecting the Responsorial Psalm

to the readings: The patriarchal context of Psalm 128 is off-putting to us who live in modern Western culture. But we must look beneath its patriarchal imagery to its promise of blessedness for all people who live according to the way of God. Living God's way means reverencing our parents throughout all the stages of their lives (first reading). It means bearing compassion and patience toward one another, offering forgiveness to those who have hurt us, and remaining faithful to the word of Christ (second reading). It means discerning the will of God for our lives, no matter the form of its deliverance or the level of self-sacrifice demanded (gospel). As Psalm 128 indicates, choosing to live in such a way will bear fruit not only for ourselves and our immediate family but for all the people of God.

to psalmist preparation: In this responsorial psalm you sing about families related by blood and about the family of the church related by baptism. How does your fidelity to God shape your family relationships? How does it shape your relationship with the church?

**ASSEMBLY &
FAITH-SHARING GROUPS**
- For me, holiness means . . .
- Joseph's example of being alert and listening helps me in my family life in that . . .
- What this gospel tells me about God is . . . ; times I have witnessed God's saving hand in my family's life are . . .

PRESIDERS
My preaching helps the assembly be alert and listen to the way God speaks to them when . . .

DEACONS
My diaconal ministry has enriched my family's holiness by . . . ; my own family's struggle with the call to holiness has shaped my diaconal service by . . .

HOSPITALITY MINISTERS
My greeting alerts others to their holiness when . . .

MUSIC MINISTERS
One way my participation in the ministry of music has helped me relate more fully to my family is . . .

ALTAR MINISTERS
In *becoming* a better servant (see second reading), the one virtue that I need to work on the most is . . . ; one way for me to develop this virtue this week would be . . .

LECTORS
My proclamation of the word alerts the members of the assembly to God's direction for my life when . . .

**EXTRAORDINARY MINISTERS
OF HOLY COMMUNION**
My distribution of Holy Communion unites me more fully to the family of the church by . . .

Model Act of Penitence

Presider: The Holy Family of Jesus, Mary, and Joseph faced hardship and danger in their lives, yet remained open to God's faithful presence and guidance. Let us prepare ourselves for this liturgy by asking God to guide us along the path of holiness . . . [pause]

Lord Jesus, you are the Word dwelling within us and calling us to holiness: Lord . . .

Christ Jesus, you are the Peace that controls our hearts: Christ . . .

Lord Jesus, you unite us as one family in the Body of Christ: Lord . . .

Homily Points

• We encounter every day many things that alert us to danger: smoke alarms, media weather alerts, emergency vehicle sirens; coughs, hives, fevers; warning labels on various bottles. The signals in themselves don't protect us; we must respond to their warnings appropriately. To ignore danger signals can result in serious harm and even death.

• What are some of the signals God sends us to which we must respond? Sometimes these come through another person's interventions and observations. Sometimes they come from our own awareness that something is amiss in our lives. The signals are always there; we, like Joseph, must be alert and responsive.

• Holiness is not defined by a perfect life but by a responsive one. To be holy is to perceive the reality of our situation, interpret this in the light of God's perspective, and act in the direction of what is right and good for ourselves and others.

Model Prayer of the Faithful

Presider: Let us bring our prayers to the God who abides with us, cares for us, and guides us.

Response:

Lord, hear our prayer.

Cantor:

we pray to the Lord,

That the family of the church always be alert and listen to God's call to holiness . . . [pause]

That the family of nations live in peace and harmony, and provide justly for all . . . [pause]

That the poor and neglected of our human family receive care and protection . . . [pause]

That our families grow in holiness by our care for each other . . . [pause]

Presider: Ever-faithful God, you call us to grow in holiness: hear these our prayers that one day we might enjoy everlasting happiness with you. We ask this through Christ our Lord. **Amen.**

℞. Blessed are those who fear the Lord and walk in his ways.

Your wife shall be like a fruitful vine
in the recesses of your home;
your children like olive plants
around your table.

℞. Blessed are those who fear the Lord and walk in his ways.

Behold, thus is the man blessed
who fears the LORD.
The LORD bless you from Zion:
may you see the prosperity of Jerusalem
all the days of your life.

℞. Blessed are those who fear the Lord and walk in his ways.

SECOND READING
Col 3:12-21

Brothers and sisters:
Put on, as God's chosen ones, holy and
beloved,
heartfelt compassion, kindness,
humility, gentleness, and patience,
bearing with one another and forgiving
one another,
if one has a grievance against another;
as the Lord has forgiven you, so must
you also do.
And over all these put on love,
that is, the bond of perfection.
And let the peace of Christ control your
hearts,
the peace into which you were also
called in one body.
And be thankful.
Let the word of Christ dwell in you richly,
as in all wisdom you teach and
admonish one another,
singing psalms, hymns, and spiritual
songs
with gratitude in your hearts to God.
And whatever you do, in word or in deed,
do everything in the name of the Lord
Jesus,
giving thanks to God the Father through
him.

Wives, be subordinate to your husbands,
as is proper in the Lord.
Husbands, love your wives,
and avoid any bitterness toward them.
Children, obey your parents in everything,
for this is pleasing to the Lord.
Fathers, do not provoke your children,
so they may not become discouraged.

or Col 3:12-17

See Appendix A, p. 268.

About Liturgy
Contextualizing Scripture: It is strongly recommended that the short form of the second reading be proclaimed. Even if verses 18 to 21 would be explained in a homily, the power of proclamation has already negatively affected a portion of the assembly. Joking about "Wives, be subordinate to your husbands" only makes matters worse and is demeaning and offensive. All Scripture must be placed in its original context. This means that we realize that Sacred Scripture was written at a particular time and in a particular place and the cultural and social mores of the time are reflected in the text. This doesn't mean that Sacred Scripture is in error; it *is* divinely inspired. However, Scripture's meaning must always be interpreted in terms of its divine message that cuts across time and cultures.

When interpreting Scripture, taking texts *literally* can often lead to misinterpretation. For a long time Catholics were discouraged from reading and praying Scripture for fear that they would misinterpret and be in error. Now we are encouraged to read and pray Scripture; if we are in question about a passage or how to interpret it, there are many fine commentaries available to guide us well.

About Liturgical Music
Music suggestions: Three hymns related directly to the Holy Family are Alan Hommerding's "Come, Sing a Home and Family" [PMB, WC, WS]; Thomas Troeger's "Our Savior's Infant Cries Were Heard" [HG]; and Mary Louise Bringle's "As Joseph Lay in Troubled Sleep" [in the GIA collection *Joy and Wonder, Love and Longing*]. In the first, concrete images show how the behavior of Mary and Joseph formed the adult who Jesus became (for example, "At Mary's table, Jesus learned to bless, give thanks, and eat, To welcome all as honored guests by washing weary feet"). This hymn would be appropriate either for the entrance procession or during the preparation of the gifts. In the second hymn we sing that God entrusted the child Jesus to human hands that we might see God's blessing upon "The care of children ev'rywhere—The bruised, the lost, the poor." This hymn would work well for the preparation of the gifts. The third hymn pays tribute to Joseph for his role in protecting the child Jesus. Using the imagery of dreams, the text moves from the troubled dreams leading Joseph to the parents of the slaughtered innocents who were "not warned by dreams"; to the "haunting dreams" that guided Jesus; to Jesus himself, "our dream that never dies." This hymn would fit well during the preparation of the gifts.

While not directly related to the feast of the Holy Family, Herman Stuempfle's "The Hills Are Still, the Darkness Deep" [found in the GIA collection *The Word Goes Forth*] is certainly related by implication. Once the celebrating surrounding Jesus' birth is over, the Holy Family faces danger and challenge. This hymn reminds us that when the glories of the Christmas season end, the daily demands of faithful living remain. When "duties fill the night, the day," we need only pray that grace will give "strength to heart and hand and will." This hymn would be suitable for the preparation of the gifts.

THE HOLY FAMILY OF JESUS, MARY, AND JOSEPH

SPIRITUALITY

GOSPEL ACCLAMATION
Heb 1:1-2

℟. Alleluia, alleluia.
In the past God spoke to our ancestors
    through the prophets;
in these last days, he has spoken to us
    through the Son.
℟. Alleluia, alleluia.

Gospel

Luke 2:16-21; L18ABC

**The shepherds went in haste to
    Bethlehem and found Mary and
    Joseph,
    and the infant lying in the
        manger.
When they saw this,
    they made known the message
    that had been told them about this
        child.
All who heard it were amazed
    by what had been told them by the
        shepherds.
And Mary kept all these things,
    reflecting on them in her heart.
Then the shepherds returned,
    glorifying and praising God
    for all they had heard and seen,
    just as it had been told to them.**

**When eight days were completed for
    his circumcision,
    he was named Jesus, the name given
        him by the angel
    before he was conceived in the
        womb.**

See Appendix A, p. 269, for the other readings.

Reflecting on the Gospel

On January 20, 2009, the largest crowd ever to gather on the National Mall witnessed the new president being sworn into office. Reporters interviewed people who had stood since five o'clock that morning in the sub-zero weather in a checkpoint line to assure they would get a place on the mall. One reporter focused on a busload of high schoolers who had traveled all night only to have the power go out at their checkpoint so they never made it to the mall. Typical of youth, they were undaunted and were moved by just being there. This was an important historical moment focused on a younger president who promised change. One charismatic man can surely draw crowds and bring out harmony and a sense of unity.

The person at the center of this feast day is Mary, but the gospel includes many other players in this Christmas story: Joseph, the infant, shepherds, all who heard the shepherds' message, an angel. Born "of a woman" (second reading), Jesus is a man born for all. He inspires all to lives of reflection, proclamation, and praise. Rather than a crowd of two million gathered to witness an oath, Jesus has drawn countless millions throughout the centuries to him—not to witness an oath but to witness an unprecedented self-giving that promised an unprecedented harmony and unity.

Many a day Mary must have stood at a window in her little house in Nazareth and watched her son play or work and wondered what would become of all this, continuing to think about it as she went about her daily chores. Already Mary was a model for Jesus of reflective self-giving for the good of another. Mary not only models for us faithful, fruitful, reflective motherhood but she also models for us the blessings of being daughters and sons of God. Mary's reflecting in her heart on all that had happened to her simply opened her heart to Jesus and, through him, to all of humanity. Mary is truly the mother of God. She is also our mother and, like a good mother, shows us how we are to live so that we can grow to full stature as sons and daughters of God. Mary leads us to her son Jesus, a man born for all.

Living the Paschal Mystery

Mary faced a great mystery she could not understand, reflected on God's will for her, and became the mother of the Savior; we face many challenges during life, must ponder God's will for us, and become children of God (see second reading). Mary's whole being proclaimed the goodness of God; we proclaim God's blessing upon us (see first reading) by choosing to do good. Mary glorified God by offering her body as a dwelling for the Son; we praise God by our own self-giving.

The name Jesus (= Savior) already points to a life of self-giving and suffering that Mary as Jesus' mother will also experience. The surprise suggested by the first two readings is that we who are God's children (second reading) also participate in this experience of self-giving and suffering; this is how we receive blessing (first reading).

The yes all of us must make to do God's will necessarily means that we cannot escape dying to ourselves. We are assured in this feast's readings, however, that we are given the grace to place ourselves in God's hands and do God's will, and in this we receive further abundant blessings. All we need is to remember that Jesus is a man born for all.

Focusing the Gospel

Key words and phrases: shepherds, Mary, Joseph, infant, made known the message, all who heard, reflecting, praising, angel

To the point: The person at the center of this feast day is Mary, but the gospel includes many other players in this Christmas story: Joseph, the infant, shepherds, all who heard the shepherds' message, an angel. Born "of a woman" (second reading), Jesus is a man born for all. He inspires all to lives of reflection, proclamation, and praise.

Model Act of Penitence

Presider: On this day when we begin our new civil year, let us open ourselves to Mary as a model of life focused on the divine Son . . . [pause]

Lord Jesus, you are the Son of God and the Son of Mary: Lord . . .
Christ Jesus, your birth gives glory and praise to the Father: Christ . . .
Lord Jesus, you are the Savior of the world: Lord . . .

Model Prayer of the Faithful

Presider: We pray now to God, that our year be prosperous and peaceful.

Response:

Lord, hear our prayer.

Cantor:

we pray to the Lord,

That the church always model Mary's self-giving for the good of others . . . [pause]

That leaders of nations work diligently toward blessings and peace for all peoples . . . [pause]

That the poor, the sick, and the dying receive an abundance of God's blessings . . . [pause]

That during this year, each of us grow in our capacity to ponder God's presence, proclaim God's blessings, and praise God with all our hearts . . . [pause]

Presider: God of blessings, you hear the prayers of those who call to you: grant us prosperity and peace that we might praise and glorify you always. Grant this through Christ our Lord. **Amen.**

FOR REFLECTION

- As "Mary kept all these things, reflecting on them in her heart," she grew in understanding and appreciation of the mystery of Jesus' birth. The fruit of my own reflection on this mystery this year is . . .
- The shepherds "made known the message that had been told them." Ways that I make known my understanding and appreciation of Jesus' birth are . . .
- My manner of living brings glory and praise to God in that . . .

Homily Points

- Myriads of people come and go throughout our lives. Some of them barely break through our consciousness; others have a profound effect on who we are and how we live. But none ought to have such a profound effect on us as Jesus. The one who models this for us is Mary.

- Like Mary, we are to ponder mysteries we do not understand and come to know Jesus more deeply. Like Mary, we are to proclaim the goodness of God and come to know God's blessings. Like Mary, we are to praise God and come to know our own glory.

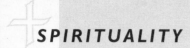

SPIRITUALITY

GOSPEL ACCLAMATION
Matt 2:2

℞. Alleluia, alleluia.
We saw his star at its rising
and have come to do him homage.
℞. Alleluia, alleluia.

Gospel   Matt 2:1-12; L20ABC

When Jesus was born in Bethlehem of
    Judea,
    in the days of King Herod,
    behold, magi from the east
        arrived in Jerusalem,
        saying,
    "Where is the newborn king
        of the Jews?
We saw his star at its rising
    and have come to do him
        homage."
When King Herod heard this,
    he was greatly troubled,
    and all Jerusalem with him.
Assembling all the chief priests and the
        scribes of the people,
    he inquired of them where the Christ
        was to be born.
They said to him, "In Bethlehem of Judea,
    for thus it has been written through the
        prophet:
    And you, Bethlehem, land of Judah,
        are by no means least among the
            rulers of Judah;
    since from you shall come a ruler,
        who is to shepherd my people Israel."
Then Herod called the magi secretly
    and ascertained from them the time of
        the star's appearance.
He sent them to Bethlehem and said,
    "Go and search diligently for the child.
When you have found him, bring me word,
    that I too may go and do him homage."
After their audience with the king they
        set out.
And behold, the star that they had seen
    at its rising preceded them,
    until it came and stopped over the
        place where the child was.

Continued in Appendix A, p. 269.

Reflecting on the Gospel

The Age of Enlightenment was a seventeenth- and eighteenth-century movement during which reason reigned; belief and motivation depended on science and mathematics with their sure methodologies. This movement eventually met its own demise because there is much more to the human spirit than pure reason. The Enlightenment could not satisfy our deeply felt hunger for mystery and awe, God's presence and the Spirit's inspiration. Indeed, the "Christian Age of Enlightenment" is a perennial movement—it is the time of the light of Christ. Ushered in by the birth of a humble baby sought by magi and threatened by king and sages, the light of Christ has not met its demise; it continues to shine brightly.

Light and darkness remain powerful symbols for us, light a time when goodness happens and darkness a time when evil occurs. The "newborn king of the Jews" was greatly troubling for those (Herod, chief priests, scribes) whose hearts were not set rightly. For those whose hearts were set rightly (magi, Mary), Jesus elicited joy and homage from them. The Light that has come into the world (see first reading) is not a star but the person of Jesus. This Light, Jesus himself, still shines upon all people, revealing either a darker side of the human heart or the radiance of God's glory.

From the very birth this Light arouses one to be "greatly troubled" or "overjoyed." The Light is a welcoming, peaceful warmth to which we surrender and are overjoyed. The Light also thickens the darkness and makes the contrast between goodness and evil that much more magnified. Those who choose to recognize the Light are drawn to give homage and open the gifts of their hearts. Those who choose darkness face a path of trouble and destruction. What does this Light reveal in our hearts?

This feast of the Epiphany celebrates the Light being manifested to all who would respond. The Light also divides our world, and this division will only be resolved when Christ comes in final glory to establish God's reign once and for all. This feast invites each of us to be among the seekers of the Light who do Christ homage. Our joy is found in the real surprise of the gospel message: we are "members of the same body" (second reading) who are now the light that shines in the darkness. Our own shining forth hastens God's reign. With such grace, no wonder all we can do is set our hearts rightly, offer homage and gifts, and follow the Light wherever it leads.

Living the Paschal Mystery

Just as Christ's birth sharpened the contrast between light and darkness, so too will our faithful discipleship magnify this contrast. The disturbing message of this gospel is that we cannot follow Christ and expect that we won't trouble others. There is a price to pay for being the light.

Each fresh look at the Christmas mystery reminds us that all Christian living is paschal mystery living; that is, the dying (darkness) precedes the rising (the Light). It ought not surprise us, then, how much darkness accompanies these beautiful Christmas season gospels; nor should it surprise us that there is a cost in our own lives for living the gospel. We continue to choose self-giving, nevertheless, because God's star always guides us and fills us with joy so long as we are surrendering to God's will. The price to pay is worth the gift: upon us the Lord's glory shines!

Focusing the Gospel
Key words and phrases: newborn king of the Jews, greatly troubled, overjoyed, homage

To the point: The "newborn king of the Jews" was greatly troubling for those (Herod, chief priests, scribes) whose hearts were not set rightly. For those whose hearts were set rightly (magi, Mary), Jesus elicited joy and homage from them. The Light which has come into the world (see first reading) is not a star, but the person of Jesus. This Light, Jesus himself, still shines upon all people, revealing either a darker side of the human heart or the radiance of God's glory. What does this Light reveal in our hearts?

Connecting the Gospel
to the second reading: A significant part of the revelation of the Spirit is that the light of Christ shines on all people of all times.

to experience: Sunny days or dark and dreary days affect us in radically different ways. Light encourages life and growth; darkness dampens spirits and inhibits growth. What life and growth is encouraged by Christ, the light of the world!

Connecting the Responsorial Psalm
to the readings: Psalm 72 was a prayer for the Israelite king. At the time of Christ, however, no king had governed Israel for nearly six hundred years (Herod was merely a figurehead, Rome the real ruler). Psalm 72, if prayed at all then, would have been a petition for the coming of the new king, the Messiah.

For us, the Messiah-King has come, and Psalm 72 is our prayer that his reign will come to fulfillment. We pray that all nations and their leaders will lay their power and wealth at the service of God's redemptive plan and that justice for the poor and afflicted will be secured. As we sing this psalm and celebrate this feast, then, we do not merely remember a nice story from the past. Rather, we commit ourselves to praying and working for the future for which Christ was born.

to psalmist preparation: Though the light of Christ may seem to be overcome at times by the dark forces that oppose it (gospel), ultimately all nations will be gathered under its banner (responsorial psalm). You lead the assembly, then, in a song of hope. How do you yourself experience this hope? What forces of darkness tempt you to lose hope? Who at these times restores your vision of the Light?

ASSEMBLY & FAITH-SHARING GROUPS
- Where the light of Christ is radiating through my life is . . .
- The darkness that Christ's light clarifies and accentuates for me is . . .
- I give Jesus homage when . . . He gives me joy by . . .

PRESIDERS
A time when I have been surprised by who was truly seeking Christ's light is . . .

DEACONS
My ministry is an epiphany of Christ's light shining into others' darkness whenever I . . .

HOSPITALITY MINISTERS
One way my hospitality announces the good news that all are invited to be "coheirs, members of the same body" (second reading) is . . .

MUSIC MINISTERS
The readings indicate that those who search for Christ will encounter darkness along the way. My music ministry has been an encounter with Christ when . . . It has been an encounter with my own darkness when . . .

ALTAR MINISTERS
The difference between serving others to call attention (glory) to myself or serving others as an act of homage to God is . . .

LECTORS
An example of where God's word was an epiphany of God's light for me is . . . ; an example where my daily living is an epiphany of God's light for others is . . .

EXTRAORDINARY MINISTERS OF HOLY COMMUNION
Distributing Holy Communion is a joyful act of homage when . . .

Model Act of Penitence

Presider: Today we celebrate the Epiphany, the feast day of the Light of Christ shining forth for all peoples to see. We pause at the beginning of this liturgy to open our hearts to receive this great Light . . . [pause]

Lord Jesus, you are the Light that shines on all peoples: Lord . . .

Christ Jesus, you are the One worthy of all homage: Christ . . .

Lord Jesus, you are the Light that dispels all darkness: Lord . . .

Homily Points

• We use metaphors such as "dark moment," "living under a cloud," "Dark Ages," etc., to describe certain troubling experiences. We use other metaphors such as "sunny disposition," "you light up my life," "shed some light on this problem," etc., to describe the opposite. The human heart grapples both with times of darkness and of light.

• The light of Christ is shining steadily in our lives, no matter what we face. The gospel invitation and reminder is that the human heart always be turned toward that Light.

• How the human heart responds to whatever life brings reveals the orientation of the human heart. Herod was troubled; so were Joseph, Mary, and the magi. The issue isn't whether we struggle with troubles and darkness; that is part of human living. The gospel call is that we remain turned toward Jesus the Light who, even in darkness, can give us joy.

Model Prayer of the Faithful

Presider: Let us make our needs known to the God who sends us Jesus our Light.

Response:

Lord,   hear   our prayer.

Cantor:

we pray to the Lord,

That the church always be a welcoming light shining in the darkness . . . [pause]

That peoples of all nations open their hearts to the salvation God offers . . . [pause]

That the troubled of heart find joy and peace in Christ the Light . . . [pause]

That each of us here remain steadfastly turned toward Christ and Light . . . [pause]

Presider: God of light and darkness, you are faithful to those who follow your Son: hear these our prayers that one day we might enjoy everlasting light and life with you. Grant this through Christ our Lord. **Amen.**

OPENING PRAYER

Let us pray
[that we will be guided by the light of faith]

Pause for silent prayer

Father,
you revealed your Son to the nations
by the guidance of a star.
Lead us to your glory in heaven
by the light of faith.

We ask this through our Lord Jesus Christ,
your Son,
who lives and reigns with you and the
Holy Spirit,
one God, for ever and ever. **Amen.**

FIRST READING
Isa 60:1-6

Rise up in splendor, Jerusalem! Your light
has come,
the glory of the Lord shines upon you.
See, darkness covers the earth,
and thick clouds cover the peoples;
but upon you the Lord shines,
and over you appears his glory.
Nations shall walk by your light,
and kings by your shining radiance.
Raise your eyes and look about;
they all gather and come to you:
your sons come from afar,
and your daughters in the arms of their
nurses.

Then you shall be radiant at what you see,
your heart shall throb and overflow,
for the riches of the sea shall be emptied
out before you,
the wealth of nations shall be brought
to you.
Caravans of camels shall fill you,
dromedaries from Midian and Ephah;
all from Sheba shall come
bearing gold and frankincense,
and proclaiming the praises of the Lord.

RESPONSORIAL PSALM
Ps 72:1-2, 7-8, 10-11, 12-13

R̸. (cf. 11) Lord, every nation on earth will adore you.

O God, with your judgment endow the
  king,
  and with your justice, the king's son;
he shall govern your people with justice
  and your afflicted ones with judgment.

R̸. Lord, every nation on earth will adore you.

Justice shall flower in his days,
  and profound peace, till the moon be no
    more.
May he rule from sea to sea,
  and from the River to the ends of the
    earth.

R̸. Lord, every nation on earth will adore you.

The kings of Tarshish and the Isles shall
    offer gifts;
  the kings of Arabia and Seba shall
    bring tribute.
All kings shall pay him homage,
  all nations shall serve him.

R̸. Lord, every nation on earth will adore you.

For he shall rescue the poor when he cries
    out,
  and the afflicted when he has no one to
    help him.
He shall have pity for the lowly and the
    poor;
  the lives of the poor he shall save.

R̸. Lord, every nation on earth will adore you.

SECOND READING
Eph 3:2-3a, 5-6

Brothers and sisters:
You have heard of the stewardship of
    God's grace
  that was given to me for your benefit,
  namely, that the mystery was made
    known to me by revelation.
It was not made known to people in other
    generations
  as it has now been revealed
  to his holy apostles and prophets by the
    Spirit:
  that the Gentiles are coheirs, members
    of the same body,
  and copartners in the promise in Christ
    Jesus through the gospel.

✠ CATECHESIS

About Liturgy

East and light as symbol: We all know that the sun rises in the east, but most of us probably don't realize what a strong symbol this has always been, both in Christian theology and architecture.

Resurrection: All four gospels mention that it was early in the morning on the first day of the week that the disciples found the empty tomb. Hence, the sun rising in the east is a natural symbol for resurrection. Morning Prayer, ideally celebrated early in the morning, is a resurrection prayer and has motifs of light and glory as well as praise.

Second Coming: From earliest times Christians looked east for Christ's second coming, the direction of light and a new dawning of life.

Church axis: Early church buildings were always constructed on an east-west axis; the altar was situated at one end so the assembly, standing facing the altar, faced east. A parallel symbolism of this axis is that as they left the building they left facing west—a symbol for darkness, sin, and evil. This was a constant reminder that the light and life showered upon the assembly at liturgy was to be taken into a world darkened with sin, and Christians were to be the light that dispels darkness.

Posture: In the early church it was customary to turn eastward for prayer. During baptisms the elect would face westward to renounce Satan and then turn eastward to recite the Creed.

About Liturgical Music

Music suggestion: Richard Wilbur's text "A Stable Lamp Is Lighted" [G2, GC, W3] uses imagery of stars and stones to express the paschal mystery reality that the Christ Child born on this day will on another day be rejected and put to death. Stones that at his birth cry out in praise will on that other day cry over "hearts made hard by sin." Stars that "bend their voices" toward earth at Christ's birth will on the day of his death "groan and darken." But both stars and stones acknowledge that in his birth as in his death "the low is lifted high" and "the worlds" of heaven and earth "are reconciled." G2 and GC use the tune ANNIKA for this hymn. David Hurd's ANDUJAR, used in W3, is much more effective. The 6/8 meter and the rocking pattern in the accompaniment place the passion predictions of the text in the context of a lullaby. The contrast is unexpected and illuminating. The hymn would work well as a choir prelude or as an assembly song during the presentation of the gifts.

It was customary in the Middle Ages, before the advent of calendars, cell phones, and the internet, to announce the date of Easter and of other important liturgical days on the feast of Epiphany. "The Proclamation of the Date of Easter," updated for the current year, is available in *Sourcebook* [LTP]. This could be proclaimed by a cantor as part of the concluding rite.

JANUARY 2, 2011
THE EPIPHANY OF THE LORD

✠ SPIRITUALITY

GOSPEL ACCLAMATION
cf. Mark 9:7

R̸. Alleluia, alleluia.
The heavens were opened and the voice of the
    Father thundered:
This is my beloved Son, listen to him.
R̸. Alleluia, alleluia.

Gospel

Matt 3:13-17; L21A

Jesus came from Galilee to John at the
    Jordan
  to be baptized by him.
John tried to prevent him, saying,
  "I need to be baptized by you,
  and yet you are coming to me?"
Jesus said to him in reply,
  "Allow it now, for thus it is fitting
    for us
  to fulfill all righteousness."
Then he allowed him.
After Jesus was baptized,
  he came up from the water and
    behold,
  the heavens were opened for him,
  and he saw the Spirit of God
    descending like a dove
  and coming upon him.
And a voice came from the heavens,
    saying,
  "This is my beloved Son, with whom
    I am well pleased."

Reflecting on the Gospel

Any parent of adolescents can attest to the reality of tension in relationships! As young ones grow toward adulthood, they begin to assert their independence. Staying out past curfew, saying they are going one place and then going to another, and being secretive about who their real friends are can all be behaviors that thrill youth and frustrate and anger parents. The youth are not yet experienced enough in life to realize the dangers behind some of their actions; they are not yet wise enough to see the broader picture and long-range implications of their actions. Parents want to protect them; youth want the thrill of being daring, trying new things, traveling uncharted waters. The tension has a good side to it as well. For the youth, it means they are growing up, learning to handle new experiences, stretching their wings. For parents, it means they have an opportunity to show real concern and care, to be responsible parents, to instill wholesome values and attitudes in their children. In this Sunday's gospel there is a tension between John and Jesus. But this tension is different from that between parents and adolescents. The gospel's portrayal of tension is between lesser and greater, between sinner and one without sin, between a ministry of reconciliation and one characterized by the Spirit, between precursor and "beloved Son."

Jesus comes to John for baptism; John wants to "prevent him." The tension this exchange reveals is resolved by a mutual self-giving: Jesus says, "Allow it"; John does what Jesus asks and baptizes him, whereby "the heavens were opened" and the Spirit of God came upon Jesus to reveal who he is—the beloved Son. Like John, we must hear Jesus say, "Allow it," and our own baptism must impel us to live self-giving lives in the Spirit.

With mutual self-giving, the sign that reveals the meaning of Jesus' baptism could happen. Our own baptism also calls us to mutual self-giving. Baptism is about more than being washed of sin; it is about being committed to the kind of self-giving that happens with the Spirit's indwelling. We give ourselves for the good of others and this is Spirit-filled gospel living. But just as with parents and adolescents, gospel living often brings misunderstanding and tension in its wake. How often as baptized followers of Jesus do we experience tension between others and ourselves over gospel values? How often do we experience tension between ourselves and what Jesus is asking us to do? John tried to prevent Jesus from coming to him for baptism. Sometimes we try to prevent Jesus from coming to us too. This gospel calls us to open ourselves and even seek Jesus' coming. *His* presence enables us to live by gospel values. In giving ourselves over to Jesus the tension is resolved, the power of the Spirit is unleashed, and the identity of Jesus is revealed to the world.

Living the Paschal Mystery

Here is the paradox of gospel living: by self-giving we are self-fulfilled. By self-giving we align ourselves with our baptismal call to identify with Jesus. By self-giving we embrace the mystery of being plunged into his dying and rising, pledging ourselves to lives of goodness and holiness. In face of the great good God gives us—being pleased with us as beloved daughters and sons—whatever tensions we might encounter in being faithful to the Spirit's indwelling seem small, indeed.

Focusing the Gospel

Key words and phrases: Jesus came . . . to John, John tried to prevent him, Allow it, Spirit of God . . . coming upon him, my beloved Son

To the point: There is a tension in the gospel between John and Jesus. Jesus comes to John for baptism; John wants to "prevent him." Jesus says, "Allow it"; John does what Jesus asks. How often as baptized followers of Jesus do we experience tension between ourselves and what Jesus is asking us to do? In giving ourselves over to Jesus the tension is resolved, the power of the Spirit is unleashed, and the identity of Jesus is revealed to the world.

Connecting the Gospel

to the first and second readings: In whom is God well pleased? In the first reading, "my chosen one" who "bring[s] forth justice." In the gospel, this "chosen one" is revealed as the "beloved Son" who "went about doing good" (second reading).

to experience: Our natural response to tension is to try to eliminate it. In fact, tension often can be a call to growth, catalyst for new self-understanding, and source of revelation of our own goodness.

Connecting the Responsorial Psalm

to the readings: At first glance these verses from Psalm 29 seem too dramatic for their context. In them God's voice is mighty, majestic, and thunderous. In unused verses from the psalm (5-9), God's voice shatters cedars, splits oak trees, strips forests, and rocks the wilderness. It is in response to this thundering that the people shout back, "Glory!" And the louder God gets, the louder they shout back.

But the readings are not full of shouts and shatterings. They speak instead of a quiet presence that protects and heals (first reading), of a divine word of peace (second reading), and of an intimate proclamation of sonship (gospel). So why all the shouting in the responsorial psalm? Because the One who leads the shouting has come to undergird the people with strength, bless them with peace, and lead them to freedom. Because the voice of God wears flesh, and speaks human words, and submits to human customs (gospel). Because in the mission of Christ the kingdom of darkness is shattered. The psalm reminds us—and the powers of evil—not to be misled by the gentleness of God's entry. It is God's own "beloved Son" who has arrived.

to psalmist preparation: In singing this psalm you name Christ as God's blessing sent to heal and save. How are you blessed in Christ? How do you share this blessing with others?

**ASSEMBLY &
FAITH-SHARING GROUPS**
- Some of the tensions I have experienced in my life that have led me to give myself over to Jesus more faithfully are . . .
- When I acknowledge that I am God's "beloved" in whom God is "well pleased," the power of the Spirit is revealed in these ways . . .
- I am grateful that I am baptized because . . .

PRESIDERS
Tension in my ministry helps me to grow and better serve my community when . . . It inhibits growth and service when . . .

DEACONS
Through my ministry I announce to others, especially the disadvantaged, that they are God's beloved when I . . .

HOSPITALITY MINISTERS
My hospitality announces to the assembly that "God shows no partiality" (second reading) by . . .

MUSIC MINISTERS
The tensions I experience in my music ministry are . . . They lead me to Jesus when . . . They separate me from Jesus when . . .

ALTAR MINISTERS
Serving others is making me more like Jesus, God's beloved, in that . . .

LECTORS
Listening to the tensions in my life enables me to proclaim God's word more effectively in that . . .

**EXTRAORDINARY MINISTERS
OF HOLY COMMUNION**
I experience that I am God's "beloved . . . with whom [God is] well pleased" during Eucharist when . . . In my distribution of Holy Communion, I help others experience themselves in this way when . . .

Model Rite of Blessing and Sprinkling Holy Water

Presider: Dear friends, we ask God to bless this water and use it as a reminder of our baptism and how beloved we are . . . [pause]

[continue with form A or B of the blessing of water]

Homily Points

• Typically, we try to eliminate tension in our lives by avoiding it, suppressing it, ignoring it, compensating for it, forcefully trying to overcome it. Many times the best way to deal with tension is to befriend it, learn from it, and make it work for us.

• John was judging the situation of Jesus' coming to him for baptism from his narrow perspective of how he felt he should be in relation to Jesus—he was the one needing baptism, not Jesus. By listening to Jesus and thus befriending the tension he felt, John opened himself up to a broader vision of his relationship with Jesus.

• When we cling to preset expectations, we can create tensions and fail to hear God inviting us to new ways things might be. We break out of our narrow expectations when we more perfectly align ourselves with our baptismal call—listening to Jesus—and allow the Spirit room to work through us, ease tensions, and reveal Jesus in new ways.

Model Prayer of the Faithful

Presider: As baptized members of the Body of Christ, let us make known our needs to the God who calls us beloved.

Response:

Lord, hear our prayer.

Cantor:

we pray to the Lord,

That all members of the church faithfully live as the beloved of God . . . [pause]

That all peoples grow in their dignity as God's children . . . [pause]

That those who are treated unjustly and without dignity be strengthened by God's love . . . [pause]

That each of us here live our baptismal call to be loved by God and to love others . . . [pause]

Presider: Loving God, you call us to be your beloved children: hear these our prayers that one day we might enjoy everlasting life with you. We ask this through Christ our Lord. **Amen**.

Let us pray
[that we be faithful to our baptism]

Pause for silent prayer

Almighty, eternal God,
when the Spirit descended upon Jesus
at his baptism in the Jordan,
you revealed him as your own beloved
  Son.
Keep us, your children born of water and
  the Spirit,
faithful to our calling.

We ask this through our Lord Jesus Christ,
  your Son,
who lives and reigns with you and the
  Holy Spirit,
one God, for ever and ever. **Amen.**

FIRST READING
Isa 42:1-4, 6-7

Thus says the LORD:
Here is my servant whom I uphold,
  my chosen one with whom I am pleased,
upon whom I have put my spirit;
  he shall bring forth justice to the
    nations,
not crying out, not shouting,
  not making his voice heard in the street.
A bruised reed he shall not break,
  and a smoldering wick he shall not
    quench,
until he establishes justice on the earth;
  the coastlands will wait for his teaching.

I, the LORD, have called you for the victory
  of justice,
  I have grasped you by the hand;
I formed you, and set you
  as a covenant of the people,
  a light for the nations,
to open the eyes of the blind,
  to bring out prisoners from confinement,
  and from the dungeon, those who live in
    darkness.

RESPONSORIAL PSALM

Ps 29:1-2, 3-4, 9-10

℟. (11b) The Lord will bless his people with peace.

Give to the LORD, you sons of God,
   give to the LORD glory and praise,
give to the LORD the glory due his name;
   adore the LORD in holy attire.

℟. The Lord will bless his people with peace.

The voice of the LORD is over the waters,
   the LORD, over vast waters.
The voice of the LORD is mighty;
   the voice of the LORD is majestic.

℟. The Lord will bless his people with peace.

The God of glory thunders,
   and in his temple all say, "Glory!"
The LORD is enthroned above the flood;
   the LORD is enthroned as king forever.

℟. The Lord will bless his people with peace.

SECOND READING

Acts 10:34-38

Peter proceeded to speak to those gathered
   in the house of Cornelius, saying:
"In truth, I see that God shows no
      partiality.
Rather, in every nation whoever fears him
      and acts uprightly
   is acceptable to him.
You know the word that he sent to the
      Israelites
   as he proclaimed peace through Jesus
      Christ, who is Lord of all,
what has happened all over Judea,
   beginning in Galilee after the baptism
   that John preached,
   how God anointed Jesus of Nazareth
   with the Holy Spirit and power.
He went about doing good
   and healing all those oppressed by the
      devil,
   for God was with him."

About Liturgy

Baptism and epiphany: Epiphany originates in the Eastern Church where they celebrated both the birth of Jesus and his baptism on January 6 (their theology holds that Jesus was "manifested" or "given birth" by the announcement at his baptism that he is the beloved Son). By the late fourth century the Western Church had added this date to its liturgical calendar and celebrated three events, captured beautifully in the *Magnificat* antiphon for Epiphany: "Three mysteries mark this day: today the star leads the Magi to the infant Christ; today water is changed into wine for the wedding feast; today Christ wills to be baptized by John in the river Jordan to bring us salvation." These three events link together the one identity and mission of Jesus.

At Epiphany we read in the gospel how the magi are led by a star to the newborn King of the Jews; thus is Jesus manifested to all nations. Jesus' identity is further revealed at his baptism where the heavens open and the voice of God announces Jesus as the beloved Son. This identity is further manifested in Jesus' ministry to others—at his first miracle at Cana where he changes water into wine and saves the wedding couple embarrassment and in all his ministry when he reaches out to anyone in need.

About Liturgical Music

Music suggestions: One of the most magnificent chant hymns of our tradition, "Of the Father's Love Begotten," beautifully expresses our praise for the mystery we celebrate this day: Jesus' identity as God's begotten, as the beginning and ending of all things, and as the fulfillment of all prophecy. The meditative style of the hymn makes it suitable for the presentation of the gifts or for the Communion procession with interludes added to lengthen it if necessary.

Delores Dufner's "In the Cycle of the Seasons" links the conclusion of the Christmas season with the call to daily paschal mystery living that marks our journey through the liturgical year. This hymn would be excellent either as a post-Communion assembly song or as a recessional. The text can be found in *The Glimmer of Glory in Song* [GIA].

Hymns directly related to the gospel text and suitable for either the entrance procession or the preparation of the gifts include "When Jesus Came to Jordan," "Jesus at the Jordan Baptized," "When John Baptized by Jordan's River," and "Down Galilee's Slow Roadways." Bob Moore has composed a choral arrangement of this last hymn [GIA G-5502] that would make an excellent choral prelude. The continuous arpeggios in the keyboard communicate that the journey of discipleship is urgent and never ending; the tight dissonances in the choral writing express the intensity of discipleship and its inherent tensions.

Ordinary Time I

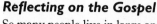

✝ SPIRITUALITY

GOSPEL ACCLAMATION
John 1:14a, 12a

℟. Alleluia, alleluia.
The Word of God became flesh and dwelt
    among us.
To those who accepted him,
he gave power to become children of God.
℟. Alleluia, alleluia.

Gospel

John 1:29-34; L64A

John the Baptist saw Jesus
    coming toward him
    and said,
    "Behold, the Lamb of
        God, who takes
        away the sin of the
        world.
He is the one of whom I said,
    'A man is coming after me who ranks
        ahead of me
    because he existed before me.'
I did not know him,
    but the reason why I came baptizing
        with water
    was that he might be made known to
        Israel."
John testified further, saying,
    "I saw the Spirit come down like a
        dove from heaven
    and remain upon him.
I did not know him,
    but the one who sent me to baptize
        with water told me,
    'On whomever you see the Spirit
        come down and remain,
    he is the one who will baptize with
        the Holy Spirit.'
Now I have seen and testified that he is
    the Son of God."

Reflecting on the Gospel

So many people live in large apartment buildings and intricately laid out condo communities that "porch dwelling" is quickly becoming a lost art. Consider what has happened to our housing in just the last decades: we have gone from mostly single-family dwellings arranged in neighborhoods where neighbors are truly neighbors to multiunit complexes where we remain impersonal strangers to one another. In the past, many houses had large porches—now we find "porch" furniture has become "deck" or "patio" furniture. The furniture is still functional, but the venue has changed. We tend now to gather in private, enclosed spaces. In times past, sitting on the porch for a while in the evening opened us to the wide vistas of neighbors and other lives. If guests were expected, we might have sat on the porch actively watching for their arrival. Sitting and waiting for someone is a kind of hospitable preparation to receive another, to open oneself to new possibilities, to empty oneself of distractions.

In this Sunday's gospel John is portrayed as one actively watching for the Messiah. Faithful to his mission to baptize all those who came to him, John readily recognized Jesus as the Messiah when the Spirit came down and rested upon him. John's fidelity to watching for the Messiah prepared him to recognize the Messiah. The way he fulfilled his mission—expanding his own horizon to receive anyone who came to him for baptism—opened him to being ready for the coming of the Messiah, being able to recognize him and to testify to his presence. This description of John's life and mission is a description of our own life and mission.

We too recognize Jesus when we actively watch for his coming into our lives and remain faithful to the mission God has given us to testify to his presence. Our active watching broadens our own vistas so we can see Jesus' presence in people and circumstances right before our eyes. Like John, the more we get to know Jesus, the more we are compelled to testify to his identity and mission. But the testimony is preceded by being good Christian "porch dwellers." We must widen our vistas to include neighbors and other lives. We must be in a constant state of expectation so when the "Son of God" comes, we are ready to receive him.

Living the Paschal Mystery

We live in a society and culture that values quick results. When it comes to what is most important to us—recognizing Jesus in our midst—we cannot expect quick results; learning to recognize Jesus in the many ways he comes to us requires patient waiting that opens our eyes wide to new possibilities. Watching for Jesus is a lifelong process. We all probably take two steps forward and then a few more steps backward and can get mightily discouraged on the way. We don't always recognize him in the person who annoys us or the mundane, everyday tasks that bore us.

In the gospel the Lord speaks to John, telling him how he would recognize Jesus (the one on whom the Spirit descends). Our "porch dwelling" affords us the quiet moments we need to listen to God speaking to us, to open ourselves to the message, to prepare ourselves to encounter Jesus and embrace the mission of testifying and gospel living that he asks. All this is possible because the Spirit descends upon us too. We testify to Jesus' presence because the Spirit within prompts us, guides us, opens us.

Focusing the Gospel

Key words and phrases: John . . . saw Jesus, baptizing with water, one who sent me, see the Spirit come down and remain

To the point: John was actively watching for the Messiah. Faithful to his mission to baptize all those who came to him, John readily recognized Jesus as the Messiah when the Spirit came down and rested upon him. We too recognize Jesus when we actively watch for his coming into our lives and remain faithful to the mission God has given us.

Connecting the Gospel

to the first reading: Israel, God's servant, shines with the glory of God and leads all nations to salvation. In the gospel Jesus is the glorified One upon whom the Spirit rests and who leads all nations to salvation.

to experience: We see what we look for. If we look for Jesus, we will see him.

Connecting the Responsorial Psalm

to the readings: In the first strophe (stanza) of this responsorial psalm we "wait" for the Lord. We keep watch, and we expect. In the final strophe we "announce" that we have found the Lord. We testify, and we proclaim. Like John the Baptist, part of our mission as disciples is to keep on the lookout for the appearance of Christ and then testify to his presence when he does appear. And this is the obedience we sing about in the middle strophes of the psalm.

As we begin once more our discipleship journey through Ordinary Time, we offer ourselves to God as obedient servants (first reading). We set out to find Jesus in every aspect of life. We begin "not knowing" entirely where and how he will appear (gospel). We end meeting him face-to-face and showing others who he is. The "I" who sings "Here I am, Lord, I come to do your will" (refrain) is not only Jesus, not only John the Baptist, but also we.

to psalmist preparation: In the context of this Sunday's readings, doing God's will means searching for Christ and then announcing his presence to others. As part of your preparation this week, choose a specific place to search for Christ, that is, within your family, in a situation at work, with someone who is suffering, etc., so that the assembly can hear in your voice the testimony of a heart speaking from experience.

ASSEMBLY & FAITH-SHARING GROUPS
- I look for Jesus in . . . I look for Jesus by . . . I find Jesus . . .
- I see the Holy Spirit resting upon . . .
- I testify to others about my encounters with Jesus by . . . when . . .

PRESIDERS
Like John the Baptist, I remain faithful to my call to make known the Messiah among us when . . .

DEACONS
My service is a way to watch for the Messiah in that . . .

HOSPITALITY MINISTERS
My hospitality is most fruitful when I watch for . . .

MUSIC MINISTERS
Like John the Baptist, my role is to turn attention away from myself to Jesus (gospel). In the ministry of music this is easy to do when . . . It is difficult to do when . . .

ALTAR MINISTERS
My serving at the altar requires a careful watching of persons and things. This leads me to Jesus when . . .

LECTORS
Preparing to proclaim the word well means that I watch for how Jesus reveals himself to me in my daily living. My watching is fruitful when . . .

EXTRAORDINARY MINISTERS OF HOLY COMMUNION
I am able to see the Spirit of the Lord resting upon each communicant when I . . .

Model Act of Penitence

Presider: In today's gospel John the Baptist watches for the Messiah on whom the Spirit will rest. Let us prepare for this liturgy by opening our hearts to recognize Jesus among us . . . [pause]

Lord Jesus, you are the One upon whom the Spirit rests: Lord . . .

Christ Jesus, you are the Lamb of God: Christ . . .

Lord Jesus, you are the Son of God: Lord . . .

Homily Points

• Active watching can lead to exciting new discoveries. For example, bird watchers pay close attention to every bird that comes into view. Because of their tireless attentiveness, sometimes a whole new species is discovered. In the gospel John the Baptist gives us another example of active watching. His attentiveness allowed him to recognize Jesus when he came into view.

• What John recognized about Jesus was surely something exciting and new. This One is the Lamb of God and the Son of God who will take away sin and baptize with the Holy Spirit. We can recognize this One too if we actively watch for him.

• We are able to see Jesus when we put on the mind of Christ. Our active watching, then, is a matter of living as Jesus did: when we see Jesus' face in the poor and needy, when we reach out a helping hand to those who are overburdened, when we encourage the discouraged. This is how we remain faithful to the mission God gave us. Indeed, actively watching for Jesus in the many people and myriad circumstances of our lives *is* our mission.

Model Prayer of the Faithful

Presider: Our active watching helps us see the needs of others. And so we pray.

Response:

Lord, hear our prayer.

Cantor:

we pray to the Lord,

That all members of the church faithfully watch for the presence of Jesus in their lives . . . [pause]

That leaders of the world are attentive and responsive to the needs of their people . . . [pause]

That those in need of food, clothing, or shelter be recognized as the presence of Jesus calling out for response . . . [pause]

That each of us be faithful to our baptismal call and open ourselves to the Spirit working through us . . . [pause]

Presider: Gracious God, you sent your Son to baptize with the Holy Spirit: hear these our prayers that we might faithfully live our baptismal promises and one day live forever with you. Grant this through Christ our Lord. **Amen.**

ALTERNATIVE OPENING PRAYER

Let us pray

Pause for silent prayer

Almighty and ever-present Father,
your watchful care reaches from end to
    end
and orders all things in such power
that even the tensions and the tragedies
    of sin
cannot frustrate your loving plans.
Help us to embrace your will,
give us the strength to follow your call,
so that your truth may live in our hearts
and reflect peace to those who believe in
    your love.

We ask this in the name of Jesus the Lord.
    Amen.

FIRST READING

Isa 49:3, 5-6

The LORD said to me: You are my servant,
    Israel, through whom I show my glory.
Now the LORD has spoken
    who formed me as his servant from the
        womb,
    that Jacob may be brought back to him
    and Israel gathered to him;
    and I am made glorious in the sight of
        the LORD,
    and my God is now my strength!
It is too little, the LORD says, for you to be
        my servant,
    to raise up the tribes of Jacob,
    and restore the survivors of Israel;
I will make you a light to the nations,
    that my salvation may reach to the ends
        of the earth.

RESPONSORIAL PSALM

Ps 40:2, 4, 7-8, 8-9, 10

R̸. (8a and 9a) Here am I, Lord; I come to do your will.

I have waited, waited for the LORD,
   and he stooped toward me and heard
      my cry.
And he put a new song into my mouth,
   a hymn to our God.

R̸. Here am I, Lord; I come to do your will.

Sacrifice or offering you wished not,
   but ears open to obedience you gave me.
Holocausts or sin-offerings you sought not;
   then said I, "Behold I come."

R̸. Here am I, Lord; I come to do your will.

"In the written scroll it is prescribed for
   me,
   to do your will, O my God, is my
      delight, and your law is within my
      heart!"

R̸. Here am I, Lord; I come to do your will.

I announced your justice in the vast
     assembly;
   I did not restrain my lips, as you, O
   LORD, know.

R̸. Here am I, Lord; I come to do your will.

SECOND READING

1 Cor 1:1-3

Paul, called to be an apostle of Christ Jesus
     by the will of God,
   and Sosthenes our brother,
   to the church of God that is in Corinth,
   to you who have been sanctified in
     Christ Jesus,
     called to be holy,
   with all those everywhere who call upon
     the name of our Lord
     Jesus Christ, their Lord and ours.
Grace to you and peace from God our
     Father
   and the Lord Jesus Christ.

About Liturgy

"Sacrifice" of the Mass: Prior to Vatican II almost the only way we referred to the Mass was as Christ's "unbloody" sacrifice of Calvary. Since the council we almost never speak of Mass as a sacrifice, preferring other paradigms, especially that of a meal. No one way of talking about the Mass can capture the complexity and richness of this sacred action. In the context of this Sunday's readings we might want to reconsider Mass as a sacrifice.

Surely at Mass we celebrate the paschal mystery—the sacrifice of Jesus in his passion and death but also the new life of his resurrection. We share in this dying and rising by placing ourselves on the altar, to be offered along with the gifts of bread and wine. Thus, every celebration of Mass requires of us a *ritual* self-sacrifice, made fruitful when we *live* this sacrifice in our daily lives by imitating Jesus' self-giving. The transformation of liturgy is a *making sacred* that enables us to conform our lives more perfectly with Jesus'. Here is the real gift of Eucharist: God loves us so much that we ourselves become not only sharers in salvation for ourselves but coworkers with Christ in bringing God's salvation to all the world.

When we refer to the Mass as a sacrifice, then, we are committing ourselves to gospel/paschal mystery living. Perhaps we are reluctant to refer to Mass as a sacrifice because we know the demands this paradigm makes of us.

About Liturgical Music

Music suggestions: This is the Sunday to return to service music suitable for Ordinary Time. The feasting is over; it is the hour to "go back to work." So we take down the Christmas environment and set aside the festive music. The style of the Mass setting, the Glory to God, and the gospel acclamation we sing need to pull us into this season of quiet, faithful, daily discipleship.

A metrically strong hymn well suited for the entrance procession is Bernadette Farrell's "Praise to You, O Christ, Our Savior," found in many hymnals. The text expresses both the identity of Christ and our call to follow him in mission as we reenter our journey through Ordinary Time. "Glorious in Majesty" [G2, GC, RS, W3] would also be an excellent entrance song for this return to Ordinary Time. Martin Willett's "Behold the Lamb" [BB, G2, GC, GC2, JS2, OFUV] uses the image of Lamb of God found in the gospel and would be a good choice either for Communion or for a choir prelude. A hymn directly related to the gospel text and suitable for either the entrance procession or the preparation of the gifts is Fred Pratt Green's "When Jesus Came to Jordan." Lynn Trapp has set this hymn for choir, adding the refrain: "Behold the Lamb of God, who takes away the sins of the world. This is God's Chosen One" [GIA G-5266]; his setting would make an excellent choral prelude or a choir-only piece during the preparation of the gifts.

Hymns expressing the desire to know Jesus more intimately and follow him more closely include "Christ Be Beside Me" [BB, JS2, WC, WS], which would function well for either the preparation of the gifts or the recessional; and "Christ Be in Your Senses" [GC2], which could be sung by the assembly during the preparation of the gifts or by the choir as a prelude using the octavo setting [GIA octavo G-5708].

✝ SPIRITUALITY

GOSPEL ACCLAMATION
cf. Matt 4:23

R̸. Alleluia, alleluia.
Jesus proclaimed the Gospel of the kingdom
and cured every disease among the people.
R̸. Alleluia, alleluia.

Gospel   Matt 4:12-23; L67A

When Jesus heard that John had been
    arrested,
  he withdrew to Galilee.
He left Nazareth and went to live in
    Capernaum by the sea,
  in the region of Zebulun and
    Naphtali,
  that what had been said through
    Isaiah the prophet
  might be fulfilled:
    Land of Zebulun and land of Naphtali,
      the way to the sea, beyond the
        Jordan,
    Galilee of the Gentiles,
    the people who sit in darkness have
      seen a great light,
    on those dwelling in a land
      overshadowed by death
    light has arisen.
From that time on, Jesus began to preach
    and say,
  "Repent, for the kingdom of heaven is at
    hand."

As he was walking by the Sea of Galilee, he
    saw two brothers,
  Simon who is called Peter, and his
    brother Andrew,
  casting a net into the sea; they were
    fishermen.
He said to them,
  "Come after me, and I will make you
    fishers of men."
At once they left their nets and followed
    him.
He walked along from there and saw two
    other brothers,
  James, the son of Zebedee, and his
    brother John.

Continued in Appendix A, p. 269,
or Matt 4:12-17 in Appendix A, p. 269.

Reflecting on the Gospel

Candles come in all shapes, sizes, and fragrances. Judging from the amount of space given for candle displays in even inexpensive stores, candles are popular as decorations in our homes. When we invite someone over for a special dinner we probably have candles burning on the set table and perhaps one or more in the living room. All these candles lend a pleasant glow to the atmosphere. But when the electricity goes out after dark and a single candle is lit, this little light makes all the difference in the world. Isn't it amazing how one little candle can shine so brightly in darkness but be barely noticed in light?

In the gospel for this Sunday Jesus goes to "the region of Zebulun and Naphtali," land of the Gentiles and, therefore, considered a land of darkness to the Jews of that time. It is as though Jesus goes to a place of darkness so the light of his Good News won't be missed but can shine brightly. Here in this region of darkness he begins his saving work. In the darkness he shines brightly, reminding us that God desires all of us to see "a great light." God desires all of us to repent of the darkness in our lives and come to the Light who is Savior.

As Jesus begins his public ministry, he issues two commands: "Repent" and "Come after me." The gospel suggests that both repentance and following Jesus are ways to walk in the light that reveal the kingdom of heaven at hand. The kingdom of heaven is neither earthly realm nor distant place. The kingdom of heaven is present in our response to Jesus. It is our willing obedience to hear him call, to leave everything, to follow him without counting the cost. The "kingdom of heaven is at hand" when we turn from darkness and not only walk in the light but also become that light ourselves.

How does "repent" open one to heed Jesus' call to follow him and become the light? We must be able to see the light who is our Savior before we can be light for others. To see and embrace the light is already following Jesus. So, one way to think about repentance is that it is turning from darkness so we can see the light. By changing our minds about the behaviors that bring darkness, we are able to focus on the light that then shines brightly enough for us to follow—becoming the light ourselves. To follow means to be light.

Living the Paschal Mystery

We shrink from darkness; we don't like it. We shrink from repentance; we don't like it either, because to repent means that we must embrace a life of self-giving. Seeing the light is actually much easier than following the light! John's faithfulness in preaching Jesus as the Messiah led him to prison and death. Jesus' preaching about God's kingdom at hand led him to the cross and death. If we follow the light, we know what awaits us: dying to self. Yet dying is the only way we ourselves can become the light that shines for others. Following the light is a metaphor for repentance because the light takes us where we would rather not go. But it is only this light that brings us everlasting life. This is why we repent and follow.

Just as one candle can dispel darkness, so can the little light each of us is dispel the darkness of sin and confusion, indifference and selfishness, greed and despair that tend to surround us. All we need to do is heed Jesus' two commands: repent and follow.

Focusing the Gospel

Key words and phrases: great light, repent, Come after me, kingdom of heaven, immediately

To the point: As Jesus begins his public ministry, he issues two commands: "Repent" and "Come after me." The gospel suggests that both repentance and following Jesus are ways to walk in the light that reveal the kingdom of heaven at hand. The kingdom of heaven is neither earthly realm nor distant place. The kingdom of heaven is present in our response to Jesus.

Connecting the Gospel

to the first reading: Matthew presents Jesus as the fulfillment of Isaiah's prophecy: Jesus is the light that comes into darkness.

to experience: We take light for granted; it is easily available with a flick of a switch. Walking in the light of Christ, however, is not so easy.

Connecting the Responsorial Psalm

to the readings: In the first reading the God of salvation has acted: the people who dwelt in darkness (i.e., death, destruction, despair) now dwell in light (i.e., life, prosperity, hope). The responsorial psalm acknowledges the gift of God's luminous and saving presence. The psalmist asks to dwell more deeply in this presence in order to contemplate the works and beauty of God and to gain the courage needed to remain faithful.

In the psalm the psalmist asks to dwell with God, but in the gospel it is Jesus who invites the apostles to "come" and be with him. Jesus invites them to see in him the luminous and saving presence of God. Like the apostles we too are called to acknowledge Jesus as "light" and "salvation" (psalm). We too are invited to dwell within the circle of Jesus' presence and to participate in his mission. This will require a change in our way of living—a gospel-driven repentance—but it will bring the light of salvation to all the world.

to psalmist preparation: The responsorial psalm invites you to see in Jesus the light of God's presence on earth and the coming of salvation to all peoples. Your singing of these verses must arise from your real desire to see God and to know salvation. When are you most aware of experiencing this desire? What supports this desire in you? What impedes it?

ASSEMBLY & FAITH-SHARING GROUPS
- Jesus' message that "the kingdom of heaven is at hand" means to me . . .
- What I must repent of to see or realize that the "kingdom of heaven is at hand" is . . .
- Simon, Andrew, James, and John all left something to follow Jesus. At this point in my life what I have to leave in order to follow Jesus more perfectly is . . .

PRESIDERS
What is difficult about repenting for me is . . . When I do repent, my ministry looks like . . .

DEACONS
My service helps others walk in the light of Christ by . . .

HOSPITALITY MINISTERS
My gracious hospitality is like a light shining for people that opens them to . . .

MUSIC MINISTERS
Jesus calls me to follow him by leading the music during liturgy. I find it is easy to respond to this call when I . . . I find it difficult to respond when I . . .

ALTAR MINISTERS
Like Jesus' first disciples, serving others well demands that I leave behind . . .

LECTORS
One way my life proclaims to others that "the kingdom of heaven is at hand" is . . .

EXTRAORDINARY MINISTERS OF HOLY COMMUNION
When I distribute Holy Communion, the faces of those who come shine with the light of Christ and this moves me to . . .

Model Act of Penitence

Presider: In today's gospel Jesus issues two commands: to repent and to follow him. Let us pause at the beginning of this liturgy and ask God for the strength to respond faithfully . . . [pause]

Lord Jesus, you are the Light that dispels darkness: Lord . . .

Christ Jesus, you reveal the presence of the kingdom of heaven: Christ . . .

Lord Jesus, you call us to follow you: Lord . . .

Homily Points

• "Lose thirty pounds in two weeks without dieting or exercising!" How alluring such "come-ons" are, and some people are foolishly taken in. Yet most of us know how misleading these claims are. For Jesus' followers, walking in the light of Christ alerts us to what is falsely alluring and strengthens us for what is rightly demanding.

• The promise of the "kingdom of heaven is at hand" is indeed alluring. This promise, however, is not misleading, but rather can be realized in our response to Jesus' commands to repent and follow him. We are to be people of the light whose way of living reveals the "kingdom of heaven is at hand."

• We reveal the immediacy of God's kingdom when we, for example, offer light to those trapped in the darkness of doubt, offer hope to those struggling with the shadow of despair, bring the wayward to repentance, affirm others that they are on the path of light and truth. Our response to others—which is our response to Jesus—reveals God's kingdom is at hand.

Model Prayer of the Faithful

Presider: We pray now for the grace to repent and follow Jesus.

Response:

Cantor:

That the church continue to be the light of Christ dispelling darkness . . . [pause]

That all people of the world find salvation through repentance . . . [pause]

That the lowly, the downcast, the hungry, and the poor be led into the light of God's kingdom . . . [pause]

That all of us here courageously follow Jesus through lives of self-giving . . . [pause]

Presider: God of darkness and light, you sent Jesus to bring all people to salvation: hear these our prayers that we might be light to those we meet and one day join the Light who is Christ in eternal glory. We pray through that same Jesus Christ our Lord. **Amen.**

OPENING PRAYER

Let us pray

Pause for silent prayer

All-powerful and ever-living God,
direct your love that is within us,
that our efforts in the name of your Son
may bring mankind to unity and peace.

We ask this through our Lord Jesus Christ,
    your Son,
who lives and reigns with you and the
    Holy Spirit,
one God, for ever and ever. **Amen.**

FIRST READING

Isa 8:23–9:3

First the LORD degraded the land of
    Zebulun
  and the land of Naphtali;
  but in the end he has glorified the
      seaward road,
  the land west of the Jordan,
  the District of the Gentiles.

Anguish has taken wing, dispelled is
    darkness:
  for there is no gloom where but now
    there was distress.

The people who walked in darkness
  have seen a great light;
  upon those who dwelt in the land of
    gloom a light has shone.
You have brought them abundant joy
  and great rejoicing,
  as they rejoice before you as at the
    harvest,
  as people make merry when dividing
    spoils.
For the yoke that burdened them,
  the pole on their shoulder,
  and the rod of their taskmaster
  you have smashed, as on the day of
    Midian.

RESPONSORIAL PSALM
Ps 27:1, 4, 13-14

R̷. (1a) The Lord is my light and my salvation.

The LORD is my light and my salvation;
  whom should I fear?
The LORD is my life's refuge;
  of whom should I be afraid?

R̷. The Lord is my light and my salvation.

One thing I ask of the LORD;
  this I seek:
to dwell in the house of the LORD
  all the days of my life,
that I may gaze on the loveliness of the
  LORD
  and contemplate his temple.

R̷. The Lord is my light and my salvation.

I believe that I shall see the bounty of the
  LORD
  in the land of the living.
Wait for the LORD with courage;
  be stouthearted, and wait for the LORD.

R̷. The Lord is my light and my salvation.

SECOND READING
1 Cor 1:10-13, 17

I urge you, brothers and sisters, in the
    name of our Lord Jesus Christ,
  that all of you agree in what you say,
  and that there be no divisions among
    you,
  but that you be united in the same mind
    and in the same purpose.
For it has been reported to me about you,
    my brothers and sisters,
  by Chloe's people, that there are
    rivalries among you.
I mean that each of you is saying,
  "I belong to Paul," or "I belong to
    Apollos,"
  or "I belong to Cephas," or "I belong to
    Christ."
Is Christ divided?
Was Paul crucified for you?
Or were you baptized in the name of Paul?
For Christ did not send me to baptize but
    to preach the gospel,
  and not with the wisdom of human
    eloquence,
  so that the cross of Christ might not be
    emptied of its meaning.

About Liturgy
Ordinary Time, second reading, and repentance: During Ordinary Time of Year A the second readings from the apostolic writings are taken from 1 Corinthians, Romans, Philippians, and 1 Thessalonians. Since these readings are assigned in a semi-continuous way (but with verses omitted because there is more Scripture than could fit into the number of Sundays in Ordinary Time), we ought not expect that these second readings will exactly correspond to the gospel as they do during festal seasons.

However, since the thrust of Ordinary Time is to walk with Jesus through a synoptic gospel to Jerusalem and during this find out the meaning of discipleship and the cost of Christian self-sacrifice, the second readings in a generic way can help us to know what living the gospel means. Often they spell out concrete Christian behaviors (or warn against what should be avoided) that enable a practical interpretation of the gospel.

These second readings, then, help us to instruct ourselves so that we can repent and follow Jesus the Light as light that brings others joy and well-being. Although the second readings aren't the focus of our attention and preaching, they are not unimportant. They are still God's word addressed to us in the here and now.

About Liturgical Music
Music suggestions: Contemporary hymns that deal with the call to discipleship and participation in the mission of Jesus include Sylvia Dunstan's "You Walk along Our Shoreline" [RS, SS, WC, WS], which would be suitable for either the entrance procession or the recessional; John Bell's "The Summons" [in most hymnals], which because of its introspective text would be appropriate for the preparation of the gifts; Suzanne Toolan's "Two Fishermen" [GC, GC2, RS, W3], which could be sung as a choir prelude or as an assembly song during the preparation of the gifts; and Joy F. Patterson's "You Call to Us, Lord Jesus" [HG], which would make an excellent entrance song.

Hymns that address Christ as light are also appropriate for this Sunday. Bernadette Farrell's "Christ, Be Our Light" [BB, GC2, JS2, OFUV, SS, WS], which combines the image of Christ as light with our call to discipleship, would be suitable for either the preparation of the gifts or the Communion procession. Suzanne Toolan's "Jesus Christ, Inner Light" [BB, JS2], which invites us to welcome the light and love of Christ as antidote to our own darkness, is meant to be sung Taizé style, with cantor singing the verses over an ostinato refrain. This piece would make an effective choral prelude [GIA octavos G-1668 and 5326], with assembly joining the choir on the refrain, or it could be sung during the Communion procession. "I Want to Walk as a Child of the Light" [in most hymnals] would work well either for the preparation of the gifts or Communion.

✠ SPIRITUALITY

GOSPEL ACCLAMATION
Matt 5:12a

R⁄. Alleluia, alleluia.
Rejoice and be glad;
your reward will be great in heaven.
R⁄. Alleluia, alleluia.

Gospel

Matt 5:1-12a; L70A

When Jesus saw the crowds, he
    went up the mountain,
and after he had sat down, his
    disciples came to him.
He began to teach them, saying:
    "Blessed are the poor in
        spirit,
    for theirs is the kingdom of
        heaven.
Blessed are they who mourn,
    for they will be comforted.
Blessed are the meek,
    for they will inherit the land.
Blessed are they who hunger and
        thirst for righteousness,
    for they will be satisfied.
Blessed are the merciful,
    for they will be shown mercy.
Blessed are the clean of heart,
    for they will see God.
Blessed are the peacemakers,
    for they will be called children of
        God.
Blessed are they who are persecuted
        for the sake of righteousness,
    for theirs is the kingdom of
        heaven.
Blessed are you when they insult you
        and persecute you
    and utter every kind of evil against
        you falsely because of me.
Rejoice and be glad,
    for your reward will be great in
        heaven."

Reflecting on the Gospel

Those who are into quilting know what a find sometimes can be made in fabric shops among remnants. Here among the "leftovers" they might discover just the right pattern and color to complete an original design perfectly. Whole quilts are sometimes even made from remnants, and these often become special family heirlooms, witnessing to years of loving stitching by a caring ancestor. Carefully piecing together different colors and patterns—small bits of cloth though each is—can create a beautiful harmony in the whole, a harmony that is a blessing to be passed on to all generations. This Sunday's first reading speaks of God's leaving a "remnant of Israel" who are humble and just, a patchwork of faithful people who abide in God's abundance and peace. They are the blessed ones of God—they are faithful, and God cares for them.

What identifies God's chosen "remnant" is not wealth, possessions, or power over others but lowliness, humility, justice, and truthfulness (see first reading). In this gospel Jesus elaborates God's call to this way of living when he proclaims the Beatitudes to his disciples. Our blessedness is both a quality of who we are and a blueprint for how we are to live as followers of Jesus. We are to be the "remnant" who carry forth God's eternal plan for establishing a just reign. The signs of this reign are abundance and peace.

Yet this kind of faithful living that makes God's reign present always invites insults and persecution, precisely because it challenges selfishness and self-promotion. Gospel living—taking seriously the Beatitudes—turns upside down the relationships people have with each other and invites a new world order that is the presence of God's kingdom of heaven. And this presence of God's kingdom is not so much our own doing as what God is accomplishing in us. To be blessed is to receive from God all good things. God never forsakes those who are in need. The goodness of our lives is made up of the bits and pieces of God's blessings that God patches together into a harmonious whole—the peace of the "kingdom of heaven."

Living the Paschal Mystery

The Beatitudes seem to describe behaviors and attitudes that we generally ascribe to those we call "saints." Yet all of us can name good people we know—truly *good* people. We can name the qualities and actions that lead us to judge them truly *good*. These (and we ourselves) are truly *good*—the blessed.

It is awesome to think that our own halting efforts at being really *good*—at extending mercy, justice, and righteousness to others as God has extended them to us—are one means for bringing God's blessedness to others! Simply sharing in God's work of salvation—providing for those in need—is a blessing in itself that brings unequaled happiness. Our deepest happiness comes not from fulfilling our own wants and desires (except for hearts desiring God) but from reaching out to others as God reaches out to us in blessing. Happiness that comes from our own desires and efforts is fleeting; the blessings of God that are showered upon us as we live humbly, justly, and faithfully last forever. Here's the truly amazing part: the happiness we share now is but a taste of our great reward in heaven!

Focusing the Gospel

Key words and phrases: Blessed are . . . , for theirs is the kingdom of heaven

To the point: What identifies God's chosen "remnant" is not wealth, possessions, or power over others but lowliness, humility, justice, and truthfulness (see first reading). Jesus elaborates God's call to this way of living when he proclaims the Beatitudes to his disciples. Our blessedness is both a quality of who we are and a blueprint for how we are to live as followers of Jesus. We are to be the "remnant" who carry forth God's eternal plan for establishing a just reign.

Connecting the Gospel

to the first reading: The blessings Jesus announces continue an ancient tradition reflected in the first reading: God extends protection and refuge to the "humble and lowly."

to our experience: When hearing these Beatitudes, many of us would not count ourselves among the poor in spirit, the meek, the merciful, etc. Nor do we tend to see ourselves as blessed. However, our very living of the Gospel is a revelation of our blessedness and of the presence of God's reign.

Connecting the Responsorial Psalm

to the readings: We can interpret this Sunday's psalm refrain either as a call to become blessed or as a celebration of blessedness already given. Both interpretations fit Christian discipleship, but the verses chosen from Psalm 146 to accompany this refrain seem to support the second one. The focus of the verses is on God and God's actions on our behalf. Phrase after phrase describes what God does for us: lifts oppression, feeds the hungry, frees captives, heals the blind, raises up the bowed down, protects strangers, etc. How blessed by God we are! And the final verse indicates that God's blessing of us will never cease but will continue "through all generations."

We bring these two interpretations together when we acknowledge how "poor" we are (gospel) and stand humbly before God (first reading), able to receive. It is then that we allow God to become the source of all that we need; it is then that we discover the blessedness we already possess.

to psalmist preparation: When you sing this Sunday's responsorial psalm refrain, you acclaim the assembly blessed, poor in spirit, members of God's kingdom. A good way to prepare yourself would be to think about and give thanks for members of your family and your parish who are examples of blessedness given and blessedness lived.

**ASSEMBLY &
FAITH-SHARING GROUPS**
- I experience the Beatitudes being lived in my family, in my neighborhood, in my workplace when . . . by . . .
- When my parish really lives these Beatitudes, what happens is . . .
- Hearing Jesus name me blessed makes me feel . . . calls me to . . .

PRESIDERS
What keeps me humble while experiencing blessedness is . . . This is evident in my ministry in that . . .

DEACONS
My ministry incarnates Jesus' message of blessedness to the disadvantaged whenever I . . .

HOSPITALITY MINISTERS
I see and respond to the blessedness of the people gathering whenever I . . .

MUSIC MINISTERS
My music ministry challenges me to live the Beatitudes by . . . Music ministry gives me a taste of the kingdom of heaven by . . .

ALTAR MINISTERS
My ministry is a summary of the Beatitudes and blueprint for living in that . . .

LECTORS
My proclamation is an announcement of God's love for the "remnant" when . . .

**EXTRAORDINARY MINISTERS
OF HOLY COMMUNION**
In distributing Holy Communion I offer the Blessed to the blessed and this fills me with . . .

Model Act of Penitence

Presider: In the gospel today we hear the familiar Beatitudes. Jesus reminds us that God blesses abundantly those who choose to live God's ways. Let us open ourselves to the blessedness God offers . . . [pause]

Lord Jesus, you are the Blessed One of God: Lord . . .

Christ Jesus, you show us the way to the kingdom of heaven: Christ . . .

Lord Jesus, you promise great reward for those who follow you: Lord . . .

Homily Points

• "Count your blessings!" How often people think of blessings only in terms of things—winning the lottery, owning a nice home, having a secure job. The Beatitudes assess blessings in an entirely different way: as attitudes and behaviors that are a sign of the presence of God's kingdom. Even more: the Beatitudes identify *us* as God's primary blessing in the world.

• In teaching the Beatitudes, Jesus calls us to a new way of being and living—indeed, he teaches a new covenant. He reverses our normal expectations of what will make us happy (blessed) in this world. It is not what we *have* but who we are, how we live, and how we relate to others that lead us to the ultimate satisfaction: our blessedness as those who dwell within the kingdom of heaven.

• All advertising is based on the enticement that what will make us happy is just this one more and better thing—the latest model car, the newest iPod, the most recent upgrade. Yet experience tells us that once we have these things, we still want more. The Beatitudes call for a radical rethinking of our needs, wants, and pleasures. Real happiness lies in the gift of blessedness that only God gives.

Model Prayer of the Faithful

Presider: We pray with confidence to a God who gives us every good blessing.

Response:

Lord, hear our prayer.

Cantor:

we pray to the Lord,

That all members of the church so live that their blessedness is evident to others . . . [pause]

That the leaders of nations lead their people to the justice and righteousness of God's reign . . . [pause]

That those who are poor in spirit, those who mourn, and those who suffer persecution for the gospel remember that they are God's blessed ones . . . [pause]

That our parish community continue to grow in blessedness . . . [pause]

Presider: God of blessings, you shower us with every good thing: hear these our prayers that one day we might enjoy everlasting life with you in heaven. Grant this through Christ our Lord. **Amen.**

ALTERNATIVE OPENING PRAYER

Let us pray

Pause for silent prayer

Father in heaven,
from the days of Abraham and Moses
until this gathering of your Church in
    prayer,
you have formed a people in the image of
    your Son.
Bless this people with the gift of your
    kingdom.
May we serve you with our every desire
and show love for one another
even as you have loved us.

Grant this through Christ our Lord.
    Amen.

FIRST READING
Zeph 2:3; 3:12-13

Seek the LORD, all you humble of the earth,
    who have observed his law;
seek justice, seek humility;
    perhaps you may be sheltered
    on the day of the LORD's anger.

But I will leave as a remnant in your midst
    a people humble and lowly,
who shall take refuge in the name of the
    LORD:
    the remnant of Israel.
They shall do no wrong
    and speak no lies;
nor shall there be found in their mouths
    a deceitful tongue;
they shall pasture and couch their flocks
    with none to disturb them.

RESPONSORIAL PSALM
Ps 146:6-7, 8-9, 9-10

℟. (Matthew 5:3) Blessed are the poor in
spirit; the kingdom of heaven is theirs!
    or:
℟. Alleluia.

The LORD keeps faith forever,
    secures justice for the oppressed,
    gives food to the hungry.
The LORD sets captives free.

℟. Blessed are the poor in spirit; the
kingdom of heaven is theirs!
    or:
℟. Alleluia.

The LORD gives sight to the blind;
  the LORD raises up those who were
    bowed down.
The LORD loves the just;
  the LORD protects strangers.

R⁊. Blessed are the poor in spirit; the
kingdom of heaven is theirs!
  or:
R⁊. Alleluia.

The fatherless and the widow the LORD
    sustains,
  but the way of the wicked he thwarts.
The LORD shall reign forever;
  your God, O Zion, through all
    generations. Alleluia.

R⁊. Blessed are the poor in spirit; the
kingdom of heaven is theirs!
  or:
R⁊. Alleluia.

SECOND READING
1 Cor 1:26-31

Consider your own calling, brothers and
    sisters.
Not many of you were wise by human
    standards,
  not many were powerful,
  not many were of noble birth.
Rather, God chose the foolish of the world
    to shame the wise,
  and God chose the weak of the world to
    shame the strong,
  and God chose the lowly and despised
    of the world,
  those who count for nothing,
  to reduce to nothing those who are
    something,
  so that no human being might boast
    before God.
It is due to him that you are in Christ
    Jesus,
  who became for us wisdom from God,
  as well as righteousness, sanctification,
    and redemption,
  so that, as it is written,
  "Whoever boasts, should boast in the
    Lord."

About Liturgy

Final blessing and dismissal: From a very early time the shape of the Mass included the two great parts of word and sacrament. Communion was really the final act of Mass, but early on there was a felt need to formalize the dismissal of the people. The simplest way to do this was in a kind of second post-Communion prayer called the "prayer over the people" (which is now a choice that is given with some Mass formularies). Paralleling the blessings of those who were dismissed earlier in Mass (and still present in the prayers accompanying the dismissal of the catechumens in parishes implementing the R.C.I.A.), there eventually developed a simple blessing over the people. The import of this concluding blessing is to call down God's help and protection on the people as they leave to take up their daily tasks.

We might interpret this concluding blessing as a kind of shorthand for the Beatitudes. Thus, we are sent forth from every liturgy armed with God's presence, knowing that whatever difficulties (persecutions) we might encounter in living the Gospel, we are not alone but always accompanied by God. Brief though it is, this final blessing at Mass sums up a message that Scripture often reminds us of: our God wishes us all good things.

About Liturgical Music

Importance of the psalm refrain: This is a good Sunday to reflect on the importance of paying attention to the responsorial psalm refrains given in the Lectionary. Whether taken from the psalm or from another source (as for this Sunday), the text of the refrain is intended to cast a specific light upon the psalm verses being sung. The refrain often reveals how the verses relate to the readings of the day. The text of the refrain, then, has an important function. This points out a problem with responsorial psalm settings that use a refrain different from the one given in the Lectionary. For example, a setting of Psalm 146 (this Sunday's psalm) with the refrain "I will praise the Lord all my days, make music to my God while I live . . ." or "Lord, come and save us" changes how the psalm relates to this specific set of readings. The psalm then becomes merely a piece of incidental music rather than a means of helping us enter more deeply into these readings and into this particular Sunday or solemnity of the liturgical year.

✝ SPIRITUALITY

GOSPEL ACCLAMATION
John 8:12

R⁊. Alleluia, alleluia.
I am the light of the world, says the Lord;
whoever follows me will have the light of life.
R⁊. Alleluia, alleluia.

Gospel

Matt 5:13-16; L73A

Jesus said to his disciples:
 "You are the salt of the earth.
But if salt loses its taste, with
  what can it be seasoned?
It is no longer good for anything
  but to be thrown out and
    trampled underfoot.
You are the light of the world.
A city set on a mountain cannot be
  hidden.
Nor do they light a lamp and then
  put it under a bushel basket;
  it is set on a lampstand,
  where it gives light to all in the
    house.
Just so, your light must shine before
  others,
  that they may see your good deeds
  and glorify your heavenly Father."

Reflecting on the Gospel

"To thine own self be true," Polonius advises his son in act 1 of Hamlet. How difficult this is for us sometimes! We are so often caught up in social, peer, and religious pressures that it is easy to lose sight of our identity and what we are about. Yet the bard said in his own words over half a millennium ago what Jesus taught over two millennia ago: To thine own self be true!

In the gospel this Sunday Jesus uses the examples of salt and light to help us understand how vital it is for us to be faithful to who we are. We are salt—we enhance others; we are light—we shine for others. Yet, eaten by itself, salt is bitter; it is meant to be in relation to something else; for example, to meat as a preservative, to food as a flavor enhancer. A lighthouse beacon shines, but it fulfills its purpose most clearly when it is seen by crew members of a ship and guides them safely home. The underlying message of these metaphors is that who we are as disciples always finds its deepest meaning in who we are in relationship to God and others. Just as salt and light are no good in and of themselves, so the good that disciples do is measured in their relationship to others. Discipleship is for the sake of others.

We can be faithful instruments—salt and light—when, as the disciples in the gospel did, we listen to Jesus and allow him to guide us. The first relationship we foster is with Jesus. This relationship ensures that we are not just any salt or any light but that of Christ. Disciples do not act alone but are always instruments in God's hand who, through God's power acting in them, do good for others. Disciples glorify God simply by opening themselves to God's working in and through them.

Isn't it interesting that in this gospel Jesus uses inanimate things—salt, light—to describe who disciples are? Disciples, however, are to be anything but inanimate. Through God's power, disciples are to bring out the good latent in the world (salt) and are to show forth by their good deeds the splendor of God's presence (light). Our discipleship is not to go unnoticed. Who we are and our relationship to God and others are at stake. Discipleship is being salt and shining forth in relation to others. It is being true to ourselves.

Living the Paschal Mystery

While the gospel uses metaphors to help us understand who we are as disciples of Jesus, this is not simply pretty language that may give us a poetic thrill but then be forgotten. The first reading makes the gospel metaphors very concrete. We are vindicated and glorify God when we act decisively as God acts: we are to feed the hungry, "shelter the oppressed and homeless, clothe the naked," remove oppression, and refrain from "malicious speech." Practically speaking for us today, this might mean that we get involved in some of the parish ministries directed to social outreach; or we might tutor one of the school children. Maybe being salty or shining forth simply means that we take stock of our already too-busy days and reflect on what has value or meaning for the good of others and what has become habit to no real avail. Discipleship always involves ongoing discernment about how we are in relation to God and others. Anything short of being the best person we can be as God's instruments of salvation is selling short being true to ourselves.

Focusing the Gospel

Key words and phrases: disciples, salt, light, good deeds

To the point: Isn't it interesting that in this gospel Jesus uses inanimate things—salt, light—to describe who disciples are? Disciples, however, are to be anything but inanimate. Through God's power, disciples are to bring out the good latent in the world (salt), and are to show forth by their good deeds the splendor of God's presence (light). Our discipleship is not to go unnoticed.

Connecting the Gospel

to the first reading: The first reading makes clear that by doing good works (sharing bread with the hungry, sheltering the homeless, etc.) we are the light shining forth God's presence and salvation.

to experience: Both salt and light are valuable to us because they serve so many household purposes. Our Christian discipleship is valuable when we serve the purpose of Jesus' mission.

Connecting the Responsorial Psalm

to the readings: In this Sunday's gospel Jesus commands us to let our light shine. The first reading identifies that light as right relationships (feeding the hungry, sheltering the homeless, clothing the naked, removing oppression) and tells us that a person who treats others in these ways will be so treated by God. But the psalm implies even more: the one who acts graciously and mercifully and justly is behaving exactly as God behaves. To act as God acts is the deepest meaning of righteous living. Such living shines in the darkness of the world for all to see.

Jesus tells us unequivocally that we have the capacity for such living: "you *are* the light of the world" (gospel). We shine simply by being faithful to who we already are. In a sense, then, we sing of ourselves in this responsorial psalm, not with arrogance but with humble acknowledgment of the power of God's grace working within us.

to psalmist preparation: How over the years have you come to understand what it means to live as a just person? Who stands for you as examples of truly just persons? What stands in the way of your being a just person?

ASSEMBLY & FAITH-SHARING GROUPS
- My discipleship is in need of "salt" when . . . I have been "salt" for the discipleship of others by . . .
- God's light shines forth in me when . . . This makes a difference in the world because . . .
- A time when the light of another's good works drew me to live the Gospel better was . . . ; a time when this drew me to glorify God was . . .

PRESIDERS
Ways my ministry is a "seasoning" within the parish are . . . ; ways my personal life shines forth Gospel values to others are . . .

DEACONS
I am light in the darkness of those in need because . . .

HOSPITALITY MINISTERS
Good hospitality, like salt, preserves and enriches the life of the community in that . . .

MUSIC MINISTERS
My music ministry is an appropriate "seasoning" for the liturgy when . . .

ALTAR MINISTERS
Serving is like salt: when properly proportioned it only enhances and never dominates. The way my service enhances the lives of others is . . .

LECTORS
The word of God that I need to shine forth in my workplace is . . . What causes me to keep my Gospel values "under a bushel basket" is . . .

EUCHARISTIC MINISTERS
My manner of distributing Holy Communion leads others to be light for the world when . . .

Model Act of Penitence

Presider: Jesus admonishes us today to be salt that seasons and light that shines. Let us prepare ourselves to celebrate these mysteries by asking for the grace to be faithful disciples . . . [pause]

Lord Jesus, you are the Light of the world: Lord . . .

Christ Jesus, you are the glory of the Father: Christ . . .

Lord Jesus, you call us to be faithful disciples: Lord . . .

Homily Points

• When the well-known humorist Erma Bombeck took a university writing course as a young student, one of her assignments was returned with the simple but powerful note, "You can write!" That comment launched Bombeck's successful writing career. How often our latent talents are unleashed because of the encouragement of someone else who sees in us what we do not yet recognize!

• We are to do what we are called by baptism to do—season the earth with the taste of God and shine forth on the earth the "good deeds" of salvation. As faithful disciples we call forth from each other the gifts God has given us for the sake of the kingdom. If we are not faithful to our mission as disciples, we become worthless.

• Calling forth the potential in others is often something we just naturally do. For example, parents encourage their children; teachers mentor students; friends bring to light the potential good that can come from a difficult situation. This gospel calls us to see such ordinary, everyday actions as ways God acts through us to bring the world to its fullest potential in Christ.

Model Prayer of the Faithful

Presider: We make known our needs to God, that we might be faithful disciples who are salt of the earth and light for the world.

Response:

Lord,—— hear our prayer.

Cantor:

we pray to the Lord,

That the church always be a light shining forth and leading others to fullness in Christ . . . [pause]

That world and church leaders always have the courage to call forth the potential in others . . . [pause]

That those caught in the distress of darkness and alienation be led by our good deeds to the light of Christ . . . [pause]

That each of us here be faithful disciples who live up to our potential to shine forth God's presence for all to see . . . [pause]

Presider: Faithful God, you are worthy of all glory: hear these our prayers that one day we might live with you for ever and ever. **Amen.**

OPENING PRAYER
Let us pray

Pause for silent prayer

Father,
watch over your family
and keep us safe in your care,
for all our hope is in you.

Grant this through our Lord Jesus Christ,
  your Son,
who lives and reigns with you and the
  Holy Spirit,
one God, for ever and ever. **Amen.**

FIRST READING
Isa 58:7-10

Thus says the LORD:
 Share your bread with the hungry,
  shelter the oppressed and the homeless;
 clothe the naked when you see them,
  and do not turn your back on your
   own.
 Then your light shall break forth like
   the dawn,
  and your wound shall quickly be
   healed;
 your vindication shall go before you,
  and the glory of the LORD shall be
   your rear guard.
 Then you shall call, and the LORD will
   answer,
  you shall cry for help, and he will say:
   Here I am!
 If you remove from your midst
  oppression, false accusation and
   malicious speech;
 if you bestow your bread on the hungry
  and satisfy the afflicted;
 then light shall rise for you in the
   darkness,
  and the gloom shall become for you
   like midday.

RESPONSORIAL PSALM
Ps 112:4-5, 6-7, 8-9

R̸. (4a) The just man is a light in darkness
to the upright.
　or:
R̸. Alleluia.

Light shines through the darkness for the
　　upright;
　he is gracious and merciful and just.
Well for the man who is gracious and
　　lends,
　who conducts his affairs with justice.

R̸. The just man is a light in darkness to
the upright.
　or:
R̸. Alleluia.

He shall never be moved;
　the just one shall be in everlasting
　　　remembrance.
An evil report he shall not fear;
　his heart is firm, trusting in the LORD.

R̸. The just man is a light in darkness to
the upright.
　or:
R̸. Alleluia.

His heart is steadfast; he shall not fear.
　Lavishly he gives to the poor;
his justice shall endure forever;
　his horn shall be exalted in glory.

R̸. The just man is a light in darkness to
the upright.
　or:
R̸. Alleluia.

SECOND READING
1 Cor 2:1-5

When I came to you, brothers and sisters,
　proclaiming the mystery of God,
　I did not come with sublimity of words
　　or of wisdom.
For I resolved to know nothing while I was
　　with you
　except Jesus Christ, and him crucified.
I came to you in weakness and fear and
　　much trembling,
　and my message and my proclamation
　　were not with persuasive words of
　　　wisdom,
　but with a demonstration of Spirit and
　　　power,
　so that your faith might rest not on
　　human wisdom
　but on the power of God.

About Liturgy

Use of candles at Mass: The liturgical requirement for the use of candles at Mass simply states that at least two lit candles should be on or next to the altar and even four or six may be used (especially at festival times) and these may be the candles carried in procession (GIRM, no. 117). The origin of lit candles, of course, was functional: before the time of electricity, candles were necessary even in daytime because the churches tended to be rather dark. Now candles are no longer functional but symbolic: they remind us of Christ, the Light of the world; in the context of this Sunday's gospel they also remind us that we are to be light that shines in the darkness.

One pastoral practice that has sprung up is that some churches have candle stands both at the altar and at the ambo. Since this fulfills the requirement of the law, it is no problem and underscores the importance of both the table ("ambo" comes from the Greek meaning "reading table") of the word and the table of the Eucharist. Questionable symbolism arises, however, when four candles are used (two at ambo, two at altar), and the two at the ambo are blown out at the conclusion of the Liturgy of the Word and the two at the altar lit, or when just two lit candles are used and they are carried from the ambo to be placed in empty candle stands at the altar. The problem with this is that we give the impression that one part is "over" and the next part "begins." In terms of the *chronology* of the ritual, this is true because we humans live in space and time. However, in terms of the *meaning* of the rite, the Liturgy of the Word cannot be separated from the Liturgy of the Eucharist and, indeed, neither are "finished" but continue into our Christian living. It would be best to omit these kinds of added rituals.

About Liturgical Music

Music suggestions: "Bring Forth the Kingdom" [G2, GC, GC2, RS] is an energetic verse-refrain song about being the salt, the light, the seed that brings forth the kingdom of God. The call-response structure of the verses gives the text added declarative power. The piece would work well for either the entrance procession or the recessional. Sylvia Dunstan's "Build Your City on a Hill," found in the collection *In Search of Hope and Grace* [GIA], draws its text directly from this Sunday's gospel and would be a good way of reflecting on this reading during the preparation of the gifts. Paul Tate's "You Are the Light of the World" [SS, WC, WS], a verse-refrain piece reminding us we are light of the world and salt of the earth, would work well during the preparation of the gifts or during the Communion procession.

In an exceptionally well-conceived poetic text, Carl Daw begins the successive verses of "Take Us as We Are, O God" [HG] with the four verbs that characterize the eucharistic rite: take, bless, break, give. The fourth verse marks the hymn as especially applicable for this Sunday: "Give us to the world you love As light and salt and yeast, That we may nourish in your name The last, the lost, the least, Until at length you call us all To your unending feast." The hymn would be appropriate during the preparation of the gifts.

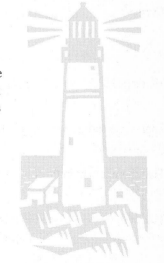

✠ SPIRITUALITY

GOSPEL ACCLAMATION
cf. Matt 11:25

R7. Alleluia, alleluia.
Blessed are you, Father, Lord of heaven and
   earth;
you have revealed to little ones the
   mysteries of the kingdom.
R7. Alleluia, alleluia.

Gospel   Matt 5:17-37; L76A

Jesus said to his disciples:
   "Do not think that I have come
      to abolish the law or the
      prophets.
I have come not to abolish but to
   fulfill.
Amen, I say to you, until heaven and
   earth pass away,
   not the smallest letter or the
      smallest part of a letter
   will pass from the law,
   until all things have taken place.
Therefore, whoever breaks one of the least
   of these commandments
   and teaches others to do so
   will be called least in the kingdom of
      heaven.
But whoever obeys and teaches these
   commandments
   will be called greatest in the kingdom of
      heaven.
I tell you, unless your righteousness
   surpasses
   that of the scribes and Pharisees,
   you will not enter the kingdom of heaven.

"You have heard that it was said to your
   ancestors,
   *You shall not kill; and whoever kills will
      be liable to judgment.*
But I say to you,
   whoever is angry with brother
   will be liable to judgment;
   and whoever says to brother, 'Raqa,'
   will be answerable to the Sanhedrin;
   and whoever says, 'You fool,'
   will be liable to fiery Gehenna.

*Continued in Appendix A, p. 270
or Matt 5:20-22a, 27-28, 33-34a, 37 in Appendix
A, p. 270.*

Reflecting on the Gospel

A father of a family of five children was fighting terminal cancer. His middle daughter had cerebral palsy. The father's relationship with his daughter was one of patience, gentleness, and obvious love and devotion as he guided her through the Mass postures, helped her to Communion, encouraged her to respond. After Mass the pastoral minister was listening to him talk about his most recent decision to choose life over death: he had joined a new cancer research group and had just begun a new form of chemotherapy. Because he spoke about his great desire as a young father to live, the pastoral minister expected his drive for a healthy life was because of his physically and mentally challenged daughter. Yet when the father asked for prayer, it wasn't for either him or his middle daughter. He asked for prayers for his oldest daughter who was now a teenager! How challenging these years can be for parents! The pastoral minister shared with him about finding a balance between setting parameters she may not cross and respecting her need to make decisions for herself. The gospel this Sunday is not about Jesus dealing with teenagers. He does remind us, though, how important the law is for us to know our parameters and to be faithful to them. He reminds us too that basic to law is a love relationship, certainly shown by this father toward both his daughters.

Jesus is not setting aside the old law. He categorically states that he has "come not to abolish but to fulfill" that law. While the world exists, we still need God's law to guide us because we are imperfect, coming only slowly to the fulfillment that Jesus promises. However, Jesus makes clear that simply keeping the law—as the scribes and Pharisees were so careful about doing—is not enough. The gospel is a lengthy comparison between the law of the Old Covenant (especially as the scribes and Pharisees to whom Jesus refers in the gospel interpreted and lived it) and a new law—a New Covenant—Jesus offers. The point of Jesus' lengthy discourse is clear: he is challenging us to a whole new covenantal basis for interpreting God's law. Rather than looking at the minimal letter of the law, we are to look at the spirit of the law, which calls us to a much fuller way of relating to God and one another. Jesus' new covenant is built on right relationships that extend beyond the letter of the law. The kingdom of heaven belongs only to those who fulfill the law by choosing fullness of life, goodness, and justice (see first reading).

No law—whether divine or human—can cover all the right choices we are to make as we journey through life. Both the gospel and first reading point to more that is needed: "trust in God," right choices that bring life to ourselves and others, relying on the wisdom and understanding of God who knows us better than we know ourselves. Our own choices for good—for life—can only come when we open ourselves to God's guidance and wisdom. In this is the promise of fullness of life.

Living the Paschal Mystery

Four times in the gospel Jesus says these or similar words: "You have heard it said . . . But I say to you . . ." How easy it is for us to do just the minimum! Jesus invites us to rethink our relationships with others, now on his terms. We are to act with the same loving-kindness as God has acted toward us. We must say and mean yes often—a yes that is a choice for life and goodness.

Focusing the Gospel

Key words and phrases: You have heard . . . But I say to you

To the point: The point of Jesus' lengthy discourse is clear: he is challenging us to a whole new covenantal basis for interpreting God's law. Rather than looking at the minimal letter of the law, we are to look at the spirit of the law, which calls us to a much fuller way of relating to God and one another. Jesus' new covenant is built on right relationships that extend beyond the letter of the law. The kingdom of heaven belongs only to those who fulfill the law by choosing fullness of life, goodness, and justice (see first reading).

Connecting the Gospel

to the first reading: Twice in the first reading we are asked to choose. We are choosing to live not by our own paltry understanding of law and life but by the "[i]mmense" and "all-seeing" wisdom of God.

to experience: Hundreds of choices face us each day; some are easy, some are hard. Rather than making choices because of personal convenience or something of our liking, Jesus challenges us to make choices that lead to the fullness of life.

Connecting the Responsorial Psalm

to the readings: Psalm 119 is the longest psalm in the psalter and includes within its carefully planned framework many types of psalm genres all woven together in praise of God's law. The relationship between the verses of Psalm 119 selected for this responsorial psalm and the first reading and gospel are readily evident. Those who keep the commandments of God are choosing life over death, good over evil (first reading). Those who understand the deepest intent of the law see it not as a list of external rubrics but as an invitation to more just and loving relationships (gospel). In the psalm we ask God to give us the kind of discernment Jesus brings to the law. We pray also for the kind of obedience to the law Jesus exemplifies: obedience flowing from a heart tempered by compassion, forgiveness, truth, and mercy.

to psalmist preparation: Wholehearted obedience to God's law leads not to a rigid heart but to a warm one. How have you grown over the years in your understanding of God's law? How has God's law made you more compassionate, more merciful, more truthful, more just? Where do you need to continue growing?

**ASSEMBLY &
FAITH-SHARING GROUPS**
- I find myself living by the letter of the law when . . . What frees me to live the spirit of the law is . . .
- A fuller way I am called to relate to those around me is . . .
- I choose life when . . . I choose goodness when . . . I choose justice when . . .

PRESIDERS
I have heard . . . But I say to the assembly . . .

DEACONS
My service ministry brings the fullness of life, goodness, and justice to others when I . . .

HOSPITALITY MINISTERS
My manner of greeting those gathering invites them to choose fullness of life when . . .

MUSIC MINISTERS
My music ministry opens me to a fuller relationship with God by . . . with other music ministers by . . . with the assembly by . . .

ALTAR MINISTERS
My humble ministry of service is life-giving for me when . . .

LECTORS
The assembly hears in my proclamation the call to choose life, goodness, and justice when I . . .

**EXTRAORDINARY MINISTERS
OF HOLY COMMUNION**
I convey to communicants the fullness God offers in Holy Communion by . . .

Model Act of Penitence

Presider: In today's gospel Jesus challenges us to live God's law in such a way that we are choosing the fullness of life God offers us. Let us call upon the Spirit of life and holiness to transform us during this celebration . . . [pause]

    Lord Jesus, you are the Wisdom of God: Lord . . .

    Christ Jesus, you are the fullness of life: Christ . . .

    Lord Jesus, you are the fulfillment of the law: Lord . . .

Homily Points

• We often ignore the letter of the law when it is to our advantage or liking; for example, we roll through stop signs, speed through yellow lights, pay the minimum income tax. Jesus also tells us to ignore the letter of the law, but for a very different reason: to deepen relationships by loving God and each other more fully.

• Jesus never said to ignore the law, and he surely did not come to abolish it. Rather, he does challenge us to go beyond the face of the law to redefine the way we live and relate to God and each other. The examples Jesus gives in this Sunday's gospel illustrate ways to open ourselves up to act toward others in the gracious way God acts toward us.

• What does the spirit of God's law invite us to choose? For example, the metaphor of plucking out one's eye challenges us to see things differently. The metaphor of cutting off one's right hand challenges us to grasp a different direction for our lives. The command to seek reconciliation with someone whom we have wronged frees us to offer ourselves more fully to God and others. It is for us to say yes or no; what do we choose?

Model Prayer of the Faithful

Presider: Let us ask God for the grace we need to choose life, goodness, and justice for all.

Response:

Lord, hear our prayer.

Cantor:

we pray to the Lord,

That the people of God be a source of life and holiness for others . . . [pause]

That world leaders work to establish laws that truly bring justice for all . . . [pause]

That those who are unjustly imprisoned, persecuted, or wronged find justice through the goodness of others . . . [pause]

That each of us here come to the fullness of life through the care we have for each other . . . [pause]

Presider: God of life, goodness, and justice, you hear the prayers of those who cry to you. Grant us our requests and bring us to the fullness of life everlasting. We ask this through Christ our Lord. **Amen.**

ALTERNATIVE OPENING PRAYER

Let us pray

Pause for silent prayer

Father in heaven,
the loving plan of your wisdom took flesh
    in Jesus Christ,
and changed mankind's history
by his command of perfect love.
May our fulfillment of his command reflect
    your wisdom
and bring your salvation to the ends of the
    earth.

We ask this through Christ our Lord.
    Amen.

FIRST READING

Sir 15:15-20

If you choose you can keep the
    commandments, they will save you;
    if you trust in God, you too shall live;
he has set before you fire and water;
    to whichever you choose, stretch forth
      your hand.
Before man are life and death, good and
    evil,
    whichever he chooses shall be given
      him.
Immense is the wisdom of the Lord;
    he is mighty in power, and all-seeing.
The eyes of God are on those who fear
    him;
    he understands man's every deed.
No one does he command to act unjustly,
    to none does he give license to sin.

RESPONSORIAL PSALM

Ps 119:1-2, 4-5, 17-18, 33-34

℟. (1b) Blessed are they who follow the law of the Lord!

Blessed are they whose way is blameless,
    who walk in the law of the LORD.
Blessed are they who observe his decrees,
    who seek him with all their heart.

℟. Blessed are they who follow the law of the Lord!

You have commanded that your precepts
    be diligently kept.
Oh, that I might be firm in the ways
    of keeping your statutes!

℟. Blessed are they who follow the law of the Lord!

Be good to your servant, that I may live
    and keep your words.
Open my eyes, that I may consider
    the wonders of your law.

℟. Blessed are they who follow the law of the Lord!

Instruct me, O LORD, in the way of your
     statutes,
   that I may exactly observe them.
Give me discernment, that I may observe
     your law
   and keep it with all my heart.

R̸. Blessed are they who follow the law of
the Lord!

SECOND READING
1 Cor 2:6-10

Brothers and sisters:
We speak a wisdom to those who are
     mature,
   not a wisdom of this age,
   nor of the rulers of this age who are
        passing away.
Rather, we speak God's wisdom,
     mysterious, hidden,
   which God predetermined before the
        ages for our glory,
   and which none of the rulers of this age
        knew;
   for, if they had known it,
   they would not have crucified the Lord
        of glory.
But as it is written:
   What eye has not seen, and ear has not
        heard,
     and what has not entered the human
        heart,
     what God has prepared for those who
        love him,
   this God has revealed to us through
        the Spirit.

For the Spirit scrutinizes everything, even
     the depths of God.

✝ CATECHESIS

About Liturgy

The spirit of liturgical law: Some people interpret the myriads of laws governing
the right celebration of liturgy too narrowly. They think that they restrict and constrain. While a mechanical approach to liturgical law may well seem like this, there is a
different intention about why we have so many laws.

When liturgical law is kept to the letter but without its spirit—without any pastoral
concern—then the law does no service to the people. The ritual is reduced to mere
rubrics with no life, and people have a right to complain about such application of the
law. On the other hand, when liturgical law is almost completely disregarded, then
we run a high risk of the liturgy becoming the captive of a few people in the community who shape it to their own understanding rather than God's wisdom and understanding. In this liturgical scenario liturgy can become quite idiosyncratic, dependent
upon the likes and dislikes of a few.

Liturgical law is not about putting our worship in a straightjacket. It is about drawing on the wisdom of the Tradition to best enact the paschal mystery. Fidelity to the
spirit of liturgical law ensures that we celebrate the one liturgy of the whole church. It
ensures that we are more than a local expression of the Body of Christ, but that we are,
indeed, a visible presence of the church.

Finding a balance between respecting the law and implementing its spirit for the
good of the community is not always easy. This is one reason why regular evaluation
of the whole liturgical endeavor (rubrics, music choices, postures, environment, etc.) is
so important. Ultimately, the criteria for good liturgy is not whether one keeps laws;
the criteria is whether the community prays, grows, and decides together to be a community choosing fullness of life, goodness, and justice.

About Liturgical Music

Music suggestions: "What Does the Lord Require" [RS, W3] combines a strong text
with an equally strong tune challenging us to "fulfill God's law so hard and high" by
acting in ways that lead us to "Do justly; Love mercy; Walk humbly with your God."
The hymn would be suitable during the preparation of the gifts as a meditation on
the gospel reading or as a recessional sending us out the door to live the way of God's
law. "The Stars Declare His Glory" [W3] reminds us that just as the stars, the vault of
heaven, the "silences of space," the rising sun, and all of creation declare the glory of
God, so too does the law of God. God's commandments are "A law of love within our
hearts, A light before our eyes." The lyrical tune suggests
this song be sung during the preparation of the gifts.
"Choose Life" [WC] is an attractive verse-refrain setting of
the text of the first reading. This song could be used during the Communion procession, with cantor or choir
singing the verses and assembly the refrain. A choral
octavo is available from WLP.

✚ SPIRITUALITY

GOSPEL ACCLAMATION
1 John 2:5

℟. Alleluia, alleluia.
Whoever keeps the word of Christ,
the love of God is truly perfected in him.
℟. Alleluia, alleluia.

Gospel   Matt 5:38-48; L79A

Jesus said to his disciples:
"You have heard that it was
    said,
*An eye for an eye and a tooth
    for a tooth.*
But I say to you, offer no
    resistance to one who is evil.
When someone strikes you on
    your right cheek,
turn the other one as well.
If anyone wants to go to law with you
    over your tunic,
hand over your cloak as well.
Should anyone press you into service
    for one mile,
go for two miles.
Give to the one who asks of you,
    and do not turn your back on one
    who wants to borrow.

"You have heard that it was said,
*You shall love your neighbor and
    hate your enemy.*
But I say to you, love your enemies
    and pray for those who persecute
    you,
that you may be children of your
    heavenly Father,
for he makes his sun rise on the bad
    and the good,
and causes rain to fall on the just and
    the unjust.
For if you love those who love you,
    what recompense will you have?
Do not the tax collectors do the same?
And if you greet your brothers only,
    what is unusual about that?
Do not the pagans do the same?
So be perfect, just as your heavenly
    Father is perfect."

Reflecting on the Gospel

Living with a perfectionist can drive us crazy! Often these "perfect" people are not only hard on themselves but also hard on everyone else around them. We tend to avoid perfectionists and perfectionism because we know we humans are anything but perfect. Quite frankly, we often drive each other crazy! And yet in this Sunday's gospel Jesus bids us to "be perfect, just as [our] heavenly Father is perfect." Had we been among his disciples so long ago, we might have responded to Jesus, "Get a life!"

Yes, Jesus' gospel command to "be perfect . . . as [our] heavenly Father is perfect" is, at first hearing, too much for us humans who are bent on revenge, minimal giving, the law of least resistance. No wonder the saying, "an eye for an eye and a tooth for a tooth" came about! In fact, the original intent of the saying was to prevent exacting exorbitant retribution from another for having been wronged. It was a law that kept things contained, reasonable. One could go only so far to pay back, get even, punish, make things right, equal things out. We still all too often think and behave as if this were our code of conduct. In the gospel Jesus is teaching us to act otherwise. We are to love as God has first loved us, to become holy as God is holy, even to be perfect as our heavenly Father.

To act toward others as God acts toward us takes quite a bit of readjusting in our thinking and doing. We must squelch our first impulses to strike out with hand and word. Rather than negatively judging another who doesn't do as we think he or she should, we must look beyond our narrow perception of things and give the other the benefit of the doubt. However, just as with the early disciples, this readjustment does not happen overnight, nor does it happen automatically.

In our treatment of one another—even those who are our enemies—Jesus (as Moses in the first reading) challenges us to go beyond what is expected, beyond what we might think is reasonable or even achievable. We are to go beyond what is human to what is divine: "Be holy" as God is holy (first reading), "be perfect" as God is perfect (gospel). On our own, this is impossible! Only because of God's love for us expressed in the life of Jesus who teaches us rightly, is this possible. Only when we experience God's love for us first, is this possible.

Living the Paschal Mystery

"Well, that will have to do for now." How often this is our cry in daily tasks. We have only a little bit of time to clean the house, so what we do will just have to do. We must write a sympathy card and can't seem to find the right words for a young widow with children, and so we do our best and say that will just have to do. A "that will just have to do" attitude is hardly the way of living to which this gospel challenges us! On the other hand, the gospel examples seem way out of proportion to our ordinary responses, and to the ordinary demands daily living places upon us. Jesus is not asking us, however, to go looking for folks without coats (although there are plenty in our neighborhoods and cities), or for those who need us to go the extra mile for them (there are plenty who need such help), or to give our money away willy-nilly. What Jesus is asking us to do is look upon every other person, whether friend or foe, family member or stranger, as the beloved of God. Acting in this manner is being holy and perfect as God is, and is done not in dramatic ways but in simple everyday gestures of love, respect, and care.

Focusing the Gospel

Key words and phrases: offer no resistance, go for two miles, love your enemies, be perfect . . . as . . . your heavenly Father

To the point: In our treatment of one another—even those who are our enemies—Jesus (as Moses in the first reading) challenges us to go beyond what is expected, beyond what we might think is reasonable or even achievable. We are to go beyond what is human to what is divine: "Be holy" as God is holy (first reading), "be perfect" as God is perfect (gospel). On our own, this is impossible! Only because of God's love for us expressed in the life of Jesus who teaches us rightly, is this possible.

Connecting the Gospel

to the first reading: In the gospel God speaks through Jesus; in the first reading, God speaks through Moses. Both messages are the same: what it means to be perfect like God (gospel) and holy like God (first reading) is to love others even at a price to ourselves.

to experience: The examples of responses to others given in the gospel seem way beyond our experience. Yet the simple things we do for one another every day—the ways we truly love one another—are what Jesus is asking of us and ways we can be holy and perfect.

Connecting the Responsorial Psalm

to the readings: We begin this responsorial psalm commanding our whole being to bless the God who pardons our sins, heals our ills, and redeems us from destruction. Rather than the justice our human hearts so readily understand and measure out, our God offers us mercy far beyond the horizon of our comprehension ("as far as the east is from the west"). Such attitudes and actions describe the holiness of God. This divine holiness is not an attribute but a state of being: God *is* holy. And we are to be holy as God is (first reading), perfect as God is (gospel). Jesus spells out the details. We are to relate to one another as God relates to us, going beyond the expected, loving without reserve, forgiving even what is unforgivable. Can we do this? Yes, because the God who is kind and merciful will nudge us with parental compassion (psalm) until we reach full stature as children of the Holy One.

to psalmist preparation: In singing this responsorial psalm you tell the assembly about the holiness of God who is compassionate, merciful, and forgiving. This is the holiness to which they are called (see first reading and gospel). Where do you see this holiness in them? In yourself?

**ASSEMBLY &
FAITH-SHARING GROUPS**
- I find myself wanting an "eye for an eye" when . . . What helps me turn the other cheek is . . .
- I find it easy to love my "neighbor" when . . . I find it difficult to love my enemies because . . .
- I struggle with the thought that I am holy because . . . with the thought that I am perfect as God in heaven because . . .

PRESIDERS
My proclamation helps others accept themselves as holy when . . .

DEACONS
My service takes me beyond what is expected when . . . beyond what is reasonable when . . . to holiness when . . .

HOSPITALITY MINISTERS
My greeting of the gathering assembly members goes beyond what is expected of me when I . . .

MUSIC MINISTERS
When music ministry requires I go the extra mile, I . . .

ALTAR MINISTERS
The very demands of this ministry can bring me to the holiness and perfection of God because . . .

LECTORS
By going beyond what is expected of me to love with God's love, my proclamation becomes . . .

**EXTRAORDINARY MINISTERS
OF HOLY COMMUNION**
My manner of distributing Holy Communion is a stronger sign of God's lavish love for us if I . . .

Model Act of Penitence

Presider: In today's gospel Jesus challenges us to love others and be perfect as our heavenly Father. As we prepare to celebrate this liturgy, let us open ourselves to God's love and mercy . . . [pause]

Lord Jesus, you are the holiness of God: Lord . . .

Christ Jesus, you call us to holiness: Christ . . .

Lord Jesus, you teach us how to love by your care for others: Lord . . .

Homily Points

• Most of us are so busy every day that we barely complete the basic demands and tasks of daily living. We might even find ourselves thinking/saying/being satisfied with taking care of life with a "lick and a promise." The gospel challenges us to go about living with a greater purpose.

• Jesus is hardly a model for giving things a "lick and a promise," but rather for walking the extra mile. For example, he looked at the hated Romans and pagans and saw not enemies but children of God. He saw lepers not as outcasts but as those deserving compassion and care. He handed over not his cloak but his very life. In all these and other ways he made visible the Father's holiness and perfection.

• Gospel living calls us to readjust radically how we live. We are not to be satisfied with minimums, not to be stuck in socially accepted ways of responding to others, not to be limited in our loving. We readjust our way of living by paying much more attention to the way Jesus himself lived. The poor, the sick, the downtrodden, the needy, enemies, those who persecute us—indeed, our very family members, coworkers, friends—all cry out to us for our love and care. This is how, concretely, we respond to Jesus' command to "be perfect."

Model Prayer of the Faithful

Presider: Let us pray to our heavenly Father for what we need to be holy and perfect.

Response:

Lord, hear our prayer.

Cantor:

we pray to the Lord,

That the church embody the gospel challenge to reach out to others with the kind of love Jesus taught us . . . [pause]

That world leaders always embody the gospel challenge to respond to the needs of the poor and downtrodden . . . [pause]

That enemies be reconciled, those in need be heard, and those who persecute others be transformed by love . . . [pause]

That each of us here grow in the holiness to which God calls us . . . [pause]

Presider: Holy God, you call us to be one with you in our love for one another. Help us to grow in the spirit of Jesus and one day share the perfection of everlasting life. We ask this through Christ our Lord. **Amen.**

ALTERNATIVE OPENING PRAYER

Let us pray

Pause for silent prayer

Almighty God,
Father of our Lord Jesus Christ,
faith in your word is the way to wisdom,
and to ponder your divine plan is to grow
   in the truth.
Open our eyes to your deeds,
our ears to the sound of your call,
so that our every act may increase our
   sharing
in the life you have offered us.

Grant this through Christ our Lord.
   Amen.

FIRST READING
Lev 19:1-2, 17-18

The LORD said to Moses,
   "Speak to the whole Israelite community
      and tell them:
   Be holy, for I, the LORD, your God, am
      holy.

"You shall not bear hatred for your
      brother or sister in your heart.
Though you may have to reprove your
      fellow citizen,
   do not incur sin because of him.
Take no revenge and cherish no grudge
      against any of your people.
You shall love your neighbor as yourself.
I am the LORD."

RESPONSORIAL PSALM
Ps 103:1-2, 3-4, 8, 10, 12-13

R̸. (8a) The Lord is kind and merciful.

Bless the LORD, O my soul;
   and all my being, bless his holy name.
Bless the LORD, O my soul,
   and forget not all his benefits.

R̸. The Lord is kind and merciful.

He pardons all your iniquities,
   heals all your ills.
He redeems your life from destruction,
   crowns you with kindness and
      compassion.

R̸. The Lord is kind and merciful.

Merciful and gracious is the LORD,
   slow to anger and abounding in
      kindness.
Not according to our sins does he deal
      with us,
   nor does he requite us according to our
      crimes.

R̸. The Lord is kind and merciful.

As far as the east is from the west,
   so far has he put our transgressions
     from us.
As a father has compassion on his
   children,
   so the Lord has compassion on those
     who fear him.

R̞. The Lord is kind and merciful.

SECOND READING

1 Cor 3:16-23

Brothers and sisters:
Do you not know that you are the temple
   of God,
   and that the Spirit of God dwells in you?
If anyone destroys God's temple, God will
   destroy that person;
   for the temple of God, which you are,
     is holy.

Let no one deceive himself.
If any one among you considers himself
   wise in this age,
   let him become a fool, so as to become
     wise.
For the wisdom of this world is foolishness
   in the eyes of God,
   for it is written:
     God catches the wise in their own
       ruses,
and again:
     The Lord knows the thoughts of the
       wise,
     that they are vain.

So let no one boast about human beings,
   for everything belongs to you,
Paul or Apollos or Cephas,
   or the world or life or death,
   or the present or the future:
   all belong to you, and you to Christ, and
     Christ to God.

About Liturgy

Matthew's Sermon on the Mount: One of the great advantages of the revised Lectionary is its three-year cycle of readings by which we hear much more of Sacred Scripture. One of the great advantages of Ordinary Time is that in each respective year of the cycle we read semi-continuously from one of the Synoptic Gospels. This means that important sections of the gospel are heard over consecutive Sundays. For just two examples, during Year B we hear most of John 6, the Bread of Life discourse, on the seventeenth to twenty-first Sundays in Ordinary Time; in Year A (this year) we hear almost all of the Sermon on the Mount from the third to ninth Sundays in Ordinary Time. Unfortunately, we only hear Matthew's Sermon on the Mount—one of the most complete, challenging, and beautiful codes of conduct we could hear and reflect on— every three years, and most years (depending on the moveable date of Easter) we only hear part of it. This year we hear the full Sermon. It is always a challenge for homilists to relate these Sundays so the assembly has some sense of the whole.

Unlike Luke, where Jesus preaches while on a plain, Matthew has Jesus going up a mountain before he sits down (a common posture at that time for a teacher) to teach. The mountain is not named, but it surely has a parallel with Mount Sinai. Moses climbed Mount Sinai to encounter the Lord and receive the Decalogue. Jesus climbs a mountain and teaches a new commandment that will lead to the fulfillment of the first. More than simply keeping laws, the Sermon on the Mount is a lengthy exhortation about ways we ought to be in relationship with each other beyond the expected relationships of the law. The relationships Jesus teaches are modeled by his own way of living and are a sign of how God relates to us. More than simply setting high standards for ethical behavior, Jesus is teaching us how to be holy as God is holy, to be perfect as our heavenly Father is perfect. Jesus is teaching us what God's kingdom looks like and how its citizens behave toward one another.

About Liturgical Music

Music suggestions: Songs acclaiming God's holiness as well as songs calling us to holiness would be most suitable this Sunday. "Holy, Holy, Holy, Lord God Almighty" [in most hymnals] would make a good hymn for the entrance procession, as would "God Is Love," set either to ABBOT'S LEIGH [BB, JS2] or to Gerard Chiusano's engaging melody [BB]. "Church of God, Elect and Glorious" [SS], in which we sing "Church of God, elect and glorious, holy nation, chosen race; called as God's own special people, royal priests and heirs of grace: know the purpose of your calling, show to all God's mighty deeds; tell of love which knows no limits, grace which meets all human needs," would be appropriate either for the entrance or for the preparation of the gifts. Also suitable for the preparation of the gifts would be "Forgive Our Sins as We Forgive" [in most hymnals], which calls us to move beyond bitterness and brooding to the forgiveness God models. Songs calling us to love one another as God loves us would be good choices for Communion. Examples include "Where Charity and Love Prevail" [in most hymnals]; David Haas's "God Is Love" [G2, GC, GC2, RS, SS]; "Love One Another" [G2, GC, RS]; and "God of Love, Make Us One" [WC, WS].

SPIRITUALITY

GOSPEL ACCLAMATION
Heb 4:12

℟. Alleluia, alleluia.
The word of God is living and effective;
discerning reflections and thoughts of the heart.
℟. Alleluia, alleluia.

Gospel   Matt 6:24-34; L82A

Jesus said to his disciples:
  "No one can serve two masters.
He will either hate one and love the other,
  or be devoted to one and despise the other.
You cannot serve God and mammon.

"Therefore I tell you, do not worry about
    your life,
  what you will eat or drink,
  or about your body, what you will wear.
Is not life more than food and the body more
    than clothing?
Look at the birds in the sky;
  they do not sow or reap, they gather
      nothing into barns,
  yet your heavenly Father feeds them.
Are not you more important than they?
Can any of you by worrying add a single
    moment to your life-span?
Why are you anxious about clothes?
Learn from the way the wild flowers grow.
They do not work or spin.
But I tell you that not even Solomon in all
    his splendor
  was clothed like one of them.
If God so clothes the grass of the field,
  which grows today and is thrown into the
      oven tomorrow,
  will he not much more provide for you, O
      you of little faith?
So do not worry and say, 'What are we to
    eat?'
  or 'What are we to drink?' or 'What are
      we to wear?'
All these things the pagans seek.
Your heavenly Father knows that you need
    them all.
But seek first the kingdom of God and his
    righteousness,
  and all these things will be given you
      besides.
Do not worry about tomorrow; tomorrow
    will take care of itself.
Sufficient for a day is its own evil."

Reflecting on the Gospel

Aesop tells the tale of a goatherd who was caught in a snow storm. Driving his goats to a nearby cave for shelter, the goatherd found the cave already occupied by a herd of wild goats—many more than his own. Greedy and desiring to increase in wealth, the goatherd took great care of the wild goats, even giving them the fodder intended for his own goats. In time the storm passed. Alas, the goatherd found he had nothing—his own goats had perished from neglect and the wild goats had run off to the hills and woods whence they came. The foolish man had made a pretty hapless choice—neglecting what was securely his own to gain what would only be lost anyway. He had chosen the wrong priority—greed over care and faithful duty. His shortsightedness and greed brought him to the very place he didn't want to be—impoverished.

We tend to worry about immediate things that affect our daily living, like food and shelter, job security and paying bills. We usually don't worry about ultimate things. Our shortsightedness can leave us quite impoverished. Jesus challenges us to a longer view: "seek first the kingdom of God and his righteousness." With that priority, our wealth is assured, but it is not a wealth measured by goats or other possessions. The wealth God offers is that God is ever faithful and will never forsake us (see first reading), that we are always embraced by God's tender love.

This Sunday's gospel begins by first challenging us to a stark, either-or choice: which master to choose, God or "mammon." Jesus categorically states that we cannot serve both. Then the gospel presents us with another, even more difficult, choice—not even to worry about our life! The gospel raises a stark contrast: do we worry excessively about everyday matters such as food, drink, and clothing, etc., or are we attentive to God's assurance that there is so much more to life than these everyday needs?

Worrying comes from serving the wrong master and having misguided priorities. The journey from worry to assurance is made by relying on the God who knows what we need and offers us so much more: fullness of life in the kingdom of God. The real value of our life and the only real wealth that we need seek is the "kingdom of God and [God's] righteousness."

Living the Paschal Mystery

Our own priorities are revealed to us in many ways. We need only look at our possessions, preoccupations, what drives us, what motivates us. When we become caught up in serving our social status or image, our acquisition of things, our professional success, even our own self-righteousness, we afflict ourselves with the anxieties such priorities always engender. When we choose to serve God—make God the center of our lives—we enter a realm of internal freedom and wealth beyond calculation.

The gospel invites us to turn our attention to what truly matters—the life only God can give. What is Jesus telling us must be our first concern in life? While being attentive to having the food and clothing, etc., that is normal and necessary, our priority must be what God offers and only God can give: eternal care, eternal life.

Focusing the Gospel

Key words and phrases: two masters, do not worry, Are you not more important, heavenly Father knows, seek first the kingdom of God

To the point: This gospel raises a stark contrast: do we worry excessively about everyday matters such as food, drink, and clothing, etc., or are we attentive to God's assurance that there is so much more to life than these everyday needs? Worrying comes from serving the wrong master and having misguided priorities. The journey from worry to assurance is made by relying on the God who knows what we need and offers us so much more: fullness of life in the kingdom of God.

Connecting the Gospel

to the first reading: With great tenderness God assures us that we will never be forsaken in what really matters—having an abiding, intimate relationship with God. Divine tenderness draws us to choose the right Master.

to experience: We tend to worry most when we are uncertain of an outcome or not in control of a situation: for example, whether we will have a job next week, whether we will be able to pay the month's bills, whether our children will grow up with good values. While these cares and worries are always part of our everyday struggles, the gospel reminds us that the ultimate outcome of life is in God's hand.

Connecting the Responsorial Psalm

to the readings: The first reading, psalm, and gospel present us with the same message: we are not to worry about our well-being, for God is the rock of our salvation (psalm), the mother who will never forget us (first reading), and the father who will provide for our every need (gospel). Knowing this, Jesus chides us to put our priorities in order and pursue God's kingdom and God's righteousness above all other goods.

But doing this is not easy! Placing pursuit of God's kingdom above all other concerns requires immense trust in God. And this is precisely Jesus' point. He is calling us to see more clearly how intimately God is involved in our lives, both in its daily unfolding and in its ultimate outcome. He is inviting us to choose as master One who is our father, mother, rock, and refuge, One who perceives our deepest needs and never fails to fill them. Yes, let us "Rest in God alone," and all else will be given to us.

to psalmist preparation: Your singing of this responsorial psalm needs to come from being filled with confidence and trust in God. When are you most able to "rest in God"? What leads you to become restless and worried? How in the midst of worry do you refocus on God?

**ASSEMBLY &
FAITH-SHARING GROUPS**
- I find myself worrying most when . . . What I worry most about is . . .
- I have been deeply touched by God's assurance of care when . . .
- Some everyday choices that have led me to fullness of life are . . .

PRESIDERS
My preaching can challenge the members of the assembly to reflect on their daily choices and whether those choices lead to fullness of life when . . .

DEACONS
In my ministry, I am the assurance that God cares for ordinary human needs when . . .

HOSPITALITY MINISTERS
The manner of my greeting instills a sense of assurance in those gathering that God cares for them when I . . .

MUSIC MINISTERS
What helps me keep my music ministry focused on the right priority is . . .

ALTAR MINISTERS
My ministry goes beyond choices about the mundane tasks of serving and reminds me of God's care for me when . . .

LECTORS
When I reflect on the tenderness God shows me, my proclamation sounds like . . .

**EXTRAORDINARY MINISTERS
OF HOLY COMMUNION**
The manner of my distribution of Holy Communion helps communicants realize that this Food and Drink is the "more" God continually gives us when . . .

CELEBRATION

Model Act of Penitence

Presider: As we prepare to celebrate this liturgy, let us open our hearts to the assurance of love and care God gives to those who seek first God's kingdom . . . [pause]

Lord Jesus, you are the fullness of life: Lord . . .

Christ Jesus, you lead us to the Father: Christ . . .

Lord Jesus, you open the way to God's kingdom: Lord . . .

Homily Points

• At face value, it would seem that many people have chosen mammon as their "master"—bigger homes, designer clothes, and the latest gadgets. It is amazing, however, that some of those who seem to "have it all" also show right priorities: for example, the thousands of people who volunteer for Doctors without Borders, Habitat for Humanity, going to New Orleans to help Katrina victims. In this we see the tender love and care of God at work.

• What does Jesus tell us should be our first concern in life? While worrying about food, drink, and clothing is normal and necessary, our priority must be the "kingdom of God and [God's] righteousness." What helps us set *this* priority is the experience of God's love and care for us and the assurance this brings.

• If we want to know what rules our lives, we need only examine how we spend our time and money. The gospel pushes us beyond everyday worries to reflect on the priorities that lead to ultimate happiness and security—fullness of life in God's kingdom. We are happiest when we give ourselves over to God's care for us and share that same care with others.

Model Prayer of the Faithful

Presider: We are confident to lift our prayers and needs to the God who loves and cares for us.

Response:

Cantor:

That the church make visible God's love and care through her ministry to all who come for help . . . [pause]

That world leaders always have the good of all as their first priority . . . [pause]

That those imprisoned by anxieties and worry be freed to seek God's love and care . . . [pause]

That each of us here reflect in our manner of living the assurance that God always cares for us . . . [pause]

Presider: Gracious God, you love and care for us beyond what we can imagine or desire. Hear these our prayers that one day we might share the everlasting fullness of life with you. We ask this through Christ our Lord. **Amen.**

Let us pray

Pause for silent prayer

Father in heaven,
form us in the likeness of your Son
and deepen his life within us.
Send us as witnesses of gospel joy
into a world of fragile peace and broken
    promises.
Touch the hearts of all men with your love
that they in turn may love one another.

We ask this through Christ our Lord.
    Amen.

FIRST READING
Isa 49:14-15

Zion said, "The LORD has forsaken me;
    my Lord has forgotten me."
Can a mother forget her infant,
    be without tenderness for the child of
        her womb?
Even should she forget,
    I will never forget you.

RESPONSORIAL PSALM

Ps 62:2-3, 6-7, 8-9

R̲). (6a) Rest in God alone, my soul.

Only in God is my soul at rest;
    from him comes my salvation.
He only is my rock and my salvation,
    my stronghold; I shall not be disturbed
        at all.

R̲). Rest in God alone, my soul.

Only in God be at rest, my soul,
    for from him comes my hope.
He only is my rock and my salvation,
    my stronghold; I shall not be disturbed.

R̲). Rest in God alone, my soul.

With God is my safety and my glory,
    he is the rock of my strength; my refuge
        is in God.
Trust in him at all times, O my people!
    Pour out your hearts before him.

R̲). Rest in God alone, my soul.

SECOND READING

1 Cor 4:1-5

Brothers and sisters:
Thus should one regard us: as servants of
    Christ
    and stewards of the mysteries of God.
Now it is of course required of stewards
    that they be found trustworthy.
It does not concern me in the least
    that I be judged by you or any human
        tribunal;
    I do not even pass judgment on myself;
I am not conscious of anything against
    me,
    but I do not thereby stand acquitted;
    the one who judges me is the Lord.
Therefore do not make any judgment
    before the appointed time,
    until the Lord comes,
    for he will bring to light what is hidden
        in darkness
    and will manifest the motives of our
        hearts,
    and then everyone will receive praise
        from God.

About Liturgy

Liturgy's priorities: Just as it is so easy to get caught up in the wrong everyday concerns and end up fretting and worrying about many things, so it is easy to get caught up in the wrong liturgical priorities and lose sight of what we are really doing when we gather to worship. Because liturgy comprises a rather complex ritual with many details, it is easy to lose sight of the bigger picture: we are assembled primarily to give God thanks and praise.

Rather than whether we like the choice of music, the personality of the presider, the friendliness of the hospitality ministers, the informal atmosphere, etc. (and none of these elements is unimportant!), liturgy calls us to a different set of priorities. God is first, and our attention is directed there through surrender to the ritual prayer, encountering God through many divine presences, making a good effort to hear God's words spoken to us in the proclamations, entering into remembering God's saving deeds on our behalf, offering ourselves as a pleasing gift along with the bread and wine, opening ourselves to being transformed by God's presence and grace, praying for the living and dead of the whole world, accepting the disciple's duty to live the celebration upon dismissal.

It is actually much easier to be more concerned with right music, postures, movement, etc., than it is to be concerned about focusing on God and the fullness of life that God offers us each time we gather to celebrate liturgy. The former can be quickly forgotten upon leaving the church building; the latter shapes a life.

About Liturgical Music

Music suggestions: Songs about trust in God and God's providence abound. "O God, Our Help in Ages Past" [in most hymnals] and "Who Can Measure Heaven and Earth" [RS, SS] would be suitable for the entrance procession or during the preparation of the gifts. Also appropriate for the preparation of the gifts would be "Seek Ye First" [in most hymnals]; "Only in God," both John Foley's setting [GC, GC2] and John Michael Talbot's [BB, JS2, OFUV, VO]; and "You Are All We Have" [G2, GC, GC2, RS, SS]. A good choice for Communion would be Steve Warner's "Be Still and Know That I Am God" [WC; choir arrangement in WLP *Choral Companion*], with cantor verses sung either in alternation with the assembly refrain or over the refrain treated as an ostinato. Another fitting choice for Communion would be Steve Warner's "All Will Be Well" [WC, WS, VO]. Two choices that would be lovely prelude pieces with the assembly joining the choir or cantors are Taizé's "Nada Te Turbe/Nothing Can Trouble" [G2, GC, GC2, RS] and John Bell's "Be Still and Know That I Am God" G2, GC, RS], with its canonic arrangement gradually increased to a multilayered, but quietly sung, harmonic fullness.

✝ SPIRITUALITY

GOSPEL ACCLAMATION
John 15:5

R♪. Alleluia, alleluia.
I am the vine, you are the branches, says the
    Lord;
whoever remains in me and I in him will
    bear much fruit.
R♪. Alleluia, alleluia.

Gospel

Matt 7:21-27; L85A

Jesus said to his disciples:
    "Not everyone who says to me,
        'Lord, Lord,'
    will enter the kingdom of
        heaven,
    but only the one who does the
        will of my Father in heaven.
Many will say to me on that day,
    'Lord, Lord, did we not prophesy in
        your name?
Did we not drive out demons in your
    name?
Did we not do mighty deeds in your
    name?'
Then I will declare to them solemnly,
    'I never knew you. Depart from me,
        you evildoers.'

"Everyone who listens to these words
        of mine and acts on them
    will be like a wise man who built his
        house on rock.
The rain fell, the floods came,
    and the winds blew and buffeted the
        house.
But it did not collapse; it had been set
        solidly on rock.
And everyone who listens to these
        words of mine
    but does not act on them
    will be like a fool who built his house
        on sand.
The rain fell, the floods came,
    and the winds blew and buffeted the
        house.
And it collapsed and was completely
        ruined."

Reflecting on the Gospel

Eighteenth-century lawyer and American statesman James Otis coined the phrase "A man's [sic] house is his castle." The context of his remark was his response to the English Parliament's law allowing searches of colonists' homes for smuggled goods that avoided taxation. His adage raises a wider concern that our homes are more than a storehouse of goods and a place of price and ownership for us. Homes are where we presume to be free from interference, can be ourselves, can find protection. In a real sense our homes are physical embodiments of ourselves and the life and virtues we value most. We need them to be secure, lasting, intact.

In the gospel for this Sunday Jesus tells a parable about a wise man who built his house on rock. Neither rain nor floods, wind nor buffeting could topple the house. It remained solid, stable, livable. The parable is doing far more than telling us how and where we are to build our homes. Jesus is instructing us about where our true home is (the kingdom of heaven) and how we ensure that we enter into and remain in this home (by doing more than simply listening to his words).

In the first reading Moses admonishes the Israelites to take God's word into their hearts and souls—into their very being. God's will cannot be something external to us. Even merely conforming to God's will is not enough. Doing something simply because it is law is lifeless and not life-giving. If God's will is to lead to fullness of life—entering the kingdom of heaven—it must be embraced, made our own, become for us a blessing rather than a burden. As it was with Jesus, our words and deeds must coincide, be in agreement, be one because they well up from deep within ourselves. The solid rock of our very selves is found in listening to Jesus' words, acting on them, and thus building lives consistent with who he is.

Not everyone builds on solid rock. Some lives are built on the slippery and changing sands of fickleness, showiness, ignoring the everyday responsibilities we ought to face and do well. The solid rock upon which Jesus invites us to build our home is nothing less than doing "the will of [the] Father in heaven." Words are not enough. Jesus makes clear that it is *deeds* that set the direction for our life. The bedrock of our life is doing God's will as revealed to us through Jesus' words. Indeed, Jesus is the rock upon which we build our lives, and it is our encounters with him that teach us to do as he did. Surely, *this* Word is enough.

Living the Paschal Mystery

Jesus' words must become our words; his deeds must become our deeds. This process of our words and deeds coalescing and aligning with Jesus' words and deeds can only happen when we truly *listen* to Jesus. This active listening is not a matter of merely hearing words; the active listening is *encountering* Jesus so that his words are internalized as a deeper relationship with him. The listening is conforming ourselves to Christ.

We encounter and listen to Jesus though the words of Scriptures we read in our private prayer as well as those proclaimed at liturgy. Jesus' words come to us through the advice and admonition of others. We might hear his word in an encouraging remark that nudges us to try harder or in the warning comment that brings us to reevaluate our choices and behaviors.

Focusing the Gospel

Key words and phrases: Not everyone who says, does the will of my Father, listens to these words of mine and acts

To the point: Words are not enough. Jesus makes it clear that it is *deeds* that set the direction for our life. The bedrock of our life is doing God's will as revealed to us through Jesus' words. Indeed, Jesus is the rock upon which we build our lives, and it is our encounters with him that teach us to do as he did. Surely, *this* Word is enough.

Connecting the Gospel

to the first reading: Moses admonishes the people to take God's word into their very "heart and soul," into their very being. We must *become* God's Word.

to experience: We are inundated with words; for example, millions of text messages are sent daily, advertising surrounds us, bulletin boards are cluttered with notices. With so many words, there may be a tendency to disregard them. The gospel warns us that we cannot disregard Jesus' words, for they teach us the manner of living that leads to fullness of life.

Connecting the Responsorial Psalm

to the readings: It is not enough merely to know God's commandments (first reading) or to hear Jesus' words (gospel). We must put them into action. Faith demands action, for it is action that proves the mettle of faith and stands up to the pressures prevailing against it. Yet Jesus' warning, and Moses' warning before him to the Israelites, implies awareness of how difficult we human beings find it to make the choice necessary to put faith into action. We'd rather play in sand where no demands can be made of us because nothing holds from one day to the next. Aware of our propensity to avoid the hard work of building rock-solid faith, we turn in the psalm to the One who is already rock-sure. "Be [our] rock," we beg God, be our foundation and our rampart. Then we will stand steady, ready to put God's will into action (gospel).

to psalmist preparation: Singing this psalm requires awareness of how much you need to rely on God to make the very choice to do God's will. When do you find yourself most in need of God's rock-fastness? How does God respond to you at these times?

ASSEMBLY & FAITH-SHARING GROUPS

- The bedrock of my life is . . . when . . . because . . .
- A word of Jesus that has really spoken to me is . . . It has made a difference in my life in that . . .
- A deed that has really spoken to me is . . . What my deeds tell others is . . .

PRESIDERS

The words of my preaching lead members of the assembly to encounter Jesus in their midst when . . .

DEACONS

My service ministry is the Word made flesh through deed when . . .

HOSPITALITY MINISTERS

My greeting is more than mere words and becomes the presence of the Word when . . .

MUSIC MINISTERS

My music ministry leads me to encounter Jesus and do God's will by. . .

ALTAR MINISTERS

My ministry of doing becomes a presence of the Word when . . .

LECTORS

The manner of my proclamation teaches the assembly what God's will is whenever I . . .

EXTRAORDINARY MINISTERS OF HOLY COMMUNION

My manner of distributing Holy Communion allows Word and deed to come together for the communicants whenever I . . .

Model Act of Penitence

Presider: In today's gospel Jesus challenges us to do God's will by listening to him and putting his words into action. Let us open ourselves to building our lives on the solid foundation of Jesus' word . . . [pause]

Lord Jesus, you are the Rock of our salvation: Lord . . .

Christ Jesus, you are the Word made flesh: Christ . . .

Lord Jesus, you show us the will of the Father: Lord . . .

Homily Points

• Words are cheap, we say. But this was not so for the parents who received a $35,000 bill for their teenage daughter's text messaging. Adding to their aggravation, the girl's messaging was, no doubt, pointless prattle. Jesus' words to us, on the other hand, are never pointless but always communications leading us to fullness of life. These words are worth any cost.

• We learn Jesus' words through our encounters with him, encounters made accessible because Jesus lived the everyday life we ourselves live. He used simple language (like talking about building a house) with which we could identify. Jesus' words came out of his lived experience—first out of his own doing of his Father's will and, second, out of his awareness of who we are and what we really need in order to hear and understand the fullness of life that is God's will for us.

• Coming to fullness of life by doing God's will does not mean performing extraordinary feats (prophesying, driving out demons, doing mighty deeds). These feats can, in fact, be expressions of turning away from God. Doing God's will means doing the ordinary things of every day as Jesus would do them.

Model Prayer of the Faithful

Presider: Let us pray that we may hear Jesus' words and live them faithfully.

Response:

Lord,—— hear our prayer.

Cantor:

we pray to the Lord,

That all members of the church continue to listen to the words of Jesus to know and do God's will . . . [pause]

That leaders of nations build peace on the solid foundation of justice . . . [pause]

That the poor and needy, the downtrodden and oppressed hear Jesus' word promising fullness of life . . . [pause]

That each of us here ever more deeply encounter Jesus in one another, hear his word more clearly, and live more perfectly as he did . . . [pause]

Presider: O God, you speak to us in the depth of our hearts. Open us to hear your Word, do your will, and come to fullness of life. We ask this through the Word made flesh, Jesus Christ our Lord. **Amen.**

Let us pray

Pause for silent prayer

God our Father,
teach us to cherish the gifts that surround us.
Increase our faith in you
and bring our trust to its promised fulfillment
in the joy of your kingdom.

Grant this through Christ our Lord.
Amen.

FIRST READING
Deut 11:18, 26-28

Moses told the people,
"Take these words of mine into your heart and soul.
Bind them at your wrist as a sign,
and let them be a pendant on your forehead.

"I set before you here, this day, a blessing and a curse:
a blessing for obeying the commandments of the LORD, your God,
which I enjoin on you today;
a curse if you do not obey the commandments of the LORD, your God,
but turn aside from the way I ordain for you today,
to follow other gods, whom you have not known.
Be careful to observe all the statutes and decrees that I set before you today."

RESPONSORIAL PSALM

Ps 31:2-3, 3-4, 17, 25

℟. (3b) Lord, be my rock of safety.

In you, O LORD, I take refuge;
    let me never be put to shame.
In your justice rescue me,
    incline your ear to me,
    make haste to deliver me!

℟. Lord, be my rock of safety.

Be my rock of refuge,
    a stronghold to give me safety.
You are my rock and my fortress;
    for your name's sake you will lead and
        guide me.

℟. Lord, be my rock of safety.

Let your face shine upon your servant;
    save me in your kindness.
Take courage and be stouthearted,
    all you who hope in the LORD.

℟. Lord, be my rock of safety.

SECOND READING

Rom 3:21-25, 28

Brothers and sisters,
Now the righteousness of God has been
    manifested apart from the law,
    though testified to by the law and the
        prophets,
    the righteousness of God through faith
        in Jesus Christ
for all who believe.
For there is no distinction;
    all have sinned and are deprived of the
        glory of God.
They are justified freely by his grace
    through the redemption in Christ Jesus,
    whom God set forth as an expiation,
    through faith, by his blood.
For we consider that a person is justified
    by faith
    apart from works of the law.

About Liturgy

Liturgy's many words: The words of liturgy are many, indeed, and they seem to be multiplying. At one time all the words of Mass for the whole year could be contained in one book. Now it takes many, many books and most of them are large and weighty: the U.S. Lectionary is multiple volumes; the Book of Gospels is rich and ornate; the Sacramentary is heavy; music books are numerous. We need ritual books for the celebration of sacraments and for other occasions, such as the dedication of a church. We have the Book of Blessings that includes "official" blessings as well as many household prayers and devotional practices. All these words are good and needed. But how do they cease to be only words? How do these words also become our deeds?

The danger of so many words is that we begin to "tune them out." We cease to listen. In order to minimize this tendency, a number of things need to be kept in mind. First of all, we ought not to increase the words of our liturgies! Commentaries, announcements, introductions are best kept to a minimum. Second, the words of our liturgies are not all the same, so they ought not be uttered the same; for example, narrations should be voiced as the stories they are, and acclamations need to be sung with full throat. Third, if there is a balance between sound and silence, then the spoken words can be heard with more meaning; if there is never silence during liturgy, there is never a pause in our words. Fourth, besides words, liturgy makes use of numerous postures, gestures, and movements. When these are done well, they help inform the words and allow them to come to fuller life within us.

About Liturgical Music

Music suggestions: "The Will of Your Love" [JS2, S&S] is a Taizé-style piece by Suzanne Toolan. While the assembly sings the ostinato refrain, "The will of your love, the will of your love be done on earth as it is in heaven," the cantor sings verses such as "Blessed are you, blessed and holy. Teach me your way, the way of your love" and "A lamp to my feet, a light to my path is your word, your word of truth." This piece would make a lovely, reflective Communion song in keeping with the gospel of the day. The South African song "Mayenziwe/Your Will Be Done" is a mantra on "Your will be done on earth" from the Our Father. Meant to be sung meditatively with layers of harmony moving in and out, this piece would also work well at the preparation of the gifts or during Communion. Songs about Christ as the foundation of our lives appear in various hymn resources and would be good choices for the entrance procession, the preparation of the gifts, or the recessional. These include "Christ Is Made the Sure Foundation," "How Firm a Foundation," "O Christ the Great Foundation," and "The Church's One Foundation."

Season of Lent

✝ SPIRITUALITY

GOSPEL ACCLAMATION
cf. Ps 95:8

If today you hear his voice,
harden not your hearts.

Gospel   Matt 6:1-6, 16-18; L219

Jesus said to his disciples:
    "Take care not to perform righteous
        deeds
    in order that people may see
        them;
    otherwise, you will have no
        recompense from your
        heavenly Father.
When you give alms,
    do not blow a trumpet before
        you,
    as the hypocrites do in the synagogues
        and in the streets
    to win the praise of others.
Amen, I say to you,
    they have received their reward.
But when you give alms,
    do not let your left hand know what
        your right is doing,
    so that your almsgiving may be secret.
And your Father who sees in secret
    will repay you.

    "When you pray,
    do not be like the hypocrites,
    who love to stand and pray in the
        synagogues and on street corners
    so that others may see them.
Amen, I say to you,
    they have received their reward.
But when you pray, go to your inner
        room,
    close the door, and pray to your
        Father in secret.
And your Father who sees in secret
    will repay you.

Continued in Appendix A, p. 270.

See Appendix A, p. 271, for other readings.

Reflecting on the Gospel

There is a kind of traditional fascination with Lent that doesn't seem to be limited to the spiritually fervent. Great numbers of us make great effort to receive the ashes, give up something we enjoy, get to church more often, or give to the poor during these special forty days. Just like springtime with its promise of new life (the word "Lent," we think, is derived from the Old English "lengthen," noting that the days are getting longer and spring is coming), Lent is our church time for getting things in order so that we may receive new life. Lent is a time for spring spiritual housecleaning. However good the discipline of Lenten practices might help us feel about ourselves, mere discipline is not the aim of Lent. However much penance we do, the only value in them is if they ultimately lead to renewed life.

Penitential practices in themselves don't guarantee a spiritual springtime of new life. All too many of us spend too much of life just going through the motions of what we are required to do. Sometimes this is no problem; for example, when brushing our teeth, the job gets done quite adequately without giving it any thought. Spiritual housecleaning is another matter. It takes a great deal of awareness—of that from which we wish to turn (our sinfulness) and toward Whom we want to turn (the God who gives us life)—for Lent to yield its promised new life. Although all of us are called to perform penance throughout the year (for example, each Friday), Lent is a special time the church gives us to concentrate and focus ourselves—not just on penance but on the whole process of conversion, of coming to new life.

Penance and conversion aren't negative aspects of our spiritual life that we tolerate because they are somehow good for us. Penance and conversion take us to our center—our open hearts—so that there we can discover God and the graciousness, mercy, and kindness that can only be ours when we turn toward God anew. There is much at stake during Lent—nothing less than encountering God in new and most intimate ways. "Now is the very acceptable time" (second reading) for us to open our hearts to the new life God offers.

Why, then, do we really perform Lenten deeds of penance (almsgiving, prayer, fasting)? Not for the passing reward of public acclaim, as the gospel warns, but for the everlasting reward of God's transforming grace (see second reading) of new life. Our penance is thus "rewarded" by a springtime life-relationship with God and each other that comes from returning to God with our whole heart (see first reading). And the reward is given now.

Living the Paschal Mystery

The readings on this, the first day of Lent, caution us to make our Lenten penance more than mere practices. It is far better to do a little well than to take on a whole lot and in the end not have deepened our relationship with God and renewed our relationships with others. Along these same lines, Lent isn't an endurance contest, either. The question we might ask ourselves on Holy Saturday as we prepare to celebrate the Easter mystery ought not be whether we succeeded in not eating our favorite junk food or in the effort to get to Mass every day (as laudable as these sacrifices might be) but whether we have discovered God in new and more life-giving ways. Our dying during Lent is for the sole purpose of finding a springtime of new life in the God who is "gracious and merciful . . . slow to anger, rich in kindness, and relenting in punishment" (first reading).

Focusing the Gospel

Key words and phrases: righteous deeds . . . recompense, When you give alms . . . pray . . . fast, Father . . . will repay you

To the point: Why do we perform Lenten deeds of penance (almsgiving, prayer, fasting)? Not for the passing reward of public acclaim but for the everlasting reward of God's transforming grace (see second reading). Our penance is thus "rewarded" by a deeper relationship with God and each other that comes from returning to God with our whole heart (see first reading). And the reward is given now.

Model Prayer of the Faithful

Presider: We pray that during this Lent we might journey through death to new life.

Response:

Lord, hear our prayer.

Cantor:

we pray to the Lord,

That members of the Body of Christ open their hearts through deeper prayer to God's transforming grace . . . [pause]

That all peoples of the world find salvation in God . . . [pause]

That our Lenten almsgiving lift up those in need, feed the hungry, and ease the burdens of the poor . . . [pause]

That our Lenten fasting bring us to hunger for deeper relationships with God and one another . . . [pause]

Presider: Gracious and merciful God, you desire that our hearts turn toward you: hear these our prayers that our Lenten penance may be sincere and our Easter joy complete. Grant this through Christ our Lord. **Amen.**

Special Features of the Rite

The act of penitence is omitted because the blessing and distribution of ashes (which occurs after the homily) takes its place. One might wonder why this rite with ashes would not open Mass and simply replace the penitential act there. One suggestion is that the blessing and distribution of ashes is best understood within the context of the readings assigned to this day.

The distribution of ashes harkens back to the Order of Penitents in the early church, but wearing sackcloth and ashes as a sign of penance is already found in the Old Testament (for example, Isa 58:5; Jer 6:26; Dan 9:3; Jonah 3:6) and in some pagan religious practices. The practice of burning the palms from the previous Palm Sunday dates at least to the twelfth century; the Sacramentary still has a rubrical note on this.

FOR REFLECTION

• The way I can perform almsgiving, prayer, and fasting so that I return to God with my whole heart is . . .

• One way I need to rend my heart (see first reading) this Lent is . . . I know God will reward me in this way . . .

• At Easter, I hope my relationship with God looks like . . . I hope my relationship with my family looks like . . . I hope my relationship with . . .

Homily Points

• Ash Wednesday is neither a Sunday nor a holy day of obligation, yet our churches are packed; we want to be marked with ashes. But ashes are the product of death—dead palm branches have been burned. Paradoxically, we use this sign of death at the beginning of Lent to mark our journey to new life.

• When we think about Lent, we generally think in terms of giving something up—a kind of "dying" to self. But the readings for this day suggest to us that merely "giving up" cannot be an end in itself. Lent is about beginnings: coming to new life, deepening our relationship with God and others, and transforming who we are and how we live.

✚ SPIRITUALITY

GOSPEL ACCLAMATION
Matt 4:4b

One does not live on bread alone,
but on every word that comes forth from the
mouth of God.

Gospel   Matt 4:1-11; L22A

At that time Jesus was led by the Spirit
into the desert
to be tempted by the devil.
He fasted for forty days and forty nights,
and afterwards he was hungry.
The tempter approached and said to him,
"If you are the Son of God,
command that these stones become
loaves of bread."
He said in reply,
"It is written:
One does not live on bread alone,
but on every word that comes forth
from the mouth of God."

Then the devil took him to the holy city,
and made him stand on the parapet of the
temple,
and said to him, "If you are the Son of
God, throw yourself down.
For it is written:
He will command his angels concerning
you
and with their hands they will support
you,
lest you dash your foot against a stone."
Jesus answered him,
"Again it is written,
You shall not put the Lord, your God, to
the test."
Then the devil took him up to a very high
mountain,
and showed him all the kingdoms of the
world in their magnificence,
and he said to him, "All these I shall give
to you,
if you will prostrate yourself and worship
me."
At this, Jesus said to him,
"Get away, Satan!
It is written:
The Lord, your God, shall you worship
and him alone shall you serve."

Then the devil left him and, behold,
angels came and ministered to him.

Reflecting on the Gospel
The devil certainly traveled a great distance and went to great lengths to tempt Jesus to give in to enticing treasure—satisfying food, commanding power, far-reaching wealth. It would seem as though the devil was desperate; he offered Jesus far more than what we receive when we give in to temptations. In the end, however, the issue is the same. In the final analysis, the gospel's account of Jesus' temptation in the desert (and our own temptations) is a face-off between "the kingdoms of the world" and the rule of God. Jesus, always obedient to the Father, resists the temptations and keeps himself focused on what enabled him and helps each of us to continue to choose to do God's will: never losing sight of the God who created us, breathing God's own divine life within us (see first reading).

The choice between the realm of God and the realm of evil is a choice to *personally* serve God and God alone or not; it is a choice about whose cause will be advanced in this world. Ultimately, both our human condition and all temptations ask of us, whom will we serve? Lent is a time of discernment of our choices that bring us death or life. This is our lifelong struggle and lifelong temptation. The good news is that God "will support" us in making right choices.

On one level the story of the temptations are about *the choice* between good and evil, between self-will and the will of God, between obedience and disobedience. But there is more at stake. The gospel's face-off between the devil and Jesus reveals temptation as a conflict between "the kingdoms of the world" and the rule of God. Ultimately temptation asks all of us, whom will you serve?

Because Jesus fasted and was hungry, he knew that for which he really hungered. For this reason, none of the temptations—for satisfaction, power, wealth—caused him to yield. He never lost sight of the God whom he served and whose will he came to fulfill. The purpose of our fasting during Lent is to lead us, like Jesus, to hunger only for God and, like Jesus, to choose to serve only God.

Living the Paschal Mystery
Temptation is something we usually think of as facing alone. In the first reading, Eve was not alone; Adam "was with her." It seems as though Adam did nothing to help Eve resist the temptation. Neither of them could withstand the temptation of the serpent alone, *nor did either of them help each other*. Neither should Lent be a time for us to withstand temptation alone. Rather, it is a wonderful time to get involved with others spiritually and help each other to grow in goodness and the ability to resist temptation and come to a deeper realization of what it means to serve God and God alone.

Most of us tend to keep our spiritual growth and struggles pretty much to ourselves. One marvelous way to help each other is to take some time with those we are in significant relationships with to do some in-depth faith sharing. When we share our own temptations as well as spiritual blessings with others, we are not alone in *choosing* and *serving* this God who gives us life—at creation and through "the one Jesus Christ" (second reading).

Focusing the Gospel

Key words and phrases: fasted . . . he was hungry, tempter approached, God . . . alone shall you serve

To the point: Because Jesus fasted and was hungry, he knew that for which he really hungered. For this reason, none of the temptations—for satisfaction, power, wealth—caused him to yield. He never lost sight of the God whom he served and whose will he came to fulfill. The purpose of our fasting during Lent is to lead us, like Jesus, to hunger only for God and, like Jesus, to choose to serve only God.

Connecting the Gospel

to the first and second readings: Adam and Eve, who wanted to be "like gods," said yes when tempted to make themselves equal to God. Jesus, who willingly gave up his equality with God in order to become human, said no when tempted and, indeed, through his obedience "the many [are] made righteous" (second reading).

to experience: The three temptations described in the gospel are extraordinary and not part of our everyday experience. Lent is about growing in the ability to recognize the everyday temptations that cause us to wander from serving God alone.

Connecting the Responsorial Psalm

to the readings: The readings for this Sunday indicate we are alone neither in sin nor in the struggle with temptations to abandon loyalty to God for seemingly easier paths of life. Above all, we are not alone in the victory over sin; no, we are united with the One who knows the struggle and brings the victory.

Lest we think, however, that sin and salvation are someone else's responsibilities (Adam and Eve's for the one, Christ's for the other), Psalm 51 intervenes to remind us that we are full participants in both. Through Psalm 51 we admit our participation in human sinfulness and begin a journey back to God. Furthermore, we make this admission and undertake this journey together as Body of Christ. We begin the season of Lent, then, singing together the theme song of our entire lives: "Be merciful, O Lord, for we have sinned" (psalm refrain).

to psalmist preparation: In Psalm 51 you acknowledge that you have sinned and ask God for forgiveness. In singing it you stand before the community as a living embodiment of both sides of the story of salvation: human sinfulness and God's ever-redeeming mercy. Such witness demands a great deal of vulnerability. Can you do it? How can God help you do it?

ASSEMBLY & FAITH-SHARING GROUPS
- I most hunger for . . . when . . . What satisfies me is . . .
- The temptations I need to address this Lent are . . .
- What distracts me from serving God faithfully is . . . Who or what helps me serve God faithfully is . . .

PRESIDERS
My manner of relating to the parishioners strengthens them to say no to temptations in that . . .

DEACONS
My service ministry helps others to serve God faithfully when . . .

HOSPITALITY MINISTERS
My gracious hospitality helps those gathering for liturgy recognize that for which they truly hunger when . . .

MUSIC MINISTERS
My participation in music ministry helps me resist the temptation to be self-serving and self-centered by . . . My collaboration with others in this ministry helps me remain faithful to serving God by . . .

ALTAR MINISTERS
My manner of serving at the altar witnesses to my life of serving God alone in that . . .

LECTORS
What helps me go beyond knowing (or quoting) the Scriptures to truly living God's word is . . .

EXTRAORDINARY MINISTERS OF HOLY COMMUNION
In distributing Holy Communion, I feed those who hunger for God by . . . This humbles me because . . .

Model Act of Penitence

Presider: Jesus is led out into the desert to be tempted. At this, the beginning of Lent, we pause to look within ourselves and see what it is that tempts us from keeping God at the center of our lives and serving God alone . . . [pause]

    Confiteor: I confess . . .

Homily Points

• We are only tempted by what we want, what is appealing, what we think will make us happy. The vaudevillian queen and last of the Red Hot Mamas, Sophie Tucker, once said, "I've been rich and I've been poor. Believe me, honey, rich is better." For followers of Jesus, however, "rich is better" has a very different meaning.

• The wealth offered us in Christ Jesus is "the abundance of grace," the "gift of justification," the "life [that comes] to all" (second reading). This is the rich gift for which we ought to hunger and which is given to those who serve God faithfully.

• Our society constantly tempts us to pursue at any cost—sometimes even at the expense of others—the riches of wealth, possessions, power, status, and success. In resisting the temptations in the desert, Jesus shows us how to put other riches first—the ones only God can give. We receive these riches now when we show care and love for one another in our families, in the workplace, in our neighborhoods. These riches are, indeed, better!

Model Prayer of the Faithful

Presider: Let us place our needs before God, asking God to strengthen us to resist temptations and serve God alone.

Response:

Lord, hear our prayer.

Cantor:

we pray to the Lord,

That all members of the Body of Christ support each other in the call to serve God alone . . . [pause]

That all people of the world faithfully respond to God's will and receive the riches of salvation . . . [pause]

That those in need of strength, protection, and courage be enriched by the love and care of this community . . . [pause]

That our Lenten practices empty us so that we hunger only for God . . . [pause]

Presider: God of creation, you breathed divine life into us: keep us faithful to your ways that one day we might enjoy everlasting life with you. Grant this through Christ our Lord. **Amen**.

ALTERNATIVE OPENING PRAYER

Let us pray

Pause for silent prayer

Lord our God,
you formed man from the clay of the earth
and breathed into him the spirit of life,
but he turned from your face and sinned.

In this time of repentance
we call out for your mercy.
Bring us back to you
and to the life your Son won for us
by his death on the cross,
for he lives and reigns for ever and ever.
    Amen.

FIRST READING
Gen 2:7-9; 3:1-7

The Lord God formed man out of the clay
    of the ground
    and blew into his nostrils the breath of
    life,
    and so man became a living being.

Then the Lord God planted a garden in
    Eden, in the east,
    and placed there the man whom he had
    formed.
Out of the ground the Lord God made
    various trees grow
    that were delightful to look at and good
    for food,
    with the tree of life in the middle of the
    garden
    and the tree of the knowledge of good
    and evil.

Now the serpent was the most cunning of
    all the animals
    that the Lord God had made.
The serpent asked the woman,
    "Did God really tell you not to eat
    from any of the trees in the garden?"
The woman answered the serpent:
    "We may eat of the fruit of the trees in
    the garden;
    it is only about the fruit of the tree
    in the middle of the garden that God said,
    'You shall not eat it or even touch it, lest
    you die.'"
But the serpent said to the woman:
    "You certainly will not die!
No, God knows well that the moment you
    eat of it
    your eyes will be opened and you will
    be like gods
    who know what is good and what is evil."
The woman saw that the tree was good
    for food,
    pleasing to the eyes, and desirable for
    gaining wisdom.

So she took some of its fruit and ate it;
 and she also gave some to her husband,
 who was with her,
 and he ate it.
Then the eyes of both of them were
 opened,
 and they realized that they were naked;
 so they sewed fig leaves together
 and made loincloths for themselves.

RESPONSORIAL PSALM

Ps 51:3-4, 5-6, 12-13, 17

R7. (cf. 3a) Be merciful, O Lord, for we have
sinned.

Have mercy on me, O God, in your
 goodness;
 in the greatness of your compassion
 wipe out my offense.
Thoroughly wash me from my guilt
 and of my sin cleanse me.

R7. Be merciful, O Lord, for we have sinned.

For I acknowledge my offense,
 and my sin is before me always:
"Against you only have I sinned,
 and done what is evil in your sight."

R7. Be merciful, O Lord, for we have sinned.

A clean heart create for me, O God,
 and a steadfast spirit renew within me.
Cast me not out from your presence,
 and your Holy Spirit take not from me.

R7. Be merciful, O Lord, for we have sinned.

Give me back the joy of your salvation,
 and a willing spirit sustain in me.
O Lord, open my lips,
 and my mouth shall proclaim your praise.

R7. Be merciful, O Lord, for we have sinned.

SECOND READING

Rom 5:12-19

Brothers and sisters:
Through one man sin entered the world,
 and through sin, death,
 and thus death came to all men,
 inasmuch as all sinned—
 for up to the time of the law, sin was in
 the world,
 though sin is not accounted when there
 is no law.
But death reigned from Adam to Moses,
 even over those who did not sin
 after the pattern of the trespass of
 Adam,
 who is the type of the one who was to
 come.

Continued in Appendix A, p. 271.

About Liturgy

Longer or shorter second reading: During Lent and the festal seasons the second reading is not a semi-continuous reading of one of the apostolic writings (as during Ordinary Time), but it is chosen specifically to relate to the season or gospel. Often the second reading contains in a nutshell the theology of the feast or season. For this reason we ordinarily recommend that the longer form of the second reading be chosen for proclamation during Lent and the festal seasons, and the short form be proclaimed during Ordinary Time.

This principle being stated, on this particular Sunday we recommend the shorter reading because the point is more easily grasped. The longer reading is a marvelous piece of typology; that is, there is an extended comparison or analogy made between Adam and Christ. However, the argument is one that is better *studied* than *proclaimed*.

About Liturgical Music

Less celebrative music for Lent: The longstanding practice of making our music during the liturgies of Lent less celebrative is grounded in the penitential simplicity that is meant to mark these celebrations. The directive concerning music during Lent appears in GIRM; no. 313 begins by stating that musical instruments should be used with moderation during the season of Advent. The directive is an application of the principle of progressive solemnity—the music of Advent is not to overshadow the "full joy" that is to characterize the celebration of Christmas. Applying the same principle further, GIRM restricts the use of musical instruments even more during Lent—they are to be used only to the extent an assembly needs them to support their singing. Through these directives GIRM is inviting us to enter the rhythm of the seasons that marks the liturgical year. During Advent and Lent we "hold back," one time in hope, the other time in penance. By holding back in this way we allow the paschal mystery dynamic of the liturgical year—its built-in rhythm of not yet-already, of anticipation-celebration, of dying-rising—to have its formative effect upon us. This rhythm is no inconsequential thing, for it is the broad year-after-year immersion in the mystery that marks our identity and forms us for mission as Body of Christ. It is important to remember, however, that the church's tradition has been to make less use of instruments, not to sing less. We must always maintain the nature of liturgy as a sung celebration.

✠ SPIRITUALITY

GOSPEL ACCLAMATION
Ps 84:5

Blessed are those who dwell in your house, O Lord;
they never cease to praise you.

Gospel

Matt 1:16, 18-21, 24a; L543

Jacob was the father of Joseph,
    the husband of Mary.
Of her was born Jesus who is
    called the Christ.

Now this is how the birth of Jesus
    Christ came about.
When his mother Mary was
    betrothed to Joseph,
    but before they lived together,
    she was found with child through the
      Holy Spirit.
Joseph her husband, since he was a
    righteous man,
    yet unwilling to expose her to shame,
    decided to divorce her quietly.
Such was his intention when, behold,
    the angel of the Lord appeared to him
      in a dream and said,
    "Joseph, son of David,
    do not be afraid to take Mary your
      wife into your home.
For it is through the Holy Spirit
    that this child has been conceived in
      her.
She will bear a son and you are to
    name him Jesus,
    because he will save his people from
      their sins."
When Joseph awoke,
    he did as the angel of the Lord had
      commanded him
    and took his wife into his home.

or Luke 2:41-51a in Appendix A, p. 272.

See Appendix A, p. 272, for the other readings.

Reflecting on the Gospel

"Shame on you!" is an expression parents sometimes use with their small children to teach them that one of their choices or behaviors is just not acceptable. Child psychologists, however, warn us of using such expressions. "Shame" can instill feelings of humiliation and contribute to a loss of respect, resulting in damaging a fragile self-esteem. We have a sixth sense about such things. Our duty to each other requires that we build up, not tear down. We want to see the good in each other and reinforce that. Sensitivity toward others and encouraging goodness in them is a way of building right relationships—it is a way of expressing righteousness. It is a way of modeling our lives after St. Joseph, whose festival we celebrate this day.

The gospel depicts Joseph as "unwilling to expose [Mary] to shame" after she became pregnant. We admire and extol Joseph for such sensitivity and care. At the same time, this festival honoring the husband of Mary and the foster father of Jesus reminds us of something even more significant about Joseph: he was actively engaged in fulfilling God's plan of salvation. No passive "supporting actor," Joseph's decisions and responses to God's initiatives show us that he was a "righteous man" because he did what God asked of him. Joseph believed the message of the angel and obeyed the command of God. Imagine this: a simple man, by obeying God, became one of God's instruments bringing salvation to all!

When we think of the conception of Jesus, we picture Mary saying yes to the angel Gabriel. This gospel (and solemnity) shows us how Joseph also uttered a yes in response to an angelic visit. Joseph's involvement in the incarnation, then, is much more than taking Mary as his wife and saving her from shame. His yes to the angel was a significant act of faith and obedience by which he participated directly in God's work of salvation. Joseph's role (as portrayed in the infancy accounts in Matthew's and Luke's gospels) is to be one who is totally obedient to God and who, by that obedience, was able to protect the Holy Family no matter what the cost. Such obedience shows that he had a remarkably close relationship with God. Without this kind of relationship, Joseph could not have faithfully said yes to all God asked of him. Yet Joseph's righteousness goes beyond even this total obedience—it includes the willingness to surrender his very life in all its details to God, no matter what hardships that surrender might bring.

No wonder we honor Joseph on this festival! He was a man who enjoyed the relationship with God that we work to have for ourselves. He was a man who was sensitive and caring. He was a man who said yes to God in things small and great. He was a man who was righteous.

Living the Paschal Mystery

Joseph in this gospel models for us how *we* are involved in the mystery of the incarnation in at least two ways. First, we are committed to God through our baptism, and fidelity to that commitment means saying yes to what God asks of us. Like Joseph, our own yes (obedience to God), care for others, sensitivity to the circumstances and plight of others are all ways that we also cooperate with God's plan of salvation. Second, by being open to God and the gift of grace God bestowed on us, the Word is made flesh within us too. Like Joseph, we need to surrender ourselves to God and let God work marvelous things in us too.

Focusing the Gospel

Key words and phrases: Joseph . . . did as . . . commanded

To the point: When we think of the conception of Jesus, we picture Mary saying yes to the angel Gabriel. This gospel (and solemnity) shows us how Joseph also uttered a yes in response to an angelic visit. Joseph's involvement in the incarnation, then, is much more than taking Mary as his wife and saving her from shame. His yes to the angel was a significant act of faith and obedience by which he participated directly in God's work of salvation.

Model Act of Penitence

Presider: We pause this day to honor St. Joseph, who cooperated fully with God's plan of salvation. Let us prepare for this liturgy by opening ourselves in faith and obedience to God's presence . . . [pause]

Lord Jesus, you were conceived by the Holy Spirit: Lord . . .

Christ Jesus, you came to save your people from their sins: Christ . . .

Lord Jesus, you learned faith and obedience from Joseph: Lord . . .

Model Prayer of the Faithful

Presider: We pray for our needs, that we might say yes to God as did Joseph.

Response:

Lord, hear our prayer.

Cantor:

we pray to the Lord,

That church leadership always model for us what it means to say yes to God's plan for salvation . . . [pause]

That leaders of nations make good choices that bring about justice and peace . . . [pause]

That those struggling with making right choices for their lives be guided by God's will . . . [pause]

That all of us, through the intercession of St. Joseph, faithfully say yes to the invitations of God . . . [pause]

Presider: God of salvation, you called St. Joseph to cooperate with your plan of salvation: hear these our prayers that we, like Joseph, might enjoy everlasting life with you. We ask this through Christ our Lord. **Amen.**

OPENING PRAYER
Let us pray
Pause for silent prayer
Father,
you entrusted our Savior to the care of
St. Joseph.
By the help of his prayers
may your Church continue to serve its Lord,
Jesus Christ,
who lives and reigns with you and the Holy
Spirit,
one God, for ever and ever. **Amen.**

FOR REFLECTION
- Like Joseph, I have set aside my plans to follow God's commands when . . .
- Joseph's yes cost him . . . It brought him . . . My yes cost me . . . It brings me . . .
- I participate directly in God's work of salvation when I . . .

Homily Points

- Isn't it interesting that we speak of the "terrible twos" with "no!" being the operative word, but don't speak of an age when "yes" is the operative word? We humans know that sometimes a yes is costly, demanding, and life-changing. Nonetheless, we all find ourselves often saying yes.

- Joseph, open to the world of dreams, did not, however, live in a dream world. His life was grounded in his ongoing yes to the earthly choices of taking Mary to be his wife and Jesus to be his foster child. In this ongoing yes Joseph was a key player in God's plan of salvation. So too our own yes in obedience and faith is our way of participating directly in God's work of salvation.

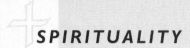

SPIRITUALITY

GOSPEL ACCLAMATION

cf. Matt 17:5

From the shining cloud the Father's voice is
   heard:
This is my beloved Son, hear him.

Gospel   Matt 17:1-9; L25A

Jesus took Peter, James,
   and John his brother,
   and led them up a
      high mountain by
      themselves.
And he was transfigured
   before them;
   his face shone like the
      sun
   and his clothes became white as light.
And behold, Moses and Elijah appeared
   to them,
   conversing with him.
Then Peter said to Jesus in reply,
   "Lord, it is good that we are here.
If you wish, I will make three tents here,
   one for you, one for Moses, and one
      for Elijah."
While he was still speaking, behold,
   a bright cloud cast a shadow over
      them,
   then from the cloud came a voice that
      said,
   "This is my beloved Son, with whom I
      am well pleased;
   listen to him."
When the disciples heard this, they fell
   prostrate
   and were very much afraid.
But Jesus came and touched them,
   saying,
   "Rise, and do not be afraid."
And when the disciples raised their
   eyes,
   they saw no one else but Jesus alone.

As they were coming down from the
   mountain,
   Jesus charged them,
   "Do not tell the vision to anyone
   until the Son of Man has been raised
      from the dead."

Reflecting on the Gospel

We've all met folks who are a stick in the mud. Earthquakes, tornadoes, twenty-foot waves couldn't move them. Content and satisfied, they stay put doing the same things, eating the same foods, watching the same TV shows. Often these folks have few friends. For most of us, our natural instinct is to move on, searching for new experiences, new possibilities, new challenges. Peter in this gospel is acting like a stick in the mud. His first response to Jesus' transfigured glory is to stay put: "Lord, it is good that we are here." He wants to erect tents; he wants to stay on the mountain top. Jesus has other plans.

Yes, when Jesus takes his three closest disciple friends "up a high mountain" and is "transfigured before them," the disciples are eager to stay. But when the voice from heaven announces who Jesus is and commands them to "listen to him," their mood shifts: they became afraid. Why are they afraid? Because listening to Jesus means not staying put, but moving onward into the unknown (see first reading). The destiny is transfiguration, but the journey is a costly one.

The first reading is about venturing forth and the cost to Abram—kinsfolk and homeland. Abram is commanded by God to leave his homeland and live on a promise of future blessing. Abram lives on a promise; so do we. This promise does more than better the condition of humankind; it offers us a share in divine life. It does have its cost; we must *listen* to Jesus, follow him, carry forth his saving mission, even when it leads to Jerusalem. The radiance of the transfiguration of Jesus overwhelms the disciples and even makes the greatness of Moses and Elijah—symbols for the law and prophets—pale in comparison. Yet the call of God to us is the same as that to Abram and to Peter, James, and John: be willing to leave everything to go where God wills. Be willing to *listen* to Jesus, learn of his ways, and embrace his journey.

Our journey as disciples leads us to eternal glory—foreshadowed by Jesus' transfiguration. This is worth any cost. In comparison to the glory that God offers us in Christ, the offering of our lives as disciples is puny in comparison. All we need do is *listen* to Jesus.

Living the Paschal Mystery

Jesus commands the disciples to "Rise, and do not be afraid." The journey of discipleship has its dangers (temptations), but we still venture forth on the journey to eternal glory. We trust in God's guidance (given through the law, prophets, teachings of Jesus, Gospel living modeled by others) and surrender ourselves into God's hands. All we need do is *listen*.

Listening to God can come through the readings and homily on Sunday. It can come through our practice of taking some time every day to read God's word in Scripture. It might come through the good modeling of discipleship by another. It might come through the guidance we seek in spiritual direction. It might come through the disciplines we choose for Lent. There are many ways God makes known the divine will for us. Listening means all these things but, most important, it means that we keep our eyes focused on the vision of Jesus transfigured and know that God, in great love and divine mercy, intends that we share in that same glory. We cannot lose sight of Jesus himself.

Focusing the Gospel

Key words and phrases: Jesus . . . transfigured, good that we are here, listen to him, very much afraid, disciples

To the point: When Jesus takes his three closest disciple friends "up a high mountain" and is "transfigured before them," the disciples are eager to stay. But when the voice from heaven announces who Jesus is and commands them to "listen to him," their mood shifts: they became afraid. Why are they afraid? Because listening to Jesus means not staying put, but moving onward into the unknown (see first reading). The destiny is transfiguration, but the journey is a costly one.

Connecting the Gospel

to the second reading: Paul encourages Timothy to "[b]ear your share of hardship for the gospel" and assures him that God will give him the necessary strength. Listening to Jesus means embracing the hardship of emptying self and loving others as he did.

to our experience: When we prepare for a journey (for example, vacation, business), we are in control of the destination, the route, the means to get there. On the Christian journey of discipleship we don't have this kind of control but must surrender to Jesus in trust: we must "listen to him."

Connecting the Responsorial Psalm

to the readings: Part of the "hardship" we bear as disciples (second reading) is that like Abram (first reading) we must leave behind what we know and love and journey into an unknown future. Part of the blessing of discipleship is that like Peter, James, and John in the gospel we are given glimpses along the way of the glory which is to come. Called to be faithful to the journey and strengthened along the way by flashes of glory, we live in the in-between time of hope.

Our hope, like Abram's, like Christ's, like the apostles', lies in the awareness that the One calling us forward will be faithful to the promise. Through the trudging and the temptations (last Sunday) we see this promise shining through even now, fleeting but with overwhelming clarity (this Sunday). The promise of future glory is real and this merciful God who keeps a tender eye upon us (psalm) grants us the vision we need to keep moving on.

to psalmist preparation: As you sing these verses from Psalm 33 you express the hope fulfilled in the gospel reading. The unseen future to which Abram was called (first reading) is fully manifest in the shining face of Jesus on the mountaintop. You sing of the trust we can hold in the God who promises such a future to us. You are a beacon of hope to the assembly. How can you also be this beacon in your daily living to those who lack hope or need encouragement?

ASSEMBLY & FAITH-SHARING GROUPS

- Where I have glimpsed the glory of Jesus is . . .
- The ways I regularly listen to Jesus, God's beloved Son, are . . . My daily living is different when I listen to Jesus because . . .
- The cost of discipleship for me is . . . The glory is . . .

PRESIDERS

The assembly listens to Jesus through my ministry of preaching; as I listen to Jesus through the lives of the assembly what I hear is . . .

DEACONS

I have witnessed glimpses of Christ's glory on the faces of others when . . . My life shines with the glory of Christ for others whenever I . . .

HOSPITALITY MINISTERS

My hospitality prepares the assembly truly to listen to Jesus in word and sacrament when . . .

MUSIC MINISTERS

Collaborating in the ministry of music strengthens me to face "hardship for the gospel" (second reading) by . . . It offers me a glimpse of the glory to which I am called when . . .

ALTAR MINISTERS

When I am motivated to serve others as a response to listening to Jesus, my service is different in that . . .

LECTORS

God's promise of future blessing (see first reading) directs my daily living in that . . . This affects how I proclaim God's word in that . . .

EXTRAORDINARY MINISTERS OF HOLY COMMUNION

The Eucharist manifests Christ's glory to me by . . . The way I share this glory with those I meet in my daily life is . . .

Model Act of Penitence

Presider: In today's gospel we hear that Peter, James, and John accompany Jesus up a mountain where they see him transfigured. Let us prepare ourselves to encounter the glory of Christ by calling to mind all that keeps us from listening to him . . . [pause]

   Confiteor: I confess . . .

Homily Points

• It's always tempting and easier just to slog along as we are. However, even in situations where we have achieved a certain success and glory (e.g., getting into the college we want, winning a tournament, getting a promotion), we realize that we cannot just sit back on our laurels; continued success means continued hard work.

• Peter, James, and John want to rest on their laurels, basking in the glory of Jesus. The divine voice from heaven brings them back to stark reality: they cannot stay there, but must go back "down the mountain," listen to Jesus, and live what they hear. Their own transfiguration into glory can only happen when they accept the unknown costs of the journey of daily discipleship.

• The season of Lent invites us to undertake personal penance as a way to discipline ourselves to better handle the costs of discipleship. But at the same time, Lent calls us to recognize the glory God offers us now (e.g., in the brightened face of someone whom we've helped, in the enriched spiritual understanding we gain through a more fervent liturgical and prayer life). Such glimpses of glory quicken our journey to Easter—a celebration of renewed life now and the promise of eternal glory.

Model Prayer of the Faithful

Presider: We ask God to strengthen us on our journey to Easter glory.

Response:

Lord, hear our prayer.

Cantor:

we pray to the Lord,

That each member of the church have the strength to venture forth on the Lenten journey of discipleship with courage . . . [pause]

That all peoples be shown God's glory and strive to live according to God's will . . . [pause]

That those living in the darkness of poverty and injustice be led to the light of God's glory . . . [pause]

That each of us listen to Jesus as he daily teaches us how to be better disciples . . . [pause]

Presider: Loving God, you were well pleased with your divine Son and made him shine with the radiance of your glory: hear these our prayers that one day we might share fully in that same glory. We ask this through that same Son, Jesus Christ our Lord. **Amen**.

OPENING PRAYER
Let us pray

Pause for silent prayer

God our Father,
help us to hear your Son.
Enlighten us with your word,
that we may find the way to your glory.

We ask this through our Lord Jesus Christ,
   your Son,
who lives and reigns with you and the
   Holy Spirit,
one God, for ever and ever. **Amen.**

FIRST READING
Gen 12:1-4a

The LORD said to Abram:
   "Go forth from the land of your kinsfolk
   and from your father's house to a land
      that I will show you.

   "I will make of you a great nation,
      and I will bless you;
   I will make your name great,
      so that you will be a blessing.
   I will bless those who bless you
      and curse those who curse you.
   All the communities of the earth
      shall find blessing in you."

Abram went as the LORD directed him.

RESPONSORIAL PSALM
Ps 33:4-5, 18-19, 20, 22

R̸. (22) Lord, let your mercy be on us, as we place our trust in you.

Upright is the word of the LORD,
　and all his works are trustworthy.
He loves justice and right;
　of the kindness of the LORD the earth is
　　full.

R̸. Lord, let your mercy be on us, as we place our trust in you.

See, the eyes of the LORD are upon those
　who fear him,
　upon those who hope for his kindness,
to deliver them from death
　and preserve them in spite of famine.

R̸. Lord, let your mercy be on us, as we place our trust in you.

Our soul waits for the LORD,
　who is our help and our shield.
May your kindness, O LORD, be upon us
　who have put our hope in you.

R̸. Lord, let your mercy be on us, as we place our trust in you.

SECOND READING
2 Tim 1:8b-10

Beloved:
Bear your share of hardship for the gospel
　with the strength that comes from God.

He saved us and called us to a holy life,
　not according to our works
　but according to his own design
　and the grace bestowed on us in Christ
　　Jesus before time began,
　but now made manifest
　through the appearance of our savior
　　Christ Jesus,
　who destroyed death and brought life
　　and immortality
　to light through the gospel.

About Liturgy

Lectio divina: It has been a spiritual practice from earliest times in the church to do *lectio divina*, or divine reading. The ancient vigils—keeping watch throughout the night before an important feast day and reading about God's mighty deeds of salvation from Sacred Scripture—were a form of *lectio divina*, as is still our Easter Vigil. We cannot *listen* to God's voice unless we learn to take time out of our busy schedules to pay attention to one of the most important ways God speaks to us—through Scripture.

　Lectio divina isn't concerned with reading a great amount of Scripture or reading the whole Bible over a given period of time. It is concerned with *attentiveness* while we are reading, so that God's word invites us to listen in a new way. We may only read one verse from Scripture (from the Sunday's gospel or from one of the daily readings, for example) and spend time asking what God is saying and how God wishes us to respond to this word. This reading, listening, and meditation has as its purpose to lead us to deeper prayer and contemplation of God's loving, merciful presence to us.

　If we begin a practice of regular *lectio divina*, we will also be teaching ourselves how better to listen to the proclamation of God's word during liturgy. It is as though we become familiar with the voice of our Beloved and can more obediently listen to him.

About Liturgical Music

Music suggestions: "O Sun of Justice" [RS, SS, W3] and "O Christ, Bright Sun of Justice" [JS2 and *Awake, My Soul*, the OCP collection of Harry Hagan hymns] would be excellent entrance hymns for this Sunday when the transfigured Christ lights the way through our Lenten journey. For the same reason, "Christ Be Our Light" [BB, GC2, JS2, OFUV, SS, WS] and "Beyond the Days" [BB, JS2] would be good choices for Communion. In "Transform Us" [HG, RS, SS] we ask Christ to "transform us," to "search us with revealing light," and to "lift us from where we have fallen." This contemporary text would be well suited for the time during the preparation of the gifts or as a choir prelude using the David Haas arrangement [GIA G-5664]. "'Tis Good, Lord, to Be Here" [in many hymn books] would be an excellent entrance hymn or hymn of praise after Communion. The text fits the story of the transfiguration as well as the season of Lent. Part of "being here" is the transformation that takes place in us during the eucharistic celebration. But, as with the disciples in the gospel, we cannot remain on this mountain; we must return to the arena of daily living. Thanks, however, to the promise of this gospel and the Eucharist, we know the glory to which fidelity in daily living will lead us.

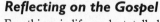

✝ SPIRITUALITY

GOSPEL ACCLAMATION
John 1:14ab

The Word became flesh and made his dwelling
among us
and we saw his glory.

Gospel Luke 1:26-38; L545

The angel Gabriel was sent
from God
to a town of Galilee called
Nazareth,
to a virgin betrothed to a
man named Joseph,
of the house of David,
and the virgin's name was
Mary.
And coming to her, he said,
"Hail, full of grace! The
Lord is with you."
But she was greatly troubled
at what was said
and pondered what sort of greeting this
might be.
Then the angel said to her,
"Do not be afraid, Mary,
for you have found favor with God.
Behold, you will conceive in your womb
and bear a son,
and you shall name him Jesus.
He will be great and will be called Son of
the Most High,
and the Lord God will give him the
throne of David his father,
and he will rule over the house of Jacob
forever,
and of his Kingdom there will be no
end."
But Mary said to the angel,
"How can this be,
since I have no relations with a man?"
And the angel said to her in reply,
"The Holy Spirit will come upon you,
and the power of the Most High will
overshadow you.
Therefore the child to be born
will be called holy, the Son of God.

Continued in Appendix A, p. 273.

See Appendix A, p. 273, for the other readings.

Reflecting on the Gospel

Few things in life can be totally hidden from others. Our faces generally tell everything. For example, when little Bobby is caught with his proverbial hand in the cookie jar, a guilty look comes over his face. Or when Melissa aces a big exam, the triumphant look on her face is evident as she bursts into the house eager to tell her parents. A promotion is accompanied by a glow of success; winning the lottery big brings a look of excitement. Sometimes what happens to us is so life-changing that our whole demeanor changes. The death of a loved one can bring a pained look not only to our faces, but even our shoulders might droop in heartsickness, our walk might slow down, our ambition to do anything at all might disappear. A clear CAT scan that assures us cancer is in remission might bring a spring to our step, a flurry of making new plans, a new determination to deepen relationships.

Like so many other things in life, pregnancy can rarely be hidden! Maternity clothes sections in department stores remind us how much the body alters during these months of growing new life. Yet, nothing is so telling as the luminescent ebullience that shows all over a mother-to-be. There is a real transformation in the mother—not just in body shape, but in her relationship to life itself. She is cooperating with God to bring forth God's greatest gift—life. She is transfigured in body and soul—a look of joy and expectancy on her face, a quiet peace and contentment deep within.

In this annunciation gospel Gabriel appears "to a virgin" to bring a singular invitation. Mary's yes to God transforms and transfigures her. Had we been there, we might have noticed a different look on her face: first, one of concern ("How can this be"), then one of committed resolve ("May it be done to me"), and then, no doubt, one of sheer joy as her months of "confinement" go by. But Mary's "transfiguration" is unprecedented! She is invited to conceive by the Holy Spirit and give birth to the "Son of God." Her faith-filled "May it be done to me according to your word" changed not only her life but that of everyone born thereafter. What a transfiguration!

The real surprise of this gospel is that because of Mary's obedience and transfiguration, what we can see clearly is God's great desire that we too share in divine life. This is why Jesus was conceived and became human in the womb of Mary. This is why Mary was transfigured. This is why we ourselves are transfigured: God desires to dwell within each of us, if only we say yes. The divine presence within us transfigures us too—Christians are marked by the radiance of divine presence. May it be done to us!

Living the Paschal Mystery

Mary said, "Behold . . . may it be done to me according to your word." Christ came into the world and said, "Behold, I come to do your will." The only way we can truly be a transfigured people and share in risen life is by saying, with both Mary and Jesus, that we willingly give ourselves over to whatever God asks of us.

For most of us it's not the big things God asks of us but the little things coming along every day that challenge and transfigure us. A gesture of kindness brings a look of satisfaction with a good choice. Volunteering our time and talent for those in need brings a look of gentle care to our face. Big or little, doing God's will always leads to a deeper share in divine life, with an accompanying deeper glow of transfiguration radiating God's presence within us.

Focusing the Gospel

Key words and phrases: conceive in your womb, Holy Spirit will come upon you, Son of God, May it be done to me

To the point: Mary's "transfiguration" is unprecedented! She is invited to conceive by the Holy Spirit and give birth to the "Son of God." Her faith-filled "May it be done to me according to your word" changed not only her life but that of everyone born thereafter. What a transfiguration!

Model Act of Penitence

Presider: We celebrate today Mary's conceiving Jesus in her womb by assenting to do God's will. Let us pray that our Lenten practices might bring us the courage and strength to do God's will and thus share in divine life . . . [pause]

Lord Jesus, you were conceived by the Holy Spirit: Lord . . .

Christ Jesus, you are our Savior and the Son of God: Christ . . .

Lord Jesus, you were born of the Virgin Mary: Lord . . .

Model Prayer of the Faithful

Presider: Let us now ask God for a deeper faith and a more committed yes to doing the divine will.

Response:

Lord, hear our prayer.

Cantor:

we pray to the Lord,

That all members of the church open themselves to God's transforming grace . . . [pause]

That all peoples of the world say yes to God's will and cooperate in God's offer of salvation . . . [pause]

That those struggling to nurture life might find strength in Mary's faithfulness . . . [pause]

That each of us here embrace with hearts filled with faith the many possibilities for newness God offers us . . . [pause]

Presider: God of life, you sent Gabriel to announce to Mary that she would conceive your divine Son: hear these our prayers that one day we might share fully in that same divine life. We ask this through that same Son, Jesus Christ our Lord. **Amen.**

OPENING PRAYER

Let us pray

Pause for silent prayer

God our Father,
your Word became man and was born of
the Virgin Mary.
May we become more like Jesus Christ
whom we acknowledge as our redeemer,
God and man.

We ask this through our Lord Jesus Christ,
your Son,
who lives and reigns with you and the Holy
Spirit,
one God, for ever and ever. **Amen.**

FOR REFLECTION

• It is easy for me to say to God, "May it be done to me," when . . . It is difficult for me to say this when . . .

• What it means to me to have the Holy Spirit overshadow me is . . .

• I am transfigured because of Mary's yes in that . . .

Homily Points

• Occasionally we all experience unprecedented and life-changing events: for example, the 1969 first landing of human beings on the moon, the 2008 Olympic achievement of Michael Phelps, the 2009 inauguration of the first African American U.S. president. This gospel tells of an even more singular and unprecedented event: Mary conceives by the Holy Spirit. With this there is a whole new and unimaginable in-breaking of God into human history.

• These unprecedented events (human and divine) share two common elements: they all required acting on belief and being open to new and unheard of possibilities. This celebration invites us to the same belief and the same openness about how God works in our own lives and changes us.

THIRD SUNDAY OF LENT

✠ SPIRITUALITY

GOSPEL ACCLAMATION
cf. John 4:42, 15

Lord, you are truly the Savior of the world;
give me living water, that I may never thirst again.

Gospel John 4:5-42; L28A

Jesus came to a town of Samaria
  called Sychar,
  near the plot of land that Jacob
    had given to his son Joseph.
Jacob's well was there.
Jesus, tired from his journey,
  sat down there at the well.
It was about noon.

A woman of Samaria came to
  draw water.
Jesus said to her,
  "Give me a drink."
His disciples had gone into the town to
  buy food.
The Samaritan woman said to him,
  "How can you, a Jew, ask me, a
    Samaritan woman, for a drink?"
—For Jews use nothing in common
    with Samaritans.—
Jesus answered and said to her,
  "If you knew the gift of God
  and who is saying to you, 'Give me a
    drink,'
  you would have asked him
  and he would have given you living
    water."
The woman said to him,
  "Sir, you do not even have a bucket
    and the cistern is deep;
  where then can you get this living
    water?
Are you greater than our father Jacob,
  who gave us this cistern and drank
    from it himself
  with his children and his flocks?"

Continued in Appendix A, p. 274,
or John 4:5-15, 19b-26, 39a, 40-42 in Appendix A,
p. 275.

Reflecting on the Gospel

Conversations can be life-giving. They can bring about new insight. They can call forth new self-understanding. This gospel conversation begins with a Jewish man and thirst, a well and a bucket. It leads to something much deeper that brought the Samaritan woman to new insight, a new self-understanding—this conversation came to be life-giving for her, and for us. Indeed, the whole gospel unfolds as an insight into who/what is life-giving: encountering Another who takes time to speak to us, facing the truth of one's way of living, the most satisfying "food" of doing God's will, proclaiming the excitement of discovering Jesus as "the savior of the world," coming to belief upon hearing the word, desiring with all one's heart for Jesus to "stay with" us.

The conversation that unfolds between Jesus and the Samaritan woman reveals what happens when we drink the life-giving water Jesus offers: we come face-to-face with the Savior of the world, we admit the truth of our own lives, we run to proclaim Jesus' presence and message to all who will hear. Encounter, truth, proclamation—this is the movement of our Lenten journey toward transformation and new life.

Jesus promises the Samaritan woman living water and the disciples food that satisfies beyond mere hunger. What is this living water that Jesus gives? It is himself as Savior, the "love of God . . . poured out into our hearts" (second reading) as the gift of the Spirit. Jesus helps the woman at the well go from a literal understanding of water to his gift of living water (the Spirit) by telling her everything she had done. He helps her come to a new self-understanding that enables her to witness to Jesus as the Messiah. She began her "Lenten journey" at the well with an encounter with Jesus, faced the truth about herself that she needed to change, and eagerly proclaimed her newfound lease on life. She models for us what happens when we drink the life-giving water Jesus offers. She models for us insight and new self-understanding of a depth only God can give.

Living the Paschal Mystery

Coming to know Jesus as the Savior of the world requires a constant deepening of faith, a faith that comes from the "gift of God." Our lives constantly play out the struggle to deepen our faith and get to know Jesus better; the journey of all disciples is to come to deeper belief, which leads to a deeper self-understanding as those who follow Jesus faithfully.

One way to deepen our faith and come to know Jesus better is by spending more time with him as a friend. Lent is an opportune time to become more attentive to Jesus' presence—especially in prayer—and encounter him as One who loves us, teaches us, and gives us life-giving water. Another way is to enumerate the blessings God has already given us and remember that these truly are gifts from God. Yet another way to deepen our faith and come to know Jesus better is to increase our self-understanding as Body of Christ and make concrete efforts to act like Christ's Body. Things like saying thank you and smiling at another who looks sad or depressed are simple acts, but they remind us of who we are: Christ for others. These kinds of everyday acts remind us that, like the Samaritan woman, we proclaim Jesus' presence by the truth of our own lives.

Focusing the Gospel

Key words and phrases: Jesus said to her . . . The Samaritan woman said to him, What you have said is true, woman . . . went into the town and said to the people

To the point: The conversation that unfolds in this gospel between Jesus and the Samaritan woman reveals what happens when we drink the life-giving water Jesus offers: we come face-to-face with the Savior of the world, we admit the truth of our own lives, we run to proclaim Jesus' presence and message to all who will hear. Encounter, truth, proclamation—this is the movement of our Lenten journey toward transformation and new life.

Connecting the Gospel

to the first reading: The water God provided the Israelites in the desert satisfied their bodily thirst. The living water Jesus gives satisfies our spiritual thirst. Both gifts reveal the presence of God in our very midst.

to the catechumenal experience: The Samaritan woman's deepening understanding of who Jesus is and her coming to believe in him as the Savior of the world prefigures the catechumens' journey in coming to know Jesus, believe in him, and approach the living waters of baptism.

Connecting the Responsorial Psalm

to the readings: In the escape from Egypt God gave the Israelites everything they needed and more. Yet at the first moment of hardship they whined against God, calling God a trickster (first reading). God has also given us everything we need and more: grace and the Holy Spirit (second reading), Jesus himself as living water within us (gospel).

In his encounter with the woman at the well, Jesus challenges us to "know the gift of God." The gradual, halting manner through which the woman discovers who Jesus is mimics our progress in coming to recognize him and all that we have been given in him. We sing Psalm 95 to remind ourselves and one another that we can enter this process or we can close our hearts to it. We can cut it off when it does not meet our preconceived expectations, as did the Israelites in the desert, or we can stick with it no matter how challenging, as did the woman at the well. The choice is ours; the reward is Jesus and fullness of life.

to psalmist preparation: Psalm 95 is quite a challenge to sing. The first two strophes are easy because you invite the assembly to praise and worship God. But the third is not so easy. How do you challenge the community for having closed its heart to God? You can only do so with integrity if you have applied the message of the psalm to yourself. When do you close your heart against God? Who challenges you to reopen your heart?

**ASSEMBLY &
FAITH-SHARING GROUPS**
- What I am thirsty for is . . . Jesus satisfies my thirst with . . .
- My Lenten encounters with Jesus bring me to this truth about myself . . .
- The manner of my daily living proclaims Jesus' life-giving presence when . . . It hides Jesus' life-giving presence when . . .

PRESIDERS
My proclamation gently leads others to truth about themselves and their daily living when . . .

DEACONS
My service shares the living water that is Jesus with those in need by . . .

HOSPITALITY MINISTERS
My gift of hospitality invites those gathering to drink of Jesus' living water when I . . .

MUSIC MINISTERS
One way I have come to know Jesus better through my participation in the ministry of music is . . . Sometimes I experience my encounter with others in the ministry of music as an encounter with Jesus because . . .

ALTAR MINISTERS
The self-emptying my service requires makes room for me to drink the living water of Jesus in that . . .

LECTORS
Praying, preparing, and proclaiming God's word satisfies my thirst for "living water" by . . .

**EXTRAORDINARY MINISTERS
OF HOLY COMMUNION**
My gift of time and ministry to the homebound satisfies their thirst for Christ when . . . My own thirst for Christ is satisfied by their faith when . . .

Model Act of Penitence

Presider: In today's gospel Jesus gives the living water of himself to the Samaritan woman at the well. During this liturgy Jesus offers us this same living water. We pause to be mindful of whatever hinders us from drinking deeply and ask God for pardon and mercy . . . [pause]

    Confiteor: I confess . . .

Homily Points

• In today's world we are justifiably concerned about access to the life-giving natural resource, water. For example, water pipes are filled with lead and crumbling; many waterways no longer teem with marine life; the plenitude of safe water we've enjoyed for so long is threatened. While the need to protect this essential and life-giving natural resource is imperative, Lent calls us to an even greater imperative: to encounter Jesus and receive the life-giving water *he* offers.

• The Samaritan woman encounters Jesus as life-giving water—the unreserved gift of himself. Jesus' self-giving and openness nourish the woman's capacity to respond with openness and honesty. Filled to the brim with new insight and life, she runs to the towns-people to proclaim the identity of this amazing Man she has encountered.

• We also encounter and hear Jesus: every day in the goodness and honesty of others, every time we hear Jesus' word proclaimed during worship, through our Lenten penitential practices that bring us closer to Jesus and each other as well as to the truth about ourselves. Filled to the brim with new insight and life, we share in the very life of Jesus. This compels us to proclaim his life-giving presence by the very way we live.

Model Prayer of the Faithful

Presider: Let us make our needs known to God, so that we can encounter Jesus more faithfully and proclaim the life he offers.

Response:

Lord, hear our prayer.

Cantor:

we pray to the Lord,

That the church always be a well of living water for all those who thirst to encounter Jesus . . . [pause]

That all peoples of the world encounter the living God and be granted salvation . . . [pause]

That encounter with Jesus lead those who have sinned to honest self-assessment and conversion of heart . . . [pause]

That each of us grow in our thirst for Jesus as the living water who sustains our efforts to proclaim his presence . . . [pause]

Presider: Living God, you desire that all people be saved: hear these our prayers and draw us to yourself where one day we might live for ever and ever. **Amen.**

OPENING PRAYER

Let us pray

Pause for silent prayer

Father,
you have taught us to overcome our sins
by prayer, fasting and works of mercy.
When we are discouraged by our
    weakness,
give us confidence in your love.

We ask this through our Lord Jesus Christ,
    your Son,
who lives and reigns with you and the
    Holy Spirit,
one God, for ever and ever. **Amen.**

FIRST READING
Exod 17:3-7

In those days, in their thirst for water,
    the people grumbled against Moses,
    saying, "Why did you ever make us
      leave Egypt?
Was it just to have us die here of thirst
    with our children and our livestock?"
So Moses cried out to the LORD,
    "What shall I do with this people?
A little more and they will stone me!"
The LORD answered Moses,
    "Go over there in front of the people,
    along with some of the elders of Israel,
    holding in your hand, as you go,
    the staff with which you struck the
      river.
I will be standing there in front of you on
    the rock in Horeb.
Strike the rock, and the water will flow
    from it
    for the people to drink."
This Moses did, in the presence of the
    elders of Israel.
The place was called Massah and Meribah,
    because the Israelites quarreled there
    and tested the LORD, saying,
    "Is the LORD in our midst or not?"

CATECHESIS

RESPONSORIAL PSALM
Ps 95:1-2, 6-7, 8-9

R̼. (8) If today you hear his voice, harden not your hearts.

Come, let us sing joyfully to the Lᴏʀᴅ;
    let us acclaim the Rock of our salvation.
Let us come into his presence with
        thanksgiving;
    let us joyfully sing psalms to him.

R̼. If today you hear his voice, harden not your hearts.

Come, let us bow down in worship;
    let us kneel before the Lᴏʀᴅ who made
        us.
For he is our God,
    and we are the people he shepherds, the
        flock he guides.

R̼. If today you hear his voice, harden not your hearts.

Oh, that today you would hear his voice:
    "Harden not your hearts as at Meribah,
    as in the day of Massah in the desert,
where your fathers tempted me;
    they tested me though they had seen my
        works."

R̼. If today you hear his voice, harden not your hearts.

SECOND READING
Rom 5:1-2, 5-8

Brothers and sisters:
Since we have been justified by faith,
    we have peace with God through our
        Lord Jesus Christ,
    through whom we have gained access
        by faith
    to this grace in which we stand,
    and we boast in hope of the glory of
        God.

And hope does not disappoint,
    because the love of God has been poured
        out into our hearts
    through the Holy Spirit who has been
        given to us.
For Christ, while we were still helpless,
    died at the appointed time for the
        ungodly.
Indeed, only with difficulty does one die
    for a just person,
    though perhaps for a good person one
        might even find courage to die.
But God proves his love for us
    in that while we were still sinners Christ
        died for us.

About Liturgy

Use of John's gospel in the Lectionary: During the third, fourth, and fifth Sundays of Lent in Year A, we hear three lengthy stories from John's gospel that are placed there specifically to lead us to reflect on baptism and its effects for fruitful discipleship. The revised Lectionary does not have a specific year devoted to reading John semi-continuously during Ordinary Time as we do with the Synoptic Gospels of Matthew, Mark, and Luke. The Lectionary hardly ignores John, though, but assigns selections from this "theological" gospel at key points in the year.

During Lent in Year A we hear three baptismal stories, as mentioned above. In Year B, from the seventeenth to twenty-first Sundays in Ordinary Time, we read almost all of the sixth chapter of John, the Bread of Life discourse. And during all three years we draw heavily from John's gospel when we hear Jesus' Last Supper discourse to his disciples on the fifth through seventh Sundays of Easter.

All of these blocks of passages from John's gospel are kept together and so presented because they give us bright imagery and solid theological commentary on the mystery of salvation being presented. It is as though we draw on the Synoptic Gospels to carry us on the journey to Jerusalem, but we draw on John to break open the meaning of the paschal mystery in our lives.

Prayers for the elect: Those to be baptized at Easter were enrolled on the first Sunday of Lent and now are called the "elect"—they are on their final journey to initiation. The gospel readings for the third, fourth, and fifth Sundays of Lent during Year A are three lengthy stories drawn from John's gospel and all have baptismal overtones: the life-giving water Jesus offers the Samaritan woman at the well, the sign Jesus offers the blind man who comes to faith and worship, the raising of Lazarus to new life. During these Sundays it would be particularly appropriate to add a fifth intention to the prayers of the faithful, specifically for the elect.

About Liturgical Music

Music suggestions: An excellent song for this Sunday would be "I've Just Come from the Fountain" [G2, GC, LMGM]. This African American spiritual identifies the "fountain" as the person of Jesus and celebrates the joy of "drinking from that fountain." The song is in verse-refrain style, with verses intended for choir (with a strong lead soprano) and refrain for the assembly. This one would be a joy to sing at Communion. Another fine text for Communion would be Delores Dufner's "Come to Me" [JS2, SS, WC]. In the verses Jesus calls us to come to him for rest, refreshment, satisfaction. In the refrain we respond by naming him the "everflowing fountain" and asking for water from his well. The song needs to be sung in dialogue fashion, with cantor or choir singing the words of Jesus and the assembly the refrain. A third good Communion choice would be "Come to Me and You Shall Never Hunger" [PS, SS], in which assembly responses of "We come to you, we trust in you" and "We drink from the stream of your delight" are intermingled with the cantor's singing of the psalm verses.

Herman Stuempfle's "The Thirsty Cry for Water, Lord" [HG, SS] calls us to the mission of sharing the living water and living bread that is Jesus with all who hunger and thirst. Set to NEW BRITAIN, the tune associated with "Amazing Grace," this song would be fitting for either the preparation of the gifts or the Communion procession.

MARCH 27, 2011
THIRD SUNDAY OF LENT

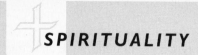

SPIRITUALITY

GOSPEL ACCLAMATION
John 8:12

I am the light of the world, says the Lord;
whoever follows me will have the light of life.

Gospel

John 9:1-41; L31A

As Jesus passed by he saw a man
    blind from birth.
His disciples asked him,
    "Rabbi, who sinned, this man or
        his parents,
    that he was born blind?"
Jesus answered,
    "Neither he nor his parents
        sinned;
    it is so that the works of God
        might be made visible through
        him.
We have to do the works of the one
    who sent me while it is day.
Night is coming when no one can work.
While I am in the world, I am the light
    of the world."
When he had said this, he spat on the
    ground
    and made clay with the saliva,
    and smeared the clay on his eyes,
        and said to him,
    "Go wash in the Pool of Siloam"—
        which means Sent—.
So he went and washed, and came back
    able to see.

His neighbors and those who had seen
    him earlier as a beggar said,
    "Isn't this the one who used to sit
        and beg?"
Some said, "It is,"
    but others said, "No, he just looks
        like him."
He said, "I am."

*Continued in Appendix A, pp. 275–276,
or John 9:1, 6-9, 13-17, 34-38 in Appendix A,
p. 276.*

Reflecting on the Gospel

Unusual events, surprising twists, or unbridled creativity might lead us to exclaim, "I can hardly believe it!" Sometimes we check out preposterous statements for ourselves to see if they have any basis in facts. Facts: verifiable, concrete, indisputable. Yet, how many facts or signs does it sometimes take us to come to belief? And, surely, the more astounding the thing we are dealing with, the slower we are to grasp the signs, the facts. A half dozen times in this gospel the blind man is questioned about his cure. How exasperating! What does it take for us to come to belief? How many signs? How many facts?

This long gospel describes a back-and-forth contestation over a sheer statement of fact—"I was blind and now I see"—and the implications of that fact. The obtuse Pharisees in this gospel refuse to see the implications to which the fact points and refuse to believe in Jesus as the "Son of Man." The blind man, however, is open to much more than the amazing fact of his having been healed. He sees its implications: he comes to recognize Jesus, believe in him, and worship him. This dynamic of healing encounter, belief, and worship defines our own Lenten and lifelong journey to new life.

Ideally, Lent leads us to encounter Jesus, sharpens our vision of his saving mission, and challenges us to more authentic worship. Lent is also a time when the darkness of our ignorance is challenged by the One who is the light of the world. This gospel challenges those who are preparing for baptism or full reception into the church to greater faith; it challenges all of us to deepen our faith so that our "enthusiasm" enables us to be possessed by our God. Then, like the blind man whom Jesus helps to see, we can exclaim "I do believe" and worship with raised hearts and voices. Worship may not lead to believing (seeing), but true believing always leads to worship.

The worship prompted by faith is wholehearted participation in divine presence by those who have seen the Lord and been disciplined in the challenges of discipleship. This gospel teaches us that faith always moves the believer to action: confessing Jesus as Lord and worshiping him.

Living the Paschal Mystery

Baptism is a ritual sign of coming to belief and admits one to full participation in worship. This statement doesn't imply that those who have not been baptized or fully received into the church haven't worshiped God. They have or they probably wouldn't be seeking to be initiated into the Catholic Church. Initiation changes the way one can worship, and the sign of this is admittance to Eucharist and reception of the Body and Blood of our Lord.

Worship, however, is far more than attendance and involvement in ritual acts, as important as that is. Worship includes a mission to reach out to others who are in need of spiritual insight, a deepened faith, or healing in any way. Authentic worship always requires a response of charity on behalf of others. Authentic worship includes an encounter with the One who gives us sight, but then it must lead us to reach out to others with a healing hand, bringing them to see and believe too.

Focusing the Gospel

Key words and phrases: blind, now I can see, I do believe, worshiped him

To the point: This long gospel describes a back-and-forth contestation over a sheer statement of fact—"I was blind and now I see"—and the implications of that fact. The obtuse Pharisees in this gospel refuse to see the implications to which the fact points and refuse to believe in Jesus as the "Son of Man." The blind man, however, is open to much more than the amazing fact of his having been healed. He sees its implications: he comes to recognize Jesus, believe in him, and worship him. This dynamic of healing encounter, belief, and worship defines our own Lenten and life-long journey to new life.

Connecting the Gospel

to the second reading: All of us are a little obtuse—we all choose at times to live "in darkness." All of us are also "children of light," continually learning "what is pleasing to the Lord." The contestation described in the gospel continues within our own hearts.

to our experience: Struggles can do us in or help us grow. In either case, they clarify our values and who we are.

Connecting the Responsorial Psalm

to the readings: In all three readings for this Sunday God seeks someone out. God sends Samuel to find David (first reading); Jesus sees the blind man as he passes by, and later comes to find him when the authorities have thrown him out (gospel); Christ comes to us with light while we are hidden in darkness (second reading). Truly this is a shepherding God (psalm).

We, however, must choose to be shepherded. Part of the self-examination involved in this Sunday's R.C.I.A. scrutinies is that despite God's movements toward us, we can still choose not to see (gospel). Will we shun darkness, or will we, like the Pharisees, only pretend to see? Will we undergo the conversion to which the seeing invites us? Will we stand by what we have seen even when, like the blind man, we face opposition? The good news of the psalm is that our shepherd God will be with us even while we struggle with darkness in ourselves and in others. We can continue the journey into light because God will provide all the strength, protection, and courage we need.

to psalmist preparation: One aspect of the gospel story of the man born blind seems to contradict the shepherd imagery of Psalm 23. Jesus heals the man, then seems to abandon him to the ire of the temple authorities. The man must stand on his own while even his parents cower. Beneath the story line, however, is the hidden presence of Jesus, who knows what is happening and seeks the man out when his ordeal is over. The shepherd God about whom you sing, then, is not one who shields you from the cost of discipleship but one who trusts your ability to deal with it. At what difficult points in life has God seemed absent from you? How have these experiences strengthened your sense of God's confidence in you? Who or what has helped you discover this hidden confidence?

ASSEMBLY & FAITH-SHARING GROUPS

- I tend to be obtuse in matters of belief when . . . Who and what help me become more open are . . .
- Lent is sharpening my vision to see Jesus more clearly in my daily living by . . .
- Like the man born blind, my own seeing (believing in) Jesus has led me to witness to him by . . . ; has led me to authentic worship in that . . .

PRESIDERS

My ministry helps the assembly gain insight into Jesus by . . . ; the assembly is helping me gain insight into Jesus by . . .

DEACONS

To "live as [a child] of light" (second reading) I must . . . I am helping others live as "children of light" when . . .

HOSPITALITY MINISTERS

Attentive hospitality is like a healing balm that prepares others for authentic worship whenever I . . .

MUSIC MINISTERS

Doing music ministry has opened my eyes to . . . It has deepened my participation in worship by . . .

ALTAR MINISTERS

When I recognize Christ in those I serve, my ministry is like . . . ; when I am closed to his presence, my serving others becomes . . .

LECTORS

Proclamation is a healing ministry when . . .

EXTRAORDINARY MINISTERS OF HOLY COMMUNION

My manner of distributing Holy Communion invites people to look beyond the ritual action to . . .

Model Act of Penitence

Presider: In today's gospel Jesus heals a blind beggar who comes to believe in and worship him. As we prepare to celebrate this liturgy, let us ask Christ to remove from our hearts whatever blocks our coming to deeper faith . . . [pause]

    Confiteor: I confess . . .

Homily Points

• All of us are a little obtuse at times. Our lack of openness can be caused by defensiveness, prejudice, fear of change or the unknown, complacency, etc. What might shake us out of our narrowness is confrontation with another's point of view, new knowledge or experiences, discovering that we have lost out on life because we have been locked within ourselves. As with the blind man in the gospel, Jesus finds us where we are and takes us to a place of new vision and life.

• The back-and-forth contestation in the gospel alerts us to the fact that conversion of heart, coming to belief, and encountering Jesus as the "Son of Man" do not happen once-and-for-all or quickly. Several times the blind man had to tell the story of how he was healed, and he never wavered from the truth, even when threatened. His steadfastness about his encounter with Jesus prepared him for a final encounter: Jesus found him and brought him to belief and worship.

• Sometimes we are the obtuse ones who need to be jolted out of our frozen ways of thinking and acting; sometimes we are the presence of Christ who call others to a broader vision and deeper faith. At all times Jesus, who has come to offer us life, pursues us and gives us all we need to believe.

Model Prayer of the Faithful

Presider: With confidence we raise our prayers to God who helps all of us see with the eyes of faith.

Response:

Lord, hear our prayer.

Cantor:

we pray to the Lord,

That during this season of Lent all members of the church encounter Jesus in new ways that deepen their faith in him . . . [pause]

That all peoples of the world walk as children of the Light . . . [pause]

That the sick and suffering encounter the healing presence of Christ . . . [pause]

That all of us here be more open to encountering Jesus in the many people and circumstances of our daily living . . . [pause]

Presider: Merciful God, you desire to heal all those who come to you: hear these our prayers that one day we might worship you for ever at the heavenly banquet table. Grant this through Christ our Lord. **Amen.**

Let us pray

Pause for silent prayer

Father of peace,
we are joyful in your Word,
your Son Jesus Christ,
who reconciles us to you.
Let us hasten toward Easter
with the eagerness of faith and love.

We ask this through our Lord Jesus Christ,
    your Son,
who lives and reigns with you and the
    Holy Spirit,
one God, for ever and ever. **Amen.**

FIRST READING
1 Sam 16:1b, 6-7, 10-13a

The LORD said to Samuel:
    "Fill your horn with oil, and be on your
        way.
I am sending you to Jesse of Bethlehem,
    for I have chosen my king from among
        his sons."

As Jesse and his sons came to the sacrifice,
    Samuel looked at Eliab and thought,
    "Surely the LORD's anointed is here
        before him."
But the LORD said to Samuel:
    "Do not judge from his appearance or
        from his lofty stature,
    because I have rejected him.
Not as man sees does God see,
    because man sees the appearance
    but the LORD looks into the heart."
In the same way Jesse presented seven
    sons before Samuel,
    but Samuel said to Jesse,
    "The LORD has not chosen any one of
        these."
Then Samuel asked Jesse,
    "Are these all the sons you have?"
Jesse replied,
    "There is still the youngest, who is
        tending the sheep."
Samuel said to Jesse,
    "Send for him;
    we will not begin the sacrificial banquet
        until he arrives here."
Jesse sent and had the young man brought
    to them.
He was ruddy, a youth handsome to behold
    and making a splendid appearance.
The LORD said,
    "There—anoint him, for this is the one!"
Then Samuel, with the horn of oil in hand,
    anointed David in the presence of his
        brothers;
    and from that day on, the spirit of the
        LORD rushed upon David.

RESPONSORIAL PSALM
Ps 23:1-3a, 3b-4, 5, 6

R⁄. (1) The Lord is my shepherd; there is nothing I shall want.

The LORD is my shepherd; I shall not want.
    In verdant pastures he gives me repose;
beside restful waters he leads me;
    he refreshes my soul.

R⁄. The Lord is my shepherd; there is nothing I shall want.

He guides me in right paths
    for his name's sake.
Even though I walk in the dark valley
    I fear no evil; for you are at my side
with your rod and your staff
    that give me courage.

R⁄. The Lord is my shepherd; there is nothing I shall want.

You spread the table before me
    in the sight of my foes;
you anoint my head with oil;
    my cup overflows.

R⁄. The Lord is my shepherd; there is nothing I shall want.

Only goodness and kindness follow me
    all the days of my life;
and I shall dwell in the house of the LORD
    for years to come.

R⁄. The Lord is my shepherd; there is nothing I shall want.

SECOND READING
Eph 5:8-14

Brothers and sisters:
You were once darkness,
    but now you are light in the Lord.
Live as children of light,
    for light produces every kind of
        goodness
    and righteousness and truth.
Try to learn what is pleasing to the Lord.
Take no part in the fruitless works of
        darkness;
    rather expose them, for it is shameful
        even to mention
the things done by them in secret;
but everything exposed by the light
    becomes visible,
for everything that becomes visible is
        light.
Therefore, it says:
    "Awake, O sleeper,
    and arise from the dead,
    and Christ will give you light."

About Liturgy

Authentic worship, participation, and Body of Christ: In the four decades after Vatican Council II there have been many calls for full, conscious, and active participation in the church's liturgy. This is probably one of the best known of the council's decisions. But participating in the ritual actions themselves is only one aspect of what the council fathers desired.

The council fathers also called for the renewal of our identity as those baptized in Christ, the Body of Christ who participates in Jesus' paschal mystery. One sign of authentic worship and participation, then, is how we are together the Body of Christ (that is, the church). Authentic worship always calls us outside of ourselves into something bigger than any one of us. Authentic worship demands of us the willingness to surrender ourselves—which means even our personal tastes and desires in how we might want to worship—in order for the Body of Christ to be strengthened.

This may seem a contradiction because worship, in one sense, is a deeply personal act—so why should we give up our personal tastes and desires? The real issue here is that the *surrender* is intensely personal, and that is far more important than our personal tastes and desires. The Body of Christ comes to full stature when our own *surrender* is joined to others' surrender and something new—Christ's life—bursts forth. This is when worship is exciting and fruitful: when worship calls us beyond ourselves, we receive gifts from God through others and then return those gifts to the community in mission.

About Liturgical Music

Music suggestions: "I Am the Light of the World" [BB, JS2, OFUV] would make an energetic and appropriate entrance song for this Sunday. The meditative "Jesus Christ, Inner Light" [BB, JS2] with ostinato assembly refrain and cantor verses would work very well either as a choral prelude or during the Communion procession. This text fits the gospel reading particularly well because through it we pray that Jesus "not let our own darkness conquer us." "I Want to Walk as a Child of the Light" [in most hymnals] would be appropriate this Sunday for either the preparation of the gifts or Communion. Using it during Communion would probably necessitate extending it with instrumental interludes between the verses, or by having the choir softly hum the SATB arrangement as an additional "verse." "Awake, O Sleeper" [GC, RS] would be a fitting recessional, sending us forth as those who "Once . . . were darkness" but "now . . . are children of light."

Fred Pratt Green's "He Healed the Darkness of My Mind" [G2, RS, W3] is based directly on this Sunday's gospel story. The tune ARLINGTON [used in G2 and RS] flows easily and could be sung by the entire assembly. The tune DUNEDIN [used in W3] is more dramatic, with large downward and upward leaps that capture well the roller coaster ride the blind man must have experienced emotionally as he went through this experience. This tune will be unfamiliar to most assemblies, so it could be sung by cantor and/or choir, either as a prelude or during the preparation of the gifts.

✠ SPIRITUALITY

GOSPEL ACCLAMATION
John 11:25a, 26

I am the resurrection and the life, says the Lord;
whoever believes in me will never die.

Gospel
John 11:1-45; L34A

Now a man was ill, Lazarus from
      Bethany,
   the village of Mary and her
      sister Martha.
Mary was the one who had
      anointed the Lord with
      perfumed oil
   and dried his feet with her
      hair;
   it was her brother Lazarus
      who was ill.
So the sisters sent word to Jesus
      saying,
   "Master, the one you love is ill."
When Jesus heard this he said,
   "This illness is not to end in death,
   but is for the glory of God,
   that the Son of God may be glorified
      through it."
Now Jesus loved Martha and her sister
      and Lazarus.
So when he heard that he was ill,
   he remained for two days in the place
      where he was.
Then after this he said to his disciples,
   "Let us go back to Judea."
The disciples said to him,
   "Rabbi, the Jews were just trying to
      stone you,
   and you want to go back there?"
Jesus answered,
   "Are there not twelve hours in a day?
If one walks during the day, he does
      not stumble,
   because he sees the light of this
      world.

Continued in Appendix A, p. 277,
or John 11:3-7, 17, 20-27, 33b-45 in Appendix A,
p. 278.

Reflecting on the Gospel

Often when a jetliner crashes, news reports carry a story about someone who had been booked to be on the flight but missed it for some reason. We think, how lucky for that person, but how sad for those who lost their lives. The relatives of the deceased might be thinking, "If only . . ." In less grave situations, we all find ourselves occasionally saying, "If only . . ." If only I had not spent so much money eating out, I wouldn't be so far behind in my bills. If only I had paid more attention to the school zone, I wouldn't have a steep traffic ticket to pay. If only I could lose weight, I would fit into all those clothes in my closet. If only . . . If only . . .

In this Sunday's gospel, both Martha and Mary greet Jesus with an "If only" statement: "Lord, if you had been here . . ." They were thinking of the immediate situation—Jesus has proved over and over again that he has the power to heal. Their brother Lazarus is ill and dying. Why didn't Jesus, their dear friend, come and heal their brother? Why did Jesus wait two days to go to Bethany? The answer to these painful questions is that Jesus was thinking and acting beyond the immediate situation. More is at stake than Lazarus recovering his health. If Jesus had chosen to go to Bethany when first called, he could have healed Lazarus. But this would have been a very different sign. The raising of Lazarus is the sign of a new revelation that death is not final. Life is.

Ultimately, the raising of Lazarus has more to do with Jesus, us, and believing than it has to do with Lazarus. Two deaths are evident in the gospel—Lazarus's, very clearly ("Lazarus has died"); but also Jesus' impending dying. Thomas has an inkling of this when he tells the other disciples after Jesus' decision to go to Bethany (near Jerusalem): "Let us also go to die with him." Thomas's presumption, however, is that death is a final end. Jesus works an even greater miracle than healing Lazarus. By raising him from the dead he gives a clear sign that he has power over death and life. The raising of Lazarus is a new kind of statement about life. Jesus' sign in this miracle is the power of the Spirit (see second reading) bringing life out of death. The new life he brings is risen and eternal. Do we believe this sign? Do we live like we believe it? Are we willing, like Jesus, to stake our lives on it?

Living the Paschal Mystery

Mary and Martha's long relationship with Jesus had brought them to believe in him. It must be comforting for us to know that their belief was still less than perfect. So is ours. And, like Mary and Martha, our belief is strengthened by encounters with Jesus. Jesus' presence means new life.

One conspicuous way we encounter Jesus is at Mass when we expressly take time out of our busy schedules to be present. Other prayer times during the day and week are also times when we consciously strive to encounter Jesus. Perhaps less evident as encounters with Jesus would be all those times when we meet him through faith-strengthening and hope-giving encounters with other people. When our discouragement is lessened by a kind remark or when our sinfulness is forgiven by a smile and welcome, we encounter Jesus in the other and are brought to new life. Jesus loves each of us as deeply as he loved Mary, Martha, and Lazarus, and he gives each of us new life too.

Focusing the Gospel

Key words and phrases: remained for two days, Lazarus has died, Let us also go to die with him, lives and believes in me will never die, The dead man came out

To the point: Why did Jesus wait two days to go to Bethany? If Jesus had chosen to go to Bethany when first called, he could have healed Lazarus. But this would have been a very different sign. The raising of Lazarus is the sign of a new revelation that death is not final. Life is. Do we believe this sign? Do we live like we believe it? Are we willing, like Jesus, to stake our lives on it?

Connecting the Gospel

to the second reading and baptism: Paul promises the Romans that "through the Spirit dwelling in [them]," their "mortal bodies" would receive life. It is in baptism that we receive this Spirit who dwells within us and gives us new life.

to our experience: Frequently a shortened form of this gospel is used at funerals, and so we tend to think of the life that Jesus gives us in terms of the resurrection and eternal life. We must become more aware that we already share in this new life now.

Connecting the Responsorial Psalm

to the readings: Psalm 130 is an individual lament arising from some un-named anguish so profound that the psalmist feels buried in the bowels of the earth. There is some sense that the underlying cause of the anguish, indeed of all human anguish, is sin. If God were to tally our sins, we would never rise from the pit. But because God does not tally sin but forgives it, the psalmist has hope. God's kindness is greater than Israel's iniquities; redemption is assured. We have only to wait.

And for what do we wait? The redemption not only of our souls but of our bodies, promised metaphorically in the first reading, foreseen in the future in the second, and experienced here and now in the gospel when Jesus calls Lazarus forth from the tomb. The closer Jesus moves to his own death in Jeru-salem, the more clearly he reveals his power over death. The closer we move to Jesus, the more we rise from the pit. In him the mercy of God is made flesh and our hope of redemption is made real.

to psalmist preparation: The depth of hope you express in singing Psalm 130 will be determined by the depth of your experience of human anguish, both your own and that of the whole world. Ask Christ for a heart wide enough to contain this, compassionate enough to weep over it, and trusting enough to count on God to turn suffering and death into redemption and new life.

**ASSEMBLY &
FAITH-SHARING GROUPS**
- I struggle with belief in life coming from death when . . . I have experienced Jesus bringing life out of death when . . .
- What it means to me to say that new life begins *now* is . . .
- Persons who have witnessed to me their willingness to stake their lives on belief in Jesus' gift of new life are . . . I witness this to others in that . . .

PRESIDERS
When confronted by death and "mini-deaths" (for example, failures, difficulties, crises, etc.), what helps me grow in believ-ing in the Spirit's power to bring new life is . . .

DEACONS
My ministry manifests Christ as "resurrec-tion and life" whenever I . . .

HOSPITALITY MINISTERS
My reaching out to others is life-giving when . . . is death-giving when . . .

MUSIC MINISTERS
Others with whom I share the ministry of music strengthen my belief in Jesus' promise of new life when . . . I strengthen their belief when . . .

ALTAR MINISTERS
God's new life rises in me whenever I serve others because . . .

LECTORS
Living my belief in Jesus' gift of new life has an impact on my proclamation in that . . . My prayerful tending to the word has helped me grow in belief by . . .

**EXTRAORDINARY MINISTERS
OF HOLY COMMUNION**
My daily living witnesses to God's own Spirit living in me whenever I . . . This af-fects the way I distribute Holy Communion in that . . .

Model Act of Penitence

Presider: In today's gospel Jesus raises Lazarus from the dead as a sign of his power over death. Let us look into our hearts and see what choices bring us death rather than life, and ask God for pardon and forgiveness . . . [pause]

   Confiteor: I confess . . .

Homily Points

• How often better outcomes come about only because we defer action: for example, parents hold back from tying a child's shoes in order to give the youngster the space needed to learn how to do this on her or his own. How often better outcomes result because we choose action, even a dangerous one: for example, a firefighter rushes into a burning building to save the life of someone trapped inside. In both examples, there is a kind of dying to self for the sake of new life.

• In this gospel Jesus defers action when he waits two days to go to Bethany and allows Lazarus to die, this, so that he can perform the even greater sign of raising him to new life. Jesus chooses action when he deliberately goes to Bethany, knowing that it places him directly on the path to Jerusalem, the place of his own death. In both instances, he shows us that new life always comes through death.

• We are called to live what we are called to believe: that new life comes from dying to self. Discipleship challenges us to make the kinds of choices about action that Jesus made. Sometimes these choices mean holding back, sometimes they mean forging ahead— always they entail some kind of dying to self. But, oh, the Life we receive in exchange!

Model Prayer of the Faithful

Presider: We now offer our prayers to God, who promises us fullness of new life.

Response:

Lord, hear our prayer.

Cantor:

we pray to the Lord,

May all members of the church choose to die to self and receive ever more abundantly God's gift of new life . . . [pause]

May all leaders of nations choose actions that give fuller life to their people . . . [pause]

May those suffering diminished life receive hope and strength from our dying to self for the good of others . . . [pause]

May each of us constantly encounter Jesus and grow in the gift of new life he offers . . . [pause]

Presider: God of new life, you heard your Son Jesus' prayer and raised Lazarus from the dead: hear these our prayers that one day we too might enjoy fullness of life with you. We ask this through that same Son, Jesus Christ our Lord. **Amen.**

OPENING PRAYER

Let us pray

Pause for silent prayer

Father,
help us to be like Christ your Son,
who loved the world and died for our
      salvation.
Inspire us by his love,
guide us by his example,
who lives and reigns with you and the
      Holy Spirit,
one God, for ever and ever. **Amen.**

FIRST READING
Ezek 37:12-14

Thus says the Lord GOD:
   O my people, I will open your graves
   and have you rise from them,
   and bring you back to the land of Israel.
Then you shall know that I am the LORD,
   when I open your graves and have you
      rise from them,
   O my people!
I will put my spirit in you that you may
   live,
   and I will settle you upon your land;
   thus you shall know that I am the LORD.
I have promised, and I will do it, says the
   LORD.

RESPONSORIAL PSALM
Ps 130:1-2, 3-4, 5-6, 7-8

℟. (7) With the Lord there is mercy and
fullness of redemption.

Out of the depths I cry to you, O LORD;
   LORD, hear my voice!
Let your ears be attentive
   to my voice in supplication.

℟. With the Lord there is mercy and
fullness of redemption.

If you, O LORD, mark iniquities,
   LORD, who can stand?
But with you is forgiveness,
   that you may be revered.

℟. With the Lord there is mercy and
fullness of redemption.

I trust in the LORD;
   my soul trusts in his word.
More than sentinels wait for the dawn,
   let Israel wait for the LORD.

℟. With the Lord there is mercy and
fullness of redemption.

For with the LORD is kindness
   and with him is plenteous redemption;
and he will redeem Israel
   from all their iniquities.

℟. With the Lord there is mercy and
fullness of redemption.

SECOND READING
Rom 8:8-11

Brothers and sisters:
Those who are in the flesh cannot please
   God.
But you are not in the flesh;
   on the contrary, you are in the spirit,
   if only the Spirit of God dwells in you.
Whoever does not have the Spirit of Christ
   does not belong to him.
But if Christ is in you,
   although the body is dead because of
      sin,
   the spirit is alive because of
      righteousness.
If the Spirit of the One who raised Jesus
   from the dead dwells in you,
   the One who raised Christ from the dead
will give life to your mortal bodies also,
   through his Spirit dwelling in you.

About Liturgy

Choosing funeral and wedding readings: A shorter form of this Sunday's gospel is frequently used at funerals. Clearly, it brings us hope in risen life. Sometimes when pastors or pastoral ministers meet with the family of a deceased person to prepare a funeral liturgy or meet with a wedding couple to prepare the marriage liturgy, the issue is "favorite passages" when it comes to choosing the readings for the Liturgy of the Word. This tends to turn the liturgy into something about those who prepare the liturgy rather than about what God is doing in the mystery of offering us salvation.

In the case of funeral liturgies, the readings ought to speak of new and eternal life with God and bring hope and comfort to those who mourn. The readings are not chosen to capture a good quality of the deceased or simply to be a favorite passage of the deceased or other family member or friend. What is helpful for the family of the deceased to understand is that the rite of Christian burial is a dynamic movement through a number of different stages, with rituals for each stage and processions connecting the stages. Catechesis is helpful here. The vigil for the deceased (the wake) is a better place to focus on bereavement, and here much more latitude is given for choosing Scripture to be shared. When this is done well, then the family is ready to "shift gears," so to speak, so that the funeral service can be focused on resurrection and new life.

For wedding liturgies, the readings ought to speak about fidelity, unity, love for one another (but love that is beyond just the love of the couple for each other). Liturgy always draws us out of ourselves toward something bigger than ourselves, even when it is to bring us comfort or joy.

About Liturgical Music

Music suggestions: Herman Stuempfle's excellent text "Martha, Mary, Waiting, Weeping" [HG] touches on Martha's struggle to believe in Jesus despite the death of Lazarus and on our struggle today to believe in his presence and power when we are grieving. A two-voiced choral setting with optional oboe is also available [GIA G-5583]. The hymn version would be appropriate during the preparation of the gifts; the choral setting would work well either at this time or as a choir prelude. Jeremy Young's "We Shall Rise Again" [G2, GC, GC2, RS] would be a good choice for the Communion procession, with cantor or choir singing the verses and assembly the refrain. The text connects hope in God's mercy (responsorial psalm) with Jesus' promise that we shall rise with him (gospel) and with the communion we share with all those who have already passed from death to life. Marty Haugen's "Awake, O Sleeper" [GC, RS] would be appropriate for either the preparation of the gifts or Communion, as would Bland Tucker's "Awake, O Sleeper, Rise from Death" [RS, WC, W3, WS]. Finally, the uplifting Swahili call and response "Jesus Has Conquered Death" [LMGM] would be excellent for the preparation of the gifts, Communion, or as a recessional.

✝ SPIRITUALITY

GOSPEL ACCLAMATION
Phil 2:8-9

Christ became obedient to the point of death,
even death on a cross.
Because of this, God greatly exalted him
and bestowed on him the name which is
above every name.

Gospel at the procession with palms

Matt 21:1-11; L37A

When Jesus and the disciples
    drew near Jerusalem
    and came to Bethphage on the
        Mount of Olives,
    Jesus sent two disciples, saying
        to them,
    "Go into the village opposite you,
    and immediately you will find
        an ass tethered,
    and a colt with her.
Untie them and bring them here
    to me.
And if anyone should say
    anything to you, reply,
'The master has need of them.'
Then he will send them at once."
This happened so that what had been
    spoken through the prophet
    might be fulfilled:
    "Say to daughter Zion,
    'Behold, your king comes to you,
        meek and riding on an ass,
        and on a colt, the foal of a beast
            of burden.'"
The disciples went and did as Jesus
    had ordered them.
They brought the ass and the colt and
    laid their cloaks over them,
    and he sat upon them.
The very large crowd spread their
    cloaks on the road,
    while others cut branches from the
        trees
    and strewed them on the road.

Continued in Appendix A, p. 278.

*See Appendix A, pp. 279–281, for the
Gospel at Mass.*

Reflecting on the Gospel

Matthew's passion account is unique in that he shows how much Jesus seems to be alone in his darkest hour. In our direst of times it would be difficult for us even to imagine the utter abandonment Jesus experienced at his trial, during his suffering, while dying on the cross. At his hour of need Jesus is left alone to face the ultimate abandonment—death itself. Alone.

Jesus' abandonment actually has two faces. The first face of abandonment: Jesus suffers abandonment not only by his followers but even seemingly by God. First, "all the disciples left him and fled." Then, he utters that heart-piercing, plaintive cry from the cross: "My God, my God, why have you forsaken me?"

In the second reading Paul presents another face of abandonment: at the incarnation Jesus chooses to abandon his divinity ("did not regard equality with God something to be grasped") and even his human dignity ("taking the form of a slave . . . humbled himself"). By so abandoning anything that might have brought him exaltation, Jesus demonstrates how completely he chose to identify with us humans. Jesus freely chooses this second face of abandonment: he let go of his rightful claim to "equality with God" (second reading), to his human dignity, and even to life itself. For his choice to abandon all, God lifts Jesus in exaltation. This is more than the "plot" of Holy Week; it is the core of Christian life.

By accepting the two faces of abandonment—abandoning and being abandoned—Jesus already was showing us the cost of dying to self. Only by emptying ourselves can we share in the exaltation of new life. Only by abandoning the fleeting things that we think will lift us up, such as human status, comfort, or success, can we be lifted up by God to grasp a share of divinity and "confess that Jesus Christ is Lord, to the glory of God the Father." Holy Week reminds us of these demands of self-giving. All of our daily living throughout the year reminds us that, ultimately, like Jesus, we must give ourselves over to God so that we might share in divine life.

Living the Paschal Mystery

We cry this day "Hosanna!" but, unlike the people of the city of Jerusalem long ago, we need not ask "Who is this?" This is the one who models for us the mystery of life: dying to self so that we might be exalted, raised to new life. This week we celebrate in pointed liturgies the meaning of our whole Christian living: dying to self so that God can raise us up too. This dying can be as simple as setting aside the time to participate in all the Triduum liturgies or as demanding as to recognize what in our lives we still need to abandon to be exalted as sons and daughters of God living new life.

Perhaps what we need to abandon is a habit of thinking of ourselves and our own needs first, ahead of others. Perhaps it means not making ourselves the center of attention. Perhaps what we need to abandon is a lot of clutter we've accumulated that can tend to take our minds off of what is really important. Perhaps we need to abandon the frenetic pace of our lives and cut some things out so we can concentrate on our loved ones more, or help out those in need more. In all of these cases what we give up—what we abandon—leads to a new lease on life. Most important, it leads to new and deeper relationships and richer experiences. This is all new life for us.

Focusing the Gospel

Key words and phrases: all the disciples left him and fled, why have you forsaken me?

To the point: Abandonment has two faces. On the one hand, Jesus suffers abandonment not only by his followers but even seemingly by God. On the other hand, Jesus freely chooses an abandonment of his own: letting go of his rightful claim to "equality with God" (second reading), to his human dignity, and to life itself. For his choice to abandon all, God lifts Jesus in exaltation. This is more than the "plot" of Holy Week; it is the core of Christian life.

Connecting the Passion Gospel

to the gospel at the procession: The two gospels in this Sunday's liturgy move from exaltation ("Hosanna!") to abandonment ("why have you forsaken me?"). The Christian mystery, however, moves from abandonment (dying to self) to exaltation (rising to new life).

to our experience: We tend to think about the cross in the narrow terms of an instrument of torture and death. The second reading this Sunday reminds us that the cross is also the means of exaltation.

Connecting the Responsorial Psalm

to the readings: The Liturgy of the Word this Sunday invites us to grapple with the relationship between abandonment and exaltation. Because Jesus freely chose to abandon glory already his (second reading) and to abandon himself to the pain and degradation of the cross (second reading, gospel), God lifted his name in glory forever (second reading). Because Jesus understood that hanging on the arms of the cross was surrender into the arms of God, he could lift God's name in glory even as he suffered (psalm). The readings and psalm show us not only that we cannot have the glory of the resurrection unless we undergo the abandonment of the cross but also that what appears to be our destruction is, in fact, our deliverance. And so on this Palm Sunday of the Lord's Passion we sing Psalm 22, surrendering ourselves into the arms of God where we find both our cross and our glory.

to psalmist preparation: In these verses of Psalm 22 you sing not only about Jesus' suffering but also about his exaltation into glory through this suffering. You sing also about your own suffering and exaltation, for through baptism you participate in Jesus' death and resurrection. How willing are you to undergo the death required for exaltation? How willing are you to ask the assembly to do so?

ASSEMBLY & FAITH-SHARING GROUPS

- Like Jesus, times when I have been abandoned by others are . . .; what enabled me not to lose hope was . . .
- Like Jesus, I am called to give my life for others when I . . .
- When I seek exaltation, what I find is . . .; when I seek self-emptying, what I find is . . .

PRESIDERS

Ways my ministry *and* life guide others through the path of dying to self to exaltation (rising to new life) are . . .

DEACONS

The kind of self-abandonment that diaconal service requires is . . .; the fruit of such abandonment is . . .

HOSPITALITY MINISTERS

The parts of hospitality that require self-abandonment are . . .; the exaltation within hospitality is . . .

MUSIC MINISTERS

One way music ministry challenges me to die to myself is . . . I have experienced this dying as an exaltation to new life in Christ when . . .

ALTAR MINISTERS

God exalts me in my serving others by . . .

LECTORS

While proclaiming the word, the temptations toward self-exaltation are . . .; the kind of self-abandonment that genuine proclamation demands is . . .

EXTRAORDINARY MINISTERS OF HOLY COMMUNION

Distributing the Eucharist requires a kind of self-abandonment in that . . . It also brings exaltation in that . . .

Model Act of Penitence [only at Masses with the simple entrance]

Presider: We begin this holiest of all weeks by hearing in Matthew's passion account how the disciples abandoned Jesus in his hour of need. Let us pause to beg God for forgiveness for the times we have abandoned Jesus . . . [pause]

    Confiteor: I confess . . .

Homily Points

• We humans have a natural fear of being abandoned: for example, if a toddler wanders off while in a store and then realizes mom or dad has "disappeared," frantic terror sets in. Can we even imagine the sense of abandonment Jesus experienced on the cross?

• Jesus' choice to give his life for our salvation meant abandoning himself into the arms of a God who promises life out of death. What we celebrate on this Palm Sunday and during all of Holy Week—indeed, all of Christian life—is the call to unite ourselves with Jesus in his act of trust and self-giving.

• Our self-abandonment for the good of others, in union with Jesus, does not generate in us the frantic terror of the lost child. Rather, it floods our hearts with courage based on absolute trust in God's ultimate presence, protection, and gift of new life. Into your hands, O God . . .

Model Prayer of the Faithful

Presider: At his hour of need Jesus cried out to his heavenly Father. In confidence let us also make our needs known to God.

Response:

Lord, hear our prayer.

Cantor:

we pray to the Lord,

That Christians everywhere choose self-giving as their way of relating to others . . . [pause]

That leaders of nations be courageous in making decisions for the good of all . . . [pause]

That those suffering pain, humiliation, or injustice receive comfort and peace through their trust in God's love and care . . . [pause]

That each of us here walk the Holy Week journey from embracing the cross to celebrating Easter joy . . . [pause]

Presider: Merciful and ever-present God, you hear the prayers of those who cry out to you in their need: never abandon us but answer our prayers and bring us to share in your life. We ask this through Christ our Lord. **Amen.**

OPENING PRAYER

Let us pray

Pause for silent prayer

Almighty, ever-living God,
you have given the human race Jesus
    Christ our Savior
as a model of humility.
He fulfilled your will by becoming man
    and giving his life on the cross.
Help us to bear witness to you
by following his example of suffering
and make us worthy to share in his
    resurrection.
We ask this through our Lord Jesus Christ,
    your Son,
who lives and reigns with you and the
    Holy Spirit,
one God, for ever and ever. **Amen.**

FIRST READING

Isa 50:4-7

The Lord God has given me
    a well-trained tongue,
that I might know how to speak to the
    weary
    a word that will rouse them.
Morning after morning
    he opens my ear that I may hear;
and I have not rebelled,
    have not turned back.
I gave my back to those who beat me,
    my cheeks to those who plucked my
      beard;
my face I did not shield
    from buffets and spitting.

The Lord God is my help,
    therefore I am not disgraced;
I have set my face like flint,
    knowing that I shall not be put to
      shame.

RESPONSORIAL PSALM

Ps 22:8-9, 17-18, 19-20, 23-24

R̸. (2a) My God, my God, why have you abandoned me?

All who see me scoff at me;
    they mock me with parted lips, they
      wag their heads:
"He relied on the Lord; let him deliver him,
    let him rescue him, if he loves him."

R̸. My God, my God, why have you abandoned me?

Indeed, many dogs surround me,
   a pack of evildoers closes in upon me;
they have pierced my hands and my feet;
   I can count all my bones.

R℣. My God, my God, why have you
abandoned me?

They divide my garments among them,
   and for my vesture they cast lots.
But you, O LORD, be not far from me;
   O my help, hasten to aid me.

R℣. My God, my God, why have you
abandoned me?

I will proclaim your name to my brethren;
   in the midst of the assembly I will
      praise you:
"You who fear the LORD, praise him;
   all you descendants of Jacob, give glory
      to him;
   revere him, all you descendants of Israel!"

R℣. My God, my God, why have you
abandoned me?

SECOND READING
Phil 2:6-11

Christ Jesus, though he was in the form
   of God,
   did not regard equality with God
      something to be grasped.
Rather, he emptied himself,
   taking the form of a slave,
   coming in human likeness;
   and found human in appearance,
   he humbled himself,
   becoming obedient to the point of death,
      even death on a cross.
Because of this, God greatly exalted him
   and bestowed on him the name
   which is above every name,
   that at the name of Jesus
   every knee should bend,
   of those in heaven and on earth and
      under the earth,
   and every tongue confess that
Jesus Christ is Lord,
   to the glory of God the Father.

About Liturgy

Introduction to the Passion account: GIRM permits that the "priest may, very briefly, introduce the faithful to the Liturgy of the Word" (no. 128). This does not mean that the priest gives a "mini homily" after the collect and this would never take the place of the homily itself. Nor is it wise to say something like "Today the readings tell us . . ." This latter example might stifle the action of the Spirit in the minds and hearts of the hearers.

However, on this day and Good Friday when we hear the very long passion accounts, it would not be wrong to help the members of the assembly focus better on a point, especially if this will be developed in the homily. The text of the first bullet under Homily Points (see facing page) might serve well, with a line added: "We humans have a natural fear of being abandoned. For example, if a toddler wanders off while in a store and then realizes mom or dad has 'disappeared,' frantic terror sets in. Can we even imagine the sense of abandonment Jesus experienced on the cross? Let us listen for the ways Jesus faces abandonment in the readings we are about to hear."

About Liturgical Music

Singing Psalm 22: To highlight the movement within Psalm 22 from abandonment to praise, the cantor might sing the first three strophes a cappella, then the fourth strophe with accompaniment. If needed, the assembly's singing of the refrain throughout could be supported with simple open chords.

Music suggestions: The most appropriate hymns for this day are ones in which we express our willingness to enter the passion with Christ and to walk with him through Holy Week to the cross and resurrection. "Wherever He Leads, I'll Go" [LMGM] is particularly appropriate and would be suitable either during the preparation of the gifts or Communion. Suggestions for Communion that could be repeated during the veneration of the cross on Good Friday are "We Acclaim the Cross of Jesus" [PMB, WC, WS] and Francis Patrick O'Brien's "Tree of Life and Glory," set for choir verses and assembly refrain [GIA G-5452]. Other songs appropriate for the preparation of the gifts include "Take Up Your Cross," "What Wondrous Love" [both in most hymnals], "The Cross of Jesus" [SS], and "Only This I Want" [BB, CBW3, G2, GC, GC2, JS2].

Easter Triduum

Hence you must have
one prayer, one petition, one mind, one hope,
dominated by love and unsullied joy—
that means you must have Jesus Christ.
You cannot have anything better than that.

—Ignatius to Magnesians, 7:1

Reflecting on the Triduum

During the Easter Season the first reading on all the Sundays is taken from the Acts of the Apostles, not from the Old Testament as is usually the case. During this time of celebrating the resurrection of the Lord, we hear how the early church responded to this Good News of new life and how they responded in faith to the presence of the risen Lord. Our joyous celebrations might lead us to think that the early church had no problems; they were so taken up with Jesus' risen presence. Yet where there are human beings living together, there tend to be differences. This contrast between fidelity to Easter faith and struggling with the foibles and sometimes even the infidelity of each other can actually help us keep in mind the reason we celebrate the Triduum and, indeed, celebrate throughout the liturgical year. Jesus came to be one with us and to bring us to oneness in him "and through him God was pleased to reconcile to himself all things . . . by making peace through the blood of his cross" (Col 1:20).

In all of Scripture St. Paul has the most to say about reconciliation; he reiterates over and over again that our reconciliation with the Father is brought about in Christ through his saving work of redemption. Since in baptism we are made members of Christ's Body and plunged into his paschal mystery, our work is also one of reconciliation. Being members of the one Body of Christ, we are to relate to each other as brothers and sisters in Christ, a well-knit unity of faithful servants to care for each other. Our being reconcilers, then, is really a matter of *being who we are*, of being faithful to our identity as members of Christ's Body. To be reconcilers is one way to make visible the presence of the risen Christ. To be reconcilers is one way we continue Jesus' saving ministry.

In Christ we share in divine life; the work of reconciliation, then, is none other than bringing about the unity that is expressed in the divine Trinity and that belongs to the Body of Christ because of our share in that same life. Divisions, even more than causing wrangling and rancor, undermine who we are and the common life that we share. Because we are human, there will be divisions. The challenge of the gospel is constantly to open ourselves to the life God gives, to surrender to God's transforming us to be ever more perfect members of the Body of Christ, to experience new relationships with each other and with God through the unity of this Body, and to enjoy the peace that comes from unity. To be reconcilers is to be faithful to the identity God has given us and trusted us to live.

Living the Paschal Mystery

At stake in the work of reconciliation is always the unity of the church. We cannot take our harmful human actions lightly but must always admit when we weaken or break our relationship with God and others and then strive to restore the unity that is at the very heart of who we are. Reconciliation is, therefore, the work of salvation because it is concerned with how we are one with God and each other. How we are with God is indicated by how we are with each other. Disunity in our families, among our friends, at the workplace sows discord beyond these groups because it sows discord within our own hearts. As members of Christ's body, our basic work is to be true to ourselves—true to our own surrender to live in Christ.

During these holy days we celebrate Jesus' self-giving so that we might be reconciled, be one in Christ. In this we learn how we ought to live—being reconciled with one another—so that our unity is preserved and brings God glory and praise through, with, and in Christ.

TRIDUUM

"Triduum" comes from two Latin words (*tres* and *dies*) that mean "a space of three days." But since we have four days with special names—Holy Thursday, Good Friday, Holy Saturday, and Easter Sunday—the "three" may be confusing to some.

The confusion is cleared up when we understand how the days are reckoned. On all high festival days the church counts a day in the same way as Jewish people count days and festivals, that is, from sundown to sundown. Thus, the Triduum consists of *three* twenty-four-hour periods that stretch over four calendar days.

Therefore, the Easter Triduum begins at sundown on Holy Thursday with the Mass of the Lord's Supper and concludes with Easter Evening Prayer at sundown on Easter Sunday; its high point is the celebration of the Easter Vigil (GNLYC no. 19).

SOLEMN PASCHAL FAST

According to the above calculation, Lent ends at sundown on Holy Thursday; thus, Holy Thursday itself is the last day of Lent. This doesn't mean that our fasting concludes on Holy Thursday, however; the church has traditionally kept a solemn forty-hour fast from the beginning of the Triduum (Holy Thursday evening, thus the solemn fast is contiguous with the Lenten fast) until the fast is broken at Communion during the Easter Vigil.

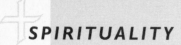

SPIRITUALITY

GOSPEL ACCLAMATION
John 13:34

I give you a new commandment, says the Lord:
love one another as I have loved you.

Gospel John 13:1-15; L39ABC

Before the feast of Passover, Jesus
    knew that his hour had come
to pass from this world to the
    Father.
He loved his own in the world and he
    loved them to the end.
The devil had already induced Judas,
    son of Simon the Iscariot, to hand
    him over.
So, during supper,
    fully aware that the Father had put
        everything into his power
    and that he had come from God and
        was returning to God,
    he rose from supper and took off his
        outer garments.
He took a towel and tied it around his waist.
Then he poured water into a basin
    and began to wash the disciples' feet
    and dry them with the towel around his
        waist.
He came to Simon Peter, who said to him,
    "Master, are you going to wash my feet?"
Jesus answered and said to him,
    "What I am doing, you do not understand
        now,
    but you will understand later."
Peter said to him, "You will never wash my
    feet."
Jesus answered him,
    "Unless I wash you, you will have no
        inheritance with me."
Simon Peter said to him,
    "Master, then not only my feet, but my
        hands and head as well."
Jesus said to him,
    "Whoever has bathed has no need except
        to have his feet washed,
        for he is clean all over;
    so you are clean, but not all."
For he knew who would betray him;
    for this reason, he said, "Not all of you
        are clean."

Continued in Appendix A, p. 282.
See Appendix A, p. 282, for the other readings.

Reflecting on the Gospel and Living the Paschal Mystery

Key words and phrases: he loved them to the end, he knew who would betray him, I have given you a model

To the point: Although most of Jesus' beloved disciples "betrayed" him, he still "loved them to the end." We are able to love those who wrong us because Jesus has already reconciled us to God and each other by giving himself in self-sacrifice. We prove our love by doing likewise and serving others—even those who wrong us.

Reflection: The night before important happenings, we tend to be focused on ourselves and preparing for the next day. The night before a big final exam, students cram. The night before surgery, we fast and pack and do whatever is necessary to go to the hospital. The night before a job interview, we press the clothes, touch up the resume, get a good night's sleep. We tend to be single minded before important events. We hardly have time to think of others.

The first Holy Thursday night was the night before Jesus' death. Rather than plot about how to escape or prepare an iron-clad defense, Jesus is not focused on himself but on his disciples. Rather than thinking about himself, he is thinking about teaching, modeling love for his disciples. He gives himself to them—twice: he gives his Body and Blood, he gives himself in humble service as a model for how we should also be toward one another. In both of these acts of giving Jesus showed how "he loved them to the end."

Yes, Jesus loves his disciples—followers who are anything but perfect. This night, when he gives himself so unexpectedly, he does so in face of the unexpected: these disciples betray him! This gospel for Holy Thursday explicitly names one betrayer but implies others. Not only Judas but eventually most of the disciples "betrayed" Jesus by abandoning him in his last hour (only his mother, the beloved disciple, and some women stood by him at the cross, according to John 19:25-26). Yet Christ shows us a truly remarkable model: "he loved them to the end."

The model Jesus gave us to follow is a love so other-centered and so complete that it overlooks the weakness of others and instead draws out the good in them. In spite of the disciples' betrayal and weakness, Jesus still works to strengthen his relationship to them. Jesus still makes it known that his mission is to reconcile all things to his Father. Indeed, the two acts of self-giving are truly both acts of reconciliation. By sharing in his Body and Blood, we are made one with him. By taking up his service ministry, we are made one with each other.

Under the umbrella of reconciliation Eucharist and service are two faces of the same coin; they both are actions that draw us to focus on the good of the other in self-giving. Relationships are healed and strengthened in such activity—giving oneself for the sake of another. We are able to love those who wrong us because Jesus has given us the example: "he loved them to the end." We prove our love by doing likewise. We are to love others by serving them and being reconciled with each other. Although most of Jesus' beloved disciples "betrayed" him, he still "loved them to the end." We are able to love those who wrong us because Jesus has already reconciled us to God and each other by giving himself in self-sacrifice. We prove our love by doing likewise and serving others—even those who wrong us.

Model Act of Penitence

Presider: This night we celebrate Jesus' great love—so great that he sat at table even with the one who would betray him. As we begin Eucharist *this* night, we pause to open our hearts to the healing that Jesus brings and the unity with him and each other that Jesus makes possible . . . [pause]

Lord Jesus, you love your disciples even to the end: Lord . . .

Christ Jesus, you reconcile us to God by your self-giving: Christ . . .

Lord Jesus, you give us an example of serving others: Lord . . .

Model Prayer of the Faithful

Presider: We bring our prayers to a God who loves us, confident that we will be heard.

Response:

Lord, hear our prayer.

Cantor:

we pray to the Lord,

That all members of the church may love with great compassion and serve others with unquenchable zeal . . . [pause]

That leaders of nations may serve their people with integrity and love . . . [pause]

That those who are hungry be fed, those who are alienated be reconciled, and those who plot evil be turned toward God . . . [pause]

That each of us here nourish others through our self-giving and loving service . . . [pause]

Presider: God of love, you gave us your divine Son as a model of self-giving: hear these our prayers that we might serve you through others. We ask this through Christ our Lord. **Amen.**

OPENING PRAYER

Let us pray

Pause for silent prayer

God our Father,
we are gathered here to share in the supper
which your only Son left to his Church to
    reveal his love.
He gave it to us when he was about to die
and commanded us to celebrate it as the
    new and eternal sacrifice.
We pray that in this eucharist
we may find the fullness of love and life.

Grant this through our Lord Jesus Christ,
    your Son,
who lives and reigns with you and the Holy
    Spirit,
one God, for ever and ever. **Amen.**

FOR REFLECTION

• I am apt to betray another when . . . I betray Jesus when . . . What brings me to reconciliation is . . .
• Eucharist nourishes me to love others more deeply because . . .
• I find it easy to serve others in need when . . . I find it most challenging when . . .

Homily Points

• As Juvenal Urbino lies dying in the arms of his beloved wife Fermina in Gabriel Garcia Marquez's best-selling novel *Love in the Time of Cholera*, he speaks these words to her: "Only God knows how much I have loved you." If we have a hard time expressing and knowing deep love for each other, how much more challenging it is to know God's love for us!

• At the Last Supper, the God-man Jesus models for us exactly how much God loves us: he, the "master and teacher," stoops to wash the feet of those he has led and taught—those very disciples who will betray and deny him in his hour of need. To "love to the end" means that even the deepest hurt ought not prevent us from giving ourselves to one another. Jesus' giving of his Body and Blood and his self-giving service both model his unsurpassed love. By doing as Jesus did—loving and serving others—do we know God's love for us. Then can we truly love one another.

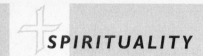

SPIRITUALITY

GOSPEL ACCLAMATION
Phil 2:8-9

Christ became obedient to the point of death,
even death on a cross.
Because of this, God greatly exalted him
and bestowed on him the name which is above
    every other name.

Gospel

John 18:1–19:42; L40ABC

Jesus went out with his
    disciples across the
    Kidron valley
to where there was a
    garden,
into which he and his
    disciples entered.
Judas his betrayer also
    knew the place,
because Jesus had often met there
    with his disciples.
So Judas got a band of soldiers and
    guards
from the chief priests and the
    Pharisees
and went there with lanterns, torches,
    and weapons.
Jesus, knowing everything that was
    going to happen to him,
went out and said to them, "Whom are
    you looking for?"
They answered him, "Jesus the
    Nazorean."
He said to them, "I AM."
Judas his betrayer was also with them.
When he said to them, "I AM,"
    they turned away and fell to the
    ground.
So he again asked them,
    "Whom are you looking for?"
They said, "Jesus the Nazorean."
Jesus answered,
    "I told you that I AM.
So if you are looking for me, let these
    men go."
This was to fulfill what he had said,
    "I have not lost any of those you gave
    me."

Continued in Appendix A, pp. 283–284.
See Appendix A, p. 285, for the other readings.

Reflecting on the Gospel and Living the Paschal Mystery
Key words and phrases: betrayer, mother, Mary, Mary, It is finished

To the point: All of us betray Jesus like those disciples so long ago. The encouragement of this day is that Jesus does not count betrayal as the last word; his last words, "It is finished," indicate that he had accomplished all that was necessary to heal our divisions—to bring reconciliation among us, and between humanity and his Father. He overcame death and turned bitterness into a sweet wood that is the promise of life.

Reflection: We use the word "dead" more than we sometimes think, especially since death is not usually a welcome topic. For example, we see dead end signs when driving, we have a place for dead files in offices, we know journalists are always rushing to meet deadlines. In all these cases, the word "dead" implies an end of some kind: end of the road, end of an order or program, end of time to write an article. And "dead" means just that: no more, finished, done, over. No doubt, when the soldiers came to Jesus' cross "and saw that he was already dead," they too thought no more, finished, done, over. No point in breaking legs to speed the onset of death. This One is gone. Just do a perfunctory thrust of a sword. How wrong they were! With Jesus, "already dead" isn't the end. The cross is not only the instrument of the death of Jesus but also the sweet wood of exaltation, salvation, and reconciliation. "It is [not] finished"!

It is interesting to note that in John's account three women were "[s]tanding by the cross of Jesus," all of whom are named "Mary." In Hebrew Mary means "bitter." Unlike the synoptic tradition where the women and others stand at a distance, Jesus' mother, his aunt, and Mary Magdalene stand near the cross. Rather than "betray" him, they experience the bitterness of death up close and personal. Jesus draws those he loves near to him. In his final act of compassion, Jesus gives his mother and his beloved disciple into each other's hands. The bitterness and disunity that death can bring is healed one more time. The faithfulness and obedience of Jesus begets the reconciliation that brings unity and peace.

For a second time during this Triduum we are reminded that Jesus is betrayed. Betrayal spawns divisions, suffering, and misery. Here, we are not speaking about Jesus' suffering but about the bitter suffering and misery our own human weakness bring upon us. Betrayal and the cross point to both the baseness and exaltation of humanity, to both the divisions and unity. The only way that we can truly heal our divisions is if each of us is willing to die to ourselves and love others with the same compassion and mercy Jesus faithfully showed. The cross—and the mystery of this day—calls us to the transformation of self that is the only way to social harmony and to lasting peace. This day is a reminder that the road to peace is paved by a cross. This day is a reminder that "dead" is no longer the end. Death opens the way for new life, unity, and peace.

All of us betray Jesus like those disciples so long ago. The encouragement of this day is that Jesus does not count betrayal as the last word; his last words, "It is finished," indicate that he had accomplished all that was necessary to heal our divisions, to bring reconciliation among us, and between humanity and his Father. He overcame death and turned bitterness into a sweet wood that is the promise of life.

Suggestions for Music

Singing the solemn prayers: Just as the Easter Vigil is the mother of all vigils, so the Good Friday solemn prayers are the mother and model of all prayers of the faithful. Because of their solemnity, they are meant to be sung, using the simple chant given in the Sacramentary, and to include short periods of silent prayer after each statement of intention. If it is not possible that these prayers be sung, they should be spoken with solemnity and with sufficient time allowed for the appropriate silent pauses for fervent prayer.

Music during the veneration of the cross: As the title of this part of this day's liturgy—"Veneration of the Cross"—indicates, what we honor in this procession is not the One crucified but the cross that embodies the mystery of his—and our—redemptive triumph over sin and death. Because we are not *historicizing* or reenacting a past event but *ritualizing* the meaning of this event for our lives here and now, this procession is not one of sorrow or expiation but of gratitude, of triumph, and of quiet and confident acceptance (the very sentiments expressed in the final verse of the responsorial psalm).

The music used during this procession needs, then, to sing about the mystery and triumph of the cross rather than about the details of Jesus' suffering and death. Singing a hymn such as "Were You There," for example, misdirects the focus of the Good Friday liturgy and is more appropriate for Palm Sunday. Singing the Reproaches also misdirects our attention toward Christ's suffering and our sinfulness rather than toward the cross as mystery and means of exaltation. The inclusion of the Reproaches in the Lectionary simply indicates that as a church we have not yet made the full transition to a post–Vatican II understanding of what the liturgy of Good Friday is about.

Examples of appropriate music include "We Acclaim the Cross of Jesus" [PMB, WC, WS]; "O Cross of Christ, Immortal Tree" [CBW3, PMB, WC, SS]; "Behold, Before Our Wond'ring Eyes" [BB, JS2]; Ricky Manalo's "We Should Glory in the Cross" [JS2; choir octavo OCP #11355CC]; Francis Patrick O'Brien's "Tree of Life and Glory" [GIA G-5452]; "We Venerate Your Cross/To Cruz Adoramos" [OFUV]; "Only This I Want" [BB, GC, GC2, JS2]. Gerard Chiusano's choral setting of the entrance antiphon for Holy Thursday, "We Should Glory in the Cross" (OCP octavo #10884), would be an excellent piece for the choir to sing, as would Steve Janco's "Glory in the Cross" (GIA octavo G-4213). If already sung as part of the Holy Thursday liturgy, repeating either of these selections would emphasize the unity of these celebrations.

OPENING PRAYER

Let us pray

Pause for silent prayer

Lord,
by shedding his blood for us,
your Son, Jesus Christ,
established the paschal mystery.
In your goodness, make us holy
and watch over us always.

We ask this through Christ our Lord. **Amen.**

FOR REFLECTION

- I betray Jesus when . . . I betray others when . . . This leaves me . . .
- I find it easiest to be faithful and obedient to Jesus when . . . This sows unity and peace in that . . .
- The cross leaves me bitter when . . . It brings me peace when . . . It is sweet for me when . . .

Homily Points

- When we are in pain (for example, have a headache or arthritis), as the pain becomes more severe it becomes all consuming. It is all we think about. Traditionally on Good Friday we have emphasized the suffering and pain of Jesus hanging on the cross. In fact, Jesus' pain and suffering were not all consuming for him—he pays attention to Mary and the beloved disciple. This day is not about pain and suffering; it is about love and exaltation.

- The cross is not the end but the necessary entry to the fullness of life. The cross (painful, yes) is not bitter but sweet. Perhaps the bitterness we experience, captured in the three Marys ("bitter") standing at the foot of the cross, indicates the human limitation we bring to this mystery. Jesus, in giving himself over to the arms of his Father, explodes our limitations. "It is [not] finished"! New life has begun!

✠ SPIRITUALITY

Gospel   Matt 28:1-10; L41ABC

After the sabbath, as the first day of
   the week was dawning,
   Mary Magdalene and the other Mary
      came to see the tomb.
And behold, there was a great
   earthquake;
   for an angel of the Lord
      descended from
      heaven,
   approached, rolled back the
      stone, and sat upon it.
His appearance was like
   lightning
   and his clothing was white
      as snow.
The guards were shaken with
   fear of him
   and became like dead men.
Then the angel said to the women in
   reply,
   "Do not be afraid!
I know that you are seeking Jesus the
   crucified.
He is not here, for he has been raised
   just as he said.
Come and see the place where he lay.
Then go quickly and tell his disciples,
   'He has been raised from the dead,
   and he is going before you to Galilee;
   there you will see him.'
   Behold, I have told you."
Then they went away quickly from the
   tomb,
   fearful yet overjoyed,
   and ran to announce this to his
      disciples.
And behold, Jesus met them on their
   way and greeted them.
They approached, embraced his feet,
   and did him homage.
Then Jesus said to them, "Do not be
   afraid.
Go tell my brothers to go to Galilee,
   and there they will see me."

Readings in Appendix A, pp. 286–291.

Reflecting on the Gospel and Living the Paschal Mystery
Key words and phrases: Very early, He has been raised, you will see him

To the point: In this night we gather to hear how God has faithfully called us chosen ones to salvation. In this night we gather to sing our alleluias, after being silent for forty days. In this night we gather to hear the Easter proclamation: "He has been raised."

Reflection: Countless parents over many, many years have tucked their little ones securely in bed and said to them, "nighty-night, don't let the bed bugs bite." Now, bed bugs are real and every now and then we hear of an outbreak of them. But the really interesting part of this bed time leave-taking is the "nighty-night." We wish our children (and each other) a good night— "nighty-night" seems to double that wish. Nighttime can be a time of terror, and it is for those unfortunate people who become victims of crime under the cover of darkness. Or nighttime can be a time of sweet dreams, of pleasant and refreshing rest, of leisure away from demands and troubles.

How many times during *this night* do we hear the word "night"? Over and over again we hear "this night." This night is like so many others—its darkness can hide treachery and evil intent. But this night is different for us Christians, for this night we deliberately enter into the darkness, we embrace it, we welcome it. In the darkness we celebrate together "nighty-night"—a doubling of goodness, joy, life. In this night we gather to hear how God has faithfully called us chosen ones to salvation. In this night we gather to sing our alleluias, after being silent for forty days. In this night we gather to hear the Easter proclamation: "He has been raised."

All the weeks of Lent we have been fasting, praying, and acting charitably toward one another—waiting to hear the Good News that is announced *this night*: "He has been raised." "Very early" the women went to the tomb, undoubtedly with heavy hearts, bringing spices to anoint their beloved dead. "Very early"—somewhere between the darkness of "nighty-night" and the promising light of a new dawn. When the women come to the tomb an angel bids them not to be afraid and then speaks even better Good News: the disciples are to go to Galilee and there they "will see him."

This night, however, other even more startling news is announced. We hear St. Paul (in the epistle) tell the Romans (and us) that we who have been "baptized into [Jesus'] death" will be "united with him in the resurrection." This night we celebrate not only the Good News of Jesus' resurrection but also the Good News that *we* now live in the risen Christ. Our bond of unity is the shared life of the risen Christ. This night announces why we work so hard at being faithful disciples, at being a reconciling community so the bonds of unity are not diminished: through baptism we already share in Jesus' risen life.

We too ought not be afraid. We ought not fear helping another overcome weakness or mend sinful ways. We ought not fear venturing out to welcome someone who seems alone into our warm circle of friends. We ought not fear healing divisions where we see them or having the courage to admit where we ourselves have caused them. We ought not fear the goodness and power of this new life we've been given. We ought not fear the terrors of the night, for *this night* new life bursts forth: the Lord Jesus "has been raised." And we share in that risen life. Alleluia!

Model Prayer of the Faithful

Presider: In Easter joy we welcome for the first time the newly baptized to pray with us for the needs of the church and world.

Response:

Lord, hear our prayer.

Cantor:

we pray to the Lord,

That the church dispel the terrors of the night by the light of a new dawn of risen glory . . . [pause]

That all peoples of the world not be afraid to welcome God's offer of reconciliation for lasting peace . . . [pause]

That the poor and downtrodden not be afraid to trust in God's lavish gifts that promise new life . . . [pause]

That each of us here radiate the new life of the risen glory we share through baptism . . . [pause]

Presider: Wondrous God, you raised up your Son to new life: hear these our prayers that we might one day share that same life with you for ever and ever. **Amen**.

OPENING PRAYER

Let us pray

Pause for silent prayer

Lord God,
you have brightened this night
with the radiance of the risen Christ.
Quicken the spirit of sonship in your Church;
renew us in mind and body
to give you whole-hearted service.

Grant this through our Lord Jesus Christ,
your Son,
who lives and reigns with you and the Holy Spirit,
one God, for ever and ever. **Amen.**

FOR REFLECTION
• I am terrified of night when . . . *This night* brings me joy because . . .
• I am overcome by the sheer joy of my sharing in Christ's risen life when . . .
• I see the risen Christ when . . . Others see the risen Christ in me when . . .

Homily Points

• Some people look forward to the beginning of night, others to its end. Some people fear the terrors of the night, others celebrate its blessings. Some people party through the night, others sleep it away. What are we, the Body of Christ, to do with *this night*?

• *This night* we pause (for a long time!) to remember the story of God's patient and enduring love for us. *This night* culminates in the first proclamation of the Easter mystery: "He has been raised." *This night* new members are initiated into the Body of the risen Christ. *This night* is like no other night: *this night* holds no terrors but only new life. *This night* we dance until the dawn.

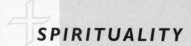

SPIRITUALITY

GOSPEL ACCLAMATION
cf. 1 Cor 5:7b-8a

℟. Alleluia, alleluia.
Christ, our paschal lamb, has been sacrificed;
let us then feast with joy in the Lord.
℟. Alleluia, alleluia.

Gospel

John 20:1-9; L42ABC

On the first day of the week,
  Mary of Magdala came to the
    tomb early in the morning,
  while it was still dark,
  and saw the stone removed from
    the tomb.
So she ran and went to Simon Peter
  and to the other disciple whom
    Jesus loved, and told them,
  "They have taken the Lord from
    the tomb,
  and we don't know where they put him."
So Peter and the other disciple went out
  and came to the tomb.
They both ran, but the other disciple ran
  faster than Peter
  and arrived at the tomb first;
  he bent down and saw the burial cloths
    there, but did not go in.
When Simon Peter arrived after him,
  he went into the tomb and saw the
    burial cloths there,
  and the cloth that had covered his
    head,
  not with the burial cloths but rolled up
    in a separate place.
Then the other disciple also went in,
  the one who had arrived at the tomb
    first,
  and he saw and believed.
For they did not yet understand the
    Scripture
  that he had to rise from the dead.

or

Matt 28:1-10; L41A *in Appendix A, p. 292*

or, at an afternoon or evening Mass
Luke 24:13-35; L46 *in Appendix A, p. 292*

See Appendix A, p. 293, for the other readings.

Reflecting on the Gospel and Living the Paschal Mystery

Key words and phrases: saw and believed, did not yet understand, he had to rise from the dead

To the point: We can identify easily with the apostles who "saw and believed," who wanted with all their hearts to know their beloved Lord was alive. Yet they "did not understand." This mystery is preposterous, unbelievable, absurd. Who ever heard of someone rising from the dead?

Reflection: Everywhere we turn at this time of the year there they are: bunnies and eggs. Stuffed ones and plastic ones, edible ones and blown up ones—they are everywhere. We enjoy the bright colors and fuzzy softness and scrumptious goodness of these annual treats. But we better not think too hard about it, or think too clearly, or think too rationally. For bunnies and eggs just don't go together. Bunnies don't lay eggs! This is a fantastic, impossible, ludicrous pairing for any right-thinking person. Bunnies just don't lay eggs! And maybe this is exactly the point. Easter and its mystery cannot be rationalized or approached logically. The Easter mystery is truly preposterous, unbelievable, absurd. Who ever heard of someone rising from the dead? We can identify easily with the apostles who "saw and believed," who wanted with all their hearts to know their beloved Lord was alive. Yet they "did not understand." This mystery is preposterous, unbelievable, absurd. Who ever heard of someone rising from the dead?

Here is the mystery of Easter: we want to see and believe, but since resurrection is so out of our human experience we simply can't understand. Belief came gradually to those first witnesses, and then only when they had a personal encounter with Jesus (some disciples "ate and drank with him"; see first reading). Our own belief in the risen Jesus gradually grows throughout our life as we continually encounter him in our own eating and drinking with him. We encounter the risen Jesus in Eucharist when we eat and drink *with him*—when Jesus' very Body and Blood become our nourishment. We also encounter the risen Jesus in each other when we witness by the goodness of our lives to Gospel values. We encounter the risen Jesus in the sure joy that comes from reconciled relationships with each other that witness to our reconciled relationship with God. We encounter the risen Jesus when we "clear out the old yeast" (second reading from 1 Cor) and "receive forgiveness of sins." All of this assures us that we are a new creation in this resurrection life—the source of our Easter joy.

We take for granted that bunnies and eggs go together at Easter; we don't have to be logical about it. The fun is precisely in the illogic. So it is with the Easter mystery. The Easter mystery is something we accept in faith. We can't be logical about it. The grace is precisely in the illogic. True, Jesus had raised people from the dead, for example, the son of the widow of Nain and his own friend Lazarus. But they were only resuscitated and would face death again. Jesus is not merely resuscitated; he is raised up from the grave to new life, never to die again. Our belief enables us to share in this same risen life. Yes, our mortal bodies will die like Jesus' and Lazarus's. But this risen life that is already within us is forever. It defies logic. It is preposterous. We do not understand it. But we believe it, we live it, we embrace it. *The* mystery: we share in eternal life—risen life with no end.

Model Act of Penitence

Presider: Today we are filled with Easter joy; our Lord is risen! During this celebration we will renew our baptismal promises and state our belief in the risen Lord. As we prepare to celebrate this great mystery, let us reflect on why we believe and how we might come to stronger belief . . . [pause]

  Lord Jesus, you are the paschal lamb that was sacrificed: Lord . . .

  Christ Jesus, you were raised from the dead on the third day: Christ . . .

  Lord Jesus, you bring the peace and joy of new life: Lord . . .

Model Prayer of the Faithful

Presider: We lift our needs confidently to a God who lavishly bestows new and eternal life on those who believe.

Response:

Lord, hear our prayer.

Cantor:

we pray to the Lord,

That the church share generously with all who come the joy of participating in the risen life Jesus offers . . . [pause]

That all people in the world open themselves to the salvation that God offers so generously . . . [pause]

That the saddened and oppressed be lifted up by the joy of the resurrection and anticipation of a better life . . . [pause]

That all of us share in the joy of the newly baptized as they eat and drink with us at the table of the Lord . . . [pause]

Presider: Glorious God, you raised your Son to new life: hear these our prayers that we might one day share eternal life with you. Grant this through your risen Son, Jesus Christ our Lord. **Amen.**

FOR REFLECTION
- For me, the absurdity of Easter is . . . Those who help me to see and believe are . . . because . . .
- I find it easiest to encounter the risen Jesus when . . .
- For me, the joy of new life is . . .

Homily Points

- Part of the fun of Easter is children searching for and finding hidden eggs. Not only are they hidden, but they are hidden in both familiar and unexpected places. The eggs are always hidden with love and always meant to be found.

- So too the new life offered us at Easter is hidden in both familiar and unexpected places, waiting to be found. This is a hunt that never ends, as our capacity to seek, find, and recognize the risen Christ within and among us increases as we grow in believing. Believing is a doing—identifying with the risen Christ and loving and serving as he did.

Season of Easter

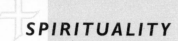

SPIRITUALITY

GOSPEL ACCLAMATION
John 20:29

℟. Alleluia, alleluia.
You believe in me, Thomas, because you have
    seen me, says the Lord;
blessed are those who have not seen me, but still
    believe!
℟. Alleluia, alleluia.

Gospel   John 20:19-31; L43A

On the evening of that first day
    of the week,
    when the doors were locked,
        where the disciples
        were,
    for fear of the Jews,
    Jesus came and stood in their
        midst
    and said to them, "Peace be with
        you."
When he had said this, he showed them
        his hands and his side.
The disciples rejoiced when they saw
        the Lord.
Jesus said to them again, "Peace be
    with you.
As the Father has sent me, so I send
    you."
And when he had said this, he breathed
        on them and said to them,
    "Receive the Holy Spirit.
Whose sins you forgive are forgiven
        them,
    and whose sins you retain are
        retained."

Thomas, called Didymus, one of the
        Twelve,
    was not with them when Jesus came.
So the other disciples said to him, "We
        have seen the Lord."
But he said to them,
    "Unless I see the mark of the nails in
        his hands
    and put my finger into the nailmarks
    and put my hand into his side, I will
        not believe."

Continued in Appendix A, p. 294.

Reflecting on the Gospel

"Aw, go on!" "Get out of here!" "You're kidding!" "You're pulling my leg!" "You don't say!" "I don't believe it!" With these and other expressions we exclaim our disbelief at something that has been said or reported to us as having been done. The sheer multiplicity of these expressions reminds us that we are quite comfortable with and prefer direct, tangible proofs. Thomas seems to be doing only the human thing when he asked for proof from the disciples who had claimed to see the Lord. He got way more than he bargained for!

Thomas refuses to believe that Jesus is alive without the physical proof of seeing and touching his wounds. Seemingly quite willing to accommodate, Jesus returns the next week and invites Thomas to see, touch, and believe. We too, like Thomas, need to encounter the risen Jesus in tangible ways. We share with him this basic human tendency to want tangible proofs. The risen Lord is relentless in bringing us to the same belief he coaxed out of Thomas. Today that "proof" comes in his being present to us and in his offer of peace. It comes to us through the community of believers who reinforce for each other that Jesus is, indeed, alive and among us because his Spirit is within us. Jesus offers us our "proofs" in our encounters with his risen presence through the "many wonders and signs" (first reading) the Spirit works within the community of believers. Blessed are we, indeed! Our blessedness rests in our realization that the resurrection is not merely believing in Jesus' new life, but through the Spirit we ourselves share in this life as we are sent forth to continue Jesus' saving ministry. Our belief is strengthened by our doing.

The struggle to believe is no less than the struggle to recognize and encounter the risen Christ. This is really what our Christian life is all about—encountering the risen Christ who lives now within the Christian community and living the reality that risen life is given to us to share with others. Our Easter joy doesn't come from proofs; it comes from persons who are willing to struggle with the mystery because what the mystery promises is so much: new life.

Living the Paschal Mystery

Not just Thomas, but all the disciples came to believe because they had "seen the Lord." Yet we are not disadvantaged because we have not seen; the advantage comes not from seeing but from *believing*. Because of believing we can say we "have seen the Lord."

Another twist to this seeing/believing issue is hinted at in the first reading. These early Christians enjoyed "favor with all the people." While other New Testament texts tell us that all wasn't peaches and cream, this passage does point to the extraordinarily good life the early Christians led, with no one in their midst in need. One way we might say that we have truly "seen the Lord," then, is in the good works performed by those who claim his name. Jesus' risen presence was different from his physical presence before the resurrection (the gospel makes a point about Jesus coming through a locked door). Therefore, even though we are removed from the historical reality of Jesus' presence, we are no less able to "see" and be present to the risen Lord. The challenge for Christian living, of course, is that we see the risen Lord in the goodness of others.

Focusing the Gospel

Key words and phrases: Receive the Holy Spirit; Unless I see . . . I will not believe; do not be unbelieving, but believe; Blessed are those

To the point: Thomas refuses to believe that Jesus is alive without the physical proof of seeing and touching his wounds. Jesus returns the next week and invites Thomas to see, touch, and believe. We too, like Thomas, need to encounter the risen Jesus in tangible ways. Jesus offers us this encounter with his risen presence through the "many wonders and signs" (first reading) the Spirit works within the community of believers. Blessed are we, indeed!

Connecting the Gospel

to the first reading: Faith begins with personal encounter with the risen Christ and leads to membership in a community of faith that witnesses through concrete actions to the presence of Christ.

to our experience: Our human senses—seeing, touching, feeling, tasting, hearing—are the doorways to knowledge. So it is not unreasonable to want tangible, sensible proof that Jesus is alive. The good news is that we experience Jesus alive and among us through one another, good works, the quiet of prayer, etc.

Connecting the Responsorial Psalm

to the readings: In the final strophe of the responsorial psalm we proclaim that redemption has been wrought by God and "it is wonderful in our eyes." We do see the redemption. The question is where and how. The disciples (Thomas-come-lately included) were shown Jesus' risen body (gospel). The crowds in the days of the early church saw "signs and wonders done through the apostles" (first reading). We might be tempted to classify as second-rate the signs provided for us—the words of Scripture (gospel), the ritual of the Eucharist, social justice for the poor (first reading), the granting of forgiveness (gospel). But these wondrous works are actually first-rate signs that redemption is real, practical, and everyday. The readings call us to see and believe. The psalm calls us to give thanks to the God from whom this redemption comes (psalm).

to psalmist preparation: This Sunday's readings remind you that the reality of the resurrection is made manifest in the manner in which Christians break bread, care for the needy, pray together, and forgive one another. As preparation for singing the responsorial psalm, you might select one of these actions to live in some specific way this week. For example, you might consciously make a family meal a true breaking of Christ's bread. Or you might share some possession with someone in need. By doing so your singing of the psalm will come from a heart that believes in the resurrection because you have made it visible in your own life.

ASSEMBLY & FAITH-SHARING GROUPS
- Some signs I have seen that help me believe in the presence to me of the risen Christ are . . .
- I know I have missed seeing and touching the risen Christ in others because . . .
- I am a sign of the many wonders God is working within my faith community when I . . .

PRESIDERS
I see, touch, and come to greater belief in Christ working through me when my ministry looks like . . .

DEACONS
I see and touch the wounds of Christ today in . . .

HOSPITALITY MINISTERS
I am a sign of the presence of the risen Christ greeting those who gather when I . . .

MUSIC MINISTERS
My singing helps me experience the new life of the risen Christ when I . . .

ALTAR MINISTERS
My serving others is a sign to the community that Christ is "My Lord and my God" when . . .

LECTORS
When I discern the presence of the risen Christ in the people and events of my daily life, my proclamation becomes . . .

EXTRAORDINARY MINISTERS OF HOLY COMMUNION
The manner of my distributing Holy Communion helps communicants see, touch, and believe in the risen Christ when I . . .

Model Rite of Blessing and Sprinkling Holy Water

Presider: Dear friends, we are sprinkled with these waters so that through them we might encounter the risen Christ and come to believe in his presence to us. We pause now to ready ourselves to celebrate these Easter mysteries . . . [pause]

   [continue with form C of the blessing of water]

Homily Points

• We've all experienced the absence of loved ones and the uncontainable joy that wells up in us when they return. For example, a parent returns from a six-month Navy tour and the children jump into his or her arms. While Jesus sometimes may seem absent to us, he is actually present to us at all times, even when we are unaware of it—we need only open our eyes to see him.

• The risen Jesus is persistent in making himself present to his disciples. This presence is essential for his continued mission. Through his gifts of peace and the Holy Spirit, he empowers his disciples to continue the mission of his saving presence.

• How do we experience Jesus' risen presence among us? Jesus is present in the stranger who reaches out to help us. Jesus is present in the person who recognizes in us and calls forth talent we didn't know we had. Jesus is present when we listen to another who longs to unburden his or her heart. Jesus is present when we forgive those who hurt us. Jesus is present in the person whose encouragement frees us from fear. Our belief in the presence of the risen Christ is strengthened through such tangible good acts. Through these acts, what happened for Thomas happens for us today.

Model Prayer of the Faithful

Presider: Let us pray for the gift of peace and the strength of the Holy Spirit to continue faithfully Jesus' saving ministry.

Response:

Lord, hear our prayer.

Cantor:

we pray to the Lord,

That all members of the church grow in believing in the presence of the risen Christ in their midst . . . [pause]

That all peoples of the world grow in believing in the goodness and forgiveness of God . . . [pause]

That the sick and suffering, the doubting and despairing be lifted up by the ministry of this believing community . . . [pause]

That each of us here be a source of forgiveness, an instrument of peace, and a faithful temple of the Holy Spirit . . . [pause]

Presider: God who promises new life to all those who believe, hear these our prayers that one day we may share the fullness of life with you and the risen Son, Jesus Christ our Lord. **Amen**.

Let us pray

Pause for silent prayer

Heavenly Father and God of mercy,
we no longer look for Jesus among the dead,
for he is alive and has become the Lord
   of life.
From the waters of death you raise us with
   him
and renew your gift of life within us.

Increase in our minds and hearts
the risen life we share with Christ
and help us to grow as your people
toward the fullness of eternal life with you.

We ask this through Christ our Lord.
   Amen.

FIRST READING
Acts 2:42-47

They devoted themselves
   to the teaching of the apostles and to the
      communal life,
   to the breaking of bread and to the
      prayers.
Awe came upon everyone,
   and many wonders and signs were done
      through the apostles.
All who believed were together and had all
      things in common;
   they would sell their property and
      possessions
   and divide them among all according to
      each one's need.
Every day they devoted themselves
   to meeting together in the temple area
   and to breaking bread in their homes.
They ate their meals with exultation and
      sincerity of heart,
   praising God and enjoying favor with
      all the people.
And every day the Lord added to their
      number those who were being saved.

RESPONSORIAL PSALM
Ps 118:2-4, 13-15, 22-24

℟. (1) Give thanks to the Lord for he is
good, his love is everlasting.
   or:
℟. Alleluia.

Let the house of Israel say,
   "His mercy endures forever."
Let the house of Aaron say,
   "His mercy endures forever."
Let those who fear the LORD say,
   "His mercy endures forever."

℟. Give thanks to the Lord for he is good,
his love is everlasting.
   or:
℟. Alleluia.

I was hard pressed and was falling,
  but the Lord helped me.
My strength and my courage is the Lord,
  and he has been my savior.
The joyful shout of victory
  in the tents of the just.

R. Give thanks to the Lord for he is good,
his love is everlasting.
  or:
R. Alleluia.

The stone which the builders rejected
  has become the cornerstone.
By the Lord has this been done;
  it is wonderful in our eyes.
This is the day the Lord has made;
  let us be glad and rejoice in it.

R. Give thanks to the Lord for he is good,
his love is everlasting.
  or:
R. Alleluia.

SECOND READING
1 Pet 1:3-9

Blessed be the God and Father of our Lord
    Jesus Christ,
  who in his great mercy gave us a new
      birth to a living hope
  through the resurrection of Jesus Christ
      from the dead,
  to an inheritance that is imperishable,
      undefiled, and unfading,
  kept in heaven for you
  who by the power of God are
      safeguarded through faith,
  to a salvation that is ready to be
      revealed in the final time.
In this you rejoice, although now for a
    little while
  you may have to suffer through various
      trials,
  so that the genuineness of your faith,
  more precious than gold that is
      perishable even though tested by
      fire,
  may prove to be for praise, glory, and
      honor
  at the revelation of Jesus Christ.
Although you have not seen him you love
    him;
  even though you do not see him now yet
      believe in him,
  you rejoice with an indescribable and
      glorious joy,
  as you attain the goal of your faith, the
      salvation of your souls.

About Liturgy

Seeing, believing, and devotional items: The church has for centuries helped us to believe what we cannot see by using things perceptible to our sense of sight, hearing, touch, taste, and feel. The most obvious examples are our sacraments that use water, oil, imposition of hands, bread, wine, etc.—visible signs—to lead us to the invisible grace God is offering us. The gospel this Sunday also reminds us that our belief is strengthened when we surround ourselves with other visible signs of Jesus' risen presence and caring love for us.

Without turning our homes into veritable shrines, we might look around where we live and determine if there are *any* signs at all of our belief. When guests come into our home, do they know that we take religion seriously? Do they see a crucifix or statue of a favorite saint? Do they see a well-used Bible? Perhaps a nice Easter present for ourselves might be to go to a religious article store and buy something that is good art that can also speak to us and others that we are believers.

These religious articles in our homes can also remind us that religion isn't simply an hour-on-Sunday deal with God. They can help us turn our lives toward God and express our belief in charitable actions on behalf of others. Belief, after all, is strengthened within the community of believers and the good we do for each other.

About Liturgical Music

Singing Psalm 118: In keeping with the structure of Psalm 118, the cantor might lead the first strophe as a litany with the assembly responding on "His mercy endures forever," sing the second strophe as a solo, and have the choir join in singing the final strophe.

Connecting hymns to the Easter season: In all three years the Lectionary readings for the weeks of Easter show the same progression. The first three weeks relate appearance stories—Christ truly risen from the dead; the fourth Sunday presents Christ as the Good Shepherd; and the last weeks, including Pentecost, deal with our call to participate in the mission of the risen Christ. The hymns we sing over these weeks can help us enter more consciously into this progression. For the first three weeks the hymns need to simply exult over Christ's resurrection (most Easter hymns do this). Hymns on the fourth Sunday need to speak of Christ's enduring presence, tender nurture, and unflagging support as we live out our discipleship (for example, "Sing of One Who Walks Beside Us" [CBW3]). For the final weeks the hymns need to challenge us to participate fully in our mission to bring risen life to all people (for example, "We Know That Christ Is Raised" [CBW3, RS, WC, SS, W3], "Now We Remain" [BB, G2, RS, WC, WS], and "Go to the World" [CBW3, RS, SS, WC, WS]).

MAY 1, 2011
SECOND SUNDAY OF EASTER
or DIVINE MERCY SUNDAY

✠ SPIRITUALITY

GOSPEL ACCLAMATION

cf. Luke 24:32

℟. Alleluia, alleluia.
Lord Jesus, open the Scriptures to us;
make our hearts burn while you speak to us.
℟. Alleluia, alleluia.

Gospel   Luke 24:13-35; L46A

That very day, the first day of the week,
  two of Jesus' disciples were going
  to a village seven miles from
    Jerusalem called Emmaus,
  and they were conversing
    about all the things that
    had occurred.
And it happened that while they
    were conversing and debating,
  Jesus himself drew near and
    walked with them,
  but their eyes were prevented
    from recognizing him.
He asked them,
  "What are you discussing as you walk
    along?"
They stopped, looking downcast.
One of them, named Cleopas, said to him
    in reply,
  "Are you the only visitor to Jerusalem
  who does not know of the things
  that have taken place there in these
    days?"
And he replied to them, "What sort of
    things?"
They said to him,
  "The things that happened to Jesus the
    Nazarene,
  who was a prophet mighty in deed and
    word
  before God and all the people,
  how our chief priests and rulers both
    handed him over
  to a sentence of death and crucified him.
But we were hoping that he would be the
    one to redeem Israel;
  and besides all this,
  it is now the third day since this took
    place.

Continued in Appendix A, p. 294.

Reflecting on the Gospel

It's easy to be so intent on a thought or a destination or a task that we miss an insight or new possibility that might present itself. For example, children might be so intent on telling their mom or dad about an incident at school that they miss its deeper import—perhaps that a classmate is offering friendship or a teacher is indirectly complimenting them. Or a busy coworker might be so intent on getting to the mail room to pick up a parcel that he or she misses meeting the new person in the office. Or someone is so lost in downloading computer program updates that he or she misses an appointment. While many tasks demand our full attention, no task is so important that we close ourselves off from the newness that always surrounds us.

The disciples on the road to Emmaus were rehashing mere facts about the One they thought would "redeem Israel." Blinded by their own disappointment, they missed the deeper insight. They could not even accept what some women had reported: "that he was alive." Though they were spellbound by the Stranger's interpreting for "them what referred to him in all the Scriptures," they still lacked insight. They needed the further sign of the "breaking of bread." They needed a catalyst to break them out of their narrow perception and open up for them insight and new possibilities. Only then did they recognize Jesus as the One for whom they longed, the One whom they thought they had lost.

The two disciples on the road to Emmaus experience an overwhelming transformation in moving from unbelief to belief—not because of any new facts or hearsay but because of personal encounter with the risen Christ in the Scriptures and the breaking of the bread. Further, after returning to Jerusalem, their newfound belief is confirmed by a community of eyewitnesses who had seen the risen Jesus too: "The Lord has truly been raised." The same is true for us today: we are transformed by encountering the risen Christ in word and sacrament, and by the testimony of the community of believers. Word and sacrament and community have the power to shake us out of complacency and see for ourselves the new life that is being offered us.

Though we cannot see Jesus now in the same way as the disciples on the road to Emmaus did, he responds to *our* request to "Stay with us" in our "breaking of bread." He responds to our need to have new experiences that shake us out of our unbelief into grasping the new insight and new life that the risen One offers.

Living the Paschal Mystery

No wonder the early church from the very beginning chose the first day of the week for breaking bread—celebrating Eucharist. This is why, for us, Eucharist—"breaking of bread"—is so pivotal; here we encounter the risen Jesus, share in his meal, and become ourselves the risen presence for others. Here we engage the dying and rising that is the pattern of our everyday living. Here we engage the mystery of salvation so powerfully that we are shaken out of our limited vision and begin to see ourselves and others as God sees us.

Others in our faith community reflect back to us the reality that Jesus is alive and among us, because he is within us. The vision of others, their deep faith, their caring and sharing are all recognizable signs that "The Lord has truly been raised."

Focusing the Gospel

Key words and phrases: they were conversing, he interpreted . . . the Scriptures, he took bread . . . recognized him, returned to Jerusalem, The Lord has truly been raised

To the point: The two disciples on the road to Emmaus experience an overwhelming transformation in moving from unbelief to belief—not because of any new facts or hearsay but because of personal encounter with the risen Christ in the Scriptures and the breaking of the bread. Further, after returning to Jerusalem, their newfound belief is confirmed by a community of eyewitnesses who had seen the risen Jesus too: "The Lord has truly been raised." The same is true for us today: we are transformed by encountering the risen Christ in word and sacrament, and by the testimony of the community of believers.

Connecting the Gospel

to the first reading: Peter's proclamation to the people of Jerusalem is an eyewitness account of the Jesus event: "God raised this Jesus; of this we are all witnesses." Moreover, Peter spoke on behalf of the entire community of believers (he "stood up with the Eleven").

to our experience: It's easier to believe anything when we do not stand alone. This is even truer of the mystery of salvation revealed in the Jesus event.

Connecting the Responsorial Psalm

to the readings: Psalm 16 is more than an argument drawn from the Old Testament to prove Jesus' resurrection (first reading). It is a profession of faith that the same life after death granted Jesus will be given to us. Our "faith and hope" rest in God (second reading) who shows us the "path to life" (psalm). Nonetheless, like the disciples on the road to Emmaus, we struggle with doubts and misunderstandings about the mystery of the resurrection (gospel). The gospel shows us the many ways Christ comes to keep us walking along the "path to life"—in prayer and conversation, in reflection on Scripture, in the breaking of the bread. Are these chance encounters? Psalm 16 is our affirmation that they are not.

to psalmist preparation: In this responsorial psalm you acknowledge that God shows you the "path of life." The gospel reveals that this path is one of personal encounter with Christ who leads you through Scripture, Eucharist, and prayerful conversation to faith in his resurrection. When and how have you encountered Christ in these ways? Who has helped you see and hear him? How in singing this psalm can you help the assembly to see and hear him?

ASSEMBLY & FAITH-SHARING GROUPS
- The kind of conversing that leaves me downcast (like the disciples) is . . . The kind of faith sharing that leads my heart to burn within me is . . .
- One of the stories about when my eyes were opened to recognize the risen Lord is . . .
- I find support from my faith community to . . . when I . . . because . . .

PRESIDERS
The risen Lord transforms my "slow heart to believe" into a "burning heart of recognition" when . . . My parish community helps me come to this transformation when . . .

DEACONS
My ministry of service witnesses to my faith in the risen Christ when . . . It helps those I serve to . . .

HOSPITALITY MINISTERS
My hospitality ministry prepares those who are assembling to encounter the risen Lord when . . .

MUSIC MINISTERS
I have encountered the risen Christ while doing the ministry of music when . . . The questions I have asked him are . . . He has answered . . .

ALTAR MINISTERS
The breaking of the bread not only reveals the risen Lord to me but also challenges me to break open my life in service to others by . . .

LECTORS
The risen Jesus opens the Scriptures for me by . . . My daily life is an opening of the Scriptures to others in that . . .

EXTRAORDINARY MINISTERS OF HOLY COMMUNION
The opening of the Scriptures prepares me to encounter the risen Christ in the breaking of the bread when . . . in the distribution of Holy Communion when . . .

✝ CELEBRATION

Model Rite of Blessing and Sprinkling Holy Water

Presider: Dear friends, through the sprinkling of this water, let us prepare ourselves to encounter the risen Christ in the Scriptures and the breaking of bread . . . [pause]

> [continue with form C of the blessing of water]

Homily Points

• Often, overwhelming transformations occur in community. For example, successful recovery for an alcoholic depends upon regular and very honest interaction with an AA group. A troubled marriage is often given new life through Retrouvaille. The success of Kairos or other encounter-based retreats depends on a community of peers witnessing faith to one another.

• The two disciples in this gospel story came to believe in Jesus' resurrection in two ways. First, they encountered Jesus himself on the road and came to recognize him. Second, their newfound faith was reinforced by the witness of other members of the community of disciples. Christian belief and life grows to fullness within a community of believers.

• The community of believers is sometimes the liturgical assembly where we hear Jesus' word in the Scriptures and encounter him in the breaking of the bread. At other times this community is the family where we call each other to growth in Christian living. At still other times, the most unexpected community (e.g., colleagues at work, people standing together in a line, strangers responding together to an emergency) can bring about an encounter with the presence of the risen Christ.

Model Prayer of the Faithful

Presider: As a community of believers, we pray for our own needs and those of others.

Response:

Lord, hear our prayer.

Cantor:

we pray to the Lord,

For the church, to always be a welcoming and supporting community for all who come seeking faith . . . [pause]

For all peoples of the world, to hear in their sacred scriptures the challenge to lead good lives . . . [pause]

For the homeless, for those without friends or family, for those without a community of support . . . [pause]

For each of us here, to lovingly support one another on our journey to deeper faith in the risen Christ . . . [pause]

Presider: Gracious God, you hear the prayers of those who call to you: be with us as we break bread in memory of your risen Son and help us to live the new life you give us to the fullest. We ask this through that same Son, Jesus Christ the Lord. **Amen.**

OPENING PRAYER

Let us pray

Pause for silent prayer

God our Father,
may we look forward with hope to our
    resurrection,
for you have made us your sons and
    daughters,
and restored the joy of our youth.

We ask this through our Lord Jesus Christ,
    your Son,
who lives and reigns with you and the
    Holy Spirit,
one God, for ever and ever. **Amen.**

FIRST READING
Acts 2:14, 22-33

Then Peter stood up with the Eleven,
    raised his voice, and proclaimed:
    "You who are Jews, indeed all of you
        staying in Jerusalem.
Let this be known to you, and listen to my
    words.
You who are Israelites, hear these words.
Jesus the Nazarene was a man commended
    to you by God
    with mighty deeds, wonders, and signs,
    which God worked through him in your
        midst, as you yourselves know.
This man, delivered up by the set plan and
    foreknowledge of God,
    you killed, using lawless men to crucify
        him.
But God raised him up, releasing him from
    the throes of death,
    because it was impossible for him to be
        held by it.
For David says of him:
    *'I saw the Lord ever before me,
        with him at my right hand I shall not
        be disturbed.*
    *Therefore my heart has been glad and
        my tongue has exulted;*
    my flesh, too, will dwell in hope,
    *because you will not abandon my soul to
        the netherworld,*
        *nor will you suffer your holy one to
        see corruption.*
    *You have made known to me the paths
        of life;*
        *you will fill me with joy in your
        presence.'*

"My brothers, one can confidently say to you
    about the patriarch David that he died
        and was buried,
    and his tomb is in our midst to this day.

But since he was a prophet and knew that
God had sworn an oath to him
that he would set one of his descendants
upon his throne,
he foresaw and spoke of the resurrection
of the Christ,
that neither was he abandoned to the
netherworld
nor did his flesh see corruption.
God raised this Jesus;
of this we are all witnesses.
Exalted at the right hand of God,
he received the promise of the Holy
Spirit from the Father
and poured him forth, as you see and
hear."

RESPONSORIAL PSALM
Ps 16:1-2, 5, 7-8, 9-10, 11

R℟. (11a) Lord, you will show us the path of
life. or: R℟. Alleluia.

Keep me, O God, for in you I take refuge;
    I say to the LORD, "My Lord are you."
O LORD, my allotted portion and my cup,
    you it is who hold fast my lot.

R℟. Lord, you will show us the path of life.
    or:
R℟. Alleluia.

I bless the LORD who counsels me;
    even in the night my heart exhorts me.
I set the LORD ever before me;
    with him at my right hand I shall not be
    disturbed.

R℟. Lord, you will show us the path of life.
    or:
R℟. Alleluia.

Therefore my heart is glad and my soul
    rejoices,
    my body, too, abides in confidence;
because you will not abandon my soul to
    the netherworld,
    nor will you suffer your faithful one to
    undergo corruption.

R℟. Lord, you will show us the path of life.
    or:
R℟. Alleluia.

You will show me the path to life,
    abounding joy in your presence,
    the delights at your right hand forever.

R℟. Lord, you will show us the path of life.
    or:
R℟. Alleluia.

SECOND READING
1 Pet 1:17-21

See Appendix A, p. 294.

✝ # CATECHESIS

About Liturgy

Mother's Day: This second Sunday of May is traditionally observed as Mother's Day. Although it would be very inappropriate to focus the liturgy on mothers, two ritual elements are always appropriate.

1. The following model intercession based on the gospel might be used as a fifth intercession during the prayer of the faithful: That all mothers be strengthened by the companionship of Jesus as they strive to bring their children to fuller life . . . [pause]. Three other model intercessions are given in BofB, chapter 55, no. 1727.

2. In BofB, chapter 55, no. 1728 a prayer over the people is given and may replace the prayer over the people given in the Sacramentary for the Third Sunday of Easter.

Eucharistic breaking of bread: Few parishes have a single loaf of bread that they break at Eucharist. Nonetheless, when the host (usually a large one) is broken during the singing of the Lamb of God, this gesture has more than practical import. The breaking of bread might symbolize for us the call to surrender our own bodies in dying to self for the sake of others as did Jesus. The breaking of bread also reminds us that we do share in the same loaf—the risen Christ himself. This one loaf makes of us, the community of believers, the one Body of Christ.

It is helpful if presiders hold the bread up when they break it so that it can be easily seen by members of the assembly. The singing of the Lamb of God accompanies this gesture and ends when the bread is broken. "Lamb of God" is another phrase that reminds us that this simple rite just before Communion calls us to salvation and new life.

About Liturgical Music

Music suggestion: A number of songs have been written to coincide with this Sunday's gospel. Marty Haugen's "On the Journey to Emmaus" [GC2, RS] builds particularly on Jesus' coming as a stranger and the disciples' discovery that in accepting the stranger they "welcomed the Lord." Text and tune would be appropriate for the preparation of the gifts. Bob Hurd's "Two Were Bound for Emmaus" [BB, JS2] would be a good choice for either the preparation of the gifts or Communion. Herman Stuempfle's "On Emmaus Journey," sometimes titled "On Emmaus' Road" [HG, PMB, SS, WC, WS], develops its thought through a progression of identity questions: "Who are you" we ask the disciples on this journey (verse 1); "Who is this" we ask when a Stranger joins them (and us) on the way (verse 2); "Who are you" we ask when we recognize the Stranger as Christ (verse 3); "Who are we" we ask when we recognize ourselves as the ones who have joined Christ on the journey "through life to death" (verse 4). In the final verse we celebrate our identity as the church, Christ's Body sent into the world. This hymn would be suitable for the preparation of the gifts or for the Communion procession.

Another song suitable for this Sunday would be John Bell's "Christ Has Risen" [GC, GC2], which speaks of the certainty of the resurrection despite disciples' struggle with doubt. As usual Bell's imagery has an immediacy that quickly hits home. Sung to ABBOT'S LEIGH or HYFRYDOL, the text would make a strong entrance hymn. Sung to Bell's given tune or to the more familiar HOLY MANNA, the song would suit the preparation of the gifts.

THIRD SUNDAY OF EASTER

SPIRITUALITY

GOSPEL ACCLAMATION
John 10:14

℟. Alleluia, alleluia.
I am the good shepherd, says the Lord;
I know my sheep, and mine know me.
℟. Alleluia, alleluia.

Gospel   John 10:1-10; L49A

Jesus said:
"Amen, amen, I say to you,
  whoever does not enter a
    sheepfold through the gate
  but climbs over elsewhere is a
    thief and a robber.
But whoever enters through the gate
  is the shepherd of the sheep.
The gatekeeper opens it for him, and
  the sheep hear his voice,
  as the shepherd calls his own sheep by
    name and leads them out.
When he has driven out all his own,
  he walks ahead of them, and the sheep
    follow him,
  because they recognize his voice.
But they will not follow a stranger;
  they will run away from him,
  because they do not recognize the voice
    of strangers."
Although Jesus used this figure of speech,
  the Pharisees did not realize what he
    was trying to tell them.

So Jesus said again, "Amen, amen, I say
    to you,
I am the gate for the sheep.
All who came before me are thieves and
    robbers,
  but the sheep did not listen to them.
I am the gate.
Whoever enters through me will be
    saved,
  and will come in and go out and find
    pasture.
A thief comes only to steal and slaughter
    and destroy;
  I came so that they might have life and
    have it more abundantly."

Reflecting on the Gospel

Five-year-old Aaron was "teaching" Grandma how to use the radio in her car and showing her what the other buttons meant. Then he exclaimed, "Grandma, you're missing buttons! You don't have the GPS ones like on Dad's car that show us where to go. How do you know where to go?" Grandma had just bought a new AAA atlas in preparation for a trip, and so when they got home she showed him the printed maps, pointed to where Mom and Dad were, where she and Grandpa were going on their trip, and where the capital of their state was. Aaron was completely fascinated by the "paper" map—he spent over an hour studying it, asking questions, paging through it. Then he exclaimed, "Grandma, this is cool! Is it newer than Dad's GPS?" Aaron had never seen a printed, paper map before! He only knew of one guide—the GPS. This Sunday's gospel points us to another guide, one not new at all, but one that will never be outdated and never mislead us. This guide is Jesus himself, the Good Shepherd.

Jesus can only be our guiding Shepherd if we become familiar enough with his "voice" so that we can follow. Following his voice is the only way to new and abundant life. The Shepherd continues to call, and it is only through repeated exposure to his voice (encountering the risen Lord) that we become so accustomed to his voice that we can follow him faithfully. Jesus is our Shepherd and guide—he knows exactly where he is leading us.

We are willing to follow Jesus' guiding ways because he has completely identified with us—even to accepting suffering and death—that he knows perfectly what we face. So on this Sunday when we celebrate Jesus' care for us and the unfailing certainty that he will not leave us, we are also poignantly reminded that following him to the green and restful pasture of risen, new life means accepting suffering and the cross.

Only by completely identifying with his suffering and death can we share in the abundance of the new life he offers us. We have been made sinless because of Jesus' saving care; we remain sinless when we follow our Good Shepherd in a life of "doing what is good" (second reading). Practice in doing good is practice in hearing our Shepherd's voice.

In this gospel Jesus promises us his continued care and protection. He also tells us *why* we can rely on him: as our guide-Shepherd, Jesus seeks only our good while protecting us from the real harm of "thieves and robbers." It is crucial that we listen to the voice of the Shepherd and stay close to him for protection, yes. But more important, we stay close to him because he guides us to the abundant life he wishes to give us. Jesus assures us twice—"Amen, amen, I say to you"—of the strength of his promise and the clarity of his mission. He is our sure guide.

Living the Paschal Mystery

Even at Easter when we celebrate the new, risen life of Jesus and share in joy and sing unending alleluias, we cannot stray too far from reflecting on the cost of this new life: self-emptying for the sake of another. During times when we seem to be overwhelmed by the demands of dying, God assures us of new life. During this Easter time when we are overjoyed at the new life, God assures us of Jesus' faithful guidance that leads us through death to new life. Yes, Jesus is our sure guide—he leads us through death on our way to a share in his new life.

Focusing the Gospel

Key words and phrases: Amen, amen, I say to you; shepherd; hear his voice; follow him; have life . . . abundantly

To the point: In this gospel Jesus promises us his continued care and protection. He tells us *why* we can rely on him: as the Good Shepherd, Jesus seeks only our good while protecting us from "thieves and robbers." It is crucial that we listen to the voice of the Shepherd and stay close to him for protection, yes. But more important, we stay close to him for the abundant life he wishes to give us. Jesus assures us twice—"Amen, amen, I say to you"—of the strength of his promise and the clarity of his mission.

Connecting the Gospel

to the second reading: Although following Jesus often entails hardship, the Shepherd doesn't lead us anyplace that he hasn't gone first: "Christ also suffered for you" and "you shall follow in his footsteps."

to our experience: Today there are many competing and contrary voices vying for our attention. This gospel challenges us to become familiar with the voice of our Shepherd so that we choose him and the life he offers.

Connecting the Responsorial Psalm

to the readings: The readings this Sunday challenge us to be realistic about the journey of discipleship. Many voices compete for our loyalty (gospel). At times we have the courage to "suffer for doing what is good"; at other times we choose to go astray (second reading). At times we hear and heed Christ's voice; at other times we do not even recognize what he is saying to us (gospel). Even with our sights fixed on fields of nourishment and streams of fresh water, we sometimes find ourselves in the valley of death (psalm). But the readings also offer us the good news that Jesus, having walked the path ahead of us, knows well its dangers and pitfalls and guards our footsteps every step of the way (second reading). When we falter or stray, he calls us by name (gospel) back to the path of life.

to psalmist preparation: Psalm 23 promises you Christ's loving and protective presence as you continue on your journey of discipleship. This journey is a long one and the possibilities of becoming lost, losing hope, being misled are real. But there is a Shepherd who is both by your side and ahead of you, one who has already journeyed the way of death and resurrection and knows its path. As you sing, take his hand and walk confidently.

ASSEMBLY & FAITH-SHARING GROUPS

- I experience Jesus' continued care and protection when . . . This leads me to . . .
- The "thieves and robbers" I encounter in my daily life are . . .
- What helps me recognize (discern) Jesus' voice amid all the competing voices in my life is . . .

PRESIDERS

My ministry is a reflection of Jesus as the Good Shepherd in that . . . Where I am falling short in embodying Jesus as the Good Shepherd is . . .

DEACONS

My daily living is the Good Shepherd's voice to and for others whenever I . . .

HOSPITALITY MINISTERS

My hospitality embodies a glimpse of the Good Shepherd's abundant life for others whenever I . . .

MUSIC MINISTERS

Some of the competing voices I deal with in doing music ministry are . . . What helps me keep my ear attuned to the voice of Jesus is . . .

ALTAR MINISTERS

Imitating the Good Shepherd in serving others helps me recognize his voice because . . .

LECTORS

The words of Scripture come alive for me when I . . . My proclamation then becomes the voice of the Good Shepherd to the assembly because . . .

EXTRAORDINARY MINISTERS OF HOLY COMMUNION

My "Body [Blood] of Christ" declared to communicants is the voice of the Good Shepherd calling them to new life when I . . .

Model Rite of Blessing and Sprinkling Holy Water

Presider: Dear friends, we sprinkle this water as a reminder of our baptism, when we became members of the Good Shepherd's flock. Let us prepare ourselves to hear his voice during this liturgy . . . [pause]

[continue with form C of the blessing of water]

Homily Points

• When we are unsure or confused about a critical decision to be made, an ethical choice, or a new direction for our life, we instinctively turn for guidance to others whose personal experience has brought them to a depth of wisdom about life. Both their experience and guidance bring us to greater strength and a new understanding and appreciation of our own life.

• Jesus assures us that *his* guidance will always lead us to the fullness of life because of the depth of his experience of human living and dying. His wisdom is unsurpassable and his voice is true.

• Jesus' voice is heard in many ways and through many persons. For example, he speaks to us in the voice of someone choosing to do the right thing, even at personal cost. He speaks to us in the voices of those who cry out passionately against injustices. He speaks to us in the self-giving of parents who choose to shepherd their children toward right values and actions. These everyday experiences teach us to listen better to the Good Shepherd's voice that leads us to greater strength and fuller life.

Model Prayer of the Faithful

Presider: Listening to Jesus' voice and with hearts filled with confidence, we now make our needs known to our loving God.

Response:

Cantor:

That all leaders of the church may be the faithful voice of the Good Shepherd. . .[pause]

That all leaders of nations may lead their people to an abundance of life . . . [pause]

That those who are sick, suffering, or searching for life be comforted by the caring voice of the Good Shepherd . . . [pause]

That each of us here grow in recognizing the voice of the Good Shepherd calling us to new and abundant life . . . [pause]

Presider: Loving and caring God, you sent your only Son to be our Good Shepherd: hear these prayers that we might always know his voice and follow him to everlasting life. We ask this through that same Christ our Lord. **Amen.**

Let us pray

Pause for silent prayer

Almighty and ever-living God,
give us new strength
from the courage of Christ our shepherd,
and lead us to join the saints in heaven,
where he lives and reigns with you and the
      Holy Spirit,
one God, for ever and ever. **Amen.**

FIRST READING
Acts 2:14a, 36-41

Then Peter stood up with the Eleven,
      raised his voice, and proclaimed:
"Let the whole house of Israel know for
      certain
      that God has made both Lord and Christ,
      this Jesus whom you crucified."

Now when they heard this, they were cut
      to the heart,
      and they asked Peter and the other
      apostles,
      "What are we to do, my brothers?"
Peter said to them,
      "Repent and be baptized, every one of
      you,
      in the name of Jesus Christ for the
      forgiveness of your sins;
      and you will receive the gift of the Holy
      Spirit.
For the promise is made to you and to
      your children
      and to all those far off,
      whomever the Lord our God will call."
He testified with many other arguments,
      and was exhorting them,
      "Save yourselves from this corrupt
      generation."
Those who accepted his message were
      baptized,
      and about three thousand persons were
      added that day.

RESPONSORIAL PSALM
Ps 23:1-3a, 3b-4, 5, 6

℟. (1) The Lord is my shepherd; there is
nothing I shall want.
      or: ℟. Alleluia.

The LORD is my shepherd; I shall not want.
      In verdant pastures he gives me repose;
beside restful waters he leads me;
      he refreshes my soul.

℟. The Lord is my shepherd; there is
nothing I shall want.
      or: ℟. Alleluia.

He guides me in right paths
    for his name's sake.
Even though I walk in the dark valley
    I fear no evil; for you are at my side
with your rod and your staff
    that give me courage.

R℣. The Lord is my shepherd; there is
nothing I shall want.
    or: R℣. Alleluia.

You spread the table before me
    in the sight of my foes;
you anoint my head with oil;
    my cup overflows.

R℣. The Lord is my shepherd; there is
nothing I shall want.
    or: R℣. Alleluia.

Only goodness and kindness follow me
    all the days of my life;
and I shall dwell in the house of the Lord
    for years to come.

R℣. The Lord is my shepherd; there is
nothing I shall want.
    or: R℣. Alleluia.

SECOND READING
1 Pet 2:20b-25

Beloved:
If you are patient when you suffer for
    doing what is good,
    this is a grace before God.
For to this you have been called,
    because Christ also suffered for you,
    leaving you an example that you should
        follow in his footsteps.
He committed no sin, and no deceit was
    found in his mouth.

When he was insulted, he returned no insult;
    when he suffered, he did not threaten;
    instead, he handed himself over to the
        one who judges justly.
He himself bore our sins in his body upon
    the cross,
    so that, free from sin, we might live for
        righteousness.
By his wounds you have been healed.
For you had gone astray like sheep,
    but you have now returned to the
        shepherd and guardian of your
        souls.

About Liturgy

Conflicting voices of liturgy: Many people are disturbed by the seemingly endless and conflicting voices speaking out on liturgy. Who or what to follow? It would be easy if there were an invariable set of rules for liturgy; while there are plenty of guidelines and some pretty specific rules, there are many options and decisions that must be made at the level of the whole church (in Rome), for a country, diocese, and even parish. So who/what determines good liturgy?

First of all, whatever takes place during liturgy must be completely directed to worship of the Father through Christ in the Holy Spirit. All worship is directed to God and has God at the center. Second, all liturgy enacts the paschal mystery, Jesus' dying and rising into which we enter at baptism and celebrate and live throughout our lives. Third, all liturgy transforms the worshipers into being more perfect members of the Body of Christ. Fourth, all liturgy leads to more just, charitable, and faith-filled Christian living. If all decisions about liturgy were measured against these four principles, a parish would already have taken a great step toward ensuring good and authentic Christian liturgy.

About Liturgical Music

Music suggestions: Examples of songs that express our need for God's shepherding attention as we struggle with the demands of discipleship include Genevieve Glen's "Shepherd, Lead Us to the Place" [in OCP's *The Listening Heart*] and her "Be Glad of Heart, All You Who Seek" [in OCP's *Voices from the Valley*], both suitable in text and tune for the preparation of the gifts; James Chepponis' "With a Shepherd's Care" [G2, GC, GC2, RS], appropriate either during the preparation of the gifts or Communion; "Shepherd of Souls, in Love, Come Feed Us" [WC] and "Shepherd of Souls/ Shepherd of Souls, Refresh and Bless" [BB, GC, GC2, JS2, OFUV, WC, WS], both intended for Communion.

While the verses of Francis Patrick O'Brien's "Shepherd of My Heart" [GC, GC2, SS] repeat Psalm 23 used as the responsorial psalm, the lovely refrain ("Guide me, O shepherd of my heart; lead me homeward through the dark, into everlasting day. Show me the way of truth and light; keep me always in your sight. May my life never part from the shepherd of my heart") makes the psalm worth repeating, either as a choral prelude (GIA octavo G-3770] or during Communion. The same can be said of Rory Cooney's "Heart of a Shepherd" [GIA octavo G-6720]. This setting uses the classic Gelineau tone for Psalm 23, with a refrain connecting our being shepherded by Christ with his call that we shepherd and care for others ("If you love me, feed my lambs; Be my heart, my voice, my hands. If you love me, feed my sheep. As for my part, I give you the heart of a shepherd.")

MAY 15, 2011
FOURTH SUNDAY OF EASTER

✝ SPIRITUALITY

GOSPEL ACCLAMATION
John 14:6

R̸. Alleluia, alleluia.
I am the way, the truth and the life, says the
   Lord;
no one comes to the Father, except through me.
R̸. Alleluia, alleluia.

Gospel   John 14:1-12; L52A

Jesus said to his disciples:
   "Do not let your hearts be troubled.
You have faith in God; have faith also
   in me.
In my Father's house there are
   many dwelling places.
If there were not,
   would I have told you that I am
      going to prepare a place for
      you?
And if I go and prepare a place for you,
   I will come back again and take you to
      myself,
   so that where I am you also may be.
Where I am going you know the way."
Thomas said to him,
   "Master, we do not know where you
      are going;
   how can we know the way?"
Jesus said to him, "I am the way and the
   truth and the life.
No one comes to the Father except
   through me.
If you know me, then you will also know
   my Father.
From now on you do know him and have
   seen him."
Philip said to him,
   "Master, show us the Father, and that
      will be enough for us."
Jesus said to him, "Have I been with you
   for so long a time
   and you still do not know me, Philip?
Whoever has seen me has seen the
   Father.
How can you say, 'Show us the Father'?
Do you not believe that I am in the
   Father and the Father is in me?

Continued in Appendix A, p. 295.

Reflecting on the Gospel

When little children stray away from their parents and feel abandoned and lost, they do an interesting thing: they stay put and just cry. When adults become lost (for example, when driving in a strange city), they become proactive: they take out a map or stop and ask for directions. In this gospel Jesus is inviting the disciples (and us) to become proactive about believing in him and doing his works, and thus finding our true way.

Thomas and Philip completely miss Jesus' point. They are looking for a roadmap—they ask Jesus to show them the way. They haven't grasped what they have encountered all along: Jesus is "the way and the truth and the life." When asked "how can we know the way?" to the Father's house, Jesus does not provide us a roadmap. Instead Jesus' answer is a surprisingly personal one: "*I am* the way and the truth and the life." Here Jesus himself is equated with risen life. Believing in Jesus and doing his works is the way to the Father. We today must encounter and come to know Jesus in our daily living, and by so identifying with him become for others "the way and the truth and the life."

Jesus' claim to be "the way and the truth and the life" lays claims on us: to have faith in him, to follow him to the Father, to do the works he does, to *be* who he is—"the way and the truth and the life." With the first disciples, we too struggle to understand these claims and the implications they have for changing the way we live. Jesus makes clear that the only way to eternal life is through belief in him. It seems like such simple, clear direction. Yet we spend our whole lives coming to the kind of belief that truthfully shows us the way.

Jesus' disclosure about himself requires, in turn, an equally personal response from us: "have faith . . . *in me*." It is only with our Easter faith that we can move from the struggle to understand to a fruitful response to Jesus' claims on us. Easter faith is more than creed; it is expressed in a relationship with the risen One. The ongoing struggle to come to faith, then, is the ongoing struggle to come to know Jesus and become more like him. This risen Jesus is not illusive; he is encountered in the "ministry of the word," in the breaking of bread, in taking care of the needs of others (see first reading), in allowing God to act in us to build us into a "chosen and precious" Body of Christ, in our announcing God's praises (see second reading). The real challenge of this gospel, then, is to expand our seeing and believing to recognize the many, varied, and surprising ways he comes to us—and to become for others those ways.

Living the Paschal Mystery

Jesus' claim that he is "the way and the truth and the life" is a sweeping one that dares us to see Jesus as everything we need to come to the fullness of risen life ourselves. The "way" is not always appealing—dying to ourselves, self-emptying for the sake of others. The good news and truth is that we follow Jesus' way in less dramatic, everyday ways. Our simple acts of reaching out to others, alleviating their suffering, or eliminating their need (whatever it might be) is how we follow Jesus' way. But more: this is how we ourselves become the way! As we do Jesus' works, we become more like him—we take on his care, his love, his passion for others. As we do his works, we ourselves become the way to the Father for others. No greater work can we do!

Focusing the Gospel

Key words and phrases: the way and the truth and the life, know me, believe, do the works that I do

To the point: In the gospel Thomas and Philip completely miss Jesus' point—they haven't grasped what they have encountered all along: Jesus is "the way and the truth and the life." Believing in Jesus and doing his works is the way to the Father. We today must encounter and come to know Jesus in our daily living, and by so identifying with him become for others "the way and the truth and the life."

Connecting the Gospel

to the second reading: Peter reminds us that we have been called "out of darkness into . . . wonderful light." We are the light of Christ because the Holy Spirit dwells within us, enabling us to be the presence of the risen Lord ("the way and the truth and the life") for others.

to our experience: It's easy for us to identify with Thomas and Philip, because many of our conversations have more than one meaning. Even our knowing what Jesus has taught us doesn't make understanding or living it any easier.

Connecting the Responsorial Psalm

to the readings: With its cry for mercy, the refrain for this Sunday's responsorial psalm sounds more fitting for the season of Lent than Easter. But it captures well one of the realities that the Lectionary movement from the resurrection appearances of Jesus (first three Sundays of Easter) to Good Shepherd Sunday (fourth) to the departure of Jesus (Ascension) and the mission given us to continue his work (Pentecost) embodies: that we always struggle with discipleship. The first reading reveals that even those historically close to the resurrection of Jesus quickly experienced rifts and conflicts among themselves. From the earliest days the church has needed God's mercy and direction if it was to remain faithful to its mission to be God's holy ones (second reading).

The psalm assures us that God gives us all we need to be faithful: an "upright word," "trustworthy" works, and a "kindness" that reaches the ends of the earth. The gospel adds the revelation that these marvelous gifts of God abide in the very *person* of Jesus, where "the Father . . . dwells [and] is doing his work." Jesus is our way, our truth, and our life. We need only trust in him.

to psalmist preparation: These verses from Psalm 33 convey utmost trust in God whose word is true, whose works are reliable, and whose kindness is granted to all who hope. In the gospel Jesus invites you to place this trust in him, for whoever knows him knows God. How has your celebration of this Easter season helped you grow in your knowledge of Jesus? What struggles with faith in him do you still experience? Who/what helps you to trust in him even in the midst of these struggles?

**ASSEMBLY &
FAITH-SHARING GROUPS**
- I miss the point about being a follower of Jesus when I . . .
- I respond to Jesus' challenge to believe in him when I . . . I do his works when I . . . This makes a difference in my world in that . . .
- Jesus is my *way, truth,* and *life* in that . . .

PRESIDERS
Where others can truly see/know the Father in seeing/knowing me is . . . Conversely, where my ministry and living fall short in showing the Father is . . .

DEACONS
My diaconal service models for others the *way* of Jesus by . . . My daily life announces to others the *truth* of Jesus in that . . .

HOSPITALITY MINISTERS
My manner of welcoming the community to liturgy opens them to know better Jesus and the Father when I . . .

MUSIC MINISTERS
My music ministry does the works of Jesus when . . .

ALTAR MINISTERS
My manner of serving at the altar shows others a way to the Father when . . .

LECTORS
I proclaim God's word with truth when I . . .

**EXTRAORDINARY MINISTERS
OF HOLY COMMUNION**
My manner of distributing Holy Communion is life-giving for those who come when I . . .

CELEBRATION

Model Rite of Blessing and Sprinkling Holy Water

Presider: Dear friends, this water reminds us of our baptism, when we were grafted onto Christ, our way and truth and life. Let us surrender ourselves into God's care so that we can be faithful followers of Jesus . . . [pause]

> [continue with form C of the blessing of water]

Homily Points

• How often we hear the exclamation, "Oh, my, I look at you and I see your father [or mother]!" The likeness becomes even more pronounced as the child learns to live the father's values, takes on the father's way of doing things, even emulates the father's mannerisms. The similarity, then, is more than skin deep. It becomes a way of being and living.

• Jesus is really asking the disciples to transfer their believing in and knowing God to him: "You have faith in God; have faith also in me." Amazingly, Jesus passes on "If you know me, then you will also know my Father" to us. Just as the presence of God was made flesh in Jesus, so is that same presence made flesh today in us—by our believing in Jesus and through our doing his works. Jesus must become our way of being and living.

• What kind of life do we need to live so that when others see us, they see Jesus and, therefore, the Father?

Model Prayer of the Faithful

Presider: We pray now that we always follow Jesus' way to the Father and eternal life.

Response:

Lord, hear our prayer.

Cantor:

we pray to the Lord,

That all members of the church deepen their believing in Jesus so that they might more perfectly do his works . . . [pause]

That all peoples of the world find the way of salvation . . . [pause]

That the lost find their way, those struggling for justice witness to truth, and all come to a greater respect for life . . . [pause]

That each of us continually grow in our relationship with the risen Christ so that we might be his risen presence for others . . . [pause]

Presider: God of salvation, through your Son Jesus we know the way to you: hear these our prayers that one day we might enjoy everlasting life with you. We ask this through Christ our Lord. **Amen.**

OPENING PRAYER

Let us pray

Pause for silent prayer

God our Father,
look upon us with love.
You redeem us and make us your children
    in Christ.
Give us true freedom
and bring us to the inheritance you
    promised.

We ask this through our Lord Jesus Christ,
    your Son,
who lives and reigns with you and the
    Holy Spirit,
one God, for ever and ever. **Amen.**

FIRST READING

Acts 6:1-7

As the number of disciples continued to
    grow,
    the Hellenists complained against the
        Hebrews
    because their widows
    were being neglected in the daily
        distribution.
So the Twelve called together the
    community of the disciples and said,
    "It is not right for us to neglect the word
        of God to serve at table.
Brothers, select from among you seven
    reputable men,
    filled with the Spirit and wisdom,
    whom we shall appoint to this task,
    whereas we shall devote ourselves to
        prayer
    and to the ministry of the word."
The proposal was acceptable to the whole
    community,
    so they chose Stephen, a man filled with
        faith and the Holy Spirit,
    also Philip, Prochorus, Nicanor, Timon,
        Parmenas,
    and Nicholas of Antioch, a convert to
        Judaism.
They presented these men to the apostles
    who prayed and laid hands on them.
The word of God continued to spread,
    and the number of the disciples in
        Jerusalem increased greatly;
    even a large group of priests were
        becoming obedient to the faith.

RESPONSORIAL PSALM

Ps 33:1-2, 4-5, 18-19

℟. (22) Lord, let your mercy be on us, as
we place our trust in you.
    or: ℟. Alleluia.

Exult, you just, in the LORD;
  praise from the upright is fitting.
Give thanks to the LORD on the harp;
  with the ten-stringed lyre chant his
    praises.

R℣. Lord, let your mercy be on us, as we
place our trust in you.
  or: R℣. Alleluia.

Upright is the word of the LORD,
  and all his works are trustworthy.
He loves justice and right;
  of the kindness of the LORD the earth is
    full.

R℣. Lord, let your mercy be on us, as we place
our trust in you.
  or: R℣. Alleluia.

See, the eyes of the LORD are upon those
    who fear him,
  upon those who hope for his kindness,
to deliver them from death
  and preserve them in spite of famine.

R℣. Lord, let your mercy be on us, as we place
our trust in you.
  or: R℣. Alleluia.

SECOND READING
1 Pet 2:4-9

Beloved:
Come to him, a living stone, rejected by
    human beings
  but chosen and precious in the sight of
    God,
  and, like living stones,
  let yourselves be built into a spiritual
    house
  to be a holy priesthood to offer spiritual
    sacrifices
  acceptable to God through Jesus Christ.
For it says in Scripture:
  Behold, I am laying a stone in Zion,
  a cornerstone, chosen and precious,
  and whoever believes in it shall not be
    put to shame.
Therefore, its value is for you who have
    faith, but for those without faith:
  The stone that the builders rejected
  has become the cornerstone,
  and
  A stone that will make people stumble,
  and a rock that will make them fall.
They stumble by disobeying the word, as
    is their destiny.

You are "a chosen race, a royal priesthood,
  a holy nation, a people of his own,
  so that you may announce the praises"
    of him
  who called you out of darkness into his
    wonderful light.

✠ CATECHESIS

About Liturgy

Easter Lectionary turning point: The Lectionary is a book of selections from Sacred Scripture to be proclaimed at liturgies—not just any random selections but carefully chosen ones to serve the paschal mystery dynamic of the liturgical year. Thus the Lectionary opens up for us the whole mystery of Christ as we walk each year through the events that are the paschal mystery—his life, ministry, suffering, death, resurrection, ascension, sending of the Spirit.

As we might expect, in the first part of the Easter season the Lectionary focuses on Jesus' resurrection appearances and captures for us one part of the meaning of this season. Now, on the Fifth Sunday of Easter, the Lectionary alerts us to the fact that this season is now at a turning point. Rather than a focus on the risen Christ, the Lectionary focuses on Jesus' instructions and prayer for his disciples—all this clearly with an eye to Pentecost and the celebration of the coming of the Spirit. With the indwelling of the Holy Spirit we are empowered to take up Jesus' saving mission, to continue his ministry, to be his presence for others. Thus, the last part of the Easter season is teaching us how to be good disciples.

Another part of the meaning of this season put forward in the Lectionary selections is that the resurrection is more than a glorious event for Jesus. Jesus' being raised up from the dead invites us to a new way to be disciples—to have a personal relationship with him through shared risen life. By our discipleship we already share in Jesus' risen life, we already share in the fruits of the resurrection.

About Liturgical Music

Music suggestions: The readings for this Sunday invite us to contemplate and deepen the intimacy we share with the person of Christ. One hymn that comes immediately to mind is "Come, My Way, My Truth, My Life" [GC, JS2, RS, WC, W3]. The text is taken from the writings of the seventeenth-century British poet George Herbert. With but one exception Herbert uses words of only a single syllable throughout the text to express the reality that the disciple and Christ are one, bound in a mystical union that is at once profound and utterly simple. This hymn would be appropriate during the preparation of the gifts or as an assembly song after Communion.

"You Are the Way" [WC, WS] responds directly to Jesus as the way, the truth, and the life, and would be suitable during the preparation of the gifts. Appropriate for either the preparation of the gifts or Communion, "The Way Is Jesus" [LMGM] is a Swahili piece alternating unison verses with a harmonized refrain. Improvising extra verses as needed should be easy. Bernadette Farrell's "The Stone Which the Builders Rejected" [JS2] would be an excellent responsorial song for Communion on this Sunday (as well as for other Sundays in the Easter season). The energetic repetitions of "Alleluia" in the refrain express well the joy we feel at being called to the banquet table of the risen Christ.

Ralph Wright's "Sing of One Who Walks Beside Us" [CBW3 and GIA's *Hymnal for the Hours*] would be a good choice for the preparation of the gifts or for the recessional song.

SPIRITUALITY

GOSPEL ACCLAMATION
John 14:23

R⁊. Alleluia, alleluia.
Whoever loves me will keep my word, says the
    Lord,
and my Father will love him and we will come
    to him.
R⁊. Alleluia, alleluia.

Gospel

John 14:15-21; L55A

Jesus said to his
    disciples:
"If you love me, you
    will keep my
    commandments.
And I will ask the
    Father,
and he will give you
    another Advocate
    to be with you always,
the Spirit of truth, whom the world
    cannot accept,
because it neither sees nor knows
    him.
But you know him, because he remains
    with you,
    and will be in you.
I will not leave you orphans; I will come
    to you.
In a little while the world will no longer
    see me,
    but you will see me, because I live
    and you will live.
On that day you will realize that I am in
    my Father
    and you are in me and I in you.
Whoever has my commandments and
    observes them
    is the one who loves me.
And whoever loves me will be loved by
    my Father,
    and I will love him and reveal myself
    to him."

Reflecting on the Gospel

A parent or grandparent may ask a small child, "How much do you love me?" and the child will respond with stretched-wide-open arms and an enthusiastic "This much!" Real love has no bounds. As wide as the child can open his or her arms—this is a whole universe to a small child. This is the unboundedness of responsive love that nurtures, strengthens, helps build strong character and values. In this Sunday's gospel Jesus begins the discourse to the disciples with "If you love me . . ." Of course we love Jesus! And, as with a small child, we might want to open our arms wide and exclaim "This much!"—as much as the whole universe. Yet Jesus seems to put a limit on how much we can love him: "*If* you love me, you will keep my commandments." Commandments are finite and measurable. Is it true that Jesus is limiting our love? Of course not!

There is more to what Jesus is saying than meets the eye, and what he is saying surely is not limiting our love. Instead, it expands our love to include the whole of our living. When Jesus says to keep *his* commandments as a sign of our love for him, he is not only speaking about the Ten Commandments (obeying the Ten Commandments is actually the easy part). He is saying that *if* we love him, we will *live as he lived*. Loving Jesus as he asks requires us to *live* in such a way that others *know* the resurrection is real, that Jesus is really present, that Jesus still cares for us deeply ("I will not leave you orphans").

Our love for Jesus is shown in the same way as the early disciples showed their love—by practical doing in our everyday living. Like Philip and Peter and John (see first reading), we are to proclaim the living Christ by the way we heal hurts in others; bring a healing touch to those who are ailing in any way; strengthen those who are weak or paralyzed by fear, doubt, or selfishness; encourage those weighed down with too much stress, work, or indecision. All this is keeping Jesus' commandments by living *his* way of life—a life characterized by deep care for others. The most encouraging aspect of this gospel is that Jesus even sends us the help we need to love and live in this way.

Our capacity to love Jesus and live as he lived is a gift. We are able to live in this way (and, therefore, show our love for him) because he sends his Spirit to dwell within us. This is the same Spirit who was showered upon the Samaritans (see first reading). The indwelling Advocate-Spirit enables us to *be* like Jesus and to love him.

Living the Paschal Mystery

So much of our life seems anything but connected to Jesus and expressive of our love for him. Our sheer busyness hardly leaves us with a moment to catch our breath, let alone be concerned about loving Jesus!

Loving Jesus doesn't require that we pray all the time or that we are consciously aware of Jesus' presence. Loving Jesus is a simple matter of keeping his commandments—being gentle and reverent toward others, having a clear conscience, doing good (see second reading). Most of us are already doing what we need to do to be good Christians; but we also need to recognize that these good actions are the way we keep his commandments. In other words, his commandments are pretty simple to know: love as he loved, be self-giving as he was, receive others as he did, do the Father's will as he did. Most of all, keeping his commandments means opening ourselves to the Spirit who dwells within us and makes us like him.

Focusing the Gospel

Key words and phrases: If you love me, his commandments, give you . . . Advocate

To the point: Jesus begins this discourse to the disciples with "If you love me . . ." Of course we love Jesus! But there is more to what Jesus is saying than meets the eye. When Jesus says to keep his commandments as a sign of our love for him, he is not speaking only about the Ten Commandments (obeying the Ten Commandments is actually the easy part). He is saying that *if* we love him, we will live as he lived. We are able to live in this way (and, therefore, show our love for him) because he sends his Spirit to dwell within us.

Connecting the Gospel

to the first reading: We are not only given the Spirit by the Father, we are also given the power to share that Spirit with others, as Peter and John went to Samaria to do.

to experience: We share spirit with others in many ways: passing on family spirit, school spirit, national spirit. Living the gospel is the way we pass on the Spirit of Jesus.

Connecting the Responsorial Psalm

to the readings: We continue in the verses of this responsorial psalm to celebrate the marvel of Jesus' death and resurrection, the culmination of God's "tremendous deeds" done among us. We also celebrate the "tremendous deed" of the gift of the Spirit poured into our hearts and flowing out, as the readings indicate, into our actions. We have a great deal to sing about.

The readings remind us, however, that we are to do more than sing about God's redemptive acts. We are to witness to them both with conviction and power (first reading) and with "gentleness and reverence" (second reading). We are to do good because of them, even if this brings us suffering (second reading). Above all, we are to reveal what God has wrought for humankind by keeping Jesus' commandments (gospel). Just as God's saving actions are the cause of our joyful singing, may our actions be cause for the whole world to sing.

to psalmist preparation: This responsorial psalm reminds you that singing God's praises for the gift of redemption is not a private activity but a public proclamation. You invite "all on earth" to "hear" what you have to declare, to "come and see" what God has done, to join you in "glorious praise" of God. Your ministry as cantor, then, reaches far beyond the ears of the assembly gathered before you. Its dimensions are cosmic. As part of your preparation this week, you might take some time to reflect on the awesome reach of your role and to ask the Spirit to give you the capacity to meet it.

ASSEMBLY & FAITH-SHARING GROUPS
- I know I love Jesus when . . . I struggle to love Jesus when . . .
- I have experienced the presence and the power of the Spirit within me when . . . within another when . . .
- Living Jesus' commandments means to me . . .

PRESIDERS
I witness to the assembly that the Spirit dwells within me when I . . .

DEACONS
My service ministry is a sign of Jesus' love for those in need when I . . .

HOSPITALITY MINISTERS
My manner of greeting those who gather communicates to them that the Spirit dwells in me and them when I . . .

MUSIC MINISTERS
Music ministry calls me to greater intimacy with Jesus by . . . I sometimes struggle with this intimacy because . . .

ALTAR MINISTERS
My serving at the altar conveys that I am doing more than the task requires (fulfilling the "law") when I . . .

LECTORS
The works I do that proclaim to others my belief in Christ and his resurrection (see first reading) are . . .

EXTRAORDINARY MINISTERS OF HOLY COMMUNION
The manner of my distributing Holy Communion is a proclamation of Jesus' love for each communicant when I . . .

Model Rite of Blessing and Sprinkling Holy Water

Presider: Dear friends, in today's gospel Jesus calls us to keep his commandments, but he also promises the gift of his Spirit who strengthens us in discipleship. May this sprinkling remind us of the Spirit who first came to dwell within us at baptism . . . [pause]

   [continue with form C of the blessing of water]

Homily Points

• Families pass on more than just a possible inheritance of material riches; more important, they pass on the sure inheritance of a way of viewing and dealing with life—a family spirit. Sometimes this spirit is life-giving, sometimes it is unhealthy; sometimes this spirit is lived, sometimes it is rejected.

• Jesus promises us: I will leave you but not abandon you; I will live always in you; I will continue to show myself to you; the Father and I will send you our Spirit of truth to guide and nurture you. The Spirit Jesus passes on to us is *always* life-giving. We are faced daily with this life-giving choice: to live in the Spirit or reject this way of living.

• In the Spirit, we are to live as Jesus lived, following his commandments: forgiving one another, healing one another, nourishing one another, offering a second coat, walking the extra mile, loving our enemies, washing one another's feet, laying down our life for the sake of the other. As difficult as living this way sometimes is, we are empowered to do so because of Jesus' continued Love.

Model Prayer of the Faithful

Presider: The God who sends us the Spirit listens to our needs and empowers us to be faithful disciples.

Response:

Lord, hear our prayer.

Cantor:

we pray to the Lord,

That the church always reveal to the world the abiding love God has for all people . . . [pause]

That all peoples of the world share equitably in the abundant life God offers . . . [pause]

That those who are down and dispirited, abandoned and unloved, be embraced by the Spirit-filled community of the church . . . [pause]

That each of us here grow in our intimate relationship with Jesus so that we can continue to choose to live in his Spirit . . . [pause]

Presider: God of Spirit and life, we celebrate the resurrection of your Son: hear these our prayers that we might share always in his risen life. We ask this through Christ our Lord. **Amen.**

Let us pray

Pause for silent prayer

Ever-living God,
help us to celebrate our joy
in the resurrection of the Lord
and to express in our lives
the love we celebrate.

Grant this through our Lord Jesus Christ,
   your Son,
who lives and reigns with you and the
   Holy Spirit,
one God, for ever and ever. **Amen.**

FIRST READING
Acts 8:5-8, 14-17

Philip went down to the city of Samaria
   and proclaimed the Christ to them.
With one accord, the crowds paid attention
   to what was said by Philip
   when they heard it and saw the signs he
      was doing.
For unclean spirits, crying out in a loud
   voice,
   came out of many possessed people,
   and many paralyzed or crippled people
      were cured.
There was great joy in that city.

Now when the apostles in Jerusalem
   heard that Samaria had accepted the
      word of God,
   they sent them Peter and John,
   who went down and prayed for them,
   that they might receive the Holy Spirit,
   for it had not yet fallen upon any of
      them;
   they had only been baptized in the name
      of the Lord Jesus.
Then they laid hands on them
   and they received the Holy Spirit.

RESPONSORIAL PSALM
Ps 66:1-3, 4-5, 6-7, 16, 20

R̸. (1) Let all the earth cry out to God with
joy.
   or:
R̸. Alleluia.

Shout joyfully to God, all the earth,
   sing praise to the glory of his name;
   proclaim his glorious praise.
Say to God, "How tremendous are your
      deeds!"

R̸. Let all the earth cry out to God with
joy.
   or:
R̸. Alleluia.

"Let all on earth worship and sing praise
    to you,
    sing praise to your name!"
Come and see the works of God,
    his tremendous deeds among the
        children of Adam.

R⁊. Let all the earth cry out to God with
joy.
    or:
R⁊. Alleluia.

He has changed the sea into dry land;
    through the river they passed on foot.
Therefore let us rejoice in him.
    He rules by his might forever.

R⁊. Let all the earth cry out to God with
joy.
    or:
R⁊. Alleluia.

Hear now, all you who fear God, while I
    declare
    what he has done for me.
Blessed be God who refused me not
    my prayer or his kindness!

R⁊. Let all the earth cry out to God with
joy.
    or:
R⁊. Alleluia.

SECOND READING
1 Pet 3:15-18

Beloved:
Sanctify Christ as Lord in your hearts.
Always be ready to give an explanation
    to anyone who asks you for a reason for
        your hope,
    but do it with gentleness and reverence,
    keeping your conscience clear,
    so that, when you are maligned,
    those who defame your good conduct
        in Christ
    may themselves be put to shame.
For it is better to suffer for doing good,
    if that be the will of God, than for doing
        evil.
For Christ also suffered for sins once,
    the righteous for the sake of the
        unrighteous,
    that he might lead you to God.
Put to death in the flesh,
    he was brought to life in the Spirit.

About Liturgy

Memorial Day: May 30 is Memorial Day in the United States. While we don't want to turn the Sunday liturgy into a patriotic celebration (as worthy as remembering our fallen heroes is), it would be remiss on our part to let this Sunday go by without any mention of the Monday holiday. It is always appropriate to mention as part of the prayer of the faithful an intention to mark such occasions. A model intention might be worded, "That those who have died out of loving service to their country may now enjoy everlasting peace."

Baptism—first sacrament of belonging: For too many Christians baptism is something that happened in the past and rids us of original sin. While that is true, there is more. The most startling effect of baptism is that we are not left orphans (as Jesus promised in the gospel)—God makes us sons and daughters (members of the Body of Christ) by sharing divine life with us. It is at baptism that we first receive the indwelling of the Holy Spirit—the Advocate who helps us live as Jesus did and thus show our love for him.

All of the goodness we do in our life flows from this basic relationship with the Almighty. Growing in our love for Jesus means that we are growing in our ability to live as Jesus lived. Thus baptism is a sacrament that permeates all we are and everything we do. At Easter we renewed our baptismal promises and all through the Easter season we use the blessing and sprinkling of water to remind us of our baptism. All this takes place at this particular time of the year for good reason—that we equate our resurrection faith with growing in our love of Jesus.

About Liturgical Music

Music suggestions: Any of the songs recommended for last Sunday would be worth repeating this week. Additional possibilities for Communion include David Haas's "We Have Been Told" [BB, RS, G2, GC, GC2, SS, WC], which invites us to live in Jesus' love and to keep his commands, and Bernadette Farrell's "Bread of Life" [BB, CBW3, G2, GC, JS2, OFUV], which speaks of Jesus' promise to return and prays that Jesus hold us "in unity, in love for all to see." Hymns that call upon the Spirit to fill our hearts with love and power would be appropriate. "Come Down, O Love Divine" [BB, CBW3, GC2, JS2, RS, WC, W3]; "O Breathe on Me, O Breath of God" [in most hymnals]; and "Holy Spirit, Flow through Me" [LMGM] are examples of hymns that are somewhat meditative in content and style and would suit the preparation of the gifts. "Into our Hearts, O Spirit, Come" [WC], with its more energetic melody, could be used for either the presentation of the gifts or the recessional. Finally, Thomas Tallis's classic "If Ye Love Me" would be an excellent choir prelude.

SPIRITUALITY

GOSPEL ACCLAMATION
Matt 28:19a, 20b

R∫. Alleluia, alleluia.
Go and teach all nations, says the Lord;
I am with you always, until the end of the world.
R∫. Alleluia, alleluia.

Gospel

Matt 28:16-20; L58A

The eleven disciples went to Galilee,
   to the mountain to which Jesus had
      ordered them.
When they saw him, they worshiped,
   but they doubted.
Then Jesus approached and said to
   them,
   "All power in heaven and on earth
      has been given to me.
Go, therefore, and make disciples of all
   nations,
   baptizing them in the name of the
      Father,
   and of the Son, and of the Holy
      Spirit,
   teaching them to observe all that I
      have commanded you.
And behold, I am with you always, until
   the end of the age."

Reflecting on the Gospel

Climbing a mountain is quite an achievement—not many of us have had such an experience, at least of a very high mountain. Some of us even huff and puff to make it to the top of a rather small hill! In this gospel Jesus had summoned the disciples to Galilee, to a mountain. Jesus' resurrection indicates that Jesus has arrived; the disciples are only beginning their journey.

Galilee: the locale for the beginning and ending of Jesus' public ministry. In between the inauguration of his public ministry and the ascension that marks the end of Jesus' time on earth, a whole history of salvation happened—Jesus called followers, taught, preached, healed, worked other miracles, made promises, kept them. Now he calls the disciples to a mountain—a place where the Beatitudes were given, the transfiguration occurred, and now a commissioning takes place. A mountain: something important in the ministry of Jesus is happening. Jesus passes on his ministry to his disciples. Now they (and we) are to take up the "Great Commission": to make disciples, to baptize in the name of the Trinity, to teach, to do all Jesus has commanded "until the end of the age."

This gospel makes it clear that Jesus doesn't call on disciples who are perfect to continue his mission—the disciples saw him and worshiped, "but they doubted." What did the disciples doubt? That Jesus had risen? No, they "saw him." That he was God? No, they "worshiped [him]." Then what did the disciples doubt? Perhaps, knowing Jesus was leaving, they doubted their own strength to carry forth Jesus' mission. What they hadn't yet come fully to believe was that Jesus would always remain with them, giving them strength. Through the Spirit. There was a startling newness to what Jesus was doing and the message he was conveying. Never before had someone been present among us who could "fill all things in every way" (second reading). Never before had someone so completely shared power.

Jesus' power isn't something that gives Jesus everything he wants at the snap of his fingers; his power isn't even used to help Jesus accomplish his goals easily. Jesus' power isn't a power *over* but a power *to*. The power given to Jesus is now handed over to his disciples, and the new thing about this power is that it is a divine Person—the Holy Spirit who is sent to dwell within us, make us one with divinity. This Spirit given to us is the way Jesus remains with us "always, until the end of the age." We have the power *to* make disciples, baptize, and teach; but more important, we have the power *to be*—to be the presence of the risen Christ through the indwelling of the Holy Spirit. With that Power and Presence, our doubts are dispelled. Yes, with the Holy Spirit we *can* faithfully continue Jesus' ministry.

Living the Paschal Mystery

We are like the disciples not only in our doubting but also in that we have been given the power to continue the work of Jesus. In a society in which healthy self-esteem is so difficult for so many people, consider what Jesus does for us: he gives us the power to continue his work and, even more, he remains within us so we are his risen presence for others. How healthy should our self-esteem be! We carry within us the Holy Spirit, the risen presence of Christ!

Focusing the Gospel

Key words and phrases: doubted, Go, I am with you always

To the point: What did the disciples doubt? That Jesus had risen? No, they "saw him." That he was God? No, they "worshiped [him]." Then what did the disciples doubt? Perhaps, knowing Jesus was leaving, they doubted their own strength to carry forth Jesus' mission. What they hadn't yet come fully to believe was that Jesus would always remain with them, giving them strength through the Spirit.

Connecting the Gospel

to the second reading: The second reading is a prayer for disciples to have all they need to carry forth Jesus' mission: Spirit of wisdom and revelation, enlightenment, hope, community of the Body, fullness.

to experience: We all know what it is like to doubt our own abilities, so we can readily identify with the doubting disciples who are about to take on the enormous mission of Jesus: "Go, therefore, and make disciples of *all* nations."

Connecting the Responsorial Psalm

to the readings: Psalm 47 is an enthronement psalm used when the ark of the covenant was carried in procession into the temple. The Israelites clapped and shouted as they celebrated God's ascendancy over all heaven and earth. We use this psalm on this day to acclaim that Christ has been given "all power in heaven and earth" (gospel). We sing it confident that Christ reigns even though we do not know the "time" when his kingdom will be fully manifest (first reading). We sing it even when the kingdom's delay generates doubts within us (gospel) for we "know what is the hope" to which we are called (second reading). We sing it even though Christ has disappeared from our midst because we know he nonetheless remains with us (gospel) and that his power flows through us (first reading). We sing it because we know Christ has won the victory over sin and death and nothing can prevail against him.

to psalmist preparation: Psalm 47 is used for the celebration of the Ascension in all three Lectionary years and can easily be interpreted as referring only to this historical event in the life of Christ. The challenge is to move beyond historicizing to the broader picture of what the church is celebrating when she sings this psalm on this day. What does it mean that Christ is head of his church (second reading)? What does it mean that through the gift of the Spirit the church shares in the power of Christ (first reading)? What does it mean that Christ who is enthroned in heaven also remains among us (gospel)? Reflecting on questions such as these as you prepare will enable you to sing this psalm for the assembly with far deeper understanding.

**ASSEMBLY &
FAITH-SHARING GROUPS**

- I am most able to "see" Jesus when . . . This leads me to worship him by . . .
- Jesus' commissioning of the disciples also applies to me in that . . .
- Jesus' promise "I am with you always" encourages me to . . .

PRESIDERS
My preaching eases doubt and instills courage to carry forth Jesus' saving mission when . . .

DEACONS
My ministry embodies for others Jesus' promise "I am with you always" whenever I . . .

HOSPITALITY MINISTERS
My manner of greeting the gathering assembly members leaves no doubt in their minds that Jesus is with them when I . . .

MUSIC MINISTERS
I experience my music ministry as a participation in the mission of Christ when . . . I sometimes doubt my ability to participate in Christ's mission because . . . What gives me courage even in my doubt is . . .

ALTAR MINISTERS
Serving at the altar is an act of worshiping Jesus; serving others also can be an act of worship in that . . .

LECTORS
My proclamation enables the assembly to see Jesus when . . . to worship him when . . . to have faith in themselves when . . .

EXTRAORDINARY MINISTERS OF HOLY COMMUNION
My manner of distributing Holy Communion helps others to "see" Jesus in a different way when I . . .

Model Rite of Blessing and Sprinkling Holy Water

Presider: Dear friends, we sprinkle this water as a reminder of our baptismal commission to carry forth Jesus' saving mission. May he strengthen us to continue his work . . . [pause]

[continue with form C of the blessing of water]

Homily Points

• We are familiar with transfers of power. For example, we experience a lengthy formal process every time a new president takes office, a company gets a new CEO, or a new principal takes over a school. Giving someone power of attorney over our affairs is another kind of transfer of power. In less formal ways, a transfer of power happens when a patient gives him- or herself over to medical staff for care or when a parent entrusts a child with a chore.

• In this gospel Jesus is transferring power to his disciples. In essence he says, I can't stay here, but neither can you; as I go *out* of the world, you must go *into* the world. Further, his transfer of power is actually the transfer of himself to us in the Spirit.

• We accept Jesus' transfer of power when we make these kinds of choices: to forgive others and to trust that others will forgive us, to extend a healing hand to others and to ask for others' help when we need healing, to encourage others to develop their God-given gifts, to lead others to encounter Jesus, to pray for others, to preach the word, to stand up for justice, to donate time and talent to charity. Indeed, all these and other saving actions are the work of the Spirit—Jesus' risen presence dwelling within us.

Model Prayer of the Faithful

Presider: Continuing the mission of Jesus, let us pray for our needs.

Response:

Lord, hear our prayer.

Cantor:

we pray to the Lord,

That all members of the church strengthen and support one another in choosing to do the works of Jesus . . . [pause]

That all peoples of the world may have the Gospel preached to them . . . [pause]

That those who are powerless to provide the necessities of life for themselves and their families receive what they need . . . [pause]

That each one of us here choose to do the works of the risen Jesus by opening ourselves more fully to the power of the Spirit . . . [pause]

Presider: Eternal God, your risen Son Jesus Christ ascended into heaven and now sits at your right hand: hear these our prayers that one day we might enjoy life everlasting. We ask this through that same Son, Jesus Christ our Lord. **Amen.**

OPENING PRAYER

Let us pray

Pause for silent prayer

God our Father,
make us joyful in the ascension of your
    Son Jesus Christ.
May we follow him into the new creation,
for his ascension is our glory and our
    hope.

We ask this through our Lord Jesus Christ,
    your Son,
who lives and reigns with you and the
    Holy Spirit,
one God, for ever and ever. **Amen.**

FIRST READING
Acts 1:1-11

In the first book, Theophilus,
    I dealt with all that Jesus did and taught
    until the day he was taken up,
    after giving instructions through the
        Holy Spirit
    to the apostles whom he had chosen.
He presented himself alive to them
    by many proofs after he had suffered,
    appearing to them during forty days
    and speaking about the kingdom of
        God.
While meeting with them,
    he enjoined them not to depart from
        Jerusalem,
    but to wait for "the promise of the
        Father
    about which you have heard me speak;
    for John baptized with water,
    but in a few days you will be baptized
        with the Holy Spirit."

When they had gathered together they
        asked him,
    "Lord, are you at this time going to
        restore the kingdom to Israel?"
He answered them, "It is not for you to
        know the times or seasons
    that the Father has established by his
        own authority.
But you will receive power when the Holy
        Spirit comes upon you,
    and you will be my witnesses in
        Jerusalem,
    throughout Judea and Samaria,
    and to the ends of the earth."
When he had said this, as they were
        looking on,
    he was lifted up, and a cloud took him
        from their sight.

While they were looking intently at the
sky as he was going,
   suddenly two men dressed in white
   garments stood beside them.
They said, "Men of Galilee,
   why are you standing there looking at
   the sky?
This Jesus who has been taken up from
   you into heaven
   will return in the same way as you have
   seen him going into heaven."

RESPONSORIAL PSALM

Ps 47:2-3, 6-7, 8-9

Ry. (6) God mounts his throne to shouts of
joy: a blare of trumpets for the Lord.
   or:
Ry. Alleluia.

All you peoples, clap your hands,
   shout to God with cries of gladness,
for the Lord, the Most High, the awesome,
   is the great king over all the earth.

Ry. God mounts his throne to shouts of joy:
a blare of trumpets for the Lord.
   or:
Ry. Alleluia.

God mounts his throne amid shouts of joy;
   the Lord, amid trumpet blasts.
Sing praise to God, sing praise;
   sing praise to our king, sing praise.

Ry. God mounts his throne to shouts of joy:
a blare of trumpets for the Lord.
   or:
Ry. Alleluia.

For king of all the earth is God;
   sing hymns of praise.
God reigns over the nations,
   God sits upon his holy throne.

Ry. God mounts his throne to shouts of joy:
a blare of trumpets for the Lord.
   or:
Ry. Alleluia.

SECOND READING

Eph 1:17-23

See Appendix A, p. 295.

About Liturgy

Blessing and sprinkling on Sundays: The blessing and sprinkling of water
is one of the options for the introductory rites, but the fact that GIRM reserves this
to Sundays, especially during the Easter season (no. 51), suggests that this rite has
special meaning. During the Easter season we are still celebrating with the neophytes
(the newly baptized) their new life in the risen Christ and initiation into the Christian
community, and so it is natural to recall our own baptism as well. Further, since all of
us renewed our baptismal promises at Easter, and since Easter extends for the full fifty
days until Pentecost, it is also fitting that we continue this rite to unify all the Sundays.

For those dioceses that celebrate the Ascension on Thursday rather than transfer
it to the following Sunday, a good choice might be to use Form C.vii of the penitential
rite. However, since the Masses for solemnities have the character of Sunday Masses
(Gloria, three readings, creed, etc.) we might also think of this day as "functioning"
like a Sunday, in which case a sprinkling rite would still be appropriate. In the United
States Ascension is a holy day of obligation when celebrated on Thursday, so we
might presume that the numbers at Mass would be fairly large. Using the sprinkling
rite even on Thursday could serve to draw the celebration into the unity of the season.

About Liturgical Music

Music suggestions: General hymns celebrating the Ascension are readily marked
in most hymnals. Examples of hymns that speak of Christ's commission to "Go . . .
and make disciples" include Sylvia Dunstan's "Go to the World" [CBW3, RS, SS, WC,
WS]; "Lord, You Give the Great Commission" [in many hymnals]; and Ruth Duck's "As
a Fire Is Meant for Burning" [G2, GC, RS], all of which would be excellent recessional
songs. Duck's "You Are Called to Tell the Story" [G2, GC, RS] would work for the
preparation of the gifts if sung to the tune (GHENT) given in the hymnals cited. The
more strongly metered 4/4 tune (REGENT SQUARE) used in the collection *Dancing
in the Universe* [GIA G-3833] would be just right for a post-Communion hymn or the
recessional. An excellent choice for either the preparation of the gifts or Communion
would be the Teresa of Avila text "Christ Has No Body Now But Yours" [VO2, WC;
choral arrangement by Steven Warner, WLP 007284; choral arrangement by David
Ogden, GIA G-6127]. The South African song "Halleluya! We Sing Your Praises" [G2,
GC, GC2, RS] expresses both our willingness to take up our commission as church and
our movement through doubt to faith (see gospel). This energetic piece would make an
excellent recessional song.

JUNE 2, 2011 (Thursday) or JUNE 5, 2011
THE ASCENSION OF THE LORD

✠ SPIRITUALITY

GOSPEL ACCLAMATION
cf. John 14:18

℞. Alleluia, alleluia.
I will not leave you orphans, says the Lord.
I will come back to you, and your hearts will
    rejoice.
℞. Alleluia, alleluia.

Gospel   John 17:1-11a; L59A

Jesus raised his eyes to heaven and said,
    "Father, the hour has come.
Give glory to your son, so that your
        son may glorify you,
    just as you gave him authority over all
        people,
    so that your son may give eternal life to
        all you gave him.
Now this is eternal life,
    that they should know you, the only true
        God,
    and the one whom you sent, Jesus Christ.
I glorified you on earth
    by accomplishing the work that you gave
        me to do.
Now glorify me, Father, with you,
    with the glory that I had with you before
        the world began.

"I revealed your name to those whom you
        gave me out of the world.
They belonged to you, and you gave them to
        me,
    and they have kept your word.
Now they know that everything you gave me
        is from you,
    because the words you gave to me I have
            given to them,
    and they accepted them and truly
            understood that I came from you,
    and they have believed that you sent me.
I pray for them.
I do not pray for the world but for the ones
        you have given me,
    because they are yours, and everything of
        mine is yours
    and everything of yours is mine,
    and I have been glorified in them.
And now I will no longer be in the world,
    but they are in the world, while I am
        coming to you."

Reflecting on the Gospel

Some professions are inherently dangerous, and yet people still choose them. Without such generosity and self-giving, we would not have police or firefighters, soldiers or sailors, storm chasers or miners. Clearly, these people do not choose such professions because they do not value their own lives. Sometimes these lines of work are chosen because it is in the "family" to do so; sometimes they are chosen because there's good pay; sometimes they are chosen because they might be looked upon as "heroes." In the gospel for this Sunday Jesus is praying for his disciples. They are being invited into a dangerous mission—to continue the saving mission of Jesus. It's "in the family" to do so; the pay is good (everlasting life!); they are heroes glorified for what they take up. Yet none of this really explains why people follow Christ.

The disciples, so often the beneficiaries of Jesus' instruction, are now the beneficiaries of Jesus' prayer for them. But his instruction and his prayer are part of his overall work that reaches a climax when he is glorified at the hour of his death and resurrection. We who belong to the family of Jesus continue his work and share in his glory as we share in his death and resurrection. This takes us to the second reading, which uses the word "glory" three times but connects sharing in this glory with "shar[ing] in the sufferings of Christ." The multiple references to glory in both the gospel and second reading situate us squarely in this Easter season, yet in their midst we are reminded that suffering is the door through which we attain glory. We can never separate resurrection from suffering—interpreted as dying to self for the good of others. Taking up Jesus' mission can be dangerous, indeed! It means self-emptying. It means self-giving. It means suffering. No wonder Jesus prays for his disciples! Taking up Jesus' work means taking up his suffering.

Sharing in the sufferings of Christ, however, doesn't mean suffering for suffering's sake. Jesus suffered by his passion and death, yes. But the greater suffering Jesus accepted was to bear (the etymology of the word "suffer" comes from the Latin "to bear") the teaching and preaching, the healing and miracle-working, the fidelity to his Father's will that brought him to the cross in the first place. In all his life Jesus showed us a model for the kind of self-giving that persisted between him and his Father. The gospel is ultimately about the mutual giving between Jesus and the Father, and our being called into the same life of mutual self-giving. We are to give ourselves to God and one another in love and service. In this is God's glory and ours. Suffering—self-giving—is but merely the way.

Living the Paschal Mystery

Our society glorifies being our own person and doing all we can to make our lives easy. This gospel and second reading make clear that to live the paschal mystery (Jesus' dying and rising) and continue Jesus' work means that we must be like Jesus and his Father in our willingness to accept self-giving. Jesus' prayer for his disciples, then, doesn't make our lives easier, but harder! It's the share in glory that makes the choice to be a faithful disciple living the paschal mystery worthwhile. It's the share in glory that draws us to this dangerous profession of discipleship—a profession that invites us each day to put our lives on the line for the good of others.

Focusing the Gospel

Key words and phrases: give, glory, ones you have given me

To the point: The gospel is about mutual giving between Jesus and the Father, and our being called into the same life of self-giving. We are to give ourselves to God and one another in love and service. In this is God's glory and ours.

Connecting the Gospel

to the second reading: This Sunday we are reminded that glory comes to us only through our sharing "in the sufferings of Christ" (second reading).

to experience: Tired of always reporting bad news, when a national news center asked viewers to share stories of good news, reports of deeds of extraordinary self-giving for the good of others poured in by the thousands. The mutual self-giving to which the gospel calls us is more abundant and evident than we sometimes think. God's glory abounds.

Connecting the Responsorial Psalm

to the readings: After Jesus' ascension the disciples find themselves in an in-between time of waiting for the descent of the Spirit. They immerse themselves in prayer (first reading). We too live in an in-between time, waiting not for the coming of the Spirit but for the return of Christ in glory and for the full flowering of his kingdom. The second reading warns that if we remain faithful to Christ during this time of waiting, we will be made to suffer for it. Because he is fully aware of what our waiting and our fidelity will entail, Jesus prays for us (gospel).

The responsorial psalm captures the content of our prayer in response. We tell Christ that we believe in the "good things" he has promised. We tell Christ that we fear nothing, for in this time of long darkness he is our "light and our salvation." We tell Christ that we desire only one thing: to dwell with him and to know him more intimately. And we beg him to have compassion on us. For we know, as he does, the costs of discipleship and the dangers to faith that this long wait holds. May our prayer remain ever joined with his.

to psalmist preparation: The confidence in God the responsorial psalm expresses is couched in intimations of danger: "whom should I fear?" and "Hear, O Lord, the sound of my call." As the second reading indicates, the glory to be yours because of faithful discipleship comes only because you have first suffered for Christ. When you sing this psalm, then, you are acknowledging the real challenge of discipleship and asking for God's help in meeting it. When you reflect on this challenge, what makes you afraid? How does Christ help you with this fear?

ASSEMBLY & FAITH-SHARING GROUPS

- God gives to me . . . I give to God . . .
- The self-giving I do that brings God glory is . . .
- My love for . . . calls me to self-giving when . . .

PRESIDERS

I lead the assembly beyond rote prayers or routine ritual to the work of glorifying God (through worship and daily living) when I . . .

DEACONS

My serving others brings them glory when . . . this is God's glory because . . .

HOSPITALITY MINISTERS

My hospitality welcomes and directs the assembly toward the work of glorifying God by . . .

MUSIC MINISTERS

I am most aware of glorifying Jesus in my music ministry when . . . What sometimes gets in the way of my glorifying Jesus is . . .

ALTAR MINISTERS

The kind of self-giving to which my serving at the altar calls me is . . .

LECTORS

My daily living proclaims to others that to share in Jesus' glory I must first share in his suffering (see second reading) when I . . .

EXTRAORDINARY MINISTERS OF HOLY COMMUNION

In my daily living, I share Jesus' self-gift to others when I . . .

✠ CELEBRATION

Model Rite of Blessing and Sprinkling Holy Water

Presider: Dear friends, we sprinkle this water to remind us of our baptism, when we first were given a share in Jesus' glory. Let us prepare ourselves to celebrate this liturgy by opening ourselves to God's glorious presence . . . [pause]

    [continue with form C of the blessing of water]

Homily Points

• The well-known and beloved Prayer of St. Francis challenges us to seek "not so much . . . to be loved as to love" and reminds us that "it is in giving that we receive." While these values are not what our society says will make us happy, they are what the Gospel preaches.

• The model for self-giving derives from the inner life of the Trinity itself. In the gospel Jesus calls his followers into the mutual love and glory of the Father and Son. Our response in the Spirit is love and service of others.

• By loving as Jesus loved and giving of ourselves as God gives to us, we increase our capacity to receive God and others. It is in giving that we receive; the more we give, the more we receive. God's glory is in this unbounded capacity.

Model Prayer of the Faithful

Presider: We pray that we might continue Jesus' work and thus give God glory.

Response:

Lord, hear our prayer.

Cantor:

we pray to the Lord,

That all members of the church preach the Gospel through lives of self-giving . . . [pause]

That all peoples of the world might share in God's glory . . . [pause]

That those bound by selfishness break free, and those shackled by an inability to love others experience God's love . . . [pause]

That each of us here serve others with an unbounded love . . . [pause]

Presider: God of glory, you raised your Son to new life: hear these our prayers that one day we might share that same life of glory with you and your Son in the Holy Spirit for ever and ever. **Amen.**

OPENING PRAYER

Let us pray

Pause for silent prayer

Father,
help us keep in mind that Christ our
    Savior
lives with you in glory
and promised to remain with us until the
    end of time.
We ask this through our Lord Jesus Christ,
    your Son,
who lives and reigns with you and the
    Holy Spirit,
one God, for ever and ever. **Amen.**

FIRST READING
Acts 1:12-14

After Jesus had been taken up to heaven
    the apostles
    returned to Jerusalem
    from the mount called Olivet, which is
        near Jerusalem,
a sabbath day's journey away.

When they entered the city
    they went to the upper room where they
        were staying,
    Peter and John and James and Andrew,
    Philip and Thomas, Bartholomew and
        Matthew,
    James son of Alphaeus, Simon the
        Zealot,
    and Judas son of James.
All these devoted themselves with one
        accord to prayer,
    together with some women,
    and Mary the mother of Jesus, and his
        brothers.

RESPONSORIAL PSALM

Ps 27:1, 4, 7-8

R̸. (13) I believe that I shall see the good things of the Lord in the land of the living.
or:
R̸. Alleluia.

The LORD is my light and my salvation;
whom should I fear?
The LORD is my life's refuge;
of whom should I be afraid?

R̸. I believe that I shall see the good things of the Lord in the land of the living.
or:
R̸. Alleluia.

One thing I ask of the LORD; this I seek:
to dwell in the house of the LORD
all the days of my life,
that I may gaze on the loveliness of the
LORD
and contemplate his temple.

R̸. I believe that I shall see the good things of the Lord in the land of the living.
or:
R̸. Alleluia.

Hear, O LORD, the sound of my call;
have pity on me, and answer me.
Of you my heart speaks; you my glance
seeks.

R̸. I believe that I shall see the good things of the Lord in the land of the living.
or:
R̸. Alleluia.

SECOND READING

1 Pet 4:13-16

Beloved:
Rejoice to the extent that you share in the
sufferings of Christ,
so that when his glory is revealed
you may also rejoice exultantly.
If you are insulted for the name of Christ,
blessed are you,
for the Spirit of glory and of God rests
upon you.
But let no one among you be made to
suffer
as a murderer, a thief, an evildoer, or as
an intriguer.
But whoever is made to suffer as a
Christian should not be ashamed
but glorify God because of the name.

About Liturgy

Types of prayer: We often pray for ourselves and for others, especially at times of difficulties or great need. Spiritual writers tell us that this *intercessory prayer* forms the major portion of how we pray to God. And surely there is nothing wrong in this! It does point to the "not yet" of this life and that we still must share in the suffering of Christ.

At the same time, knowing that our suffering brings glory to God ought to bring us at times to a *prayer of adoration, praise, and thanksgiving*, especially since we already share in God's glory ourselves because we already share in divine life. It's fairly easy for us to utter prayers of thanksgiving—especially in face of the many blessings God has given to us. Sometimes our intercessory prayers are clearly answered in terms of what we asked and this too often prompts thanksgiving. Most of us probably need to make a more conscious effort to offer God prayers of adoration and praise, not so much because of God's blessings but because we become more aware of the awesome goodness and love of God. One way to make sure this kind of prayer is a regular part of our spiritual exercises is to set aside Sunday as a day when we primarily offer God prayers of adoration and praise.

About Liturgical Music

Music suggestions: On this last Sunday before Pentecost it would be appropriate for the assembly to sing a post-Communion hymn as a communal petition/prayer for the Spirit's coming. One possibility would be the Taizé "Veni Sancte Spiritus" [G2, GC, GC2, LMGM, RS, W3], with choir or cantor(s) singing the verses over the assembly refrain. Another good choice would be "O Holy Spirit, Come to Bless" [CBW3], the opening verse of which is especially fitting: "O Holy Spirit, come to bless your waiting Church, we pray: We long to grow in holiness as children of the day." A third choice would be "Spirit of the Living God" [LMGM], which could be sung several times as a mantra. A fourth possibility would be Paul Page's lovely "Come, Spirit, Come" [in *Mantras for the Seasons*, WLP 007195], with ostinato assembly refrain under cantored verses.

JUNE 5, 2011
SEVENTH SUNDAY OF EASTER
or CELEBRATION OF ASCENSION

✝ SPIRITUALITY

GOSPEL ACCLAMATION
℟. Alleluia, alleluia.
Come, Holy Spirit, fill the hearts of your faithful
and kindle in them the fire of your love.
℟. Alleluia, alleluia.

Gospel

John 20:19-23; L63A

On the evening of that first day of the
    week,
  when the doors were locked, where
    the disciples were,
  for fear of the Jews,
  Jesus came and stood in their midst
  and said to them, "Peace be with
    you."
When he had said this, he showed them
    his hands and his side.
The disciples rejoiced when they saw
    the Lord.
Jesus said to them again, "Peace be
    with you.
As the Father has sent me, so I send
    you."
And when he had said this, he breathed
    on them and said to them,
  "Receive the Holy Spirit.
Whose sins you forgive are forgiven
    them,
  and whose sins you retain are
    retained."

Reflecting on the Gospel

Many of the elder members of our families and communities speak of times gone by when locking doors (even in big cities) was simply not something people did. Neighborhoods were communities that looked out for each other. Strangers coming into the midst were noted. But beyond this, there was a trust and companionship that marked the atmosphere and made locking doors seem unnecessary. Today our neighborhoods tend to be marked by fear. Doors are not only locked, but double and triple locked. We pay thousands of dollars for the latest in alarm systems and then a monthly fee for the service. Fear has become, sadly enough, a way of life for us. But fear is nothing new. The disciples were in a locked room because they were afraid. Fear marks a serious breakdown in relationships. Forgiveness marks a serious attempt to rebuild relationships. It is no surprise, then, that in his resurrection night appearance Jesus bestows on this fearful group the gift of peace, of the Holy Spirit, then sends them out on a mission of forgiveness.

By linking the sending of the Spirit and the commission to forgive sins, John is accenting the disciples' share in risen life. Forgiveness heals the breach between two persons or groups, heals the divergence of lives, ensures that we remain "one body" in Christ (second reading). The only way we can share risen life is that there be no breach among us—"whether Jews or Greeks, slaves or free persons" (second reading). Forgiveness, then, stands as a duty for those sharing in risen life.

Twice in this gospel Jesus says, "Peace be with you." Peace is the fruit of the Spirit (cf. Gal 5:22). It is the effect of our taking up the mission of Jesus. Peace is indicative of the presence of the Spirit in those whose lives are characterized by forgiveness. Peace is a way we witness to healed relationships within us and the larger community.

What, then, is the forgiveness of sins for which the Spirit empowers us? It is our being with the Holy Spirit—a way of *being* together in risen life. It is both an intimate sharing of *life* as well as Jesus' commissioning us to continue his work. This forgiveness is about building right relationships or not, about opening doors between ourselves and others or closing them, about allowing the peace of Christ to replace the fears that stifle our connecting to one another. The risen Christ breathes into us the Spirit—this capacity to forgive—then sends us out into the world to unleash this Spirit. Every day is a Pentecost.

Living the Paschal Mystery

Pentecost is more than celebrating the "birthday" of the church—it celebrates our "birth" into risen life ("he breathed on them"; cf. Gen 2:7) and being sent to forgive others. We can speak of a "birthday" of the church (the church being the Body of Christ) only when we make the church a reality through forgiveness of one another. Then every day is a "birthday"—a birthing of the risen life of Christ in each other.

Forgiveness is sometimes the most difficult thing we do; so many simple acts in our everyday living demand that we seek and give forgiveness. This is why Jesus sent the Spirit: to empower us, through the common risen life we share, to forgive, to heal divisions in the community, to be peacemakers. We overcome our fears and unlock the doors of our closed relationships when we reach out to others in forgiveness.

Focusing the Gospel

Key words and phrases: I send you, Receive the Holy Spirit, forgive

To the point: What is the forgiveness of sins for which the Spirit empowers us? This forgiveness is about building right relationships or not, about opening doors between ourselves and others or closing them, about allowing the peace of Christ to replace the fears that stifle our connecting to one another. The risen Christ breathes into us the Spirit—this capacity to forgive—then sends us out into the world to unleash this Spirit. Every day is a Pentecost.

Connecting the Gospel

to the second reading: The second reading explicitly describes life in the Spirit: we receive different spiritual gifts, different forms of service; we are one Body with many parts. None of these manifestations of the Spirit are given for ourselves but for the purpose of the mission of the church—the unleashing of the Spirit for the growth of the whole human community.

to experience: Because we commemorate the giving of the Holy Spirit on Pentecost Sunday, we tend to limit the Spirit's coming to a single day. In fact, the Spirit is present and empowering us from the beginning of our life in God. Every day is Pentecost.

Connecting the Responsorial Psalm

to the readings: Psalm 104 is deliberately patterned after the story of creation as recounted in Genesis 1. The psalm unfolds in seven sections dealing with different aspects of God's mighty creative acts. In the verses we use for Pentecost, we proclaim that God's works are manifold. We pray that God's works ("glory") "endure forever" and that God be "glad in [them]."

The good news is that the "mighty acts of God" (first reading) will endure because we have been empowered to continue them (gospel). Jesus has breathed upon us his very Spirit and sent us to carry out the Spirit's greatest work: the granting of peace through forgiveness of sins. The work of the Spirit is the constant renewal of relationship between us and God, us and one another, us and the whole of the created world. Truly God is glad in this work and glad in us who do it.

to psalmist preparation: The gospel for Pentecost this Lectionary year indicates that the primary power Jesus gives the disciples through the Spirit is the power to forgive sins. How does forgiveness bring about renewal? How have you yourself experienced the renewing power of forgiveness? Where in your life right now do you need to ask the Spirit for this power?

ASSEMBLY & FAITH-SHARING GROUPS

- I experience the Spirit within me prompting me to forgive when . . .
- The Spirit has unleashed in me . . . Others experience this Pentecost when . . .
- The Spirit removes these fears . . . opens these doors . . . strengthens these relationships . . .

PRESIDERS

Some of the ways I assist each member of the assembly to realize his or her "manifestation of the Spirit" (second reading) for the benefit of all are . . .

DEACONS

My ministry of service unlocks fearful hearts whenever I . . .

HOSPITALITY MINISTERS

My welcome and care (whether at home or at liturgy) embodies for others how our different-ness is united in "one Spirit" (see second reading) by . . .

MUSIC MINISTERS

My blending with other members of the choir is a manifestation of the presence of the Spirit in that . . .

ALTAR MINISTERS

My humble serving at the altar and in my daily living is a true manifestation of the Spirit whenever I . . .

LECTORS

My daily living proclaims the manifestation of the Spirit whenever I . . .

EXTRAORDINARY MINISTERS OF HOLY COMMUNION

As a minister of Communion some of the ways that I am healing the tension and uniting diversity within the Body of Christ (see second reading) are . . .

Model Rite of Blessing and Sprinkling Holy Water

Presider: Dear friends, as we sprinkle this water we are reminded of our baptism, when we first received the Holy Spirit. Let us prepare to celebrate through these sacred mysteries this divine Presence among us . . . [pause]

[continue with form C of the blessing of water]

Homily Points

• Sometimes saying "I'm sorry" is simply the socially correct thing to do, but it carries no real intent and entails no change of behavior or attitude. For example, when we are stopped for speeding and the officer comes up to the car window, the first words we utter are "I'm sorry," but the next day (or next hour!) we speed again. Or when big sister hits little brother, the parent might make the big sister say "I'm sorry," but this is no guarantee she will stop hitting her brother.

• We can limit reconciliation to moments of apology that entail no change in behavior toward or relationship with the person we have hurt. Jesus makes it clear that the sending of the Spirit among us means an essential change in who and how we are in relationship with God and each other.

• In a real sense the whole mission of Jesus—of the church—can be summed up in the act of forgiveness. Forgiveness is not just about simply apologizing for having done something hurtful to another but it is about the change of heart needed to be in right relationship with God and one another. Change of heart opens the door for peace within the family, the church, and the world. Forgiveness and peace are the fruit of the Spirit's presence within and among us.

Model Prayer of the Faithful

Presider: Let us pray that we might be in right relationship with God and others through the power of the Holy Spirit given us.

Response:

Lord, hear our prayer.

Cantor:

we pray to the Lord,

That the church always be a community of peace welcoming all who come seeking forgiveness . . . [pause]

That leaders of the world be models of forgiving others and preserving world peace . . . [pause]

That those who lead violent lives may be transformed into persons of peace . . . [pause]

That all of us here be quick to forgive so that our unity in the Body of Christ is evident to all . . . [pause]

Presider: God of peace and forgiveness, your risen Son sent the Holy Spirit upon the disciples: hear these our prayers that we might forgive and be forgiven, and live always in right relationship with you and each other. We ask this through Christ our Lord. **Amen.**

OPENING PRAYER
Let us pray

Pause for silent prayer

God our Father,
let the Spirit you sent on your Church
to begin the teaching of the gospel
continue to work in the world
through the hearts of all who believe.

We ask this through our Lord Jesus Christ,
     your Son,
who lives and reigns with you and the
     Holy Spirit,
one God, for ever and ever. **Amen.**

FIRST READING
Acts 2:1-11

When the time for Pentecost was fulfilled,
     they were all in one place together.
And suddenly there came from the sky
     a noise like a strong driving wind,
     and it filled the entire house in which
          they were.
Then there appeared to them tongues as
     of fire,
     which parted and came to rest on each
          one of them.
And they were all filled with the Holy
     Spirit
     and began to speak in different tongues,
     as the Spirit enabled them to proclaim.

Now there were devout Jews from every
          nation under heaven
          staying in Jerusalem.
At this sound, they gathered in a large
          crowd,
     but they were confused
     because each one heard them speaking
          in his own language.
They were astounded, and in amazement
          they asked,
     "Are not all these people who are
          speaking Galileans?
Then how does each of us hear them in his
     native language?
We are Parthians, Medes, and Elamites,
     inhabitants of Mesopotamia, Judea and
          Cappadocia,
     Pontus and Asia, Phrygia and
          Pamphylia,
     Egypt and the districts of Libya near
          Cyrene,
     as well as travelers from Rome,
     both Jews and converts to Judaism,
     Cretans and Arabs,
     yet we hear them speaking in our own
          tongues
of the mighty acts of God."

RESPONSORIAL PSALM

Ps 104:1, 24, 29-30, 31, 34

R̸. (cf. 30) Lord, send out your Spirit, and renew the face of the earth.
  or: R̸. Alleluia.

Bless the LORD, O my soul!
  O LORD, my God, you are great indeed!
How manifold are your works, O LORD!
  The earth is full of your creatures.

R̸. Lord, send out your Spirit, and renew the face of the earth.
  or: R̸. Alleluia.

If you take away their breath, they perish
  and return to their dust.
When you send forth your spirit, they are
  created,
  and you renew the face of the earth.

R̸. Lord, send out your Spirit, and renew the face of the earth.
  or: R̸. Alleluia.

May the glory of the LORD endure forever;
  may the LORD be glad in his works!
Pleasing to him be my theme;
  I will be glad in the LORD.

R̸. Lord, send out your Spirit, and renew the face of the earth.
  or: R̸. Alleluia.

SECOND READING

1 Cor 12:3b-7, 12-13

Brothers and sisters:
No one can say, "Jesus is Lord," except by
  the Holy Spirit.

There are different kinds of spiritual gifts
  but the same Spirit;
  there are different forms of service but
  the same Lord;
  there are different workings but the
  same God
  who produces all of them in everyone.
To each individual the manifestation of
  the Spirit
  is given for some benefit.

As a body is one though it has many parts,
  and all the parts of the body, though
  many, are one body,
  so also Christ.
For in one Spirit we were all baptized into
  one body,
  whether Jews or Greeks, slaves or free
  persons,
  and we were all given to drink of one
  Spirit.

SEQUENCE

See Appendix A, p. 295.

About Liturgy

Beware of novelty in liturgy: The early Christian community members experienced many unusual occurrences, and we hear about many of them during these weeks of Easter when we read from the Acts of the Apostles. The first reading for this solemnity—the Lucan account of the giving of the Spirit on that first Pentecost—includes such a phenomenal account: those who received the Holy Spirit "began to speak in different tongues." Taking this passage literally, it is popular for parishes to proclaim this reading from Acts or the intentions at the prayer of the faithful in the various languages represented by the assembly members. The problem with this approach is that the novelty obscures the power of the proclamation in terms of its real message. We focus on the *phenomenon* rather than on the *hearing* of the "mighty acts of God" or understanding the announcement of an intention so one can really enter into the prayer. The real power of liturgy doesn't come from what we *do* to the ritual but how we receive God's presence acting to transform us.

About Liturgical Music

Music suggestions: Hymns to the Holy Spirit abound, so the task is to use them judiciously. For example, "O Breathe on Me, O Breath of God" would be suitable for the preparation of the gifts, but the tune to which it is set is too gentle for the entrance procession. For another example, even though the refrain of David Haas's "Send Us Your Spirit" is almost identical to the refrain of the responsorial psalm for this day, it would not be suitable for the psalm because its verses are not the psalm text. This song would be better used as a prayerful prelude, with assembly joining in on the canonic refrain.

A second caution is not to overuse Holy Spirit hymns on this day. Singing one for the entrance and another one for the preparation of the gifts would be enough. For Communion, songs such as "We Are Many Parts" that refer to the work of the Spirit in making us one Body would be appropriate. For the recessional, songs about the mission of the church would be most appropriate, such as "Lord, You Give the Great Commission"; "Go to the World"; and "The Church of Christ in Every Age."

JUNE 12, 2011
PENTECOST SUNDAY

Ordinary Time II

SPIRITUALITY

GOSPEL ACCLAMATION
Rev 1:8

℟. Alleluia, alleluia.
Glory to the Father, the Son, and the Holy Spirit;
to God who is, who was, and who is to come.
℟. Alleluia, alleluia.

Gospel

John 3:16-18; L164A

**God so loved the world that he gave his
only Son,
so that everyone who believes in him
might not perish
but might have eternal life.
For God did not send his Son into the
world to condemn the world,
but that the world might be saved
through him.
Whoever believes in him will not be
condemned,
but whoever does not believe has
already been condemned,
because he has not believed in the
name of the only Son of God.**

Reflecting on the Gospel

Mysteries intrigue us. Sometimes they frustrate us. Always they elude solving. The mystery of the Holy Trinity may be intriguing to us, probably doesn't frustrate us, but does always elude solving. We cannot—ought not—ignore it, for it is the source of our own life and holiness.

God chose to create and redeem humanity in an unequaled act of love. The readings this Sunday remind us that God is gracious, sharing divine life with us: "God so loved" us that God "gave his only Son" so that "the world might be saved" (gospel). Yes, God sent the Son so that we might have life. Divine life and love extend beyond the inner intimacy of the three Persons of the Holy Trinity to us. Much more than a theological concept, the Trinity is the mystery of a lived Presence within and among us, made visible as mercy and graciousness (see first reading) and as joy, encouragement, and peace (see second reading).

In the second reading St. Paul admonishes the community to behave with concrete manifestations of trinitarian living: rejoice, mend our ways, "encourage one another, agree with one another, live in peace." All of us know how difficult it can be to live with others. What makes community possible is that divine life is already within us. We can be a community of persons because the Holy Trinity shares their divine life with us. So when we perform gracious acts, it is really God working in and through us. In this way our lives, then, can become manifestations of the Holy Trinity itself. While the Trinity remains a great mystery, it is nonetheless manifested in the way we live with each other.

The model for our community living is God's very own saving acts on our behalf from the very beginning of time. God "pardon[s] our wickedness" because God is "merciful and gracious" (first reading). The challenge here runs in two directions. First, we must move beyond ourselves in self-giving in order to act with the graciousness and mercy of God. Second, we must cultivate an inner life centered on God. The mystery of the Trinity calls us to go both beyond ourselves and deeper into ourselves—to an intimacy with God that turns us outward in mercy and graciousness to others. Thus is the trinitarian grace, love, and fellowship manifested in our midst. God is triune mystery, yes! But it is even more mystery laden that God shares divine Self with us in such a gracious manner and "receives us" as God's very own.

Living the Paschal Mystery

It is awesome to think that God invites us to share in such a great mystery as the Holy Trinity! It seems as though God's graciousness never ends—not only with sending the Son but, further, with inviting us into God's saving work. In this context we might think of the simple, ordinary ways we reach out to others—a smile, a helping hand, a kind word—as ways we actually manifest the mystery and majesty of our triune God. Such love as this can only be matched by those who share in divine life!

We are to be in relationship with each other as the three divine Persons of the Holy Trinity are in relationship with each other. This sounds impossible to us humans who experience hurts, broken relationships, lack of graciousness so much of the time. Perhaps this is why the mystery of the Holy Trinity has been revealed to us: as God's beloved who have been saved by the Son and given life in the Spirit, as those created in God's image, we can aspire to healing unity.

Focusing the Gospel

Key words and phrases: God so loved, gave his only Son, have eternal life

To the point: God sent the Son so that we might have life. Divine life and love extend beyond the inner intimacy of the three Persons of the Holy Trinity to us. Much more than a theological concept, the Trinity is the mystery of a lived Presence within and among us, made visible as mercy and graciousness (see first reading) and as joy, encouragement, and peace (see second reading).

Connecting the Gospel

to the first and second readings: The gospel and these two readings together point to the trinitarian mystery. The first reading emphasizes the presence of the first Person of the Trinity; the second reading mentions the fellowship of the Holy Spirit; the gospel identifies the saving work of the Son.

to experience: All of us know how difficult it can be to live with others. What makes community possible is, not asserting individual rights, but granting one another the love, mercy, and graciousness God freely grants to us.

Connecting the Responsorial Psalm

to the readings: Daniel 3:52-56 is an addition (included in Roman Catholic but not Jewish or Protestant versions of the Old Testament) to the story of the three men thrown into the fiery furnace because they would not worship the Babylonian gods. The verses are part of a lengthy song of praise sung by the men as they moved about in the furnace, untouched by the flames. When king Nebuchadnezzar peered inside, he was amazed to see that they were alive and unharmed, and that a fourth "person" walked among them. He immediately released them, declaring their God mighty above all others.

The first and second readings tell us that God reveals divine might not through displays of power but through acts of love. Without limit, God offers us mercy, kindness, patience, and peace. Even more, God gives us "his only Son" that we might have fullness of life (gospel). What better response can we make than "Blessed are you . . . Glory and praise forever!" (psalm).

to psalmist preparation: An excellent preparation for leading this canticle would be to use part of it (e.g., "Blessed are you, God!" or, "Glory and praise to you, God!") as a personal prayer every day this week. Sing it as you rise each morning, as you see new spring life pushing up from the ground, as you look upon the face of a loved one, as you share a meal. Sing it wherever you see pain eased, forgiveness given, hope rekindled. You will be celebrating the God in whom you believe, and the assembly will hear this in your singing on Sunday.

**ASSEMBLY &
FAITH-SHARING GROUPS**
- I experience God's love and presence when . . . This helps me love and be present to others in that . . .
- I experience God as a loving trinity of Persons when . . .
- My life becomes fuller when . . . My life seems diminished when . . .

PRESIDERS
How my ministry mediates "the grace of the Lord Jesus Christ" (second reading) to the community is . . . How it manifests "the love of God" is . . . How it promotes "the fellowship of the Holy Spirit" is . . .

DEACONS
My service makes God's mercy and graciousness present to those in need whenever I . . .

HOSPITALITY MINISTERS
I am modeling a generosity of graciousness *within* and *to* the community (see first reading) by . . .

MUSIC MINISTERS
I experience "grace . . . love . . . fellowship" (second reading) with other music ministers when . . . I thank them for this Trinity-like behavior by . . . I contribute to this behavior when I . . .

ALTAR MINISTERS
My serving witnesses to God's gracious and merciful desire for fuller life for us when . . .

LECTORS
My proclamation manifests God's desire that we have fuller life through the saving work of the Son when . . .

**EXTRAORDINARY MINISTERS
OF HOLY COMMUNION**
When I distribute Holy Communion, I participate in God's giving of the Son to those who believe in these ways . . .

Model Act of Penitence

Presider: We honor today the Most Blessed Trinity, the community of divine Persons who loves and saves us. We pause at the beginning of this liturgy to open ourselves to such a gracious God . . . [pause]

Lord Jesus, you are the only-begotten Son of God: Lord . . .

Christ Jesus, you are present in majesty and glory: Christ . . .

Lord Jesus, you did not come to condemn the world but to save it: Lord . . .

Homily Points

• Dealing with a person who is two-faced puts us on edge because we don't know who we're dealing with, which face we're looking at, whether or not we are being toyed with. We react strongly to such duplicity, manipulation, and lack of personal integrity. We want those to whom we relate to have one face—a face of honesty and integrity. We can't even imagine someone putting on three faces!

• Yet, the God who called us into being is three Persons with the "face" of a gracious and merciful God, the "face" of a saving God who sacrifices Self for our sake, the "face" of a loving God who desires fellowship with us. These three "faces," however, have no duplicity about them. They are triune wholeness and goodness.

• We all have been taught (and, hopefully, believe) that we are created in the image of God. Guess what? This means we are to show the world three "faces."

Model Prayer of the Faithful

Presider: With confidence we make our needs known to our gracious, merciful, and triune God.

Response:

Lord, hear our prayer.

Cantor:

we pray to the Lord,

That the church might always be a community of persons who act graciously for the good of others . . . [pause]

That all peoples of the world come to lasting peace through mutual respect and love for one another . . . [pause]

That those who lack love be loved, those who lack forgiveness be forgiven, those who need mercy be shown graciousness . . . [pause]

That each one of us rejoice always in the community of persons and divine life we share . . . [pause]

Presider: God of mercy and graciousness, you sent your Son to save the world: hear these our prayers that we might one day be with you in everlasting life and love. We ask this through Jesus Christ our Lord, who with the Holy Spirit is one God, for ever and ever. **Amen.**

Let us pray
[to our God who is Father, Son, and Holy Spirit]

Pause for silent prayer

God, we praise you:
Father all-powerful, Christ Lord and
    Savior, Spirit of love.
You reveal yourself in the depths of our
    being,
drawing us to share in your life and your
    love.
One God, three Persons,
be near to the people formed in your
    image,
close to the world your love brings to life.

We ask this, Father, Son, and Holy Spirit,
one God, true and living, for ever and ever.
    Amen.

FIRST READING
Exod 34:4b-6, 8-9

Early in the morning Moses went up
    Mount Sinai
    as the LORD had commanded him,
    taking along the two stone tablets.

Having come down in a cloud, the LORD
    stood with Moses there
    and proclaimed his name, "LORD."
Thus the LORD passed before him and
    cried out,
    "The LORD, the LORD, a merciful and
        gracious God,
    slow to anger and rich in kindness and
        fidelity."
Moses at once bowed down to the ground
    in worship.
Then he said, "If I find favor with you, O
    LORD,
    do come along in our company.
This is indeed a stiff-necked people; yet
    pardon our wickedness and sins,
    and receive us as your own."

RESPONSORIAL PSALM
Dan 3:52, 53, 54, 55

R. (52b) Glory and praise forever!

Blessed are you, O Lord, the God of our
fathers,
praiseworthy and exalted above all
forever;
and blessed is your holy and glorious
name,
praiseworthy and exalted above all for
all ages.

R. Glory and praise forever!

Blessed are you in the temple of your holy
glory,
praiseworthy and glorious above all
forever.

R. Glory and praise forever!

Blessed are you on the throne of your
kingdom,
praiseworthy and exalted above all
forever.

R. Glory and praise forever!

Blessed are you who look into the depths
from your throne upon the cherubim,
praiseworthy and exalted above all
forever.

R. Glory and praise forever!

SECOND READING
2 Cor 13:11-13

Brothers and sisters, rejoice. Mend your
ways, encourage one another,
agree with one another, live in peace,
and the God of love and peace will be
with you.
Greet one another with a holy kiss.
All the holy ones greet you.

The grace of the Lord Jesus Christ
and the love of God
and the fellowship of the Holy Spirit be
with all of you.

About Liturgy

Father's Day: The Mass of the Sunday is to be respected even if this Sunday is Father's Day. A fifth intention might be added at the prayer of the faithful (see BofB 1732), and a blessing for fathers may be given in place of the prayer over the people for the Sunday (see BofB 1733).

A model intention at the prayer of the faithful might be "That all fathers, grandfathers, and godfathers model the graciousness, mercy, and love of our triune God."

The greeting at the beginning of Mass: The end of the second reading for this solemnity is one of the greetings that the presider may choose to use after the Sign of the Cross at the beginning of Mass (form A: "The grace of our Lord Jesus Christ and the love of God and the fellowship of the Holy Spirit be with you all"). The other two choices given in the Sacramentary are also taken from Scripture: "The grace and peace of God our Father and the Lord Jesus Christ be with you" (form B; cf. Gal 1:3) and "The Lord be with you" (form C; cf. Ruth 2:4). Our response ("And with your spirit"; new Roman Missal translation) is also from Scripture (cf. Gal 6:18), though it is a paraphrase. GIRM gives us the reason for this greeting: "through his greeting the priest declares to the assembled community that the Lord is present. This greeting and the people's response express the mystery of the gathered Church" (no. 50).

In actual pastoral practice, it seems as though form A is the one most often chosen and perhaps this is as it should be. This is the only one of the three greetings that expressly names all three Persons of the Holy Trinity. This emphasizes for us not only that the "Lord is present" but also that the *Trinity* is present. All liturgy is trinitarian; that is, all three Persons of the Holy Trinity are present and working in our celebration of liturgy. All three Persons of the Holy Trinity help form us into the one Body of Christ, the church. Care must be taken that this greeting isn't something we respond to by rote. It is a reminder that we celebrate liturgy because the Holy Trinity is present and calls us to share in this divine action.

About Liturgical Music

Service music: Since the celebration of Pentecost last Sunday marked our return to Ordinary Time, this is the Sunday to "retire" the festive service music of the Easter season until next year. However, because this Sunday and next (Solemnity of the Most Holy Body and Blood of Christ) are solemnities, a celebratory Mass setting is called for. One way to mark the shift from Easter season to these solemnities and on into Ordinary Time is to sing a setting different from that reserved for the Easter season yet more festive in style from whatever will be sung during Ordinary Time.

Responsorial psalm: Another way to mark the solemnity of this day would be to sing the canticle from Daniel used as the responsorial psalm as a litany led by the psalmist (or two psalmists in alternation). Gelineau's excellent, energetic setting in this fashion can be found in RS, W3, and GIA's *Lectionary Psalms: Grail/Gelineau.*

✝ SPIRITUALITY

GOSPEL ACCLAMATION
cf. Luke 1:76

℟. Alleluia, alleluia.
You, child, will be called prophet of the Most High,
for you will go before the Lord to prepare his
    way.
℟. Alleluia, alleluia.

Gospel   Luke 1:57-66, 80; L587

When the time arrived for Elizabeth to have
    her child
    she gave birth to a son.
Her neighbors and relatives heard
    that the Lord had shown his
        great mercy toward her,
    and they rejoiced with her.
When they came on the
        eighth day to circum-
        cise the child,
    they were going to call
        him Zechariah after
        his father,
    but his mother said in reply,
    "No. He will be called John."
But they answered her,
    "There is no one among your relatives
        who has this name."
So they made signs, asking his father what
    he wished him to be called.
He asked for a tablet and wrote, "John is
    his name,"
    and all were amazed.
Immediately his mouth was opened, his
    tongue freed,
    and he spoke blessing God.
Then fear came upon all their neighbors,
    and all these matters were discussed
    throughout the hill country of Judea.
All who heard these things took them to
    heart, saying,
    "What, then, will this child be?"
For surely the hand of the Lord was with
    him.

The child grew and became strong in spirit,
    and he was in the desert until the day
    of his manifestation to Israel.

See Appendix A, p. 296, for the other readings.

Reflecting on the Gospel

This solemnity celebrates the birth of John the Baptist; to this end the readings alert us to the wonder of humanity as God's created work (see responsorial psalm). The selection from Isaiah captures two unique aspects of John's birth: "from my mother's womb he gave me my name" and "formed me as his servant from my mother's womb." At a most unexpected time and in a most unexpected way God brought mercy to Elizabeth and Zechariah. Although these two co-operated with God's plan of salvation and gave John the name commanded by the angel, little could they have known that his destiny was more than bringing vindication to an elderly couple who were childless. John's destiny was more than being born under miraculous and wondrous circumstances; his destiny was to herald the Messiah of Israel who would bring salvation.

As wondrous as the events of John's birth may be, his greatness comes not from how he was born but from who he becomes—a "light to the nations," (first reading), a herald of repentance (second reading). His identity as light and herald is revealed and confirmed in his mission. Thus, his greatness derives from his fidelity to his mission: "I am not he. Behold, one is coming after me." It is impossible to speak of John's birth without noting his fidelity to his mission and his relationship to the Messiah.

John the Baptist's birth and mission remind us that God is always working—John is the manifestation of God's working on behalf of all the world. From the most intimate circumstances (formed and nurtured in the womb) to the global ("manifestation to Israel"), God is always knitting together salvation. Ultimately, then, this celebration remembering the nativity of John is really a salvation feast remembering that God reaches "to the ends of the earth."

Why should John's neighbors and relatives have been "amazed" when Zechariah wrote "John is his name"? There was no law that he should be named Zechariah after his father. But the radically new name ("There is no one among your relatives who has this name.") indicates that John is not about Elizabeth and Zechariah but about God, for John is the manifestation of God's favor. John's very birth cannot be separated from the mission he was given: to manifest the Messiah to Israel.

Living the Paschal Mystery

All of us manifest the wonder of humanity and God's gracious gift of creation, because birth is always a miracle. Life is such a gift—its mystery reveals God's desire to be in intimate relationship with creation. All of us, then, share with John the Baptist the cause for rejoicing at birth; through all of us God has shown "great mercy." Like John the Baptist, each of us must be willing to manifest our identity as children belonging to God in our own mission to be a light dispelling the darkness of evil in our world and heralds of Christ's presence among us. Each of us reveals and confirms our own identity in our mission.

We herald the Messiah when we live the paschal mystery. By dying to ourselves for the sake of others we manifest the goodness of God and God's desire that salvation reach the ends of the earth. We also herald the Messiah when our lives witness to the joy of the divine life that God has shared with us. We ourselves become "strong in spirit" when we develop our own relationship with God through prayer and good works. Then, like John, the Lord's hand will be with us too.

Focusing the Gospel

Key words and phrases: What, then, will this child be?; became strong in spirit; manifestation

To the point: As wondrous as the events of John's birth may be, his greatness comes not from how he was born but from who he becomes—God's servant (see first reading), a herald of repentance (second reading). His identity as servant and herald is revealed and confirmed in his mission. Thus, his greatness derives from his fidelity to his mission.

Model Act of Penitence

Presider: Today we celebrate the birth of John the Baptist who announced the coming of the Messiah. We pause now to reflect on how God uses us to announce the presence of Jesus to others . . . [pause]

Lord Jesus, you are a Light to the nations: Lord . . .

Christ Jesus, you are the Messiah heralded by John: Christ . . .

Lord Jesus, you bring salvation and peace to all: Lord . . .

Model Prayer of the Faithful

Presider: Let us pray that we might be faithful to our identity and mission as was John the Baptist.

Response:

Lord, hear our prayer.

Cantor:

we pray to the Lord,

That the church may always be a faithful herald of the presence of Jesus in the world . . . [pause]

That John the Baptist may inspire leaders to herald repentance and peace among the people they serve . . . [pause]

That the lowly may be lifted up and those in need might find mercy . . . [pause]

That each of us here, like John the Baptist, grow strong in Spirit and faithful in mission . . . [pause]

Presider: Merciful God, you knit us wondrously in our mother's womb to praise you for your mighty deeds of salvation: hear these our prayers that one day we might enjoy eternal life with you. We ask this through your Son, Jesus Christ our Lord. **Amen.**

OPENING PRAYER
Let us pray

Pause for silent prayer

God our Father,
you raised up John the Baptist
to prepare a perfect people for Christ the Lord.
Give your Church joy in spirit
and guide those who believe in you
into the way of salvation and peace.

We ask this through our Lord Jesus Christ,
your Son,
who lives and reigns with you and the Holy Spirit,
one God, for ever and ever. **Amen.**

FOR REFLECTION
• Like John I live out my destiny as a herald of Christ's salvation for others whenever I . . .
• Those who have been John the Baptist for me are . . .
• I am aware that, like John the Baptist, the hand of the Lord is with me when . . .

Homily Points

• The current generation of youth is sometimes referred to as the "entitlement" generation—they expect everything they need to be given to them without their putting out effort, as if these things are "owed" them. Many young adults have yet to learn that life is demanding, and meeting these demands means they must grow into identity, adult responsibilities, and purpose.

• Given the miraculous circumstances surrounding John's birth, we would surely think he would have grown up feeling "entitled." Yet John went to the desert to learn his identity and mission and how to be faithful to both. He did not fear taking up the hard work of calling people to repentance and heralding the coming of the Messiah. For this he sacrificed his life. For this he is counted among our most honored prophets.

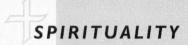

SPIRITUALITY

GOSPEL ACCLAMATION
John 6:51

R⎔. Alleluia, alleluia.
I am the living bread that came down from heaven,
  says the Lord;
whoever eats this bread will live forever.
R⎔. Alleluia, alleluia.

Gospel

John 6:51-58; L167A

Jesus said to the Jewish crowds:
  "I am the living bread that came
    down from heaven;
  whoever eats this bread will
    live forever;
  and the bread that I will give
  is my flesh for the life of the world."

The Jews quarreled among themselves,
  saying,
  "How can this man give us his flesh
    to eat?"
Jesus said to them,
  "Amen, amen, I say to you,
  unless you eat the flesh of the Son of
    Man and drink his blood,
  you do not have life within you.
Whoever eats my flesh and drinks my
    blood
  has eternal life,
  and I will raise him on the last day.
For my flesh is true food,
  and my blood is true drink.
Whoever eats my flesh and drinks my
    blood
  remains in me and I in him.
Just as the living Father sent me
  and I have life because of the Father,
  so also the one who feeds on me
  will have life because of me.
This is the bread that came down from
  heaven.
Unlike your ancestors who ate and still
    died,
  whoever eats this bread will live
    forever."

Reflecting on the Gospel

Change is very difficult for most of us. Even small interruptions in our daily routines can throw us off track. Sometimes the change affects everything about our daily living, as with a move to another city or state, a change of employment, or getting married. Sometimes change affects us personally and radically; for example, stage-four cancer requires aggressive treatment that totally disrupts our lives. But no change we humans can imagine or encounter equals the change proposed by Jesus in this gospel and implied by our celebration of this solemnity.

Jesus invites us to a change that makes a difference in *who we are*. Real change means transformation of self. It means no longer clinging to who we are or acting as we wish but letting go. The real challenge of this solemnity is that we are invited to change. And what is at stake is life everlasting.

Jesus' call to eat his Body and drink his Blood is a call to participate in (see second reading) his very life: "the one who feeds on me will have life because of me." Nourished by and on him, we ourselves become, with him, "the living bread" given unreservedly for others. We *are* the Body of Christ (see second reading) already sharing in eternal life. The real change Jesus invites us to participate in is changing ourselves into who he is: living bread, true food and drink.

In the gospel Jesus *is* the bread that is the *living* bread; this is *all* we need to "live forever." The reasoning is simple enough: by partaking of Jesus' Body and Blood we *become* what we eat—we become the "one body" (second reading) in which we all share. All this is good and inviting. This is the "Holy Communion" that assures us of who we are as baptized Christians—the Body of Christ. This is why Eucharist is (and remains throughout our life) a sacrament of *initiation*: we are constantly being fed on the Bread of Life and constantly drawn more deeply into being who we are—members of the one Body of Christ.

The challenge of this solemnity is to change. We are given the invitation to partake in the Body and Blood of Christ so that we are changed—transformed so that we can more readily embrace Jesus' very identity that brings us everlasting life. This change, however, must be lived. We are to be his life poured out in our everyday good living. We are to give our life—his life!—unreservedly for others. The sacramental eating and drinking of Jesus' Body and Blood is the culmination and ritual manifestation of the self-giving of our everyday living. The change ultimately invited by this solemnity is to be as giving as Jesus is. This is the way to eternal life.

Living the Paschal Mystery

It is far too easy for us to file out of our pews or chairs into the Communion line, receive, return, leave after Mass is over, and get on with our lives. The food and drink that Jesus offers us in this memorial celebration requires of us conscious preparation, deliberate partaking, and ongoing savoring by how we live. Eucharist *changes* us to live more holy and self-giving lives. We can't just put on a costume or cloak of being Jesus' followers; sharing in the Body and Blood of Christ means that we share in Jesus' life of self-giving. This means becoming more aware of others' needs and responding to them; it means doing our everyday tasks well and out of love; it means being honest, just, and forgiving. Eternal life is the fruit of our transformation in Christ. We are to remain in him and are sent to be his presence in the world.

Focusing the Gospel

Key words and phrases: living bread, unless you eat, have life because of me

To the point: Jesus' call to eat his Body and drink his Blood is a call to participate in (see second reading) his very life: "the one who feeds on me will have life because of me." Nourished by and on him, we ourselves become, with him, "the living bread" given unreservedly for others. We *are* the Body of Christ (see second reading) already sharing in eternal life.

Connecting the Gospel

to the first reading: The bread (manna) given the Israelites in the desert is perishable; those who eat perishable bread, themselves perish. In the gospel Jesus gives us living bread—himself; those who eat this bread live forever.

to experience: In our society so much of our food intake is "on the run." The food and drink that Jesus offers requires of us conscious preparation, deliberate partaking, and ongoing savoring by how we live.

Connecting the Responsorial Psalm

to the readings: In the first reading Moses admonishes the Israelites never to forget all that God has done for them. God has freed them from slavery, directed their steps through the desert, taught them patiently to obey the commands of the covenant, and, in the midst of great hunger, fed them with a "food unknown" to their ancestors.

In the gospel Jesus also offers a food previously unknown to any on earth: his very flesh and blood to eat and drink. Jesus' immediate hearers are stunned by his words and become divided and fractious (gospel). But we who believe in his words and choose to partake of his flesh become one with him and with each other (second reading). We participate in the very mystery of Christ and become his Body. We eat the "best of wheat" (psalm) and are born into eternal life.

to psalmist preparation: God fills you "with the best of wheat" (psalm), the very person of Jesus. But God is also nourishing you to participate in the death and resurrection of Jesus (see second reading). What does the gift of the Eucharist mean to you? How can you grow in your willingness to die with Jesus so that you can rise with him?

**ASSEMBLY &
FAITH-SHARING GROUPS**
- What it means to me to "have life because of [Jesus]" is . . .
- Participating in Jesus' Body and Blood challenges me to . . .
- I find it easy to be "living bread" for others when . . . I find it most difficult when . . .

PRESIDERS
The ordinary daily tasks of my ministry are a participation in the Body and Blood of Christ in that . . .

DEACONS
My ministry is "true food and drink" for those in need because . . .

HOSPITALITY MINISTERS
My hospitality points the assembly beyond participation in the eucharistic ritual to the deeper significance of participating in Jesus' dying and rising whenever I . . .

MUSIC MINISTERS
My participation in the Body and Blood of Christ deepens my participation in music ministry by . . . My participation in music ministry prepares me for deeper participation in the Body and the Blood by . . .

ALTAR MINISTERS
My participation in the Body and Blood of Christ directs and motivates my serving others in that . . .

LECTORS
My proclaiming God's word reveals that I live "by every word that comes forth from the mouth of the Lord" (first reading) when I . . .

**EXTRAORDINARY MINISTERS
OF HOLY COMMUNION**
My ministry helps me become more perfectly "living bread" for others whenever I . . .

CELEBRATION

Model Act of Penitence

Presider: Today we celebrate the mystery of our sharing in Jesus' life by partaking of his Body and Blood. Let us prepare ourselves to celebrate well this great mystery . . . [pause]

Lord Jesus, you are the living Bread come down from heaven: Lord . . .

Christ Jesus, you are our eternal Life: Christ . . .

Lord Jesus, you nourish us with your Body and Blood: Lord . . .

Homily Points

• We often use imagery of eating and drinking. For example, we might say we are "starved for affection" or we "thirst for attention" or we "hunger for praise." All of these "hungers" can only be fed by others. Jesus is the Other who promises to feed us with something far more lasting and nourishing—his very self.

• Eating and drinking are so everyday and necessary, it is not surprising that Jesus uses food and drink as a most profound act of giving and most astounding promise. He continually gives us his Body and Blood in the Eucharist as well as through each other (his Body). And for those who eat his Body and drink his Blood, his astounding promise of eternal life is already being fulfilled.

• By eating this Body and drinking this Blood, we take on Jesus' consciousness, his values, his way of living and relating. Like Jesus, we must be "living bread," choosing to lay down our own lives for others. More often than not, this self-giving happens through small, seemingly inconsequential acts of kindness. Paradoxically, this self-giving does not empty us but fills us with the very life (eternal life!) of Jesus.

Model Prayer of the Faithful

Presider: We make our needs known to a loving God who nourishes us with living Bread for life everlasting.

Response:

Lord, hear our prayer.

Cantor:

we pray to the Lord,

That all members of the church, the Body of Christ, continually offer themselves in self-giving for the good of others . . . [pause]

That all peoples of the world have sufficient bread to sustain their lives . . . [pause]

That the hungry be fed, the thirsty receive their fill, and all those in need be nourished by Christ's promise of life . . . [pause]

That we who are gathered here, through our sharing together in the Body and Blood of Christ, grow as a self-giving, eucharistic people . . . [pause]

Presider: Gracious God, you give us your only Son as our Food and Drink: hear these our prayers, that as we share in Jesus' Body and Blood, we also share in his promise of eternal life. We ask this through that same Son, Jesus Christ our Lord. **Amen.**

ALTERNATIVE OPENING PRAYER

Let us pray

[for the willingness to make present in our world the love of Christ shown to us in the eucharist]

Pause for silent prayer

Lord Jesus Christ,
we worship you living among us
in the sacrament of your body and blood.

May we offer to our Father in heaven
a solemn pledge of undivided love.
May we offer our brothers and sisters
a life poured out in loving service of that kingdom
where you live with the Father and the Holy Spirit,
one God, for ever and ever. **Amen.**

FIRST READING

Deut 8:2-3, 14b-16a

Moses said to the people:
"Remember how for forty years now the LORD, your God,
has directed all your journeying in the desert,
so as to test you by affliction
and find out whether or not it was your intention
to keep his commandments.
He therefore let you be afflicted with hunger,
and then fed you with manna,
a food unknown to you and your fathers,
in order to show you that not by bread alone does one live,
but by every word that comes forth from the mouth of the LORD.

"Do not forget the LORD, your God,
who brought you out of the land of Egypt,
that place of slavery;
who guided you through the vast and terrible desert
with its saraph serpents and scorpions,
its parched and waterless ground;
who brought forth water for you from the flinty rock
and fed you in the desert with manna,
a food unknown to your fathers."

RESPONSORIAL PSALM
Ps 147:12-13, 14-15, 19-20

R̸. (12) Praise the Lord, Jerusalem.
or:
R̸. Alleluia.

Glorify the LORD, O Jerusalem;
　praise your God, O Zion.
For he has strengthened the bars of your
　　gates;
　he has blessed your children within you.

R̸. Praise the Lord, Jerusalem.
or:
R̸. Alleluia.

He has granted peace in your borders;
　with the best of wheat he fills you.
He sends forth his command to the earth;
　swiftly runs his word!

R̸. Praise the Lord, Jerusalem.
or:
R̸. Alleluia.

He has proclaimed his word to Jacob,
　his statutes and his ordinances to Israel.
He has not done thus for any other nation;
　his ordinances he has not made known
　　to them. Alleluia.

R̸. Praise the Lord, Jerusalem.
or:
R̸. Alleluia.

SECOND READING
1 Cor 10:16-17

Brothers and sisters:
The cup of blessing that we bless,
　is it not a participation in the blood of
　　Christ?
The bread that we break,
　is it not a participation in the body of
　　Christ?
Because the loaf of bread is one,
　we, though many, are one body,
　for we all partake of the one loaf.

[OPTIONAL] SEQUENCE

See Appendix A, p. 297.

About Liturgy

Communion procession: We usually think of the Communion procession as a pragmatic action that gets us from our place in church to where Communion is distributed and back again. It is that, but so much more.

In most churches the Communion procession moves *forward* in the church; this direction has symbolic meaning. *Forward* is toward the altar, which symbolizes Christ and the messianic banquet. In other words, our moving forward in the Communion procession is a gesture reminding us that in our very lives we are moving forward to that day of our eternal participation in the heavenly banquet—we are moving forward to eternal life. This procession, then, is symbolic of our journey to salvation.

As a moving forward to the messianic table, the Communion procession also might symbolize our whole life's journey—what we do ritually in this moment is what, really, all our Christian living is about—moving toward eternal union with God. To process and receive Communion is already a witness on our part that we wish to change and live our very lives according to God's ways. This symbolizes for us the relationship between celebrating Eucharist and living Eucharist—God nourishes us for the journey to eternal life. To live Eucharist fully we must live our lives as Jesus did—dying to self so that one day we will share in the eternal life promised by the resurrection.

About Liturgical Music

Music appropriate for the Communion procession: This solemnity provides a good opportunity to reflect on the songs we sing during the Communion procession. GIRM indicates that the purpose of the Communion song is to enable the assembly to express their union of spirit through the unity of their voices, to express joy of heart, and to emphasize more clearly the communal nature of the procession (no. 86). This means that songs expressing private devotion, such as "Jesus, My Lord, My God, My All" and "O Jesus, We Adore Thee" are not appropriate at this time. Appropriate Communion songs lead us to reflect on our participation with Christ in the mystery of his death and resurrection, on our shared identity as Body of Christ, and on our call to be the Body of Christ in the world.

GIRM directs that the Communion song is to begin when the presider receives Communion (no. 86). This is because it is the presider who leads us in the procession to the messianic banquet. The song is to continue until everyone in the assembly has received. Singing from the Communion of the presider to the Communion of the last person in line expresses our awareness that everyone present is part of the Body of Christ and our desire that everyone be included. And is this not the deepest meaning of the Eucharist?

JUNE 26, 2011

THE SOLEMNITY OF THE MOST HOLY BODY AND BLOOD OF CHRIST

✠ SPIRITUALITY

GOSPEL ACCLAMATION
Matt 16:18

R⍭. Alleluia, alleluia.
You are Peter and upon this rock I will build my
   church,
and the gates of the netherworld shall not
   prevail against it.
R⍭. Alleluia, alleluia.

Gospel

Matt 16:13-19; L591

When Jesus went into the region
   of Caesarea Philippi
he asked his disciples,
   "Who do people say that the
      Son of Man is?"
They replied, "Some say John the
   Baptist, others Elijah,
still others Jeremiah or one of the
   prophets."
He said to them, "But who do you say
   that I am?"
Simon Peter said in reply,
   "You are the Christ, the Son of the
      living God."
Jesus said to him in reply, "Blessed are
   you, Simon son of Jonah.
For flesh and blood has not revealed
   this to you, but my heavenly
   Father.
And so I say to you, you are Peter,
   and upon this rock I will build my
      Church,
   and the gates of the netherworld
      shall not prevail against it.
I will give you the keys to the Kingdom
   of heaven.
Whatever you bind on earth shall be
   bound in heaven;
   and whatever you loose on earth
      shall be loosed in heaven."

See Appendix A, p. 298, for the other readings.

Reflecting on the Gospel

We usually use the word "dramatic" to indicate events or experiences that are earthshaking, emotionally intense, bolts of lightening in our lives. The stories about Peter and Paul in the first and second readings surely include dramatic events and images. Neither double chains, nor a multitude of guards, nor secure locks, nor impending death, nor any "evil threat" could deter Peter and Paul from pursuing the mission given them by Christ. Peter and Paul were "rocks" of the early church. Today, we are the "rocks" commissioned by that same Christ—strengthened, protected, and helped just as dramatically as they.

To understand how we ourselves are "rocks" of the church, we must understand that God's work is always dramatic. This, because what God is accomplishing in Christ through us is simply beyond our imagination, contrary to the norm, totally extraordinary. Thus, the focus of the readings and this solemnity isn't so much on Peter's and Paul's rescue through supernatural means as it is on what God is doing through them—and continues to do through us.

God does everything necessary to bring salvation to all humankind, even when we face great adversity. The witness of these two great apostles is the bedrock upon which this church is built: upon confession that Jesus is "the living God" and upon self-giving that arises from a deep and abiding faith. The everyday routine of daily discipleship is dramatic in its quiet fidelity and in the ongoing presence of God who is continually acting in our favor.

Just as God acts, so must we act: we, like Paul, must pour out our lives and, like Peter, confess that Jesus is "the Christ, the Son of the living God." Like Peter and Paul we must not shrink from adversity but act boldly because we know that God delivers us from harm so the mission of Christ can be fulfilled. If Peter is the rock and Paul is the libation, then each of us is called to be rock and libation. Christ didn't choose the holiest or smartest or bravest of disciples. He chose ordinary people who would be open to the strength he provides. On this festival we not only honor Peter and Paul but also raise our voices to bring Christ "glory for ever and ever. Amen." This is dramatic, indeed!

Living the Paschal Mystery

Sometimes we really don't understand just how powerfully God acts through us. Most of us won't be imprisoned like Peter or proclaim the gospel in the same way Paul did. But all of us can take their example and love Jesus even when we've betrayed him (sinned). The mystery and drama of this festival is that God always hears when we call out (responsorial psalm) and transforms us so that we too can be worthy disciples. All we need is to be faithful.

Like Peter, we confess that Jesus is "the Christ, the Son of the living God" when we take the time to teach our children their prayers and that God loves them. We confess that Jesus is at the center of our lives when we are consistent in the Gospel values we live and aren't afraid to talk about them with others. Like Paul, we pour out our lives as a libation when we speak out against injustices or when we go the extra mile for someone in need. We are like Paul when we encourage another and compliment another for a task well done. The dramatic reality of being Jesus' followers is that we are "rocks" when we do the little things of our everyday lives well, as Jesus would do them.

Focusing the Gospel

Key words and phrases: Christ, you are, upon this rock, netherworld shall not prevail

To the point: Peter and Paul were "rocks" of the early church. Neither double chains, nor a multitude of guards, nor secure locks, nor impending death, nor any "evil threat" could deter Peter and Paul from pursuing the mission given them by Christ. Today, we are the "rocks" commissioned by that same Christ—strengthened, protected, and helped just as dramatically as they.

Model Act of Penitence

Presider: Today we celebrate the faithfulness of the great apostles Peter and Paul. Let us ask God that we remain faithful to our part in furthering the work of salvation . . . [pause]

   Lord Jesus, you are the Son of Man: Lord . . .

   Christ Jesus, you are the Christ, the Son of the living God: Christ . . .

   Lord Jesus, you called your apostles Peter and Paul to continue your saving work: Lord . . .

Model Prayer of the Faithful

Presider: Through the intercession of Sts. Peter and Paul we raise our prayers to God.

Response:

Lord,   hear   our   prayer.

Cantor:

we pray to   the Lord,

That the church may always be a rock upon which people can find strength to be faithful disciples . . . [pause]

That all peoples have the Good News of salvation preached to them . . . [pause]

That those in any need receive strength, encouragement, and help . . . [pause]

That each of us grow in recognizing the many ways God strengthens, supports, and helps us as we cooperate in the work of salvation . . . [pause]

Presider: Redeeming God, you sent your Son to bring us salvation: through the intercession of Sts. Peter and Paul hear these our prayers and bring us one day to share with them your everlasting life. We ask this through Christ our Lord. **Amen.**

OPENING PRAYER

Let us pray

Pause for silent prayer

God our Father,
today you give us the joy
of celebrating the feast of the apostles Peter
   and Paul.
Through them your Church first received
   the faith.
Keep us true to their teaching.

Grant this through our Lord Jesus Christ,
   your Son,
who lives and reigns with you and the Holy
   Spirit,
one God, for ever and ever. **Amen.**

FOR REFLECTION

- Those who have been rocks of faith for me are . . . I am a rock of faith for others when . . .
- The difficulties I have faced in being faithful to Jesus are . . . What has helped me overcome them is . . .
- I receive strength from God to . . . God protects me in these ways . . . I experience God's help when . . .

Homily Points

- The circumstances of Peter's release from prison and Paul's boast about his missionary work are pretty dramatic. Yet both would acknowledge that whatever they accomplished, they did so with the power and strength of the Spirit of Jesus: "The Lord stood by me and gave me strength" (second reading).

- God is working in, through, and for us to bring about salvation just as dramatically as God did with Peter and Paul. Rather than removing chains and unlocking doors, however, God's help is experienced when someone unexpectedly comes along to support and encourage us; when clear insight about how to get out of a difficult situation moves us in the right direction; when, seemingly totally exhausted from daily demands, we find a reserve of strength to help the children.

✚ SPIRITUALITY

GOSPEL ACCLAMATION
Matt 11:29ab

R⁊. Alleluia, alleluia.
Take my yoke upon you, says the Lord;
and learn from me, for I am meek and humble of
    heart.
R⁊. Alleluia, alleluia.

Gospel

Matt 11:25-30; L170A

At that time Jesus exclaimed:
  "I give praise to you, Father, Lord of
      heaven and earth,
    for although you have hidden these
        things
    from the wise and the learned
      you have revealed them to little ones.
  Yes, Father, such has been your
      gracious will.
  All things have been handed over to me
      by my Father.
  No one knows the Son except the Father,
    and no one knows the Father except
        the Son
    and anyone to whom the Son wishes
        to reveal him.

  "Come to me, all you who labor and are
      burdened,
    and I will give you rest.
  Take my yoke upon you and learn from
      me,
    for I am meek and humble of heart;
    and you will find rest for yourselves.
  For my yoke is easy, and my burden
      light."

See Appendix A, p. 299, for the other readings.

Reflecting on the Gospel

With today's advances in medical science we no longer determine death by the cessation of a heartbeat; in so many cases CPR can restart a stopped heart. Only when someone is brain-dead do we lose all sense of hope that life remains. Yet despite this medical sophistication, we still think of the heart as the center and source of life. The heart symbolizes for us so much more than a muscle that pumps blood throughout our body; it symbolizes healing, "kindness and compassion," mercy and graciousness (see responsorial psalm), but most of all the heart symbolizes love. No wonder the church celebrates a festival in honor of the Sacred Heart of Jesus! We grasp in this festival the mystery of God's gracious love for us (see second reading), the call to belong to God as God's own (see first reading), and the desire of Jesus that we know the Father as intimately as he knows God (gospel).

God "set his heart on" Israel and chose them not because Israel was a large or great nation but simply because God loved them (first reading). Neither does God's love for us depend on our being "wise and . . . learned" but only upon our coming to Jesus in whose "meek and humble" heart we find rest. This gracious will of God in offering us so much love can only be matched by the graciousness of our own will in returning that love. Sometimes we return that love in fidelity; sometimes we don't.

The consequence of choosing infidelity to God's love is destruction (see first reading); the consequence of choosing fidelity to God's love is that we become yoked to Christ (see gospel), who makes the burden of loving both God and one another (see second reading) easier for us. Whether we respond with faithfulness or unfaithfulness, however, God's love remains everlasting and the Sacred Heart's care remains unfailing.

It would seem impossible that we could return love so great as God's; yet by choosing to be yoked to Christ we actually do return God's great love. Being yoked to Christ, we journey in tandem with him. His will becomes more perfectly our own will. His love becomes our love. By loving each other we are loving with the same heart as Jesus. This festival is a pledge that through God's great love and our own returning of that love we "little ones" are raised up to the dignity of sharing in God's very life.

Living the Paschal Mystery

The centenarian had wandered out of his assisted-living facility room into the group of elderly folks gathered around the TV. Very gently one of the staff took him by the elbow, began talking with him, and led him away from the crowd into a small room, ostensibly to show him a picture. There she lovingly pulled up the zipper on his pants, rebuttoned his cockeyed shirt and tucked it in, and made him more presentable. This little scene is an example of God's love being manifested, of the caring heart of that staff person manifesting Jesus' Sacred Heart. Rather than embarrass him, she took him aside. Rather than scold him, she treated him with dignity. Rather than hurry him, she matched her heart to his. We might live the mystery of this festival in so many little ways—all we need do is open our hearts to the needs around us and respond with love, reverence, and care to all God's "little ones."

Focusing the Gospel

Key words and phrases: Take my yoke

To the point: The consequence of choosing infidelity to God's love is destruction (see first reading); the consequence of choosing fidelity to God's love is that we become yoked to Christ (see gospel), who makes the burden of loving both God and one another (see second reading) easier for us. Whether we respond with faithfulness or unfaithfulness, however, God's love remains everlasting and the Sacred Heart's care remains unfailing.

Model Act of Penitence

Presider: We celebrate today the solemnity of the Sacred Heart of Jesus. We pause to open ourselves to such great love . . . [pause]

Lord Jesus, you reveal the Father's great love for us: Lord . . .

Christ Jesus, you love us even to death: Christ . . .

Lord Jesus, your yoke is easy and your burden is light: Lord . . .

Model Prayer of the Faithful

Presider: We make our needs known to the God who loves us beyond compare.

Response:

Lord, hear our prayer.

Cantor:

we pray to the Lord,

That all members of the church open their hearts to all who come to be unburdened . . . [pause]

That all peoples of the world receive God's great love as a pledge of salvation. . . [pause]

That those who are burdened by the cares of life find rest in Jesus . . . [pause]

That each of us here faithfully reach out to others with the gracious heart of Jesus . . . [pause]

Presider: Gracious God, your Son loved us even to dying for us: hear these our prayers that we may grow in our love for you and one day share in your everlasting life. We make our prayer through the loving heart of Jesus Christ our Lord. **Amen.**

OPENING PRAYER

Let us pray

Pause for silent prayer

Father,
we rejoice in the gifts of love
we have received from the heart of Jesus
    your Son.
Open our hearts to share his life
and continue to bless us with his love.

We ask this through our Lord Jesus Christ,
    your Son,
who lives and reigns with you and the Holy
    Spirit,
one God, for ever and ever. **Amen.**

FOR REFLECTION

- Whenever I remember that God has loved me first, set the divine heart on me, and has chosen me (see first reading), I am prompted to . . .
- For me, being yoked to Christ means . . . This is a burden when . . . This is easy when . . .
- I know I am choosing to love God and others when I . . . I know I am not choosing to love when . . .

Homily Points

• We naturally shy away from persons whom we judge to be "coldhearted." We are naturally attracted to persons who have a "warm heart." What would it mean for us if others regarded us as having a "Sacred Heart"?

• Having a "Sacred Heart" means that we choose to be yoked to Christ, loving God and others as Christ loves. This is not a sentimental love that glosses over human infidelity. It is a mature love expressing faithful choices to care for others, rooted in our continued experience of God's unfailing love and care for us.

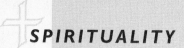

✠ SPIRITUALITY

GOSPEL ACCLAMATION
cf. Matt 11:25

℞. Alleluia, alleluia.
Blessed are you, Father, Lord of heaven and earth;
you have revealed to little ones the
    mysteries of the kingdom.
℞. Alleluia, alleluia.

Gospel

Matt 11:25-30; L100A

At that time Jesus exclaimed:
 "I give praise to you, Father,
     Lord of heaven and earth,
 for although you have hidden
     these things
 from the wise and the learned
 you have revealed them to little ones.
Yes, Father, such has been your
     gracious will.
All things have been handed over to me
     by my Father.
No one knows the Son except the
     Father,
   and no one knows the Father except
     the Son
   and anyone to whom the Son wishes
     to reveal him.

"Come to me, all you who labor and are
     burdened,
   and I will give you rest.
Take my yoke upon you and learn from
     me,
   for I am meek and humble of heart;
   and you will find rest for yourselves.
For my yoke is easy, and my burden
     light."

Reflecting on the Gospel

Sons often imitate their fathers (it's also true for daughters and mothers, but in a different way). What Dad does, Son does. If Dad is out mowing the lawn, Son wants to be riding along with Dad. If Dad is working in the garage, Son wants to be right there pounding away on a piece of wood. If Dad is carrying something heavy, Son grabs a corner and wants to help, to ease the burden. Sometimes we might see the son carrying a much-too-heavy bag of rubbish, pretending he is just as strong as his dad. Someday, though, the son grows up and learns that heavy burdens are not desirable. We don't go through life looking for heavy burdens to shoulder. They all too often weigh us down, break our back, can even break our spirit.

Heavy burdens—either in daily life or in discipleship—are not what God desires for us. God's "gracious will" is that we recognize divine presence coming to us (see first reading) in the person of Jesus. Jesus is not a strong, conquering warrior king but a "meek and humble" Savior. Not in the things of war (first reading: chariots, horses, bows) but in the things of peace (gospel: learning, meekness, praise) does this Savior come. He comes to place on our shoulders not burdens but his own yoke, not a weight or shackle but a freeing relationship of love and care. Burdened we are, yes. But alone, no.

God's gracious will is that God comes to us (first reading) and, in turn, invites us to come to Christ ("Come to me, all you who labor and are burdened"). As meek and humble of heart, Jesus is accessible to us. But if we choose to come to him, we also share the burden that Jesus himself carries. This burden is that of utter fidelity to doing the Father's will; it is self-giving for the sake of others; it is seeing the face of our meek and humble Savior in the face of the dying and needy. Yet Jesus promises that his burden is easy and light. The burden is easy and light because Jesus shares the burden of carrying it with us who are yoked to him. We do not shoulder the yoke or carry the burden alone. All we need do is rest in Jesus.

Living the Paschal Mystery

Sheer force of outside power cannot usually ease life's burdens; but the gentle breeze of a helping hand, a good listener, an unexpected bonus can. We all know how quickly a task can be accomplished when we have help. What a relief it is for someone to come along to help us shovel our car out of a deep snow drift, or stop to share some gas if we run out on the highway, or open a door for us when our arms are full of packages. Light burdens are the result of sharing, of relationships that are dependable and honest, self-giving and loving.

In order to faithfully take up our mission to make God known, we must hand our lives over to Jesus such that the risen One can dwell within us. This means that all our actions must conform to how Jesus himself lived. We must be constantly open to the revelation Jesus makes to us, be open to the many ways Jesus comes to us. The "rest" Jesus offers, then, really carries great demand—to share in Jesus' mission to make known the Father.

To be yoked to Jesus means that we are yoked to his saving mission. This doesn't mean that we all become missionaries! It does mean that we make a concerted effort to live as Jesus did. Only in this way is our burden truly light.

Focusing the Gospel

Key words and phrases: gracious will, Come to me, meek and humble

To the point: Heavy burdens—either in daily life or in discipleship—are not what God desires for us. God's "gracious will" is that we recognize divine presence coming to us (see first reading) in the person of Jesus. Jesus is not a strong, conquering warrior king but a "meek and humble" Savior. He comes to place on our shoulders not burdens but his own yoke, not a weight or shackle but a freeing relationship of love and care. Life will burden us, yes. But we do not carry these burdens alone.

Connecting the Gospel

to the first reading: The meek, savior king for whom Zechariah longs is fulfilled in Jesus, the humble presence of God.

to experience: The world instinctively uses power, weapons, and warfare to achieve freedom and peace. But Jesus teaches us another way: take up his yoke (be disciples) and find true and lasting peace.

Connecting the Responsorial Psalm

to the readings: In this Sunday's gospel Jesus invites us to take up the yoke of revealing to the world who God is. This God whom we are to reveal comes humbly (first reading and gospel) to raise up those who are bowed down (psalm). The commission given us by Jesus, then, does not add burdens to the backs of people but lifts them. Nor does it add burdens to our own shoulders, for the very work, Jesus promises, will bring us rest (gospel).

In a subtle way the responsorial psalm shows us how this promise is fulfilled. By alternating between shouting God's praises (strophes 1 and 3) and proclaiming God's nature (strophes 2 and 4), the psalm indicates that the very work of acknowledging God to the world leads to deeper knowledge of who God is. The very mission itself leads us closer to the God of mercy and compassion. Such work is, then, ultimately freeing and easeful. May we take it up with joy.

to psalmist preparation: In a sense, every time you sing a responsorial psalm you reveal some aspect of God and God's "gracious will" (gospel) to the assembly. How has this ministry led you to know God more deeply? How has it offered you "rest" (gospel)?

**ASSEMBLY &
FAITH-SHARING GROUPS**
- God's gracious will for me is . . . I recognize God's presence when . . .
- What God reveals to me in Jesus is . . . What I reveal to others because I have taken his yoke upon me is . . .
- I come to Jesus when burdened and find rest in him by . . .

PRESIDERS
My ministry embodies Jesus as meek and humble of heart whenever I . . .

DEACONS
When I serve out of humility and meekness, my ministry looks like . . .

HOSPITALITY MINISTERS
My ministry gives rest and lightens the burden of my sisters and brothers when I greet them in this way . . .

MUSIC MINISTERS
Some of the burdens of music ministry are . . . When these burdens weigh heavily Jesus offers me refreshment through . . .

ALTAR MINISTERS
My manner of serving at the altar with gentleness and humility lends a sense of peace to the celebration in that . . .

LECTORS
When I am at peace (see first reading) in my daily living with God and others, my proclamation sounds like . . .

**EXTRAORDINARY MINISTERS
OF HOLY COMMUNION**
I live the Eucharist and in that nurture others to be "meek and humble of heart" whenever I . . .

Model Act of Penitence

Presider: In the gospel today Jesus invites us to come to him because his yoke is easy and his burden is light. We pause now to ready ourselves to respond to his gracious invitation . . . [pause]

Lord Jesus, you are meek and humble of heart: Lord . . .

Christ Jesus, you bring peace and everlasting life: Christ . . .

Lord Jesus, you ease our burdens and grant us rest: Lord . . .

Homily Points

• Our heaviest burdens are not measured in pounds like those bags full of groceries we lug into the house. Rather, our heaviest burdens are measured in emotional and spiritual toll that wears us down and bends us over, and sometimes even breaks our spirit. For example, we shoulder the burden of loss at the death of a loved one, of ill health, of a missing child, of impending or real war, of insecurity in the future with waning savings, of the pain of broken or strained relationships, of feeling unforgiven, of discouragement in the work we do.

• Jesus does not promise to remove our burdens. What he does promise is to always remain present with us. The burdens are not eased because the problems go away; the burdens become light because Jesus is always with us, helping us carry them.

• Jesus comes to us as a Person who knows what it means to carry the burdens of human living. We encounter him in the person who understands the weight we are carrying and reaches out to us, in the new insight that comes from taking some time alone to be silent, in the meekness and humility that bring us to let go of our tendency to rugged individualism. Burdened we are, yes. But alone, no.

Model Prayer of the Faithful

Presider: We make our needs known to a loving God who wills to ease our burdens.

Response:

Lord, hear our prayer.

Cantor:

we pray to the Lord,

That all members of the church reach out with care and love toward those who are heavy-burdened . . . [pause]

That our nation conduct its affairs with meekness, humility, and justice and promote peace in the world . . . [pause]

That those who are at the breaking point in carrying the burdens of life find ease and rest . . . [pause]

That each of us gladly put on the yoke binding us to Christ and one another . . . [pause]

Presider: Gracious God, you sent your meek and humble Son to share our burdens: hear these our prayers that one day we might enjoy the fullness of life with you. We ask this through that same Son, Jesus Christ our Lord. **Amen.**

Let us pray

Pause for silent prayer

Father,
in the rising of your Son
death gives birth to new life.
The sufferings he endured restored hope
    to a fallen world.
Let sin never ensnare us
with empty promises of passing joy.
Make us one with you always,
so that our joy may be holy,
and our love may give life.

We ask this through Christ our Lord.
    Amen.

FIRST READING
Zech 9:9-10

Thus says the LORD:
Rejoice heartily, O daughter Zion,
    shout for joy, O daughter Jerusalem!
See, your king shall come to you;
    a just savior is he,
meek, and riding on an ass,
    on a colt, the foal of an ass.
He shall banish the chariot from Ephraim,
    and the horse from Jerusalem;
the warrior's bow shall be banished,
    and he shall proclaim peace to the
        nations.
His dominion shall be from sea to sea,
    and from the River to the ends of the
        earth.

RESPONSORIAL PSALM
Ps 145:1-2, 8-9, 10-11, 13-14

℟. (cf. 1) I will praise your name forever,
my king and my God.
    or:
℟. Alleluia.

I will extol you, O my God and King,
    and I will bless your name forever and
        ever.
Every day will I bless you,
    and I will praise your name forever and
        ever.

℟. I will praise your name forever, my
king and my God.
    or:
℟. Alleluia.

The LORD is gracious and merciful,
  slow to anger and of great kindness.
The LORD is good to all
  and compassionate toward all his
  works.

R̸. I will praise your name forever, my
king and my God.
  or:
R̸. Alleluia.

Let all your works give you thanks, O
  LORD,
  and let your faithful ones bless you.
Let them discourse of the glory of your
  kingdom
  and speak of your might.

R̸. I will praise your name forever, my
king and my God.
  or:
R̸. Alleluia.

The LORD is faithful in all his words
  and holy in all his works.
The LORD lifts up all who are falling
  and raises up all who are bowed down.

R̸. I will praise your name forever, my
king and my God.
  or:
R̸. Alleluia.

SECOND READING
Rom 8:9, 11-13

Brothers and sisters:
You are not in the flesh;
  on the contrary, you are in the spirit,
  if only the Spirit of God dwells in you.
Whoever does not have the Spirit of Christ
  does not belong to him.
If the Spirit of the one who raised Jesus
  from the dead dwells in you,
  the one who raised Christ from the dead
  will give life to your mortal bodies also,
  through his Spirit that dwells in you.
Consequently, brothers and sisters,
  we are not debtors to the flesh,
  to live according to the flesh.
For if you live according to the flesh, you
  will die,
  but if by the Spirit you put to death the
  deeds of the body,
  you will live.

✝ CATECHESIS

About Liturgy

Monday is July 4th: It would be inappropriate to turn Sunday's Mass into a patriotic celebration in lieu of the Monday holiday. At the same time, it would be remiss not to include something of the holiday in the Mass. A fifth intention might be added at the prayer of the faithful. A model would be: "That our great nation share its wealth and resources with all those heavily burdened by poverty, injustices, or oppression."

Repeated gospel—Lectionary hermeneutic: This year it just so happens that the solemnity of the Sacred Heart falls on the Friday before this Fourteenth Sunday in Ordinary Time. This means that exactly the same gospel is proclaimed three days apart. Since most of the Sunday assembly would not have been at Mass on Friday, this repetition is probably not even noted. However, this year it does give us an opportunity to comment on what is called a "Lectionary hermeneutic."

The schema of readings in the Lectionary have a marvelous order and purpose to them. The riches of the Lectionary are more clearly shown when the readings are interpreted (the word "hermeneutic" means the art of interpretation) according to pairings with other readings, the festival being celebrated, where we are in the liturgical year. In the case of Friday's and Sunday's gospel, each is paired with a very different first reading. Friday's pairing and festival led us to reflect on and interpret God's great love for us, to pay attention to the tenderness of the Sacred Heart, to pay attention to our response in love. Sunday's pairing of the gospel with first reading leads us to focus more specifically on the meekness and humility of Jesus, God's enduring presence, and how that presence lightens all our burdens.

About Liturgical Music

Music suggestions: "Come to Me, O Weary Traveler" [G2, GC, GC2, JS2, RS] expresses the content of this Sunday's gospel with great effectiveness. The text captures the sensitivity of Jesus to our needs as tired disciples, and the tune pulls us into the very restfulness Jesus promises. An effective way to sing it would be to have a cantor sing verse 1, everyone join in at verse 2, choir add SATB at verse 3, then everyone sing verse 4 (still SATB) softly and a cappella. The hymn is appropriate for either the preparation of the gifts or Communion. If used during Communion, the song can be lengthened by interspersing instrumental only verses, or choir only verses, singing the SATB arrangement on a soft "ooo."

Another good choice for the Communion procession is Delores Dufner's "Come to Me/Come to Me, All Pilgrims Thirsty" [JS2, SS, WC]. Because this is a verse-refrain piece in which the verses express the words of Jesus and the refrain speaks our response, the hymn needs to be sung with cantor or choir doing the verses and the assembly singing only the refrain.

A great temptation this Sunday will be to sing patriotic songs because of the 4th of July on Monday, but we need to remember that liturgy is a celebration of the universal church, not of our national identity. The patriotic songs are best reserved for the civic prayer services and other social gatherings held this weekend.

✝ SPIRITUALITY

GOSPEL ACCLAMATION

R⁊. Alleluia, alleluia.
The seed is the word of God, Christ is the sower.
All who come to him will have life forever.
R⁊. Alleluia, alleluia.

Gospel   Matt 13:1-23; L103A

On that day, Jesus went out of the
    house and sat down by the sea.
Such large crowds gathered around
    him
    that he got into a boat and sat
        down,
    and the whole crowd stood along
        the shore.
And he spoke to them at length in
    parables, saying:
"A sower went out to sow.
And as he sowed, some seed fell on the
    path,
    and birds came and ate it up.
Some fell on rocky ground, where it had
    little soil.
It sprang up at once because the soil was
    not deep,
    and when the sun rose it was scorched,
    and it withered for lack of roots.
Some seed fell among thorns, and the thorns
    grew up and choked it.
But some seed fell on rich soil, and
    produced fruit,
    a hundred or sixty or thirtyfold.
Whoever has ears ought to hear."

The disciples approached him and said,
    "Why do you speak to them in parables?"
He said to them in reply,
    "Because knowledge of the mysteries of
        the kingdom of heaven
    has been granted to you, but to them it
        has not been granted.
To anyone who has, more will be given and
    he will grow rich;
    from anyone who has not, even what he
        has will be taken away.
This is why I speak to them in parables,
    because
    *they look but do not see and hear but do
        not listen or understand.*

Continued in Appendix A, p. 300.

Continued in Appendix A, p. 300.

Reflecting on the Gospel

We pragmatic Americans tend to be people who do not live with abandon. Although we are often a wasteful people (consider, for example, the amount of food thrown away in school cafeterias and restaurants!), we tend to be measured and calculated in many areas of our lives. We are married to our day planners, spreadsheets, and GPS devices. The parable in this Sunday's gospel is about sowing seed. Farmers today would simply shake their heads incredulously at the farmer in the gospel. It's kind of stupid for the sower to throw seed on soil that clearly will not produce much! The parable mentions four kinds of soil, but only the last, that which is "rich," bears fruit. Why sow three-fourths of the seed on nonproductive soil? How wasteful!

The amazing surprise of this parable is that even if only one-fourth of the seed that is sown produces fruit, that one-fourth still produces much! The sower can sow with abandon because the harvest will be abundant—this is assured by God! God's seed, however, is not wheat or corn. The harvest cannot be measured by bushels. God's seed does not produce a harvest that can be eaten. God's seed is of another kind and produces a harvest that nourishes in even more lavish ways than food made from human hands. As the first reading from Isaiah reminds us, God's word is likened to a seed, and this word "goes forth . . . achieving the end for which [God] sent it."

Because God's word challenges us to conform ourselves more perfectly to God's will, we tend to close our ears to hearing it and to limit our response to living it. Yes, there is resistance to God's word, and only God can overcome it. God sows the seed (word) lavishly and with abandon. God's desire that the divine word be heard and lived (bear fruit) is so great that God is willing to "waste" three-fourths in order that at least one-fourth be heard and evoke response from us. Now we are to take up God's word and keep sowing. Now we are to scatter God's word with abandon and with hope. Even though only a small portion of what is sown bears fruit, God nonetheless assures an abundant harvest.

Living the Paschal Mystery

Only seed that sinks into rich soil can produce fruit. Our daily gospel living is about tilling and fertilizing and constantly preparing the "soil" of our hearts so that we can receive God's word and nurture it to bear fruit. We must let God's word sink deep within us so that it can bear fruit in our daily living, "achieving the end for which [God] sent it"!

Most of us hear God's word proclaimed primarily during the Liturgy of the Word at Mass on Sundays. It is naive to think that we can go to Mass cold, without having prepared the readings, and be attuned enough to God's word to hear and remember the message well enough to live it. One way to deepen our gospel living is to take quality time each week—alone or with others—to sit with God's word and become attuned to the message. This is how we cultivate our hearts to hear God's word, so it is not wasted on barren hearts.

We also hear God's word through the words of others. A challenging remark that moves us to new action on behalf of others, a critical remark that causes us to look at our own behavior and choices, a kind remark that brings us joy are all ways God's word comes to us, and ways we can sow the seed of God's word in the hearts of others.

Focusing the Gospel

Key words and phrases: Sow, some seed fell, some fell, some seed fell, some seed fell, yields a hundred or sixty or thirtyfold

To the point: There is resistance to God's word that only God can overcome. God sows the seed (word) lavishly and with abandon. Now we are to keep sowing. Now we are to scatter God's word with abandon and with hope. Even though only a small portion of what is sown bears fruit, God nonetheless assures an abundant harvest.

Connecting the Gospel

to the first reading: The promise God makes through Isaiah is that God's word will achieve "the end for which [God] sent it." Thus both the first reading and gospel promise that the harvest will be fruitful and abundant.

to experience: We are so inundated with words—for example, multisectioned daily newspapers, twenty-four-hour radio and TV, internet, text messaging—that we can easily tune them out so they actually lose their impact. We cannot let this happen with God's word, but we must keep ourselves attuned to the varied ways God's word comes to us.

Connecting the Responsorial Psalm

to the readings: In the first reading Isaiah compares God's word to the rain and snow that come down from heaven. Both inevitably accomplish the purpose for which they are sent. In the parable of the sower and the seed, however, we hear that God's word does not always achieve its goal (gospel). God's plan can be blocked by the circumstances of human living and the choices of human hearts.

Bridging the contradiction between these two readings is the confidence of Psalm 65. We must be honest about the resistance to God's word that is ever present within the world and within our own hearts, but we need not lose hope because of it. The psalm assures us that no matter how slow we are to receive the seed, how reticent to let it grow, how distracted from the task, God who has prepared both the grain and the land, "softening it with showers, blessing its yield," will bring what has been planted to abundant harvest. We have only to let God do this work, and to join all the world's fields and valleys in shouting for joy over God's indomitable power.

to psalmist preparation: While the parable of the sower and the seed confronts you with the very real possibility of resisting God's word and work, the psalm turns your focus away from self to the graciousness of God who continuously waters and tills the earth and makes it fruitful. No matter what resistance you put up against the word of God, God persists in working the "land" of your heart until you yield to receive what God desires to plant there. What "tilling" do you need to ask God to do? What fruitfulness can you already thank God for?

ASSEMBLY & FAITH-SHARING GROUPS
- What helps me to be rich soil for God's word is . . .
- In my life the harvest of attending to God's word has been . . .
- The ways I sow God's word abundantly are . . . with abandon are . . .

PRESIDERS
As presider, I receive the word of God from . . . I sow the word of God by . . .

DEACONS
My ministry prepares soil to receive God's word when . . . My ministry attends to God's seed once planted when . . .

HOSPITALITY MINISTERS
My hospitality tills the soil of the assembly, making it ready for God's seed in that . . .

MUSIC MINISTERS
My music ministry reveals how God's word is bearing fruit in me when . . . in the assembly when . . .

ALTAR MINISTERS
Serving cultivates in me a rich soil to receive God's word when . . .

LECTORS
I have witnessed my proclamation of the word "achieving the end for which [God] sent it" (first reading) when . . .

EXTRAORDINARY MINISTERS OF HOLY COMMUNION
I receive the Eucharist fruitfully when I . . . My distribution is an extravagant sowing of the Eucharist when I . . .

Model Act of Penitence

Presider: God sows the seed of the divine word so that salvation can spread to the ends of the earth. Let us pause to open our hearts to receive fruitfully God's word . . . [pause]

Lord Jesus, you are the Word of God: Lord . . .

Christ Jesus, you teach us to hear God's word and live it: Christ . . .

Lord Jesus, you bless us with knowledge and understanding of your ways: Lord . . .

Homily Points

• A strange example of seed growing in a most unpredictable place was once reported in the news. Operating on a man's lung, surgeons were amazed to find, not a tumor, but a three-inch fir tree! Somewhere, somehow this man had apparently inhaled a seed and in the deep, dark, moist environment of his lung this seed took hold and grew. Had this sprouted seed been left to grow, it might ultimately have killed the man. The seed of God's word, however, never kills but always gives life.

• The seed of God's word also takes root in unpredictable places—in both the faithful who hear it and in the unfaithful who reject it. In those who give the seed shelter and nourishment, God produces an unexpectedly abundant harvest: new and lasting life.

• God's word is sown in the proclamation of the word at liturgy, to be sure. But it also is sown in other and sometimes most unpredictable places and ways. God's word is sown at the family dinner table where the day's joys and challenges are shared. God's word is sown in extending expressions of endearment, in expressing understanding and forgiveness, in speaking encouragement, in challenging injustice. In all these ways, through us, God's word achieves the end for which it was sent.

Model Prayer of the Faithful

Presider: Our God is lavish and patient, and will hear these needs that we present in prayer.

Response:

Lord, hear our prayer.

Cantor:

we pray to the Lord,

That the church sow the word of God with lavishness and hope in God's abundant harvest . . . [pause]

That all peoples of the world be fertile soil in which the seed of God's word takes root and bears fruit . . . [pause]

That those with stony hearts might open themselves to hear the good news of God's word of salvation . . . [pause]

That each of us here scatter God's word with conviction and abandon . . . [pause]

Presider: Generous and patient God, you sent your Son as Word made flesh to take root in our hearts: hear these our prayers that one day we may live with you for ever and ever. **Amen**.

Let us pray

Pause for silent prayer

God our Father,
your light of truth
guides us to the way of Christ.
May all who follow him
reject what is contrary to the gospel.

We ask this through our Lord Jesus Christ,
    your Son,
who lives and reigns with you and the
    Holy Spirit,
one God, for ever and ever. **Amen**.

FIRST READING
Isa 55:10-11

Thus says the LORD:
Just as from the heavens
    the rain and snow come down
and do not return there
    till they have watered the earth,
    making it fertile and fruitful,
giving seed to the one who sows
    and bread to the one who eats,
so shall my word be
    that goes forth from my mouth;
my word shall not return to me void,
    but shall do my will,
    achieving the end for which I sent it.

RESPONSORIAL PSALM
Ps 65:10, 11, 12-13, 14

R̸. (Luke 8:8) The seed that falls on good ground will yield a fruitful harvest.

You have visited the land and watered it;
    greatly have you enriched it.
God's watercourses are filled;
    you have prepared the grain.

R̸. The seed that falls on good ground will yield a fruitful harvest.

Thus have you prepared the land:
        drenching its furrows,
    breaking up its clods,
softening it with showers,
    blessing its yield.

R̸. The seed that falls on good ground will yield a fruitful harvest.

You have crowned the year with your
        bounty,
    and your paths overflow with a rich
        harvest;
the untilled meadows overflow with it,
    and rejoicing clothes the hills.

R̸. The seed that falls on good ground will yield a fruitful harvest.

The fields are garmented with flocks
    and the valleys blanketed with grain.
    They shout and sing for joy.

R̸. The seed that falls on good ground will yield a fruitful harvest.

SECOND READING
Rom 8:18-23

Brothers and sisters:
I consider that the sufferings of this
        present time are as nothing
    compared with the glory to be revealed
        for us.
For creation awaits with eager expectation
    the revelation of the children of God;
    for creation was made subject to futility,
    not of its own accord but because of the
        one who subjected it,
    in hope that creation itself
    would be set free from slavery to
        corruption
    and share in the glorious freedom of the
        children of God.
We know that all creation is groaning in
        labor pains even until now;
    and not only that, but we ourselves,
    who have the firstfruits of the Spirit,
    we also groan within ourselves
    as we wait for adoption, the redemption
        of our bodies.

About Liturgy

Interpreting Scriptures: This Sunday's gospel is one example of a time when Jesus gives an interpretation of a parable. His interpretation at the end of the long form of the gospel is part of the conversation he has with his disciples about who is able to hear Jesus' message. In this interpretive context, then, Jesus' explanation of the parable centers around who can or cannot hear.

Although an interpretation of the parable is actually given in the gospel itself, interpreting Scripture need not be strictly limited to such explanations, which more likely arose from the community where the gospel text was written than from the mouth of Jesus himself. Scripture truly is the word of God, yet it always has layers and layers of meaning, and this is why year after year we keep coming back to these Scripture passages.

The nature of Jesus' parables is to be evocative. Parables have many layers of meaning, which is why we can come back to them year after year and still learn from them. While we surely do not discount the interpretation given in the gospels for some of Jesus' parables, we must keep in mind that the cultural and community context that gave rise to that particular interpretation is of another time and people. These interpretations might tweak our imaginations to think in other ways about the word Jesus is giving us.

Consequently, there are different, valid approaches to understanding the gospel parables. While acknowledging the interpretation of the parable given by the early community where the gospel text arose, the Lectionary structure suggests that this is not the only valid interpretation and application of the parable. Indeed, all the interpretations together keep opening up new meanings of God's word for us so that it can achieve "the end for which [God] sent it" (first reading).

About Liturgical Music

Music suggestions: An excellent prelude piece for the choir this Sunday would be "A Sower Came from Ancient Hills" [GIA G-5074]. Herman Stuempfle's insightful text identifies the seed as Christ himself cast upon the stony ground of Calvary where he dies to rise in superabundant harvest.

The opening verse of "Word of God, Come Down on Earth" [CBW3, RS, W3, WC] is particularly relevant for this Sunday: "Word of God, come down on earth, living rain from heav'n descending; Touch our hearts and bring to birth Faith and hope and love unending. Word almighty, we revere you; Word made flesh, we long to hear you." The strong tune suggests its appropriateness for the entrance procession. "The Word Is in Your Heart" [G2, GC] would work well as a quiet song during the preparation of the gifts. An appropriate Communion song would be "Seed, Scattered and Sown" [BB, CBW3, G2, GC, GC2, JS2, OFUV, RS]. Ricky Manalo's "Many and Great" [BB] uses the imagery of seeds and wheat and would also be well suited for Communion. A fitting recessional song would be "Sent Forth by God's Blessing" [BB, CBW3, JS2, OFUV, PMB, WC, WS], which uses the image of the seed of God's teaching blossoming into action in our lives (verse 1).

JULY 10, 2011
FIFTEENTH SUNDAY IN ORDINARY TIME

✝ SPIRITUALITY

GOSPEL ACCLAMATION
cf. Matt 11:25

℟. Alleluia, alleluia.
Blessed are you, Father, Lord of heaven and
      earth;
you have revealed to little ones the
      mysteries of the kingdom.
℟. Alleluia, alleluia.

Gospel   Matt 13:24-43; L106A

Jesus proposed another parable to
      the crowds, saying:
"The kingdom of heaven may be
      likened
   to a man who sowed good seed in
      his field.
While everyone was asleep his
      enemy came
   and sowed weeds all through the
      wheat, and then went off.
When the crop grew and bore fruit,
      the weeds appeared as well.
The slaves of the householder came to
      him and said,
   'Master, did you not sow good seed in
      your field?
Where have the weeds come from?'
He answered, 'An enemy has done this.'
His slaves said to him,
   'Do you want us to go and pull them
      up?'
He replied, 'No, if you pull up the weeds
   you might uproot the wheat along with
      them.
Let them grow together until harvest;
   then at harvest time I will say to the
      harvesters,
   "First collect the weeds and tie them in
      bundles for burning;
   but gather the wheat into my barn."'"

He proposed another parable to them.
"The kingdom of heaven is like a mustard
      seed
   that a person took and sowed in a field.
It is the smallest of all the seeds,
   yet when full-grown it is the largest of
      plants.

Continued in Appendix A, p. 300.

Reflecting on the Gospel

Patience is, indeed, a virtue. We admire parents who seemingly have endless patience with their two-year-old's constant "No!" We respect supervisors who are patient with mistakes while a trainee is learning. We imitate good teachers who patiently coax their students to stretch their learning curve and achieve all their talent allows. Patience allows us to tolerate self-willfulness or mistakes or lack of understanding even as we encourage growth, goodness, and wisdom. Patience is a virtue that enables us to wait for the maturing of persons and abilities and ideas.

The "kingdom of heaven" is continually being established by a God who is amazingly patient. This Sunday's three gospel parables illustrate this well. In the first, God exercises patience until the wheat grows enough so the weeds can be pulled without destroying the wheat. In the second, God waits patiently until the tiny seed grows into a large enough plant to welcome the birds of the sky. In the third, God patiently allows time for the yeast to work its leavening effect on the dough. God has all the patience in the world, and so must we if we are truly to be God's servants.

Jesus describes the kingdom of heaven as having room for growth and maturation: there are weeds among the wheat, a bush is in growth, the dough is rising. The wheat, bush, and dough are not finished products; it takes time and patience to bring forth the desired good end. In this present age we are to live with patience and confident assurance that the kingdom of heaven will become fully manifest: there will be a harvest, there will be a large bush, there will be a loaf of bread. The mystery of the kingdom, of course, is that while the end is guaranteed—life will come forth—all of us must live faithfully and work diligently if we wish to reap the fruits of God's patience—life everlasting. In the meantime, we must contend with the temptations (weeds: evils) that keep us from being faithful.

In the end it is less important to understand God's kingdom with our minds than it is to live according to the values of the kingdom. The first reading lists some of these values for us: the children of the kingdom are to live like the Master of the kingdom—showing the kind of care, leniency, clemency, justice, and kindness that instill in others hope rather than despair, fecundity rather than barrenness, the desire to do good rather than evil. We can come confidently to the day of judgment by being good disciples of the Master. As we grow in our discipleship, it is patience and hope in the final outcome that sustains us so that in the end we will be counted among the "righteous [who] shine like the sun."

Living the Paschal Mystery

The impulse of the first parable is to pull the weeds. The impulse during our whole Christian living is to be impatient with ourselves as we grow in our discipleship. Part of living the paschal mystery is to be patient with ourselves, especially when we have failed. The mercy, forgiveness, leniency, justice, and patience of God encourage repentance (see first reading). Even our mistakes are ways that we have "ears . . . to hear" and learn better the ways of God. God's final judgment comes at the "end of the age" when, hopefully, all of us have lived the ways of patience and faithfulness and have borne fruit.

Focusing the Gospel

Key words and phrases: kingdom of heaven; weeds all through the wheat
. . . if you pull; smallest of all the seeds . . . full-grown; yeast . . . whole batch
was leavened

To the point: The "kingdom of heaven" is continually being established by a
God who is amazingly patient. This Sunday's three gospel parables illustrate
this well. In the first, God exercises patience until the wheat grows enough so
the weeds can be pulled without destroying the wheat. In the second, God waits
patiently until the tiny seed grows into a large enough plant to welcome the
birds of the sky. In the third, God patiently allows time for the yeast to work
its leavening effect on the dough. God has all the patience in the world, and so
must we if we are truly to be God's servants.

Connecting the Gospel

to the first reading: Children of the kingdom are to be like the Master of the
kingdom. Our patience must show the same care, leniency, clemency, justice,
kindness, and hope.

to experience: We tend to be impatient for immediate outcomes. However,
the length and height and breadth and richness of the "kingdom of heaven"
cannot be rushed, immediately at hand, or under our control.

Connecting the Responsorial Psalm

to the readings: In these verses from Psalm 86 we beg God to listen to our
pleading and give us strength. The parables told by Jesus in the gospel make
clear the cause of our begging: alongside the good God has planted in the
church and the world, so much bad exists; so many starts toward the coming of
the kingdom are just insignificant, tiny seeds; a little yeast leavens a measure
of flour, but the work of kneading must first be done if the bread is to rise. We
need the grace of patience and persistence. And we need the kindness of God,
this God who understands how slow growth can be (gospel) and who leaves
needed room for repentance (first reading). In singing this psalm we ask this
"good and forgiving" God (psalm refrain) to give us a share in the divine leniency, patience, and strength.

to psalmist preparation: As you prepare to sing this responsorial psalm,
you might talk with God about your own longing for the coming of the kingdom and your struggles with its delay. When do you feel discouraged? Who or
what helps you maintain hope?

**ASSEMBLY &
FAITH-SHARING GROUPS**
- I am patient like God when . . . I am im-
patient unlike God when . . .
- The challenge these parables present for
the way I live every day is . . .
- My daily life embodies the values of the
Master of the kingdom (e.g., care, leni-
ency, clemency, justice, kindness, and
hope; see first reading) in that . . .

PRESIDERS
What makes me hopeful and patient about
the growth of the wheat in the midst of the
weeds is . . .

DEACONS
My ministry inspires others to remain
patient as they labor to produce the fruitfulness of God's kingdom when . . .

HOSPITALITY MINISTERS
Good hospitality within a community is like
yeast in flour because . . .

MUSIC MINISTERS
In my music ministry one way I have seen
the kingdom of heaven come is . . . I experience the need to grow in patience and
compassion as I wait for this kingdom to
come when . . .

ALTAR MINISTERS
Serving others points to the hidden presence
and activity of the kingdom because . . .

LECTORS
When I am patient with myself in living
God's word, my proclamation looks like . . .

**EXTRAORDINARY MINISTERS
OF HOLY COMMUNION**
My manner of distributing Holy Communion
is a leaven bringing hope and life when . . .

Model Act of Penitence

Presider: In today's gospel we hear about God's amazing patience with us in establishing the kingdom of heaven. Let us open our hearts to God's presence and patience . . . [pause]

Lord Jesus, you are the Master encouraging patience in your followers: Lord . . .

Christ Jesus, you are the Sower fostering us to full growth: Christ . . .

Lord Jesus, you are the Leaven raising us to new life: Lord . . .

Homily Points

• We twenty-first century Americans would not have done well with the centuries it took medieval people to build their magnificent cathedrals. But had these people rushed the project, the buildings would not be standing today in all their glory. Worthwhile and lasting things take time and cannot be rushed.

• The kingdom of heaven is guaranteed by the God who patiently cultivates even when the field produces weeds as well as wheat, the God who confidently plants even when the seed seems inconsequential, the God who capably raises batches of bread from a mere bit of yeast. This is a God who knows that worthwhile and everlasting things take time and cannot be rushed.

• If God is patient with wheat and seed and leaven, how much more is God patient with us! God's patience in teasing goodness out of us is how the kingdom of heaven grows among us. Being patient with testy children and helping them be good, being patient trying to teach another some skill, being patient with one another's foibles and weaknesses are all ways God's patience is present through us. God's patience abounds, as does the kingdom of heaven.

Model Prayer of the Faithful

Presider: We present our needs to a patient God who always hears us.

Response:

Cantor:

That the church extend patience and understanding to all those who are seeking the kingdom of heaven . . . [pause]

That leaders of nations patiently teach those they govern virtuous living and model for them life-giving values . . . [pause]

That all those without the necessities of life receive all they need through the patient goodness of those working for the coming of the kingdom . . . [pause]

That each of us here patiently persevere in the fruitfulness of our own good living . . . [pause]

Presider: Patient God, you sent your Son to teach us how to live: hear these our prayers that one day we might be judged worthy to share everlasting life with you. We ask this through Christ our Lord. **Amen.**

RESPONSORIAL PSALM

Ps 86:5-6, 9-10, 15-16

R̸. (5a) Lord, you are good and forgiving.

You, O Lᴏʀᴅ, are good and forgiving,
    abounding in kindness to all who call
        upon you.
Hearken, O Lᴏʀᴅ, to my prayer
    and attend to the sound of my pleading.

R̸. Lord, you are good and forgiving.

All the nations you have made shall come
    and worship you, O Lᴏʀᴅ,
    and glorify your name.
For you are great, and you do wondrous
        deeds;
    you alone are God.

R̸. Lord, you are good and forgiving.

You, O Lᴏʀᴅ, are a God merciful and
        gracious,
    slow to anger, abounding in kindness
        and fidelity.
Turn toward me, and have pity on me;
    give your strength to your servant.

R̸. Lord, you are good and forgiving.

SECOND READING

Rom 8:26-27

Brothers and sisters:
The Spirit comes to the aid of our
        weakness;
    for we do not know how to pray as we
        ought,
    but the Spirit himself intercedes with
        inexpressible groanings.
And the one who searches hearts
    knows what is the intention of the
        Spirit,
    because he intercedes for the holy ones
    according to God's will.

About Liturgy

Liturgical catechesis takes patience: Like the slaves in the gospel, most of us have little patience when it comes to learning more about liturgy so we can celebrate it better. Sometimes too much change too fast confuses us and we have a hard time entering wholeheartedly into liturgy. Sometimes we don't have the patience to discipline ourselves to read bulletin inserts or buy and read a good book on liturgy. Sometimes we don't agree with what is being said or taught, and so we just don't listen, or we listen and then promptly forget what we've learned. The point is that something as important as liturgy requires constant learning, constant updating, and all this takes a great deal of patience!

One good exercise that each of us might undertake is to resolve once a month to learn something new about liturgy. This can be something as simple as coming to Mass a little early or staying a little longer to read slowly and thoughtfully through one of the hymn texts or one of the eucharistic prayers. It might be something as challenging as signing up for a series of classes on the liturgy. The real trick to updating ourselves liturgically is not to bite off too much but be patient with ourselves. Take one step at a time and it is amazing how fruitful this can be. The challenge is to take that first step!

About Liturgical Music

Distinguishing liturgical from devotional songs, part 1: Since hymn books are used for more than liturgy, most of them contain devotional as well as liturgical songs. Although uplifting and prayerful, devotional hymns are not appropriate for liturgy because they cannot support the kind of prayer that the liturgy requires, prayer that leads us to our communal identity as Body of Christ and helps us surrender to the liturgy's enactment of the paschal mystery.

How do we distinguish liturgical hymn texts from devotional ones? We need to begin by considering the difference between devotional and liturgical prayer itself. Both are necessary for full Christian living, but they differ in their focus. Devotional prayer centers on our immediate needs and concerns and adapts as these needs change. Liturgical prayer, on the other hand, focuses on the rhythm of the paschal mystery as it unfolds in the life of the church throughout the liturgical year. Liturgical prayer, then, does not change with our needs but draws us beyond them to the broader context of the mystery of Christ dying and rising within us.

JULY 17, 2011
SIXTEENTH SUNDAY
IN ORDINARY TIME

✠ SPIRITUALITY

GOSPEL ACCLAMATION
cf. Matt 11:25

℞. Alleluia, alleluia.
Blessed are you, Father, Lord of heaven and earth;
you have revealed to little ones the mysteries of
the kingdom.
℞. Alleluia, alleluia.

Gospel   Matt 13:44-52; L109A

Jesus said to his disciples:
"The kingdom of heaven is like a
treasure buried in a field,
which a person finds and
hides again,
and out of joy goes and
sells all that he has
and buys that field.
Again, the kingdom
of heaven is like a
merchant
searching for fine pearls.
When he finds a pearl of great price,
he goes and sells all that he has and
buys it.
Again, the kingdom of heaven is like a
net thrown into the sea,
which collects fish of every kind.
When it is full they haul it ashore
and sit down to put what is good into
buckets.
What is bad they throw away.
Thus it will be at the end of the age.
The angels will go out and separate the
wicked from the righteous
and throw them into the fiery furnace,
where there will be wailing and
grinding of teeth.

"Do you understand all these things?"
They answered, "Yes."
And he replied,
"Then every scribe who has been
instructed in the kingdom of
heaven
is like the head of a household
who brings from his storeroom both the
new and the old."

or Matt 13:44-46 in Appendix A, p. 301.

Reflecting on the Gospel

Someone's true values can easily be discovered, especially by simply observing what is around the home. If every corner is filled with things, the person values inanimate objects. If the walls shine forth with pictures of family and friends, the person values relationships. If there are healthy green plants about (and perhaps fresh flowers), the person values growth and life. If the space is uncluttered, the person values simplicity and silence. This Sunday's gospel speaks to the value of the kingdom of heaven. How might this be captured in one's home? Perhaps by a crucifix on a wall or a piece of religious art or a statue. But more important, we know the kingdom of heaven is present when God is present, and this is manifested by the "treasures" of God: hospitality and kindness, joy and love, wisdom and understanding. These expressions of divine presence are no less real than the furniture, decorations, and dishes about the house.

All three comparisons in the gospel point to the incomparable value of "the kingdom of heaven." But God's kingdom is not fully revealed by images such as earthly treasure, priceless gems, an abundance of sumptuous seafood, or the things we might have about the house. The kingdom of heaven is fully revealed in those people with "heart[s] so wise and understanding" (first reading) that they know what is right and judge justly. Discipleship means searching for this treasure of incomparable value and giving all we have to become part of it. We disciples seek continually for that which we want more than anything else.

The treasure we go out to seek isn't some *thing* in some *place*; it is nothing less than the very *presence of God* that is breaking in upon us now but is only fully realized in the future. Now here is where the surprise of the gospel comes in: the kingdom of heaven isn't some object or realm that we can identify *physically*; instead it is the gift of divine presence God gives us (see first reading, where Solomon asks for wisdom). God's presence to us is a free, unexpected, and invaluable gift.

Isn't it a beautiful thing that God even asks us what we want (first reading: "Ask something of me and I will give it to you.")? This shows how much God cares for us. It confirms that God chooses to be involved in the affairs of humankind. It reveals God's abiding presence to us. This is the kingdom of heaven: God's presence. We already have the very understanding (wisdom) we need to recognize the kingdom (the wisdom that Solomon requested and received): it is a gift of the Holy Spirit first given us in baptism. God gives us the gift to understand; all we need do is use it to seek God's loving presence within us and among us.

Living the Paschal Mystery

This "treasure" does have its cost: we must actively search for it, recognize it when we find it, and sort out all the distractions that keep us from recognizing it. In the gospel the seekers go out in obvious places to find the treasure. For us, the discovery of the kingdom of heaven is most often in our everyday circumstances when we experience overwhelmingly the in-breaking of God's presence. This may be something so simple as the smile of a person's grateful thanks or the sense of rightness that comes with fidelity to daily prayer. It may be something more challenging, as admitting that we've hurt another. It may be demanding, such as committing time to help those in need. The issue is to recognize that God chooses to be present to us and wants us to seek that presence with all our hearts!

Focusing the Gospel

Key words and phrases: kingdom of heaven; buried . . . finds; searching . . . finds; net thrown . . . full; Do you understand . . . ?

To the point: All three comparisons in the gospel point to the incomparable value of "the kingdom of heaven." But God's kingdom is not fully revealed by images such as earthly treasure, priceless gems, or an abundance of sumptuous seafood. The kingdom of heaven is fully revealed in those people with "heart[s] so wise and understanding" (first reading) that they know what is right and judge justly. Discipleship means searching for this treasure of incomparable value and giving all we have to become part of it.

Connecting the Gospel

to the first reading: The "scribe who has been instructed in the kingdom of heaven" is modeled by Solomon in the first reading. The wisdom and understanding that Solomon requested and received is essential for us to become people who more fully reveal God's kingdom.

to experience: We are easily fooled about what has true value for us. For example, we max out credit cards buying things we covet, yet none of these things in themselves bring us wisdom, understanding, happiness, lasting satisfaction, knowledge of right and wrong, just judgments. Only living in the presence of God (that is, in God's kingdom) has true and lasting value.

Connecting the Responsorial Psalm

to the readings: Psalm 119, the longest psalm in the Bible (176 verses), is an extended meditation on the law of God and is not intended to be prayed in one sitting but savored, section by section, over the course of a lifetime. The verses we sing this Sunday reveal that the treasure we seek (gospel) and the wisdom for which we ask (first reading) are found through obedience to the law of God. The law of God helps us discern what is of true worth and sort out good from evil. Like the people in this Sunday's gospel parables, we do not know where the kingdom is before we find it. But we have been given a roadmap to guide our path forward and save us from taking false steps (psalm). We have only to love the law (psalm refrain) and follow where it leads.

to psalmist preparation: As you prepare to sing this Sunday's psalm, you might spend some time examining how you see God's law. Do you see the law as a list of "do's" and "don't's" that puts limits on what you would like to have and to do, or do you see it as a guide to rich, relational living? Your answer depends on where you believe true treasure lies. Pray for the grace to look where Solomon, and Jesus, point.

ASSEMBLY & FAITH-SHARING GROUPS
- What I value most in life is . . . What I need to reevaluate in my life is . . .
- To become part of the kingdom of heaven, I am willing to give my all to . . .
- Those who have taught me wisdom and understanding are . . . These enable me to . . .

PRESIDERS
I best lead people to a treasure of incomparable value when I . . .

DEACONS
The kind/quality of service required of me in order to further the kingdom of heaven is . . .

HOSPITALITY MINISTERS
My manner of greeting those gathering invites them to seek the incomparable treasure offered in liturgy when . . .

MUSIC MINISTERS
The price I have to pay to do my music ministry well is . . . The treasure I receive as reward is . . .

ALTAR MINISTERS
My service is a value that draws me more deeply into the kingdom of heaven in that . . .

LECTORS
My prayer and preparation of the word are ways of seeking "an understanding heart to judge . . . people and to distinguish right from wrong" (first reading) when . . .

EXTRAORDINARY MINISTERS OF HOLY COMMUNION
My manner of distributing Holy Communion makes visible the incomparable value of the kingdom of heaven in that . . .

Model Act of Penitence

Presider: In the gospel Jesus teaches us about the incomparable value of the kingdom of heaven. Let us open ourselves to God's presence so that we are worthy members of God's kingdom . . . [pause]

Lord Jesus, you are the presence of the kingdom of heaven: Lord . . .

Christ Jesus, you are the wisdom and understanding of God: Christ . . .

Lord Jesus, you judge us justly: Lord . . .

Homily Points

• We humans are very clever about how and what we seek as treasure. Some people endanger their lives to plumb the depths of the seas to recover treasure from sunken ships. Some people spend every weekend going to garage sales and flea markets. Some people comb beaches or garbage dumps or city parks with metal detectors to find things of value.

• We can't use a metal detector to find the kingdom of God! What we need is a wise and understanding heart. Such a heart does not take us to a place or to things but leads us to seek and treasure the people who mediate for us God's loving and abiding presence. This divine presence is the kingdom of heaven among us.

• Our actions and ways of relating to people reveal our true values. To be faithful disciples, we must be willing to give our all to encounter God's presence in the goodness we share with others and in their goodness extended to us. We also encounter God's presence in our self-giving response to the needs of others. In everyday experiences and encounters such as these, we find lasting treasure—the kingdom of heaven among us.

Model Prayer of the Faithful

Presider: Let us ask God for wisdom and understanding, that we might discover the kingdom of heaven among us.

Response:

Lord, hear our prayer.

Cantor:

we pray to the Lord,

That members of the church reveal the presence of the kingdom of heaven through the good works they do . . . [pause]

That all peoples of the world seek God and the kingdom of heaven diligently . . . [pause]

That those in any need receive from the storehouse of God's treasures . . . [pause]

That our parish community be wise in our decisions and just in our judgments . . . [pause]

Presider: Ever-present God, you will to be found by those who seek you: hear these our prayers that one day we might live forever in your presence. We ask this through Christ our Lord. **Amen.**

Let us pray
[for the faith to recognize God's presence in our world]

Pause for silent prayer

God our Father,
open our eyes to see your hand at work
in the splendor of creation,
in the beauty of human life.
Touched by your hand our world is holy.
Help us to cherish the gifts that surround us,
to share your blessings with our brothers and sisters,
and to experience the joy of life in your presence.

We ask this through Christ our Lord.
   Amen.

1 Kgs 3:5, 7-12

The LORD appeared to Solomon in a dream at night.
God said, "Ask something of me and I will give it to you."
Solomon answered:
   "O LORD, my God, you have made me, your servant, king
   to succeed my father David;
   but I am a mere youth, not knowing at all how to act.
I serve you in the midst of the people whom you have chosen,
   a people so vast that it cannot be numbered or counted.
Give your servant, therefore, an understanding heart
   to judge your people and to distinguish right from wrong.
   For who is able to govern this vast people of yours?"

The LORD was pleased that Solomon made this request.
So God said to him:
   "Because you have asked for this—
   not for a long life for yourself,
   nor for riches,
   nor for the life of your enemies,
   but for understanding so that you may know what is right—
   I do as you requested.
I give you a heart so wise and understanding
   that there has never been anyone like you up to now,
   and after you there will come no one to equal you."

RESPONSORIAL PSALM

Ps 119:57, 72, 76-77, 127-128, 129-130

R7. (97a) Lord, I love your commands.

I have said, O LORD, that my part
   is to keep your words.
The law of your mouth is to me more
   precious
     than thousands of gold and silver
      pieces.

R7. Lord, I love your commands.

Let your kindness comfort me
   according to your promise to your
     servants.
Let your compassion come to me that I
   may live,
   for your law is my delight.

R7. Lord, I love your commands.

For I love your commands
   more than gold, however fine.
For in all your precepts I go forward;
   every false way I hate.

R7. Lord, I love your commands.

Wonderful are your decrees;
   therefore I observe them.
The revelation of your words sheds light,
   giving understanding to the simple.

R7. Lord, I love your commands.

SECOND READING

Rom 8:28-30

Brothers and sisters:
We know that all things work for good for
   those who love God,
   who are called according to his purpose.
For those he foreknew he also predestined
   to be conformed to the image of his Son,
   so that he might be the firstborn
   among many brothers and sisters.
And those he predestined he also called;
   and those he called he also justified;
   and those he justified he also glorified.

About Liturgy

Liturgy as great treasure: It is true that we experience God's presence in the many circumstances of our daily lives. But surely one of the most sublime ways we experience God's presence is in the very celebration of liturgy. The Constitution on the Sacred Liturgy tells us that in liturgy Christ is present in his word, in the presider, in the assembly, and in the eucharistic bread and wine (no. 7). Thus liturgy itself is a great treasure trove of God's presence. This presents both a caution and a challenge for us in celebrating liturgy.

The caution that we must always keep in mind is that liturgy first and foremost is our entry into the dying and rising of Christ, and in that very act of surrender of self we give God praise and thanks. There is sometimes a tendency in liturgy to celebrate in a way that pleases *us* and, thus, subtly turns liturgy toward ourselves rather than toward God. When we do this we run a risk of misunderstanding God's presence to us.

The challenge is that we must *surrender* to God's action during the liturgy so that we see the many ways God is present in the celebration. It is too easy to let our minds wander or be distracted by restlessness around us or the things we must do when we get home. Liturgy asks of us a single-minded presence *to* God so that we can experience God's loving and abiding presence to us. This is liturgy's great treasure: that we celebrate God's presence to us and among us.

About Liturgical Music

Distinguishing liturgical from devotional songs, part 2: In order for devotional and liturgical prayer to fulfill their respective roles, each has its own form. Devotional prayer is free-form; it is shaped by us, and rightly so. Whether we are praying alone or with a group, devotional prayer allows us to pour out our personal needs and concerns before God. Liturgical prayer, on the other hand, is highly structured. Its content is decided by the church and spelled out in designated ritual books. Its purpose is to take us beyond our individual, immediate concerns and immerse us in the prayer of the universal church and in our vocation to be the Body of Christ dying and rising for the salvation of the world.

Once we understand the difference between devotional and liturgical prayer, it becomes easier to distinguish between songs that are appropriate for liturgy and those that are better suited for devotional prayer. Devotional song texts speak of personal salvation in terms of our individual relationship with Jesus. Liturgical hymn texts, on the other hand, use ecclesial terminology: they sing of the church, of the sacraments, of our identity as Body of Christ. They are paschal mystery-oriented, that is, they speak not so much about being saved by the blood of Jesus as about choosing to participate with Christ in the mystery of death and resurrection. They use sacramental rather than devotional language, speaking of Eucharist and baptism in terms of ecclesial relationships rather than in terms of individual salvation and healing.

JULY 24, 2011
SEVENTEENTH SUNDAY
IN ORDINARY TIME

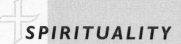

SPIRITUALITY

GOSPEL ACCLAMATION
Matt 4:4b

R℣. Alleluia, alleluia.
One does not live on bread alone,
but on every word that comes forth from the
mouth of God.
R℣. Alleluia, alleluia.

Gospel   Matt 14:13-21; L112A

When Jesus heard of the death of
    John the Baptist,
  he withdrew in a boat to a
    deserted place by himself.
The crowds heard of this and
    followed him on foot from their
    towns.
When he disembarked and saw the
    vast crowd,
  his heart was moved with pity for
    them, and he cured their sick.
When it was evening, the disciples
    approached him and said,
  "This is a deserted place and it is
    already late;
  dismiss the crowds so that they can
    go to the villages
  and buy food for themselves."
Jesus said to them, "There is no need
    for them to go away;
  give them some food yourselves."
But they said to him,
  "Five loaves and two fish are all we
    have here."
Then he said, "Bring them here to me,"
  and he ordered the crowds to sit
    down on the grass.
Taking the five loaves and the two fish,
    and looking up to heaven,
  he said the blessing, broke the loaves,
  and gave them to the disciples,
  who in turn gave them to the crowds.
They all ate and were satisfied,
  and they picked up the fragments left
    over—
  twelve wicker baskets full.
Those who ate were about five
    thousand men,
  not counting women and children.

Reflecting on the Gospel

He was well past ninety years old, and his mind had receded into the empty murkiness of advanced Alzheimer's disease. He no longer knew family members, could not feed or dress himself, could barely speak or see. His family came to visit faithfully every week and always made sure there was on hand chocolate candy, his favorite. As soon as the box was brought out and opened and he smelled the sweet delight, he would hold out his open hand, palm turned up, and say, "I'll have some of that." This was the one touch point with reality that he somehow managed to maintain. We might surmise that the hungry crowd in this Sunday's gospel probably held out their hands to the disciples as they distributed the blessed bread and fish and said, "I'll have some of that." What the disciples were able to give them through the power and compassion of Jesus, however, was much more than food to satisfy physical hunger. They were given a share in the abundance and fullness of life only Jesus can offer. Jesus opens the disciples' and crowd's hopes to a fullness they do not expect: the *future* banquet of eternal life.

To the disciples' concern about the isolated place, late hour, and crowd's hunger, Jesus replies, "give them some food yourselves." Hampered by the scarcity of food they have at hand, the disciples are unable to feed the hungry crowd. Jesus takes and blesses the loaves and fish, the disciples themselves do feed the crowd, and "all ate and were satisfied." This miracle is essentially a sign of God's kingdom. In that kingdom there is never scarcity or lack of power to respond to others but always the superabundance of God's nourishing and satisfying presence among and within us. There were twelve baskets left over—an image of the abundance God gives us and the fullness of life we are offered.

The gospel tells us that those in the crowd "were satisfied." Jesus' compassion not only filled their immediate needs but gave them a glimpse of what truly satisfies—eternal life. In the crowd's seeking Jesus they "were satisfied." In our continually seeking Jesus, we too will be satisfied—one day, with eternal life. This gospel orients us to a most satisfying future!

Living the Paschal Mystery

Jesus' response to the crowd's needs was an in-breaking of God's kingdom, embodied by the very person and presence of Jesus whom the crowd sought. If *we* are the presence of the risen Christ today, then we too are an in-breaking of God's kingdom when we reach out in compassion to satisfy the needs of others.

One challenge, then, of our everyday living of the paschal mystery is to see in the self-sacrificing dying we embrace for the sake of others an in-breaking of God's presence and kingdom. In other words, our compassion and care for others is more than simply satisfying another's need (as important even as that is in itself); like Jesus, our compassion carries with it the foretaste of eternal life. This places our everyday self-sacrificing in a whole different context, and so we are better able to see how our dying to self leads to rising and eternal life.

At the same time, sometimes we must hold our own hands out and say, "I'll have some of that." We must be willing to receive the life that divine presence brings, whether that comes through liturgy and prayer or through the goodness of others. And, always, we are given life in abundance.

Focusing the Gospel

Key words and phrases: give them some food yourselves, gave them to the crowds, all ate and were satisfied, twelve wicker baskets full

To the point: To the disciples' concern about the isolated place, late hour, and crowd's hunger, Jesus replies, "give them some food yourselves." Hampered by the scarcity of food they have at hand, the disciples are unable to feed the hungry crowd. Jesus takes and blesses the loaves and fish, the disciples themselves do feed the crowd, and "all ate and were satisfied." This miracle is essentially a sign of God's kingdom. In that kingdom there is never scarcity or lack of power to respond to others but always the superabundance of God's nourishing and satisfying presence among and within us.

Connecting the Gospel

to the first reading: The future banquet of abundance that Isaiah had envisioned is made present in Jesus' response to the hungry crowd. Both Isaiah and Jesus point to the significance of this banquet: "that you may have life" (first reading).

to experience: Sometimes we have more power to accomplish things than we realize; for example, a single human might lift a car off an injured child. In God's kingdom, our power as faithful followers of Jesus to feed the world's "hungers" is utterly limitless.

Connecting the Responsorial Psalm

to the readings: What does the crowd in this Sunday's gospel seek? Here-and-now healing, here-and-now satisfaction of their needs. What does Jesus give them? Jesus opens up their immediate here-and-now hopes to an eschatological fullness they cannot imagine: the feasting of the messianic banquet where all are fed and where what appears to be far too little becomes much more than is needed.

Isaiah already hints at this eschatological fullness in the first reading. Come, he says, receive without pay far more than you have ever expected. In the verses of the responsorial psalm we sing confidently of this fullness that is offered us: God "answers all our needs" and fills "the desire" of "every living thing." Moreover, the psalm's use of the present tense indicates that God does so here-and-now. It is *today*—now—that we sit at the eschatological banquet. We have only to eat and believe.

to psalmist preparation: In this Sunday's gospel the disciples give to the crowd the food Jesus has given them. As a psalmist, what "food" does Jesus give you? How do you pass this nourishment on to the assembly?

ASSEMBLY & FAITH-SHARING GROUPS
- The "five loaves and two fish" that I have to satisfy the needs of others are . . .
- Some occasions when I have glimpsed the super-abundance of God's presence ("twelve wicker baskets full") are . . .
- I am aware of God's power acting through me when . . . I distrust that God's power is within me when . . .

PRESIDERS
Like the disciples, I want to dismiss others to take care of their own needs when . . . Like Jesus, I am moved with pity to respond to human needs when . . .

DEACONS
My own limited giftedness (the "five loaves and two fish" of my life) was enough in Christ to satisfy others when . . .

HOSPITALITY MINISTERS
My hospitality embodies the Lord's invitation to the people to "come . . . heed" (see first reading) whenever I . . .

MUSIC MINISTERS
I find myself being fed by Christ through my music ministry when . . . I see others being fed by Christ through my music ministry when . . .

ALTAR MINISTERS
My serving others is done with the compassion of Jesus whenever I . . .

LECTORS
When I come to the word seeking to "have life" (first reading), my proclamation is like . . .

EXTRAORDINARY MINISTERS OF HOLY COMMUNION
My distribution of Holy Communion is a participation in Jesus' power to nourish and satisfy the "hungers" of those who come when I . . .

Model Act of Penitence

Presider: In today's gospel Jesus draws abundance out of the seeming scarcity of a few loaves and fish. Let us open ourselves to receive God's abundance during this liturgy so that we may be empowered to satisfy the hungers of others . . . [pause]

Lord Jesus, you satisfy all hungers: Lord . . .

Christ Jesus, you are the Bread of Life: Christ . . .

Lord Jesus, you give us the rich banquet of eternal life: Lord . . .

Homily Points

• We talk about the two worldviews of whether the glass is half empty or half full. We often fixate on what we don't have while overlooking an abundance that we do have. For example, we might covet the latest electronic gadget while missing the loving glance of a child. True satisfaction does not come from what we acquire, but is freely, abundantly, and sometimes surprisingly given to us through our relationships with others.

• Withdrawing to a deserted place to grieve the death of John the Baptist, Jesus still provides life-giving nourishment for the hungry crowd that comes to him. Where the disciples perceive scarcity of food and powerlessness to act (the glass half empty), Jesus reveals to them not only his unlimited capacity to nourish the crowd but also the disciples' capacity to act *with him* in doing so (the glass half full).

• God's kingdom is neither half empty nor even half full but is always a "full glass." God continually graces us with a share in divine life, incorporates us into the community of those filled with the Spirit of Jesus, and empowers us to satisfy the "hungers" of others. Wherever fullness of life is lacking, we bring life, for example, by donating to charity or volunteering at the local soup kitchen; by taking time to help youngsters with their homework, calm a person who is upset, encourage someone afraid to make a change in their lives, forgive another, say thank you. These many ways of relating to others make present the life of God's kingdom and God's promise of fullness.

Model Prayer of the Faithful

Presider: Filled with the abundance of life and power God offers us, we pray for those in need.

Response:

Lord, hear our prayer.

Cantor:

we pray to the Lord,

That all members of the church faithfully witness to the presence of God's kingdom among us . . . [pause]

That all people of the world seek God and eternal life . . . [pause]

That the sick be cured and the hungry be filled . . . [pause]

That each of us here have confidence in the abundance God has given us and seek satisfaction in spending ourselves for others . . . [pause]

Presider: Lavish God, you are gracious beyond compare: hear these our prayers that one day all people might enjoy fullness of life with you. We ask this through Christ our Lord. **Amen.**

Let us pray
[to the Father whose kindness never fails]

Pause for silent prayer

God our Father,
gifts without measure flow from your goodness
to bring us your peace.
Our life is your gift.
Guide our life's journey,
for only your love makes us whole.
Keep us strong in your love.

We ask this through Christ our Lord.
Amen.

FIRST READING
Isa 55:1-3

Thus says the LORD:
All you who are thirsty,
come to the water!
You who have no money,
come, receive grain and eat;
come, without paying and without cost,
drink wine and milk!
Why spend your money for what is not bread;
your wages for what fails to satisfy?
Heed me, and you shall eat well,
you shall delight in rich fare.
Come to me heedfully,
listen, that you may have life.
I will renew with you the everlasting covenant,
the benefits assured to David.

RESPONSORIAL PSALM
Ps 145:8-9, 15-16, 17-18

R̸. (cf. 16) The hand of the Lord feeds us; he answers all our needs.

The LORD is gracious and merciful,
　　slow to anger and of great kindness.
The LORD is good to all
　　and compassionate toward all his
　　　　works.

R̸. The hand of the Lord feeds us; he answers all our needs.

The eyes of all look hopefully to you,
　　and you give them their food in due
　　　　season;
you open your hand
　　and satisfy the desire of every living
　　　　thing.

R̸. The hand of the Lord feeds us; he answers all our needs.

The LORD is just in all his ways
　　and holy in all his works.
The LORD is near to all who call upon him,
　　to all who call upon him in truth.

R̸. The hand of the Lord feeds us; he answers all our needs.

SECOND READING
Rom 8:35, 37-39

Brothers and sisters:
What will separate us from the love of
　　Christ?
Will anguish, or distress, or persecution,
　　or famine,
　　or nakedness, or peril, or the sword?
No, in all these things we conquer
　　overwhelmingly
　　through him who loved us.
For I am convinced that neither death, nor
　　life,
　　nor angels, nor principalities,
　　nor present things, nor future things,
　　nor powers, nor height, nor depth,
　　nor any other creature will be able to
　　　　separate us
　　from the love of God in Christ Jesus our
　　　　Lord.

About Liturgy

Homiletic challenge and fullness of life: It has become popular to preach the gospels on the multiplication of loaves from a sociological point of view, that is, the miracle consists in Jesus' inspiring the crowds to open up their picnic baskets and share with one another so that all "were satisfied." The attractiveness of this interpretive approach is that people can readily identify with it (it is within their human experience), and the interpretation also contains an inherent challenge: the gospel calls all of us to share what we have with others who have less.

The downside of this interpretation is that the homilist misses an opportunity to make the real point: God's continual blessing of us with abundance beyond our ability to imagine. This miracle points to the abundance of the fullness of life we share now. By focusing on the miracle as part of God's self-revelation through Jesus, we are invited to place God's abundant gifts in the larger context of divine life that is already ours and will be ours one day in utter fullness. Two elements of the gospel point to this interpretation: the actions of Jesus (take, bless, break, give) parallel the actions that we do at Eucharist, and the twelve baskets of fragments left over point to the messianic banquet and eternal life. It is a greater homiletic challenge to preach the fullness of eternal life.

About Liturgical Music

Distinguishing liturgical from devotional songs, part 3: As ritual enactment of the paschal mystery, liturgy is demanding prayer. We are often tempted to slip into devotional prayer during the course of liturgy because it is easier. The challenge, however, is to remain faithful to liturgical prayer, and to do so we must be discerning about the music we choose to use at liturgy. Page through your parish music resource(s) and determine which songs are devotional and which are liturgical. Earmark those that can support liturgical prayer, and then gradually phase out of use *at liturgy* those that are better suited for devotional prayer. Unless they are theologically unsound, however, these songs needn't be—nor should they be—removed from the parish repertoire. The issue is not with their value, or with our need for them in our spiritual lives, but with where and how we use them.

If people are hungry for devotional hymn texts, the parish needs to assess what opportunities for devotional prayer it provides. Are they sufficient to meet the needs of the people? Are they scheduled throughout the year? Do they correlate with and support the liturgical feasts and seasons? One of the responsibilities of every parish is to offer the devotional prayer experiences people need and to use these as the appropriate times for singing devotional hymns.

JULY 31, 2011
EIGHTEENTH SUNDAY IN ORDINARY TIME

✚ SPIRITUALITY

GOSPEL ACCLAMATION
cf. Ps 130:5

℟. Alleluia, alleluia.
I wait for the Lord;
my soul waits for his word.
℟. Alleluia, alleluia.

Gospel   Matt 14:22-33; L115A

After he had fed the people, Jesus
    made the disciples get into a
    boat
and precede him to the other
    side,
    while he dismissed the crowds.
After doing so, he went up on the
    mountain by himself to pray.
When it was evening he was there
    alone.
Meanwhile the boat, already a few
    miles offshore,
    was being tossed about by the waves,
    for the wind was against it.
During the fourth watch of the night,
    he came toward them walking on the
    sea.
When the disciples saw him walking on
    the sea they were terrified.
"It is a ghost," they said, and they cried
    out in fear.
At once Jesus spoke to them, "Take
    courage, it is I; do not be afraid."
Peter said to him in reply,
    "Lord, if it is you, command me to
        come to you on the water."
He said, "Come."
Peter got out of the boat and began to
    walk on the water toward Jesus.
But when he saw how strong the wind
    was he became frightened;
    and, beginning to sink, he cried out,
        "Lord, save me!"
Immediately Jesus stretched out his hand
    and caught Peter,
    and said to him, "O you of little faith,
        why did you doubt?"
After they got into the boat, the wind
    died down.
Those who were in the boat did him
    homage, saying,
    "Truly, you are the Son of God."

Reflecting on the Gospel

When beloved grandparents or a favorite aunt or uncle come to visit, little children's faces light up with delight, and they usually run and jump into the adults' arms to receive a tight hug and kiss. There is instant recognition and expectation. In this Sunday's gospel the disciples' faces did not light up with delight when Jesus came to them across the stormy sea, but "they were terrified." They did not come running to him, but they "cried out in fear." Even when Jesus assures them who it is they are seeing, Peter challenges him: "*if* it is you . . ."

What does it take for us to recognize Jesus?

This gospel selection follows immediately upon last Sunday's episode of healing and feeding the five thousand. The disciples don't get it—they had just witnessed the miracle of the loaves and fish, but they still don't recognize Jesus in all his power. Moreover, Peter has the audacity to challenge Jesus' word: "Lord, *if* it is you . . ." No wonder he sank! How many encounters with Jesus must we have to know that "Truly, [he is] the Son of God," to trust in his power, and to come to him with confidence? Endless! How many times will Jesus keep coming to us? Endless!

This Jesus, whom the disciples have seen heal and work other miracles, now walks on the stormy sea—Jesus even has power over nature and, by implication, over the evil that the stormy seas symbolize. When Peter dares Jesus to reveal who he is by challenging him to command him to come to him on the water, it's not only Jesus' identity that is at stake but Peter's trust. His challenge ("*if* it is you") results in disastrous fright. Peter drops all pretensions of courage and cries out to be saved. Jesus' command, "Come," challenges more than Peter's courage—it is an opportunity for Jesus' self-revelation ("it is I") that calls forth deeper trust and confidence from Peter.

Only Jesus can remove the stumbling blocks that keep us from recognizing him and coming to him. Here is why Peter's challenge to Jesus is so exposing: Jesus' identity is assured (he saved Peter); Peter's (our) trust in Jesus' power is still weak, still needs to be strengthened (Peter "became frightened"). The good news of this gospel is that challenge doesn't lead to "drowning" but to a revelation of who Jesus is.

Living the Paschal Mystery

Most of us will not have the experience of Peter—nothing in our human experience leads us to expect that we will ever walk on water! But that is not the goal of trust in Jesus or of Christian living. The real challenge is to see in this gospel the many ways Jesus comes to us and how we might encounter Jesus in our everyday lives—not as One walking on water, but as One who dwells in the other in need. We are called to see Jesus in anyone who is calling out for help, anyone who seems to be "drowning" in the chaos of everyday living, anyone who cries out to be saved.

It takes more trust and confidence to see Jesus in the other than to walk on water! This, because it demands a great self-emptying on our part to see dignity in those in need. But this is also the glimpse of the life that comes out of our dying—serving another is an encounter with Jesus, the One who saves. Jesus comes to us endlessly in recognizable circumstances (liturgy and prayer, for example) and in unexpected ways (in those in need, in good surprises, in the visits of loved ones). We need only reach out to him and let him touch us and save us.

Focusing the Gospel

Key words and phrases: if it is you; sink; Jesus . . . caught; Truly, you are the Son of God

To the point: The disciples don't get it—they had just witnessed the miracle of the loaves and fish, but they still don't recognize Jesus in all his power. Moreover, Peter has the audacity to challenge Jesus' word: "Lord, *if* it is you . . ." No wonder he sank! How many encounters with Jesus must we have to know that "Truly, [he is] the Son of God," to trust in his power, and to come to him with confidence? Endless! How many times will Jesus keep coming to us? Endless!

Connecting the Gospel

to the first reading: Elijah does not encounter God in the expected ways divine power is manifested but in "a tiny whispering sound." Peter, by contrast, does encounter Jesus in a raging storm. Whether in dramatic or unassuming ways, God continually moves toward us. It is we who must move toward God in trust.

to experience: Nothing in our human experience leads us to expect that we will ever walk on water! But that is not the goal of faith. Encounter with God's abiding and saving presence is.

Connecting the Responsorial Psalm

to the readings: Psalm 85 was probably written at the time when the Israelites returned from their exile in Babylon and found their homeland devastated and their hearts unable to believe they could restore it. In the second half of the psalm—the verses we sing this Sunday—the people listen to "what God proclaims" and begin to see that God will replenish their land and restore justice and peace to their nation.

In the first reading Elijah must listen for God amid a great deal of clamor. In the gospel the disciples must see Jesus through a fog of hesitant recognition and quavering belief. In the responsorial psalm we declare "[Lord, we] will hear" and beg "Lord, let us see . . ." What is it that we hear and see? We hear God's presence even when its manifestation seems insignificant (first reading). We see God's redemption even when chaos and destruction have had their day (psalm) and our own cloudy vision makes us slow to perceive who God is and what God is doing (gospel). The psalm reminds us that we can hear and see God; we have only to listen and look with faith.

to psalmist preparation: In the psalm refrain the community begs God to show them kindness and grant them salvation. In the verses you proclaim that what they pray for—peace, kindness, truth, justice—will be given to them. As you prepare to sing these verses, you might use the refrain as part of your daily prayer. Where do you (does the world) need to see God's kindness? Where do you (does the world) need to see salvation being granted?

ASSEMBLY & FAITH-SHARING GROUPS

- My life has been like the disciples'—tossed about by wind and waves, sometimes even sinking—when . . . At those times the ways I have experienced Jesus' "stretched out . . . hand" to save me were . . .
- What distracts me from recognizing Jesus' presence to me is . . . What helps me encounter Jesus is . . .
- I am most inclined to trust Jesus when . . . I tend to distrust Jesus when . . . What helps me grow in my trust is . . .

PRESIDERS

I reach out with a saving hand to those struggling to encounter Jesus when I . . .

DEACONS

My diaconal service lifts up those drowning in the burdens of life whenever I . . .

HOSPITALITY MINISTERS

My welcoming those who gather for liturgy can help them encounter Jesus coming to them when I . . .

MUSIC MINISTERS

My music ministry helps me see more clearly who Jesus is when . . . My music ministry helps the assembly see Jesus more clearly when . . .

ALTAR MINISTERS

My manner of serving at the altar witnesses to others that I have encountered Jesus and do believe in him in that . . .

LECTORS

My time preparing the word is an experience of "the Lord . . . passing by" (first reading) in that . . .

EXTRAORDINARY MINISTERS OF HOLY COMMUNION

My distribution of Holy Communion is a share in Jesus' endless coming to the people he loves, and this leads me to . . .

Model Act of Penitence

Presider: In this Sunday's gospel Jesus bids Peter to come to him across the stormy sea. Let us prepare ourselves to come to Jesus across the stormy seas of our own faith journey . . . [pause]

Lord Jesus, you are our Savior in the midst of doubt and fear: Lord . . .

Christ Jesus, you truly are the Son of God: Christ . . .

Lord Jesus, you save those who cry out to you: Lord . . .

Homily Points

• Children learning how to play ball are constantly admonished by their coaches, "Keep your eye on the ball!" Losing focus on the ball leads to missed hits, dropped catches, and lost games. How simple the directive is, yet how hard for some players to learn!

• Jesus commands Peter to come to him across the raging sea. Peter doubts who Jesus is, this man with the power to walk on water. Peter becomes distracted by the rage of the storm, the fear in his heart, and his doubt in Jesus' power. Peter has not yet learned to keep his eye on Jesus. Had he kept his focus on Jesus, Peter would never have begun to sink.

• Jesus never takes his eye off Peter but invites him—despite his doubt—to keep moving toward him in confidence and trust. As with Peter, Jesus invites us to come to him in times of doubt and fear, discouragement and distress, lack of confidence in his abiding presence and help. Jesus never takes his eye off us and never fails to come to us in the challenges of discipleship, the varied circumstances of our daily living, and in the people we encounter each day.

Model Prayer of the Faithful

Presider: In faith let us make our needs known to the God who reaches out to us with loving presence.

Response:

Lord, hear our prayer.

Cantor:

we pray to the Lord,

That the church may always be a haven of safety for all those who cry out for help . . . [pause]

That all peoples of the world come to a deeper faith in the God who saves . . . [pause]

That those who are drowning in the burdens of life be lifted up by new strength and courage . . . [pause]

That each of us here overcome our own doubts and fears by more perfectly opening ourselves to Jesus' presence within and among us . . . [pause]

Presider: God of power and might, you save those who cry out to you: hear these our prayers that one day we might enjoy fullness of life with you. We ask this through Christ our Lord. **Amen.**

ALTERNATIVE OPENING PRAYER

Let us pray
[that through us others may find the
way to life in Christ]

Pause for silent prayer

Father,
we come, reborn in the Spirit,
to celebrate our sonship in the Lord Jesus
Christ.
Touch our hearts,
help them grow toward the life you have
promised.
Touch our lives,
make them signs of your love for all men.

Grant this through Christ our Lord.
Amen.

FIRST READING
1 Kgs 19:9a, 11-13a

At the mountain of God, Horeb,
Elijah came to a cave where he took
shelter.
Then the LORD said to him,
"Go outside and stand on the mountain
before the LORD;
the LORD will be passing by."
A strong and heavy wind was rending the
mountains
and crushing rocks before the LORD—
but the LORD was not in the wind.
After the wind there was an earthquake—
but the LORD was not in the earthquake.
After the earthquake there was fire—
but the LORD was not in the fire.
After the fire there was a tiny whispering
sound.
When he heard this,
Elijah hid his face in his cloak
and went and stood at the entrance of
the cave.

RESPONSORIAL PSALM

Ps 85:9, 10, 11-12, 13-14

℟. (8) Lord, let us see your kindness, and grant us your salvation.

I will hear what God proclaims;
    the LORD—for he proclaims peace.
Near indeed is his salvation to those who
    fear him,
    glory dwelling in our land.

℟. Lord, let us see your kindness, and grant us your salvation.

Kindness and truth shall meet;
    justice and peace shall kiss.
Truth shall spring out of the earth,
    and justice shall look down from
    heaven.

℟. Lord, let us see your kindness, and grant us your salvation.

The LORD himself will give his benefits;
    our land shall yield its increase.
Justice shall walk before him,
    and prepare the way of his steps.

℟. Lord, let us see your kindness, and grant us your salvation.

SECOND READING

Rom 9:1-5

Brothers and sisters:
I speak the truth in Christ, I do not lie;
    my conscience joins with the Holy Spirit
      in bearing me witness
    that I have great sorrow and constant
      anguish in my heart.
For I could wish that I myself were
      accursed and cut off from Christ
    for the sake of my own people,
    my kindred according to the flesh.
They are Israelites;
    theirs the adoption, the glory, the
      covenants,
    the giving of the law, the worship, and
      the promises;
    theirs the patriarchs, and from them,
    according to the flesh, is the Christ,
who is over all, God blessed forever.
    Amen.

About Liturgy

Faith and creed: The ancient name for a creed is *symbolum*—the formula of profession recapitulates (is a symbol for) the mysteries of our faith that we celebrate in the Eucharist (see GIRM no. 67). Following immediately after the silence after the homily, the Creed is our *response* to our encounter with Christ in the Liturgy of the Word. Parallel with this Sunday's gospel account, in the proclamation of the gospel (and in the other readings as well since they accord with the gospel), we hear the challenge of Jesus' walking toward us and bidding us to come to him; the recitation of the Creed is our response to Jesus' bid to come. It symbolizes our readiness to hand our lives over to him in faith, trust, and confidence.

The Nicene Creed (the usual creed recited on Sundays and solemnities) recounts the works of all the persons of the Trinity, but the entire centerpiece of the Creed is a profound profession of Christ's divinity. The rubrics prescribe that we bow our heads while reciting the lines "by the power of the Holy Spirit he was born of the Virgin Mary, and became man." In addition to helping us keep our minds on what we are saying, this gesture is an act of homage toward the divine Son who announced his identity as "I am," one with God from all eternity.

About Liturgical Music

Music suggestions: The venerable history of a hymn like "How Firm a Foundation" [in most hymnals] lends strength to its appropriateness for this Sunday. The text first appeared in John Rippon's 1787 British collection, *A Selection of Hymns.* The tune FOUNDATION was widely printed in nineteenth-century American shape-note hymnals. Thus the faith on which this hymn stands is an aged one, tested by tribulation and confirmed by real experience of God's never failing intervention to save. Typical of its birthplace and time, the tune is a pentatonic one (only five notes are used) with a driving cut-time meter (some hymnals give the meter as 4/4, but the real feel is two beats to the bar). Utterly simple yet strong and durable—is this not what characterizes faith? The hymn could be used either for the entrance procession or during the preparation of the gifts. It would also make a fitting assembly hymn of praise after Communion.

Other songs well suited to this Sunday's readings include "How Can I Keep from Singing" [in most hymnals]; "This Day God Gives Me" [in most hymnals]; "O God, Our Help in Ages Past" [in most hymnals]; "Be Not Afraid" [in most hymnals]; John Bell's "Be Still and Know That I Am God" [G2, GC, RS]; Steve Warner's "Be Still and Know That I Am God" [VO2, WC]; "Be Still, My Soul" [BB, JS2]; "All Will Be Well" [VO, WC, WS]; and "Precious Lord, Take My Hand" [in most hymnals].

AUGUST 7, 2011
NINETEENTH SUNDAY IN ORDINARY TIME

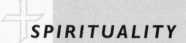

SPIRITUALITY

GOSPEL ACCLAMATION
cf. Matt 4:23

℟. Alleluia, alleluia.
Jesus proclaimed the Gospel of the kingdom
and cured every disease among the people.
℟. Alleluia, alleluia.

Gospel

Matt 15:21-28; L118A

At that time, Jesus withdrew
    to the region of Tyre and
    Sidon.
And behold, a Canaanite woman
    of that district came and
    called out,
    "Have pity on me, Lord, Son of
        David!
My daughter is tormented by a demon."
But Jesus did not say a word in answer
    to her.
Jesus' disciples came and asked him,
    "Send her away, for she keeps calling
        out after us."
He said in reply,
    "I was sent only to the lost sheep of
        the house of Israel."
But the woman came and did Jesus
    homage, saying, "Lord, help me."
He said in reply,
    "It is not right to take the food of the
        children
    and throw it to the dogs."
She said, "Please, Lord, for even the
        dogs eat the scraps
    that fall from the table of their
        masters."
Then Jesus said to her in reply,
    "O woman, great is your faith!
Let it be done for you as you wish."
And the woman's daughter was healed
    from that hour.

Reflecting on the Gospel

It seems as though the dearer something or someone is to us or the greater the need, the greater our efforts are to achieve what we want. Most parents sacrifice greatly so their children can have a better life than they did growing up. Young adults give up free time to study for college exams so they can improve their GPAs, retain their scholarships, and graduate with good hope for secure jobs. Those who are serious about losing weight and maintaining good health exercise daily and eat nutritious food that is perhaps not especially to their liking. In this Sunday's gospel a Canaanite woman (a foreigner) approaches Jesus with a heartfelt request to heal her daughter. Jesus' reply seems anything but welcoming! She does anything but give up!

This is a harsh gospel: Jesus initially excludes the Canaanite woman from his ministry. But the woman isn't daunted, so great is her desire that her daughter be healed. The woman wins! The life of her daughter is at stake, and this gives her the courage to challenge who are to be the recipients of Jesus' ministry. In this gospel Jesus initially declares that his mission is only to "the house of Israel" and, consequently, harshly rebuffs the Canaanite woman. Subsequent dialogue between Jesus and this persistent woman leads Jesus to extol her great faith and heal her daughter. The gospel challenges us to be persons of strong faith who are persistent in prayer and courageous in asking for salvation. For such people God's salvation is already given. The encounter between Jesus and the woman reveals the unrestricted mercy of Jesus, the power of great faith, and the universality of salvation for those who believe.

There is even more good news in this gospel: even "scraps" in God's kingdom are sufficient to meet our needs! The inclusiveness of salvation doesn't just embrace all people; it embraces and meets all needs. "Great faith" also recognizes that even a little bit from God is sufficient. Such faith sees the great worth that even a little bit from God holds. For, after all, what God offers us is *life*. And this life is more than even our own human life; God offers us a share in divine life, now and for all eternity.

Living the Paschal Mystery

The Canaanite woman's single-mindedness on behalf of her daughter is rewarded with her being healed. This gospel challenges us to be just as single-minded about placing our requests before God, and also just as single-minded about our own inclusive ministry to others.

It's interesting that the Canaanite woman's cry to Jesus was that he "have pity on *me*" (not on her daughter, although that is surely implied in the request). Her love for her daughter and her great desire that she be healed could not be separated from herself—she and her daughter were one in the need for healing and life.

This gives us an insight into our inclusivity and ministry: we must be so "at one" with others that their plight is our own plight. Ministry is more than *doing* for another; it implies an empathy with another that discloses the unity we share as members of the Body of Christ. One dimension of living the gospel is that we work to increase our unity with one another, which in turn draws us to reach out to others in mercy and compassion, no matter who they are.

Focusing the Gospel

Key words and phrases: only . . . the house of Israel, great is your faith, daughter was healed

To the point: In this gospel Jesus initially declares that his mission is only to "the house of Israel" and, consequently, harshly rebuffs the Canaanite woman. Subsequent dialogue between Jesus and this persistent woman leads Jesus to extol her great faith and heal her daughter. The gospel challenges us to be persons of strong faith who are persistent in prayer and courageous in asking for salvation. For such people God's salvation is already given.

Connecting the Gospel

to the first reading: How shocking Isaiah's prophecy must have been to the ancient Jews still searching for their identity during the Babylonian captivity, these people who understood themselves to be God's chosen ones! The gospel shows that the disciples are still struggling with this same issue: to whom God extends salvation. Both Isaiah and Jesus make clear that salvation is for all.

to experience: We sometimes think that our words to God must be correct, the "right ones," polite, holy, loving. We have a hard time "arguing" with God in the manner the Canaanite woman used with Jesus. Our conversations with God must be as real and honest as our conversations with each other.

Connecting the Responsorial Psalm

to the readings: Psalm 67 was a song of thanksgiving for the harvest (the Lectionary omits verse 7, "The earth has yielded its harvest; God, our God, blesses us"), expressing the ever-widening reach of God's blessings from the people of Israel, to all nations, to the ends of the earth.

The first reading also proclaims that God's blessings and salvation are for all peoples, not just the Israelites. In the gospel Jesus makes this revelation concrete when he responds to the Canaanite woman's persistent plea and heals her daughter. In singing Psalm 67 we pray, then, that all peoples be brought into the circle of God's embrace. We stretch our hearts to take in God's unlimited expansiveness. We act like Christ.

to psalmist preparation: As you prepare to sing this responsorial psalm, you might spend some time reflecting on your own understanding of the reach of God's salvation. Whom do you find it hard to see within God's saving embrace? Whose cries of need seem more a bother to you than an opportunity to show God's saving desire (gospel)? How, on the other hand, have you grown in your understanding and in your ability to respond? How has your heart been widened?

**ASSEMBLY &
FAITH-SHARING GROUPS**
- When I speak to God, I use words like . . . I wish I could use words like . . .
- I need to ask God for salvation when . . . I experience salvation right now in my life when . . .
- What I could learn from the Canaanite mother when I am faced with resistance or rebuff is . . .

PRESIDERS
In my ministry, sometimes I harshly rebuff another when . . . I am most kind and compassionate when . . .

DEACONS
I am like the Canaanite mother and advocate for those in need whenever I . . .

HOSPITALITY MINISTERS
In my ministry I sometimes rebuff others whenever I . . . My ministry most warmly welcomes others when . . .

MUSIC MINISTERS
When I persist in practicing my music, I gain . . . When I persist in practicing my faith, I gain . . .

ALTAR MINISTERS
My serving is really a kind of persistent prayer expressing my great faith when I . . .

LECTORS
My care and persistence in preparing to lector expresses great faith in that . . .

**EXTRAORDINARY MINISTERS
OF HOLY COMMUNION**
My manner of distributing Holy Communion extols the communicants' great faith whenever I . . .

Model Act of Penitence

Presider: God's mercy is unbounded—even to Jesus' reaching out to the bold and persistent Canaanite woman who asks for her daughter to be healed in today's gospel. As we prepare for liturgy, let us recall God's mercy to us . . . [pause]

Lord Jesus, you are the Son of God and Son of David: Lord . . .

Christ Jesus, you are merciful and compassionate: Christ . . .

Lord Jesus, you offer salvation to those who call to you in need: Lord . . .

Homily Points

• We have many ways to keep other people "in their place." We use put-down words, we ignore them as if they were not there, we turn our backs on them, we are sarcastic, we criticize them to their face, etc. The gospel portrays Jesus as a typical Jewish male of his time who puts the Canaanite woman in her place. The Canaanite woman in turn puts Jesus in his place!

• For the Canaanite woman, Jesus is the one who can heal, that is, the One who brings salvation. Nothing deters her from reminding him of his role as the "Son of David." Amazed by her great faith, he grants her request to heal her daughter and in this demonstrates who he really is—the Savior. He thus acknowledges her rightful place among the saved.

• It would seem strange if we prayed persistently to ask God to put us in our place! Our place is both to be Jesus' presence bringing salvation into our midst as well as to be the Canaanite woman asking for wholeness—salvation—for ourselves. For example, at times our place is to feed the hungry, clothe the naked, visit the imprisoned, care for the sick. At other times our place is to receive in our own need caring actions from others. This is exactly where great faith leads us. This is the best place to be!

Model Prayer of the Faithful

Presider: We make our needs known to God with steadfast persistence and great faith.

Response:

Lord, hear our prayer.

Cantor:

we pray to the Lord,

That all members of the church strive to deepen their faith and express it through good works for others . . . [pause]

That all peoples come to the salvation God offers . . . [pause]

That the sick be healed, the rejected find acceptance, and the rebuffed receive courage . . . [pause]

That each of us here share with others the gift of life we have received so abundantly from God . . . [pause]

Presider: Merciful God, you offer life and salvation to all who cry out to you: hear these our prayers that one day we might enjoy the fullness of life with you in heaven. We ask this through Christ our Lord. **Amen.**

ALTERNATIVE OPENING PRAYER

Let us pray
   [with humility and persistence]

Pause for silent prayer

Almighty God, ever-loving Father,
your care extends beyond the boundaries
      of race and nation
to the hearts of all who live.

May the walls, which prejudice raises
      between us,
crumble beneath the shadow of your
      outstretched arm.

We ask this through Christ our Lord.
   Amen.

FIRST READING

Isa 56:1, 6-7

Thus says the LORD:
Observe what is right, do what is just;
   for my salvation is about to come,
   my justice, about to be revealed.

The foreigners who join themselves to the
      LORD,
   ministering to him,
loving the name of the LORD,
   and becoming his servants—
all who keep the sabbath free from
      profanation
   and hold to my covenant,
them I will bring to my holy mountain
   and make joyful in my house of prayer;
their burnt offerings and sacrifices
   will be acceptable on my altar,
for my house shall be called
   a house of prayer for all peoples.

RESPONSORIAL PSALM
Ps 67:2-3, 5, 6, 8

R︎. (4) O God, let all the nations praise you!

May God have pity on us and bless us;
   may he let his face shine upon us.
So may your way be known upon earth;
   among all nations, your salvation.

R︎. O God, let all the nations praise you!

May the nations be glad and exult
   because you rule the peoples in equity;
   the nations on the earth you guide.

R︎. O God, let all the nations praise you!

May the peoples praise you, O God;
   may all the peoples praise you!
May God bless us,
   and may all the ends of the earth fear
      him!

R︎. O God, let all the nations praise you!

SECOND READING
Rom 11:13-15, 29-32

Brothers and sisters:
I am speaking to you Gentiles.
Inasmuch as I am the apostle to the
   Gentiles,
   I glory in my ministry in order to make
      my race jealous
   and thus save some of them.
For if their rejection is the reconciliation of
   the world,
   what will their acceptance be but life
      from the dead?

For the gifts and the call of God are
   irrevocable.
Just as you once disobeyed God
   but have now received mercy because of
      their disobedience,
   so they have now disobeyed in order
      that,
   by virtue of the mercy shown to you,
   they too may now receive mercy.
For God delivered all to disobedience,
   that he might have mercy upon all.

About Liturgy
Second reading and revelation to the Gentiles: During Ordinary Time the second readings for Sundays and solemnities follow their own order, with semi-continuous readings from New Testament apostolic letters. This Sunday is one of the Sundays when by coincidence the second reading not only fits the gospel, first reading, and responsorial psalm but actually offers an interpretive insight.

These readings must be understood in the cultural context of Jesus and his time: the Jewish nation understood the Messiah as One who would come to save *them* and by so doing all nations would come to receive salvation *through* God's mighty deeds for Israel. This Sunday's gospel and Paul's mission to the Gentiles underscore the radically different and challenging understanding of the Messiah this inclusivity brings—salvation is for all. It would surely be appropriate this Sunday to include reference to the second reading in the homily.

About Liturgical Music
Music suggestions: Some widely available hymns that express the inclusivity of salvation proclaimed in this Sunday's Liturgy of the Word are "There's a Wideness in God's Mercy" (suitable for the entrance or the preparation of the gifts), "Gather Us In" (intended as an entrance song), and "In Christ There Is No East or West" (which would work well either as the entrance song or as the recessional). Less-broadly published but exceptionally suited to this Sunday is "Help Us Accept Each Other" [W3, RS], which could be used for the entrance or the preparation of the gifts.

"O Lord, Hear My Prayer" [G2, GC, GC2, LMGM, RS, SS] would be effective during the preparation of the gifts as an echo of both the Canaanite woman's pleading (first text) and her joy when Jesus finally responds (alternate text). An excellent Communion choice would be Sylvia Dunstan's "All Who Hunger" [G2, GC, GC2, RS]. Like the Canaanite woman, all who hunger because of any need are "never strangers" but "welcome guest[s]" at the table of God's goodness. Because the HOLY MANNA setting of this hymn is through-composed, it may be difficult for the assembly to sing while processing. Bob Moore's setting makes the last two phrases a refrain that can be sung easily without book in hand. Another excellent choice for Communion would be "At the Table of the World" [PMB, VO, WC, WS, choral octavo WLP 2612].

AUGUST 14, 2011
TWENTIETH SUNDAY
IN ORDINARY TIME

SPIRITUALITY

GOSPEL ACCLAMATION

℟. Alleluia, alleluia.
Mary is taken up to heaven;
a chorus of angels exults.
℟. Alleluia, alleluia.

Gospel   Luke 1:39-56; L622

Mary set out
    and traveled to the hill country
        in haste
    to a town of Judah,
    where she entered the house of
        Zechariah
    and greeted Elizabeth.
When Elizabeth heard Mary's
        greeting,
    the infant leaped in her womb,
    and Elizabeth, filled with the
        Holy Spirit,
    cried out in a loud voice and said,
    "Blessed are you among women,
    and blessed is the fruit of your womb.
And how does this happen to me,
    that the mother of my Lord should come
        to me?
For at the moment the sound of your greet-
        ing reached my ears,
    the infant in my womb leaped for joy.
Blessed are you who believed
    that what was spoken to you by the Lord
    would be fulfilled."

And Mary said:
    "My soul proclaims the greatness of the
        Lord;
        my spirit rejoices in God my Savior
        for he has looked upon his lowly ser-
            vant.
    From this day all generations will call me
        blessed:
        the Almighty has done great things for
            me,
        and holy is his Name.
    He has mercy on those who fear him
        in every generation.
    He has shown the strength of his arm,
        and has scattered the proud in their
            conceit.

Continued in Appendix A, p. 301.
See Appendix A, p. 301, for the other readings.

Reflecting on the Gospel

This festival honoring Mary reminds us of an intimate love relationship—that between Mary and her divine son. Humanity and divinity kiss—not only in the womb between the Virgin and her divine son but also in the singular unity of the humanity and divinity of her son. Such a singular privilege, we would think, would leave Mary far above us. Not so! Mary remains ever the humble one who does God's will and is open to however God wishes to use her to bring about salvation for all.

Even as "mother of [the] Lord" Mary remained a "lowly" one. Having said yes to God's grace within her, she visits the pregnant Elizabeth. Thus Mary demonstrates for us faithful discipleship—yes to God and generous hospitality of self. Mary's self-giving, then, is more than her body being the first temple for the Lord; her self-giving means that she brings that presence of her Lord to others. She could sing her *Magnificat* with full-throated faith because she herself had experienced the marvels God had brought about in her. She herself had been "lifted up" to become the mother of God.

It is for this faithful discipleship that Mary "belong[ed] to Christ" (second reading). This discipleship began when she consented to the pregnancy and gave birth "to a son . . . destined to rule all the nations" (first reading), but it didn't end there. Mary's whole life—even to standing beneath the cross—was focused on her son, continuing a growth in intimacy—love relationship—with the One who was both Son and Lord.

This festival celebrates that God has indeed "lifted up the lowly"—Mary has been assumed body and soul into heaven. Mary was lifted up by God because of her faithfulness to God's saving mystery, her generosity of life toward others, and her acknowledgment of God as the source of her grace and goodness. When we too are faithful, humble, and generous as Mary models for us, like her we are lifted up to share in "a place prepared by God" (first reading) where "in Christ shall all be brought to life" (second reading).

This festival reminds us, therefore, that Mary was not *unique* in her faithful discipleship—all of us can "belong to Christ" and bring others life as well as receive life ourselves. Like Mary, we must say yes to whatever God asks of us. Then, like Mary also, we bear Christ for others and are blessed! We too are "lowly ones" who are lifted up to share in divine life!

Living the Paschal Mystery

Mary had a singular privilege of giving birth to the divine son; yet in another way, we as children of God also give birth to the presence of the risen Christ for others. This is perhaps the first and most important meaning of discipleship: that we nurture Christ within ourselves so that through us others can encounter him. Discipleship is fruitful to the extent that our love relationship with the One whom we follow grows into the kind of mature love that knows no bounds in its self-giving.

In order to be Christ-bearers we must unceasingly return to the source of our blessedness—our loving God. This begins in fidelity to the intimacy of daily prayer and continues in recognizing that God dwells in us and in those we meet in the everyday circumstances of our lives. Our love for each other reflects our love for God. Our generosity toward each other reflects the generosity of God toward us in giving us the divine Son as our brother and Mary as our heavenly mother.

Focusing the Gospel

Key words and phrases: Blessed are you who believed, lifted up the lowly, remained with her about three months

To the point: This festival celebrates that God has indeed "lifted up the lowly"—Mary has been assumed body and soul into heaven. Mary was lifted up by God because of her faithfulness to God's saving mystery, her generosity of life toward others, and her acknowledgment of God as the source of her grace and goodness. When we too are faithful, humble, and generous as Mary models for us, like her we are lifted up to share in "a place prepared by God" (first reading) where "in Christ shall all be brought to life" (second reading).

Model Act of Penitence

Presider: Today we celebrate the singular privileges Mary enjoyed: the lowly one who was raised up to be the mother of the Savior and the one who was raised up body and soul into heaven. Let us reflect on the graces God has bestowed on us . . . [pause]

Lord Jesus, you are the blessed fruit of Mary's womb: Lord . . .

Christ Jesus, you are the fulfillment of God's promise of salvation: Christ . . .

Lord Jesus, you are God our Savior: Lord . . .

Model Prayer of the Faithful

Presider: With confidence that God hears the prayer of the lowly, we make our needs known.

Response:

Cantor:

That the church proclaim by gracious words and generous deeds the greatness of God . . . [pause]

That all peoples receive the salvation offered in Christ . . . [pause]

That the lowly be raised up, the hungry be fed, and those needing any kind of help be remembered . . . [pause]

That each of us here grow in believing that we too are bearers of the presence of the risen Christ to all we meet . . . [pause]

Presider: Loving God, you blessed Mary because she bore your divine Son: hear these our prayers that we might one day be with her in heaven to sing your everlasting praises. We ask this through that same Son, Jesus Christ our Lord. **Amen.**

FOR REFLECTION

• Mary's faithfulness inspires me to . . .
Mary's generosity of life inspires me to
. . . Mary's humility inspires me to . . .

• I experience being lifted up by God
when . . .

• I proclaim the greatness of God by . . .
God has done these great things for
me . . .

Homily Points

• We often give public citations and recognition to individuals who show remarkable fidelity to their responsibilities of life and generosity toward others. How much we admire recipients of these awards when they acknowledge others who have helped them grow into this kind of fidelity and generosity!

• In response to Elizabeth's words praising her, Mary immediately sings a hymn of praise honoring God's greatness and fidelity. True humility does not lie in denying that we can do great things. True humility lies in our acknowledging the Source of all the goodness we do.

SPIRITUALITY

GOSPEL ACCLAMATION
Matt 16:18

℟. Alleluia, alleluia.
You are Peter and upon this rock I will build my Church
and the gates of the netherworld shall not prevail against it.
℟. Alleluia, alleluia.

Gospel

Matt 16:13-20; L121A

Jesus went into the
    region of Caesarea
    Philippi and
he asked his
    disciples,
    "Who do people say
        that the Son of
        Man is?"
They replied, "Some say John the
        Baptist, others Elijah,
    still others Jeremiah or one of the
        prophets."
He said to them, "But who do you say
        that I am?"
Simon Peter said in reply,
    "You are the Christ, the Son of the
        living God."
Jesus said to him in reply,
    "Blessed are you, Simon son of
        Jonah.
For flesh and blood has not revealed
        this to you, but my heavenly
        Father.
And so I say to you, you are Peter,
    and upon this rock I will build my
        church,
    and the gates of the netherworld
        shall not prevail against it.
I will give you the keys to the kingdom
        of heaven.
Whatever you bind on earth shall be
        bound in heaven;
    and whatever you loose on earth
        shall be loosed in heaven."
Then he strictly ordered his disciples
    to tell no one that he was the Christ.

Reflecting on the Gospel

Without thinking about it too much, we have all kinds of expectations about buildings. We associate adobe and one-floor plans especially with western homes and we associate basements and multiple stories especially with mid-west farm homes. We expect a court building to have rooms with judges' benches, jury boxes, witness stands, and defendant and prosecution tables. A museum has galleries and a theater has a large auditorium. Some people expect churches to have columns and statues and ornate architecture. This Sunday's gospel is about a special kind of building, but neither the disciples in the gospel nor we are totally prepared for what Jesus reveals about this kind of building.

The gospel begins with a seemingly straightforward question that Jesus puts to his disciples about his identity, and it ends with Jesus revealing how he will build his church. Jesus uses people, not bricks and mortar, as the "rocks" of his foundation. Jesus builds his church out of the community of believers who continually acknowledge him as "the Christ" and remain ever faithful to his saving mission. Rather than a fixed edifice, the church is a fluidity of persons cemented together in the mystery of Christ. And nothing shall "prevail against it."

Today when we hear the word "church" we often think of it as the building down the street or as institutional—its organizational structure, power, wealth, prestige, hierarchy, etc. This gospel challenges us to keep before our eyes the more important understanding of church as the community of believers who constantly make present the risen Christ. Jesus makes a vital connection between his self-identity and the reality of the church. The church rests in Jesus, derives from who he is and his ministry, and is built up only by our own participation in the identity of Jesus. The church is the Body of Christ made visible in the community of believers who carry forward Jesus' saving mission. The church will prevail because Jesus' saving mission will prevail to the end of time when all will be gathered back to the Father.

The question in the gospel about the identity of Jesus really goes beyond even the identity of Jesus! Jesus is doing a wonderful thing in this gospel—he is telling us that by being church we participate in his identity (as children of God) and his saving mission. Nothing will prevail against this church so long as we keep ourselves turned toward Jesus and remember that our own identity as members of the Body of Christ is bound up in who Jesus is: "the Christ, the Son of the living God."

Living the Paschal Mystery

Without detracting from the primacy of Peter and the Chair of Peter, nonetheless we also share in building up the church each time we are faithful to who Jesus is. Church isn't something we *go to* once a week, but it is an *identity* we share as members of the Body of Christ into which we were initiated at baptism. We build up this Body, the church, any time we reach out to another in need and respond as Christ would. We build up this Body, the church, every time we gather as a liturgical assembly to give God praise and thanks. We build up his Body, the church, any time we forgive, offer an encouraging word, show mercy and compassion. In all these and many other ways we are not only building up the church but also witnessing to our identity as church—as the presence of the risen Christ made visible in and through us. Such an identity we share!

Focusing the Gospel

Key words and phrases: You are the Christ, upon this rock, build my church

To the point: This gospel begins with a seemingly straightforward question that Jesus puts to his disciples about his identity, and it ends with Jesus revealing how he will build his church. Jesus uses people, not bricks and mortar, as the "rocks" of his foundation. Jesus builds his church out of the community of believers who continually acknowledge him as "the Christ" and remain ever faithful to his saving mission. Rather than a fixed edifice, the church is a fluidity of persons cemented together in the mystery of Christ. And nothing shall "prevail against it."

Connecting the Gospel

to the first reading: The church is the community of those people whom God has placed "like a peg in a sure spot" (first reading). God absolutely assures that the church will continue as God wills it to be.

to experience: There is a tendency to think of faith in Jesus only as a personal commitment. The gospel reminds us that faith finds its deepest expression in the community of the church.

Connecting the Responsorial Psalm

to the readings: In some versions of Psalm 138 the word "angels" found in the first strophe is translated "other gods," for the Hebrew term used ('*elohim*) variously meant "God," "gods," or "godlike beings." These multiple meanings emerged as Israel slowly groped toward belief in one God. As their faith in the one God '*Elohim* grew, they dethroned their notion of other gods. Compared to the one God, other gods were mere angels or idols, and it is before these shadows of former power that the psalmist stands and sings God's praises.

It is fitting that we sing this psalm on the Sunday when we celebrate Peter's coming to recognize who Jesus is. As with Israel, his recognition was a slow process. As with Israel, his movement toward faith was a gift of God's revelation. As with Israel, his faith would be the foundation of the faith of many others. So too for us. We pray in this psalm that God never forsake the work of revelation and salvation begun within us.

to psalmist preparation: The "work of [God's] hands" you sing about in this Sunday's psalm is the gift of revelation, the gift of faith, the gift of the church founded upon the person Peter, who grew in faith through experience and grace. You could pick any one of these—revelation, faith, the church—to pray about this week. How have you, through experience and grace, come to hear God's revelation? How have you grown in your faith? How have you strengthened your identity with the church?

**ASSEMBLY &
FAITH-SHARING GROUPS**
- I would answer Jesus' question about his identity by saying he is . . .
- My understanding of Jesus' identity determines and purifies my understanding of the church in that . . .
- I experience Jesus continuing to build his church on me when . . . by . . .

PRESIDERS
My identity as an ordained minister has matured as my encounters with Jesus have deepened in that . . .

DEACONS
My manner of serving builds up the church when . . . It tears down the church when . . .

HOSPITALITY MINISTERS
Good hospitality cements the community of believers to . . .

MUSIC MINISTERS
My music ministry has brought me to deeper knowledge of and faith in Jesus when . . .

ALTAR MINISTERS
My serving others is a revelation of Jesus' identity to the community in that . . .

LECTORS
Those who observe how I live would come to know Jesus as . . .

**EXTRAORDINARY MINISTERS
OF HOLY COMMUNION**
I remind the assembly (through my ministry and daily living) of its identity as the Body of Christ whenever I . . .

Model Act of Penitence

Presider: In today's gospel we hear Peter acknowledge that Jesus is the Christ, the Son of the living God. As we prepare ourselves for this liturgy let us open our hearts to encounter this same Christ who is present among us, his church gathered in his name . . . [pause]

Lord Jesus, you are the Christ, the Son of the living God: Lord . . .

Christ Jesus, you are the revelation of the heavenly Father: Christ . . .

Lord Jesus, you build your church upon the community of the faithful: Lord . . .

Homily Points

• Parents cringe when children ask seemingly simple questions like "Where do babies come from?" or "Where did Grandma go when she died?" They answer with an age-appropriate response and breathe a sigh of relief if the child is satisfied with what they say. Some questions, however, have no age-appropriate answer, nor can any answer ever leave us completely satisfied. Jesus asks just such a question in this gospel.

• "[W]ho do you say that I am?" is not a question that can be answered easily because it really asks about the very mystery of God and salvation. Further, Jesus' response to Peter's answer reveals another mystery: that of his church built upon *us*, an imperfect people, yet a church that will prevail.

• This gospel intrigues us with the mystery of our own identity as church built of a community of believers. If the identity of the church and its saving mission fell on our shoulders as individuals, we would be crushed under its weight. But this is a shared identity: we rely on one another in our strengths and our weaknesses, in our failures and our victories, in our gifts and our limitations. In all, Christ is the center who assures our continued growth in our faithfulness to him and constantly helps us as we take up his saving mission and journey to fullness of life.

Model Prayer of the Faithful

Presider: As the church of Christ, let us pray for our needs and those of the whole world.

Response:

Lord, hear our prayer.

Cantor:

we pray to the Lord,

That we members of the church always be faithful to our identity as Christ's Body and our sharing in his saving mission . . . [pause]

That all peoples of the world receive the salvation Christ offers . . . [pause]

That those suffering any need be filled through the generosity of Christ's church . . . [pause]

That each of us here grow in our faithfulness to Christ and one another . . . [pause]

Presider: God of salvation, you call us to be the community of the church: hear these our prayers that as we share now in the identity and mission of Christ we might one day share in his everlasting life. We ask this through that same Christ our Lord. **Amen.**

OPENING PRAYER

Let us pray

Pause for silent prayer

Father,
help us to seek the values
that will bring us lasting joy in this
 changing world.
In our desire for what you promise
make us one in mind and heart.

Grant this through our Lord Jesus Christ,
 your Son,
who lives and reigns with you and the
 Holy Spirit,
one God, for ever and ever. **Amen.**

FIRST READING
Isa 22:19-23

Thus says the LORD to Shebna, master of
 the palace:
"I will thrust you from your office
 and pull you down from your station.
On that day I will summon my servant
 Eliakim, son of Hilkiah;
I will clothe him with your robe,
 and gird him with your sash,
 and give over to him your authority.
He shall be a father to the inhabitants of
 Jerusalem,
 and to the house of Judah.
I will place the key of the House of David
 on Eliakim's shoulder;
 when he opens, no one shall shut;
 when he shuts, no one shall open.
I will fix him like a peg in a sure spot,
 to be a place of honor for his family."

RESPONSORIAL PSALM

Ps 138:1-2, 2-3, 6, 8

R⁊. (8bc) Lord, your love is eternal; do not forsake the work of your hands.

I will give thanks to you, O LORD, with all my heart,
    for you have heard the words of my mouth;
    in the presence of the angels I will sing your praise;
I will worship at your holy temple.

R⁊. Lord, your love is eternal; do not forsake the work of your hands.

I will give thanks to your name,
    because of your kindness and your truth:
when I called, you answered me;
    you built up strength within me.

R⁊. Lord, your love is eternal; do not forsake the work of your hands.

The LORD is exalted, yet the lowly he sees,
    and the proud he knows from afar.
Your kindness, O LORD, endures forever;
    forsake not the work of your hands.

R⁊. Lord, your love is eternal; do not forsake the work of your hands.

SECOND READING

Rom 11:33-36

Oh, the depth of the riches and wisdom and knowledge of God!
How inscrutable are his judgments and how unsearchable his ways!
For who has known the mind of the Lord
    or who has been his counselor?
Or who has given the Lord anything that he may be repaid?
For from him and through him and for him are all things.
To him be glory forever. Amen.

About Liturgy

Liturgy and the identity of Christ: Each liturgy includes numerous times when we acknowledge the identity and presence of Christ. For example, we begin Mass with the Sign of the Cross—an acknowledgment not simply of the presence of "Christ, the Son of the living God," but of the other two persons of the Trinity as well. Even more telling is our language preceding and concluding the proclamation of the gospel. In both acclamations we utter praise: "Glory to *you*, O Lord"; "Praise to *you*, Lord Jesus Christ." It is telling that we use second-person pronouns in these two acclamations: *you* (we don't do so at the conclusion of the first and second readings). Our language itself is saluting the very person of Christ, whom we address as really present to us in this assembly, during this gospel proclamation.

These acclamations say something more: by our *common* acknowledgment of the presence of Christ in the very proclamation of the gospel, we also are binding ourselves together as one community; the "glue" that binds us is none other than our shared identity as the Body of Christ, which we ourselves proclaim by acknowledging Christ's presence. The proclamation of the gospel is a particular moment for building up the Body of Christ, the church!

About Liturgical Music

Music suggestions: This would also be a good week to repeat a hymn used on the Nineteenth Sunday when Peter struggled with fear and doubt and the disciples first proclaimed Jesus as Son of God. Repeating a hymn such as "How Firm a Foundation" helps us see the progression in the Lectionary gospel readings as well as the progression in our own faith as we move through this long season of Ordinary Time.

Bernadette Farrell's "Praise to You, O Christ Our Savior" [BB, CBW3, G2, GC, JS2, RS] would make a good choice for the entrance song. The text's assertion of faith in Christ is well supported by a strong melodic line and sturdy 4/4 meter. Sylvia Dunstan's "Who Is This Who Walks Among Us?" [in *Where the Promise Shines* from GIA] was written to be used on this Sunday when Peter makes his profession of faith in Jesus as Son of God. Set to a strong 8787 tune (such as STUTTGART or MERTON), this hymn would make an excellent entrance song. Other appropriate choices for this Sunday include "O Christ, the Great Foundation" [CBW3, CH, GC2, RS, SS, W3]; "Church of God" [GC, PMB, RS]; and "Christ's Church Shall Glory" [CH, RS, SS, W3].

AUGUST 21, 2011
TWENTY-FIRST SUNDAY IN ORDINARY TIME

SPIRITUALITY

GOSPEL ACCLAMATION
See Eph 1:17-18

℟. Alleluia, alleluia.
May the Father of our Lord Jesus Christ
enlighten the eyes of our hearts,
that we may know what is the hope
that belongs to our call.
℟. Alleluia, alleluia.

Gospel

Matt 16:21-27; L124A

Jesus began to show his
    disciples
  that he must go to
      Jerusalem and suffer
      greatly
  from the elders, the chief
      priests, and the scribes,
  and be killed and on the third day be
      raised.
Then Peter took Jesus aside and began
    to rebuke him,
  "God forbid, Lord! No such thing
      shall ever happen to you."
He turned and said to Peter,
  "Get behind me, Satan! You are an
      obstacle to me.
You are thinking not as God does, but
    as human beings do."

Then Jesus said to his disciples,
  "Whoever wishes to come after me
      must deny himself,
  take up his cross, and follow me.
For whoever wishes to save his life will
    lose it,
  but whoever loses his life for my
      sake will find it.
What profit would there be for one to
    gain the whole world
  and forfeit his life?
Or what can one give in exchange for
    his life?
For the Son of Man will come with his
    angels in his Father's glory,
  and then he will repay all according
      to his conduct."

Reflecting on the Gospel

None of us likes to be rebuffed by another. If a child is trying to help a parent and the parent pushes the little one aside because he or she is getting in the way of doing the task quickly, the child is hurt; constant rebuffing can even greatly damage the child's self-esteem. If a boss rebuffs a worker, the worker might develop resentment and not care about doing his or her best. If a friend rebuffs a friend to pursue some selfish interest, the friend is rightfully hurt. In this gospel Jesus harshly rebuffs Peter. The gospel doesn't record Peter's feelings or response, but he must have been hurt. Jesus, however, didn't rebuff Peter because Jesus wanted to pursue some selfish interest. Jesus is single-minded about the purpose for which he came—to be faithful to doing the Father's will in bringing us salvation—and Peter's rebuke was counter to Jesus' integrity.

This gospel begins with a clear statement of what we call the paschal mystery: Jesus will "suffer," "be killed," and "be raised." Peter recoils at this statement of Jesus' fate. So do we! Suffering and death is hardly an attraction that we would seek and make central in our daily lives. Yet it must be, for Jesus attests that the only way to have our life is to lose it. Why would we want to make losing our life—suffering and death—something central to our daily living? Like Peter, we tend to limit our vision by focusing only on the suffering and death. The fullness of the paschal mystery always leads through suffering and death to new life.

"Jesus *began* to show . . ." The disciples can only gradually grasp and accept the demanding truth Jesus relates: "suffer greatly . . . and be killed." Peter recoils at the import—who wouldn't? Jesus' curt command to Peter—"Get behind me, Satan!"—points to the crux of the challenge: we are to think like God, not like humans. In God's saving plan, life comes through death. No human instinctively understands or embraces this. God's love alone reveals this mystery, makes it happen, and embraces us as we surrender ourselves to this truth.

If we focus only on the cost of discipleship—dying to self; losing one's life for the sake of another; daring to be a countercultural sign in a culture overtaken with more and better possessions, constant entertainment, self-indulgence—we'll become as disillusioned and discouraged as Jeremiah in the first reading. We always need to hear Jesus' *whole* message about the paschal mystery: we must lose our life in order to find it. The suffering and death *always* lead to new life. We know this because Jesus has already shown us the way. His prophecy about his passion and death *includes* his announcement of being raised to new life. This is what is central to who we are as Christians, what is to be all-absorbing in our lives.

Living the Paschal Mystery

Authentic discipleship doesn't require us to hunt for suffering. Being faithful to Jesus will bring enough as it is. This is so because living and witnessing to gospel values challenges so many values that society touts as ones that will bring us happiness. Ultimately, though, we find that only living gospel values brings us lasting happiness, even though we must die to self in the process. All who wish to be faithful to Jesus' call to gospel living must be prepared to suffer—and also be prepared to receive new life. The life Jesus offers is worth any price!

Focusing the Gospel

Key words and phrases: Jesus began to show; suffer greatly; be killed; Get behind me, Satan; loses his life . . . find it

To the point: "Jesus *began* to show . . ." The disciples can only gradually grasp and accept the demanding truth Jesus relates: "suffer greatly . . . and be killed." Peter recoils at the import—who wouldn't? Jesus' curt command to Peter—"Get behind me, Satan!"—points to the crux of the challenge: we are to think like God, not like humans. In God's saving plan, life comes through death. No human instinctively understands or embraces this. God's love alone reveals this mystery, makes it happen, and embraces us as we surrender ourselves to this truth.

Connecting the Gospel

to the first reading: Jeremiah suffered for being faithful to God's call. All who choose such fidelity must be prepared to suffer. Jesus promises that those who surrender their lives for God's "sake" will be saved.

to experience: Authentic discipleship does not mean that we hunt for suffering. Choosing to be faithful to gospel living (the mission of Jesus) will bring enough as it is.

Connecting the Responsorial Psalm

to the readings: Jesus does not hedge what he has to say to the disciples: "I must go to Jerusalem and be killed and then raised, and you must follow in my footsteps." Peter reacts as did Jeremiah in his day: "Lord, you have 'duped' me; I thought we were heading for glory and now you promise degradation and death." Jeremiah cries, "What kind of God are you?" Peter cries, "What kind of Messiah are you?"

To these questions the responsorial psalm replies: You are the God for whom we thirst, the God whose kindness is "greater . . . than life itself," the God who alone ultimately satisfies us. If we maintain our focus on this God, we will have, as did Jeremiah, as did Jesus, as ultimately did Peter, the courage to lose our life. For we will have learned that in our very thirsting for God we have already tasted the greater life promised us.

to psalmist preparation: In Hebrew, Psalm 63 reads "My *nephesh* [= throat] is thirsting for you, O Lord my God." The sense is that the psalmist cries out to God from the place that receives breath and nourishment, the place through which life enters the body. When you open your throat to sing this psalm, do you realize that you will be crying out to God for life? How can you help the assembly hear your thirst for God? How can you help them taste your satisfaction?

**ASSEMBLY &
FAITH-SHARING GROUPS**
- At the call to deny self, take up the cross, and follow Jesus, I respond with mere human thinking ("God forbid, Lord!") when I . . . I respond according to God's way of thinking when I . . .
- I've experienced life coming from "death" when . . .
- In the midst of the challenges and difficulties of faithfully following Jesus, I have experienced God's loving embrace when . . .

PRESIDERS
My preaching is honest about the real cost/demands of discipleship in that . . . My preaching helps people experience the new life God offers when . . .

DEACONS
Diaconal service has challenged me (sometimes painfully) to deny and lose self by . . . My ministry has also helped me find life in that . . .

HOSPITALITY MINISTERS
Extending genuine hospitality is an embrace of God's love when I . . .

MUSIC MINISTERS
My fidelity to music ministry calls me to die to myself when . . . This same fidelity brings me new life when . . .

ALTAR MINISTERS
Serving others is a way of losing my life for the sake of Jesus in that . . .

LECTORS
My time with the word challenges my thinking "as humans do" and develops my thinking "as God does" in that . . .

**EXTRAORDINARY MINISTERS
OF HOLY COMMUNION**
In Holy Communion Jesus freely gives himself to us. I give myself to others in these ways . . .

Model Act of Penitence

Presider: In today's gospel Jesus tells the disciples that he must suffer and be killed before he will be raised up. As followers of Jesus, we can expect no less in our own lives. We pause at the beginning of this liturgy to ask God for the strength to be faithful . . . [pause]

Lord Jesus, you are the Savior who gave your life that we might have life: Lord . . .

Christ Jesus, you reign forever in risen glory: Christ . . .

Lord Jesus, you are the revelation of God's love for us: Lord . . .

Homily Points

• What parent hasn't had the experience of holding a squirming and crying child while putting stinging antiseptic on a cut? The parent's action causes pain for the child, surely not because the parent wants to hurt the child but because the parent fears infection or even greater harm. The parent desires only good for the child.

• God does not desire pain for pain's sake. What God desires for us is new life, the life that comes only through conforming ourselves to God's will (as Jeremiah does in the first reading and Jesus in the gospel). This always entails "pain." We embrace the pain of dying to self, losing our life, self-giving for the sake of others to the extent that we think like God: see beyond the immediate "death" and seek the only thing that is lasting—a share in the new life God offers.

• Our instinctive reaction, like Peter's, is to recoil in the face of the demands of living the gospel. What motivates us to choose to be faithful despite the cost to self is Jesus' promise of new life and God's continued love and presence as we journey toward the fullness of life.

Model Prayer of the Faithful

Presider: The life of a disciple is demanding; we ask God now for the strength to be faithful.

Response:

Lord, hear our prayer.

Cantor:

we pray to the Lord,

That all members of the church grow in the courage needed to follow Jesus through death to life . . . [pause]

That all world leaders work to relieve the suffering and pain of others . . . [pause]

That those suffering in any way be comforted by the loving embrace of God . . . [pause]

That this community of faith support one another in our struggle to live the gospel faithfully, and rejoice together in the new life we are given even now . . . [pause]

Presider: Gracious God, you raised your divine Son to new life through his suffering and death: hear these our prayers, strengthen us to be faithful disciples, and bring us one day to enjoy the fullness of life with you. We ask this through Christ our Lord. **Amen.**

OPENING PRAYER

Let us pray

Pause for silent prayer

Almighty God,
every good thing comes from you.
Fill our hearts with love for you,
increase our faith,
and by your constant care
protect the good you have given us.

We ask this through our Lord Jesus Christ,
    your Son,
who lives and reigns with you and the
    Holy Spirit,
one God, for ever and ever. **Amen.**

FIRST READING
Jer 20:7-9

You duped me, O LORD, and I let myself be
    duped;
    you were too strong for me, and you
    triumphed.
All the day I am an object of laughter;
    everyone mocks me.

Whenever I speak, I must cry out,
    violence and outrage is my message;
the word of the LORD has brought me
    derision and reproach all the day.

I say to myself, I will not mention him,
    I will speak in his name no more.
But then it becomes like fire burning in
    my heart,
    imprisoned in my bones;
I grow weary holding it in, I cannot endure
    it.

RESPONSORIAL PSALM
Ps 63:2, 3-4, 5-6, 8-9

R̴. (2b) My soul is thirsting for you, O
Lord my God.

O God, you are my God whom I seek;
    for you my flesh pines and my soul
        thirsts
    like the earth, parched, lifeless and
        without water.

R̴. My soul is thirsting for you, O Lord my
God.

Thus have I gazed toward you in the
        sanctuary
    to see your power and your glory,
for your kindness is a greater good than
        life;
    my lips shall glorify you.

R̴. My soul is thirsting for you, O Lord my
God.

Thus will I bless you while I live;
    lifting up my hands, I will call upon
        your name.
As with the riches of a banquet shall my
        soul be satisfied,
    and with exultant lips my mouth shall
        praise you.

R̴. My soul is thirsting for you, O Lord my
God.

You are my help,
    and in the shadow of your wings I shout
        for joy.
My soul clings fast to you;
    your right hand upholds me.

R̴. My soul is thirsting for you, O Lord my
God.

SECOND READING
Rom 12:1-2

I urge you, brothers and sisters, by the
        mercies of God,
    to offer your bodies as a living sacrifice,
    holy and pleasing to God, your spiritual
        worship.
Do not conform yourselves to this age
    but be transformed by the renewal of
        your mind,
    that you may discern what is the will
        of God,
    what is good and pleasing and perfect.

About Liturgy

Paschal mystery central: The challenge in reading about or reflecting on the paschal mystery is to take it from being a theological concept to a celebrated and lived reality in our daily lives. This means seeing how the paschal mystery unfolds in the very structure of the liturgy as well as in the challenges of daily Christian living.

Liturgical structure: Each liturgy embodies within its very shape or structure the dying and rising dynamic of the paschal mystery. For example, at Mass the Liturgy of the Word's prophetic challenge to living the gospel reminds us that our everyday living is to be united with Christ's ministry of reaching out to others. In the Liturgy of the Eucharist we praise and thank God for the gift of new life and salvation, and for the nourishing strength given us as we come to the eucharistic table. Within the very unfolding of the liturgy the balance of dying and rising is presented, always reminding us that the dying leads us to new life.

Daily living: In daily living the balance between dying and rising isn't always so apparent because they usually don't flow one into the other, as is true with the ritual structure of liturgy. In other words, we can't approach the mystery with the attitude, "OK, I've done my suffering; now where's the new life?" However, there are even hints of the balance in our daily lives. For example, parents generally give of themselves unreservedly for their children's welfare. At the same time they experience great pride and joy in watching their children grow into healthy, happy, productive adults. Another way to consider the dying and rising is that in the very dying is the new life. This is so because in dying to ourselves—by conforming our wills to God's, by committing ourselves to the good of others, etc.—we are becoming more like Christ onto whom we were grafted at baptism. Becoming more like Christ, we share more abundantly in the risen life he offers. As the gospel this Sunday teaches us, by dying to self we receive new life. What God offers us when we surrender our life to living gospel values is unimaginable to us humans. God offers us a share in the risen life of the Son.

About Liturgical Music

Music suggestions: This Sunday introduces a dramatic shift in the content of the gospel readings. Jesus begins to walk toward Jerusalem and death, and challenges his disciples—meaning us—to walk with him. One way to express this shift musically is to change the service music we have been singing. Changing the service music expresses our willingness to change direction with Jesus and walk with him to the cross and resurrection. We then need to keep this set of service music in place for the rest of Ordinary Time so that it can support us on our ongoing journey.

Songs speaking of our call and our willingness to carry the cross certainly fit this Sunday. "Take Up Your Cross" [in most hymnals], Bernadette Farrell's "Unless a Grain of Wheat" [BB, G2, GC, GC2, JS2, OFVU, RS], "Only This I Want" [BB, G2, GC, GC2, JS2, OFUV], appropriate verses of Dan Schutte's "Glory in the Cross" [BB, JS2, OFUV], and "Lift High the Cross" [in most hymnals] are some examples.

AUGUST 28, 2011
TWENTY-SECOND SUNDAY IN ORDINARY TIME

✠ SPIRITUALITY

GOSPEL ACCLAMATION
2 Cor 5:19

℟. Alleluia, alleluia.
God was reconciling the world to himself in Christ
and entrusting to us the message of
reconciliation.
℟. Alleluia, alleluia.

Gospel

Matt 18:15-20; L127A

Jesus said to his disciples:
"If your brother sins
    against you,
  go and tell him his fault
    between you and him
    alone.
If he listens to you, you have won over
    your brother.
If he does not listen,
  take one or two others along with
    you,
  so that 'every fact may be
    established
  on the testimony of two or three
    witnesses.'
If he refuses to listen to them, tell the
    church.
If he refuses to listen even to the
    church,
  then treat him as you would a Gentile
    or a tax collector.
Amen, I say to you,
  whatever you bind on earth shall be
    bound in heaven,
  and whatever you loose on earth
    shall be loosed in heaven.
Again, amen, I say to you,
  if two of you agree on earth
  about anything for which they are to
    pray,
  it shall be granted to them by my
    heavenly Father.
For where two or three are gathered
    together in my name,
  there am I in the midst of them."

Reflecting on the Gospel

Wouldn't life be great if we could take Jesus' words in this Sunday's gospel at face value, literally? Getting two people to agree about some things we might pray for is not difficult at all, especially if the outcome of our prayer is exactly as we envision it. Without any effort whatsoever, we could find dozens of people who would join us in praying to win a mega lottery (provided, of course, we share it equally!). We could find scores of people who would join us in praying for world peace, an end to hunger, an equitable and responsible distribution and use of the world's resources. So, is Jesus' seeming promise just hyperbole? No, not exactly. Jesus' teaching in the first part of the gospel and his condition for having our prayers answered (captured in the last line) provide the context and rationale for his promise that our prayers will be heard.

Both our human life and our life in Christ call attention to the fact that we are never totally alone nor ever act alone: we are members of our families, neighborhoods, social groups, the Body of Christ. We find our deepest identity not in ourselves but in community with God and others. What this gospel teaches us about sinning against each other and seeking reconciliation rests on the final statement: Jesus abides in the midst of the church, the community of believers who commit themselves to him and live as he did. A sin of one member against another affects the life of the whole community of the church. In the church we are accountable to and for one another because our manner of relating, reconciling, and praying together reveals both our commitment to Jesus and his living presence among us.

Praying in Jesus' name means so much more than ending our prayers with "we ask this through Christ our Lord." It means living the kind of loving relationship befitting those who have been made members of Jesus' community of believers. What is ultimately at stake in our community relationships is the presence of Jesus in the church: when reconciliation takes place and where two or three gather in his name, Jesus is "in the midst of them." This helps us understand that we don't have church without the presence of Jesus in our midst. The church is nothing less than the presence of the risen Christ in and among us. This very community of persons makes present Christ. When rifts disrupt the community, it weakens our potency to make visible this risen presence. This is no small matter that Jesus addresses in the gospel! At stake is whether we are being true to ourselves and to the persons God has called us to be in Christ. At stake is whether we care enough about having Christ in our midst that we seek reconciliation with anyone we have harmed in any way.

Living the Paschal Mystery

Facing another about hurts is one of the most difficult "dyings" we undertake—a dying that requires us to risk relationships, let go of self-righteousness, perhaps face angry reaction. From the other side, admitting that we have hurt another—even something so simple as apologizing to another for an inadvertent hurt—takes great humility and honesty. Neither facing another nor facing ourselves about sinfulness is easy!

The good news and strength to be reconcilers come from Jesus' promise that he is in the midst of two or three gathered in his name. The challenge of this gospel is to grow in the consciousness that we and others are the presence of the risen Christ for one another, and then to act accordingly.

Focusing the Gospel

Key words and phrases: sins against you, two of you agree, two or three of you gathered, I in the midst of them

To the point: What this gospel teaches us about sinning against each other and seeking reconciliation rests on the final statement: Jesus abides in the midst of the church, the community of believers who commit themselves to him and live as he did. A sin of one member against another affects the life of the whole community of the church. In the church we are accountable to and for one another because our manner of relating, reconciling, and praying together reveals both our commitment to Jesus and his living presence among us.

Connecting the Gospel

to first reading: In a very dramatic prophecy ("I will hold you responsible for his death") Ezekiel reveals the word of the LORD: calling others to live rightly is truly our responsibility. In the gospel Jesus makes clear that accepting this responsibility affects the well-being of the whole community.

to experience: Traditionally, the sacrament of penance has been solely a private matter among penitent, priest, and God. The revised rite of communal reconciliation underscores the communal aspects of both sin and reconciliation.

Connecting the Responsorial Psalm

to the readings: Psalm 95 was an enthronement psalm sung while the Israelites processed to the temple. A song leader called the community to enter God's presence singing songs of praise and thanksgiving. In the midst of this call to worship, however, the leader sounded a jarring note: the people were warned not to turn against God as their ancestors did in the desert. The human heart, they were reminded, is fickle and easily hardened.

This Sunday the Lectionary applies Psalm 95 to us, the church. We are called to worship. We are called to hear the voice of God and heed it. But fidelity is not easy and so we are also called to confront one another honestly when we fail (first reading and gospel) and to handle the conflicts and hurts among us directly and openly (gospel). We are to deal with our fickle, human hearts with the grace promised us by Christ (gospel). At stake is our fidelity to God, the authenticity of our community, and the genuineness of our worship.

to psalmist preparation: When you sing this psalm, you invite the assembly to be faithful to genuine worship. The psalm indicates that human beings have a poor track record in this regard. As you sing it, then, you enact what the first reading and gospel demand: you speak honestly to the people about their behavior and invite them to conversion. As you prepare to sing this psalm, you might spend some time thanking God for those persons in your life who have challenged your behavior when it was not faithful. What gave them the courage to be so honest? What gave you the grace to hear what they were saying?

ASSEMBLY & FAITH-SHARING GROUPS
- When others sin against me, my instinctive reaction is . . . Jesus calls me to respond by . . .
- When I have sinned against another, who or what brought me to be reconciled was . . .
- I experience Jesus present where two or three are gathered in his name in these ways . . .

PRESIDERS
My manner of relating with the parish staff and committees models how to correct one another, accept correction, and be reconciled in these ways . . .

DEACONS
My serving others builds up the community of the church in that . . .

HOSPITALITY MINISTERS
My hospitality enables those who are assembling truly to gather in Jesus' name when . . .

MUSIC MINISTERS
As music ministers, what helps us pray and sing together in Christ's name is . . .

ALTAR MINISTERS
My self-giving while serving at the altar facilitates the community to pray as one Body in Christ in that . . .

LECTORS
My manner of proclaiming the word helps people face their responsibilities as members of the church when . . .

EXTRAORDINARY MINISTERS OF HOLY COMMUNION
My distribution of Holy Communion participates in Christ's work of making "holy communion" happen among church members whenever I . . .

Model Act of Penitence

Presider: We come together to pray in Jesus' name. Let us pause to look within ourselves to see if we are doing anything that disrupts our unity as the community of Jesus' followers . . . [pause]

Lord Jesus, you are the unifying presence abiding in our midst: Lord . . .

Christ Jesus, you are one with your Father and the Spirit: Christ . . .

Lord Jesus, you call us to be reconciled to you and to each other: Lord . . .

Homily Points

• Imagine sitting at the dinner table when two family members are not speaking to one another. Tension fills everyone at the table and can even make eating difficult. How courageous and risky it is for someone to speak up to resolve the tension. How disruptive it is for the family not to address the tension.

• The family sitting at the dinner table is, in the gospel, the community of the church. Jesus challenges us to deal openly with the ways we willfully or even inadvertently hurt one another lest our unity be permanently weakened. What is at stake is our identity as the Body of Christ, our capacity to pray with one another, and our ability to make decisions based on gospel values.

• Sin is not limited to breaking commandments or failing to do what we know we ought. Sin is any conscious and willful behavior or attitude that diminishes our relationship with God and others. Being a loving family means working hard at resolving differences. Being a loving church means dealing with tensions and antagonisms in honest and life-giving ways. Being good citizens of our country and world means working for justice and peace, reconciling differences across borders.

Model Prayer of the Faithful

Presider: We now make our needs known to our loving God who calls us together as one community in Christ.

Response:

Lord, hear our prayer.

Cantor:

we pray to the Lord,

That all members of the community of the church always strive to be reconciled with God and each other . . . [pause]

That nations torn by war be reconciled and come to live in harmony and peace . . . [pause]

That families torn apart by discord be reconciled . . . [pause]

That this faith community continue to witness to the unity of the Body of Christ . . . [pause]

Presider: Merciful God, you desired our reconciliation so much that you sent your only Son to live among us: hear these our prayers that we might live in harmony and peace, and one day enjoy the fullness of life with you. We ask this through Christ our Lord. **Amen.**

OPENING PRAYER

Let us pray

Pause for silent prayer

God our Father,
you redeem us
and make us your children in Christ.
Look upon us,
give us true freedom
and bring us to the inheritance you
    promised.

Grant this through our Lord Jesus Christ,
    your Son,
who lives and reigns with you and the
    Holy Spirit,
one God, for ever and ever. **Amen.**

FIRST READING
Ezek 33:7-9

Thus says the LORD:
    You, son of man, I have appointed
        watchman for the house of Israel;
    when you hear me say anything, you
        shall warn them for me.
If I tell the wicked, "O wicked one, you
        shall surely die,"
    and you do not speak out to dissuade
        the wicked from his way,
    the wicked shall die for his guilt,
    but I will hold you responsible for his
        death.
But if you warn the wicked,
    trying to turn him from his way,
    and he refuses to turn from his way,
    he shall die for his guilt,
    but you shall save yourself.

RESPONSORIAL PSALM
Ps 95:1-2, 6-7, 8-9

R̷. (8) If today you hear his voice, harden not your hearts.

Come, let us sing joyfully to the LORD;
    let us acclaim the rock of our salvation.
Let us come into his presence with
        thanksgiving;
    let us joyfully sing psalms to him.

R̷. If today you hear his voice, harden not your hearts.

Come, let us bow down in worship;
    let us kneel before the LORD who made
        us.
For he is our God,
    and we are the people he shepherds, the
        flock he guides.

R̷. If today you hear his voice, harden not your hearts.

Oh, that today you would hear his voice:
    "Harden not your hearts as at Meribah,
    as in the day of Massah in the desert,
where your fathers tempted me;
    they tested me though they had seen my
        works."

R̷. If today you hear his voice, harden not your hearts.

SECOND READING
Rom 13:8-10

Brothers and sisters:
Owe nothing to anyone, except to love one
        another;
    for the one who loves another has
        fulfilled the law.
The commandments, "You shall not
        commit adultery;
    you shall not kill; you shall not steal;
        you shall not covet,"
and whatever other commandment
        there may be,
    are summed up in this saying, namely,
    "You shall love your neighbor as
        yourself."
Love does no evil to the neighbor;
    hence, love is the fulfillment of the law.

About Liturgy
Labor Day: Labor Day isn't a liturgical day and so there is no commemoration of it in the liturgy. It is perfectly appropriate to add a fifth intercession to the prayer of the faithful, for example, "That all in our nation's workforce grow in the dignity of labor and be assured of job security and just compensation."

The dignity of labor has been brought out more than once in church teaching, even being afforded an encyclical on the subject (Pope John Paul II's *Laborem exercens*, On Human Work, issued September 14, 1981). Christian labor embraces more than an honest day's work and just compensation. Human labor parallels the work of God in creation and redemption, and so our work is a participation in God's self-giving for the good of others. Moreover, human labor is also more than making a living, as important as that is. Human labor also includes building up the church and making present God's kingdom in our world. Even the "work" of liturgy ("liturgy" comes from two Greek words meaning "the work of the people") is something to be celebrated this day!

About Liturgical Music
Music suggestions: Songs speaking of the presence of Christ binding us together as the community of the church would be very appropriate this Sunday. M.D. Ridge's "Where Two or Three Have Gathered" [in the OCP collection *Sounding Glory*] offers a beautiful text and tune written for this gospel passage. This hymn would be an excellent choice during the preparation of the gifts, or as a choir prelude piece [OCP octavo 10582C]. Another fine hymn about our unity in Christ is Brian Wren's "I Come with Joy" [in many hymnals]. The verses move progressively from the individual "I" who comes "with joy" to worship the Lord to the communal "we" who, bound together in the Eucharist, "go with joy" to "give the world The love that makes us one."

Also appropriate this Sunday would be songs that speak of the need to work for unity and reconciliation among us as well as songs that challenge us to call one another to conversion. "The Master Came to Bring Good News" [CBW3, GC, GC2, RS, W3], with its refrain, "Father, forgive us! Through Jesus hear us! As we forgive one another!" would work well for the entrance procession. "Help Us Accept Each Other" [RS, W3] would also make a good choice for the entrance procession or could be used during the preparation of gifts. In "Somebody's Knockin' at Your Door" [in many hymnals] Jesus persists in calling us to conversion and we are challenged to hear his knock; this lively spiritual would be suitable during the preparation of the gifts. In Carl Daw's text "As We Gather at Your Table" [CWB3, GC2, JS2, RS, SS] we ask to become aware of God's presence and to be given the compassion to forgive one another. The hymn would make an excellent entrance song. "Forgive Our Sins" [in many hymnals], which challenges us by asking how God's pardon can "reach and bless The unforgiving heart" and begs God to cleanse us of resentments so that we may be "bound to all in bonds of love," would be appropriate during the preparation of the gifts.

✦ SPIRITUALITY

GOSPEL ACCLAMATION
John 13:34

℟. Alleluia, alleluia.
I give you a new commandment, says the Lord;
love one another as I have loved you.
℟. Alleluia, alleluia.

Gospel

Matt 18:21-35; L130A

Peter approached
     Jesus and
     asked him,
     "Lord, if my
     brother sins
     against me,
     how often must I
     forgive?
As many as seven times?"
Jesus answered, "I say to you, not
     seven times but seventy-seven
     times.
That is why the kingdom of heaven
     may be likened to a king
who decided to settle accounts with
     his servants.
When he began the accounting,
     a debtor was brought before him who
          owed him a huge amount.
Since he had no way of paying it back,
     his master ordered him to be sold,
     along with his wife, his children, and
          all his property,
     in payment of the debt.
At that, the servant fell down, did him
     homage, and said,
     'Be patient with me, and I will pay
          you back in full.'
Moved with compassion the master of
     that servant
     let him go and forgave him the loan.
When that servant had left, he found
     one of his fellow servants
who owed him a much smaller
     amount.

Continued in Appendix A, p. 302.

Reflecting on the Gospel

Paying off debts—especially large ones—is always a cause for rejoicing. Many families throw mortgage-burning parties after they've made their last payment on a family home. Even the painful experience of filing for bankruptcy brings its own unique kind of relief—one can start over without feeling that he or she is digging out of an impossible hole. We can readily identify, then, with the king's servant-debtor—he has dug himself into a pretty deep hole because of the "huge amount" he owes the king, yet the king readily and graciously forgives the debt. We would think that this servant-debtor would gather his friends for a party. Instead, the lowdown scoundrel goes out and finds a fellow servant in debt to him, and then deals with this fellow servant in exactly the way the king did not deal with him.

The servant-debtor did not ask the king to forgive his debt but to remain patient until it was paid off. The king did *not* do what the servant begged: "Be patient with me." Instead, he immediately forgave the whole debt. Absolutely unthinkable! This overwhelming, unexpected, compassionate forgiveness of the king makes the servant's behavior toward his fellow servant all the more despicable. It also helps us understand Jesus' response to Peter's question about how often we are to forgive one another. God's forgiveness of us knows no limits and is always granted. Anything less in our forgiveness of one another brings the same judgment against us that Jesus renders against the "wicked servant."

Life in the church demands that we forgive one another not only because it is the compassionate thing to do but because this is how God acts and expects us to act (see the last line of the gospel). It belongs to the very "being" of God to forgive; if we are of God, then it is also of our very "being" to forgive. The key to understanding this is that we are in relationship both with God and with each other. By forgiving we choose not to let any offense that has happened between us control how we continue to relate to one another. By forgiving we repair the damage to the relationship and restore dignity both to the forgiver and to the forgiven. This is why counting how many times we forgive—even to the seven that Peter suggests at the beginning of the gospel—misses the point. Jesus' response to Peter is a way of reminding us that God forgives us countless times, and this is the motivation for forgiving each other equally countless times. Our "heavenly Father" has shown us the way—forgive one another "from [the] heart."

Living the Paschal Mystery

The second reading for this Sunday speaks in its own way of why we forgive one another: "None of us lives for oneself" because we "live for the Lord." Our relationship to each other is described in terms of our relationship to God. Forgiveness is absolutely central to the message of the whole gospel because it is necessary in order for our relationships with God and each other to continually grow stronger and more graceful.

Christ's dying and rising models for us our own dying and rising: "no one dies for oneself." We always die (to ourselves) for the sake of the other. Forgiving entails dying to damaged relationships so that we might all belong to the Lord and rise to every new life with him. Forgiving means God has hold of us and enables us to act in a God-like manner. Forgiving means that petty hurts or even major ruptures pale in comparison to the life-giving wholesomeness of being in healthy and strong relationships.

Focusing the Gospel

Key words and phrases: moved with compassion, master . . . forgave him, he refused, should you not have had pity . . . as I had pity

To the point: The king did *not* do what the servant begged: "Be patient with me." Instead, he immediately forgave the whole debt. Absolutely unthinkable! This overwhelming, unexpected, compassionate forgiveness of the king makes the servant's behavior toward his fellow servant all the more despicable. It also helps us understand Jesus' response to Peter's question about how often we are to forgive one another. God's forgiveness of us knows no limits and is always granted. Anything less in our forgiveness of one another brings the same judgment against us that Jesus renders against the "wicked servant."

Connecting the Gospel

to the first reading: The reading from Sirach asks, "Could anyone refuse mercy to another?" Yes! The servant in the gospel did. And so do we—all the time. But, never God!

to experience: Grudges among families, communities, nations are often passed on from generation to generation. For example, family feuds go on for decades during which time members do not speak to each other. The only thing that can break the cycle of hate, fear, and disunity is the gift of forgiveness.

Connecting the Responsorial Psalm

to the readings: The core of this Sunday's responsorial psalm is its refrain: "The Lord is kind and merciful, slow to anger, and rich in compassion." This phrase was first spoken not *about* God but *by* God as direct revelation to Moses: this is my name—Lord—and this is who I am—merciful, gracious, compassionate (cf. Exod 34:5-6). The phrase appears so often in the Old Testament that it is called "the little creed," a capsule profession of who God is and how God relates to us.

In singing this psalm we profess "the little creed" as our own. We name the nature of God. And we proclaim the nature of our covenant relationship with one another: as God forgives us, so we are to forgive one another (first reading). Like God we are to put transgressions behind us "as far as the east is from the west" (psalm). We are to forgive one another no matter how great or small the debt and no matter how many times it is necessary (gospel). The call is mandatory, not optional. May our singing of this psalm transform our hearts and our behavior.

to psalmist preparation: Last Sunday you challenged the assembly to "harden not [their] hearts." This Sunday you sing about One who has the softest of hearts—God whose forgiveness is unceasing, incalculable, and universal. How can you let God's forgiveness enter your heart? Where do you need to offer forgiveness for the seventy-seventh time (gospel)? Where do you need to receive it for the seventy-seventh time?

ASSEMBLY & FAITH-SHARING GROUPS

- I struggle with forgiving when . . . because . . .
- I experience God's compassionate forgiveness when . . . I offer this compassionate forgiveness to others when . . .
- I have been surprised by the gift of forgiveness when . . . This has drawn me to . . .

PRESIDERS

I find it easiest to preach forgiveness when . . . I am challenged in my preaching forgiveness when . . .

DEACONS

I extend God's unlimited compassion and forgiveness through my service of others in that . . .

HOSPITALITY MINISTERS

My manner of greeting those who are assembling enables them to let go of "debts" they owe one another when . . .

MUSIC MINISTERS

My music ministry softens hard hearts and helps others forgive one another in that . . .

ALTAR MINISTERS

A forgiving heart affects my relationship with others and helps me serve at the altar better in that . . .

LECTORS

My time with the word helps me release "wrath and anger" (first reading) and instead "hug . . . tight" God's way of compassion and forgiveness whenever . . .

EXTRAORDINARY MINISTERS OF HOLY COMMUNION

I offer the bread and cup of compassion and forgiveness in my daily living whenever I . . .

Model Act of Penitence

Presider: God's merciful forgiveness is generous and assured. As we prepare to celebrate well this liturgy, let us call to mind our need for forgiveness . . . [pause]

Lord Jesus, you are kind and forgiving: Lord . . .

Christ Jesus, you are slow to anger and rich in compassion: Christ . . .

Lord Jesus, you judge us justly and mercifully: Lord . . .

Homily Points

• When another person does not do something we ask, we often feel hurt, resentful, even angry. When the other person does something far superior to what we have asked, we react with astonishment, admiration, appreciation. The Master in this Sunday's gospel not only does far more than the servant asked, he does the unthinkable. Yet the servant reacted with anything but astonishment, admiration, appreciation.

• Despite having been dealt with compassionately by his Master, the hard-hearted servant fails to offer this same compassion to his fellow servant. Sinning and being sinned against is a part of human living. Forgiving and being forgiven is part of divine life. Jesus acknowledges the fact of the former and invites us into the gracefulness of the latter. He exhorts us to forgive one another in the same manner as God forgives us: from the heart, as often as necessary.

• We choose to live in one of two situations. Either we live in an atmosphere of fear or contention where we carefully calculate who and what we forgive. Or we live in the kingdom of Jesus where we run the risk of forgiving even seventy-seven times. What encourages us to choose the second way of living is the positive experience and resulting growth that come from our being forgiven by God and others. Forgiveness begets life.

Model Prayer of the Faithful

Presider: Let us pray that we have the heart to forgive others as God has forgiven us.

Response:

Lord,   hear our prayer.

Cantor:

we pray   to the Lord,

That all members of the church put on the compassionate and forgiving heart of Christ . . . [pause]

That leaders of nations be compassionate in their judgments and merciful in exacting payments . . . [pause]

That those with hardened and unforgiving hearts be moved by the loving forgiveness of God . . . [pause]

That each of us here build strong relationships with each other based on dignity and forgiveness . . . [pause]

Presider: Gracious God, you forgive us whenever we ask for your mercy: hear these our prayers that we might grow in our willingness to forgive. We ask this through Christ our Lord. **Amen.**

OPENING PRAYER

Let us pray

Pause for silent prayer

Almighty God,
our creator and guide,
may we serve you with all our heart
and know your forgiveness in our lives.

We ask this through our Lord Jesus Christ,
    your Son,
who lives and reigns with you and the
    Holy Spirit,
one God, for ever and ever. **Amen.**

FIRST READING
Sir 27:30–28:7

Wrath and anger are hateful things,
    yet the sinner hugs them tight.
The vengeful will suffer the LORD's
    vengeance,
    for he remembers their sins in detail.
Forgive your neighbor's injustice;
    then when you pray, your own sins will
        be forgiven.
Could anyone nourish anger against
    another
    and expect healing from the LORD?
Could anyone refuse mercy to another like
    himself,
    can he seek pardon for his own sins?
If one who is but flesh cherishes wrath,
    who will forgive his sins?
Remember your last days, set enmity
    aside;
    remember death and decay, and cease
        from sin!
Think of the commandments, hate not
    your neighbor;
    remember the Most High's covenant,
        and overlook faults.

RESPONSORIAL PSALM
Ps 103:1-2, 3-4, 9-10, 11-12

R̸. (8) The Lord is kind and merciful, slow to anger, and rich in compassion.

Bless the LORD, O my soul;
   and all my being, bless his holy name.
Bless the LORD, O my soul,
   and forget not all his benefits.

R̸. The Lord is kind and merciful, slow to anger, and rich in compassion.

He pardons all your iniquities,
   heals all your ills,
redeems your life from destruction,
   he crowns you with kindness and
      compassion.

R̸. The Lord is kind and merciful, slow to anger, and rich in compassion.

He will not always chide,
   nor does he keep his wrath forever.
Not according to our sins does he deal
      with us,
   nor does he requite us according to our
      crimes.

R̸. The Lord is kind and merciful, slow to anger, and rich in compassion.

For as the heavens are high above the
      earth,
   so surpassing is his kindness toward
      those who fear him.
As far as the east is from the west,
   so far has he put our transgressions
      from us.

R̸. The Lord is kind and merciful, slow to anger, and rich in compassion.

SECOND READING
Rom 14:7-9

Brothers and sisters:
None of us lives for oneself, and no one
      dies for oneself.
For if we live, we live for the Lord,
   and if we die, we die for the Lord;
      so then, whether we live or die, we are
         the Lord's.
For this is why Christ died and came to
      life,
   that he might be Lord of both the dead
      and the living.

About Liturgy
Postures during liturgy: There are a number of times during Mass when our posture indicates that we hold another in high honor. With respect to God, for example, we genuflect to the Blessed Sacrament or bow to the altar or Book of the Gospels; we bow at the words during the Creed, "by the power of the Holy Spirit he was born of the Virgin Mary, and became man"; we might bow our heads when we pronounce Jesus' name; we bow in respect before we receive Holy Communion. With respect to each other, the deacon or altar minister might bow to us before incensing us; we offer each other a sign of peace. In themselves these gestures are worthy of God, the saints, and those of us who are members of the Body of Christ, for they give evidence of the dignity we have and offer another, and our mutual respect for the relationships within community that make us one in the Body of Christ.

There is always a tendency during liturgy to do these gestures (as well as postures, responses, etc.!) out of routine. The meaning behind them suggests that we gently call ourselves to think about what we are doing. They are ways that we express honor and respect, and because we do them together we announce that we all share in God's divine life. In this is the source of our dignity, of our desire for reconciliation, of our unity in the Body of Christ.

About Liturgical Music
Music suggestions: Many of the songs suggested for last Sunday—"The Master Came to Bring Good News," "Help Us Accept Each Other," "Forgive Our Sins," "Somebody's Knockin' at Your Door"—would be appropriate choices again this week. Repeating a song helps us see the connection between one Sunday liturgy and the next. No Sunday celebration of the Eucharist is its own self-contained event. Rather, the Sundays flow one into another and work together to immerse us in the mystery of Christ as it unfolds throughout the liturgical year and in our lives.

Nonetheless, we need to be cautious in our song choices. Even two songs about forgiving one another may be too much for one liturgy, and three certainly will be. Selecting just one and using it well is the best approach.

SEPTEMBER 11, 2011
TWENTY-FOURTH SUNDAY IN ORDINARY TIME

✠ SPIRITUALITY

GOSPEL ACCLAMATION
cf. Acts 16:14b

℟. Alleluia, alleluia.
Open our hearts, O Lord,
to listen to the words of your Son.
℟. Alleluia, alleluia.

Gospel   Matt 20:1-16a; L133A

Jesus told his disciples this parable:
  "The kingdom of heaven is like a
      landowner
  who went out at dawn to hire
      laborers for his vineyard.
After agreeing with them for the usual
      daily wage,
  he sent them into his vineyard.
Going out about nine o'clock,
  the landowner saw others standing idle
      in the marketplace,
  and he said to them, 'You too go into my
      vineyard,
  and I will give you what is just.'
So they went off.
And he went out again around noon,
  and around three o'clock, and did
      likewise.
Going out about five o'clock,
  the landowner found others standing
      around, and said to them,
  'Why do you stand here idle all day?'
They answered, 'Because no one has hired
      us.'
He said to them, 'You too go into my
      vineyard.'
When it was evening the owner of the
      vineyard said to his foreman,
  'Summon the laborers and give them
      their pay,
  beginning with the last and ending with
      the first.'
When those who had started about five
      o'clock came,
  each received the usual daily wage.
So when the first came, they thought that
      they would receive more,
  but each of them also got the usual wage.

Continued in Appendix A, p. 302.

Reflecting on the Gospel

It began in 1929 and wasn't really over until a decade later. This period is known as the Great Depression. People who remember this difficult economic time are well into their senior years by now. But even today, this many decades later, mention the Great Depression and the picture that pops into most people's minds (and most people alive today did not live through it) is the breadlines.

People lined up for blocks all over the country to receive a bit of food. Parents were frantic to feed their children. Unemployment rose above 20 percent. Wages declined by about 40 percent. This was not a time of prosperity. Idleness was rampant. This was not the kind of idleness that gives us a bit of respite from a long day's work, but the kind of idleness that is borne of frustration, lack of work, inability to provide. In this Sunday's gospel a most sensitive landowner hires day laborers for his vineyard. Presumably at dawn when he went out to hire laborers, he would have hired what he thought he needed for the day. But he goes out four other times of the day and hires laborers because they were "standing idle."

More even than a desire to get the work done (the first laborers hired could have done that), the landowner shows great predisposition to *all* the laborers he meets throughout the day. He is concerned that all have a chance to labor, no matter at what hour they are hired. And this is exactly Matthew's point of the parable: that all will have a chance to be saved. We might think that the landowner in the gospel is just to those he called first and generous to those he called last. In fact, our gracious and saving Landowner-God is both just and generous to all the laborers simply because his "wages" are always a free gift, undeserved, and more than we can earn or expect. If we shift the focus of the parable away from thinking about justice and wages toward a kingdom and salvation perspective, shift the focus away from ourselves to a focus on God, then a different view of God's graciousness and saving desire opens up.

In this gospel parable the landowner's behavior is remarkable in two ways: his care for idle workers not able to put their skills and energy to good use, and his manner of paying wages. His behavior describes aptly the kingdom of heaven: God calls each of us to use whatever our gifts are to advance the growth of the kingdom; God "pays" us not in dollars and cents but with the free gift of salvation that is immeasurable, unlimited, endless, and overflowing. In God's kingdom there is no cause for idleness and no limit on "wages."

Living the Paschal Mystery

Most of us think of work as a necessity: we need a paycheck to pay the bills, procure the necessities, and maybe have a little left over for some entertainment. This parable invites us to think of work in a different way: by our labors we are building up God's kingdom, spreading God's reign in our world. God calls us to be laborers in the divine vineyard—a call we first answer at baptism and then continually answer throughout our lives each time we say yes, reach out to others in imitation of God's goodness and generosity, and cooperate with all God asks of us. This divine, saving "work" is a privilege—we actually share in God's saving deeds! God uses us to bring salvation to the world. This work has a great dignity about it. This work is a privilege. This work is a lifelong response to God's invitation to be God's laborers.

Focusing the Gospel

Key words and phrases: others standing idle, give you what is just, because I am generous

To the point: In this gospel parable the landowner's behavior is remarkable in two ways: his care for idle workers not able to put their skills and energy to good use, and his manner of paying wages. His behavior describes aptly the kingdom of heaven: God calls each of us to use whatever our gifts are to advance the growth of the kingdom; God "pays" us not in dollars and cents but with the free gift of salvation that is immeasurable, unlimited, endless, and overflowing. In God's kingdom there is no cause for idleness and no limit on "wages."

Connecting the Gospel

to the first reading: The first reading challenges us to expand our thoughts and ways to the limitless reach of God's manner of dealing with us. The gospel makes this specific by showing us a God who is merciful and generous in calling everyone to salvation.

to experience: We must limit our generosity to others because our resources are limited; for example, we have only so many dollars and so much time to contribute to those in need. God, however, is unlimited in giving us life and salvation.

Connecting the Responsorial Psalm

to the readings: Like a mother sitting at her child's bedside ready to respond to the slightest cry, God is ever near, answering our every need (psalm refrain). Once we recognize that God is giving us all that we need, we are no longer tempted to grumble about what God is giving to others (gospel). Instead we rejoice that everyone's needs are being met and bless the One who is "just in all his ways" (psalm). We turn away from our rivalries with one another to celebrate the limitless expanse of God's care and generosity. Then the "ways" and "thoughts" of God that are far above us (first reading) can find a place very near, in our own hearts. Perhaps our greatest need is to have our narrowness of heart transformed by the generosity in the heart of God. May this be that for which we call to God (refrain). It will be given to us.

to psalmist preparation: These readings and the psalm offer you many avenues of prayer and reflection as you prepare to do your ministry this weekend. For example, what ways or thoughts of God seem to elude you (first reading)? How does God bring these ways and thoughts "near" (psalm)? When have you been the recipient of God's mercy and compassion? How has this helped you offer the same mercy and compassion to others? When have you struggled with seeming unfairness in God's manner of treating yourself and others? What/who has helped you shift your understanding to God's perspective?

ASSEMBLY & FAITH-SHARING GROUPS
- The work God calls me to do for the kingdom is . . . The "hour" God called me was . . .
- I experience God's unlimited gift of life to me when . . .
- The gifts I have to offer for the growth of the kingdom are . . .

PRESIDERS
My preaching calls laborers to God's vineyard no matter what "time of the day" when I . . .

DEACONS
My ministry embodies the unimaginable generosity of God to others by . . .

HOSPITALITY MINISTERS
My hospitality models for the community that everyone (no matter how different) is "equal to us" whenever I . . .

MUSIC MINISTERS
The "wages" I receive for my participation in music ministry are . . .

ALTAR MINISTERS
When I recall God's incredible generosity, my serving others is like . . .

LECTORS
I have learned that God's ways and thoughts are high above mine (see first reading) in that . . . This is sometimes pleasing and sometimes difficult for me because . . .

EXTRAORDINARY MINISTERS OF HOLY COMMUNION
My manner of distributing Holy Communion witnesses to God's unbounded generosity toward all in that . . .

Model Act of Penitence

Presider: The gospel today reminds us of God's unbounded generosity toward us. Let us prepare to celebrate this liturgy by opening ourselves to the gift of life God is now offering us . . . [pause]

Lord Jesus, you are generous beyond measure: Lord . . .

Christ Jesus, you unfailingly give us the gift of life: Christ . . .

Lord Jesus, you generously extend salvation to all: Lord . . .

Homily Points

• Every good parent makes a list of chores for the children in order to teach them responsibility and how to be contributing members of the family community. Most children put off doing their chores until the very last hour! But even after procrastinating, they still learn the lessons of contributing their part to family life.

• There is no one among us who in at least one detail of discipleship has not started working until the eleventh hour! Jesus teaches through this parable that God nevertheless continues to call us to be laborers in the divine vineyard. God's desire is that we contribute to the growth of the kingdom according to each of our unique gifts. Our "wages" is nothing less than abundant life now and, at the final hour, salvation.

• God simply will not allow us to stand around idle because what is at stake—the kingdom of heaven and the reach of salvation—is too important. The kingdom of heaven becomes visible when each contributes according to his or her God-given gifts as needs arise. The issue isn't how long we labor or how much we give but our willingness to keep giving.

Model Prayer of the Faithful

Presider: God has given each of us gifts for building up the kingdom of heaven. Let us pray for our needs so that we labor fruitfully.

Response:

Lord, hear our prayer.

Cantor:

we pray to the Lord,

That all members of the church respond generously to God's call to work for the growth of God's kingdom . . . [pause]

That all peoples use their gifts wisely and come to fullness of life and salvation . . . [pause]

That the unemployed find work and be able to provide generously for those entrusted to their care . . . [pause]

That this faith community generously contribute their time and gifts to those in need . . . [pause]

Presider: Generous God, you sent your Son to bring us salvation: hear these our prayers and strengthen us to be faithful laborers in your vineyard. We ask this through Christ our Lord. **Amen.**

OPENING PRAYER

Let us pray
[that we may grow in the love of God and of one another]

Pause for silent prayer

Father,
guide us, as you guide creation
according to your law of love.
May we love one another
and come to perfection
in the eternal life prepared for us.

Grant this through our Lord Jesus Christ, your Son,
who lives and reigns with you and the Holy Spirit,
one God, for ever and ever. **Amen.**

FIRST READING
Isa 55:6-9

Seek the LORD while he may be found,
     call him while he is near.
Let the scoundrel forsake his way,
     and the wicked his thoughts;
let him turn to the LORD for mercy;
     to our God, who is generous in forgiving.
For my thoughts are not your thoughts,
     nor are your ways my ways, says the LORD.
As high as the heavens are above the earth,
     so high are my ways above your ways
     and my thoughts above your thoughts.

RESPONSORIAL PSALM

Ps 145:2-3, 8-9, 17-18

R. (18a) The Lord is near to all who call upon him.

Every day will I bless you,
  and I will praise your name forever and
    ever.
Great is the LORD and highly to be praised;
  his greatness is unsearchable.

R. The Lord is near to all who call upon him.

The LORD is gracious and merciful,
  slow to anger and of great kindness.
The LORD is good to all
  and compassionate toward all his
    works.

R. The Lord is near to all who call upon him.

The LORD is just in all his ways
  and holy in all his works.
The LORD is near to all who call upon him,
  to all who call upon him in truth.

R. The Lord is near to all who call upon him.

SECOND READING

Phil 1:20c-24, 27a

Brothers and sisters:
Christ will be magnified in my body,
  whether by life or by death.
For to me life is Christ, and death is gain.
If I go on living in the flesh,
  that means fruitful labor for me.
And I do not know which I shall choose.
I am caught between the two.
I long to depart this life and be with Christ,
  for that is far better.
Yet that I remain in the flesh
  is more necessary for your benefit.

Only, conduct yourselves in a way worthy
  of the gospel of Christ.

About Liturgy

Liturgical ministries as responding to God's call for laborers: Many of us take for granted those who minister at Mass each Sunday—assembly, presider, deacon, hospitality ministers (or greeters or ushers), altar ministers, music ministers, lectors, extraordinary ministers of Holy Communion. Sometimes, too, because we minister when our name appears on the schedule, we might fall into the trap of thinking we are just getting necessary jobs accomplished. GIRM no. 91 speaks of the eucharistic celebration as an action of the whole church in which different orders and offices unfold and the ordained ministers and lay Christian faithful fulfill "their office or their duty" according to what "pertains to them."

Whatever ministries are exercised by different persons during liturgy, they are always undertaken after careful discernment of one's abilities, prayer to do God's will (hear God's call to minister), and appropriate preparation for the ministry itself. In addition to fulfilling ministries at Mass, then, liturgical ministers also witness to God's persistent call to followers of Jesus to be laborers in the divine vineyard who make present the kingdom and continue Jesus' work here on earth.

About Liturgical Music

Music suggestions: One of the most fitting hymns for this Sunday's liturgy is "There's a Wideness in God's Mercy" [in many hymnals] in which we sing that there is "plentiful redemption" and "joy for all" because "the love of God is broader than the measures of our mind." The tune generally associated with this hymn, IN BABILONE, would work well for the entrance procession or during the preparation of the gifts. W3 offers a second setting by Calvin Hampton that expresses musically the metaphor that God's mercy is wide as the sea. Beneath a shifting melodic meter (the tune moves back and forth between 4/4 and 3/4), a stream of 8th notes in the tenor voice moves continuously forward over a rock-steady, half-note rhythm in the bass. Through changing rhythms the sea relentlessly rolls, vast and fluid, adaptable, but ineluctable. Such is the nature of God's mercy. The arrangement includes a flute or violin obbligato for the final verse. If the rhythmic pattern is too difficult for the assembly, the choir could sing the arrangement—it is too beautiful to pass up—either as a prelude or during the preparation of the gifts.

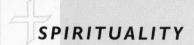

✝ SPIRITUALITY

GOSPEL ACCLAMATION
John 10:27

R⁊. Alleluia, alleluia.
My sheep hear my voice, says the Lord;
I know them, and they follow me.
R⁊. Alleluia, alleluia.

Gospel

Matt 21:28-32; L136A

Jesus said to the chief priests
    and elders of the people:
    "What is your opinion?
A man had two sons.
He came to the first and
    said,
    'Son, go out and work in the
        vineyard today.'
He said in reply, 'I will not,'
    but afterwards changed his mind and
        went.
The man came to the other son and
    gave the same order.
He said in reply, 'Yes, sir,' but did not
    go.
Which of the two did his father's will?"
They answered, "The first."
Jesus said to them, "Amen, I say to
    you,
    tax collectors and prostitutes
    are entering the kingdom of God
        before you.
When John came to you in the way of
    righteousness,
    you did not believe him;
    but tax collectors and prostitutes did.
Yet even when you saw that,
    you did not later change your minds
        and believe him."

Reflecting on the Gospel

Living with people who constantly change their minds can drive some of us batty! Such a simple thing as what to have for supper can bring ten things out of the freezer and take a half hour to decide. Planning a vacation would be painful indeed, as lists are made for things needed to go one place, only to be scrapped and started all over again when a decision is made to go someplace else. In these kinds of instances changing our mind has no serious consequences—maybe time is lost and nerves are frayed, but those are quickly forgotten as the dinner is finally served or folks actually leave for an enjoyable vacation. In this Sunday's gospel two sons change their minds about how they carry through on their response to their father's command to go out and work in his vineyard. No doubt, the work in the vineyard eventually got finished. But the point of the parable goes far beyond simply doing work. Jesus is telling us something important about "the kingdom of God" and salvation: we cannot afford to dilly-dally around. Our belief must be decisive and our actions must carry through and be consistent with our belief.

"What is your opinion?" Jesus asks in the opening line of this gospel. He asks this question not to elicit information from the "chief priests and elders" but to challenge them to do what they say they believe. Believing is doing God's will. No matter what we say, the real issue is what we do (as with the two sons in the gospel). Any change of mind we have must be about turning ourselves from mere talk to doing God's will. This is the "way of righteousness" and how we "[enter] the kingdom of God." This kind of change of mind has serious consequences: whether we gain salvation or not. No matter what we say, the issue is what we believe and how we act on that belief. Here, belief is equated with doing God's will. Any change of mind must be such that we bring our wills in conformity to God's will. This is the "way of righteousness"; this is the way of salvation.

Truth be told, all of us are a little like both sons at once. Sometimes we hear and respond faithfully to God's will, but at other times our actions don't carry through what we hear and believe. The good news in this is that God does not change the divine mind about calling us to salvation. Whether we say yes or no to God's call, God does keep calling us. We are the ones who need a change of mind. We are the ones who must believe in God's offer of salvation and faithfully do God's will.

Living the Paschal Mystery

The second reading from the letter to the Philippians gives us a hint as to how we can hear Jesus' preaching and respond in faithful obedience: "by being of the same mind, with the same love, united in heart, thinking one thing . . . regard others as more important than yourselves . . ." This is the kingdom perspective—to change our focus from ourselves to others and, in turn, our concern for others helps us focus on God and the divine will for us. Jesus himself is the model, for "he emptied himself . . . becoming obedient to the point of death, even death on a cross." Nothing was too much for Jesus so that others might be saved. So it ought to be for us. The change of mind described in the gospel entails self-emptying for the sake of others, lived every day in the little things that come our way. This gospel challenges us constantly to turn our hearts toward God, discern the divine will, and then put it into action.

Focusing the Gospel

Key words and phrases: which . . . did his father's will, entering the king-dom of God, way of righteousness, believe

To the point: "What is your opinion?" Jesus asks this question not to elicit in-formation from the "chief priests and elders" but to challenge them to do what they say they believe. Believing is doing God's will. No matter what we say, the real issue is what we do (as with the two sons in the gospel). Any change of mind we have must be about turning ourselves from mere talk to doing God's will. This is the "way of righteousness" and how we "[enter] the kingdom of God."

Connecting the Gospel

to the first reading: In this selection from Ezekiel the word of the LORD clearly calls the "house of Israel" to conversion of life. The consequences are life or death. In the gospel Jesus clearly calls us to make a choice: to choose life by putting belief into action.

to experience: We quickly learn to stop asking a favor from someone who says yes but then doesn't follow through. God, however, never writes us off but keeps coming back to give us another chance to say yes and do the divine will.

Connecting the Responsorial Psalm

to the readings: The first reading and gospel this Sunday point out that we have a tenuous hold on righteousness and easily fluctuate between saying yes and no to God. But the responsorial psalm indicates that God never wavers in the offer of forgiveness. Psalm 25 invites us to turn our attention from our own behavior to the goodness and mercy of God.

Upheld by such mercy, we can admit our sins of yesterday (psalm) and seek the conversion we need (first reading). We have only to ask, and God teaches us what we need to know to live rightly (psalm). The point is not to worry about being sinners (that is inevitable) but to be humble and honest enough to be teachable. The tax collectors and prostitutes in the gospel have been great learners; the self-righteous chief priests and elders, on the other hand, have learned nothing. God never stops inviting us to a change of heart. It rests upon us to do the necessary learning.

to psalmist preparation: What do these verses from Psalm 25 reveal about God's manner of relating to human beings? How do they invite you to relate to God in return? On a personal level, what ways do you need to ask God to teach you? How is God doing this teaching?

**ASSEMBLY &
FAITH-SHARING GROUPS**
- I say yes to God and then don't follow through when . . . I say no to God, and what brings me to change my mind is . . .
- My believing leads to faithful doing when . . .
- For me, the "way of righteousness" is . . .

PRESIDERS
My preaching confronts the assembly to put belief into action when . . . My manner of living does the same when . . .

DEACONS
By serving those in need, I put belief into action and inspire others to live in the "way of righteousness" when . . .

HOSPITALITY MINISTERS
The manner of my warm welcome helps those assembling for liturgy to hear God's word and say yes to whatever God asks when I . . .

MUSIC MINISTERS
My participation in music ministry helps me to know better God's will for me when . . . My music ministry helps me to say yes when . . .

ALTAR MINISTERS
Serving others well requires me to change my mind about . . .

LECTORS
The "turning away" (first reading) I need to live before proclaiming this word with integrity is . . .

**EXTRAORDINARY MINISTERS
OF HOLY COMMUNION**
My "Amen" at liturgy translates into a liv-ing "yes" to God's "way of righteousness" when I . . .

Model Act of Penitence

Presider: The gospel today invites us to line up our saying with our doing. As we prepare to celebrate this liturgy, let us be mindful of when our actions have strayed from doing God's will . . . [pause]

Lord Jesus, you call us to integrity of life: Lord . . .

Christ Jesus, you were ever obedient to your Father's will: Christ . . .

Lord Jesus, you lead us in the way of righteousness: Lord . . .

Homily Points

• We often say we are "of two minds" about something. For example, whether to go out for a meal or eat in; whether to vote yes for a school levy or not; whether to leave one job or to take another one. Sometimes our "two-mindedness" results from our being relatively indifferent about the final decision.

• When it comes to putting faith into action, however, we cannot be indifferent. We can have only one mind—to discern and do God's will—because the outcome is life or death.

• What does it mean to do God's will? It means to listen to the "prophets" God sends to call us to conversion of life, to change our minds about whatever blocks our believing in what they say, and to put into action what we come to believe. Doing God's will is the "way of righteousness" that leads to growth in relationships, graciousness of actions, and integrity of character.

Model Prayer of the Faithful

Presider: Let us pray that we might put on the mind of Jesus.

Response:

Lord, hear our prayer.

Cantor:

we pray to the Lord,

That the church grow in being a community of believers with one mind and heart, obedient to God's will . . . [pause]

That all peoples of the world grow in hearing God's message of salvation and living it . . . [pause]

That the poor and the needy be lifted up by the faithful actions of the community of believers . . . [pause]

That each of us here grow in our ability to listen to God's voice, discern God's will, and respond with integrity . . . [pause]

Presider: Gracious God, you call us to be faithful to carry out your divine will for our salvation: hear these our prayers that one day we might share in your everlasting life. We ask this through Christ our Lord. **Amen.**

OPENING PRAYER

Let us pray

Pause for silent prayer

Father,
you show your almighty power
in your mercy and forgiveness.
Continue to fill us with your gifts of love.
Help us to hurry toward the eternal life
    you promise
and come to share in the joys of your
    kingdom.

Grant this through our Lord Jesus Christ,
    your Son,
who lives and reigns with you and the
    Holy Spirit,
one God, for ever and ever. **Amen.**

FIRST READING

Ezek 18:25-28

Thus says the Lord:
You say, "The Lord's way is not fair!"
Hear now, house of Israel:
    Is it my way that is unfair, or rather, are
        not your ways unfair?
When someone virtuous turns away from
        virtue to commit iniquity, and dies,
    it is because of the iniquity he
        committed that he must die.
But if he turns from the wickedness he has
        committed,
    and does what is right and just,
    he shall preserve his life;
    since he has turned away from all the
        sins that he has committed,
    he shall surely live, he shall not die.

RESPONSORIAL PSALM

Ps 25:4-5, 6-7, 8-9

℟. (6a) Remember your mercies, O Lord.

Your ways, O Lord, make known to me;
    teach me your paths,
guide me in your truth and teach me,
    for you are God my savior.

℟. Remember your mercies, O Lord.

Remember that your compassion, O Lord,
    and your love are from of old.
The sins of my youth and my frailties
        remember not;
    in your kindness remember me,
    because of your goodness, O Lord.

℟. Remember your mercies, O Lord.

Good and upright is the LORD;
  thus he shows sinners the way.
He guides the humble to justice,
  and teaches the humble his way.

R⁊. Remember your mercies, O Lord.

SECOND READING
Phil 2:1-11

Brothers and sisters:
If there is any encouragement in Christ,
  any solace in love,
  any participation in the Spirit,
  any compassion and mercy,
  complete my joy by being of the same
    mind, with the same love,
  united in heart, thinking one thing.
Do nothing out of selfishness or out of
    vainglory;
  rather, humbly regard others as more
    important than yourselves,
  each looking out not for his own
    interests,
  but also for those of others.

Have in you the same attitude
  that is also in Christ Jesus,
    who, though he was in the form of
      God,
    did not regard equality with God
      something to be grasped.
  Rather, he emptied himself,
    taking the form of a slave,
    coming in human likeness;
    and found human in appearance,
    he humbled himself,
    becoming obedient to the point of
      death,
    even death on a cross.
  Because of this, God greatly exalted him
    and bestowed on him the name
    which is above every name,
    that at the name of Jesus
    every knee should bend,
    of those in heaven and on earth
      and under the earth,
    and every tongue confess that
    Jesus Christ is Lord,
    to the glory of God the Father.

or Phil 2:1-5

See Appendix A, p. 302.

About Liturgy

Ordinary Time and second reading: Whenever the second reading during Ordinary Time helps us interpret the gospel, by all means we would want to plumb its riches during Mass, for example, at the homily or drawing on its imagery for the intentions during the prayer of the faithful. This Sunday's selection from the letter to the Philippians gives us clear direction for what hearing God's will for us and changing our lives might look like: have the mind/attitude of Christ and practice self-emptying so that our focus can be on others rather than ourselves. Further, this reading reminds us that our growth in Christian living isn't dependent only upon ourselves: we hear God's message in community and live it out in community. Our relationship with Jesus helps us hear, but so does our relationship with others. Ultimately this reading is an encouragement that the difficult challenges of faithful discipleship aren't something we undertake by ourselves but with the support of the whole Christian community.

About Liturgical Music

Music suggestion: The references in Fred Pratt Green's hymn "God Is Here! As We His People" [GC, JS2, RS, WC, W3] to "our lifelong need of grace," to "what it means in daily living to believe and adore," and to "keep us faithful to the gospel" are apt connections with this Sunday's first reading, psalm, and gospel. The hymn is set to the tune ABBOT'S LEIGH, which is an excellent example of when and how a 3/4 meter can work as an entrance processional. The melody leaps dramatically through C major, takes a stepwise detour through D minor, then jumps back aboard the C major ride. Through it all the 3/4 meter is really felt as a strong 1. The trip is not meant to be taken speedily, but with a broad enough tempo that we can savor the harmonic motion and the richness of the text.

Songs that express our willingness to hear God's call to discipleship and say yes include Michael Ward's "Here I Am, Lord"—which connects particularly well with this Sunday's readings and psalm—[PMB, WC, WS]; Steven Warner's "Here I Am, O God" [VO]; and Dan Schutte's "Here I Am, Lord" [in most hymnals]. In "Done Made My Vow to the Lord" [LMGM] we hold steady to the promise we've made to God until we "see what the end will be." On the other hand, "O Breathe on Me, O Breath of God" [in many hymnals] is a prayer that we be given the grace to surrender ourselves to love what God loves and do what God would do, and "Our Father, We Have Wandered" [CH, GC2, RS, SS, W3, WC, WS] is humble confession of how we have failed in discipleship.

SEPTEMBER 25, 2011
TWENTY-SIXTH SUNDAY
IN ORDINARY TIME

SPIRITUALITY

R̸. Alleluia, alleluia.
I have chosen you from the world, says the Lord,
to go and bear fruit that will remain.
R̸. Alleluia, alleluia.

Gospel   Matt 21:33-43; L139A

Jesus said to the chief priests
     and the elders of the people:
  "Hear another parable.
There was a landowner who planted
     a vineyard,
  put a hedge around it, dug a wine
       press in it, and built a tower.
Then he leased it to tenants and went
     on a journey.
When vintage time drew near,
  he sent his servants to the tenants to
       obtain his produce.
But the tenants seized the servants and
     one they beat,
  another they killed, and a third they
       stoned.
Again he sent other servants, more
       numerous than the first ones,
  but they treated them in the same way.
Finally, he sent his son to them, thinking,
  'They will respect my son.'
But when the tenants saw the son, they
     said to one another,
  'This is the heir.
Come, let us kill him and acquire his
       inheritance.'
They seized him, threw him out of the
       vineyard, and killed him.
What will the owner of the vineyard do to
     those tenants when he comes?"
They answered him,
  "He will put those wretched men to a
       wretched death
  and lease his vineyard to other tenants
    who will give him the produce at the
       proper times."

Continued in Appendix A, p. 302.

Reflecting on the Gospel

All or nothing. I want the whole enchilada. I want to have my cake and eat it too. These kinds of expressions say much about all too many individuals in our society. Getting more, getting ahead, selfishly keeping what they have, taking but never giving, and sometimes even taking what is not rightly theirs does define some people. Thank God most people are not like this. But the tenants in the gospel parable are definitely like this. They go to great lengths to take more than the percentage of produce they deserve as tenants. They even resort to violence: they kill two different groups of servants; they even kill the landowner's son. What kind of an outcome do they expect? How unrealistic to think that they will come to own the vineyard! By wanting everything, they end up with nothing—not even their own lives. Such a price to pay for unrealistic expectations, unabated greed, unmitigated cruelty!

As a metaphor for the kingdom, the vineyard obviously belongs solely and exclusively to God: God owns it, builds it, does all that is necessary to protect it. We are the laborers invited into the kingdom to tend the divine vineyard, to produce an abundance of fruit. Ironically, the vineyard that the wicked tenants attempt to gain by violence is freely given to those of us who will work faithfully to produce its fruit. We are those new tenants who produce fruit because we surrender our self-will to God and accept Jesus as the One who shows the way. By so doing we gain everything. Apart from Jesus we tenants can do nothing on our own.

Obviously, the landowner does all that is necessary so that the produce will be assured for both himself and his tenants. But the tenants want more than their rightful share—they want the whole heritage. Ironically, their actions lead to their losing everything—even their lives. In contrast, through the death of God's Son we gain everything. We are legitimate heirs to more than our rightful share. We receive an inconceivable heritage—the fruit of the "kingdom of God," abundant life that can never be pressed out.

Living the Paschal Mystery

Many of us throw our whole hearts into what we do. We want to get ahead. We do our best if for no other reason than to look good. We can readily identify with the two vineyard owners in both the first reading and gospel. They put their whole hearts into their vineyard, doing everything they can to assure fruit. This describes aptly God's ways with us. God puts all the divine heart into coaxing us to be good and faithful tenants, cooperating with the divine will to produce an abundance of fruit.

After all this talk, what is the fruit of the kingdom? What is it we are to produce? Here is the real twist of the gospel: the fruit of the kingdom is the *life* God offers, but the only way to produce that fruit is *to die to self*! Just like the gospel tenants and the landowner's son (but for very different reasons), we get "killed" ourselves. That is, we must die to ourselves in order to do the work God asks of us and to inherit the abundance of life God offers. Finally, then, the kingdom does involve a kind of violence: our rooting out anything that keeps us from growing in relationship with God and hearing God's word, our dying to self so that we can do God's will. This may sound like more than we bargain for, but all we need do is remember that "by the Lord has this been done, and it is wonderful"!

Focusing the Gospel

Key words and phrases: planted . . . put . . . dug . . . built, sent his son, This is the heir, kill him, will produce its fruit

To the point: Obviously, the landowner does all that is necessary so that the produce would be assured for both himself and his tenants. But the tenants want more than their rightful share—they want the whole heritage. Ironically, their actions lead to their losing everything—even their lives. In contrast, through the death of God's Son we gain everything. We are legitimate heirs to more than our rightful share. We receive an inconceivable heritage—the fruit of the "kingdom of God," abundant life that can never be pressed out.

Connecting the Gospel

to the first reading: The vineyard owners in both the first reading and gospel do all they need to do to assure a good vintage. But an abundant vintage is never assured: the yield may be "wild grapes" or the yield may be stolen by greedy tenants. In both readings the outcome is judgment against infidelity.

to experience: How discouraging it is to do everything we can to ensure the successful outcome of a project or business venture, only to have it ruined by forces beyond our control. At this point, we tend simply to give up. God, however, never gives up on building the kingdom.

Connecting the Responsorial Psalm

to the readings: Psalm 80 was a communal lament written at some point in history when the nation of Israel underwent ruin at the hands of an enemy. In it the people ask God why this has been done and beg God to "once again" give "new life" to this vine transplanted from Egypt. The first reading relates the same tragedy. God destroys the vineyard Israel because, despite assiduous planning and care, it has produced nothing but "wild grapes." The gospel presents a different slant on the same scenario. In this case it is not the vineyard but its appointed caretakers that prove fruitless and unfaithful.

Central to the psalm that stands between the first reading and the gospel is the cry of "once again." Whether it is the vineyard or the ones who care for the vineyard who prove unfaithful, this is not the first time we human beings turn our back on the God who calls us into being and then sustains us. Nor will it be the last time. "Once again" and many times over must we cry out: Please, God, save us; please, God, start over with us! And God always does.

to psalmist preparation: Both last Sunday's responsorial psalm and the one for this week sing of God's mercy and care when we fail in fidelity. Our failure is no surprise; the marvel is God's unflagging efforts to redeem us. Where right now is God "once again" offering you another chance? Where is God "once again" offering it to the church? Where is God "once again" offering it to the world?

**ASSEMBLY &
FAITH-SHARING GROUPS**
- What God is doing in me to produce a good vintage is . . . How I cooperate with God to produce good fruit is . . .
- What I have received from God as an heir is . . . The obstacles in me that keep me from receiving what God offers are . . .
- I share the rich vintage of God's kingdom with others by . . . when . . .

PRESIDERS
My preaching stirs up in the assembly a desire for the rich vintage God offers them when . . .

DEACONS
My ministry of service embodies God's hard work to produce good fruit in the world whenever I . . .

HOSPITALITY MINISTERS
Caring hospitality is a way of cooperating with God to produce good fruit in the gathering assembly in that . . .

MUSIC MINISTERS
What helps me remember that God is the owner of the "vineyard" of my music ministry is . . . When I remember this, my music making sounds like . . .

ALTAR MINISTERS
My serving produces good fruit in that . . .

LECTORS
Evidence that my time with the word is producing good fruit is . . .

**EXTRAORDINARY MINISTERS
OF HOLY COMMUNION**
My manner of distributing Holy Communion helps communicants grasp God's rich vintage being given them when . . .

Model Act of Penitence

Presider: In this Sunday's readings God carefully prepares a vineyard so it will produce an abundance of fruit. Let us prepare ourselves to receive the rich vintage God offers us during this liturgy . . . [pause]

Lord Jesus, you produce rich harvest in us: Lord . . .

Christ Jesus, you died and rose to new life: Christ . . .

Lord Jesus, you make us heirs of your risen life: Lord . . .

Homily Points

• How disappointing it is to work hard at something, only to have it go wrong and have no good outcome happen! Students might spend hours studying for an exam, only to discover they've studied the wrong questions. A worker puts in long overtime hours on a project, only to have the manager scuttle the project. How disheartening this is for us, and how often it even results in our hesitating to work so hard the next time.

• God is amazingly resilient despite human forces and frailties that constantly thwart the divine plan for our salvation. Nothing—not even sparing the life of the divine Son—deters God from offering us a rich heritage in divine life itself. For our part, we are to be faithful tenants who rejoice in our heritage and acknowledge that we have been given far more than we expect or deserve.

• Being God's faithful tenants means that we do nothing to keep God's tender care from producing good fruit in and through us. As faithful tenants, we plant seeds of encouragement and hope, we water the growing fruit with prayer, we fertilize it with reflection on God's word, we cultivate it by good works, and we celebrate its abundance by sharing it with others.

Model Prayer of the Faithful

Presider: Let us pray to God, the owner of the vineyard of our lives, that we will be good and faithful tenants.

Response:

Lord, hear our prayer.

Cantor:

we pray to the Lord,

That all members of the church spend themselves generously to produce an abundant fruit of life for others . . . [pause]

That leaders of nations be responsible stewards who do all in their power to help their people live good and productive lives . . . [pause]

That those who lack what they need for healthy living be given a share in the abundance of others . . . [pause]

That each of us gathered here always be faithful tenants who celebrate and responsibly use the abundant fruits of this earth . . . [pause]

Presider: Nurturing God, you produce an abundance of good fruit for your kingdom: be with us as we feast on this abundance, share it with one another, and come to life everlasting with you. We ask this through Christ our Lord. **Amen.**

ALTERNATIVE OPENING PRAYER

Let us pray
[before the face of God in trusting faith]

Pause for silent prayer

Almighty and eternal God,
Father of the world to come,
your goodness is beyond what our spirit
    can touch
and your strength is more than the mind
    can bear.
Lead us to seek beyond our reach
and give us the courage to stand before
    your truth.

We ask this through Christ our Lord.
    Amen.

FIRST READING
Isa 5:1-7

Let me now sing of my friend,
    my friend's song concerning his vineyard.
My friend had a vineyard
    on a fertile hillside;
he spaded it, cleared it of stones,
    and planted the choicest vines;
within it he built a watchtower,
    and hewed out a wine press.
Then he looked for the crop of grapes,
    but what it yielded was wild grapes.

Now, inhabitants of Jerusalem and people
    of Judah,
    judge between me and my vineyard:
What more was there to do for my vineyard
    that I had not done?
Why, when I looked for the crop of grapes,
    did it bring forth wild grapes?
Now, I will let you know
    what I mean to do with my vineyard:
take away its hedge, give it to grazing,
    break through its wall, let it be trampled!
Yes, I will make it a ruin:
    it shall not be pruned or hoed,
    but overgrown with thorns and briers;
I will command the clouds
    not to send rain upon it.
The vineyard of the LORD of hosts is the
    house of Israel,
    and the people of Judah are his
        cherished plant;
he looked for judgment, but see,
    bloodshed!
    for justice, but hark, the outcry!

RESPONSORIAL PSALM
Ps 80:9, 12, 13-14, 15-16, 19-20

℟. (Isaiah 5:7a) The vineyard of the Lord
is the house of Israel.

A vine from Egypt you transplanted;
    you drove away the nations and planted
        it.
It put forth its foliage to the Sea,
    its shoots as far as the River.

R̤. The vineyard of the Lord is the house
of Israel.

Why have you broken down its walls,
    so that every passer-by plucks its fruit,
the boar from the forest lays it waste,
    and the beasts of the field feed upon it?

R̤. The vineyard of the Lord is the house of
Israel.

Once again, O LORD of hosts,
    look down from heaven, and see;
take care of this vine,
    and protect what your right hand has
        planted,
    the son of man whom you yourself
        made strong.

R̤. The vineyard of the Lord is the house of
Israel.

Then we will no more withdraw from you;
    give us new life, and we will call upon
        your name.
O LORD, God of hosts, restore us;
    if your face shine upon us, then we shall
        be saved.

R̤. The vineyard of the Lord is the house of
Israel.

SECOND READING
Phil 4:6-9

Brothers and sisters:
Have no anxiety at all, but in everything,
    by prayer and petition, with
        thanksgiving,
    make your requests known to God.
Then the peace of God that surpasses all
    understanding
    will guard your hearts and minds in
        Christ Jesus.

Finally, brothers and sisters,
    whatever is true, whatever is honorable,
    whatever is just, whatever is pure,
    whatever is lovely, whatever is
        gracious,
    if there is any excellence
    and if there is anything worthy of
        praise,
    think about these things.
Keep on doing what you have learned and
    received
    and heard and seen in me.
Then the God of peace will be with you.

About Liturgy

Fruit of the vine: The image of the vineyard and tenants and fruit might lead us to think that the fruit we are to produce as faithful disciples is something that only occurs in the future. In fact, God has already *given us* the fruit of the vine and with this the strength we need to produce even more abundant fruit. This image of "fruit of the vine" can have many meanings, one of them being the good works we perform for others in our daily living. More specifically, with respect to Mass, we are offered the "fruit of the vine" as Jesus' precious Blood at Holy Communion.

GIRM no. 281 states that Communion under both kinds is a "fuller sign value" (see also the June, 2001 U.S. Bishops' Norms for the Celebration and Reception of Holy Communion under Both Kinds in the Dioceses of the United States of America, no. 16). It further states that the reason for this is that the new covenant was ratified in Jesus' blood and in this the relationship between our eucharistic banquet and the messianic banquet can more clearly be seen. Everyone should be encouraged to partake in this fuller sign of God's love for us.

About Liturgical Music

Music suggestions: This Sunday's first reading, gospel, and psalm are about God's judgment against our infidelity and God's unflagging efforts to bring us back from this infidelity. An excellent choice for either the entrance or the recessional would be "God, Whose Purpose Is to Kindle" [GC, GC2, RS, W3]. Verse 3 particularly applies: "God, who still a sword delivers Rather than a placid peace, With your sharpened word disturb us, From complacency release!" "The Kingdom of God" [CH, GC, GC2, PMB, RS, W3, WC] would also make a good entrance song. Note its third verse: "The kingdom of God is challenge and choice: Believe the good news, repent and rejoice!"

Role of music: The music we sing for liturgy is not frosting on the cake but a substantive component of the liturgy. We only understand music's role when we first grasp the theological foundation for that role: the assembly's full, conscious, active participation in ritual enactment of the paschal mystery. Music fulfills its ministry only when it enables the assembly to surrender more deeply to the mystery of what it means to be the Body of Christ dying and rising for the life of the world. Whenever the music is aimed at another target (e.g., keeping the people interested, making them feel good, stroking the ego of a cantor), it distracts the people from the real purpose of the liturgy and stunts their growth to full stature as members of the Body of Christ. The only way to keep the music on target is to operate out of a clear and consistent theological understanding of the liturgy.

OCTOBER 2, 2011
TWENTY-SEVENTH SUNDAY
IN ORDINARY TIME

✦ SPIRITUALITY

GOSPEL ACCLAMATION
cf. Eph 1:17-18

R⁒. Alleluia, alleluia.
May the Father of our Lord Jesus Christ
enlighten the eyes of our hearts, so
that we may know what is the hope
that belongs to our call.
R⁒. Alleluia, alleluia.

Gospel Matt 22:1-14; L142A

Jesus again in reply spoke to the
    chief priests and elders of the
    people
  in parables, saying,
  "The kingdom of heaven may be
    likened to a king
  who gave a wedding feast for his
    son.
He dispatched his servants
  to summon the invited guests to the
    feast,
  but they refused to come.
A second time he sent other servants,
    saying,
  'Tell those invited: "Behold, I have
    prepared my banquet,
  my calves and fattened cattle are killed,
  and everything is ready; come to the
    feast."'
Some ignored the invitation and went
    away,
  one to his farm, another to his business.
The rest laid hold of his servants,
  mistreated them, and killed them.
The king was enraged and sent his troops,
  destroyed those murderers, and burned
    their city.
Then he said to his servants, 'The feast is
    ready,
  but those who were invited were not
    worthy to come.
Go out, therefore, into the main roads
  and invite to the feast whomever you
    find.'
The servants went out into the streets
  and gathered all they found, bad and
    good alike,
  and the hall was filled with guests.

Continued in Appendix A, p. 303.

Reflecting on the Gospel

This isn't just any banquet the guests are invited to in the parable in this Sunday's gospel: the invitations are sent out by the *king* and the occasion is the king's son's *wedding*. No doubt those who initially receive invitations have some kind of social status and so there is great dignity and affirmation in simply being invited—the invitation indicates a special, limited, and reserved relationship to the king. Imagine, then, the surprise and scandal at the refusals!

The refusals of the invited guests hit hard at the very relationship between the king and those invited to the feast. The refusal is a betrayal of dignity, election, and warm regard. Although the king's feast is prepared and invitations are sent, the presence of guests at the feast really isn't assured. It is scandalous enough that some invited guests give lame excuses and don't come; it is even more scandalous that others who are invited kill the king's servants. None of this deters the king: the feast will be served, a place is reserved, and the feast will take place with others as guests.

Why in the world would invited guests refuse to come to a king's feast? Perhaps they don't realize what an extraordinary banquet is being offered. Perhaps they haven't maintained their side of an ongoing relationship with the king. Perhaps they do not wish to sit down with some of the other invited guests. The problem isn't with the king, for whom this wedding feast is a priority, but with the invited guests who put their own "feast" ahead of the king's.

The parable, of course, is about being invited to God's feast. We are all invited guests. Sometimes we too refuse the invitation. The scandal of the refusal of our King's invitation indicates why sin (the refused invitation is a metaphor for sin) is so damaging (both the sin of those to whom Jesus is speaking in the gospel and our own sin). We too are invited to God's feast because we share a special, loving, covenantal relationship with God. Sin is our refusal to share in God's feast and life, and this refusal damages our relationship with God as well as with each other. A refused invitation is not simply a missed opportunity for a fine banquet. A refused invitation is a weakening in the relationship between host and guest. Like the wedding feast the king puts on for his son, God's banquet will also be served, and places are reserved for us. Will we come?

Living the Paschal Mystery

Even when we refuse to come, our King continually sends out invitations to us. This reminds us of how much God wants to share divine life and salvation with us. God sent the only Son to live among us and bring us salvation, even at the risk of the Son being killed. God's banquet of life is worth any cost to God. It ought to be worth any cost to us.

While none of us would be so foolish as to refuse, for example, an invitation to a state dinner at the White House, we do often refuse God's many invitations that are far more important. We are invited, for example, to the eucharistic feast every Sunday. We come, but do we truly participate in this banquet? We are invited to a feast of generosity through many opportunities to share our gifts with others less fortunate than ourselves. Do we willingly donate time, energy, resources to others? We are invited to a feast of relationships within family, workplace, neighborhood. Do we share our values and spirituality with others? Which is the feast we choose? Will we come?

Focusing the Gospel

Key words and phrases: king, wedding feast, invited guests, refused to come

To the point: Why would invited guests refuse to come to a king's feast? Perhaps they don't realize what an extraordinary banquet is being offered. Perhaps they haven't maintained their side of an ongoing relationship with the king. Perhaps they do not wish to sit down with some of the other invited guests. The problem isn't with the king, for whom this wedding feast is a priority, but with the invited guests who put their own "feast" ahead of the king's. Which is the feast we choose?

Connecting the Gospel

to the first reading: The first reading identifies what is given to those who come to the king's feast: rich abundance, freedom from death, an end to all tears, everlasting joy. But above all, they are given salvation.

to experience: On special occasions we hire caterers who charge by the plate. When guests don't show up, the host or hostess is charged nonetheless and suffers a loss. When we refuse to come to God's banquet, the loss is not God's, however, but ours! And what a loss!

Connecting the Responsorial Psalm

to the readings: Psalm 23 celebrates the covenant relationship we share with God. The verses sing of all that God constantly does for us—shepherd, guide, protect, nurture. The refrain is our promise to accept God's offer of life and to live always in God's presence. Yet the gospel relates two stories in which persons choose not to accept God's invitation to fullness of life. Despite all that God offers us, despite how profusely and repeatedly God makes the offer, we can and do say no. We know from personal experience how real and repetitive our refusal can be. We know from the readings and psalm how persistent God will be in inviting us to new life. May our singing of the psalm refrain be our pledge that our answer remains yes.

to psalmist preparation: The refrain for this Sunday's responsorial psalm can be seen as both a promise on God's part and a pledge on your part. In what area of your life is God calling you right now to keep your pledge to live as one who belongs to God's house?

**ASSEMBLY &
FAITH-SHARING GROUPS**

- The king's invitation to the wedding feast comes to me when . . . by . . . for . . .
- To come to the feast "dressed in a wedding garment," I need to . . .
- The most important "feast" in my life is . . .

PRESIDERS

My preaching encourages people to say yes to God's invitation to come to the feast when I . . .

DEACONS

My ministry proclaims to those I serve their invitation to the king's rich banquet whenever I . . .

HOSPITALITY MINISTERS

I am the joyful welcome to God's feast when I . . .

MUSIC MINISTERS

My music making helps the assembly savor God's feast more deeply when . . . it hinders their feasting when . . .

ALTAR MINISTERS

My faithful service at the altar helps me enter into God's feast more deeply when I . . .

LECTORS

My preparing God's word is "a feast of rich food and choice wines" (first reading) for me when . . .

**EXTRAORDINARY MINISTERS
OF HOLY COMMUNION**

My manner of distributing Holy Communion adds further joy to the feast when I . . .

Model Act of Penitence

Presider: Each Sunday we are invited to God's banquet to share in the bread of life and the cup of salvation. As we prepare to celebrate God's feast, let us come with open and hungry hearts . . . [pause]

Lord Jesus, you spread a rich feast of word and sacrament before us: Lord . . .

Christ Jesus, you are the food of everlasting life: Christ . . .

Lord Jesus, you even overlook our weaknesses to invite us to your feast: Lord . . .

Homily Points

• We hesitate to accept an invitation to a wedding (with the sometimes formidable expense that might entail) if the couple is only casually known to us. On the other hand, it is a joy to receive an invitation to a wedding of someone close to us, and we spare no expense in doing all that is customary in accepting this invitation.

• God spares no expense for the messianic banquet, and the invitation is extended to all. As we grow in our realization of the richness of this banquet—fullness of life—we ourselves spare no "expense" in accepting the invitation. We willingly put on the proper "wedding garment" of conforming our lives to what is expected of those who are friends of the King.

• As those invited to God's banquet, we must do all we can to grow into an ever more loving relationship with God and increase our desire to sit at God's table. Ultimately, the issue is whether we choose God's gracious invitation to life over our own selfish interests, whether we choose the feast God prepares for us over the one *we* prepare for ourselves. Which is the feast we choose?

Model Prayer of the Faithful

Presider: Let us pray to the God who invites us to a lavish banquet.

Response:

Lord, hear our prayer.

Cantor:

we pray to the Lord,

That all members of the church respond joyfully to God's invitation to come to the feast . . . [pause]

That all nations provide sufficient nourishment so their people are healthy and prosperous . . . [pause]

That the hungry be fed and those who are filled share with others . . . [pause]

That our parish community continually grow in our love for God and each other and in our desire to sit at God's lavish table . . . [pause]

Presider: Abundant God, you give all good things to those who come to you: hear these our prayers that one day we might sit at the everlasting banquet of your love. We ask this through Christ our Lord. **Amen.**

Let us pray

Pause for silent prayer

Lord,
our help and guide,
make your love the foundation of our lives.
May our love for you express itself
in our eagerness to do good for others.

Grant this through our Lord Jesus Christ,
        your Son,
who lives and reigns with you and the
        Holy Spirit,
one God, for ever and ever. **Amen.**

FIRST READING
Isa 25:6-10a

On this mountain the LORD of hosts
        will provide for all peoples
a feast of rich food and choice wines,
        juicy, rich food and pure, choice wines.
On this mountain he will destroy
        the veil that veils all peoples,
the web that is woven over all nations;
        he will destroy death forever.
The Lord GOD will wipe away
        the tears from every face;
the reproach of his people he will remove
        from the whole earth; for the LORD has
                spoken.
        On that day it will be said:
"Behold our God, to whom we looked to
                save us!
        This is the LORD for whom we looked;
        let us rejoice and be glad that he has
                saved us!"
For the hand of the LORD will rest on this
        mountain.

RESPONSORIAL PSALM
Ps 23:1-3a, 3b-4, 5, 6

R℣. (6cd) I shall live in the house of the Lord all the days of my life.

The LORD is my shepherd; I shall not want.
   In verdant pastures he gives me repose;
beside restful waters he leads me;
   he refreshes my soul.

R℣. I shall live in the house of the Lord all the days of my life.

He guides me in right paths
   for his name's sake.
Even though I walk in the dark valley
   I fear no evil; for you are at my side
with your rod and your staff
   that give me courage.

R℣. I shall live in the house of the Lord all the days of my life.

You spread the table before me
   in the sight of my foes;
you anoint my head with oil;
   my cup overflows.

R℣. I shall live in the house of the Lord all the days of my life.

Only goodness and kindness follow me
   all the days of my life;
and I shall dwell in the house of the LORD
   for years to come.

R℣. I shall live in the house of the Lord all the days of my life.

SECOND READING
Phil 4:12-14, 19-20

Brothers and sisters:
I know how to live in humble
      circumstances;
   I know also how to live with abundance.
In every circumstance and in all things
   I have learned the secret of being well
      fed and of going hungry,
   of living in abundance and of being in
      need.
I can do all things in him who strengthens
   me.
Still, it was kind of you to share in my
   distress.

My God will fully supply whatever you
   need,
   in accord with his glorious riches in
      Christ Jesus.
To our God and Father, glory forever and
   ever. Amen.

About Liturgy

Controversy in Matthew's gospel: In Matthew's gospel Jesus tells many parables about the kingdom after he arrives in Jerusalem (for the past four Sundays we've listened to some of these kingdom parables). The controversy between Jesus and some of the Jewish leaders is sharpening. Some of the parables even include the killing of someone; last week, for example, the wretched vineyard tenants kill the landowner's son, and this week, in the parable about the king who invites guests to his son's wedding feast, the king's servant-messengers are killed. This imagery has layers of meaning. God's own Son will likewise be killed. Those expected to have eternal reward—to sit at the messianic banquet—lose out because of their bad behavior and those least expected share in God's graciousness. Matthew seems intent on not letting his readers miss his point about inclusivity and so has Jesus tell story after story demonstrating this theme.

Over and over in these parables about the kingdom Jesus confronts us with the message that those who are expecting to enter the kingdom will not, and those thought to be kept out of the kingdom will be ushered in. The thorny issue of the historical context of Matthew's gospel is that some of the Jewish leaders (chief priests, elders, scribes, Pharisees, Sadducees) presume that they will inherit the blessing of God's promises because they meticulously keep the law. Sinners (prostitutes, tax collectors) cannot possibly be favored by God. Israel, as God's chosen people, will inherit; the Gentiles will not. Jesus' message of salvation for all is confronting, challenging, and intolerable for those who presume to know whom God does and does not favor.

About Liturgical Music

Music suggestions: Songs calling us to gather around the feast of God's table would be most appropriate this Sunday. Two particularly appropriate ones are Dan Schutte's "Gather the People" [BB], with its refrain "Gather the people! Enter the feast! All are invited, the greatest and least. The banquet is ready, now to be shared. Join in the heavenly feast that God has prepared"; and his "Table of Plenty" [BB, JS2, OFUV]. The first would work well for the entrance song and the second for the Communion procession.

More on the role of music: All who are involved in music ministry—music directors, choir members, cantors, instrumentalists, pastors—need to be familiar with the liturgical documents of the church and with the theology that shapes these documents. Without this theological vision, choices made about music can fall prey to well-meaning but misguided ignorance or, even worse, to whim.

One of the key underpinnings of the theological vision of the liturgical documents is the notion of liturgy as ritual enactment of the paschal mystery. Because of baptism, the faithful share in Christ's identity and are called to surrender consciously—in liturgy and in life—to participation in his paschal mystery. Sharing in Christ's identity and the call to paschal mystery living is the fullest meaning of the priesthood of the faithful and of the norm of full, conscious, active participation in the liturgy. This means that the goal of liturgical celebration, and of the more difficult liturgical catechesis that must accompany it, is not liturgies that engage the assembly so that they "feel good" for the moment but liturgies that challenge them in the long term to live the dying and rising mystery into which they have been baptized.

OCTOBER 9, 2011
TWENTY-EIGHTH SUNDAY IN ORDINARY TIME

✝ SPIRITUALITY

GOSPEL ACCLAMATION
Phil 2:15d, 16a

℟. Alleluia, alleluia.
Shine like lights in the world
as you hold on to the word of life.
℟. Alleluia, alleluia.

Gospel

Matt 22:15-21; L145A

The Pharisees went off
and plotted how they
might entrap Jesus in
speech.
They sent their disciples
to him, with the
Herodians, saying,
"Teacher, we know that you are a
truthful man
and that you teach the way of God in
accordance with the truth.
And you are not concerned with
anyone's opinion,
for you do not regard a person's
status.
Tell us, then, what is your opinion:
Is it lawful to pay the census tax to
Caesar or not?"
Knowing their malice, Jesus said,
"Why are you testing me, you
hypocrites?
Show me the coin that pays the census
tax."
Then they handed him the Roman coin.
He said to them, "Whose image is this
and whose inscription?"
They replied, "Caesar's."
At that he said to them,
"Then repay to Caesar what belongs
to Caesar
and to God what belongs to God."

Reflecting on the Gospel

The gospels show that the controversy between Jesus and Jewish leaders (in this Sunday's gospel, the Pharisees) gets more heated as Jesus nears Jerusalem. Some of these Jewish leaders were anything but sincere when approaching Jesus. They were trying to protect themselves, their positions, and their way of interpreting religious obligations. This is clearly opposed to the message of Jesus to be loving, caring, and forgiving, to put the other's good ahead of self, to have clear priorities toward both God and one's responsibilities in community. Such closed and hard hearts of some Jewish leaders! This gospel once again shows the Pharisees plotting to "entrap Jesus." The controversy between Jesus and the religious leaders continues and is becoming more obvious and deliberate.

With utter sarcasm and insincerity the Pharisees in this gospel attempt to entrap Jesus. Seeing through their ruse, Jesus turns the tables and entraps them "with the truth." The "way of God" is found not in opposing civil and religious authority but in acting with the integrity of Jesus in both areas of life, responding appropriately in each "kingdom." Like Jesus, we are to give ourselves for the good of others in all areas of life. Giving ourselves first to God, we will know the "way" and the "truth" of all other loyalties, and our choices and behaviors will further God's plan of salvation.

By trying to entrap Jesus, the Pharisees in the gospel are actually putting "Caesar" (that is, their own will and agenda, their own fears and obstinacy) ahead of God! Their actions have betrayed that they themselves do anything but "teach the way of God in accordance with the truth," which is why their address to Jesus is nothing else but pure sarcasm. Their lifestyle hardly indicates that they are trying to sort out obligations to Caesar and God, and they hardly have put God first.

The obligations to Caesar and God are radically different: to the state we pay taxes, but to God we give undivided service and worship. Isaiah speaks for God: "I am the LORD, there is no other" (first reading); our ultimate loyalty and self-offering is to God and so we "give to the LORD the glory due his name!" (responsorial psalm). If we keep God central in our lives, then there is no problem with giving to "Caesar" what belongs to "Caesar." Further, if we place this in the eschatological (end times and fulfillment) context of Matthew's gospel, the controversy the religious leaders confront Jesus with simply crumbles, for everything in this world ultimately belongs to God; there is nothing of this world that compares to who God is and how much God cares for us, and nothing of this world is worth more than what God offers us.

What God wants most from us isn't money! What God asks of us is the self-offering that acknowledges who God is and who we are in relation to God. In return, God gives what no emperor or state can give: a share in divine life.

Living the Paschal Mystery

Often our struggle with living this gospel is not really about two "kingdoms" presenting opposing values but about our own selfish values trumping everything else. The kind of self-giving that gives to God what is God's due and to society what is society's due necessitates that we think of others first. It truly is that simple, yet sometimes so hard to live!

Focusing the Gospel

Key words and phrases: entrap Jesus, way of God, truth, repay to Caesar
. . . and to God

To the point: With utter sarcasm and insincerity the Pharisees in this gospel
attempt to entrap Jesus. Seeing through their ruse, Jesus turns the tables and
entraps them "with the truth." The "way of God" is found not in opposing civil
and religious authority but in acting with the integrity of Jesus in both areas
of life, responding appropriately in each "kingdom." Like Jesus, we are to give
ourselves for the good of others in all areas of life. Giving ourselves first to God,
we will know the "way" and the "truth" of all other loyalties, and our choices
and behaviors will further God's plan of salvation.

Connecting the Gospel

to the first reading: There are really two issues the first reading and gospel
raise: God can (and does) use civil authority for divine purposes of salvation
(see first reading), and we are to respond appropriately in both civil and religious matters (see gospel).

to experience: Sometimes the two "kingdoms" in which we live are in conflict—our religious values clash with civil policy. As faithful followers of Jesus,
we must always choose first God's kingdom.

Connecting the Responsorial Psalm

to the readings: On the surface level the connection between this Sunday's
responsorial psalm, first reading, and gospel is readily evident. God alone is
God. Even when unrecognized, God alone is the source of all power and authority (see first reading). The psalm calls us to give God "glory and praise" and to
announce God's sovereignty to all nations. In the gospel Jesus commands us to
give God what is properly due.

A subtle irony in the readings, however, reveals that this command has
deeper than surface dimensions. While a non-Jew unknowingly cooperates with
God's plan, Jewish religious leaders knowingly work to subvert it. One who
does not know God furthers God's redemptive plan, while those reputed to be
God's servants thwart it. The message for us is that to give God proper due it
is not sufficient merely to mouth praise or to engage in public religious activity.
Rather, we are to give what Cyrus unwittingly offered and the Pharisees knowingly refused: our hearts in conscious cooperation with God's will.

to psalmist preparation: When you sing Psalm 96 this Sunday, you will
be calling the assembly to give God "glory and honor" by living in such a way
that they cooperate with God's plan of salvation. What helps you live in this
way? What hinders you?

**ASSEMBLY &
FAITH-SHARING GROUPS**
- I thwart the establishment of God's kingdom when I . . . I advance God's kingdom when I . . .
- I act with the integrity of Jesus in civil
life by . . . in church life by . . .
- What and who help me give to God what
belongs to God are . . .

PRESIDERS
My ministry helps parishioners know and
live the "way of God" best when I . . .

DEACONS
My serving others brings together the
kingdoms of the world and church in these
ways . . .

HOSPITALITY MINISTERS
My hospitality affirms and supports the
assembly's giving to God what belongs to
God in these ways . . .

MUSIC MINISTERS
Sometimes my music ministry keeps me
more in the "kingdom" of the world when
. . . What helps me keep my music ministry serving God's kingdom is . . .

ALTAR MINISTERS
My serving at the altar advances God's
kingdom when I . . .

LECTORS
Like King Cyrus in the first reading, I let
God use me to lead people home when I . . .

**EXTRAORDINARY MINISTERS
OF HOLY COMMUNION**
The self-offering that the liturgy signifies
and my ministry embodies is the "way of
God" in that . . .

Model Act of Penitence

Presider: Today's gospel raises the question of truth and integrity about giving to God what belongs to God. As we prepare to celebrate this liturgy, let us reflect on what we give to God . . . [pause]

Lord Jesus, you gave yourself to the Father in obedience and love: Lord . . .

Christ Jesus, you show us the way and the truth: Christ . . .

Lord Jesus, you lead us to integrity of life: Lord . . .

Homily Preparation

• All of us have dual citizenship—not of two countries but of two "kingdoms." We are to be both in the world yet not of the world. The world holds myriad distractions and attractions that lure us. Sometimes, indeed, we are faced with momentous choices between these two "kingdoms."

• The real issue underlying this gospel is not loyalty to God or state but truthfulness. This truthfulness is revealed in integrity of life, honesty in dealing with others, and clarity about what we are to give God and what we are to give one another.

• Jesus calls us to the same integrity that characterizes himself. We are to be forthright in our dealings with one another, whether this means, for example, honest confrontation against manipulators or making just payment of civil debts. Above all, we are to live as persons who give "God what belongs to God"—our wholehearted gift of self in obedience and love.

Model Prayer of the Faithful

Presider: Let us pray that we live with integrity, giving God what belongs to God.

Response:

Lord, hear our prayer.

Cantor:

we pray to the Lord,

That all members of the church respond with integrity to the demands of both the Gospel and civil responsibilities . . . [pause]

That all nations use their resources wisely for the good of all their people . . . [pause]

That the poor and those in need receive their just due . . . [pause]

That each of us here grow in our faithfulness to the ways of God . . . [pause]

Presider: Gracious God, you call us to integrity of life: hear these our prayers that we might one day share eternally in the fullness of your kingdom. We ask this through Christ our Lord. **Amen.**

Let us pray
  [for the gift of simplicity and joy in our
  service of God and man]

Pause for silent prayer

Almighty and ever-living God,
our source of power and inspiration,
give us strength and joy
in serving you as followers of Christ,
who lives and reigns with you and the
    Holy Spirit,
one God, for ever and ever. **Amen.**

FIRST READING
Isa 45:1, 4-6

Thus says the LORD to his anointed, Cyrus,
    whose right hand I grasp,
subduing nations before him,
    and making kings run in his service,
opening doors before him
    and leaving the gates unbarred:
For the sake of Jacob, my servant,
    of Israel, my chosen one,
I have called you by your name,
    giving you a title, though you knew me
    not.
I am the LORD and there is no other,
    there is no God besides me.
It is I who arm you, though you know me
    not,
    so that toward the rising and the setting
    of the sun
    people may know that there is none
    besides me.
I am the LORD, there is no other.

RESPONSORIAL PSALM

Ps 96:1, 3, 4-5, 7-8, 9-10

R̸. (7b) Give the Lord glory and honor.

Sing to the LORD a new song;
   sing to the LORD, all you lands.
Tell his glory among the nations;
   among all peoples, his wondrous deeds.

R̸. Give the Lord glory and honor.

For great is the LORD and highly to be
   praised;
   awesome is he, beyond all gods.
For all the gods of the nations are things
   of nought,
   but the LORD made the heavens.

R̸. Give the Lord glory and honor.

Give to the LORD, you families of nations,
   give to the LORD glory and praise;
   give to the LORD the glory due his name!
Bring gifts, and enter his courts.

R̸. Give the Lord glory and honor.

Worship the LORD, in holy attire;
   tremble before him, all the earth;
say among the nations: The LORD is king,
   he governs the peoples with equity.

R̸. Give the Lord glory and honor.

SECOND READING

1 Thess 1:1-5b

Paul, Silvanus, and Timothy to the church
   of the Thessalonians
   in God the Father and the Lord Jesus
     Christ:
   grace to you and peace.
We give thanks to God always for all of
   you,
   remembering you in our prayers,
   unceasingly calling to mind your work
     of faith and labor of love
   and endurance in hope of our Lord Jesus
     Christ,
   before our God and Father,
   knowing, brothers and sisters loved by
     God,
   how you were chosen.
For our gospel did not come to you in
   word alone,
   but also in power and in the Holy Spirit
   and with much conviction.

About Liturgy

Worship and gift of self: If there is anything we learn from the prophets of the Old Testament and from the religious leaders of the New Testament, it is that worship cannot be empty. Worship is the praise of God that is borne out by caring for others who are the beloved of God; caring for others is caring about God. Worship that stays within the four walls of a building is empty; even the very structure of liturgy itself bears this out and reminds us that God changes us during liturgy so that we can live better for the good of others. Worship begins with God's gift of Self to us; it concludes by sending us forth to be a gift of self for those we meet in our everyday living. This is how we live with the integrity of Jesus.

Every liturgy ends with some sort of mission—we are sent to love and serve the Lord in each other. These are not just ritual words at the end of Mass to which we more or less consciously respond, "Thanks be to God." Our "thanks be to God" is more than words—it requires us to give thanks to God for all God has given us by taking care of others and creation as God's gifts to us. Although the prayers and readings at liturgy change from celebration to celebration and these might give us some specific Christian actions we might try to live during the week, in a sense liturgy's dismissal is always the same: go and *live* the transformation of liturgy and the deepening of God's presence within. This is the gift of self liturgy asks of us: giving ourselves to others. This, then, is our ultimate praise and thanksgiving to God, our ultimate giving to God what is God's due.

About Liturgical Music

Music suggestions: Numerous hymns of praise abound, but particularly appropriate for this Sunday would be ones that call us to give God the glory belonging to the creator of all. "Sing Praise to God Who Reigns Above" [GC, JS2, PMB, RS, SS, WC, W3] concludes every verse with the phrase "To God all praise and glory." The sturdy tune MIT FREUDEN ZART makes this hymn very effective for the entrance procession. Other excellent choices for the entrance procession would be "God, We Praise You" [BB, JS2, PMB, RS, SS, W3, WC, WS]; Lucien Deiss's "All the Earth" [PMB, WC, WS]; and "O God beyond All Praising" [BB, CBW3, JS2, PMB, SS, W3, WC]. A lovely choice for Communion would be Paul Inwood's "Center of My Life" [BB, JS2, OFUV]. An appropriate choice for the recessional hymn would be Erik Routley's challenging "What Does the Lord Require" [RS, W3].

Carl Daw's text "Baited, the Question Rose" [HG] was written to accord with this gospel. The final verse adds a very creative dimension to the question of whose image is on the coin: "May we discern, O God, Your daily gifts of grace; Show us your image freshly coined In ev'ry heart and face." The tune to which this song is set will be unfamiliar to most assemblies, as will its dissonant harmonic structure. Both tune and structure, however, fit well this gospel's confrontation between Jesus and the Pharisees. The hymn could be used effectively as a choir prelude.

OCTOBER 16, 2011

TWENTY-NINTH SUNDAY IN ORDINARY TIME

✝ SPIRITUALITY

GOSPEL ACCLAMATION
John 14:23

℟. Alleluia, alleluia.
Whoever loves me will keep my word, says the
   Lord,
and my Father will love him and we will come
   to him.
℟. Alleluia, alleluia.

Gospel

Matt 22:34-40; L148A

When the Pharisees heard that Jesus
   had silenced the Sadducees,
   they gathered together, and one of
      them,
   a scholar of the law, tested him by
      asking,
   "Teacher, which commandment in
      the law is the greatest?"
He said to him,
   "You shall love the Lord, your God,
   with all your heart,
   with all your soul,
   and with all your mind.
This is the greatest and the first
   commandment.
The second is like it:
   You shall love your neighbor as
      yourself.
The whole law and the prophets depend
   on these two commandments."

Reflecting on the Gospel

Our priorities indicate how things are of relative importance to us. If we have only so much time in the evening, we make dinner, help the children with their homework, and make some phone calls we've been putting off before we kick off our shoes and sit back and relax. Studying for an important exam takes priority over going out with friends. Taking time to exercise daily indicates we care about our health. The things that are important to us generally have impact on our well-being and that of others. This Sunday's gospel is about priorities—and indicates what is to be the top priority for all of us.

The "scholar of the law" tests Jesus by asking him to prioritize—to identify the *greatest* law. Had Jesus answered by naming as most important one of the numerous precepts so dear to the Pharisees (and that they insisted be kept meticulously), he would have failed the "test." Jesus does state a clear priority with his answer—there is one commandment above all others: to love God with our entire being. This is the most important thing in our lives and everything else we do is measured against our love for God. He also teaches that the second commandment (love neighbor as self) is a rephrasing of the first in terms of the human beings with whom we live and relate. By loving our neighbor we are loving God and keeping the greatest commandment.

The first reading details what love of neighbor requires: we are not to "molest or oppress" strangers, widows, or orphans. This phrase (strangers or aliens, widows, orphans) identifying three categories of needy people in Israel became a metaphor referring to anyone in need. In other words, love of neighbor takes in everyone, but especially those who cannot help themselves. Why should we love our neighbor in such an extraordinary way? The first reading answers this question: because God has loved us in just the same way ("for I am compassionate"). God's love for us sets the standard for our love of neighbor—no one is excluded, no demand is too great.

Here is the surprise of the gospel: love of God and love of neighbor cannot really be separated; in loving our neighbor we love God! We cannot separate love of God and love of neighbor because our neighbor was created in God's image and bears within him or her the presence of God. Further, our love for God cannot be something only *thought* or even only *said* (for example, in prayer). Our love for God must be carried out by loving *actions* toward our neighbors. This is how God has already loved us and acted toward us!

Living the Paschal Mystery

Most of us don't have great difficulty loving those we know and care about. The first reading directs our love even toward the neighbor we don't know. In our present society this is perhaps not only challenging but sometimes it is also very risky. In a crime-laden society such as ours we tend not to trust the stranger—the one we meet on the street or the one who might come to our door. On the one hand, we must be careful and protect ourselves and our loved ones. On the other hand, we must be genuinely sensitive to others' needs.

If someone comes to our door and needs to use the phone, we can offer to make the call for them; if we see something happening that is wrong, we can take responsibility and call the police or other agency; we can do something so simple as hold a door open for someone who is package-laden. In these and countless other ways each day we not only *do* our love for our neighbor, but in those acts we also show our love for God. This is our most important priority: to love God in the neighbor we meet every day.

Focusing the Gospel

Key words and phrases: tested him, which . . . law is the greatest, You shall love God with . . ., second is like it

To the point: The "scholar of the law" tests Jesus by asking him to identify the greatest law. Had Jesus answered by naming as most important one of the numerous precepts so dear to the Pharisees, he would have failed the "test." Jesus does state a clear priority with his answer—there is one commandment above all others: to love God with our entire being. He also teaches that the second commandment (love neighbor as self) is a rephrasing of the first in terms of the human beings with whom we live and relate. By loving our neighbor we are loving God and keeping the greatest commandment.

Connecting the Gospel

to the first reading: All the LORD's exhortations in the first reading deal with concrete examples of concern and compassion for others, which are acts of love. In loving our neighbor, we are loving as God has first loved us.

to experience: Most of us don't have difficulty loving those we know and care about. The first reading directs our love even toward the neighbor we don't know.

Connecting the Responsorial Psalm

to the readings: Implied in this responsorial psalm's expression of whole-hearted love of God ("I love you, Lord, my strength") is acknowledgment that the source of our capacity to love both God and neighbor unselfishly and un-stintingly is God. It is God who gives us the strength to live according to the demands of the covenant. The first reading spells out these demands in concrete terms as acts of compassion toward real people in real need. In the gospel Jesus teaches us that fidelity to the covenant rests as much upon these acts of compassion as it does upon love of God.

This command to love wholeheartedly and concretely is demanding. The good news of the psalm is that we are not left to our own meager resources. Rather, we draw upon a reserve that is divine, unshakable, and unfailing. We can love as we are commanded because we have God as "our strength."

to psalmist preparation: You can love God with all your heart and soul and you can love your neighbor as yourself (gospel) because God gives you the strength to do so (psalm). You might take time this week to reflect on how this strength has grown in you, and give God thanks. You might also examine where this strength needs to grow, and ask for God's grace.

**ASSEMBLY &
FAITH-SHARING GROUPS**
- When asked to name the greatest commandment, Jesus named two! The way I understand how the two are related is . . .
- I have grown in being able to love God with my whole being in these ways . . .
- I have grown in loving my neighbor as myself in these ways . . .

PRESIDERS
My preaching challenges the assembly to love God above all and love neighbor compassionately when I . . . My manner of living does this when I . . .

DEACONS
My serving others makes visible my love for God when I . . .

HOSPITALITY MINISTERS
My hospitality toward the Body of Christ shows that I truly love God and neighbor when I . . .

MUSIC MINISTERS
I express my love for other music ministers when I . . . my love for the assembly when I . . .

ALTAR MINISTERS
My service at the altar enables me to love better my neighbor as myself whenever I . . .

LECTORS
My preparing to proclaim God's word is an act of loving God when . . . of loving others when . . .

**EXTRAORDINARY MINISTERS
OF HOLY COMMUNION**
My love of God gets "incarnated" into loving service for the Body of Christ whenever I . . .

Model Act of Penitence

Presider: Jesus is quite clear about the greatest commandment: love God and neighbor. We are able to love in this way because God has first loved us. We pause now and remember God's love for us . . . [pause]

Lord Jesus, you are God's love made visible: Lord . . .

Christ Jesus, you loved us even to death on a cross: Christ . . .

Lord Jesus, you care for us with kindness and compassion: Lord . . .

Homily Points

• Popular sayings such as, "Watch out for number 1!" or "Do unto others before they do unto you!" belie the message of this gospel. Self-centeredness can paint a very dark picture of our society. But this is not a complete picture of the way we live together. We know many, many generous and caring people who truly take this gospel to heart.

• The gospel sets a clear priority for how we are to act: love above all else. Jesus showed us by the way he lived what it means to love God with all one's being and love others as self. Jesus loved by his teaching, preaching, forgiving, and healing. Jesus loved by his open and welcoming encounters with all who came to him. Jesus loved by his suffering and death. Yes, Jesus loved above all else.

• While at times we fail in this kind of love, nonetheless most of us actually live out the priority Jesus models. Like Jesus, we teach, forgive, reach out a healing hand, support and care for the discouraged. We volunteer our time at soup kitchens and shelters, we build homes for the homeless, we participate in acts of justice that lead to systemic change for the good. Yes, we too seek to love with all our hearts.

Model Prayer of the Faithful

Presider: Confident of God's abiding love for us, we now make our needs known so that we can love with all our hearts.

Response:

Lord, hear our prayer.

Cantor:

we pray to the Lord,

That the church show loving concern for all who come for guidance and help . . . [pause]

That leaders of nations guide their people to love and care for one another . . . [pause]

That those who are victims of hatred, violence, or abuse be embraced by God's abiding love . . . [pause]

That our parish community grow in our love for each other and our outreach to those in need . . . [pause]

Presider: Loving-kind God, you love us beyond compare: hear these our prayers that one day we might live eternally in your love. We ask this through Christ our Lord. **Amen.**

OPENING PRAYER

Let us pray

Pause for silent prayer

Almighty and ever-living God,
strengthen our faith, hope, and love.
May we do with loving hearts
what you ask of us
and come to share the life you promise.

We ask this through our Lord Jesus Christ,
 your Son,
who lives and reigns with you and the
 Holy Spirit,
one God, for ever and ever. **Amen.**

FIRST READING

Exod 22:20-26

Thus says the LORD:
"You shall not molest or oppress an alien,
 for you were once aliens yourselves in
 the land of Egypt.
You shall not wrong any widow or orphan.
If ever you wrong them and they cry out
 to me,
 I will surely hear their cry.
My wrath will flare up, and I will kill you
 with the sword;
 then your own wives will be widows,
 and your children orphans.

"If you lend money to one of your poor
 neighbors among my people,
 you shall not act like an extortioner
 toward him
 by demanding interest from him.
If you take your neighbor's cloak as a
 pledge,
 you shall return it to him before sunset;
 for this cloak of his is the only covering
 he has for his body.
What else has he to sleep in?
If he cries out to me, I will hear him; for I
 am compassionate."

RESPONSORIAL PSALM
Ps 18:2-3, 3-4, 47, 51

R̰. (2) I love you, Lord, my strength.

I love you, O Lord, my strength,
  O Lord, my rock, my fortress, my
    deliverer.

R̰. I love you, Lord, my strength.

My God, my rock of refuge,
  my shield, the horn of my salvation, my
    stronghold!
Praised be the Lord, I exclaim,
  and I am safe from my enemies.

R̰. I love you, Lord, my strength.

The Lord lives and blessed be my rock!
  Extolled be God my savior.
You who gave great victories to your king
  and showed kindness to your anointed.

R̰. I love you, Lord, my strength.

SECOND READING
1 Thess 1:5c-10

Brothers and sisters:
You know what sort of people we were
    among you for your sake.
And you became imitators of us and of the
    Lord,
  receiving the word in great affliction,
    with joy from the Holy Spirit,
  so that you became a model for all the
    believers
  in Macedonia and in Achaia.
For from you the word of the Lord has
    sounded forth
  not only in Macedonia and in Achaia,
  but in every place your faith in God has
    gone forth,
  so that we have no need to say
    anything.
For they themselves openly declare about
    us
  what sort of reception we had among
    you,
  and how you turned to God from idols
  to serve the living and true God
  and to await his Son from heaven,
  whom he raised from the dead,
  Jesus, who delivers us from the coming
    wrath.

About Liturgy

Parish bulletins and showing love for one another: Almost all parishes distribute a bulletin each Sunday and these usually contain information necessary for the good order of the parish: Mass intentions, liturgical ministers' schedule, parish meeting schedule, other announcements. While all this is necessary, the weekly parish bulletin can also be broadened to include catechesis on various topics. Sometimes this can be in the form of inserts that afford a topic greater development (bulletin inserts are available from Liturgical Press based on *Living Liturgy*™), and at other times catechesis might be just a couple of sentences placed in a box (perhaps with a graphic) to draw attention to it.

Following up on this week's gospel from now until the end of the liturgical year (that is, for about the next month), a parish might include notices of the good things neighbors have done for one another (it may be best to omit names). In this way the parish staff would be affirming these good works, but reporting them can also be a form of catechesis—giving parishioners some ideas about how practically they might do good for one another (love one another) and how easy this really is to fit into one's daily schedule. While loving one's neighbor seems such a simple thing and we hear about it all the time, in fact it's something we need to be reminded about often.

About Liturgical Music

Music suggestions: A most fitting text during Communion this Sunday would be "Ubi Caritas." The Taizé setting [in most hymnals] provides the kind of improvisation needed to cover the length of the procession. Omer Westendorf's English paraphrase "Where Charity and Love Prevail" [the well-known setting by Paul Benoit is found in most hymnals; PMB, WC, WS contain a setting of the text by Mark Hill] will need to be lengthened either with organ or choir interludes (for example, between every two sung verses the choir could hum the tune a cappella, in a soft dynamic). Two versions of the ninth-century chant, set in verse-refrain style, are Richard Proulx's "Where True Love and Charity Are Found" [CBW3, GC, GC2, RS, W3] and Joyce Glover's "Where True Charity and Love Dwell" [BB, JS2, PMB, WC, WS]. Choir or cantor(s) could sing the verses, with assembly joining on the refrain. Bob Hurd's bilingual "Ubi Caritas" [BB, JS2, OFUV] is also set for cantor or choir on the verses and assembly on the refrain, as is Cheryl Aranda's "Tri-lingual Ubi Caritas" [OFUV, PMB, WS].

Other good choices for Communion include James Chepponis's "Love One Another" [G2, GC, RS] and "Love Is His Word" [PMB, RS, W3, WC]. "Make Us True Servants" [PMB, WC, WS] would be an appropriate text for the recessional song. Randall DeBruyn's "In Perfect Charity" [OCP octavo 8413TD] would make a lovely and fitting choral prelude.

OCTOBER 23, 2011
THIRTIETH SUNDAY IN ORDINARY TIME

SPIRITUALITY

GOSPEL ACCLAMATION
Matt 23:9b, 10b

R̸. Alleluia, alleluia.
You have but one Father in heaven
and one master, the Christ.
R̸. Alleluia, alleluia.

Gospel   Matt 23:1-12; L151A

Jesus spoke to the crowds
        and to his disciples,
        saying,
    "The scribes and the
        Pharisees
    have taken their
        seat on the chair
        of Moses.
Therefore, do and
    observe all things whatsoever they
    tell you,
    but do not follow their example.
For they preach but they do not
    practice.
They tie up heavy burdens hard to
    carry
    and lay them on people's shoulders,
    but they will not lift a finger to move
        them.
All their works are performed to be
    seen.
They widen their phylacteries and
    lengthen their tassels.
They love places of honor at banquets,
    seats of honor in synagogues,
    greetings in marketplaces, and the
        salutation 'Rabbi.'
As for you, do not be called 'Rabbi.'
You have but one teacher, and you are
    all brothers.
Call no one on earth your father;
    you have but one Father in heaven.
Do not be called 'Master';
    you have but one master, the Christ.
The greatest among you must be your
    servant.
Whoever exalts himself will be
    humbled;
    but whoever humbles himself will be
        exalted."

Reflecting on the Gospel

We tend to have great admiration for people of their word. At one time a handshake was all that was necessary to seal a contract—a person's word was the same as the deed accomplished and nothing more was needed. This kind of word-behavior is so important to us humans that the aphorism "practice what you preach" is a common part of our language. This Sunday's gospel is the source for this common saying.

After so many prior confrontations, Jesus himself now directly takes on the scribes and Pharisees by pointing to a problem in the community: "they preach but they do not practice." Jesus clearly teaches that who we are is defined by how we are with God and one another. We are to be learners of the one true Master, all children of the "one Father in heaven," humble servants of Christ and each other. How we *are* reveals most truly who we are. How we *do* reveals most truly who we are. Our word-behavior about the Gospel must be consistent. We must truly live the Gospel. Our Gospel living is our "handshake"—our promise that the deed is accomplished and nothing more is needed. Even more, the deed that is accomplished is nothing less than our own salvation—our own final exaltation, final share in Jesus' glory.

Jesus rightly criticizes those who pursue the titles rabbi, father, master. Yet this controversy over titles involves more than social prestige and honor: it reveals that how people view themselves tends to be how they live. But ultimately what really matters is how we understand ourselves in relation to God, who alone is the sure Teacher, Father, and Master. When that is clear, we know ourselves to be humble servants.

The gospel, then, isn't insisting that we not work for promotions or be called by well-deserved titles. The gospel is saying that we must always keep our eyes on God as central in our lives, doing works out of love for God and others, and act with the integrity of Jesus. Our works and example—or word-behaviors—must reveal our ultimate word-behavior: that we are disciples of Jesus, the servant of others. In this sense the humbling of ourselves isn't beyond us—it is simply living in right relationship with God and others. This means that we never forget our first and most important title: to be servant. This means that we must always practice what we preach. And what we preach is Jesus who is humble servant now exalted.

Living the Paschal Mystery

All our lives we grapple with being humble servant. Gradually on our life journey we discover that our proper "seat" is in the place of the servant and our true "place of honor" is at God's Table where all are equals. When we have this clear in our own minds, then words and deeds are not in opposition.

One way of dying to self that gospel living entails is to be servant of others; this puts title, position, wealth into perspective: all is at the service of the good of others. The new life we might experience by such living takes the form of others respecting us not because of our title or the words we speak but because of the genuine goodness of who we are and what we do. Rather than lay heavy burdens on others, we reach out to help them carry their loads. Rather than putting on symbols of prestige or taking places of honor, we spend ourselves for the least fortunate among us. Being humble servant means we place ourselves at the service of others, recognizing all as our brothers and sisters in Christ.

Focusing the Gospel

Key words and phrases: preach but they do not practice, one teacher, one Father, one master, servant, humbles himself

To the point: After so many prior confrontations, Jesus himself now directly takes on the scribes and Pharisees by pointing to a problem in the community: "they preach but they do not practice." Jesus clearly teaches that who we are is defined by how we are with God and one another. We are to be learners of the one true Master, all children of the "one Father in heaven," humble servants of Christ and each other. How we are reveals most truly who we are.

Connecting the Gospel

to the first reading: The reading from Malachi reinforces the teaching of Jesus: we must practice what we preach. We must never be the cause of others turning away from our one God and Father.

to experience: We all struggle to align what we do with what we say, especially when we are in some position of authority (e.g., parents, teachers, civic leaders). What is at stake is not only our own integrity but also the well-being of those for whom we are role models.

Connecting the Responsorial Psalm

to the readings: We have no need for any status or title other than that which has already been given us: we are God's children (see first reading and gospel). Whenever we pursue anything else as the source of our status—power, public recognition, domination—we "violate [this] covenant" (first reading). We make ourselves the masters and one another the slaves to our burdensome commands (gospel). Malachi chastises such behavior (first reading) and Jesus condemns it (gospel).

Psalm 131 expresses the self-understanding Jesus, our "one master" (gospel), wishes to teach us. The core of discipleship is humble relationship with God (psalm) leading to humble, servant-oriented relationship with one another (gospel). To learn this we must give up false strivings for glory and prestige. We must seek our true place before God. What we will discover, the psalm promises, is genuine peace and ultimate hope.

to psalmist preparation: An implied challenge in this Sunday's responsorial psalm is that you be willing to grow to your full stature as a son or daughter of God. What do you need to let go of in order for this growth to happen?

ASSEMBLY & FAITH-SHARING GROUPS
- I know I have failed to practice what I preach when . . . The strongest preaching I do by the way I live is . . .
- What my behavior reveals about who I am is . . .
- As a disciple I am genuinely a learner when . . . a child of the Father when . . . a humble servant when . . .

PRESIDERS
My practicing what I preach leads to confrontation when I . . .

DEACONS
My community of faith knows me as "servant" because . . .

HOSPITALITY MINISTERS
When hospitality is "performed to be seen" its impact on the community is . . . When hospitality is done as humble service its impact on the community is . . .

MUSIC MINISTERS
When I find myself using music ministry to gain attention and status, Christ calls me back to humble service by . . .

ALTAR MINISTERS
Serving others demands a humbling of self in that . . . Serving others also brings its own exaltation in that . . .

LECTORS
My title as "minister of the word" accurately describes my *identity* in that . . . It captures my proper *relationship* to God in that . . .

EXTRAORDINARY MINISTERS OF HOLY COMMUNION
My manner of distributing Holy Communion communicates that we are all children of the one loving Father when I . . .

Model Act of Penitence

Presider: In today's gospel Jesus challenges us to put into practice what we preach. As we prepare to celebrate this liturgy, let us recall those times when we have failed to do this . . . [pause]

Lord Jesus, you are the Master who teaches us how to live: Lord . . .

Christ Jesus, you are the exalted One who sits at the right hand of the Father: Christ . . .

Lord Jesus, you are the humble servant who shows us how to be children of the Father: Lord . . .

Homily Points

• How many parents or teachers haven't had the experience of seeing their behavior played back to them by children or youth? This is so true when it comes to language, mannerisms, habits, preferences, and prejudices. Sometimes it is young people's imitation of adult behavior that confronts the adults with the truth about who they are and brings about in them a desire for change.

• Jesus talks to the crowds and disciples about the failure of the scribes and Pharisees to live up to their preaching. Jesus' teaching hits home because his own life witnessed so completely to what he preached: he not only taught us to reach out to the poor, but he himself reached out to the marginalized; he not only preached forgiveness, but he himself forgave; he taught love as the greatest commandment, and then loved sinners, children, Gentiles, lepers.

• Practicing what we preach, as Jesus did, is not easy! We never grow out of the necessity to do so. As we journey through life and grow in maturity, graciousness, and self-understanding, we are enabled to recognize more and more any dichotomy between word and action, and resolve it. As word and deed fuse, we become who we truly are: children of the one Father, learners from Christ our master, and humble servants of others.

Model Prayer of the Faithful

Presider: Let us pray that our words and deeds be consistent and true.

Response:

Cantor:

That all members of the church grow in putting the word of God into practice . . . [pause]

That all those in religious and civic leadership positions fulfill their responsibilities as servants of the good of all . . . [pause]

That the poor and marginalized be attended to with care and love . . . [pause]

That each of us here embrace one another as children of the same Father and humble servants of one another . . . [pause]

Presider: God our Father, you sent your Son to teach us how to live: hear these our prayers that we might live graciously and humbly. We ask this through Christ our Lord. **Amen**.

OPENING PRAYER
Let us pray

Pause for silent prayer

God of power and mercy,
only with your help
can we offer you fitting service and praise.
May we live the faith we profess
and trust your promise of eternal life.

Grant this through our Lord Jesus Christ,
   your Son,
who lives and reigns with you and the
   Holy Spirit,
one God, for ever and ever. **Amen**.

FIRST READING
Mal 1:14b–2:2b, 8-10

A great King am I, says the LORD of hosts,
   and my name will be feared among the nations.
And now, O priests, this commandment is for you:
   If you do not listen,
if you do not lay it to heart,
   to give glory to my name, says the LORD of hosts,
I will send a curse upon you
   and of your blessing I will make a curse.
You have turned aside from the way,
   and have caused many to falter by your instruction;
you have made void the covenant of Levi,
   says the LORD of hosts.
I, therefore, have made you contemptible
   and base before all the people,
since you do not keep my ways,
   but show partiality in your decisions.
Have we not all the one father?
   Has not the one God created us?
Why then do we break faith with one another,
   violating the covenant of our fathers?

RESPONSORIAL PSALM
Ps 131:1, 2, 3

R̸. In you, Lord, I have found my peace.

O Lord, my heart is not proud,
　nor are my eyes haughty;
I busy not myself with great things,
　nor with things too sublime for me.

R̸. In you, Lord, I have found my peace.

Nay rather, I have stilled and quieted
　my soul like a weaned child.
Like a weaned child on its mother's lap,
　so is my soul within me.

R̸. In you, Lord, I have found my peace.

O Israel, hope in the Lord,
　both now and forever.

R̸. In you, Lord, I have found my peace.

SECOND READING
1 Thess 2:7b-9, 13

Brothers and sisters:
We were gentle among you, as a nursing
　mother cares for her children.
With such affection for you, we were
　determined to share with you
　not only the gospel of God, but our very
　　selves as well,
　so dearly beloved had you become to us.
You recall, brothers and sisters, our toil
　and drudgery.
Working night and day in order not to
　burden any of you,
　we proclaimed to you the gospel of God.

And for this reason we too give thanks to
　God unceasingly,
　that, in receiving the word of God from
　　hearing us,
　you received not a human word but, as
　　it truly is, the word of God,
　which is now at work in you who
　　believe.

About Liturgy
Second reading and second coming: In Year A for the five Sundays preceding the solemnity of Christ the King, the second reading is taken from St. Paul's First Letter to the Thessalonians. This is most likely the earliest of our New Testament writings and as such it reflects the expectation of the early Christian community that Christ would return soon to gather all things back to God. This second coming of Christ (accompanied by the end of the world as we know it, final judgment, general resurrection, and eschatological fulfillment) is a predominant motif as we conclude one liturgical year and begin another. It is fitting, therefore, that we pay attention to these second readings, which help us also to interpret the gospel and first reading. It would be appropriate to make these links in the homilies on these Sundays.

About Liturgical Music
Music suggestions: In "The Virtue of Humility" [HG] Delores Dufner creates delightful imagery to communicate the message of this Sunday's gospel (e.g., "The virtue of humility Revokes the law of gravity" and "On virtue's ladder, Gospel friend, By climbing downward we ascend"). Text and tune would be suitable for the preparation of the gifts. Also suitable for the preparation of the gifts would be the Shaker hymn "'Tis the Gift to be Simple" [GC2, RS], with its refrain "When true simplicity is gained, To bow and to bend we shan't be ashamed; To turn, turn will be our delight, Till by turning, turning we come 'round right." PMB, WC, and WS include extra verses that extend the song. (If the hymnal in use does not include these verses, choir or cantor could sing them with the assembly joining in on the refrain.)

A third appropriate choice for this Sunday would be Richard Gilliard's "The Servant Song" [in most hymnals], in which we pray to support one another in the call to servanthood: "Will you let me be your servant, let me be as Christ to you; Pray that I may have the grace to Let you be my servant, too." David Haas has developed the original SATB arrangement of this hymn into a choir-assembly piece with simple use of handbells and C instrument [GIA G-4995]. Francis Patrick O'Brien has composed a lovely SAB a cappella setting [GIA G-5451]. The gentleness of this hymn makes it suitable for the preparation of the gifts, for the Communion procession, or as a choral prelude.

OCTOBER 30, 2011
THIRTY-FIRST SUNDAY
IN ORDINARY TIME

GOSPEL ACCLAMATION
Matt 11:28

℟. Alleluia, alleluia.
Come to me, all you who labor and are burdened
and I will give you rest, says the Lord.
℟. Alleluia, alleluia.

Gospel

Matt 5:1-12a; L667

When Jesus saw the
crowds, he went up
the mountain,
and after he had sat
down, his disciples
came to him.
He began to teach them,
saying:
"Blessed are the poor in
spirit,
for theirs is the Kingdom of
heaven.
Blessed are they who mourn,
for they will be comforted.
Blessed are the meek,
for they will inherit the land.
Blessed are they who hunger and
thirst for righteousness,
for they will be satisfied.
Blessed are the merciful,
for they will be shown mercy.
Blessed are the clean of heart,
for they will see God.
Blessed are the peacemakers,
for they will be called children of
God.
Blessed are they who are persecuted
for the sake of righteousness,
for theirs is the Kingdom of heaven.
Blessed are you when they insult you
and persecute you
and utter every kind of evil against
you falsely because of me.
Rejoice and be glad,
for your reward will be great in
heaven."

See Appendix A, p. 303, for the other readings.

Reflecting on the Gospel

The children are cranky and demanding, the washing machine unexpectedly and irreparably breaks down at a time when the budget is already stretched to the limit, a phone call tells that a relative has a fast-growing and terminal cancer—these and countless other situations in life might send us scurrying to St. Jude (the patron of impossible situations) in a hurried prayer, but they hardly leave us any sense at all that we too are the blessed, beloved of God. "Yet so we are."

Blessedness is an attribute of God. In these Beatitudes Matthew lays out who and what Jesus' disciples are to be: poor in spirit, empathetic, and meek; seekers of justice, mercy, purity, and peace. Because living like this confronts and challenges others, it often brings persecution of one kind or another. Nonetheless, we still choose to live this way because any ill-treatment is far surpassed by the reward—being of God and sharing in the blessedness of divine life. How truly blessed are we! Most assuredly, as God's beloved children we celebrate that we already share in divine life.

The difference between us and the saints in heaven is not in the life we share—we all share in God's life, we are all blessed, we are all of God—but in the fact that *we* still face and must daily deal with the difficulties of life that can cause us to lose sight of God and all the blessings we have been given. We are blessed when we don't despair at the difficulties of life but meet them with the virtues of the blessed: meekness, slowness to anger, charity toward others, comfort, righteousness, mercy, peace. Our blessedness, then, rests in our relationship with God and on our responses to the situations in life that call us to die to ourselves. God's kingdom is present in our blessedness and in the good choices we make to further that life of God that is in and around us. Persecution may be faced because of the choices we make. And that persecution may stretch our courage, but it cannot take away who we are—the blessed ones of God.

Living the Paschal Mystery

Being holy and living the gospel doesn't mean that difficulties will never come our way, nor does it mean that we will always respond well to these difficulties, nor does it mean that overcoming difficulties will be easy. Neither does being holy and living the gospel mean that we need to go out looking for ways to "die" or to be persecuted so that we can be holy. In themselves, difficulties and persecution are not necessarily signs of holiness. Blessedness is best measured and achieved by the ordinary experiences of life and our way of responding to them. This means first and foremost that we act as people who belong to God, those who have been made "white in the blood of the Lamb" (first reading) and so are God's beloved children.

The saints in heaven give us courage that it is possible to spend our lives being faithful to God and charitable toward each other. They model for us gospel living—dying to self so that one day we share in God's everlasting glory. This solemnity, then, has many facets but all point to God's self-giving of divine life to us. This self-giving is the blessedness of God's kingdom that is being realized in our very own lives. There is a challenge to this solemnity as well as great joy and rejoicing: to believe and live as though blessedness is already ours and holiness is not beyond our grasp. The blessedness God offers is an unshakable peace that comes from resting in God's abiding divine presence. For this we are to "rejoice and be glad."

Focusing the Gospel

Key words and phrases: Blessed, persecute you, reward will be great

To the point: Blessedness is an attribute of God. In these Beatitudes Matthew lays out who and what Jesus' disciples are to be: poor in spirit, empathetic, and meek; seekers of justice, mercy, purity, and peace. Because living like this confronts and challenges others, it often brings persecution of one kind or another. Nonetheless, we still choose to live this way because any ill-treatment is far surpassed by the reward—being of God and sharing in the blessedness of divine life. How truly blessed are we!

Model Act of Penitence

Presider: We celebrate today the saints who share eternal life with God in heaven as well as our own blessedness as we share now in the divine life God gives us. Let us prepare to celebrate this liturgy . . . [pause]

Lord Jesus, you are the blessedness of God among us: Lord . . .

Christ Jesus, you teach us the way of holiness: Christ . . .

Lord Jesus, your grace makes us your blessed ones: Lord . . .

Model Prayer of the Faithful

Presider: Blessed be God who is all good! May this God of blessedness give us what we need to follow in the path of the Son.

Response:

Lord, hear our prayer.

Cantor:

we pray to the Lord,

That all members of the church grow in fidelity to the way of life Jesus teaches us . . . [pause]

That all people of the world be guided to salvation by the God who loves and cares . . . [pause]

That those who mourn be comforted, the persecuted find justice, and the hungry and thirsty be filled . . . [pause]

That each of us here rejoice and be glad for our share in the blessedness of God's life . . . [pause]

Presider: Blessed God, you sent your Son to show us the way to holiness: hear these our prayers that one day we might share with all the angels and saints in your everlasting life. We ask this through Christ our Lord. **Amen.**

FOR REFLECTION

• Where I recognize God's blessedness in me is . . .

• I choose to live the Beatitudes when . . . What happens to me because of this living is . . .

• The communion of all saints means to me . . . It affects my daily living in that . . .

Homily Points

• Opposition often indicates that we should change the direction we are going. For example, when parents, spouse, friends discourage us from a major job change, we take their input to heart. In the case of living the Beatitudes, however, opposition actually indicates we are going the right way.

• Jesus promises blessedness to those who are faithful to the way of life he teaches. He also warns about persecution. It is precisely our blessedness—being of God and sharing in God's life—that strengthens us and gives us hope that we have, indeed, chosen the right path. This is the path of all saints.

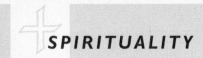

SPIRITUALITY

GOSPEL ACCLAMATION
cf. John 6:40

This is the will of my Father, says the Lord,
that everyone who sees the Son and believes
   in him
may have eternal life.

Gospel

John 6:37-40; L1016.12

Jesus said to the crowds:
"Everything that the Father
   gives me will come to me,
   and I will not reject anyone
      who comes to me,
   because I came down from
      heaven not to do my own
      will
but the will of the one who sent me.
And this is the will of the one who sent
   me,
   that I should not lose anything of
      what he gave me,
   but that I should raise it on the last
      day.
For this is the will of my Father,
   that everyone who sees the Son and
      believes in him
   may have eternal life,
   and I shall raise him up on the last
      day."

*See Appendix A, p. 304, for the other readings
or any other readings from L668 or any readings
from the Masses for the Dead (L1011–1015).*

Reflecting on the Gospel

Hope is a virtue that seems to be hard to grasp. Faith we can handle—this has to do with living our yes to God and is clearly borne out in our doing good for others. Love is within our reach as well—it is the love we extend also by doing good for others. Both faith and love imply *action*; we don't just talk about these virtues, we *do* them. But what about hope? We have a sense that it has something to do with that which is not yet—it has something to do with an outcome we wish to happen in the future. But how do we live a future when we are so completely taken up in the present? How do we get a handle on this festival, when we are talking about hope in everlasting life for the faithful departed?

We have good reason to call this festival one of the "faithful" departed. While our deceased loved ones were not perfect in their lives here on earth—none of us is—we also know them to have been good people who tried to follow God's will. So of course, then, we have hope that those who have died are not rejected by Jesus and that he will not lose any one of them but all will have eternal life.

Yes, this is a festival of hope! The ground of our hope is Jesus' promise that he will not lose anyone given to him. There is a condition, however: we must believe in Jesus who is ever faithful to his Father's will. Believing in Jesus means that we too do the will of the Father. We have been given all the guidance we need to make the right choices in this life. Each of those good choices—to "no longer be in slavery to sin" (second reading)—is a response that embodies that our lives are filled with hope. Those faithful departed whom we remember this day are not lost—they have believed in Jesus, they have done the will of God, they have gained eternal life.

Yes, this is a festival of hope! As we remember the faithful departed we are invited to look, not back on their lives, but forward to the eternal life Jesus promises them and us. This is God's gift to those who were "baptized into Christ" and who have lived with Christ; "death no longer has power over them" (second reading). On November 1st we tend to remember those saints who died long ago but with whom we probably have little or no connection. On this festival of All Souls we remember the dead who were much nearer to us, family members and friends. This is why this day is so close to many of us—it calls forth from us the hope that our loved ones are already sharing in the promise of everlasting life.

Living the Paschal Mystery

"We have grown into union with" Christ by entering into "a death like his." This is a beautiful image—our choice to die to self for the good of others is how we grow into deeper union with Christ! Our very choice to die to self is already an expression of our hope in the promise of eternal life that Jesus has given us. We couldn't be any surer of how to achieve eternal life than to die to ourselves as Jesus died to himself for us. We "grow into" resurrection and eternal life by dying to ourselves. In a sense, then, this festival is not only one of hope but also one of the faith and love we have in the present. Our yes to God and our love for one another are all concrete expressions of our hope that one day we will enjoy everlasting life. Yes, this is a festival of hope!

Focusing the Gospel

Key words and phrases: not lose anything, will of my Father, sees the Son and believes, eternal life

To the point: This is a festival of hope! The ground of our hope is Jesus' promise that he will not lose anyone given to him. There is a condition, however: we must believe in Jesus who is ever faithful to his Father's will. Believing in Jesus means that we too do the will of the Father. Those faithful departed whom we remember this day are not lost—they have believed in Jesus, they have done the will of God, they have gained eternal life.

Model Act of Penitence

Presider: We remember in a special way today our loved ones who have died, in the certain hope that they now share in God's everlasting life. Let us open ourselves to God's promise of life . . . [pause]

 Lord Jesus, you are the risen Son of the Father: Lord . . .

 Christ Jesus, you are our hope eternal: Christ . . .

 Lord Jesus, you call us to believe in you: Lord . . .

Model Prayer of the Faithful

Presider: We pray for our deceased loved ones and for ourselves, placing our needs before a merciful and gracious God.

Response:

Lord, hear our prayer.

Cantor:

we pray to the Lord,

That all members of the church deepen their faith in the risen Lord and strengthen their will to do whatever God asks of them . . . [pause]

That all peoples come to the fullness of life God promises . . . [pause]

That all the faithful departed share in the joy of everlasting life . . . [pause]

That each of us here remember our departed loved ones through prayer and good works . . . [pause]

Presider: Merciful God, you promised eternal life to those who remain faithful disciples of your Son: hear these our prayers that one day all might enjoy everlasting life with you. We ask this through that same Son, Jesus Christ our Lord. **Amen.**

OPENING PRAYER

Let us pray

Pause for silent prayer

Merciful Father,
hear our prayers and console us.
As we renew our faith in your Son,
whom you raised from the dead,
strengthen our hope that all our departed
  brothers and sisters
will share in his resurrection,
who lives and reigns with you and the Holy
  Spirit,
one God, for ever and ever. **Amen.**

FOR REFLECTION

- The words in the gospel that are most comforting and hope-filled for me are . . .
- I express my belief in Jesus by . . . God's will for me is . . .
- Some ways I remember and reverence my deceased loved ones are . . .

Homily Points

- It is deeply ingrained in people of all cultures to have a reverence and respect for the dead. For example, often when someone is killed in an auto accident, family or friends place flowers and other items at the site. Or Hispanics celebrate the *Dia de los Muertos* (the Day of the Dead) by bringing food, flowers, and favorite things to the grave site, and telling stories of their loved ones' lives. All these are ways to keep loved ones alive and present to us.

- This festival remembering all the faithful departed is our Catholic way of celebrating even more than our love for those who have died. We also celebrate God's gift of eternal life to those who have believed in the risen Lord and been faithful to doing God's will. We celebrate our certain hope that these beloved dead remain alive and present because God has promised this will be so.

✠ SPIRITUALITY

GOSPEL ACCLAMATION
Matt 24:42a, 44

℟. Alleluia, alleluia.
Stay awake and be ready!
For you do not know on what day your Lord will
    come.
℟. Alleluia, alleluia.

Gospel   Matt 25:1-13; L154A

Jesus told his disciples this parable:
    "The kingdom of heaven will be
        like ten virgins
    who took their lamps and went
        out to meet the bridegroom.
Five of them were foolish and five
    were wise.
The foolish ones, when taking
    their lamps,
    brought no oil with them,
    but the wise brought flasks of oil with
        their lamps.
Since the bridegroom was long delayed,
    they all became drowsy and fell asleep.
At midnight, there was a cry,
    'Behold, the bridegroom! Come out to
        meet him!'
Then all those virgins got up and trimmed
    their lamps.
The foolish ones said to the wise,
    'Give us some of your oil,
    for our lamps are going out.'
But the wise ones replied,
    'No, for there may not be enough for us
        and you.
Go instead to the merchants and buy
    some for yourselves.'
While they went off to buy it,
    the bridegroom came
    and those who were ready went into
        the wedding feast with him.
Then the door was locked.
Afterwards the other virgins came and
    said,
    'Lord, Lord, open the door for us!'
But he said in reply,
    'Amen, I say to you, I do not know you.'
Therefore, stay awake,
    for you know neither the day nor the
        hour."

Reflecting on the Gospel

We just know that some things we do promise delays. Many of us avoid shopping at certain stores where we know the checkout lanes are always insufferably long. Doctors' offices are notorious for long delays. When we arrive at an airport and check the flight board, we dread seeing "delayed" behind our scheduled flight. Delays annoy us because they cost us precious time, catch us off guard with nothing productive to do, keep us from meeting other appointments or deadlines, deprive us from being with loved ones, or even sometimes can mean life or death, such as when someone is being rushed to the hospital in an ambulance and the traffic is so snarled that even with sirens blaring and lights flashing, the ambulance cannot get through. Our annoyance at delays teaches us how much we live in the here-and-now and how precious time is to us. This Sunday's gospel challenges us to look with longer vision—there is more to the present than just the present. We are to become aware that every detail of what we're doing now is part of life's journey toward the future where we meet our Bridegroom and are invited into his feast.

There is no doubt that the bridegroom will come. What is unexpected is his *long delay*, which reveals the wisdom of those virgins who were prepared. In this gospel parable the five wise virgins can well afford to sleep, for they are prepared with plenty of oil. The five foolish virgins also sleep during the long delay, but they should have been busy procuring the oil they need to greet the bridegroom and enter the feast. Jesus is warning us in this parable that the here-and-now is an important readying for his second coming, and we cannot afford to sleep it away! The long delay of the bridegroom's coming reveals both the wisdom and longer vision of the five virgins who were prepared and the *loss* of those who were shortsighted and unprepared—the "door was locked" and they were not admitted to the wedding feast.

In this parable Matthew is addressing the *delay* until Christ comes again. The question for us, then, is how do we deal with the delay? Matthew is suggesting an issue beyond vigilance—that we must also be *prepared*. We can't comfortably fall asleep and await the Bridegroom's return. We are living in a crucial time of spending our lives being open to Christ's comings in the here-and-now. We must actively seek our Bridegroom, and at the same time have the long-range vision that sees Christ seeking us.

Living the Paschal Mystery

We rarely, if ever, view our daily Christian living in light of the final coming of Christ. But his final coming is, in fact, the context that gives meaning to our daily behavior and our ongoing hope. If we are not ready at the second coming of Christ (with its accompanying judgment), we can't count on anyone else to cover for us. We are provided now with all we need (e.g., wisdom, invitation to vigilance, warnings about preparedness) to be ready when Christ comes. The real challenge is not to think of this as only a future event that won't happen in our own lifetime. When Christ will come is not the important issue. We don't know when Christ will come again! And so Christian living requires that we act each day as if this were the day when our Bridegroom will come and invite us to the feast. We must be ready.

Focusing the Gospel

Key words and phrases: the bridegroom was long delayed, the bridegroom came, those who were ready went into the wedding feast

To the point: In this gospel parable the five wise virgins can well afford to sleep, for they are prepared with plenty of oil. The five foolish virgins also sleep during the long delay, but they should have been busy procuring the oil they need to greet the bridegroom and enter the feast. Jesus is warning us in this parable that the here-and-now is an important readying for his second coming, and we cannot afford to sleep it away!

Connecting the Gospel

to the first reading: The first reading reveals that wisdom is a virtue given to all those who seek her. Even before our desire and our watching for wisdom, she comes to us. In the gospel, the Bridegroom's coming is assured even before we desire or watch for the Bridegroom.

to experience: We rarely, if ever, view our daily Christian living in light of the final coming of Christ. But his final coming is, in fact, the promise that gives ultimate meaning to our daily behavior and our ongoing hope.

Connecting the Responsorial Psalm

to the readings: In these verses from Psalm 63, we consciously seek God: we pine and thirst for God, we gaze toward God, we bless God throughout life, and we remember God even at night. And we know that we will be rewarded for this seeking with a "kindness . . . greater . . . than life" and with "the riches of a banquet." Both the first reading and the psalm indicate how God/Wisdom comes to those who seek what God/Wisdom has to offer. The very seeking guarantees the reward.

The gospel reading reminds us, however, that we can be misled by the *appearance* of seeking. All ten virgins go out to meet the bridegroom, all ten participate in the role culturally assigned to them. But half of them are not really looking for the bridegroom; they are merely going through a routine. True vigilance, true seeking for God, demands ongoing preparation and work. It is not enough, then, for us merely to go through the routine of praying Psalm 63 as we celebrate this liturgy. We must pay the price of our longing and do so in practical everyday ways.

to psalmist preparation: What does it mean for you to thirst for God? How do you experience this thirst? What surface satisfactions stand in your way? What do you need to do to prepare yourself to receive even more from God?

**ASSEMBLY &
FAITH-SHARING GROUPS**
- I "sleep away" opportunities to encounter Christ when I . . .
- The second coming of Christ has an impact on the way I live daily in that . . .
- What it means to me to be "wise" during the "long delay" of the Bridegroom's coming is . . .

PRESIDERS
My preaching helps the assembly keep their lamps trimmed and burning in their daily living when I say . . .

DEACONS
My ministry spurs others to wakefulness for the presence of Christ whenever I . . .

HOSPITALITY MINISTERS
My hospitality for others teaches me about vigilance and preparation for Christ's coming whenever I . . .

MUSIC MINISTERS
One way my music ministry helps me keep my lamps trimmed and burning for the coming of Christ is . . .

ALTAR MINISTERS
Serving others is a way to be vigilant and prepare for Christ's coming because . . .

LECTORS
My preparation to lector is a preparation for the coming of the Bridegroom in that . . .

**EXTRAORDINARY MINISTERS
OF HOLY COMMUNION**
My manner of distributing Holy Communion helps communicants welcome the Bridegroom when I . . .

Model Act of Penitence

Presider: The gospel today tells the parable of the five wise virgins who have enough oil for their lamps and five foolish virgins who do not. At the beginning of this liturgy, let us consider how well we are prepared to meet Christ our Bridegroom . . . [pause]

Lord Jesus, you are the Bridegroom who comes to us: Lord . . .

Christ Jesus, you invite us to your wedding feast: Christ . . .

Lord Jesus, you admonish us to stay awake and be prepared: Lord . . .

Homily Points

• We regularly change the oil in our cars to keep the engines running smoothly. We keep our skin oiled lest it become dry and scaly. We use oil in cooking both to add flavor and to prevent sticking. This Sunday's gospel about having sufficient oil on hand is not so beyond our experience.

• Jesus warns us in this gospel parable that, while we do not know when he will come at the end of time, we cannot sleep away our lives. We must be prepared to see him whenever and wherever he comes to us. What we do now determines whether we will be able to see and greet the Bridegroom when he comes and be able to enter his feast.

• Oil provides the light that enables us to see the Bridegroom when he arrives. We need sufficient "oil" to keep our spiritual lamps trimmed and burning. We ensure that we have enough oil when we solicit the wisdom of other members of the community in decision making, keep always burning the expectation that we may see the Bridegroom at any moment and in any circumstances, and shine the light of faith wherever there is darkness. We cannot sleep; we must be prepared; we must have enough oil.

Model Prayer of the Faithful

Presider: Let us make our needs known to God so we can prepare well for Christ's coming to us.

Response:

Lord, hear our prayer.

Cantor:

we pray to the Lord,

That all members of the church support one another to prepare well for Christ's second coming . . . [pause]

That peoples of all nations be wise in seeking God . . . [pause]

That the sick receive the oil of healing, the sad receive the oil of gladness, and the poor receive the oil of plenty . . . [pause]

That our parish community be prepared for the many comings of Christ in our daily lives . . . [pause]

Presider: Gracious God, you are present to us and give us what we need: hear these our prayers that one day we might enjoy everlasting life with you. We ask this through Christ our Lord. **Amen.**

OPENING PRAYER
Let us pray

Pause for silent prayer

God of power and mercy,
protect us from all harm.
Give us freedom of spirit
and health in mind and body
to do your work on earth.

We ask this through our Lord Jesus Christ,
    your Son,
who lives and reigns with you and the
    Holy Spirit,
one God, for ever and ever. **Amen**.

FIRST READING
Wis 6:12-16

Resplendent and unfading is wisdom,
    and she is readily perceived by those
        who love her,
    and found by those who seek her.
She hastens to make herself known in
        anticipation of their desire;
    whoever watches for her at dawn shall
        not be disappointed,
    for he shall find her sitting by his gate.
For taking thought of wisdom is the
        perfection of prudence,
    and whoever for her sake keeps vigil
    shall quickly be free from care;
because she makes her own rounds,
        seeking those worthy of her,
    and graciously appears to them in the
        ways,
    and meets them with all solicitude.

RESPONSORIAL PSALM
Ps 63:2, 3-4, 5-6, 7-8

℟. (2b) My soul is thirsting for you, O Lord my God.

O God, you are my God whom I seek;
    for you my flesh pines and my soul
        thirsts
    like the earth, parched, lifeless and
        without water.

℟. My soul is thirsting for you, O Lord my God.

Thus have I gazed toward you in the
        sanctuary
    to see your power and your glory,
for your kindness is a greater good than
        life;
    my lips shall glorify you.

℟. My soul is thirsting for you, O Lord my God.

Thus will I bless you while I live;
    lifting up my hands, I will call upon
        your name.
As with the riches of a banquet shall my
      soul be satisfied,
    and with exultant lips my mouth shall
      praise you.

R̶. My soul is thirsting for you, O Lord
my God.

I will remember you upon my couch,
    and through the night-watches I will
      meditate on you:
you are my help,
    and in the shadow of your wings I shout
      for joy.

R̶. My soul is thirsting for you, O Lord
my God.

SECOND READING
1 Thess 4:13-18

We do not want you to be unaware,
    brothers and sisters,
    about those who have fallen asleep,
    so that you may not grieve like the rest,
      who have no hope.
For if we believe that Jesus died and rose,
    so too will God, through Jesus,
    bring with him those who have fallen
      asleep.
Indeed, we tell you this, on the word of the
      Lord,
    that we who are alive,
    who are left until the coming of the
      Lord,
    will surely not precede those who have
      fallen asleep.
For the Lord himself, with a word of
      command,
    with the voice of an archangel and with
      the trumpet of God,
    will come down from heaven,
    and the dead in Christ will rise first.
Then we who are alive, who are left,
    will be caught up together with them in
      the clouds
    to meet the Lord in the air.
Thus we shall always be with the Lord.
Therefore, console one another with these
      words.

or 1 Thess 4:13-14

See Appendix A, p. 304.

About Liturgy

Ministry of liturgy coordinator: One liturgical ministry that is rarely addressed is that of liturgy coordinator. Sometimes this role is fulfilled by a sacristan, sometimes by the director of music, sometimes by the director of liturgy. If liturgy is to unfold in a smooth manner someone needs to make sure that everyone and everything are present and ready—that everything is properly prepared. This means that the usual things for Sunday Mass—bread and wine, Lectionary, Sacramentary, candles, etc.—are attended to in the proper way; for example, the liturgical books already ought to have the ribbons in the proper places, with those who will use those books knowing which color ribbon to use when. If something "extra" is taking place (for example, a baptism), then there are other things that must be prepared: the proper ritual books readied; the baptismal water checked for cleanliness and amount and a pitcher (or shell) nearby; oils, candle, and white garment in place; soap, water, and towel for the presider to cleanse his hands. Too often these little things can be forgotten and then there is a disruption in the service.

One way to handle this is to have a "checklist" for each type of liturgy that a parish may celebrate. Then whoever might be appointed the liturgy coordinator (or whoever else assumes this role) can make sure that he or she hasn't forgotten anything. It's not a disaster to return to the sacristy for a forgotten item; but it does disrupt the natural flow of a liturgy. Even more disastrous is a presider who is flipping through pages of a liturgical book to find the right text! Preparedness may seem like a little thing, but it is always wise to be ready! Preparing and being ready now assures that the feast unfolds with dignity and grace, reverence and smooth flow.

About Liturgical Music

Music suggestions: An excellent choral prelude piece for this Sunday is the spiritual "Keep Your Lamps Trimmed and Burning." The Andre Thomas arrangement [Hinshaw Music HMC-577] is scored for SATB choir and conga drums and would be of easy to moderate difficulty for the average choir to learn. The arrangement by Alan Hommerding [WLP-5739], which incorporates motifs from the sixteenth-century Advent hymn "Wake, O Wake and Sleep No Longer" and the African American song "This Little Light of Mine," is more challenging. Both arrangements are lively, exciting, and worth learning, and would be useful again during the first two weeks of Advent.

A word to the music director: Preparing music for liturgy involves myriad music read-throughs, hymn searches, planning sessions, rehearsals, decisions, interpersonal interactions and communications, etc. Most of this ministry is preparation, with only a small percentage actual celebration. The good news from this Sunday's Liturgy of the Word is that as a music director seeks God in these mundane preparations, God will be seeking and finding the music director. The preparation, then, becomes the celebration, for it is the practical, everyday place where the music director and God encounter one another. And this is the real preparation for liturgy.

✠ SPIRITUALITY

GOSPEL ACCLAMATION
John 15:4a, 5b

R7. Alleluia, alleluia.
Remain in me as I remain in you, says the Lord.
Whoever remains in me bears much fruit.
R7. Alleluia, alleluia.

Gospel   Matt 25:14-30; L157A

Jesus told his disciples this parable:
   "A man going on a journey
   called in his servants and entrusted his
      possessions to them.
To one he gave five talents; to another,
      two; to a third, one—
   to each according to his ability.
Then he went away.
Immediately the one who received five
      talents went and traded with them,
   and made another five.
Likewise, the one who received two made
      another two.
But the man who received one went off
      and dug a hole in the ground
      and buried his master's money.

"After a long time
   the master of those servants came back
   and settled accounts with them.
The one who had received five talents
      came forward
   bringing the additional five.
He said, 'Master, you gave me five
      talents.
See, I have made five more.'
His master said to him, 'Well done, my
      good and faithful servant.
Since you were faithful in small matters,
   I will give you great responsibilities.
Come, share your master's joy.'
Then the one who had received two
      talents also came forward and said,
   'Master, you gave me two talents.
See, I have made two more.'
His master said to him, 'Well done, my
      good and faithful servant.

Continued in Appendix A, p. 305.

Reflecting on the Gospel

We are familiar with this parable about servants being "entrusted with [their master's] possessions" and its outcome: the industrious servants are rewarded, the lazy servant is punished. We readily recognize this parable as a story of final judgment when the master (Christ) returns, and this is yet another Sunday that invites us to reflect on Christ's second coming. But note: the parable begins with something wondrous—the master "entrusted his possessions" to his servants.

Such confidence the master had in his servants as he "entrusted his possessions to them"! But not all servants proved trustworthy—controlled by fear ("so out of fear I went off and buried your talent"), one did nothing to increase what had been given him. Fear can surely paralyze us and cause us to lose everything. As disciples who are entrusted now with the saving work of Jesus, we are to act boldly with the unmerited and generous "possessions" we have been given. Our faithfulness to the mission leads us to an even more wondrous "possession"—full participation in the "master's joy."

This parable teaches us what to do during the delay while awaiting our Master's return: we are to live in such a way that we grow in our greatest "possession"—the divine life that has been given us. If, like the lazy servant in the parable, we focus on our fear and Christ's judgment, we will be paralyzed in our ability to continue using the "talents" we have been given to continue Christ's work of salvation. However, if we focus on the promised share in the "master's joy," then we will be willing to risk what we have in order to grow in our most prized possession—our share in divine life and the relationship with Christ that entails. The Christian life and journey of discipleship begins with unmerited and unimaginable blessing—a share in God's life. When we are faithful it will end even more wondrously—we will enter fully into the "master's joy."

The issue in the parable isn't how much we have but that we put to the greatest use the blessings we have already been given. There is no greater gift than that of the risen life of the divine Son and the Spirit; through them, the divine life in which we already share is an expression of God's desire for intimacy with us (see first reading). One aspect of what we are to do during the delay in Christ's coming is to use our blessings well in faithful discipleship and in intimately loving God in return. This, in turn, increases our blessings. When the Master comes, then, we need have no fear of the judgment, for we will have been "good and faithful servant[s]." Then we too will enter fully into the Master's joy.

Living the Paschal Mystery

The master commends the two faithful servants for their industriousness and then tells them he will give them "great responsibilities." For us as Christians, our "great responsibilities" are, of course, to be faithful disciples making present the kingdom of God in our daily lives. Another part of these "great responsibilities" is to live now the Master's joy, confident that one day we will enter even more fully into that joy. Responsibility means to use our blessings to spread God's goodness as well as appreciate now the joy of those blessings. Joy isn't something only in the future; it is a fruit of the Spirit we enjoy now.

Focusing the Gospel

Key words and phrases: entrusted his possessions, you were faithful, share your master's joy, so out of fear

To the point: Such confidence the master had in his servants, for he "entrusted his possessions to them"! But not all servants proved trustworthy—controlled by fear, one did nothing to increase what had been given him. Fear can surely paralyze us and cause us to lose everything. As disciples who are entrusted now with the saving work of Jesus, we are to act boldly with the unmerited and generous "possessions" we have been given. Our faithfulness to the mission leads us to an even more wondrous "possession"—full participation in the "master's joy."

Connecting the Gospel

to the first reading: The faithful wife in the first reading uses her talents to serve both family and neighbor because she is moved to do so by the tender love of her husband who has entrusted his greatest treasure to her—his heart. We are moved to serve both God and others by the greatest treasure given to us—the love of God.

to experience: We all experience moments or situations when fear paralyzes us and we feel unable to act. What helps us get beyond our fear and inaction is discovering that we possess hidden strengths that enable us to deal with the situation.

Connecting the Responsorial Psalm

to the readings: The first reading and psalm together offer us a balanced image of a woman and a man who, each in their respective social roles, are faithful to God's desires about the manner of human living. Both texts are couched in the domestic terms that characterized Hebrew life and understanding, but the Lectionary's intent is to offer models for all sorts of lifestyles, vocations, and situations in life. Those who "fear the Lord" are faithful in carrying out the ordinary everyday demands of covenant living, and their fidelity and generosity flow back to them in abundant blessings.

In the gospel parable Jesus places the same demand on us and makes the same promise. Each of us has been given some responsibility for building up the kingdom of God. If we are faithful servants, we will be greatly rewarded. If we are irresponsible, we will have everything, even the kingdom, taken from us. May our choice be the one that leads to blessedness and a share in God's joy!

to psalmist preparation: Psalm 128 celebrates the blessedness that comes to a person who in daily living is faithful to the demands of the covenant. What demands for faithfully living the covenant do the circumstances of your life make on you? When are you tempted to avoid these demands? When do you experience the blessedness that comes from responding to them?

**ASSEMBLY &
FAITH-SHARING GROUPS**
- God has entrusted to me these "possessions" . . . I experience God's trust in me when . . .
- What causes me sometimes to be paralyzed by fear is . . . This affects how I live the gospel in that . . .
- I experience now the "master's joy" when I . . .

PRESIDERS
One of the "possessions" God has entrusted to me is the assembly and so I . . .

DEACONS
One of the "possessions" God has entrusted to me is those in need and so I . . .

HOSPITALITY MINISTERS
One of the "possessions" God has entrusted to me that helps me better do my hospitality ministry is . . .

MUSIC MINISTERS
The "master's joy" I have experienced in my music ministry is . . .

ALTAR MINISTERS
My God-given "possessions" that are increased by serving others are . . .

LECTORS
As a lector, the word is my "possession" and so I . . .

**EXTRAORDINARY MINISTERS
OF HOLY COMMUNION**
Celebrating the Eucharist is already a share in the fullness of the "master's joy" in that . . .

Model Act of Penitence

Presider: God has given us each many blessings, first among them a share in divine life. We pause at the beginning of this liturgy to recall those blessings and bring grateful hearts to this celebration . . . [pause]

Lord Jesus, you are God's blessing for us: Lord . . .

Christ Jesus, you are the fullness of joy: Christ . . .

Lord Jesus, you call us to build your kingdom: Lord . . .

Homily Points

• Suppose the servant given one talent had actually tried to increase the number of talents but had failed, losing even the one he had been given. How would the master have dealt with him? No doubt, more leniently than he did in the parable in face of the servant's inaction. Failure is not the issue—fear that keeps us from acting is.

• The first two servants in the gospel used what had been given to them to the fullest extent. Their "reward" was determined not by how much they gained (five or two talents) but by their total faithfulness and wise industriousness in acting. Likewise, God judges us not by how much or little we have but by how faithful we are in using what we have to build up God's kingdom.

• Leaving his "possessions" for us to develop is exactly what Jesus has done by entrusting to us the treasures of his very presence in word and sacrament, of his Spirit who lives in and among us, and of the blessings of one another in community. How much Jesus entrusts us with the future of the kingdom and the work of salvation! His trust places a choice before us, however: we can use these treasures he has given us or we can bury them.

Model Prayer of the Faithful

Presider: We now make our needs known to a God who has entrusted to us Christ's saving mission.

Response:

Lord, hear our prayer.

Cantor:

we pray to the Lord,

That all members of the church act fearlessly in living the Gospel faithfully . . . [pause]

That leaders of nations share the possessions of the earth equitably with their people . . . [pause]

That people locked in fear might receive courage from an awareness of the blessings God has already bestowed upon them . . . [pause]

That our parish community build up God's kingdom by always using wisely the blessings given us for the good of others . . . [pause]

Presider: Generous God, you entrust us to continue your Son's saving work: give us strength and courage to be faithful that one day we might share in the fullness of your joy. We ask this through Christ our Lord. **Amen.**

OPENING PRAYER

Let us pray

Pause for silent prayer

Father of all that is good,
keep us faithful in serving you,
for to serve you is our lasting joy.

We ask this through our Lord Jesus Christ,
     your Son,
who lives and reigns with you and the
     Holy Spirit,
one God, for ever and ever. **Amen.**

FIRST READING
Prov 31:10-13, 19-20, 30-31

When one finds a worthy wife,
     her value is far beyond pearls.
Her husband, entrusting his heart to her,
     has an unfailing prize.
She brings him good, and not evil,
     all the days of her life.
She obtains wool and flax
     and works with loving hands.
She puts her hands to the distaff,
     and her fingers ply the spindle.
She reaches out her hands to the poor,
     and extends her arms to the needy.
Charm is deceptive and beauty fleeting;
     the woman who fears the Lord is to be
          praised.
Give her a reward for her labors,
     and let her works praise her at the city
          gates.

RESPONSORIAL PSALM

Ps 128:1-2, 3, 4-5

℟. (cf. 1a) Blessed are those who fear the Lord.

Blessed are you who fear the Lord,
    who walk in his ways!
For you shall eat the fruit of your
        handiwork;
    blessed shall you be, and favored.

℟. Blessed are those who fear the Lord.

Your wife shall be like a fruitful vine
    in the recesses of your home;
your children like olive plants
    around your table.

℟. Blessed are those who fear the Lord.

Behold, thus is the man blessed
    who fears the Lord.
The Lord bless you from Zion:
    may you see the prosperity of Jerusalem
    all the days of your life.

℟. Blessed are those who fear the Lord.

SECOND READING

1 Thess 5:1-6

Concerning times and seasons, brothers
        and sisters,
    you have no need for anything to be
        written to you.
For you yourselves know very well that
        the day of the Lord will come
    like a thief at night.
When people are saying, "Peace and
        security,"
    then sudden disaster comes upon them,
    like labor pains upon a pregnant
        woman,
    and they will not escape.

But you, brothers and sisters, are not in
        darkness,
    for that day to overtake you like a thief.
For all of you are children of the light
    and children of the day.
We are not of the night or of darkness.
Therefore, let us not sleep as the rest do,
    but let us stay alert and sober.

About Liturgy

Liturgical ministries and increase of "talents": The average parish has a great many people involved actively in the various "visible" liturgical ministries: hospitality ministers, music ministers, altar ministers, lectors, extraordinary ministers of Holy Communion, and others. In all cases these ministries require some "talent" in order to fulfill them properly. In addition to learning the "job," what is also required is growth in a spirituality of the ministry that moves the "doing" toward real service to the community—herein lies the real demand for "talent."

No doubt some ministers groan at times when they see their name on the schedule for a particular Sunday. Perhaps they are not in a good space in their life and preparing well for a ministry brings an added burden. However, realizing liturgical ministry is a commitment they have made, they choose to be faithful, do the preparation, and come with a ready attitude to serve. Often this is a time when the "increase of talents" the gospel speaks about becomes so evident—perhaps a special grace is given during Mass in terms of a particularly poignant presence of Christ to the minister or a real sense of joy in the celebration because they have more fully participated and allowed God to work in and through them. Continued reflection helps all of us see how Christ is increasing our own "talents" when we remain faithful disciples. Most important, this is how we cooperate with Christ in continuing his saving mission. He uses our "talents" to further God's reign.

About Liturgical Music

Music suggestions: A textually and musically strong entrance hymn for this Sunday would be "God, Whose Giving Knows No Ending" [PMB, RS, W3, WC, WS]. Supported by a propelling tune (RUSTINGTON), phrase after phrase of the text pulls the assembly into the call of this gospel: "Gifted by you, we turn to you, Off'ring up ourselves in praise"; "Skills and time are ours for pressing Toward the goals of Christ, your Son"; "Born with talents, make us servants Fit to answer at your throne"; etc. Steven Janco's "Whenever You Serve Me / Psalm 146" [PMB, WC] expresses how richly God rewards fidelity and service and would make a fitting Communion song. The psalm verses spell out the many blessings God bestows on the faithful and the refrain repeats, "Whenever you serve me, says the Lord, my Father in heaven will honor you . . ." The song is in responsorial form, with cantor(s) or choir singing the verses and the assembly the refrain. A full score is also available [WLP 6210]. Ruth Duck's "Moved by the Gospel, Let Us Move" [G2, GC, RS, SS] calls us to use our artistic gifts and talents in varied ways to further God's kingdom and to express "the shape of holiness." The song would work well for the recessional.

Role of prelude music: GIRM 2002 directs that silence is to be observed even before the liturgy begins—in the church, the sacristy, the vesting room, and adjacent areas "so that all may dispose themselves to carry out the sacred action in a devout and fitting manner" (no. 45). The directive does not eliminate prelude music but challenges us to make liturgically sound choices about what is played or sung at this time. Instrumental or choral prelude music that draws the assembly to awareness of their identity as Body of Christ, to readiness for liturgical prayer, and to presence to the liturgical festival or season is always appropriate. On the other hand, devotional pieces that pull the assembly either into private prayer or into the personality or emotional frame of mind of the performer(s) is not. When we understand the liturgical function of the prelude music and its relationship to the silence that is to mark preparation for the celebration, we make wise musical choices that will deepen the assembly's participation in the liturgy.

NOVEMBER 13, 2011
THIRTY-THIRD SUNDAY IN ORDINARY TIME

✝ SPIRITUALITY

GOSPEL ACCLAMATION
Mark 11:9, 10

℟. Alleluia, alleluia.
Blessed is he who comes in the name of the Lord!
Blessed is the kingdom of our father David that
    is to come!
℟. Alleluia, alleluia.

Gospel   Matt 25:31-46; L160A

Jesus said to his disciples:
    "When the Son of Man comes
        in his glory,
    and all the angels with him,
    he will sit upon his glorious
        throne,
    and all the nations will be
        assembled before him.
And he will separate them one from
    another,
    as a shepherd separates the sheep from
        the goats.
He will place the sheep on his right and
    the goats on his left.
Then the king will say to those on his right,
    'Come, you who are blessed by my
        Father.
Inherit the kingdom prepared for you from
    the foundation of the world.
For I was hungry and you gave me food,
    I was thirsty and you gave me drink,
    a stranger and you welcomed me,
    naked and you clothed me,
    ill and you cared for me,
    in prison and you visited me.'
Then the righteous will answer him and
    say,
    'Lord, when did we see you hungry and
        feed you,
    or thirsty and give you drink?
When did we see you a stranger and
    welcome you,
    or naked and clothe you?
When did we see you ill or in prison, and
    visit you?'
And the king will say to them in reply,
    'Amen, I say to you, whatever you did
    for one of the least brothers of mine,
        you did for me.'

Continued in Appendix A, p. 304.

Reflecting on the Gospel

If one new TV genre is successful, then similar shows quickly spring up on all the networks. Daytime TV listings seem to schedule a ton of "judge" shows—Judge Shirley and Judge Sam and Judge You-Name-Him-or-Her. While these are supposed to be "real" cases with real consequences, the situations tend to be pretty cockamamie. There is a judgment, to be sure, but the network pays the judgment. Both parties seem to win. In the final analysis neither party wins—this is just "entertainment." The downside to these shows is that it makes judgment commonplace and shows the least among us in anything but a good light. The gospel for this special Sunday—the end of the liturgical year—shows that judgment is anything but commonplace and that the least among us are really the face of Christ for us.

The gospel for this festival honoring Christ the King presents him enthroned in glory, judging the nations. He calls forth those who are "blessed by [his] Father" to share in his "eternal life." To be blessed means nothing less than to share in God's holiness, to be *of* God, to act toward each other—especially the least among us—as God acts toward us. We hear the Son of Man's call to eternal glory now in the cry of those in need; we respond to that call by our care and compassion; and we inherit glory here and now and forever.

So much about this gospel speaks to us of Christ's glory and power ("When the Son of Man comes in his glory," "all nations will be assembled before him," "king will say") and rightfully it should. However, there is a remarkable surprise in the gospel. Christ is victorious, to be sure; he is King enthroned, to be sure; he judges all nations, to be sure; but the surprise is that on this festival honoring Christ the King both the gospel and the first reading speak about our caring for each other.

Jesus' utterance that "whatsoever you did for one of the least . . . of mine, you did for me" suggests that Christ is willing even in death and victory to be identified with us humans—even with the "least" of us humans! Christ doesn't even cling to his kingship and glory—hard won as they were with his very suffering and death—but chooses to identify with the "least" among us. How much more ought we to serve the "least" among us! Even the capacity to care for others is a gift of God, part of our being blessed.

We honor Christ the King by acknowledging that he is in others and within us. No greater honor can we give our Savior-King than to serve him in one another. In a sense, then, our focus on each other is really a focus on Christ—for it is a measure of how much we imitate his care for others. He showed us by his very life how to care for others. So must we spend our lives in this way.

Living the Paschal Mystery

One of the best ways we can begin to see Christ in others is by not judging their negative aspects first but instead looking for the good in them. This can be carried out in such a simple Christian practice as seeking always to compliment rather than to criticize another. Taking care not to spread gossip is another way. Thus do we build up the Body of Christ and bring honor to Christ our King who dwells in ourselves and others. Thus do we see the face of Christ our King in everyone we meet.

Focusing the Gospel

Key words and phrases: glory; Come, you who are blessed by my Father; whatever you did . . . you did for me; eternal life

To the point: The gospel for this festival honoring Christ the King presents him enthroned in glory, judging the nations. He calls forth those who are "blessed by [his] Father" to share in his "eternal life." To be blessed means nothing less than to share in God's holiness, to be *of* God, to act toward each other—especially the least among us—as God acts toward us. We hear the Son of Man's call to eternal glory now in the cry of those in need; we respond to that call by our care and compassion; and we inherit glory here and now and forever.

Connecting the Gospel

to the first reading: The first reading details all the caring and compassionate ways our shepherd God has acted toward us. The one who has shepherded us toward the day of judgment (see first reading) demands only that we have also shepherded one another (gospel).

to experience: We don't like being judged, but we tend to be quick to judge others. How different our judgments would be if we always realize that we are looking upon the face of Christ in the other!

Connecting the Responsorial Psalm

to the readings: In the first reading and psalm the shepherding work God does is that of nurturing, healing, tending, and feeding us who are his sheep. In the gospel the shepherding work Christ does is that of judging and sorting. In the first scenario God cares for us, in the second Christ holds us accountable for caring for one another. We are not merely sheep; we are also to be shepherds to others in need. We are to seek the lost, bind up the wounded, heal the sick, give drink to the thirsty, feed the hungry, clothe the naked because, Psalm 23 reminds us, God has been doing this for us.

Two things will happen on that day of judgment. Whether we knew it or not, we will discover that the needy to whom we reached out were Christ (gospel). And whether we knew it or not we will discover that with Christ we have conquered death (second reading). In caring for our brothers and sisters we will have been shepherded to the fullness of life. Has this not been the whole purpose of our journey through this, another liturgical year, when the whole mystery of Christ is revealed not only to us but also in us? What more could we want on this day when we acclaim Christ as our King and conclude another year of faithful discipleship?

to psalmist preparation: Our shepherd God is continually leading you to a new way of being and relating. Where has this journey taken you during this past liturgical year? Has it been easy to follow, or hard? What has helped you? What has hindered you? What graces and growths has God given you along the way?

**ASSEMBLY &
FAITH-SHARING GROUPS**
- I experience God's blessedness in me and this leads me to . . .
- The "least" to whom I most often reach out are . . . The "least" that I most often neglect are . . .
- It is easiest to see the person of Christ in others when . . .

PRESIDERS
The readings reveal Christ as Shepherd, King, and Judge. Of these three my ministry is most like . . . because . . . and least like . . . because . . .

DEACONS
The "scattered" sheep (see first reading) that I sometimes avoid or neglect are . . .; ways I could improve my tending to their needs are . . .

HOSPITALITY MINISTERS
My hospitality toward those assembling for liturgy helps me reach out to the "least" I meet in my daily life by . . .

MUSIC MINISTERS
One way I have grown in my ability to see Christ in others with whom I share music ministry, especially those whom I consider the "least," is . . .

ALTAR MINISTERS
Times when I have encountered Christ while serving his "least" are . . .

LECTORS
My manner of proclamation announces God's blessedness within us when . . .

**EXTRAORDINARY MINISTERS
OF HOLY COMMUNION**
When I look at the faces of those coming to receive Holy Communion, I see . . .

Model Act of Penitence

Presider: Today we honor Christ the King who is enthroned in eternal glory. As we prepare to celebrate his feast, let us open our hearts to being counted among his blessed ones . . . [pause]

Lord Jesus, you are our King enthroned in glory: Lord . . .

Christ Jesus, you are Judge over the living and the dead: Christ . . .

Lord Jesus, you call us to eternal life: Lord . . .

Homily Points

• Who are the "least" among us to whom Jesus admonishes us to reach out in this gospel? Certainly they are the hungry, thirsty, naked, imprisoned, etc. But they also include, for example, someone in the family who may be imprisoned by depression and needs to be set free. Or someone at work who may be hungering for a deserved compliment. Or someone at the parish who thirsts to have his or her gifts called forth. The "least" have many faces.

• Actually, the "least" among us all have one and the same face: that of Christ. The simple graciousness of responding to another's need is truly an encounter with the Christ who is always present, even when we are not conscious of this presence. When we allow ourselves to be blessed by Christ our King's presence in those in need, we inherit eternal glory and discover our own blessedness.

• Our blessedness makes demands on us—we must spend ourselves for the good of others. We enter Christ's kingdom at the end of time because we have been building his kingdom here and now in our manner of treating one another and especially the least among us. Helping others is not simple philanthropy; it is acting out of who we are: "the blessed of the Father."

Model Prayer of the Faithful

Presider: With confidence we make our needs known to our God who blesses us and calls us into the kingdom of Christ our King.

Response:

Lord, hear our prayer.

Cantor:

we pray to the Lord,

That all members of the Body of Christ respond to Christ in one another, especially the least among us . . . [pause]

That religious and civic leaders judge with the justice and compassion of Christ the King . . . [pause]

That the least among us always be treated with dignity, graciousness, and care . . . [pause]

That each one of us here grow in the blessedness God bestows upon us . . . [pause]

Presider: Blessed be God forever! You sent your Son to make known your blessedness within us: hear these our prayers that one day we might enjoy everlasting glory with you. We ask this through Christ our King. **Amen.**

ALTERNATIVE OPENING PRAYER
Let us pray

Pause for silent prayer

Father all-powerful, God of love,
you have raised our Lord Jesus Christ from
    death to life,
resplendent in glory as King of creation.
Open our hearts,
free all the world to rejoice in his peace,
to glory in his justice, to live in his love.
Bring all mankind together in Jesus Christ
    your Son,
whose kingdom is with you and the Holy
    Spirit,
one God, for ever and ever. **Amen.**

FIRST READING
Ezek 34:11-12, 15-17

Thus says the Lord GOD:
    I myself will look after and tend my
        sheep.
As a shepherd tends his flock
    when he finds himself among his
        scattered sheep,
    so will I tend my sheep.
I will rescue them from every place where
        they were scattered
    when it was cloudy and dark.
I myself will pasture my sheep;
    I myself will give them rest, says the
        Lord GOD.
The lost I will seek out,
    the strayed I will bring back,
    the injured I will bind up,
    the sick I will heal,
    but the sleek and the strong I will
        destroy,
    shepherding them rightly.

As for you, my sheep, says the Lord GOD,
    I will judge between one sheep and
        another,
    between rams and goats.

RESPONSORIAL PSALM
Ps 23:1-2, 2-3, 5-6

℟. (1) The Lord is my shepherd; there is nothing I shall want.

The LORD is my shepherd; I shall not want.
    In verdant pastures he gives me repose.

℟. The Lord is my shepherd; there is nothing I shall want.

Beside restful waters he leads me;
  he refreshes my soul.
He guides me in right paths
  for his name's sake.

R̦. The Lord is my shepherd; there is
nothing I shall want.

You spread the table before me
  in the sight of my foes;
you anoint my head with oil;
  my cup overflows.

R̦. The Lord is my shepherd; there is
nothing I shall want.

Only goodness and kindness follow me
  all the days of my life;
and I shall dwell in the house of the LORD
  for years to come.

R̦. The Lord is my shepherd; there is
nothing I shall want.

SECOND READING
1 Cor 15:20-26, 28

Brothers and sisters:
Christ has been raised from the dead,
  the firstfruits of those who have fallen
    asleep.
For since death came through man,
  the resurrection of the dead came also
    through man.
For just as in Adam all die,
  so too in Christ shall all be brought to
    life,
  but each one in proper order:
  Christ the firstfruits;
  then, at his coming, those who belong
    to Christ;
  then comes the end,
  when he hands over the kingdom to his
    God and Father,
  when he has destroyed every
    sovereignty
  and every authority and power.
For he must reign until he has put all his
    enemies under his feet.
The last enemy to be destroyed is death.
When everything is subjected to him,
  then the Son himself will also be
    subjected
  to the one who subjected everything to
    him,
  so that God may be all in all.

About Liturgy

Ongoing catechesis: Now that we have completed another liturgical year, there is perhaps some tendency to think in terms of other things we have completed: "That's finished and over with; now I can get on with the next thing." But the marvelous rhythm of the liturgical year is that we immediately begin another year and are given yet another opportunity to grow in our understanding and living of the paschal mystery, an opportunity to come ever closer to the Christ whose disciples we are.

Our catechesis about liturgy can never end, either. Liturgy, as mystery, is inexhaustible; this means that we can never get to the point where we know enough about liturgy. We can always learn more, and the more we learn, the deeper into liturgy we are taken and, consequently, the deeper into Christ's mystery. It might be a good exercise at the end of this liturgical year to think back over the past year (perhaps review some of the catechesis pages in *Living Liturgy*™) and consider what we have learned about liturgy. Then, ask the important questions: "Has this helped me celebrate better? Live better?" After all, this is the real goal of liturgy: to be transformed continually so that we are ever more perfect members of the Body of Christ.

About Liturgical Music

Music suggestions: Hymns particularly appropriate to this year's Christ the King gospel reading include Mary Louise Bringle's "See My Hands and Feet" [in the GIA collection *Joy and Wonder, Love and Longing*] in which the risen Christ calls us to "See my hands and feet" then "Be my hands and feet" touching, healing, feeding, bearing the burdens of others. This hymn would be suitable during the preparation of the gifts or during Communion, with cantor or choir singing the verses and the assembly joining in on the refrain. In Herman Stuempfle's "We Turn Our Eyes to Heaven" [in HG and the GIA collection *Redeeming the Time*], God turns our eyes from heaven to earth so that we can we see the face of Christ in the needy. This hymn would fit the preparation of the gifts. "The Church of Christ in Every Age" [GC2, JS2, RS, SS, W3, WC], which calls us to continued commitment to the mission of Christ in the world, would make a good recessional.

NOVEMBER 20, 2011
THE SOLEMNITY OF OUR LORD
JESUS CHRIST THE KING

✝ SPIRITUALITY

GOSPEL ACCLAMATION
1 Thess 5:18

℟. Alleluia, alleluia.
In all circumstances, give thanks,
for this is the will of God for you in Christ Jesus.
℟. Alleluia, alleluia.

Gospel

Luke 17:11-19; L947.6

As Jesus continued his journey
    to Jerusalem,
  he traveled through Samaria
    and Galilee.
As he was entering a village,
    ten lepers met him.
They stood at a distance from
    him and raised their voices, saying,
  "Jesus, Master! Have pity on us!"
And when he saw them, he said,
  "Go show yourselves to the priests."
As they were going they were cleansed.
And one of them, realizing he had been
    healed,
  returned, glorifying God in a loud voice;
  and he fell at the feet of Jesus and
    thanked him.
He was a Samaritan.
Jesus said in reply,
  "Ten were cleansed, were they not?
Where are the other nine?
Has none but this foreigner returned to
    give thanks to God?"
Then he said to him, "Stand up and go;
  your faith has saved you."

See Appendix A, p. 305, for the other readings.

FIRST READING
Sir 50:22-24; L943.2

RESPONSORIAL PSALM
Ps 67:2-3, 5, 7-8; L919.1

SECOND READING
1 Cor 1:3-9; L944.1

*Additional reading choices may be found in the
Lectionary for Mass, vol. IV, "In Thanksgiving to
God," nos. 943–947.*

Reflecting on the Gospel

"Now say thank-you." How many parents have said this to their children dozens of times? From the time children can talk we teach them to say thank-you. Perhaps one of the reasons why this is an early and oft-taught lesson is that giving and receiving results in a unique relationship between persons. Giving and receiving—gift and thank-you—are the exchange of mutual goodness. What is received is not owed—it is gift. But gratitude *is owed* because only thankfulness can complete the exchange of mutual goodness. This gift-thanks-exchange is really goodness-exchange.

For most of us, the gifts of God given so lavishly and for which we would be thankful are not so dramatic as being cured of leprosy, as is the case in the gospel story. For this reason some of the most generous gifts of God can easily be taken for granted: growth and new life, "joy of heart," peace, goodness, deliverance (first reading); grace, peace, knowledge, spiritual gifts, fellowship (second reading). The gifts of God are neither few nor occasional; neither should be our thanks. The Christian stance is to "give thanks . . . always" (second reading). The Samaritan leper models for us the behavior of a thankful person: he recognizes the blessing and returns to the Gift-giver to give thanks. It is easier to see and give thanks for the dramatic things; the Christian stance of thankfulness beckons us to see God's blessings not just in the big, obvious ways but in the many instances of goodness that come our way each day.

The grateful leper properly turned his heartfelt thanks to God—both by giving God glory and by saying thanks to Jesus for his healing. This leper exemplifies what ought to be our whole demeanor toward God, even without having received such a dramatic gift as being healed from leprosy. Indeed, all we have and all we are is gift from God (see second reading). Thanksgiving is a recognition of God's many and varied gifts to us as individuals, as a family, as a nation. For this we ought to give God glory and thanks always and everywhere.

Living the Paschal Mystery

Grateful people are those who are open to the simple realization that everything we have and are is pure gift. The more we give thanks—not only to God, but also to each other—the more we are able to recognize that everything about us is gift. Armed with this realization, we are much more open to the beauty of creation, and do everything we can to conserve the resources given us. We use what we need well and are conscious not to waste what we don't need or what is more than our due.

Grateful people are also conscious of the role thanks plays in strengthening relationships. Most of us have been formed from the time we've been wee little ones to say thanks when we get a birthday or Christmas gift. Now perhaps the challenge is to form ourselves to say thanks for the many little, everyday ways people are good toward us so that our thanks becomes a recognition of that goodness. Saying thanks for a good meal; saying thanks for a sunny, warm day; saying thanks for small acts of kindness are all ways we actually build positive and loving relationships. Saying thanks is such a simple but profound human activity! Cultivating the habit of gratitude bears the fruit of an ever-growing and deeper relationship with God and each other.

Focusing the Gospel
Key words and phrases: healed, glorifying God, thanked him

To the point: The grateful leper properly turned his heartfelt thanks to God—both by giving God glory and by saying thanks to Jesus for his healing. This leper exemplifies what ought to be our whole demeanor toward God, even without having received such a dramatic gift as being healed from leprosy. Indeed, all we have and all we are is gift from God (see second reading). Thanksgiving is a recognition of God's many and varied gifts to us as individuals, as a family, as a nation. For this we ought to give God glory and thanks always and everywhere.

Model Act of Penitence
Presider: We come together this Thanksgiving Day to offer God worship and thanks. We pause now to count our many blessings and open our hearts to the presence of such a generous God . . . [pause]

Lord Jesus, you deserve all glory and thanks: Lord . . .

Christ Jesus, you have done wondrous things for us: Christ . . .

Lord Jesus, you extend to us kindness and truth: Lord . . .

Model Prayer of the Faithful
Presider: We gather today with hearts filled with gratitude for the many gifts we have been given. In confidence we ask God for what we yet need.

Response:

Cantor:

That all members of the church grow in gratitude for the many gifts bestowed upon them . . . [pause]

That our national leaders ensure that our many blessings as a nation be shared equitably and kindly with all . . . [pause]

That all those in need receive what they need from the abundant goods of this earth . . . [pause]

That each of us here grow in relating to others with generous and thankful hearts . . . [pause]

Presider: Generous and gracious God, you have given us abundant blessings: hear these our prayers that we might one day share in your most wondrous promise of life everlasting. With grateful hearts we pray through Christ our Lord. **Amen.**

OPENING PRAYER
Let us pray

Pause for silent prayer

Father all-powerful,
your gifts of love are countless
and your goodness is infinite.
On Thanksgiving Day we come before you
with gratitude for your kindness:
open our hearts to concern for our fellow
	men and women,
so that we may share your gifts in loving
	service.

We ask this through our Lord Jesus Christ,
	your Son,
who lives and reigns with you and the Holy
	Spirit,
one God for ever and ever. **Amen.**

FOR REFLECTION
- This Thanksgiving Day, I am especially grateful for . . .
- Some ways I glorify God—at the eucharistic banquet and at the family banquet—are . . .
- My heart wells up in thanksgiving when . . .

Homily Points
- Grateful hearts don't rise from nowhere. They always arise from a sense of having been gifted—which implies relationship, need, and openness to receiving. Whether the gift is something so large as being healed from a life-threatening disease or so small as a glass of water, the gratitude always has the same effect: both giver and receiver are magnified.

- Both the leper and Jesus are magnified when the leper returns to give thanks. The leper is opened to glorify God and grow in faith. Jesus is opened to announce the leper's salvation and reveal that his mission is for all, even Samaritans. Gratitude extends beyond a simple exchange of gift and thanks. Gratitude opens us to an expansive and gracious way of living that permeates every moment of our lives.

261

Readings *(continued)*

Second Sunday of Advent, *December 5, 2010*

Gospel (cont.)
Matt 3:1-12; L4A

Even now the ax lies at the root of the trees.
Therefore every tree that does not bear good fruit
   will be cut down and thrown into the fire.
I am baptizing you with water, for repentance,
   but the one who is coming after me is mightier than I.
I am not worthy to carry his sandals.
He will baptize you with the Holy Spirit and fire.
His winnowing fan is in his hand.
He will clear his threshing floor
   and gather his wheat into his barn,
   but the chaff he will burn with unquenchable fire."

SECOND READING (cont.)
Rom 15:4-9

Welcome one another, then, as Christ welcomed you,
   for the glory of God.
For I say that Christ became a minister of the circumcised
   to show God's truthfulness,
   to confirm the promises to the patriarchs,
   but so that the Gentiles might glorify God for his mercy.
As it is written:
   Therefore, I will praise you among the Gentiles
     and sing praises to your name.

The Immaculate Conception of the Blessed Virgin Mary, *December 8, 2010*

FIRST READING
Gen 3:9-15, 20

After the man, Adam, had eaten of the tree,
   the LORD God called to the man and asked
     him, "Where are you?"
He answered, "I heard you in the garden;
   but I was afraid, because I was naked,
   so I hid myself."
Then he asked, "Who told you that you were
   naked?
You have eaten, then,
   from the tree of which I had forbidden you
     to eat!"
The man replied, "The woman whom you put
   here with me—
   she gave me fruit from the tree, and so I
     ate it."
The LORD God then asked the woman,
   "Why did you do such a thing?"
The woman answered, "The serpent tricked
   me into it, so I ate it."

Then the LORD God said to the serpent:
   "Because you have done this, you shall be
     banned
     from all the animals
     and from all the wild creatures;
   on your belly shall you crawl,
     and dirt shall you eat
     all the days of your life.
I will put enmity between you and the
     woman,
   and between your offspring and hers;

he will strike at your head,
   while you strike at his heel."

The man called his wife Eve,
   because she became the mother of all the
     living.

RESPONSORIAL PSALM
Ps 98:1, 2-3, 3-4

℟. (1a) Sing to the Lord a new song, for he
has done marvelous deeds.

Sing to the LORD a new song,
   for he has done wondrous deeds;
his right hand has won victory for him,
   his holy arm.

℟. Sing to the Lord a new song, for he has
done marvelous deeds.

The LORD has made his salvation known:
   in the sight of the nations he has revealed
     his justice.
He has remembered his kindness and his
     faithfulness
   toward the house of Israel.

℟. Sing to the Lord a new song, for he has
done marvelous deeds.

All the ends of the earth have seen
   the salvation by our God.
Sing joyfully to the LORD, all you lands;
   break into song; sing praise.

℟. Sing to the Lord a new song, for he has
done marvelous deeds.

SECOND READING
Eph 1:3-6, 11-12

Brothers and sisters:
Blessed be the God and Father of our Lord
   Jesus Christ,
   who has blessed us in Christ
   with every spiritual blessing in the
     heavens,
   as he chose us in him, before the foundation
     of the world,
   to be holy and without blemish before him.
In love he destined us for adoption to himself
     through Jesus Christ,
   in accord with the favor of his will,
   for the praise of the glory of his grace
   that he granted us in the beloved.

In him we were also chosen,
   destined in accord with the purpose of the
     One
   who accomplishes all things according to
     the intention of his will,
   so that we might exist for the praise of his
     glory,
   we who first hoped in Christ.

Gospel (cont.)
Luke 1:26-38; L689

And behold, Elizabeth, your relative,
    has also conceived a son in her old age,
    and this is the sixth month for her who was called barren;
    for nothing will be impossible for God."
Mary said, "Behold, I am the handmaid of the Lord.
May it be done to me according to your word."
Then the angel departed from her.

The Nativity of the Lord, *December 25, 2010 (Vigil Mass)*

Gospel (cont.)
Matt 1:1-25; L13ABC

David became the father of Solomon,
    whose mother had been the wife of Uriah.
Solomon became the father of Rehoboam,
    Rehoboam the father of Abijah,
    Abijah the father of Asaph.
Asaph became the father of Jehoshaphat,
    Jehoshaphat the father of Joram,
    Joram the father of Uzziah.
Uzziah became the father of Jotham,
    Jotham the father of Ahaz,
    Ahaz the father of Hezekiah.
Hezekiah became the father of Manasseh,
    Manasseh the father of Amos,
    Amos the father of Josiah.
Josiah became the father of Jechoniah and his brothers
    at the time of the Babylonian exile.

After the Babylonian exile,
    Jechoniah became the father of Shealtiel,
    Shealtiel the father of Zerubbabel,
    Zerubbabel the father of Abiud.
Abiud became the father of Eliakim,
    Eliakim the father of Azor,
    Azor the father of Zadok.
Zadok became the father of Achim,
    Achim the father of Eliud,
    Eliud the father of Eleazar.
Eleazar became the father of Matthan,
    Matthan the father of Jacob,
    Jacob the father of Joseph, the husband of Mary.
Of her was born Jesus who is called the Christ.

Thus the total number of generations
    from Abraham to David

is fourteen generations;
    from David to the Babylonian exile,
    fourteen generations;
    from the Babylonian exile to the Christ,
    fourteen generations.

Now this is how the birth of Jesus Christ came about.
When his mother Mary was betrothed to Joseph,
    but before they lived together,
    she was found with child through the Holy Spirit.
Joseph her husband, since he was a righteous man,
    yet unwilling to expose her to shame,
    decided to divorce her quietly.
Such was his intention when, behold,
    the angel of the Lord appeared to him in a dream and said,
    "Joseph, son of David,
    do not be afraid to take Mary your wife into your home.
For it is through the Holy Spirit
    that this child has been conceived in her.
She will bear a son and you are to name him Jesus,
    because he will save his people from their sins."
All this took place to fulfill
    what the Lord had said through the prophet:
    Behold, the virgin shall conceive and bear a son,
        and they shall name him Emmanuel,
    which means "God is with us."
When Joseph awoke,
    he did as the angel of the Lord had commanded him
    and took his wife into his home.
He had no relations with her until she bore a son,
    and he named him Jesus.

Gospel (cont.)

or Matt 1:18-25

This is how the birth of Jesus Christ came about.
When his mother Mary was betrothed to Joseph,
  but before they lived together,
  she was found with child through the Holy Spirit.
Joseph her husband, since he was a righteous man,
  yet unwilling to expose her to shame,
  decided to divorce her quietly.
Such was his intention when, behold,
  the angel of the Lord appeared to him in a dream and said,
  "Joseph, son of David,
  do not be afraid to take Mary your wife into your home.
For it is through the Holy Spirit
  that this child has been conceived in her.

She will bear a son and you are to name him Jesus,
  because he will save his people from their sins."
All this took place to fulfill
  what the Lord had said through the prophet:
    Behold, the virgin shall conceive and bear a son,
      and they shall name him Emmanuel,
    which means "God is with us."
When Joseph awoke,
  he did as the angel of the Lord had commanded him
  and took his wife into his home.
He had no relations with her until she bore a son,
  and he named him Jesus.

FIRST READING

Isa 62:1-5

For Zion's sake I will not be silent,
  for Jerusalem's sake I will not be quiet,
until her vindication shines forth like the dawn
  and her victory like a burning torch.

Nations shall behold your vindication,
  and all the kings your glory;
you shall be called by a new name
  pronounced by the mouth of the LORD.
You shall be a glorious crown in the hand of
    the LORD,
  a royal diadem held by your God.
No more shall people call you "Forsaken,"
  or your land "Desolate,"
but you shall be called "My Delight,"
  and your land "Espoused."
For the LORD delights in you
  and makes your land his spouse.
As a young man marries a virgin,
  your Builder shall marry you;
and as a bridegroom rejoices in his bride
  so shall your God rejoice in you.

RESPONSORIAL PSALM

Ps 89:4-5, 16-17, 27, 29

R̸. (2a) Forever I will sing the goodness of the
Lord.

I have made a covenant with my chosen one,
  I have sworn to David my servant:
forever will I confirm your posterity
  and establish your throne for all
    generations.

R̸. Forever I will sing the goodness of the Lord.

Blessed the people who know the joyful shout;
  in the light of your countenance, O LORD,
    they walk.
At your name they rejoice all the day,
  and through your justice they are exalted.

R̸. Forever I will sing the goodness of the Lord.

He shall say of me, "You are my father,
  my God, the rock, my savior."
Forever I will maintain my kindness toward
    him,
  and my covenant with him stands firm.

R̸. Forever I will sing the goodness of the Lord.

SECOND READING

Acts 13:16-17, 22-25

When Paul reached Antioch in Pisidia and
    entered the synagogue,
  he stood up, motioned with his hand, and
    said,
  "Fellow Israelites and you others who are
    God-fearing, listen.
The God of this people Israel chose our
    ancestors
  and exalted the people during their sojourn
    in the land of Egypt.
With uplifted arm he led them out of it.
Then he removed Saul and raised up David
    as king;
  of him he testified,
  'I have found David, son of Jesse, a man
    after my own heart;
  he will carry out my every wish.'
From this man's descendants God, according
    to his promise,
  has brought to Israel a savior, Jesus.
John heralded his coming by proclaiming a
    baptism of repentance
  to all the people of Israel;
  and as John was completing his course, he
    would say,
  'What do you suppose that I am? I am not he.
Behold, one is coming after me;
  I am not worthy to unfasten the sandals of
    his feet.'"

Gospel (cont.)
Luke 2:1-14; L14ABC

Now there were shepherds in that region living in the fields
   and keeping the night watch over their flock.
The angel of the Lord appeared to them
   and the glory of the Lord shone around them,
   and they were struck with great fear.
The angel said to them,
   "Do not be afraid;
   for behold, I proclaim to you good news of great joy
   that will be for all the people.
For today in the city of David
   a savior has been born for you who is Christ and Lord.
And this will be a sign for you:
   you will find an infant wrapped in swaddling clothes
   and lying in a manger."
And suddenly there was a multitude of the heavenly host with the
      angel,
   praising God and saying:
      "Glory to God in the highest
         and on earth peace to those on whom his favor rests."

FIRST READING
Isa 9:1-6

The people who walked in darkness
   have seen a great light;
upon those who dwelt in the land of gloom
   a light has shone.
You have brought them abundant joy
   and great rejoicing,
as they rejoice before you as at the harvest,
   as people make merry when dividing
         spoils.
For the yoke that burdened them,
   the pole on their shoulder,
and the rod of their taskmaster
   you have smashed, as on the day of Midian.
For every boot that tramped in battle,
   every cloak rolled in blood,
   will be burned as fuel for flames.
For a child is born to us, a son is given us;
   upon his shoulder dominion rests.
They name him Wonder-Counselor, God-Hero,
   Father-Forever, Prince of Peace.
His dominion is vast
   and forever peaceful,
from David's throne, and over his kingdom,
   which he confirms and sustains
by judgment and justice,
   both now and forever.
The zeal of the LORD of hosts will do this!

RESPONSORIAL PSALM
Ps 96:1-2, 2-3, 11-12, 13

Ry. (Luke 2:11) Today is born our Savior,
Christ the Lord.

Sing to the LORD a new song;
   sing to the LORD, all you lands.
Sing to the LORD; bless his name.

Ry. Today is born our Savior, Christ the Lord.

Announce his salvation, day after day.
   Tell his glory among the nations;
   among all peoples, his wondrous deeds.

Ry. Today is born our Savior, Christ the Lord.

Let the heavens be glad and the earth rejoice;
   let the sea and what fills it resound;
   let the plains be joyful and all that is in
      them!
Then shall all the trees of the forest exult.

Ry. Today is born our Savior, Christ the Lord.

They shall exult before the LORD, for he
      comes;
   for he comes to rule the earth.
He shall rule the world with justice
   and the peoples with his constancy.

Ry. Today is born our Savior, Christ the Lord.

SECOND READING
Titus 2:11-14

Beloved:
The grace of God has appeared, saving all
   and training us to reject godless ways and
         worldly desires
   and to live temperately, justly, and
         devoutly in this age,
   as we await the blessed hope,
   the appearance of the glory of our great
         God
   and savior Jesus Christ,
   who gave himself for us to deliver us from
         all lawlessness
   and to cleanse for himself a people as his
         own,
   eager to do what is good.

The Nativity of the Lord, December 25, 2010 (Mass at Dawn)

FIRST READING
Isa 62:11-12

See, the LORD proclaims
   to the ends of the earth:
say to daughter Zion,
   your savior comes!
Here is his reward with him,
   his recompense before him.
They shall be called the holy people,
   the redeemed of the LORD,
and you shall be called "Frequented,"
   a city that is not forsaken.

RESPONSORIAL PSALM
Ps 97:1, 6, 11-12

R⁊. A light will shine on us this day: the Lord
is born for us.

The LORD is king; let the earth rejoice;
   let the many isles be glad.
The heavens proclaim his justice,
   and all peoples see his glory.

R⁊. A light will shine on us this day: the Lord
is born for us.

Light dawns for the just;
   and gladness, for the upright of heart.
Be glad in the LORD, you just,
   and give thanks to his holy name.

R⁊. A light will shine on us this day: the Lord
is born for us.

SECOND READING
Titus 3:4-7

Beloved:
When the kindness and generous love
   of God our savior appeared,
not because of any righteous deeds we had
      done
   but because of his mercy,
he saved us through the bath of rebirth
   and renewal by the Holy Spirit,
whom he richly poured out on us
   through Jesus Christ our savior,
so that we might be justified by his grace
   and become heirs in hope of eternal life.

The Nativity of the Lord, December 25, 2010 (Mass during the Day)

Gospel (cont.)
John 1:1-18; L16ABC

The true light, which enlightens everyone,
   was coming into the world.

He was in the world,
   and the world came to be through him,
   but the world did not know him.
He came to what was his own,
   but his own people did not accept him.

But to those who did accept him
   he gave power to become children of God,
   to those who believe in his name,
   who were born not by natural generation
   nor by human choice nor by a man's decision
   but of God.

And the Word became flesh
   and made his dwelling among us,
   and we saw his glory,
   the glory as of the Father's only Son,
   full of grace and truth.

John testified to him and cried out, saying,
   "This was he of whom I said,
   'The one who is coming after me ranks ahead of me
   because he existed before me.'"
From his fullness we have all received,
   grace in place of grace,
   because while the law was given through Moses,
   grace and truth came through Jesus Christ.
No one has ever seen God.
The only Son, God, who is at the Father's side,
   has revealed him.

or John 1:1-5, 9-14

In the beginning was the Word,
   and the Word was with God,
   and the Word was God.
He was in the beginning with God.
All things came to be through him,
   and without him nothing came to be.
What came to be through him was life,
   and this life was the light of the human race;
the light shines in the darkness,
   and the darkness has not overcome it.
The true light, which enlightens everyone,
   was coming into the world.

He was in the world,
   and the world came to be through him,
   but the world did not know him.
He came to what was his own,
   but his own people did not accept him.

But to those who did accept him
   he gave power to become children of God,
   to those who believe in his name,
   who were born not by natural generation
   nor by human choice nor by a man's decision
   but of God.

And the Word became flesh
   and made his dwelling among us,
   and we saw his glory,
   the glory as of the Father's only Son,
   full of grace and truth.

The Nativity of the Lord, December 25, 2010 (Mass during the Day)

FIRST READING
Isa 52:7-10

How beautiful upon the mountains
    are the feet of him who brings glad tidings,
announcing peace, bearing good news,
    announcing salvation, and saying to Zion,
    "Your God is King!"

Hark! Your sentinels raise a cry,
    together they shout for joy,
for they see directly, before their eyes,
    the LORD restoring Zion.
Break out together in song,
    O ruins of Jerusalem!
For the LORD comforts his people,
    he redeems Jerusalem.
The LORD has bared his holy arm
    in the sight of all the nations;
all the ends of the earth will behold
    the salvation of our God.

RESPONSORIAL PSALM
Ps 98:1, 2-3, 3-4, 5-6

R̸. (3c) All the ends of the earth have seen the
saving power of God.

Sing to the LORD a new song,
    for he has done wondrous deeds;
his right hand has won victory for him,
    his holy arm.

R̸. All the ends of the earth have seen the
saving power of God.

The LORD has made his salvation known:
    in the sight of the nations he has revealed
        his justice.
He has remembered his kindness and his
    faithfulness
    toward the house of Israel.

R̸. All the ends of the earth have seen the
saving power of God.

All the ends of the earth have seen
    the salvation by our God.
Sing joyfully to the LORD, all you lands;
    break into song; sing praise.

R̸. All the ends of the earth have seen the
saving power of God.

Sing praise to the LORD with the harp,
    with the harp and melodious song.
With trumpets and the sound of the horn
    sing joyfully before the King, the LORD.

R̸. All the ends of the earth have seen the
saving power of God.

SECOND READING
Heb 1:1-6

Brothers and sisters:
In times past, God spoke in partial and
    various ways
    to our ancestors through the prophets;
    in these last days, he has spoken to us
        through the Son,
    whom he made heir of all things
    and through whom he created the universe,
who is the refulgence of his glory, the very
    imprint of his being,
    and who sustains all things by his
        mighty word.
When he had accomplished purification
    from sins,
    he took his seat at the right hand of the
        Majesty on high,
as far superior to the angels
    as the name he has inherited is more
        excellent than theirs.

For to which of the angels did God ever say:
    You are my son; this day I have begotten
        you?
Or again:
    I will be a father to him, and he shall be a
        son to me?
And again, when he leads the firstborn into
    the world, he says:
    Let all the angels of God worship him.

The Holy Family of Jesus, Mary, and Joseph, December 26, 2010

SECOND READING
Col 3:12-17

Brothers and sisters:
Put on, as God's chosen ones, holy and beloved,
    heartfelt compassion, kindness, humility,
        gentleness, and patience,
    bearing with one another and forgiving one
        another,
    if one has a grievance against another;
    as the Lord has forgiven you, so must you
        also do.
And over all these put on love,
    that is, the bond of perfection.
And let the peace of Christ control your hearts,
    the peace into which you were also called in
        one body.

And be thankful.
Let the word of Christ dwell in you richly,
    as in all wisdom you teach and admonish
        one another,
    singing psalms, hymns, and spiritual songs
    with gratitude in your hearts to God.
And whatever you do, in word or in deed,
    do everything in the name of the Lord Jesus,
    giving thanks to God the Father through him.

Solemnity of the Blessed Virgin Mary, Mother of God, *January 1, 2011*

FIRST READING
Num 6:22-27

The LORD said to Moses:
"Speak to Aaron and his sons and tell them:
This is how you shall bless the Israelites.
Say to them:
The LORD bless you and keep you!
The LORD let his face shine upon
you, and be gracious to you!
The LORD look upon you kindly and
give you peace!
So shall they invoke my name upon the
Israelites,
and I will bless them."

RESPONSORIAL PSALM
Ps 67:2-3, 5, 6, 8

R̸. (2a) May God bless us in his mercy.

May God have pity on us and bless us;
may he let his face shine upon us.
So may your way be known upon earth;
among all nations, your salvation.

R̸. May God bless us in his mercy.

May the nations be glad and exult
because you rule the peoples in equity;
the nations on the earth you guide.

R̸. May God bless us in his mercy.

May the peoples praise you, O God;
may all the peoples praise you!
May God bless us,
and may all the ends of the earth fear him!

R̸. May God bless us in his mercy.

SECOND READING
Gal 4:4-7

Brothers and sisters:
When the fullness of time had come, God sent
his Son,
born of a woman, born under the law,
to ransom those under the law,
so that we might receive adoption as sons.
As proof that you are sons,
God sent the Spirit of his Son into our
hearts,
crying out, "Abba, Father!"
So you are no longer a slave but a son,
and if a son then also an heir, through God.

The Epiphany of the Lord, *January 2, 2011*

Gospel (cont.)
Matt 2:1-12; L20ABC

They were overjoyed at seeing the star,
and on entering the house
they saw the child with Mary his mother.
They prostrated themselves and did him homage.
Then they opened their treasures
and offered him gifts of gold, frankincense, and myrrh.
And having been warned in a dream not to return to Herod,
they departed for their country by another way.

Third Sunday in Ordinary Time, *January 23, 2011*

Gospel (cont.)
Matt 4:12-23; L67A

They were in a boat, with their father Zebedee, mending their nets.
He called them, and immediately they left their boat and their father
and followed him.
He went around all of Galilee,
teaching in their synagogues, proclaiming the gospel of the
kingdom,
and curing every disease and illness among the people.

or Matt 4:12-17

When Jesus heard that John had been arrested,
he withdrew to Galilee.
He left Nazareth and went to live in Capernaum by the sea,
in the region of Zebulun and Naphtali,
that what had been said through Isaiah the prophet
might be fulfilled:
Land of Zebulun and land of Naphtali,
the way to the sea, beyond the Jordan,
Galilee of the Gentiles,
the people who sit in darkness have seen a great light,
on those dwelling in a land overshadowed by death
light has arisen.
From that time on, Jesus began to preach and say,
"Repent, for the kingdom of heaven is at hand."

Gospel (cont.)
Matt 5:17-37; L76A

Therefore, if you bring your gift to the altar,
  and there recall that your brother
  has anything against you,
  leave your gift there at the altar,
  go first and be reconciled with your brother,
  and then come and offer your gift.
Settle with your opponent quickly while on the way to court.
Otherwise your opponent will hand you over to the judge,
  and the judge will hand you over to the guard,
  and you will be thrown into prison.
Amen, I say to you,
  you will not be released until you have paid the last penny.

"You have heard that it was said,
  You shall not commit adultery.
But I say to you,
  everyone who looks at a woman with lust
  has already committed adultery with her in his heart.
If your right eye causes you to sin,
  tear it out and throw it away.
It is better for you to lose one of your members
  than to have your whole body thrown into Gehenna.
And if your right hand causes you to sin,
  cut it off and throw it away.
It is better for you to lose one of your members
  than to have your whole body go into Gehenna.

"It was also said,
  Whoever divorces his wife must give her a bill of divorce.
But I say to you,
  whoever divorces his wife—unless the marriage is unlawful—
  causes her to commit adultery,
  and whoever marries a divorced woman commits adultery.

"Again you have heard that it was said to your ancestors,
  Do not take a false oath,
  but make good to the Lord all that you vow.
But I say to you, do not swear at all;
  not by heaven, for it is God's throne;
  nor by the earth, for it is his footstool;
  nor by Jerusalem, for it is the city of the great King.
Do not swear by your head,
  for you cannot make a single hair white or black.
Let your 'Yes' mean 'Yes,' and your 'No' mean 'No.'
Anything more is from the evil one."

or Matt 5:20-22a, 27-28, 33-34a, 37

Jesus said to his disciples:
  "I tell you, unless your righteousness surpasses
  that of the scribes and Pharisees,
  you will not enter the kingdom of heaven.

"You have heard that it was said to your ancestors,
  You shall not kill; and whoever kills will be liable to judgment.
But I say to you,
  whoever is angry with his brother
  will be liable to judgment.

"You have heard that it was said, *You shall not commit adultery.*
But I say to you,
  everyone who looks at a woman with lust
  has already committed adultery with her in his heart.

"Again you have heard that it was said to your ancestors,
  Do not take a false oath,
  but make good to the Lord all that you vow.
But I say to you, do not swear at all.
Let your 'Yes' mean 'Yes,' and your 'No' mean 'No.'
Anything more is from the evil one."

Gospel (cont.)
Matt 6:1-6, 16-18; L219

"When you fast,
  do not look gloomy like the hypocrites.
They neglect their appearance,
  so that they may appear to others to be fasting.
Amen, I say to you, they have received their reward.
But when you fast,
  anoint your head and wash your face,
  so that you may not appear to be fasting,
  except to your Father who is hidden.
And your Father who sees what is hidden will repay you."

Ash Wednesday, *March 9, 2011*

FIRST READING
Joel 2:12-18

Even now, says the LORD,
   return to me with your whole heart,
   with fasting, and weeping, and mourning;
Rend your hearts, not your garments,
   and return to the LORD, your God.
For gracious and merciful is he,
   slow to anger, rich in kindness,
   and relenting in punishment.
Perhaps he will again relent
   and leave behind him a blessing,
Offerings and libations
   for the LORD, your God.

Blow the trumpet in Zion!
   proclaim a fast,
   call an assembly;
Gather the people,
   notify the congregation;
Assemble the elders,
   gather the children
   and the infants at the breast;
Let the bridegroom quit his room
   and the bride her chamber.
Between the porch and the altar
   let the priests, the ministers of the LORD,
      weep,
And say, "Spare, O LORD, your people,
   and make not your heritage a reproach,
   with the nations ruling over them!
Why should they say among the peoples,
   'Where is their God?'"

Then the LORD was stirred to concern for his
      land
   and took pity on his people.

RESPONSORIAL PSALM
Ps 51:3-4, 5-6ab, 12-13, 14, and 17

R̸. (see 3a) Be merciful, O Lord, for we have
sinned.

Have mercy on me, O God, in your goodness;
   in the greatness of your compassion wipe
      out my offense.
Thoroughly wash me from my guilt
   and of my sin cleanse me.

R̸. Be merciful, O Lord, for we have sinned.

For I acknowledge my offense,
   and my sin is before me always:
"Against you only have I sinned,
   and done what is evil in your sight."

R̸. Be merciful, O Lord, for we have sinned.

A clean heart create for me, O God,
   and a steadfast spirit renew within me.
Cast me not out from your presence,
   and your Holy Spirit take not from me.

R̸. Be merciful, O Lord, for we have sinned.

Give me back the joy of your salvation,
   and a willing spirit sustain in me.
O Lord, open my lips,
   and my mouth shall proclaim your praise.

R̸. Be merciful, O Lord, for we have sinned.

SECOND READING
2 Cor 5:20–6:2

Brothers and sisters:
We are ambassadors for Christ,
   as if God were appealing through us.
We implore you on behalf of Christ,
   be reconciled to God.
For our sake he made him to be sin who did
      not know sin,
   so that we might become the righteousness
      of God in him.

Working together, then,
   we appeal to you not to receive the grace of
      God in vain.
For he says:

In an acceptable time I heard you,
   and on the day of salvation I helped you.

Behold, now is a very acceptable time;
   behold, now is the day of salvation.

First Sunday of Lent, *March 13, 2011*

SECOND READING (cont.)
Rom 5:12-19

But the gift is not like the transgression.
For if by the transgression of the one, the
      many died,
   how much more did the grace of God
   and the gracious gift of the one man Jesus
      Christ
   overflow for the many.
And the gift is not like the result of the one
      who sinned.
For after one sin there was the judgment that
      brought condemnation;
   but the gift, after many transgressions,
      brought acquittal.
For if, by the transgression of the one,
   death came to reign through that one,
   how much more will those who receive the
      abundance of grace
   and of the gift of justification
   come to reign in life through the one Jesus
      Christ.

In conclusion, just as through one transgression
   condemnation came upon all,
   so, through one righteous act,
   acquittal and life came to all.
For just as through the disobedience of the
      one man
   the many were made sinners,
   so, through the obedience of the one,
   the many will be made righteous.

or Rom 5:12, 17-19

Brothers and sisters:
Through one man sin entered the world,
   and through sin, death,
   and thus death came to all men, inasmuch
      as all sinned—

For if, by the transgression of the one,
   death came to reign through that one,
   how much more will those who receive the
      abundance of grace
   and of the gift of justification

come to reign in life through the one Jesus
      Christ.
In conclusion, just as through one
      transgression
   condemnation came upon all,
   so, through one righteous act,
   acquittal and life came to all.
For just as through the disobedience of the
      one man
   the many were made sinners,
   so, through the obedience of the one,
   the many will be made righteous.

Gospel
Luke 2:41-51a; L543

Each year Jesus' parents went to Jerusalem for the feast of Passover,
    and when he was twelve years old,
    they went up according to festival custom.
After they had completed its days, as they were returning,
    the boy Jesus remained behind in Jerusalem,
    but his parents did not know it.
Thinking that he was in the caravan,
    they journeyed for a day
    and looked for him among their relatives and acquaintances,
    but not finding him,
    they returned to Jerusalem to look for him.
After three days they found him in the temple,
    sitting in the midst of the teachers,
    listening to them and asking them questions,
    and all who heard him were astounded
    at his understanding and his answers.
When his parents saw him,
    they were astonished,
    and his mother said to him,
    "Son, why have you done this to us?
Your father and I have been looking for you with great anxiety."
And he said to them,
    "Why were you looking for me?
Did you not know that I must be in my Father's house?"
But they did not understand what he said to them.
He went down with them and came to Nazareth,
    and was obedient to them.

FIRST READING
2 Sam 7:4-5a, 12-14a, 16

The LORD spoke to Nathan and said:
"Go, tell my servant David,
    'When your time comes and you rest with
        your ancestors,
    I will raise up your heir after you, sprung
        from your loins,
    and I will make his kingdom firm.
It is he who shall build a house for my name.
And I will make his royal throne firm forever.
I will be a father to him,
    and he shall be a son to me.
Your house and your kingdom shall endure
        forever before me;
    your throne shall stand firm forever.'"

RESPONSORIAL PSALM
Ps 89:2-3, 4-5, 27, and 29

R⁒. (37) The son of David will live forever.

The promises of the LORD I will sing forever,
    through all generations my mouth will
        proclaim your faithfulness,
For you have said, "My kindness is
    established forever";
    in heaven you have confirmed your
        faithfulness.

R⁒. The son of David will live forever.

"I have made a covenant with my chosen one;
    I have sworn to David my servant:
Forever will I confirm your posterity
    and establish your throne for all
        generations."

R⁒. The son of David will live forever.

"He shall say of me, 'You are my father,
    my God, the Rock my savior!'
Forever I will maintain my kindness toward
        him,
    my covenant with him stands firm."

R⁒. The son of David will live forever.

SECOND READING
Rom 4:13, 16-18, 22

Brothers and sisters:
It was not through the law
    that the promise was made to Abraham
        and his descendants
    that he would inherit the world,
    but through the righteousness that comes
        from faith.
For this reason, it depends on faith,
    so that it may be a gift,
    and the promise may be guaranteed to all
        his descendants,
    not to those who only adhere to the law
    but to those who follow the faith of Abraham,
    who is the father of all of us, as it is written,
    I have made you father of many nations.
He is our father in the sight of God,
    in whom he believed, who gives life to the
        dead
    and calls into being what does not exist.
He believed, hoping against hope,
    that he would become *the father of many
        nations,*
    according to what was said, *Thus shall
        your descendants be.*
That is why *it was credited to him as
    righteousness.*

Gospel (cont.)
Luke 1:26-38; L545

And behold, Elizabeth, your relative,
   has also conceived a son in her old age,
    and this is the sixth month for her who was called barren;
    for nothing will be impossible for God."
Mary said, "Behold, I am the handmaid of the Lord.
May it be done to me according to your word."
Then the angel departed from her.

FIRST READING
Isa 7:10-14; 8:10

The LORD spoke to Ahaz, saying:
Ask for a sign from the LORD, your God;
   let it be deep as the netherworld, or high as
    the sky!
But Ahaz answered,
   "I will not ask! I will not tempt the LORD!"
Then Isaiah said:
   Listen, O house of David!
Is it not enough for you to weary people,
   must you also weary my God?
Therefore the Lord himself will give you this
   sign:
   the virgin shall conceive, and bear a son,
   and shall name him Emmanuel,
   which means "God is with us!"

RESPONSORIAL PSALM
Ps 40:7-8a, 8b-9, 10, 11

℟. (8a and 9a) Here am I, Lord; I come to do
your will.

Sacrifice or oblation you wished not,
   but ears open to obedience you gave me.
Holocausts and sin-offerings you sought not;
   then said I, "Behold, I come."

℟. Here am I, Lord; I come to do your will.

"In the written scroll it is prescribed for me,
To do your will, O God, is my delight,
   and your law is within my heart!"

℟. Here am I, Lord; I come to do your will.

I announced your justice in the vast assembly;
   I did not restrain my lips, as you, O LORD,
    know.

℟. Here am I, Lord; I come to do your will.

Your justice I kept not hid within my heart;
   your faithfulness and your salvation I have
    spoken of;
I have made no secret of your kindness and
   your truth
   in the vast assembly.

℟. Here am I, Lord; I come to do your will.

SECOND READING
Heb 10:4-10

Brothers and sisters:
It is impossible that the blood of bulls and
   goats
takes away sins.
For this reason, when Christ came into the
   world, he said:

   "Sacrifice and offering you did not desire,
    but a body you prepared for me;
   in holocausts and sin offerings you took no
    delight.
   Then I said, 'As is written of me in the scroll,
   behold, I come to do your will, O God.'"

First he says, "Sacrifices and offerings,
   holocausts and sin offerings,
   you neither desired nor delighted in."
These are offered according to the law.
Then he says, "Behold, I come to do your will."
He takes away the first to establish the
   second.
By this "will," we have been consecrated
   through the offering of the Body of Jesus
    Christ once for all.

Gospel (cont.)
John 4:5-42; L28A

Jesus answered and said to her,
 "Everyone who drinks this water will be thirsty again;
 but whoever drinks the water I shall give will never thirst;
 the water I shall give will become in him
 a spring of water welling up to eternal life."
The woman said to him,
 "Sir, give me this water, so that I may not be thirsty
 or have to keep coming here to draw water."

Jesus said to her,
 "Go call your husband and come back."
The woman answered and said to him,
 "I do not have a husband."
Jesus answered her,
 "You are right in saying, 'I do not have a husband.'
For you have had five husbands,
 and the one you have now is not your husband.
What you have said is true."
The woman said to him,
 "Sir, I can see that you are a prophet.
Our ancestors worshiped on this mountain;
 but you people say that the place to worship is in Jerusalem."
Jesus said to her,
 "Believe me, woman, the hour is coming
 when you will worship the Father
 neither on this mountain nor in Jerusalem.
You people worship what you do not understand;
 we worship what we understand,
 because salvation is from the Jews.
But the hour is coming, and is now here,
 when true worshipers will worship the Father in Spirit and truth;
 and indeed the Father seeks such people to worship him.
God is Spirit, and those who worship him
 must worship in Spirit and truth."
The woman said to him,
 "I know that the Messiah is coming, the one called the Christ;
 when he comes, he will tell us everything."
Jesus said to her,
 "I am he, the one speaking with you."

At that moment his disciples returned,
 and were amazed that he was talking with a woman,
 but still no one said, "What are you looking for?"
 or "Why are you talking with her?"
The woman left her water jar
 and went into the town and said to the people,
 "Come see a man who told me everything I have done.
Could he possibly be the Christ?"
They went out of the town and came to him.
Meanwhile, the disciples urged him, "Rabbi, eat."
But he said to them,
 "I have food to eat of which you do not know."
So the disciples said to one another,
 "Could someone have brought him something to eat?"
Jesus said to them,
 "My food is to do the will of the one who sent me
 and to finish his work.
Do you not say, 'In four months the harvest will be here'?
I tell you, look up and see the fields ripe for the harvest.
The reaper is already receiving payment
 and gathering crops for eternal life,
 so that the sower and reaper can rejoice together.
For here the saying is verified that 'One sows and another reaps.'
I sent you to reap what you have not worked for;
 others have done the work,
 and you are sharing the fruits of their work."

Many of the Samaritans of that town began to believe in him
 because of the word of the woman who testified,
 "He told me everything I have done."
When the Samaritans came to him,
 they invited him to stay with them;
 and he stayed there two days.
Many more began to believe in him because of his word,
 and they said to the woman,
 "We no longer believe because of your word;
 for we have heard for ourselves,
 and we know that this is truly the savior of the world."

Third Sunday of Lent, *March 27, 2011*

Gospel
John 4:5-15, 19b-26, 39a, 40-42; L28A

Jesus came to a town of Samaria called Sychar,
   near the plot of land that Jacob had given to his son Joseph.
Jacob's well was there.
Jesus, tired from his journey, sat down there at the well.
It was about noon.

A woman of Samaria came to draw water.
Jesus said to her,
   "Give me a drink."
His disciples had gone into the town to buy food.
The Samaritan woman said to him,
   "How can you, a Jew, ask me, a Samaritan woman, for a drink?"
—For Jews use nothing in common with Samaritans.—
Jesus answered and said to her,
   "If you knew the gift of God
   and who is saying to you, 'Give me a drink,'
   you would have asked him
   and he would have given you living water."
The woman said to him,
   "Sir, you do not even have a bucket and the cistern is deep;
   where then can you get this living water?
Are you greater than our father Jacob,
   who gave us this cistern and drank from it himself
   with his children and his flocks?"
Jesus answered and said to her,
   "Everyone who drinks this water will be thirsty again;
   but whoever drinks the water I shall give will never thirst;
   the water I shall give will become in him
   a spring of water welling up to eternal life."
The woman said to him,
   "Sir, give me this water, so that I may not be thirsty
   or have to keep coming here to draw water."

"I can see that you are a prophet.
Our ancestors worshiped on this mountain;
   but you people say that the place to worship is in Jerusalem."
Jesus said to her,
   "Believe me, woman, the hour is coming
   when you will worship the Father
   neither on this mountain nor in Jerusalem.
You people worship what you do not understand;
   we worship what we understand,
   because salvation is from the Jews.
But the hour is coming, and is now here,
   when true worshipers will worship the Father in Spirit and truth;
   and indeed the Father seeks such people to worship him.
God is Spirit, and those who worship him
   must worship in Spirit and truth."
The woman said to him,
   "I know that the Messiah is coming, the one called the Christ;
   when he comes, he will tell us everything."
Jesus said to her,
   "I am he, the one speaking with you."

Many of the Samaritans of that town began to believe in him.
When the Samaritans came to him,
   they invited him to stay with them;
   and he stayed there two days.
Many more began to believe in him because of his word,
   and they said to the woman,
   "We no longer believe because of your word;
   for we have heard for ourselves,
   and we know that this is truly the savior of the world."

Fourth Sunday of Lent, *April 3, 2011*

Gospel (cont.)
John 9:1-41; L31A

So they said to him, "How were your eyes opened?"
He replied,
   "The man called Jesus made clay and anointed my eyes
   and told me, 'Go to Siloam and wash.'
So I went there and washed and was able to see."
And they said to him, "Where is he?"
He said, "I don't know."

They brought the one who was once blind to the Pharisees.
Now Jesus had made clay and opened his eyes on a sabbath.
So then the Pharisees also asked him how he was able to see.
He said to them,
   "He put clay on my eyes, and I washed, and now I can see."
So some of the Pharisees said,
   "This man is not from God,
   because he does not keep the sabbath."
But others said,
   "How can a sinful man do such signs?"

And there was a division among them.
So they said to the blind man again,
   "What do you have to say about him,
   since he opened your eyes?"
He said, "He is a prophet."

Now the Jews did not believe
   that he had been blind and gained his sight
   until they summoned the parents of the one who had gained his sight.
They asked them,
   "Is this your son, who you say was born blind?
How does he now see?"
His parents answered and said,
   "We know that this is our son and that he was born blind.
We do not know how he sees now,
   nor do we know who opened his eyes.
Ask him, he is of age;
   he can speak for himself."

His parents said this because they were afraid
  of the Jews, for the Jews had already agreed
  that if anyone acknowledged him as the Christ,
  he would be expelled from the synagogue.
For this reason his parents said,
  "He is of age; question him."

So a second time they called the man who had been blind
  and said to him, "Give God the praise!
We know that this man is a sinner."
He replied,
  "If he is a sinner, I do not know.
One thing I do know is that I was blind and now I see."
So they said to him,
  "What did he do to you?
  How did he open your eyes?"
He answered them,
  "I told you already and you did not listen.
Why do you want to hear it again?
Do you want to become his disciples, too?"
They ridiculed him and said,
  "You are that man's disciple;
  we are disciples of Moses!
We know that God spoke to Moses,
  but we do not know where this one is from."
The man answered and said to them,
  "This is what is so amazing,
  that you do not know where he is from, yet he opened my eyes.
We know that God does not listen to sinners,
  but if one is devout and does his will, he listens to him.
It is unheard of that anyone ever opened the eyes of a person born
    blind.
If this man were not from God,
  he would not be able to do anything."
They answered and said to him,
  "You were born totally in sin,
  and are you trying to teach us?"
Then they threw him out.

When Jesus heard that they had thrown him out,
  he found him and said, "Do you believe in the Son of Man?"
He answered and said,
  "Who is he, sir, that I may believe in him?"
Jesus said to him,
  "You have seen him,
  and the one speaking with you is he."
He said,
  "I do believe, Lord," and he worshiped him.
Then Jesus said,
  "I came into this world for judgment,
  so that those who do not see might see,
  and those who do see might become blind."

Some of the Pharisees who were with him heard this
  and said to him, "Surely we are not also blind, are we?"
Jesus said to them,
  "If you were blind, you would have no sin;
  but now you are saying, 'We see,' so your sin remains."

or John 9:1, 6-9, 13-17, 34-38; L31A

As Jesus passed by he saw a man blind from birth.
He spat on the ground and made clay with the saliva,
  and smeared the clay on his eyes, and said to him,
  "Go wash in the Pool of Siloam"—which means Sent—.
So he went and washed, and came back able to see.

His neighbors and those who had seen him earlier as a beggar said,
  "Isn't this the one who used to sit and beg?"
Some said, "It is,"
  but others said, "No, he just looks like him."
He said, "I am."

They brought the one who was once blind to the Pharisees.
Now Jesus had made clay and opened his eyes on a sabbath.
So then the Pharisees also asked him how he was able to see.
He said to them,
  "He put clay on my eyes, and I washed, and now I can see."
So some of the Pharisees said,
  "This man is not from God,
  because he does not keep the sabbath."
But others said,
  "How can a sinful man do such signs?"
And there was a division among them.
So they said to the blind man again,
  "What do you have to say about him,
  since he opened your eyes?"
He said, "He is a prophet."

They answered and said to him,
  "You were born totally in sin,
  and are you trying to teach us?"
Then they threw him out.

When Jesus heard that they had thrown him out,
  he found him and said, "Do you believe in the Son of Man?"
He answered and said,
  "Who is he, sir, that I may believe in him?"
Jesus said to him,
  "You have seen him,
  and the one speaking with you is he."
He said,
  "I do believe, Lord," and he worshiped him.

Gospel (cont.)

John 11:1-45; L34A

But if one walks at night, he stumbles,
    because the light is not in him."
He said this, and then told them,
    "Our friend Lazarus is asleep,
    but I am going to awaken him."
So the disciples said to him,
    "Master, if he is asleep, he will be saved."
But Jesus was talking about his death,
    while they thought that he meant ordinary sleep.
So then Jesus said to them clearly,
    "Lazarus has died.
And I am glad for you that I was not there,
    that you may believe.
Let us go to him."
So Thomas, called Didymus, said to his fellow disciples,
    "Let us also go to die with him."

When Jesus arrived, he found that Lazarus
    had already been in the tomb for four days.
Now Bethany was near Jerusalem, only about two miles away.
And many of the Jews had come to Martha and Mary
    to comfort them about their brother.
When Martha heard that Jesus was coming,
    she went to meet him;
    but Mary sat at home.
Martha said to Jesus,
    "Lord, if you had been here,
    my brother would not have died.
But even now I know that whatever you ask of God,
    God will give you."
Jesus said to her,
    "Your brother will rise."
Martha said to him,
    "I know he will rise,
    in the resurrection on the last day."
Jesus told her,
    "I am the resurrection and the life;
    whoever believes in me, even if he dies, will live,
    and everyone who lives and believes in me will never die.
Do you believe this?"
She said to him, "Yes, Lord.
I have come to believe that you are the Christ, the Son of God,
    the one who is coming into the world."

When she had said this,
    she went and called her sister Mary secretly, saying,
    "The teacher is here and is asking for you."
As soon as she heard this,
    she rose quickly and went to him.

For Jesus had not yet come into the village,
    but was still where Martha had met him.
So when the Jews who were with her in the house comforting her
    saw Mary get up quickly and go out,
    they followed her,
    presuming that she was going to the tomb to weep there.
When Mary came to where Jesus was and saw him,
    she fell at his feet and said to him,
    "Lord, if you had been here,
    my brother would not have died."
When Jesus saw her weeping and the Jews who had come with her
        weeping,
    he became perturbed and deeply troubled, and said,
    "Where have you laid him?"
They said to him, "Sir, come and see."
And Jesus wept.
So the Jews said, "See how he loved him."
But some of them said,
    "Could not the one who opened the eyes of the blind man
    have done something so that this man would not have died?"

So Jesus, perturbed again, came to the tomb.
It was a cave, and a stone lay across it.
Jesus said, "Take away the stone."
Martha, the dead man's sister, said to him,
    "Lord, by now there will be a stench;
    he has been dead for four days."
Jesus said to her,
    "Did I not tell you that if you believe
    you will see the glory of God?"
So they took away the stone.
And Jesus raised his eyes and said,
    "Father, I thank you for hearing me.
I know that you always hear me;
    but because of the crowd here I have said this,
    that they may believe that you sent me."
And when he had said this,
    he cried out in a loud voice,
    "Lazarus, come out!"
The dead man came out,
    tied hand and foot with burial bands,
    and his face was wrapped in a cloth.
So Jesus said to them,
    "Untie him and let him go."

Now many of the Jews who had come to Mary
    and seen what he had done began to believe in him.

Fifth Sunday of Lent, *April 10, 2011*

Gospel
John 11:3-7, 17, 20-27, 33b-45; L34A

The sisters of Lazarus sent word to Jesus saying,
"Master, the one you love is ill."
When Jesus heard this he said,
"This illness is not to end in death,
but is for the glory of God,
that the Son of God may be glorified through it."
Now Jesus loved Martha and her sister and Lazarus.
So when he heard that he was ill,
he remained for two days in the place where he was.
Then after this he said to his disciples,
"Let us go back to Judea."

When Jesus arrived, he found that Lazarus
had already been in the tomb for four days.
When Martha heard that Jesus was coming,
she went to meet him;
but Mary sat at home.
Martha said to Jesus,
"Lord, if you had been here,
my brother would not have died.
But even now I know that whatever you ask of God,
God will give you."
Jesus said to her,
"Your brother will rise."
Martha said,
"I know he will rise,
in the resurrection on the last day."
Jesus told her,
"I am the resurrection and the life;
whoever believes in me, even if he dies, will live,
and everyone who lives and believes in me will never die.
Do you believe this?"
She said to him, "Yes, Lord.
I have come to believe that you are the Christ, the Son of God,
the one who is coming into the world."

He became perturbed and deeply troubled, and said,
"Where have you laid him?"
They said to him, "Sir, come and see."
And Jesus wept.
So the Jews said, "See how he loved him."
But some of them said,
"Could not the one who opened the eyes of the blind man
have done something so that this man would not have died?"

So Jesus, perturbed again, came to the tomb.
It was a cave, and a stone lay across it.
Jesus said, "Take away the stone."
Martha, the dead man's sister, said to him,
"Lord, by now there will be a stench;
he has been dead for four days."
Jesus said to her,
"Did I not tell you that if you believe
you will see the glory of God?"
So they took away the stone.
And Jesus raised his eyes and said,
"Father, I thank you for hearing me.
I know that you always hear me;
but because of the crowd here I have said this,
that they may believe that you sent me."
And when he had said this,
he cried out in a loud voice,
"Lazarus, come out!"
The dead man came out,
tied hand and foot with burial bands,
and his face was wrapped in a cloth.
So Jesus said to them,
"Untie him and let him go."

Now many of the Jews who had come to Mary
and seen what he had done began to believe in him.

Palm Sunday of the Lord's Passion, *April 17, 2011*

Gospel (cont.) at the procession with palms
Matt 21:1-11; L37A

The crowds preceding him and those following
kept crying out and saying:
"Hosanna to the Son of David;
blessed is he who comes in the name of the Lord;
hosanna in the highest."
And when he entered Jerusalem
the whole city was shaken and asked, "Who is this?"
And the crowds replied,
"This is Jesus the prophet, from Nazareth in Galilee."

Gospel at Mass
Matt 26:14–27:66; L38A

One of the Twelve, who was called Judas Iscariot, went to the chief priests and said, "What are you willing to give me if I hand him over to you?" They paid him thirty pieces of silver, and from that time on he looked for an opportunity to hand him over.

On the first day of the Feast of Unleavened Bread, the disciples approached Jesus and said, "Where do you want us to prepare for you to eat the Passover?" He said, "Go into the city to a certain man and tell him, 'The teacher says, "My appointed time draws near; in your house I shall celebrate the Passover with my disciples."'" The disciples then did as Jesus had ordered, and prepared the Passover.

When it was evening, he reclined at table with the Twelve. And while they were eating, he said, "Amen, I say to you, one of you will betray me." Deeply distressed at this, they began to say to him one after another, "Surely it is not I, Lord?" He said in reply, "He who has dipped his hand into the dish with me is the one who will betray me. The Son of Man indeed goes, as it is written of him, but woe to that man by whom the Son of Man is betrayed. It would be better for that man if he had never been born." Then Judas, his betrayer, said in reply, "Surely it is not I, Rabbi?" He answered, "You have said so."

While they were eating, Jesus took bread, said the blessing, broke it, and giving it to his disciples said, "Take and eat; this is my body." Then he took a cup, gave thanks, and gave it to them, saying, "Drink from it, all of you, for this is my blood of the covenant, which will be shed on behalf of many for the forgiveness of sins. I tell you, from now on I shall not drink this fruit of the vine until the day when I drink it with you new in the kingdom of my Father." Then, after singing a hymn, they went out to the Mount of Olives.

Then Jesus said to them, "This night all of you will have your faith in me shaken, for it is written: / *I will strike the shepherd, / and the sheep of the flock will be dispersed;* / but after I have been raised up, I shall go before you to Galilee." Peter said to him in reply, "Though all may have their faith in you shaken, mine will never be." Jesus said to him, "Amen, I say to you, this very night before the cock crows, you will deny me three times." Peter said to him, "Even though I should have to die with you, I will not deny you." And all the disciples spoke likewise.

Then Jesus came with them to a place called Gethsemane, and he said to his disciples, "Sit here while I go over there and pray." He took along Peter and the two sons of Zebedee, and began to feel sorrow and distress. Then he said to them, "My soul is sorrowful even to death. Remain here and keep watch with me." He advanced a little and fell prostrate in prayer, saying, "My Father, if it is possible, let this cup pass from me; yet, not as I will, but as you will." When he returned to his disciples he found them asleep. He said to Peter, "So you could not keep watch with me for one hour? Watch and pray that you may not undergo the test. The spirit is willing, but the flesh is weak." Withdrawing a second time, he prayed again, "My Father, if it is not possible that this cup pass without my drinking it, your will be done!" Then he returned once more and found them asleep, for they could not keep their eyes open. He left them and withdrew again and prayed a third time, saying the same thing again. Then he returned to his disciples and said to them, "Are you still sleeping and taking your rest? Behold, the hour is at hand when the Son of Man is to be handed over to sinners. Get up, let us go. Look, my betrayer is at hand."

While he was still speaking, Judas, one of the Twelve, arrived, accompanied by a large crowd, with swords and clubs, who had come from the chief priests and the elders of the people. His betrayer had arranged a sign with them, saying, "The man I shall kiss is the one;

arrest him." Immediately he went over to Jesus and said, "Hail, Rabbi!" and he kissed him. Jesus answered him, "Friend, do what you have come for." Then stepping forward they laid hands on Jesus and arrested him. And behold, one of those who accompanied Jesus put his hand to his sword, drew it, and struck the high priest's servant, cutting off his ear. Then Jesus said to him, "Put your sword back into its sheath, for all who take the sword will perish by the sword. Do you think that I cannot call upon my Father and he will not provide me at this moment with more than twelve legions of angels? But then how would the Scriptures be fulfilled which say that it must come to pass in this way?" At that hour Jesus said to the crowds, "Have you come out as against a robber, with swords and clubs to seize me? Day after day I sat teaching in the temple area, yet you did not arrest me. But all this has come to pass that the writings of the prophets may be fulfilled." Then all the disciples left him and fled.

Those who had arrested Jesus led him away to Caiaphas the high priest, where the scribes and the elders were assembled. Peter was following him at a distance as far as the high priest's courtyard, and going inside he sat down with the servants to see the outcome. The chief priests and the entire Sanhedrin kept trying to obtain false testimony against Jesus in order to put him to death, but they found none, though many false witnesses came forward. Finally two came forward who stated, "This man said, 'I can destroy the temple of God and within three days rebuild it.'" The high priest rose and addressed him, "Have you no answer? What are these men testifying against you?" But Jesus was silent. Then the high priest said to him, "I order you to tell us under oath before the living God whether you are the Christ, the Son of God." Jesus said to him in reply, "You have said so. But I tell you: / From now on you will see 'the Son of Man / seated at the right hand of the Power' / and 'coming on the clouds of heaven.'" / Then the high priest tore his robes and said, "He has blasphemed! What further need have we of witnesses? You have now heard the blasphemy; what is your opinion?" They said in reply, "He deserves to die!" Then they spat in his face and struck him, while some slapped him, saying, "Prophesy for us, Christ: who is it that struck you?"

Now Peter was sitting outside in the courtyard. One of the maids came over to him and said, "You too were with Jesus the Galilean." But he denied it in front of everyone, saying, "I do not know what you are talking about!" As he went out to the gate, another girl saw him and said to those who were there, "This man was with Jesus the Nazarene." Again he denied it with an oath, "I do not know the man!" A little later the bystanders came over and said to Peter, "Surely you too are one of them; even your speech gives you away." At that he began to curse and to swear, "I do not know the man." And immediately a cock crowed. Then Peter remembered the word that Jesus had spoken: "Before the cock crows you will deny me three times." He went out and began to weep bitterly.

When it was morning, all the chief priests and the elders of the people took counsel against Jesus to put him to death. They bound him, led him away, and handed him over to Pilate, the governor.

Then Judas, his betrayer, seeing that Jesus had been condemned, deeply regretted what he had done. He returned the thirty pieces of silver to the chief priests and elders, saying, "I have sinned in betraying innocent blood." They said, "What is that to us? Look to it yourself." Flinging the money into the temple, he departed and went off and hanged himself. The chief priests gathered up the money, but said, "It is not lawful to deposit this in the temple treasury, for it is the price of blood." After consultation, they used it to buy the potter's field as a burial place for foreigners. That is why that field even today is called the Field of Blood. Then was fulfilled what had been said through Jeremiah the prophet, *And they took the thirty pieces of silver, the value of a man with a price on his head, a price set by some of the Israelites, and they paid it out for the potter's field just as the Lord had commanded me.*

Now Jesus stood before the governor, and he questioned him, "Are you the king of the Jews?" Jesus said, "You say so." And when he was accused by the chief priests and elders, he made no answer. Then Pilate said to him, "Do you not hear how many things they are testifying against you?" But he did not answer him one word, so that the governor was greatly amazed.

Now on the occasion of the feast the governor was accustomed to release to the crowd one prisoner whom they wished. And at that time they had a notorious prisoner called Barabbas. So when they had assembled, Pilate said to them, "Which one do you want me to release to you, Barabbas, or Jesus called Christ?" For he knew that it was out of envy that they had handed him over. While he was still seated on the bench, his wife sent him a message, "Have nothing to do with that righteous man. I suffered much in a dream today because of him." The chief priests and the elders persuaded the crowds to ask for Barabbas but to destroy Jesus. The governor said to them in reply, "Which of the two do you want me to release to you?" They answered, "Barabbas!" Pilate said to them, "Then what shall I do with Jesus called Christ?" They all said, "Let him be crucified!" But he said, "Why? What evil has he done?" They only shouted the louder, "Let him be crucified!" When Pilate saw that he was not succeeding at all, but that a riot was breaking out instead, he took water and washed his hands in the sight of the crowd, saying, "I am innocent of this man's blood. Look to it yourselves." And the whole people said in reply, "His blood be upon us and upon our children." Then he released Barabbas to them, but after he had Jesus scourged, he handed him over to be crucified.

Then the soldiers of the governor took Jesus inside the praetorium and gathered the whole cohort around him. They stripped off his clothes and threw a scarlet military cloak about him. Weaving a crown out of thorns, they placed it on his head, and a reed in his right hand. And kneeling before him, they mocked him, saying, "Hail, King of the Jews!" They spat upon him and took the reed and kept striking him on the head. And when they had mocked him, they stripped him of the cloak, dressed him in his own clothes, and led him off to crucify him.

As they were going out, they met a Cyrenian named Simon; this man they pressed into service to carry his cross.

And when they came to a place called Golgotha —which means Place of the Skull—, they gave Jesus wine to drink mixed with gall. But when he had tasted it, he refused to drink. After they had crucified him, they divided his garments by casting lots; then they sat down and kept watch over him there. And they placed over his head the written charge against him: This is Jesus, the King of the Jews. Two revolu-

tionaries were crucified with him, one on his right and the other on his left. Those passing by reviled him, shaking their heads and saying, "You who would destroy the temple and rebuild it in three days, save yourself, if you are the Son of God, and come down from the cross!" Likewise the chief priests with the scribes and elders mocked him and said, "He saved others; he cannot save himself. So he is the king of Israel! Let him come down from the cross now, and we will believe in him. He trusted in God; let him deliver him now if he wants him. For he said, 'I am the Son of God.'" The revolutionaries who were crucified with him also kept abusing him in the same way.

From noon onward, darkness came over the whole land until three in the afternoon. And about three o'clock Jesus cried out in a loud voice, *"Eli, Eli, lema sabachthani?"* which means, "My God, my God, why have you forsaken me?" Some of the bystanders who heard it said, "This one is calling for Elijah." Immediately one of them ran to get a sponge; he soaked it in wine, and putting it on a reed, gave it to him to drink. But the rest said, "Wait, let us see if Elijah comes to save him." But Jesus cried out again in a loud voice, and gave up his spirit.

(Here all kneel and pause for a short time.)

And behold, the veil of the sanctuary was torn in two from top to bottom. The earth quaked, rocks were split, tombs were opened, and the bodies of many saints who had fallen asleep were raised. And coming forth from their tombs after his resurrection, they entered the holy city and appeared to many. The centurion and the men with him who were keeping watch over Jesus feared greatly when they saw the earthquake and all that was happening, and they said, "Truly, this was the Son of God!" There were many women there, looking on from a distance, who had followed Jesus from Galilee, ministering to him. Among them were Mary Magdalene and Mary the mother of James and Joseph, and the mother of the sons of Zebedee.

When it was evening, there came a rich man from Arimathea named Joseph, who was himself a disciple of Jesus. He went to Pilate and asked for the body of Jesus; then Pilate ordered it to be handed over. Taking the body, Joseph wrapped it in clean linen and laid it in his new tomb that he had hewn in the rock. Then he rolled a huge stone across the entrance to the tomb and departed. But Mary Magdalene and the other Mary remained sitting there, facing the tomb.

The next day, the one following the day of preparation, the chief priests and the Pharisees gathered before Pilate and said, "Sir, we remember that this impostor while still alive said, 'After three days I will be raised up.' Give orders, then, that the grave be secured until the third day, lest his disciples come and steal him and say to the people, 'He has been raised from the dead.' This last imposture would be worse than the first." Pilate said to them, "The guard is yours; go, secure it as best you can." So they went and secured the tomb by fixing a seal to the stone and setting the guard.

or Matt 27:11-54; L38A

Jesus stood before the governor, Pontius Pilate, who questioned him,
"Are you the king of the Jews?"
Jesus said, "You say so."
And when he was accused by the chief priests and elders,
he made no answer.
Then Pilate said to him,
"Do you not hear how many things they are testifying against you?"
But he did not answer him one word,
so that the governor was greatly amazed.

Now on the occasion of the feast
the governor was accustomed to release to the crowd
one prisoner whom they wished.
And at that time they had a notorious prisoner called Barabbas.
So when they had assembled, Pilate said to them,
"Which one do you want me to release to you,
Barabbas, or Jesus called Christ?"
For he knew that it was out of envy
that they had handed him over.
While he was still seated on the bench,
his wife sent him a message,
"Have nothing to do with that righteous man.
I suffered much in a dream today because of him."
The chief priests and the elders persuaded the crowds
to ask for Barabbas but to destroy Jesus.
The governor said to them in reply,
"Which of the two do you want me to release to you?"
They answered, "Barabbas!"
Pilate said to them,
"Then what shall I do with Jesus called Christ?"
They all said,
"Let him be crucified!"
But he said,
"Why? What evil has he done?"
They only shouted the louder,
"Let him be crucified!"
When Pilate saw that he was not succeeding at all,
but that a riot was breaking out instead,
he took water and washed his hands in the sight of the crowd,
saying, "I am innocent of this man's blood.
Look to it yourselves."
And the whole people said in reply,
"His blood be upon us and upon our children."
Then he released Barabbas to them,
but after he had Jesus scourged,
he handed him over to be crucified.

Then the soldiers of the governor took Jesus inside the praetorium
and gathered the whole cohort around him.
They stripped off his clothes
and threw a scarlet military cloak about him.
Weaving a crown out of thorns, they placed it on his head,
and a reed in his right hand.
And kneeling before him, they mocked him, saying,
"Hail, King of the Jews!"
They spat upon him and took the reed
and kept striking him on the head.
And when they had mocked him,
they stripped him of the cloak,

dressed him in his own clothes,
and led him off to crucify him.
As they were going out, they met a Cyrenian named Simon;
this man they pressed into service
to carry his cross.

And when they came to a place called Golgotha
—which means Place of the Skull—,
they gave Jesus wine to drink mixed with gall.
But when he had tasted it, he refused to drink.
After they had crucified him,
they divided his garments by casting lots;
then they sat down and kept watch over him there.
And they placed over his head the written charge against him:
This is Jesus, the King of the Jews.
Two revolutionaries were crucified with him,
one on his right and the other on his left.
Those passing by reviled him, shaking their heads and saying,
"You who would destroy the temple and rebuild it in three days,
save yourself, if you are the Son of God,
and come down from the cross!"
Likewise the chief priests with the scribes and elders mocked him
and said,
"He saved others; he cannot save himself.
So he is the king of Israel!
Let him come down from the cross now,
and we will believe in him.
He trusted in God;
let him deliver him now if he wants him.
For he said, 'I am the Son of God.'"
The revolutionaries who were crucified with him
also kept abusing him in the same way.
From noon onward, darkness came over the whole land
until three in the afternoon.
And about three o'clock Jesus cried out in a loud voice,
"Eli, Eli, lema sabachthani?"
which means, "My God, my God, why have you forsaken me?"
Some of the bystanders who heard it said,
"This one is calling for Elijah."
Immediately one of them ran to get a sponge;
he soaked it in wine, and putting it on a reed,
gave it to him to drink.
But the rest said,
"Wait, let us see if Elijah comes to save him."
But Jesus cried out again in a loud voice,
and gave up his spirit.

(Here all kneel and pause for a short time.)

And behold, the veil of the sanctuary
was torn in two from top to bottom.
The earth quaked, rocks were split, tombs were opened,
and the bodies of many saints who had fallen asleep were raised.
And coming forth from their tombs after his resurrection,
they entered the holy city and appeared to many.
The centurion and the men with him who were keeping watch over Jesus
feared greatly when they saw the earthquake
and all that was happening, and they said,
"Truly, this was the Son of God!"

Gospel (cont.)
John 13:1-15; L39ABC

So when he had washed their feet
    and put his garments back on and reclined at table again,
    he said to them, "Do you realize what I have done for you?
You call me 'teacher' and 'master,' and rightly so, for indeed I am.
If I, therefore, the master and teacher, have washed your feet,
    you ought to wash one another's feet.
I have given you a model to follow,
    so that as I have done for you, you should also do."

FIRST READING
Exod 12:1-8, 11-14

The LORD said to Moses and Aaron in the
        land of Egypt,
    "This month shall stand at the head of your
        calendar;
    you shall reckon it the first month of the
        year.
Tell the whole community of Israel:
    On the tenth of this month every one of
        your families
    must procure for itself a lamb, one apiece
        for each household.
If a family is too small for a whole lamb,
    it shall join the nearest household in
        procuring one
    and shall share in the lamb
    in proportion to the number of persons who
        partake of it.
The lamb must be a year-old male and
        without blemish.
You may take it from either the sheep or the
        goats.
You shall keep it until the fourteenth day of
        this month,
    and then, with the whole assembly of Israel
        present,
    it shall be slaughtered during the evening
        twilight.
They shall take some of its blood
    and apply it to the two doorposts and the
        lintel
    of every house in which they partake of the
        lamb.
That same night they shall eat its roasted
        flesh
    with unleavened bread and bitter herbs.

"This is how you are to eat it:
    with your loins girt, sandals on your feet
        and your staff in hand,
    you shall eat like those who are in flight.

It is the Passover of the LORD.
For on this same night I will go through Egypt,
    striking down every firstborn of the land,
        both man and beast,
    and executing judgment on all the gods of
        Egypt—I, the LORD!
But the blood will mark the houses where you
    are.
Seeing the blood, I will pass over you;
    thus, when I strike the land of Egypt,
    no destructive blow will come upon you.

"This day shall be a memorial feast for you,
    which all your generations shall celebrate
    with pilgrimage to the LORD, as a perpetual
        institution."

RESPONSORIAL PSALM
Ps 116:12-13, 15-16bc, 17-18

R⃓. (cf. 1 Cor 10:16) Our blessing-cup is a communion with the Blood of Christ.

How shall I make a return to the LORD
    for all the good he has done for me?
The cup of salvation I will take up,
    and I will call upon the name of the LORD.

R⃓. Our blessing-cup is a communion with the Blood of Christ.

Precious in the eyes of the LORD
    is the death of his faithful ones.
I am your servant, the son of your handmaid;
    you have loosed my bonds.

R⃓. Our blessing-cup is a communion with the Blood of Christ.

To you will I offer sacrifice of thanksgiving,
    and I will call upon the name of the LORD.
My vows to the LORD I will pay
    in the presence of all his people.

R⃓. Our blessing-cup is a communion with the Blood of Christ.

SECOND READING
1 Cor 11:23-26

Brothers and sisters:
I received from the Lord what I also handed
        on to you,
    that the Lord Jesus, on the night he was
        handed over,
    took bread, and, after he had given thanks,
    broke it and said, "This is my body that is
        for you.
Do this in remembrance of me."
In the same way also the cup, after supper,
        saying,
    "This cup is the new covenant in my blood.
Do this, as often as you drink it, in
    remembrance of me."
For as often as you eat this bread and drink
        the cup,
    you proclaim the death of the Lord until he
        comes.

Gospel (cont.)
John 18:1–19:42; L40ABC

Then Simon Peter, who had a sword, drew it,
    struck the high priest's slave, and cut off his right ear.
The slave's name was Malchus.
Jesus said to Peter,
    "Put your sword into its scabbard.
Shall I not drink the cup that the Father gave me?"
So the band of soldiers, the tribune, and the Jewish guards seized Jesus,
    bound him, and brought him to Annas first.
He was the father-in-law of Caiaphas,
    who was high priest that year.
It was Caiaphas who had counseled the Jews
    that it was better that one man should die rather than the people.

Simon Peter and another disciple followed Jesus.
Now the other disciple was known to the high priest,
    and he entered the courtyard of the high priest with Jesus.
But Peter stood at the gate outside.
So the other disciple, the acquaintance of the high priest,
    went out and spoke to the gatekeeper and brought Peter in.
Then the maid who was the gatekeeper said to Peter,
    "You are not one of this man's disciples, are you?"
He said, "I am not."
Now the slaves and the guards were standing around a charcoal fire
    that they had made, because it was cold,
    and were warming themselves.
Peter was also standing there keeping warm.

The high priest questioned Jesus
    about his disciples and about his doctrine.
Jesus answered him,
    "I have spoken publicly to the world.
I have always taught in a synagogue
    or in the temple area where all the Jews gather,
    and in secret I have said nothing. Why ask me?
Ask those who heard me what I said to them.
They know what I said."
When he had said this,
    one of the temple guards standing there struck Jesus and said,
    "Is this the way you answer the high priest?"
Jesus answered him,
    "If I have spoken wrongly, testify to the wrong;
    but if I have spoken rightly, why do you strike me?"
Then Annas sent him bound to Caiaphas the high priest.

Now Simon Peter was standing there keeping warm.
And they said to him,
    "You are not one of his disciples, are you?"
He denied it and said,
    "I am not."
One of the slaves of the high priest,
    a relative of the one whose ear Peter had cut off, said,
    "Didn't I see you in the garden with him?"
Again Peter denied it.
And immediately the cock crowed.

Then they brought Jesus from Caiaphas to the praetorium.
It was morning.
And they themselves did not enter the praetorium,
    in order not to be defiled so that they could eat the Passover.

So Pilate came out to them and said,
    "What charge do you bring against this man?"
They answered and said to him,
    "If he were not a criminal,
    we would not have handed him over to you."
At this, Pilate said to them,
    "Take him yourselves, and judge him according to your law."
The Jews answered him,
    "We do not have the right to execute anyone,"
    in order that the word of Jesus might be fulfilled
    that he said indicating the kind of death he would die.
So Pilate went back into the praetorium
    and summoned Jesus and said to him,
    "Are you the King of the Jews?"
Jesus answered,
    "Do you say this on your own
    or have others told you about me?"
Pilate answered,
    "I am not a Jew, am I?
Your own nation and the chief priests handed you over to me.
What have you done?"
Jesus answered,
    "My kingdom does not belong to this world.
If my kingdom did belong to this world,
    my attendants would be fighting
    to keep me from being handed over to the Jews.
But as it is, my kingdom is not here."
So Pilate said to him,
    "Then you are a king?"
Jesus answered,
    "You say I am a king.
For this I was born and for this I came into the world,
    to testify to the truth.
Everyone who belongs to the truth listens to my voice."
Pilate said to him, "What is truth?"

When he had said this,
    he again went out to the Jews and said to them,
    "I find no guilt in him.
But you have a custom that I release one prisoner to you at Passover.
Do you want me to release to you the King of the Jews?"
They cried out again,
    "Not this one but Barabbas!"
Now Barabbas was a revolutionary.

Then Pilate took Jesus and had him scourged.
And the soldiers wove a crown out of thorns and placed it on his head,
    and clothed him in a purple cloak,
    and they came to him and said,
    "Hail, King of the Jews!"
And they struck him repeatedly.
Once more Pilate went out and said to them,
    "Look, I am bringing him out to you,
    so that you may know that I find no guilt in him."
So Jesus came out,
    wearing the crown of thorns and the purple cloak.
And he said to them, "Behold, the man!"

When the chief priests and the guards saw him they cried out,
  "Crucify him, crucify him!"
Pilate said to them,
  "Take him yourselves and crucify him.
I find no guilt in him."
The Jews answered,
  "We have a law, and according to that law he ought to die,
  because he made himself the Son of God."
Now when Pilate heard this statement,
  he became even more afraid,
  and went back into the praetorium and said to Jesus,
  "Where are you from?"
Jesus did not answer him.
So Pilate said to him,
  "Do you not speak to me?
Do you not know that I have power to release you
  and I have power to crucify you?"
Jesus answered him,
  "You would have no power over me
  if it had not been given to you from above.
For this reason the one who handed me over to you
  has the greater sin."
Consequently, Pilate tried to release him; but the Jews cried out,
  "If you release him, you are not a Friend of Caesar.
Everyone who makes himself a king opposes Caesar."

When Pilate heard these words he brought Jesus out
  and seated him on the judge's bench
  in the place called Stone Pavement, in Hebrew, Gabbatha.
It was preparation day for Passover, and it was about noon.
And he said to the Jews,
  "Behold, your king!"
They cried out,
  "Take him away, take him away! Crucify him!"
Pilate said to them,
  "Shall I crucify your king?"
The chief priests answered,
  "We have no king but Caesar."
Then he handed him over to them to be crucified.
So they took Jesus, and, carrying the cross himself,
  he went out to what is called the Place of the Skull,
  in Hebrew, Golgotha.
There they crucified him, and with him two others,
  one on either side, with Jesus in the middle.
Pilate also had an inscription written and put on the cross.
It read,
  "Jesus the Nazorean, the King of the Jews."
Now many of the Jews read this inscription,
  because the place where Jesus was crucified was near the city;
  and it was written in Hebrew, Latin, and Greek.
So the chief priests of the Jews said to Pilate,
  "Do not write 'The King of the Jews,'
  but that he said, 'I am the King of the Jews.'"
Pilate answered,
  "What I have written, I have written."

When the soldiers had crucified Jesus,
  they took his clothes and divided them into four shares,
  a share for each soldier.
They also took his tunic, but the tunic was seamless,
  woven in one piece from the top down.
So they said to one another,

"Let's not tear it, but cast lots for it to see whose it will be,"
  in order that the passage of Scripture might be fulfilled that says:
    They divided my garments among them,
      and for my vesture they cast lots.
This is what the soldiers did.
Standing by the cross of Jesus were his mother
  and his mother's sister, Mary the wife of Clopas,
  and Mary of Magdala.
When Jesus saw his mother and the disciple there whom he loved
  he said to his mother, "Woman, behold, your son."
Then he said to the disciple,
  "Behold, your mother."
And from that hour the disciple took her into his home.

After this, aware that everything was now finished,
  in order that the Scripture might be fulfilled,
  Jesus said, "I thirst."
There was a vessel filled with common wine.
So they put a sponge soaked in wine on a sprig of hyssop
  and put it up to his mouth.
When Jesus had taken the wine, he said,
  "It is finished."
And bowing his head, he handed over the spirit.

Here all kneel and pause for a short time.

Now since it was preparation day,
  in order that the bodies might not remain
    on the cross on the sabbath,
  for the sabbath day of that week was a solemn one,
  the Jews asked Pilate that their legs be broken
  and that they be taken down.
So the soldiers came and broke the legs of the first
  and then of the other one who was crucified with Jesus.
But when they came to Jesus and saw that he was already dead,
  they did not break his legs,
  but one soldier thrust his lance into his side,
  and immediately blood and water flowed out.
An eyewitness has testified, and his testimony is true;
  he knows that he is speaking the truth,
  so that you also may come to believe.
For this happened so that the Scripture passage might be fulfilled:
  Not a bone of it will be broken.
And again another passage says:
  They will look upon him whom they have pierced.

After this, Joseph of Arimathea,
  secretly a disciple of Jesus for fear of the Jews,
  asked Pilate if he could remove the body of Jesus.
And Pilate permitted it.
So he came and took his body.
Nicodemus, the one who had first come to him at night,
  also came bringing a mixture of myrrh and aloes
  weighing about one hundred pounds.
They took the body of Jesus
  and bound it with burial cloths along with the spices,
  according to the Jewish burial custom.
Now in the place where he had been crucified there was a garden,
  and in the garden a new tomb, in which no one had yet been
    buried.
So they laid Jesus there because of the Jewish preparation day;
  for the tomb was close by.

FIRST READING
Isa 52:13–53:12

See, my servant shall prosper,
  he shall be raised high and greatly exalted.
Even as many were amazed at him—
  so marred was his look beyond human
    semblance
  and his appearance beyond that of the sons
    of man—
so shall he startle many nations,
  because of him kings shall stand speechless;
for those who have not been told shall see,
  those who have not heard shall ponder it.

Who would believe what we have heard?
  To whom has the arm of the LORD been
    revealed?
He grew up like a sapling before him,
  like a shoot from the parched earth;
there was in him no stately bearing to make
    us look at him,
  nor appearance that would attract us to him.
He was spurned and avoided by people,
  a man of suffering, accustomed to infirmity,
one of those from whom people hide their faces,
  spurned, and we held him in no esteem.

Yet it was our infirmities that he bore,
  our sufferings that he endured,
while we thought of him as stricken,
  as one smitten by God and afflicted.
But he was pierced for our offenses,
  crushed for our sins;
upon him was the chastisement that makes
    us whole,
  by his stripes we were healed.
We had all gone astray like sheep,
  each following his own way;
but the LORD laid upon him
  the guilt of us all.

Though he was harshly treated, he submitted
  and opened not his mouth;
like a lamb led to the slaughter
  or a sheep before the shearers,
  he was silent and opened not his mouth.
Oppressed and condemned, he was taken away,
  and who would have thought any more of
    his destiny?
When he was cut off from the land of the living,
  and smitten for the sin of his people,
a grave was assigned him among the wicked
  and a burial place with evildoers,
though he had done no wrong
  nor spoken any falsehood.
But the LORD was pleased
  to crush him in infirmity.

If he gives his life as an offering for sin,
  he shall see his descendants in a long life,
  and the will of the LORD shall be
    accomplished through him.

Because of his affliction
  he shall see the light
    in fullness of days;
through his suffering, my servant shall justify
    many,
  and their guilt he shall bear.
Therefore I will give him his portion among
    the great,
  and he shall divide the spoils with the
    mighty,
because he surrendered himself to death
  and was counted among the wicked;
and he shall take away the sins of many,
  and win pardon for their offenses.

RESPONSORIAL PSALM
Ps 31:2, 6, 12-13, 15-16, 17, 25

℟. (Luke 23:46) Father, into your hands I
commend my spirit.

In you, O LORD, I take refuge;
  let me never be put to shame.
In your justice rescue me.
  Into your hands I commend my spirit;
you will redeem me, O LORD, O faithful God.

℟. Father, into your hands I commend my
spirit.

For all my foes I am an object of reproach,
  a laughingstock to my neighbors, and a
    dread to my friends;
  they who see me abroad flee from me.
I am forgotten like the unremembered dead;
  I am like a dish that is broken.

℟. Father, into your hands I commend my
spirit.

But my trust is in you, O LORD;
  I say, "You are my God.
In your hands is my destiny; rescue me
  from the clutches of my enemies and my
    persecutors."

℟. Father, into your hands I commend my
spirit.

Let your face shine upon your servant;
  save me in your kindness.
Take courage and be stouthearted,
  all you who hope in the LORD.

℟. Father, into your hands I commend my
spirit.

SECOND READING
Heb 4:14-16; 5:7-9

Brothers and sisters:
Since we have a great high priest who has
  passed through the heavens,
Jesus, the Son of God,
  let us hold fast to our confession.
For we do not have a high priest
  who is unable to sympathize with our
    weaknesses,
  but one who has similarly been tested in
    every way,
  yet without sin.
So let us confidently approach the throne of
    grace
  to receive mercy and to find grace for
    timely help.

In the days when Christ was in the flesh,
  he offered prayers and supplications with
    loud cries and tears
  to the one who was able to save him from
    death,
  and he was heard because of his reverence.
Son though he was, he learned obedience from
    what he suffered;
  and when he was made perfect,
  he became the source of eternal salvation
    for all who obey him.

FIRST READING
Gen 1:1–2:2

In the beginning, when God created the
     heavens and the earth,
  the earth was a formless wasteland, and
     darkness covered the abyss,
  while a mighty wind swept over the waters.

Then God said,
  "Let there be light," and there was light.
God saw how good the light was.
God then separated the light from the darkness.
God called the light "day," and the darkness
     he called "night."
Thus evening came, and morning followed—
     the first day.

Then God said,
  "Let there be a dome in the middle of the
     waters,
  to separate one body of water from the
     other."
And so it happened:
  God made the dome,
  and it separated the water above the dome
     from the water below it.
God called the dome "the sky."
Evening came, and morning followed—the
     second day.

Then God said,
  "Let the water under the sky be gathered
     into a single basin,
  so that the dry land may appear."
And so it happened:
  the water under the sky was gathered into
     its basin,
  and the dry land appeared.
God called the dry land "the earth,"
  and the basin of the water he called "the
     sea."
God saw how good it was.
Then God said,
  "Let the earth bring forth vegetation:
  every kind of plant that bears seed
  and every kind of fruit tree on earth
  that bears fruit with its seed in it."
And so it happened:
  the earth brought forth every kind of plant
     that bears seed
  and every kind of fruit tree on earth
  that bears fruit with its seed in it.
God saw how good it was.
Evening came, and morning followed—the
     third day.

Then God said:
  "Let there be lights in the dome of the sky,
  to separate day from night.
Let them mark the fixed times, the days and
     the years,

and serve as luminaries in the dome of the
     sky,
  to shed light upon the earth."
And so it happened:
  God made the two great lights,
  the greater one to govern the day,
  and the lesser one to govern the night;
  and he made the stars.
God set them in the dome of the sky,
  to shed light upon the earth,
  to govern the day and the night,
  and to separate the light from the darkness.
God saw how good it was.
Evening came, and morning followed—the
     fourth day.

Then God said,
  "Let the water teem with an abundance of
     living creatures,
  and on the earth let birds fly beneath the
     dome of the sky."
And so it happened:
  God created the great sea monsters
  and all kinds of swimming creatures with
     which the water teems,
  and all kinds of winged birds.
God saw how good it was, and God blessed
     them, saying,
  "Be fertile, multiply, and fill the water of
     the seas;
  and let the birds multiply on the earth."
Evening came, and morning followed—the
     fifth day.

Then God said,
  "Let the earth bring forth all kinds of living
     creatures:
  cattle, creeping things, and wild animals of
     all kinds."
And so it happened:
  God made all kinds of wild animals, all
     kinds of cattle,
  and all kinds of creeping things of the earth.
God saw how good it was.
Then God said:
  "Let us make man in our image, after our
     likeness.
Let them have dominion over the fish of the sea,
  the birds of the air, and the cattle,
  and over all the wild animals
  and all the creatures that crawl on the
     ground."
God created man in his image;
     in the image of God he created him;
     male and female he created them.
God blessed them, saying:
  "Be fertile and multiply;
  fill the earth and subdue it.
Have dominion over the fish of the sea, the
     birds of the air,

and all the living things that move on the
     earth."
God also said:
  "See, I give you every seed-bearing plant all
     over the earth
  and every tree that has seed-bearing fruit
     on it to be your food;
  and to all the animals of the land, all the
     birds of the air,
  and all the living creatures that crawl on
     the ground,
  I give all the green plants for food."
And so it happened.
God looked at everything he had made, and
     he found it very good.
Evening came, and morning followed—the
     sixth day.

Thus the heavens and the earth and all their
     array were completed.
Since on the seventh day God was finished
     with the work he had been doing,
  he rested on the seventh day from all the
     work he had undertaken.

or

Gen 1:1, 26-31a

In the beginning, when God created the
     heavens and the earth,
  God said: "Let us make man in our image,
     after our likeness.
Let them have dominion over the fish of the sea,
  the birds of the air, and the cattle,
  and over all the wild animals
  and all the creatures that crawl on the
     ground."
God created man in his image;
     in the image of God he created him;
     male and female he created them.
God blessed them, saying:
  "Be fertile and multiply;
  fill the earth and subdue it.
Have dominion over the fish of the sea, the
     birds of the air,
  and all the living things that move on the
     earth."
God also said:
  "See, I give you every seed-bearing plant all
     over the earth
  and every tree that has seed-bearing fruit
     on it to be your food;
  and to all the animals of the land, all the
     birds of the air,
  and all the living creatures that crawl on
     the ground,
  I give all the green plants for food."
And so it happened.
God looked at everything he had made, and
     found it very good.

RESPONSORIAL PSALM
Ps 104:1-2, 5-6, 10, 12, 13-14, 24, 35

R℣. (30) Lord, send out your Spirit, and renew
the face of the earth.

Bless the LORD, O my soul!
  O LORD, my God, you are great indeed!
You are clothed with majesty and glory,
  robed in light as with a cloak.

R℣. Lord, send out your Spirit, and renew the
face of the earth.

You fixed the earth upon its foundation,
  not to be moved forever;
with the ocean, as with a garment, you
    covered it;
  above the mountains the waters stood.

R℣. Lord, send out your Spirit, and renew the
face of the earth.

You send forth springs into the watercourses
  that wind among the mountains.
Beside them the birds of heaven dwell;
  from among the branches they send forth
    their song.

R℣. Lord, send out your Spirit, and renew the
face of the earth.

You water the mountains from your palace;
  the earth is replete with the fruit of your
    works.
You raise grass for the cattle,
  and vegetation for man's use,
producing bread from the earth.

R℣. Lord, send out your Spirit, and renew the
face of the earth.

How manifold are your works, O LORD!
  In wisdom you have wrought them all—
  the earth is full of your creatures.
Bless the LORD, O my soul!

R℣. Lord, send out your Spirit, and renew the
face of the earth.

or

Ps 33:4-5, 6-7, 12-13, 20–22

R℣. (5b) The earth is full of the goodness of the
Lord.

Upright is the word of the LORD,
  and all his works are trustworthy.
He loves justice and right;
  of the kindness of the LORD the earth is full.

R℣. The earth is full of the goodness of the Lord.

By the word of the LORD the heavens were
    made;
  by the breath of his mouth all their host.
He gathers the waters of the sea as in a
    flask;
  in cellars he confines the deep.

R℣. The earth is full of the goodness of the Lord.

Blessed the nation whose God is the LORD,
  the people he has chosen for his own
    inheritance.
From heaven the LORD looks down;
  he sees all mankind.

R℣. The earth is full of the goodness of the Lord.

Our soul waits for the LORD,
  who is our help and our shield.
May your kindness, O LORD, be upon us
  who have put our hope in you.

R℣. The earth is full of the goodness of the Lord.

SECOND READING
Gen 22:1-18

God put Abraham to the test.
He called to him, "Abraham!"
"Here I am," he replied.
Then God said:
  "Take your son Isaac, your only one, whom
    you love,
  and go to the land of Moriah.
There you shall offer him up as a holocaust
  on a height that I will point out to you."
Early the next morning Abraham saddled his
    donkey,
  took with him his son Isaac and two of his
    servants as well,
  and with the wood that he had cut for the
    holocaust,
  set out for the place of which God had told
    him.

On the third day Abraham got sight of the
    place from afar.
Then he said to his servants:
  "Both of you stay here with the donkey,
  while the boy and I go on over yonder.
We will worship and then come back to you."
Thereupon Abraham took the wood for the
    holocaust
  and laid it on his son Isaac's shoulders,
  while he himself carried the fire and the
    knife.
As the two walked on together, Isaac spoke to
    his father Abraham:
  "Father!" Isaac said.
"Yes, son," he replied.
Isaac continued, "Here are the fire and the
    wood,
  but where is the sheep for the holocaust?"
"Son," Abraham answered,
  "God himself will provide the sheep for the
    holocaust."
Then the two continued going forward.

When they came to the place of which God
  had told him,

Abraham built an altar there and arranged
  the wood on it.
Next he tied up his son Isaac,
  and put him on top of the wood on the altar.
Then he reached out and took the knife to
  slaughter his son.
But the LORD's messenger called to him from
    heaven,
  "Abraham, Abraham!"
"Here I am," he answered.
"Do not lay your hand on the boy," said the
    messenger.
"Do not do the least thing to him.
I know now how devoted you are to God,
  since you did not withhold from me your
    own beloved son."
As Abraham looked about,
  he spied a ram caught by its horns in the
    thicket.
So he went and took the ram
  and offered it up as a holocaust in place of
    his son.
Abraham named the site Yahweh-yireh;
  hence people now say, "On the mountain
    the LORD will see."

Again the LORD's messenger called to
  Abraham from heaven and said:
  "I swear by myself, declares the LORD,
  that because you acted as you did
  in not withholding from me your beloved
    son,
  I will bless you abundantly
  and make your descendants as countless
  as the stars of the sky and the sands of the
    seashore;
  your descendants shall take possession
  of the gates of their enemies,
  and in your descendants all the nations of
    the earth
    shall find blessing—
  all this because you obeyed my
    command."

or

Gen 22:1-2, 9a, 10-13, 15-18

God put Abraham to the test.
He called to him, "Abraham!"
"Here I am," he replied.
Then God said:
  "Take your son Isaac, your only one, whom
    you love,
  and go to the land of Moriah.
There you shall offer him up as a holocaust
  on a height that I will point out to you."

When they came to the place of which God
  had told him,
  Abraham built an altar there and arranged
    the wood on it.

Then he reached out and took the knife to
  slaughter his son.
But the LORD's messenger called to him from
  heaven,
  "Abraham, Abraham!"
"Here I am," he answered.
"Do not lay your hand on the boy," said the
  messenger.
"Do not do the least thing to him.
I know now how devoted you are to God,
  since you did not withhold from me your
  own beloved son."
As Abraham looked about,
  he spied a ram caught by its horns in the
  thicket.
So he went and took the ram
  and offered it up as a holocaust in place of
  his son.

Again the LORD's messenger called to
  Abraham from heaven and said:
  "I swear by myself, declares the LORD,
  that because you acted as you did
  in not withholding from me your beloved son,
  I will bless you abundantly
  and make your descendants as countless
  as the stars of the sky and the sands of the
  seashore;
  your descendants shall take possession
  of the gates of their enemies,
  and in your descendants all the nations of
  the earth
  shall find blessing—
  all this because you obeyed my command."

RESPONSORIAL PSALM
Ps 16:5, 8, 9-10, 11

R⁊. (1) You are my inheritance, O Lord.

O LORD, my allotted portion and my cup,
  you it is who hold fast my lot.
I set the LORD ever before me;
  with him at my right hand I shall not be
  disturbed.

R⁊. You are my inheritance, O Lord.

Therefore my heart is glad and my soul rejoices,
  my body, too, abides in confidence;
because you will not abandon my soul to the
  netherworld,
  nor will you suffer your faithful one to
  undergo corruption.

R⁊. You are my inheritance, O Lord.

You will show me the path to life,
  fullness of joys in your presence,
  the delights at your right hand forever.

R⁊. You are my inheritance, O Lord.

THIRD READING
Exod 14:15–15:1

The LORD said to Moses, "Why are you crying
  out to me?
Tell the Israelites to go forward.
And you, lift up your staff and, with hand
  outstretched over the sea,
  split the sea in two,
  that the Israelites may pass through it on
  dry land.
But I will make the Egyptians so obstinate
  that they will go in after them.
Then I will receive glory through Pharaoh
  and all his army,
  his chariots and charioteers.
The Egyptians shall know that I am the LORD,
  when I receive glory through Pharaoh
  and his chariots and charioteers."

The angel of God, who had been leading
  Israel's camp,
  now moved and went around behind them.
The column of cloud also, leaving the front,
  took up its place behind them,
  so that it came between the camp of the
  Egyptians
  and that of Israel.
But the cloud now became dark, and thus the
  night passed
  without the rival camps coming any closer
  together all night long.
Then Moses stretched out his hand over the
  sea,
  and the LORD swept the sea
  with a strong east wind throughout the night
  and so turned it into dry land.
When the water was thus divided,
  the Israelites marched into the midst of the
  sea on dry land,
  with the water like a wall to their right and
  to their left.

The Egyptians followed in pursuit;
  all Pharaoh's horses and chariots and
  charioteers went after them
  right into the midst of the sea.
In the night watch just before dawn
  the LORD cast through the column of the
  fiery cloud
  upon the Egyptian force a glance that
  threw it into a panic;
  and he so clogged their chariot wheels
  that they could hardly drive.
With that the Egyptians sounded the retreat
  before Israel,
  because the LORD was fighting for them
  against the Egyptians.

Then the LORD told Moses, "Stretch out your
  hand over the sea,
  that the water may flow back upon the
  Egyptians,
  upon their chariots and their charioteers."
So Moses stretched out his hand over the sea,
  and at dawn the sea flowed back to its
  normal depth.
The Egyptians were fleeing head on toward
  the sea,
  when the LORD hurled them into its midst.
As the water flowed back,
  it covered the chariots and the charioteers
  of Pharaoh's whole army
  which had followed the Israelites into the sea.
Not a single one of them escaped.
But the Israelites had marched on dry land
  through the midst of the sea,
  with the water like a wall to their right and
  to their left.
Thus the LORD saved Israel on that day
  from the power of the Egyptians.
When Israel saw the Egyptians lying dead on
  the seashore
  and beheld the great power that the LORD
  had shown against the Egyptians,
  they feared the LORD and believed in him
  and in his servant Moses.

Then Moses and the Israelites sang this song
  to the LORD:
  I will sing to the LORD, for he is gloriously
  triumphant;
  horse and chariot he has cast into the sea.

RESPONSORIAL PSALM
Exod 15:1-2, 3-4, 5-6, 17-18

R⁊. (1b) Let us sing to the Lord; he has covered
himself in glory.

I will sing to the LORD, for he is gloriously
  triumphant;
  horse and chariot he has cast into the sea.
My strength and my courage is the LORD,
  and he has been my savior.
He is my God, I praise him;
  the God of my father, I extol him.

R⁊. Let us sing to the Lord; he has covered
himself in glory.

The LORD is a warrior,
  LORD is his name!
Pharaoh's chariots and army he hurled into
  the sea;
  the elite of his officers were submerged in
  the Red Sea.

R⁊. Let us sing to the Lord; he has covered
himself in glory.

The flood waters covered them,
  they sank into the depths like a stone.
Your right hand, O LORD, magnificent in
    power,
  your right hand, O LORD, has shattered the
    enemy.

R℣. Let us sing to the Lord; he has covered
himself in glory.

You brought in the people you redeemed
  and planted them on the mountain of your
    inheritance—
the place where you made your seat, O
    LORD,
  the sanctuary, LORD, which your hands
    established.
The LORD shall reign forever and ever.

R℣. Let us sing to the Lord; he has covered
himself in glory.

FOURTH READING
Isa 54:5-14

The One who has become your husband is
    your Maker;
  his name is the LORD of hosts;
your redeemer is the Holy One of Israel,
  called God of all the earth.
The LORD calls you back,
  like a wife forsaken and grieved in spirit,
  a wife married in youth and then cast off,
  says your God.
For a brief moment I abandoned you,
  but with great tenderness I will take you
    back.
In an outburst of wrath, for a moment
  I hid my face from you;
but with enduring love I take pity on you,
  says the LORD, your redeemer.
This is for me like the days of Noah,
  when I swore that the waters of Noah
  should never again deluge the earth;
so I have sworn not to be angry with you,
  or to rebuke you.
Though the mountains leave their place
  and the hills be shaken,
my love shall never leave you
  nor my covenant of peace be shaken,
  says the LORD, who has mercy on you.
O afflicted one, storm-battered and unconsoled,
  I lay your pavements in carnelians,
  and your foundations in sapphires;
I will make your battlements of rubies,
  your gates of carbuncles,
  and all your walls of precious stones.
All your children shall be taught by the LORD,
  and great shall be the peace of your children.

In justice shall you be established,
  far from the fear of oppression,
  where destruction cannot come near you.

RESPONSORIAL PSALM
Ps 30:2, 4, 5-6, 11-12, 13

R℣. (2a) I will praise you, Lord, for you have
rescued me.

I will extol you, O LORD, for you drew me
    clear
  and did not let my enemies rejoice over me.
O LORD, you brought me up from the
    netherworld;
  you preserved me from among those going
    down into the pit.

R℣. I will praise you, Lord, for you have
rescued me.

Sing praise to the LORD, you his faithful ones,
  and give thanks to his holy name.
For his anger lasts but a moment;
  a lifetime, his good will.
At nightfall, weeping enters in,
  but with the dawn, rejoicing.

R℣. I will praise you, Lord, for you have
rescued me.

Hear, O LORD, and have pity on me;
  O LORD, be my helper.
You changed my mourning into dancing;
  O LORD, my God, forever will I give you
    thanks.

R℣. I will praise you, Lord, for you have
rescued me.

FIFTH READING
Isa 55:1-11

Thus says the LORD:
All you who are thirsty,
  come to the water!
You who have no money,
  come, receive grain and eat;
come, without paying and without cost,
  drink wine and milk!
Why spend your money for what is not bread,
  your wages for what fails to satisfy?
Heed me, and you shall eat well,
  you shall delight in rich fare.
Come to me heedfully,
  listen, that you may have life.
I will renew with you the everlasting
    covenant,
  the benefits assured to David.
As I made him a witness to the peoples,
  a leader and commander of nations,
so shall you summon a nation you knew not,

and nations that knew you not shall run
    to you,
because of the LORD, your God,
  the Holy One of Israel, who has glorified you.

Seek the LORD while he may be found,
  call him while he is near.
Let the scoundrel forsake his way,
  and the wicked man his thoughts;
let him turn to the LORD for mercy;
  to our God, who is generous in forgiving.
For my thoughts are not your thoughts,
  nor are your ways my ways, says the LORD.
As high as the heavens are above the earth,
  so high are my ways above your ways
  and my thoughts above your thoughts.

For just as from the heavens
  the rain and snow come down
and do not return there
  till they have watered the earth,
  making it fertile and fruitful,
giving seed to the one who sows
  and bread to the one who eats,
so shall my word be
  that goes forth from my mouth;
my word shall not return to me void,
  but shall do my will,
  achieving the end for which I sent it.

RESPONSORIAL PSALM
Isa 12:2-3, 4, 5-6

R℣. (3) You will draw water joyfully from the
springs of salvation.

God indeed is my savior;
  I am confident and unafraid.
My strength and my courage is the LORD,
  and he has been my savior.
With joy you will draw water
  at the fountain of salvation.

R℣. You will draw water joyfully from the
springs of salvation.

Give thanks to the LORD, acclaim his name;
  among the nations make known his deeds,
  proclaim how exalted is his name.

R℣. You will draw water joyfully from the
springs of salvation.

Sing praise to the LORD for his glorious
    achievement;
  let this be known throughout all the earth.
Shout with exultation, O city of Zion,
  for great in your midst
  is the Holy One of Israel!

R℣. You will draw water joyfully from the
springs of salvation.

SIXTH READING
Bar 3:9-15, 32–4:4

Hear, O Israel, the commandments of life:
    listen, and know prudence!
How is it, Israel,
    that you are in the land of your foes,
    grown old in a foreign land,
defiled with the dead,
    accounted with those destined for the
        netherworld?
You have forsaken the fountain of wisdom!
    Had you walked in the way of God,
    you would have dwelt in enduring peace.
Learn where prudence is,
    where strength, where understanding;
that you may know also
    where are length of days, and life,
    where light of the eyes, and peace.
Who has found the place of wisdom,
    who has entered into her treasuries?

The One who knows all things knows her;
    he has probed her by his knowledge—
the One who established the earth for all
      time,
    and filled it with four-footed beasts;
    he who dismisses the light, and it departs,
    calls it, and it obeys him trembling;
before whom the stars at their posts
    shine and rejoice;
when he calls them, they answer, "Here we
    are!"
    shining with joy for their Maker.
Such is our God;
    no other is to be compared to him:
he has traced out the whole way of
      understanding,
    and has given her to Jacob, his servant,
    to Israel, his beloved son.

Since then she has appeared on earth,
    and moved among people.
She is the book of the precepts of God,
    the law that endures forever;
all who cling to her will live,
    but those will die who forsake her.
Turn, O Jacob, and receive her:
    walk by her light toward splendor.
Give not your glory to another,
    your privileges to an alien race.
Blessed are we, O Israel;
    for what pleases God is known to us!

RESPONSORIAL PSALM
Ps 19:8, 9, 10, 11

℟. (John 6:68c) Lord, you have the words of
everlasting life.

The law of the LORD is perfect,
    refreshing the soul;
the decree of the LORD is trustworthy,
    giving wisdom to the simple.

℟. Lord, you have the words of everlasting life.

The precepts of the LORD are right,
    rejoicing the heart;
the command of the LORD is clear,
    enlightening the eye.

℟. Lord, you have the words of everlasting life.

The fear of the LORD is pure,
    enduring forever;
the ordinances of the LORD are true,
    all of them just.

℟. Lord, you have the words of everlasting life.

They are more precious than gold,
    than a heap of purest gold;
sweeter also than syrup
    or honey from the comb.

℟. Lord, you have the words of everlasting life.

SEVENTH READING
Ezek 36:16-17a, 18-28

The word of the LORD came to me, saying:
    Son of man, when the house of Israel lived
      in their land,
    they defiled it by their conduct and deeds.
Therefore I poured out my fury upon them
    because of the blood that they poured out
      on the ground,
    and because they defiled it with idols.
I scattered them among the nations,
    dispersing them over foreign lands;
    according to their conduct and deeds I
      judged them.
But when they came among the nations
    wherever they came,
    they served to profane my holy name,
    because it was said of them: "These are the
      people of the LORD,
    yet they had to leave their land."
So I have relented because of my holy name
    which the house of Israel profaned
    among the nations where they came.
Therefore say to the house of Israel: Thus
      says the Lord GOD:
    Not for your sakes do I act, house of Israel,
    but for the sake of my holy name,
    which you profaned among the nations to
      which you came.
I will prove the holiness of my great name,
    profaned among the nations,
    in whose midst you have profaned it.
Thus the nations shall know that I am the
      LORD, says the Lord GOD,
    when in their sight I prove my holiness
      through you.
For I will take you away from among the
      nations,

gather you from all the foreign lands,
    and bring you back to your own land.
I will sprinkle clean water upon you
    to cleanse you from all your impurities,
    and from all your idols I will cleanse you.
I will give you a new heart and place a new
      spirit within you,
    taking from your bodies your stony hearts
    and giving you natural hearts.
I will put my spirit within you and make you
      live by my statutes,
    careful to observe my decrees.
You shall live in the land I gave your fathers;
    you shall be my people, and I will be your
      God.

RESPONSORIAL PSALM
Ps 42:3, 5; 43:3, 4 (when baptism is celebrated)

℟. (42:2) Like a deer that longs for running
streams, my soul longs for you, my God.

Athirst is my soul for God, the living God.
    When shall I go and behold the face of God?

℟. Like a deer that longs for running streams,
my soul longs for you, my God.

I went with the throng
    and led them in procession to the house of
      God,
amid loud cries of joy and thanksgiving,
    with the multitude keeping festival.

℟. Like a deer that longs for running streams,
my soul longs for you, my God.

Send forth your light and your fidelity;
    they shall lead me on
and bring me to your holy mountain,
    to your dwelling-place.

℟. Like a deer that longs for running streams,
my soul longs for you, my God.

Then will I go in to the altar of God,
    the God of my gladness and joy;
then will I give you thanks upon the harp,
    O God, my God!

℟. Like a deer that longs for running streams,
my soul longs for you, my God.

or

Isa 12:2-3, 4bcd, 5-6 (when baptism is not
celebrated)

℟. (3) You will draw water joyfully from the
springs of salvation.

God indeed is my savior;
    I am confident and unafraid.
My strength and my courage is the LORD,
    and he has been my savior.
With joy you will draw water
    at the fountain of salvation.

℟. You will draw water joyfully from the
springs of salvation.

Give thanks to the LORD, acclaim his name;
   among the nations make known his deeds,
   proclaim how exalted is his name.

R⁊. You will draw water joyfully from the
springs of salvation.

Sing praise to the LORD for his glorious
   achievement;
   let this be known throughout all the earth.
Shout with exultation, O city of Zion,
   for great in your midst
   is the Holy One of Israel!

R⁊. You will draw water joyfully from the
springs of salvation.

or

Ps 51:12-13, 14-15, 18-19

R⁊. (12a) Create a clean heart in me, O God.

A clean heart create for me, O God,
   and a steadfast spirit renew within me.
Cast me not out from your presence,
   and your Holy Spirit take not from me.

R⁊. Create a clean heart in me, O God.

Give me back the joy of your salvation,
   and a willing spirit sustain in me.
I will teach transgressors your ways,
   and sinners shall return to you.

R⁊. Create a clean heart in me, O God.

For you are not pleased with sacrifices;
   should I offer a holocaust, you would not
      accept it.
My sacrifice, O God, is a contrite spirit;
   a heart contrite and humbled, O God, you
      will not spurn.

R⁊. Create a clean heart in me, O God.

EPISTLE
Rom 6:3-11

Brothers and sisters:
Are you unaware that we who were baptized
      into Christ Jesus
   were baptized into his death?
We were indeed buried with him through
      baptism into death,
   so that, just as Christ was raised from the
         dead
   by the glory of the Father,
   we too might live in newness of life.

For if we have grown into union with him
      through a death like his,
   we shall also be united with him in the
      resurrection.
We know that our old self was crucified with
      him,
   so that our sinful body might be done away
         with,
   that we might no longer be in slavery to sin.
For a dead person has been absolved from
      sin.
If, then, we have died with Christ,
   we believe that we shall also live with
      him.
We know that Christ, raised from the dead,
      dies no more;
   death no longer has power over him.
As to his death, he died to sin once and for
      all;
   as to his life, he lives for God.
Consequently, you too must think of
      yourselves as being dead to sin
   and living for God in Christ Jesus.

RESPONSORIAL PSALM
Ps 118:1-2, 16-17, 22-23

R⁊. Alleluia, alleluia, alleluia.

Give thanks to the LORD, for he is good,
   for his mercy endures forever.
Let the house of Israel say,
   "His mercy endures forever."

R⁊. Alleluia, alleluia, alleluia.

"The right hand of the LORD has struck with
      power;
   the right hand of the LORD is exalted.
I shall not die, but live,
   and declare the works of the LORD."

R⁊. Alleluia, alleluia, alleluia.

The stone which the builders rejected
   has become the cornerstone.
By the LORD has this been done;
   it is wonderful in our eyes.

R⁊. Alleluia, alleluia, alleluia.

Gospel

Matt 28:1-10; L41ABC

After the sabbath, as the first day of the week was dawning,
   Mary Magdalene and the other Mary came to see the tomb.
And behold, there was a great earthquake;
   for an angel of the Lord descended from heaven,
   approached, rolled back the stone, and sat upon it.
His appearance was like lightning
   and his clothing was white as snow.
The guards were shaken with fear of him
   and became like dead men.
Then the angel said to the women in reply,
   "Do not be afraid!
I know that you are seeking Jesus the crucified.
He is not here, for he has been raised just as he said.
Come and see the place where he lay.

Then go quickly and tell his disciples,
   'He has been raised from the dead,
   and he is going before you to Galilee;
   there you will see him.'
   Behold, I have told you."
Then they went away quickly from the tomb,
   fearful yet overjoyed,
   and ran to announce this to his disciples.
And behold, Jesus met them on their way and greeted them.
They approached, embraced his feet, and did him homage.
Then Jesus said to them, "Do not be afraid.
Go tell my brothers to go to Galilee,
   and there they will see me."

or, at an afternoon or evening Mass

Gospel

Luke 24:13-35; L46

That very day, the first day of the week,
   two of Jesus' disciples were going
   to a village seven miles from Jerusalem called Emmaus,
   and they were conversing about all the things that had occurred.
And it happened that while they were conversing and debating,
   Jesus himself drew near and walked with them,
   but their eyes were prevented from recognizing him.
He asked them,
   "What are you discussing as you walk along?"
They stopped, looking downcast.
One of them, named Cleopas, said to him in reply,
   "Are you the only visitor to Jerusalem
   who does not know of the things
   that have taken place there in these days?"
And he replied to them, "What sort of things?"
They said to him,
   "The things that happened to Jesus the Nazarene,
   who was a prophet mighty in deed and word
   before God and all the people,
   how our chief priests and rulers both handed him over
   to a sentence of death and crucified him.
But we were hoping that he would be the one to redeem Israel;
   and besides all this,
   it is now the third day since this took place.
Some women from our group, however, have astounded us:
   they were at the tomb early in the morning
   and did not find his body;
   they came back and reported
   that they had indeed seen a vision of angels
   who announced that he was alive.
Then some of those with us went to the tomb
   and found things just as the women had described,
   but him they did not see."

And he said to them, "Oh, how foolish you are!
How slow of heart to believe all that the prophets spoke!
Was it not necessary that the Christ should suffer these things
   and enter into his glory?"
Then beginning with Moses and all the prophets,
   he interpreted to them what referred to him
   in all the Scriptures.
As they approached the village to which they were going,
   he gave the impression that he was going on farther.
But they urged him, "Stay with us,
   for it is nearly evening and the day is almost over."
So he went in to stay with them.
And it happened that, while he was with them at table,
   he took bread, said the blessing,
   broke it, and gave it to them.
With that their eyes were opened and they recognized him,
   but he vanished from their sight.
Then they said to each other,
   "Were not our hearts burning within us
   while he spoke to us on the way and opened the Scriptures to us?"
So they set out at once and returned to Jerusalem
   where they found gathered together
   the eleven and those with them who were saying,
   "The Lord has truly been raised and has appeared to Simon!"
Then the two recounted
   what had taken place on the way
   and how he was made known to them in the breaking of bread.

FIRST READING
Acts 10:34a, 37-43

Peter proceeded to speak and said:
"You know what has happened all over
Judea,
beginning in Galilee after the baptism
that John preached,
how God anointed Jesus of Nazareth
with the Holy Spirit and power.
He went about doing good
and healing all those oppressed by the devil,
for God was with him.
We are witnesses of all that he did
both in the country of the Jews and in
Jerusalem.
They put him to death by hanging him on a
tree.
This man God raised on the third day and
granted that he be visible,
not to all the people, but to us,
the witnesses chosen by God in advance,
who ate and drank with him after he rose
from the dead.
He commissioned us to preach to the people
and testify that he is the one appointed by
God
as judge of the living and the dead.
To him all the prophets bear witness,
that everyone who believes in him
will receive forgiveness of sins through his
name."

RESPONSORIAL PSALM
Ps 118:1-2, 16-17, 22-23

℟. (24) This is the day the Lord has made; let
us rejoice and be glad.
or:
℟. Alleluia.

Give thanks to the LORD, for he is good,
for his mercy endures forever.
Let the house of Israel say,
"His mercy endures forever."

℟. This is the day the Lord has made; let us
rejoice and be glad.
or:
℟. Alleluia.

"The right hand of the LORD has struck with
power;
the right hand of the LORD is exalted.
I shall not die, but live,
and declare the works of the LORD."

℟. This is the day the Lord has made; let us
rejoice and be glad.
or:
℟. Alleluia.

The stone which the builders rejected
has become the cornerstone.
By the LORD has this been done;
it is wonderful in our eyes.

℟. This is the day the Lord has made; let us
rejoice and be glad.
or:
℟. Alleluia.

SECOND READING Col 3:1-4

Brothers and sisters:
If then you were raised with Christ, seek what
is above,
where Christ is seated at the right hand of
God.
Think of what is above, not of what is on earth.
For you have died, and your life is hidden
with Christ in God.
When Christ your life appears,
then you too will appear with him in glory.

or

1 Cor 5:6b-8

Brothers and sisters:
Do you not know that a little yeast leavens all
the dough?
Clear out the old yeast,
so that you may become a fresh batch of
dough,
inasmuch as you are unleavened.
For our paschal lamb, Christ, has been
sacrificed.
Therefore, let us celebrate the feast,
not with the old yeast, the yeast of malice
and wickedness,
but with the unleavened bread of sincerity
and truth.

SEQUENCE *Victimae paschali laudes*

Christians, to the Paschal Victim
Offer your thankful praises!
A Lamb the sheep redeems;
Christ, who only is sinless,
Reconciles sinners to the Father.
Death and life have contended in that combat
stupendous:
The Prince of life, who died, reigns
immortal.
Speak, Mary, declaring
What you saw, wayfaring.
"The tomb of Christ, who is living,
The glory of Jesus' resurrection;
Bright angels attesting,
The shroud and napkin resting.
Yes, Christ my hope is arisen;
To Galilee he goes before you."
Christ indeed from death is risen, our new life
obtaining.
Have mercy, victor King, ever reigning!
Amen. Alleluia.

Second Sunday of Easter (or Divine Mercy Sunday), May 1, 2011

Gospel (cont.)
John 20:19-31; L43A

Now a week later his disciples were again inside
    and Thomas was with them.
Jesus came, although the doors were locked,
    and stood in their midst and said, "Peace be with you."
Then he said to Thomas, "Put your finger here and see my hands,
    and bring your hand and put it into my side,
    and do not be unbelieving, but believe."
Thomas answered and said to him, "My Lord and my God!"
Jesus said to him, "Have you come to believe because you have seen
        me?
Blessed are those who have not seen and have believed."

Now Jesus did many other signs in the presence of his disciples
    that are not written in this book.
But these are written that you may come to believe
    that Jesus is the Christ, the Son of God,
    and that through this belief you may have life in his name.

Third Sunday of Easter, May 8, 2011

Gospel (cont.)
Luke 24:13-35; L46A

Some women from our group, however, have astounded us:
    they were at the tomb early in the morning
    and did not find his body;
    they came back and reported
    that they had indeed seen a vision of angels
    who announced that he was alive.
Then some of those with us went to the tomb
    and found things just as the women had described,
    but him they did not see."
And he said to them, "Oh, how foolish you are!
How slow of heart to believe all that the prophets spoke!
Was it not necessary that the Christ should suffer these things
    and enter into his glory?"
Then beginning with Moses and all the prophets,
    he interpreted to them what referred to him
    in all the Scriptures.
As they approached the village to which they were going,
    he gave the impression that he was going on farther.
But they urged him, "Stay with us,
    for it is nearly evening and the day is almost over."
So he went in to stay with them.
And it happened that, while he was with them at table,
    he took bread, said the blessing,
    broke it, and gave it to them.
With that their eyes were opened and they recognized him,
    but he vanished from their sight.
Then they said to each other,
    "Were not our hearts burning within us
    while he spoke to us on the way and opened the Scriptures to us?"
So they set out at once and returned to Jerusalem
    where they found gathered together
    the eleven and those with them who were saying,
    "The Lord has truly been raised and has appeared to Simon!"
Then the two recounted
    what had taken place on the way
    and how he was made known to them in the breaking of bread.

SECOND READING
1 Pet 1:17-21

Beloved:
If you invoke as Father him who judges impartially
    according to each one's works,
        conduct yourselves with reverence during the time of your
            sojourning,
        realizing that you were ransomed from your futile conduct,
        handed on by your ancestors,
        not with perishable things like silver or gold
        but with the precious blood of Christ
        as of a spotless unblemished lamb.

He was known before the foundation of the world
    but revealed in the final time for you,
    who through him believe in God
    who raised him from the dead and gave him glory,
    so that your faith and hope are in God.

Fifth Sunday of Easter, *May 22, 2011*

Gospel (cont.)
John 14:1-12; L52A

The words that I speak to you I do not speak on my own.
The Father who dwells in me is doing his works.
Believe me that I am in the Father and the Father is in me,
   or else, believe because of the works themselves.
Amen, amen, I say to you,
   whoever believes in me will do the works that I do,
   and will do greater ones than these,
   because I am going to the Father."

Pentecost Sunday Mass during the Day, *June 12, 2011*

SEQUENCE
Veni, Sancte Spiritus

Come, Holy Spirit, come!
And from your celestial home
   Shed a ray of light divine!
Come, Father of the poor!
Come, source of all our store!
   Come, within our bosoms shine.
You, of comforters the best;
You, the soul's most welcome guest;
   Sweet refreshment here below;
In our labor, rest most sweet;
Grateful coolness in the heat;
   Solace in the midst of woe.
O most blessed Light divine,
Shine within these hearts of yours,
   And our inmost being fill!
Where you are not, we have naught,
Nothing good in deed or thought,
   Nothing free from taint of ill.
Heal our wounds, our strength renew;
On our dryness pour your dew;
   Wash the stains of guilt away:
Bend the stubborn heart and will;
Melt the frozen, warm the chill;
   Guide the steps that go astray.
On the faithful, who adore
And confess you, evermore
   In your sevenfold gift descend;
Give them virtue's sure reward;
Give them your salvation, Lord;
   Give them joys that never end. Amen.
   Alleluia.

The Ascension of the Lord, *June 2, 2011 (Thursday) or June 5, 2011*

SECOND READING
Eph 1:17-23

Brothers and sisters:
May the God of our Lord Jesus Christ, the Father of glory,
   give you a Spirit of wisdom and revelation
   resulting in knowledge of him.
May the eyes of your hearts be enlightened,
   that you may know what is the hope that belongs to his call,
   what are the riches of glory
   in his inheritance among the holy ones,
   and what is the surpassing greatness of his power
   for us who believe,
   in accord with the exercise of his great might,
   which he worked in Christ,
   raising him from the dead
   and seating him at his right hand in the heavens,
   far above every principality, authority, power, and dominion,
   and every name that is named
   not only in this age but also in the one to come.
And he put all things beneath his feet
   and gave him as head over all things to the church,
   which is his body,
   the fullness of the one who fills all things in every way.

FIRST READING
Isa 49:1-6

Hear me, O coastlands,
    listen, O distant peoples.
The LORD called me from birth,
    from my mother's womb he gave me my
       name.
He made of me a sharp-edged sword
    and concealed me in the shadow of his arm.
He made me a polished arrow,
    in his quiver he hid me.
You are my servant, he said to me,
    Israel, through whom I show my glory.

Though I thought I had toiled in vain,
    and for nothing, uselessly, spent my
       strength,
yet my reward is with the LORD,
    my recompense is with my God.
For now the LORD has spoken
    who formed me as his servant from the
       womb,
that Jacob may be brought back to him
    and Israel gathered to him;
and I am made glorious in the sight of the
       Lord,
    and my God is now my strength!
It is too little, he says, for you to be my servant,
    to raise up the tribes of Jacob,
    and restore the survivors of Israel;
I will make you a light to the nations,
    that my salvation may reach to the ends of
       the earth.

RESPONSORIAL PSALM
Ps 139:1-3, 13-14, 14-15

R̂. (14a) I praise you for I am wonderfully made.

O LORD you have probed me and you know
    me;
    you know when I sit and when I stand;
    you understand my thoughts from afar.
My journeys and my rest you scrutinize,
    with all my ways you are familiar.

R̂. I praise you for I am wonderfully made.

Truly you have formed my inmost being;
    you knit me in my mother's womb.
I give you thanks that I am fearfully,
      wonderfully made;
    wonderful are your works.

R̂. I praise you for I am wonderfully made.

My soul also you knew full well;
    nor was my frame unknown to you
when I was made in secret,
    when I was fashioned in the depths of the
      earth.

R̂. I praise you for I am wonderfully made.

SECOND READING
Acts 13:22-26

In those days, Paul said:
    "God raised up David as their king;
    of him he testified,
    I have found David, son of Jesse, a man
       after my own heart;
    he will carry out my every wish.
From this man's descendants God, according
      to his promise,
    has brought to Israel a savior, Jesus.
John heralded his coming by proclaiming a
      baptism of repentance
    to all the people of Israel;
    and as John was completing his course, he
      would say,
'What do you suppose that I am? I am not he.
Behold, one is coming after me;
    I am not worthy to unfasten the sandals of
      his feet.'

"My brothers, children of the family of
    Abraham,
    and those others among you who are God-
      fearing,
    to us this word of salvation has been sent."

OPTIONAL SEQUENCE

Lauda Sion

Laud, O Zion, your salvation,
Laud with hymns of exultation,
   Christ, your king and shepherd true:

Bring him all the praise you know,
He is more than you bestow.
   Never can you reach his due.

Special theme for glad thanksgiving
Is the quick'ning and the living
   Bread today before you set:

From his hands of old partaken,
As we know, by faith unshaken,
   Where the Twelve at supper met.

Full and clear ring out your chanting,
Joy nor sweetest grace be wanting,
   From your heart let praises burst:

For today the feast is holden,
When the institution olden
   Of that supper was rehearsed.

Here the new law's new oblation,
By the new king's revelation,
   Ends the form of ancient rite:

Now the new the old effaces,
Truth away the shadow chases,
   Light dispels the gloom of night.

What he did at supper seated,
Christ ordained to be repeated,
   His memorial ne'er to cease:

And his rule for guidance taking,
Bread and wine we hallow, making
   Thus our sacrifice of peace.

This the truth each Christian learns,
Bread into his flesh he turns,
   To his precious blood the wine:

Sight has fail'd, nor thought conceives,
But a dauntless faith believes,
   Resting on a pow'r divine.

Here beneath these signs are hidden
Priceless things to sense forbidden;
   Signs, not things are all we see:

Blood is poured and flesh is broken,
Yet in either wondrous token
   Christ entire we know to be.

Whoso of this food partakes,
Does not rend the Lord nor breaks;
   Christ is whole to all that taste:

Thousands are, as one, receivers,
One, as thousands of believers,
   Eats of him who cannot waste.

Bad and good the feast are sharing,
Of what divers dooms preparing,
   Endless death, or endless life.

Life to these, to those damnation,
See how like participation
   Is with unlike issues rife.

When the sacrament is broken,
Doubt not, but believe 'tis spoken,
   That each sever'd outward token
     Doth the very whole contain.

Nought the precious gift divides,
Breaking but the sign betides
   Jesus still the same abides,
     still unbroken does remain.

The shorter form of the sequence begins here.

Lo! the angel's food is given
To the pilgrim who has striven;
   See the children's bread from heaven,
     Which on dogs may not be spent.

Truth the ancient types fulfilling,
Isaac bound, a victim willing,
   Paschal lamb, its lifeblood spilling,
     Manna to the fathers sent.

Very bread, good shepherd, tend us,
Jesu, of your love befriend us,
   You refresh us, you defend us,
   Your eternal goodness send us
In the land of life to see.

You who all things can and know,
Who on earth such food bestow,
   Grant us with your saints, though lowest,
   Where the heav'nly feast you show,
Fellow heirs and guests to be. Amen. Alleluia.

FIRST READING
Acts 12:1-11

In those days, King Herod laid hands upon
    some members of the church to harm
    them.
He had James, the brother of John, killed by
    the sword,
    and when he saw that this was pleasing to
        the Jews
    he proceeded to arrest Peter also.
—It was the feast of Unleavened Bread.—
He had him taken into custody and put in
    prison
    under the guard of four squads of four
        soldiers each.
He intended to bring him before the people
    after Passover.
Peter thus was being kept in prison,
    but prayer by the church was fervently
        being made
    to God on his behalf.

On the very night before Herod was to bring
    him to trial,
    Peter, secured by double chains,
    was sleeping between two soldiers,
    while outside the door guards kept watch
        on the prison.
Suddenly the angel of the Lord stood by him
    and a light shone in the cell.
He tapped Peter on the side and awakened
    him, saying,
    "Get up quickly."
The chains fell from his wrists.
The angel said to him, "Put on your belt and
    your sandals."
He did so.
Then he said to him, "Put on your cloak and
    follow me."

So he followed him out,
    not realizing that what was happening
        through the angel was real;
    he thought he was seeing a vision.
They passed the first guard, then the second,
    and came to the iron gate leading out to
        the city,
    which opened for them by itself.
They emerged and made their way down an
    alley,
    and suddenly the angel left him.
Then Peter recovered his senses and said,
    "Now I know for certain that the Lord sent
        his angel
    and rescued me from the hand of Herod
    and from all that the Jewish people had
        been expecting."

RESPONSORIAL PSALM
Ps 34:2-3, 4-5, 6-7, 8-9

℟. (8) The angel of the Lord will rescue those
who fear him.

I will bless the LORD at all times;
    his praise shall be ever in my mouth.
Let my soul glory in the LORD;
    the lowly will hear me and be glad.

℟. The angel of the Lord will rescue those
who fear him.

Glorify the LORD with me,
    let us together extol his name.
I sought the LORD, and he answered me
    and delivered me from all my fears.

℟. The angel of the Lord will rescue those
who fear him.

Look to him that you may be radiant with joy,
    and your faces may not blush with shame.
When the poor one called out, the LORD heard,
    and from all his distress he saved him.

℟. The angel of the Lord will rescue those
who fear him.

The angel of the LORD encamps
    around those who fear him, and delivers
        them.
Taste and see how good the LORD is;
    blessed the man who takes refuge in him.

℟. The angel of the Lord will rescue those
who fear him.

SECOND READING
2 Tim 4:6-8, 17-18

I, Paul, am already being poured out like a
    libation,
    and the time of my departure is at hand.
I have competed well; I have finished the race;
    I have kept the faith.
From now on the crown of righteousness
        awaits me,
    which the Lord, the just judge,
    will award to me on that day, and not only
        to me,
    but to all who have longed for his
        appearance.

The Lord stood by me and gave me strength,
    so that through me the proclamation might
        be completed
    and all the Gentiles might hear it.
And I was rescued from the lion's mouth.
The Lord will rescue me from every evil
    threat
    and will bring me safe to his heavenly
        kingdom.
To him be glory forever and ever. Amen.

The Solemnity of the Most Sacred Heart of Jesus, *July 1, 2011*

FIRST READING
Deut 7:6-11

Moses said to the people:
"You are a people sacred to the LORD, your
God;
he has chosen you from all the nations on
the face of the earth
to be a people peculiarly his own.
It was not because you are the largest of all
nations
that the LORD set his heart on you and
chose you,
for you are really the smallest of all nations.
It was because the LORD loved you
and because of his fidelity to the oath he
had sworn to your fathers,
that he brought you out with his strong
hand
from the place of slavery,
and ransomed you from the hand of
Pharaoh, king of Egypt.
Understand, then, that the LORD, your God, is
God indeed,
the faithful God who keeps his merciful
covenant
down to the thousandth generation
toward those who love him and keep his
commandments,
but who repays with destruction a person
who hates him;
he does not dally with such a one,
but makes them personally pay for it.
You shall therefore carefully observe the
commandments,
the statutes and the decrees that I enjoin on
you today."

RESPONSORIAL PSALM
Ps 103:1-2, 3-4, 6, 8, 10

℟. (cf. 17) The Lord's kindness is everlasting
to those who fear him.

Bless the LORD, O my soul;
all my being, bless his holy name.
Bless the LORD, O my soul;
and forget not all his benefits.

℟. The Lord's kindness is everlasting to those
who fear him.

He pardons all your iniquities,
heals all your ills.
He redeems your life from destruction,
crowns you with kindness and compassion.

℟. The Lord's kindness is everlasting to those
who fear him.

Merciful and gracious is the LORD,
slow to anger and abounding in kindness.
Not according to our sins does he deal with us,
nor does he requite us according to our
crimes.

℟. The Lord's kindness is everlasting to those
who fear him.

SECOND READING
1 John 4:7-16

Beloved, let us love one another,
because love is of God;
everyone who loves is begotten by God and
knows God.
Whoever is without love does not know God,
for God is love.
In this way the love of God was revealed to
us:
God sent his only Son into the world
so that we might have life through him.
In this is love:
not that we have loved God, but that he
loved us
and sent his Son as expiation for our sins.
Beloved, if God so loved us,
we also must love one another.
No one has ever seen God.
Yet, if we love one another, God remains in
us,
and his love is brought to perfection in us.

This is how we know that we remain in him
and he in us,
that he has given us of his Spirit.
Moreover, we have seen and testify
that the Father sent his Son as savior of the
world.
Whoever acknowledges that Jesus is the Son
of God,
God remains in him and he in God.
We have come to know and to believe in the
love God has for us.

God is love, and whoever remains in love
remains in God and God in him.

Fifteenth Sunday in Ordinary Time, *July 10, 2011*

Gospel (cont.)
Matt 13:1-23; L103A

Isaiah's prophecy is fulfilled in them, which says:
You shall indeed hear but not understand,
   you shall indeed look but never see.
Gross is the heart of this people,
   they will hardly hear with their ears,
   they have closed their eyes,
   lest they see with their eyes
   and hear with their ears
and understand with their hearts and be converted,
   and I heal them.

"But blessed are your eyes, because they see,
   and your ears, because they hear.
Amen, I say to you, many prophets and righteous people
   longed to see what you see but did not see it,
   and to hear what you hear but did not hear it.

"Hear then the parable of the sower.
The seed sown on the path is the one
   who hears the word of the kingdom without understanding it,
   and the evil one comes and steals away
   what was sown in his heart.
The seed sown on rocky ground
   is the one who hears the word and receives it at once with joy.
But he has no root and lasts only for a time.
When some tribulation or persecution comes because of the word,
   he immediately falls away.

The seed sown among thorns is the one who hears the word,
   but then worldly anxiety and the lure of riches choke the word
   and it bears no fruit.
But the seed sown on rich soil
   is the one who hears the word and understands it,
   who indeed bears fruit and yields a hundred or sixty or thirtyfold."

or Matt 13:1-9

On that day, Jesus went out of the house and sat down by the sea.
Such large crowds gathered around him
   that he got into a boat and sat down,
   and the whole crowd stood along the shore.
And he spoke to them at length in parables, saying:
   "A sower went out to sow.
And as he sowed, some seed fell on the path,
   and birds came and ate it up.
Some fell on rocky ground, where it had little soil.
It sprang up at once because the soil was not deep,
   and when the sun rose it was scorched,
   and it withered for lack of roots.
Some seed fell among thorns, and the thorns grew up and choked it.
But some seed fell on rich soil, and produced fruit,
   a hundred or sixty or thirtyfold.
Whoever has ears ought to hear."

Sixteenth Sunday in Ordinary Time, *July 17, 2011*

Gospel (cont.)
Matt 13:24-43; L106A

It becomes a large bush,
   and the 'birds of the sky come and dwell in its branches.'"

He spoke to them another parable.
"The kingdom of heaven is like yeast
   that a woman took and mixed with three measures of wheat flour
   until the whole batch was leavened."

All these things Jesus spoke to the crowds in parables.
He spoke to them only in parables,
   to fulfill what had been said through the prophet:
   "I will open my mouth in parables,
   I will announce what has lain hidden from the foundation
      of the world."

Then, dismissing the crowds, he went into the house.
His disciples approached him and said,
   "Explain to us the parable of the weeds in the field."
He said in reply, "He who sows good seed is the Son of Man,
   the field is the world, the good seed the children of the kingdom.
The weeds are the children of the evil one,
   and the enemy who sows them is the devil.
The harvest is the end of the age, and the harvesters are angels.
Just as weeds are collected and burned up with fire,
   so will it be at the end of the age.
The Son of Man will send his angels,
   and they will collect out of his kingdom
   all who cause others to sin and all evildoers.

They will throw them into the fiery furnace,
   where there will be wailing and grinding of teeth.
Then the righteous will shine like the sun
   in the kingdom of their Father.
Whoever has ears ought to hear."

or Matt 13:24-30

Jesus proposed another parable to the crowds, saying:
"The kingdom of heaven may be likened
   to a man who sowed good seed in his field.
While everyone was asleep his enemy came
   and sowed weeds all through the wheat, and then went off.
When the crop grew and bore fruit, the weeds appeared as well.
The slaves of the householder came to him and said,
   'Master, did you not sow good seed in your field?
Where have the weeds come from?'
He answered, 'An enemy has done this.'
His slaves said to him,
   'Do you want us to go and pull them up?'
He replied, 'No, if you pull up the weeds
   you might uproot the wheat along with them.
Let them grow together until harvest;
   then at harvest time I will say to the harvesters,
   "First collect the weeds and tie them in bundles for burning;
   but gather the wheat into my barn."'"

Seventeenth Sunday in Ordinary Time, July 24, 2011

Gospel
Matt 13:44-46; L109A

Jesus said to his disciples:
"The kingdom of heaven is like a treasure buried in a field,
which a person finds and hides again,
and out of joy goes and sells all that he has and buys that field.
Again, the kingdom of heaven is like a merchant
searching for fine pearls.
When he finds a pearl of great price,
he goes and sells all that he has and buys it."

Assumption of the Blessed Virgin Mary, August 15, 2011

Gospel (cont.)
Luke 1:39-56; L622

He has cast down the mighty from their thrones,
and has lifted up the lowly.
He has filled the hungry with good things,
and the rich he has sent away empty.
He has come to the help of his servant Israel
for he has remembered his promise of mercy,
the promise he made to our fathers,
to Abraham and his children forever."

Mary remained with her about three months
and then returned to her home.

FIRST READING
Rev 11:19a; 12:1-6a, 10ab

God's temple in heaven was opened,
and the ark of his covenant could be seen in
the temple.

A great sign appeared in the sky, a woman
clothed with the sun,
with the moon beneath her feet,
and on her head a crown of twelve stars.
She was with child and wailed aloud in pain
as she labored to give birth.
Then another sign appeared in the sky;
it was a huge red dragon, with seven heads
and ten horns,
and on its heads were seven diadems.
Its tail swept away a third of the stars in the
sky
and hurled them down to the earth.
Then the dragon stood before the woman
about to give birth,
to devour her child when she gave birth.
She gave birth to a son, a male child,
destined to rule all the nations with an iron
rod.
Her child was caught up to God and his
throne.
The woman herself fled into the desert
where she had a place prepared by God.

Then I heard a loud voice in heaven say:
"Now have salvation and power come,
and the Kingdom of our God
and the authority of his Anointed One."

RESPONSORIAL PSALM
Ps 45:10, 11, 12, 16

R̂. (10bc) The queen stands at your right
hand, arrayed in gold.

The queen takes her place at your right hand
in gold of Ophir.

R̂. The queen stands at your right hand,
arrayed in gold.

Hear, O daughter, and see; turn your ear,
forget your people and your father's house.

R̂. The queen stands at your right hand,
arrayed in gold.

So shall the king desire your beauty;
for he is your lord.

R̂. The queen stands at your right hand,
arrayed in gold.

They are borne in with gladness and joy;
they enter the palace of the king.

R̂. The queen stands at your right hand,
arrayed in gold.

SECOND READING
1 Cor 15:20-27

Brothers and sisters:
Christ has been raised from the dead,
the firstfruits of those who have fallen
asleep.
For since death came through man,
the resurrection of the dead came also
through man.
For just as in Adam all die,
so too in Christ shall all be brought to life,
but each one in proper order:
Christ the firstfruits;
then, at his coming, those who belong to
Christ;
then comes the end,
when he hands over the Kingdom to his
God and Father,
when he has destroyed every sovereignty
and every authority and power.
For he must reign until he has put all his
enemies under his feet.
The last enemy to be destroyed is death,
for "he subjected everything under his feet."

Twenty-Fourth Sunday in Ordinary Time,
September 11, 2011

Gospel (cont.)
Matt 18:21-35; L130A

He seized him and started to choke him, demanding,
  'Pay back what you owe.'
Falling to his knees, his fellow servant begged him,
  'Be patient with me, and I will pay you back.'
But he refused.
Instead, he had the fellow servant put in prison
  until he paid back the debt.
Now when his fellow servants saw what had happened,
  they were deeply disturbed, and went to their master
  and reported the whole affair.
His master summoned him and said to him, 'You wicked servant!
I forgave you your entire debt because you begged me to.
Should you not have had pity on your fellow servant,
  as I had pity on you?'
Then in anger his master handed him over to the torturers
  until he should pay back the whole debt.
So will my heavenly Father do to you,
  unless each of you forgives your brother from your heart."

Twenty-Fifth Sunday in Ordinary Time,
September 18, 2011

Gospel (cont.)
Matt 20:1-16a; L133A

And on receiving it they grumbled against the landowner, saying,
  'These last ones worked only one hour,
  and you have made them equal to us,
  who bore the day's burden and the heat.'
He said to one of them in reply,
  'My friend, I am not cheating you.
Did you not agree with me for the usual daily wage?
Take what is yours and go.
What if I wish to give this last one the same as you?
Or am I not free to do as I wish with my own money?
Are you envious because I am generous?'
Thus, the last will be first, and the first will be last."

Twenty-Sixth Sunday in Ordinary Time,
September 25, 2011

SECOND READING
Phil 2:1-5

Brothers and sisters:
If there is any encouragement in Christ,
  any solace in love,
  any participation in the Spirit,
  any compassion and mercy,
  complete my joy by being of the same mind, with the same love,
  united in heart, thinking one thing.
Do nothing out of selfishness or out of vainglory;
  rather, humbly regard others as more important than yourselves,
  each looking out not for his own interests,
  but also for those of others.

Have in you the same attitude
  that is also in Christ Jesus.

Twenty-Seventh Sunday in Ordinary Time, October 2, 2011

Gospel (cont.)
Matt 21:33-43; L139A

Jesus said to them, "Did you never read in the Scriptures:
  The stone that the builders rejected
    has become the cornerstone;
  by the Lord has this been done,
    and it is wonderful in our eyes?
Therefore, I say to you,
  the kingdom of God will be taken away from you
  and given to a people that will produce its fruit."

Gospel (cont.)
Matt 22:1-14; L142A

But when the king came in to meet the guests,
he saw a man there not dressed in a wedding garment.
The king said to him, 'My friend, how is it
that you came in here without a wedding garment?'
But he was reduced to silence.
Then the king said to his attendants, 'Bind his hands and feet,
and cast him into the darkness outside,
where there will be wailing and grinding of teeth.'
Many are invited, but few are chosen."

or Matt 22:1-10

Jesus again in reply spoke to the chief priests and elders of the people
in parables, saying,
"The kingdom of heaven may be likened to a king
who gave a wedding feast for his son.
He dispatched his servants
to summon the invited guests to the feast,
but they refused to come.

A second time he sent other servants, saying,
'Tell those invited: "Behold, I have prepared my banquet,
my calves and fattened cattle are killed,
and everything is ready; come to the feast."'
Some ignored the invitation and went away,
one to his farm, another to his business.
The rest laid hold of his servants,
mistreated them, and killed them.
The king was enraged and sent his troops,
destroyed those murderers, and burned their city.
Then he said to his servants, 'The feast is ready,
but those who were invited were not worthy to come.
Go out, therefore, into the main roads
and invite to the feast whomever you find.'
The servants went out into the streets
and gathered all they found, bad and good alike,
and the hall was filled with guests."

All Saints, *November 1, 2011*

FIRST READING
Rev 7:2-4, 9-14

I, John, saw another angel come up from the
East,
holding the seal of the living God.
He cried out in a loud voice to the four angels
who were given power to damage the land
and the sea,
"Do not damage the land or the sea or the
trees
until we put the seal on the foreheads of the
servants of our God."
I heard the number of those who had been
marked with the seal,
one hundred and forty-four thousand
marked
from every tribe of the children of Israel.

After this I had a vision of a great multitude,
which no one could count,
from every nation, race, people, and tongue.
They stood before the throne and before the
Lamb,
wearing white robes and holding palm
branches in their hands.
They cried out in a loud voice:
"Salvation comes from our God,
who is seated on the throne,
and from the Lamb."
All the angels stood around the throne
and around the elders and the four living
creatures.

They prostrated themselves before the throne,
worshiped God, and exclaimed:

"Amen. Blessing and glory, wisdom and
thanksgiving,
honor, power, and might
be to our God forever and ever. Amen."

Then one of the elders spoke up and said to
me,
"Who are these wearing white robes, and
where did they come from?"
I said to him, "My lord, you are the one who
knows."
He said to me,
"These are the ones who have survived the
time of great distress;
they have washed their robes
and made them white in the Blood of the
Lamb."

RESPONSORIAL PSALM
Ps 24:1-2, 3-4, 5-6

R̂. (cf. 6) Lord, this is the people that longs to
see your face.

The LORD's are the earth and its fullness;
the world and those who dwell in it.
For he founded it upon the seas
and established it upon the rivers.

R̂. Lord, this is the people that longs to see
your face.

Who can ascend the mountain of the LORD?
or who may stand in his holy place?
One whose hands are sinless, whose heart is
clean,
who desires not what is vain.

R̂. Lord, this is the people that longs to see
your face.

He shall receive a blessing from the LORD,
a reward from God his savior.
Such is the race that seeks for him,
that seeks the face of the God of Jacob.

R̂. Lord, this is the people that longs to see
your face.

SECOND READING
1 John 3:1-3

Beloved:
See what love the Father has bestowed on us
that we may be called the children of God.
Yet so we are.
The reason the world does not know us
is that it did not know him.
Beloved, we are God's children now;
what we shall be has not yet been revealed.
We do know that when it is revealed we shall
be like him,
for we shall see him as he is.
Everyone who has this hope based on him
makes himself pure,
as he is pure.

All Souls, *November 2, 2011*

(Other options can be found in the Lectionary for Mass, L668.)

FIRST READING

Dan 12:1-3; L1011.7

In those days, I, Daniel, mourned
   and heard this word of the Lord:
At that time there shall arise
   Michael, the great prince,
   guardian of your people;
It shall be a time unsurpassed in distress
   since nations began until that time.
At that time your people shall escape,
   everyone who is found written in the book.

Many of those who sleep in the dust of the
     earth shall awake;
Some shall live forever,
   others shall be an everlasting horror and
     disgrace.
But the wise shall shine brightly
   like the splendor of the firmament,
And those who lead the many to justice
   shall be like the stars forever.

RESPONSORIAL PSALM

Ps 27:1, 4, 7, 8b, 9a, 13-14; L1013.3

R̊. (1a) The Lord is my light and my salvation.
  or:
R̊. (13) I believe that I shall see the good
things of the Lord in the land of the living.

The LORD is my light and my salvation;
   whom should I fear?
The LORD is my life's refuge;
   of whom should I be afraid?

R̊. The Lord is my light and my salvation.
  or:
R̊. I believe that I shall see the good things of
the Lord in the land of the living.

One thing I ask of the LORD;
   this I seek:
To dwell in the house of the LORD
   all the days of my life,
That I may gaze on the loveliness of the LORD
   and contemplate his temple.

R̊. The Lord is my light and my salvation.
  or:
R̊. I believe that I shall see the good things of
the Lord in the land of the living.

Hear, O LORD, the sound of my call;
   have pity on me, and answer me.
Your presence, O LORD, I seek.
   Hide not your face from me.

R̊. The Lord is my light and my salvation.
  or:
R̊. I believe that I shall see the good things of
the Lord in the land of the living.

I believe that I shall see the bounty of the
   LORD
   in the land of the living.
Wait for the LORD with courage;
   be stouthearted, and wait for the LORD.

R̊. The Lord is my light and my salvation.
  or:
R̊. I believe that I shall see the good things of
the Lord in the land of the living.

SECOND READING

Rom 6:3-9; L1014.3

Brothers and sisters:
Are you unaware that we who were baptized
     into Christ Jesus
   were baptized into his death?
We were indeed buried with him through
     baptism into death,
   so that, just as Christ was raised from the
     dead
   by the glory of the Father,
   we too might live in newness of life.

For if we have grown into union with him
     through a death like his,
   we shall also be united with him in the
     resurrection.
We know that our old self was crucified with
     him,
   so that our sinful body might be done away
     with,
   that we might no longer be in slavery to
     sin.
For a dead person has been absolved from sin.
If, then, we have died with Christ,
   we believe that we shall also live with him.
We know that Christ, raised from the dead,
     dies no more;
   death no longer has power over him.

Thirty-Second Sunday in Ordinary Time, *November 6, 2011*

SECOND READING

1 Thess 4:13-14

We do not want you to be unaware, brothers and sisters,
   about those who have fallen asleep,
   so that you may not grieve like the rest, who have no hope.
For if we believe that Jesus died and rose,
   so too will God, through Jesus,
   bring with him those who have fallen asleep.

Solemnity of our Lord Jesus Christ the King, *November 20, 2011*

Gospel (cont.)

Matt 25:31-46; L160A

Then he will say to those on his left,
   'Depart from me, you accursed,
   into the eternal fire prepared for the devil and his angels.
For I was hungry and you gave me no food,
   I was thirsty and you gave me no drink,
   a stranger and you gave me no welcome,
   naked and you gave me no clothing,
   ill and in prison, and you did not care for me.'
Then they will answer and say,
   'Lord, when did we see you hungry or thirsty
   or a stranger or naked or ill or in prison,
   and not minister to your needs?'
He will answer them, 'Amen, I say to you,
   what you did not do for one of these least ones,
   you did not do for me.'
And these will go off to eternal punishment,
   but the righteous to eternal life."

Thirty-Third Sunday in Ordinary Time, *November 13, 2011*

Gospel (cont.)
Matt 25:14-30; L157A

Since you were faithful in small matters,
  I will give you great responsibilities.
Come, share your master's joy.'
Then the one who had received the one talent came forward and said,
  'Master, I knew you were a demanding person,
  harvesting where you did not plant
  and gathering where you did not scatter;
  so out of fear I went off and buried your talent in the ground.
Here it is back.'
His master said to him in reply, 'You wicked, lazy servant!
So you knew that I harvest where I did not plant
  and gather where I did not scatter?
Should you not then have put my money in the bank
  so that I could have got it back with interest on my return?
Now then! Take the talent from him and give it to the one with ten.
For to everyone who has,
  more will be given and he will grow rich;
  but from the one who has not,
  even what he has will be taken away.
And throw this useless servant into the darkness outside,
  where there will be wailing and grinding of teeth.'"

or Matt 25:14-15, 19-21

Jesus told his disciples this parable:
  "A man going on a journey
  called in his servants and entrusted his possessions to them.
To one he gave five talents; to another, two; to a third, one—
  to each according to his ability.
Then he went away.

After a long time
  the master of those servants came back
  and settled accounts with them.
The one who had received five talents came forward
  bringing the additional five.
He said, 'Master, you gave me five talents.
See, I have made five more.'
His master said to him, 'Well done, my good and faithful servant.
Since you were faithful in small matters,
  I will give you great responsibilities.
Come, share your master's joy.'"

Thanksgiving Day, *November 24, 2011*

FIRST READING
Sir 50:22-24; L943.2

And now, bless the God of all,
  who has done wondrous things on earth;
Who fosters people's growth from their
    mother's womb,
  and fashions them according to his will!
May he grant you joy of heart
  and may peace abide among you;
May his goodness toward us endure in Israel
  to deliver us in our days.

RESPONSORIAL PSALM
Psalm 67:2-3, 5, 7-8

R̶. (7) The earth has yielded its fruit, the Lord
our God has blessed us.
  or:
R̶. (4) O God, let all the nations praise you!

May God have pity on us and bless us;
  may he let his face shine upon us.
So may your way be known upon earth;
  among all nations, your salvation.

R̶. The earth has yielded its fruit, the Lord
our God has blessed us.
  or:
R̶. O God, let all the nations praise you!

May the nations be glad and exult
  because you rule the peoples in equity;
  the nations on the earth you guide.

R̶. The earth has yielded its fruit, the Lord
our God has blessed us.
  or:
R̶. O God, let all the nations praise you!

The earth has yielded its fruits;
  God, our God, has blessed us.
May God bless us,
  and may all the ends of the earth fear him!

R̶. The earth has yielded its fruit, the Lord
our God has blessed us.
  or:
R̶. O God, let all the nations praise you!

SECOND READING
1 Cor 1:3-9; L944.1

Brothers and sisters:
Grace to you and peace from God our Father
  and the Lord Jesus Christ.

I give thanks to my God always on your
    account
  for the grace of God bestowed on you in
    Christ Jesus,

that in him you were enriched in every
    way,
  with all discourse and all knowledge,
  as the testimony to Christ was confirmed
    among you,
  so that you are not lacking in any spiritual
    gift
  as you wait for the revelation of our Lord
    Jesus Christ.
He will keep you firm to the end,
  irreproachable on the day of our Lord Jesus
    Christ.
God is faithful,
  and by him you were called to fellowship
    with his Son, Jesus Christ our Lord.

Choral Settings for the Prayer of the Faithful

Purchasers of this volume may reproduce these choral arrangements for use in their parish or community. The music must be reproduced as given below, with composer's name and copyright line.

ORDINARY TIME, WEEKS 2-9

Cantor:

we pray to the Lord,

SATB Response:

Descant

Lord, hear our prayer.

Lord, hear our prayer.

Music: Kathleen Harmon, SNDdeN, ©1999, Institute for Liturgical Ministry, 4960 Salem Avenue, Dayton OH 45416. All rights reserved.

ORDINARY TIME, WEEKS 14-21

Cantor:

we pray to the Lord,

SATB Response:

Lord, hear our prayer.

Music: Kathleen Harmon, SNDdeN, ©1999, Institute for Liturgical Ministry, 4960 Salem Avenue, Dayton OH 45416. All rights reserved.

ORDINARY TIME, WEEKS 22-33

Cantor:

we pray to the Lord,

SATB Response:

Lord, hear our prayer.

Music: Kathleen Harmon, SNDdeN, ©1999, Institute for Liturgical Ministry, 4960 Salem Avenue, Dayton OH 45416. All rights reserved.

Lectionary Pronunciation Guide

Lectionary Word	Pronunciation
Aaron	EHR-uhn
Abana	AB-uh-nuh
Abednego	uh-BEHD-nee-go
Abel-Keramin	AY-b'l-KEHR-uh-mihn
Abel-meholah	AY-b'l-mee-HO-lah
Abiathar	uh-BAI-uh-ther
Abiel	AY-bee-ehl
Abiezrite	ay-bai-EHZ-rait
Abijah	uh-BAI-dzhuh
Abilene	ab-uh-LEE-neh
Abishai	uh-BIHSH-ay-ai
Abiud	uh-BAI-uhd
Abner	AHB-ner
Abraham	AY-bruh-ham
Abram	AY-br'm
Achaia	uh-KAY-yuh
Achim	AY-kihm
Aeneas	uh-NEE-uhs
Aenon	AY-nuhn
Agrippa	uh-GRIH-puh
Ahaz	AY-haz
Ahijah	uh-HAI-dzhuh
Ai	AY-ee
Alexandria	al-ehg-ZAN-dree-uh
Alexandrian	al-ehg-ZAN-dree-uhn
Alpha	AHL-fuh
Alphaeus	AL-fee-uhs
Amalek	AM-uh-lehk
Amaziah	am-uh-ZAI-uh
Amminadab	ah-MIHN-uh-dab
Ammonites	AM-uh-naitz
Amorites	AM-uh-raits
Amos	AY-muhs
Amoz	AY-muhz
Ampliatus	am-plee-AY-tuhs
Ananias	an-uh-NAI-uhs
Andronicus	an-draw-NAI-kuhs
Annas	AN-uhs
Antioch	AN-tih-ahk
Antiochus	an-TAI-uh-kuhs
Aphiah	uh-FAI-uh
Apollos	uh-PAH-luhs
Appius	AP-ee-uhs
Aquila	uh-KWIHL-uh
Arabah	EHR-uh-buh
Aram	AY-ram
Arameans	ehr-uh-MEE-uhnz
Areopagus	ehr-ee-AH-puh-guhs
Arimathea	ehr-uh-muh-THEE-uh
Aroer	uh-RO-er

Lectionary Word	Pronunciation
Asaph	AY-saf
Asher	ASH-er
Ashpenaz	ASH-pee-naz
Assyria	a-SIHR-ee-uh
Astarte	as-TAHR-tee
Attalia	at-TAH-lee-uh
Augustus	uh-GUHS-tuhs
Azariah	az-uh-RAI-uh
Azor	AY-sawr
Azotus	uh-ZO-tus
Baal-shalishah	BAY-uhl-shuh-LAI-shuh
Baal-Zephon	BAY-uhl-ZEE-fuhn
Babel	BAY-bl
Babylon	BAB-ih-luhn
Babylonian	bab-ih-LO-nih-uhn
Balaam	BAY-lm
Barabbas	beh-REH-buhs
Barak	BEHR-ak
Barnabas	BAHR-nuh-buhs
Barsabbas	BAHR-suh-buhs
Bartholomew	bar-THAHL-uh-myoo
Bartimaeus	bar-tih-MEE-uhs
Baruch	BEHR-ook
Bashan	BAY-shan
Becorath	bee-KO-rath
Beelzebul	bee-EHL-zee-buhl
Beer-sheba	BEE-er-SHEE-buh
Belshazzar	behl-SHAZ-er
Benjamin	BEHN-dzhuh-mihn
Beor	BEE-awr
Bethany	BEHTH-uh-nee
Bethel	BETH-el
Bethesda	beh-THEHZ-duh
Bethlehem	BEHTH-leh-hehm
Bethphage	BEHTH-fuh-dzhee
Bethsaida	behth-SAY-ih-duh
Beth-zur	behth-ZER
Bildad	BIHL-dad
Bithynia	bih-THIHN-ih-uh
Boanerges	bo-uh-NER-dzheez
Boaz	BO-az
Caesar	SEE-zer
Caesarea	zeh-suh-REE-uh
Caiaphas	KAY-uh-fuhs
Cain	kayn
Cana	KAY-nuh
Canaan	KAY-nuhn
Canaanite	KAY-nuh-nait
Canaanites	KAY-nuh-naits

Lectionary Word	Pronunciation
Candace	kan-DAY-see
Capernaum	kuh-PERR-nay-uhm
Cappadocia	kap-ih-DO-shee-u
Carmel	KAHR-muhl
carnelians	kahr-NEEL-yuhnz
Cenchreae	SEHN-kree-ay
Cephas	SEE-fuhs
Chaldeans	kal-DEE-uhnz
Chemosh	KEE-mahsh
Cherubim	TSHEHR-oo-bihm
Chislev	KIHS-lehv
Chloe	KLO-ee
Chorazin	kor-AY-sihn
Cilicia	sih-LIHSH-ee-uh
Cleopas	KLEE-o-pas
Clopas	KLO-pas
Corinth	KAWR-ihnth
Corinthians	kawr-IHN-thee-uhnz
Cornelius	kawr-NEE-lee-uhs
Crete	kreet
Crispus	KRIHS-puhs
Cushite	CUHSH-ait
Cypriot	SIH-pree-at
Cyrene	sai-REE-nee
Cyreneans	sai-REE-nih-uhnz
Cyrenian	sai-REE-nih-uhn
Cyrenians	sai-REE-nih-uhnz
Cyrus	SAI-ruhs
Damaris	DAM-uh-rihs
Damascus	duh-MAS-kuhs
Danites	DAN-aits
Decapolis	duh-KAP-o-lis
Derbe	DER-bee
Deuteronomy	dyoo-ter-AH-num-mee
Didymus	DID-I-mus
Dionysius	dai-o-NIHSH-ih-uhs
Dioscuri	dai-O-sky-ri
Dorcas	DAWR-kuhs
Dothan	DO-thuhn
dromedaries	DRAH-muh-dher-eez
Ebed-melech	EE-behd-MEE-lehk
Eden	EE-dn
Edom	EE-duhm
Elamites	EE-luh-maitz
Eldad	EHL-dad
Eleazar	ehl-ee-AY-zer
Eli	EE-lai
Eli Eli Lema Sabachthani	AY-lee AY-lee luh-MAH sah-BAHK-tah-nee

Lectionary Word	Pronunciation	Lectionary Word	Pronunciation	Lectionary Word	Pronunciation
Eliab	ee-LAI-ab	Gilead	GIHL-ee-uhd	Joppa	DZHAH-puh
Eliakim	ee-LAI-uh-kihm	Gilgal	GIHL-gal	Joram	DZHO-ram
Eliezer	ehl-ih-EE-zer	Golgotha	GAHL-guh-thuh	Jordan	DZHAWR-dn
Elihu	ee-LAI-hyoo	Gomorrah	guh-MAWR-uh	Joseph	DZHO-zf
Elijah	ee-LAI-dzhuh	Goshen	GO-shuhn	Joses	DZHO-seez
Elim	EE-lihm	Habakkuk	huh-BAK-uhk	Joshua	DZHAH-shou-ah
Elimelech	ee-LIHM-eh-lehk	Hadadrimmon	hay-dad-RIHM-uhn	Josiah	dzho-SAI-uh
Elisha	ee-LAI-shuh	Hades	HAY-deez	Jotham	DZHO-thuhm
Eliud	ee-LAI-uhd	Hagar	HAH-gar	Judah	DZHOU-duh
Elizabeth	ee-LIHZ-uh-bth	Hananiah	han-uh-NAI-uh	Judas	DZHOU-duhs
Elkanah	el-KAY-nuh	Hannah	HAN-uh	Judea	dzhou-DEE-uh
Eloi Eloi Lama	AY-lo-ee AY-lo-ee	Haran	HAY-ruhn	Judean	dzhou-DEE-uhn
Sabechthani	LAH-mah sah-	Hebron	HEE-bruhn	Junia	dzhou-nih-uh
	BAHK-tah-nee	Hermes	HER-meez	Justus	DZHUHS-tuhs
Elymais	ehl-ih-MAY-ihs	Herod	HEHR-uhd	Kephas	KEF-uhs
Emmanuel	eh-MAN-yoo-ehl	Herodians	hehr-O-dee-uhnz	Kidron	KIHD-ruhn
Emmaus	eh-MAY-uhs	Herodias	hehr-O-dee-uhs	Kiriatharba	kihr-ee-ath-AHR-buh
Epaenetus	ee-PEE-nee-tuhs	Hezekiah	heh-zeh-KAI-uh	Kish	kihsh
Epaphras	EH-puh-fras	Hezron	HEHZ-ruhn	Laodicea	lay-o-dih-SEE-uh
ephah	EE-fuh	Hilkiah	hihl-KAI-uh	Lateran	LAT-er-uhn
Ephah	EE-fuh	Hittite	HIH-tait	Lazarus	LAZ-er-uhs
Ephesians	eh-FEE-zhuhnz	Hivites	HAI-vaitz	Leah	LEE-uh
Ephesus	EH-fuh-suhs	Hophni	HAHF-nai	Lebanon	LEH-buh-nuhn
Ephphatha	EHF-uh-thuh	Hor	HAWR	Levi	LEE-vai
Ephraim	EE-fray-ihm	Horeb	HAWR-ehb	Levite	LEE-vait
Ephrathah	EHF-ruh-thuh	Hosea	ho-ZEE-uh	Levites	LEE-vaits
Ephron	EE-frawn	Hur	her	Leviticus	leh-VIH-tih-kous
Epiphanes	eh-PIHF-uh-neez	hyssop	HIH-suhp	Lucius	LOO-shih-uhs
Erastus	ee-RAS-tuhs	Iconium	ai-KO-nih-uhm	Lud	luhd
Esau	EE-saw	Isaac	AI-zuhk	Luke	look
Esther	EHS-ter	Isaiah	ai-ZAY-uh	Luz	luhz
Ethanim	EHTH-uh-nihm	Iscariot	ihs-KEHR-ee-uht	Lycaonian	lihk-ay-O-nih-uhn
Ethiopian	ee-thee-O-pee-uhn	Ishmael	ISH-may-ehl	Lydda	LIH-duh
Euphrates	yoo-FRAY-teez	Ishmaelites	ISH-mayehl-aits	Lydia	LIH-dih-uh
Exodus	EHK-so-duhs	Israel	IHZ-ray-ehl	Lysanias	lai-SAY-nih-uhs
Ezekiel	eh-ZEE-kee-uhl	Ituraea	ih-TSHOOR-ree-uh	Lystra	LIHS-truh
Ezra	EHZ-ruh	Jaar	DZHAY-ahr	Maccabees	MAK-uh-beez
frankincense	FRANGK-ihn-sehns	Jabbok	DZHAB-uhk	Macedonia	mas-eh-DO-nih-uh
Gabbatha	GAB-uh-thuh	Jacob	DZHAY-kuhb	Macedonian	mas-eh-DO-nih-uhn
Gabriel	GAY-bree-ul	Jairus	DZH-hr-uhs	Machir	MAY-kihr
Gadarenes	GAD-uh-reenz	Javan	DZHAY-van	Machpelah	mak-PEE-luh
Galatian	guh-LAY-shih-uhn	Jebusites	DZHEHB-oo-zaits	Magdala	MAG-duh-luh
Galatians	guh-LAY-shih-uhnz	Jechoniah	dzhehk-o-NAI-uh	Magdalene	MAG-duh-lehn
Galilee	GAL-ih-lee	Jehoiakim	dzhee-HOI-uh-kihm	magi	MAY-dzhai
Gallio	GAL-ih-o	Jehoshaphat	dzhee-HAHSH-uh-fat	Malachi	MAL-uh-kai
Gamaliel	guh-MAY-lih-ehl	Jephthah	DZHEHF-thuh	Malchiah	mal-KAI-uh
Gaza	GAH-zuh	Jeremiah	dzhehr-eh-MAI-uh	Malchus	MAL-kuhz
Gehazi	gee-HAY-zai	Jericho	DZHEHR-ih-ko	Mamre	MAM-ree
Gehenna	geh-HEHN-uh	Jeroham	dzhehr-RO-ham	Manaen	MAN-uh-ehn
Genesis	DZHEHN-uh-sihs	Jerusalem	dzheh-ROU-suh-lehm	Manasseh	man-AS-eh
Gennesaret	gehn-NEHS-uh-reht	Jesse	DZHEH-see	Manoah	muh-NO-uh
Gentiles	DZHEHN-tailz	Jethro	DZHEHTH-ro	Mark	mahrk
Gerasenes	DZHEHR-uh-seenz	Joakim	DZHO-uh-kihm	Mary	MEHR-ee
Gethsemane	gehth-SEHM-uh-ne	Job	DZHOB	Massah	MAH-suh
Gideon	GIHD-ee-uhn	Jonah	DZHO-nuh	Mattathias	mat-uh-THAI-uhs

Lectionary Word	Pronunciation	Lectionary Word	Pronunciation	Lectionary Word	Pronunciation
Matthan	MAT-than	Parmenas	PAHR-mee-nas	Sabbath	SAB-uhth
Matthew	MATH-yoo	Parthians	PAHR-thee-uhnz	Sadducees	SAD-dzhoo-seez
Matthias	muh-THAI-uhs	Patmos	PAT-mos	Salem	SAY-lehm
Medad	MEE-dad	Peninnah	pee-NIHN-uh	Salim	SAY-lim
Mede	meed	Pentecost	PEHN-tee-kawst	Salmon	SAL-muhn
Medes	meedz	Penuel	pee-NYOO-ehl	Salome	suh-LO-mee
Megiddo	mee-GIH-do	Perez	PEE-rehz	Salu	SAYL-yoo
Melchizedek	mehl-KIHZ-eh-dehk	Perga	PER-guh	Samaria	suh-MEHR-ih-uh
Mene	MEE-nee	Perizzites	PEHR-ih-zaits	Samaritan	suh-MEHR-ih-tuhn
Meribah	MEHR-ih-bah	Persia	PER-zhuh	Samothrace	SAM-o-thrays
Meshach	MEE-shak	Peter	PEE-ter	Samson	SAM-s'n
Mespotamia	mehs-o-po-TAY-mih-uh	Phanuel	FAN-yoo-ehl	Samuel	SAM-yoo-uhl
Micah	MAI-kuh	Pharaoh	FEHR-o	Sanhedrin	san-HEE-drihn
Midian	MIH-dih-uhn	Pharisees	FEHR-ih-seez	Sarah	SEHR-uh
Milcom	MIHL-kahm	Pharpar	FAHR-pahr	Sarai	SAY-rai
Miletus	mai-LEE-tuhs	Philemon	fih-LEE-muhn	saraph	SAY-raf
Minnith	MIHN-ihth	Philippi	fil-LIH-pai	Sardis	SAHR-dihs
Mishael	MIHSH-ay-ehl	Philippians	fih-LIHP-ih-uhnz	Saul	sawl
Mizpah	MIHZ-puh	Philistines	fih-LIHS-tihnz	Scythian	SIH-thee-uihn
Moreh	MO-reh	Phinehas	FEHN-ee-uhs	Seba	SEE-buh
Moriah	maw-RAI-uh	Phoenicia	fee-NIHSH-ih-uh	Seth	sehth
Mosoch	MAH-sahk	Phrygia	FRIH-dzhih-uh	Shaalim	SHAY-uh-lihm
myrrh	mer	Phrygian	FRIH-dzhih-uhn	Shadrach	SHAY-drak
Mysia	MIH-shih-uh	phylacteries	fih-LAK-ter-eez	Shalishah	shuh-LEE-shuh
Naaman	NAY-uh-muhn	Pi-Hahiroth	pai-huh-HAI-rahth	Shaphat	Shay-fat
Nahshon	NAY-shuhn	Pilate	PAI-luht	Sharon	SHEHR-uhn
Naomi	NAY-o-mai	Pisidia	pih-SIH-dih-uh	Shealtiel	shee-AL-tih-ehl
Naphtali	NAF-tuh-lai	Pithom	PAI-thahm	Sheba	SHEE-buh
Nathan	NAY-thuhn	Pontius	PAHN-shus	Shebna	SHEB-nuh
Nathanael	nuh-THAN-ay-ehl	Pontus	PAHN-tus	Shechem	SHEE-kehm
Nazarene	NAZ-awr-een	Praetorium	pray-TAWR-ih-uhm	shekel	SHEHK-uhl
Nazareth	NAZ-uh-rehth	Priscilla	PRIHS-kill-uh	Shiloh	SHAI-lo
nazirite	NAZ-uh-rait	Prochorus	PRAH-kaw-ruhs	Shinar	SHAI-nahr
Nazorean	naz-aw-REE-uhn	Psalm	Sahm	Shittim	sheh-TEEM
Neapolis	nee-AP-o-lihs	Put	puht	Shuhite	SHOO-ait
Nebuchadnezzar	neh-byoo-kuhd-NEHZ-er	Puteoli	pyoo-TEE-o-lai	Shunammite	SHOO-nam-ait
Negeb	NEH-gehb	Qoheleth	ko-HEHL-ehth	Shunem	SHOO-nehm
Nehemiah	nee-hee-MAI-uh	qorban	KAWR-bahn	Sidon	SAI-duhn
Ner	ner	Quartus	KWAR-tuhs	Silas	SAI-luhs
Nicanor	nai-KAY-nawr	Quirinius	kwai-RIHN-ih-uhs	Siloam	sih-LO-uhm
Nicodemus	nih-ko-DEE-muhs	Raamses	ray-AM-seez	Silvanus	sihl-VAY-nuhs
Niger	NAI-dzher	Rabbi	RAB-ai	Simeon	SIHM-ee-uhn
Nineveh	NIHN-eh-veh	Rabbouni	ra-BO-nai	Simon	SAI-muhn
Noah	NO-uh	Rahab	RAY-hab	Sin (desert)	sihn
Nun	nuhn	Ram	ram	Sinai	SAI-nai
Obed	O-behd	Ramah	RAY-muh	Sirach	SAI-rak
Olivet	AH-lih-veht	Ramathaim	ray-muh-THAY-ihm	Sodom	SAH-duhm
Omega	o-MEE-guh	Raqa	RA-kuh	Solomon	SAH-lo-muhn
Onesimus	o-NEH-sih-muhs	Rebekah	ree-BEHK-uh	Sosthenes	SAHS-thee-neez
Ophir	O-fer	Rehoboam	ree-ho-BO-am	Stachys	STAY-kihs
Orpah	AWR-puh	Rephidim	REHF-ih-dihm	Succoth	SUHK-ahth
Pamphylia	pam-FIHL-ih-uh	Reuben	ROO-b'n	Sychar	SI-kar
Paphos	PAY-fuhs	Revelation	reh-veh-LAY-shuhn	Syene	sai-EE-nee
		Rhegium	REE-dzhee-uhm	Symeon	SIHM-ee-uhn
		Rufus	ROO-fuhs	synagogues	SIHN-uh-gahgz

Lectionary Word	Pronunciation	Lectionary Word	Pronunciation	Lectionary Word	Pronunciation
Syrophoenician	SIHR-o fee-NIHSH-ih-uhn	Timon	TAI-muhn	Zebedee	ZEH-beh-dee
		Titus	TAI-tuhs	Zebulun	ZEH-byoo-luhn
Tabitha	TAB-ih-thuh	Tohu	TO-hyoo	Zechariah	zeh-kuh-RAI-uh
Talitha koum	TAL-ih-thuh-KOOM	Trachonitis	trak-o-NAI-tis	Zedekiah	zeh-duh-KAI-uh
Tamar	TAY-mer	Troas	TRO-ahs	Zephaniah	zeh-fuh-NAI-uh
Tarshish	TAHR-shihsh	Tubal	TYOO-b'l	Zerah	ZEE-ruh
Tarsus	TAHR-suhs	Tyre	TAI-er	Zeror	ZEE-rawr
Tekel	TEH-keel	Ur	er	Zerubbabel	zeh-RUH-buh-behl
Terebinth	TEHR-ee-bihnth	Urbanus	er-BAY-nuhs	Zeus	zyoos
Thaddeus	THAD-dee-uhs	Uriah	you-RAI-uh	Zimri	ZIHM-rai
Theophilus	thee-AH-fih-luhs	Uzziah	yoo-ZAI-uh	Zion	ZAI-uhn
Thessalonians	theh-suh-LO-nih-uhnz	Wadi	WAH-dee	Ziph	zihf
Theudas	THU-duhs	Yahweh-yireh	YAH-weh-yer-AY	Zoar	ZO-er
Thyatira	thai-uh-TAI-ruh	Zacchaeus	zak-KEE-uhs	Zorah	ZAWR-uh
Tiberias	tai-BIHR-ih-uhs	Zadok	ZAY-dahk	Zuphite	ZUHF-ait
Timaeus	tai-MEE-uhs	Zarephath	ZEHR-ee-fath